Dit muziekverhaal

is een herinnering aan

Jannie Willy Graeuwert

Blue
6 simple pieces of music
for various ensemble:
piano/organ, guitar duo,
wood wind/clarinet/saxophone/brass/
string quartet, string orchestra,
concert band or combinations

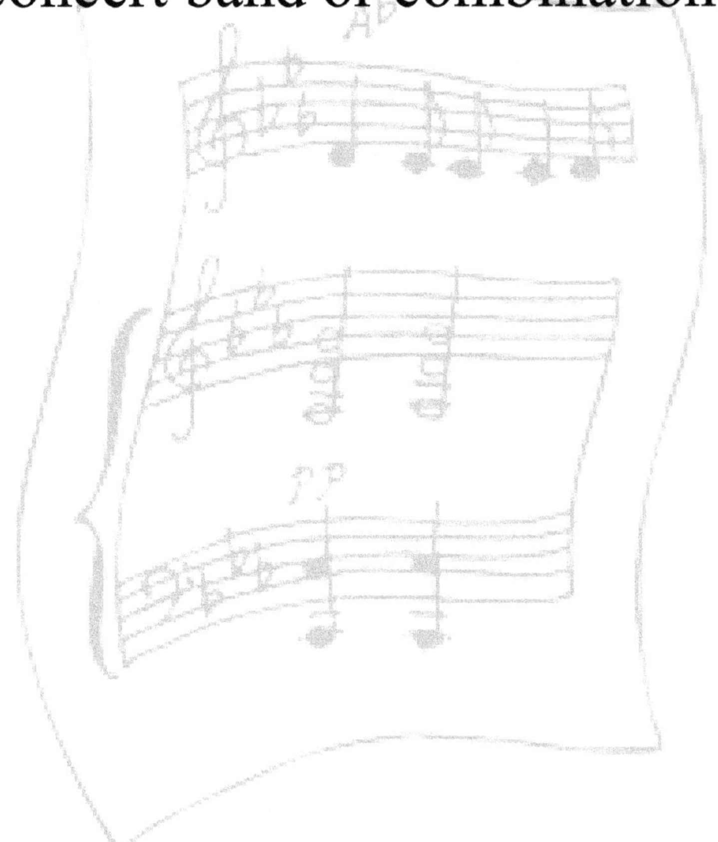

ISBN 978-90-78808-22-0

www.uitgeverijmuz.com

Contents

J

Joost de Groo

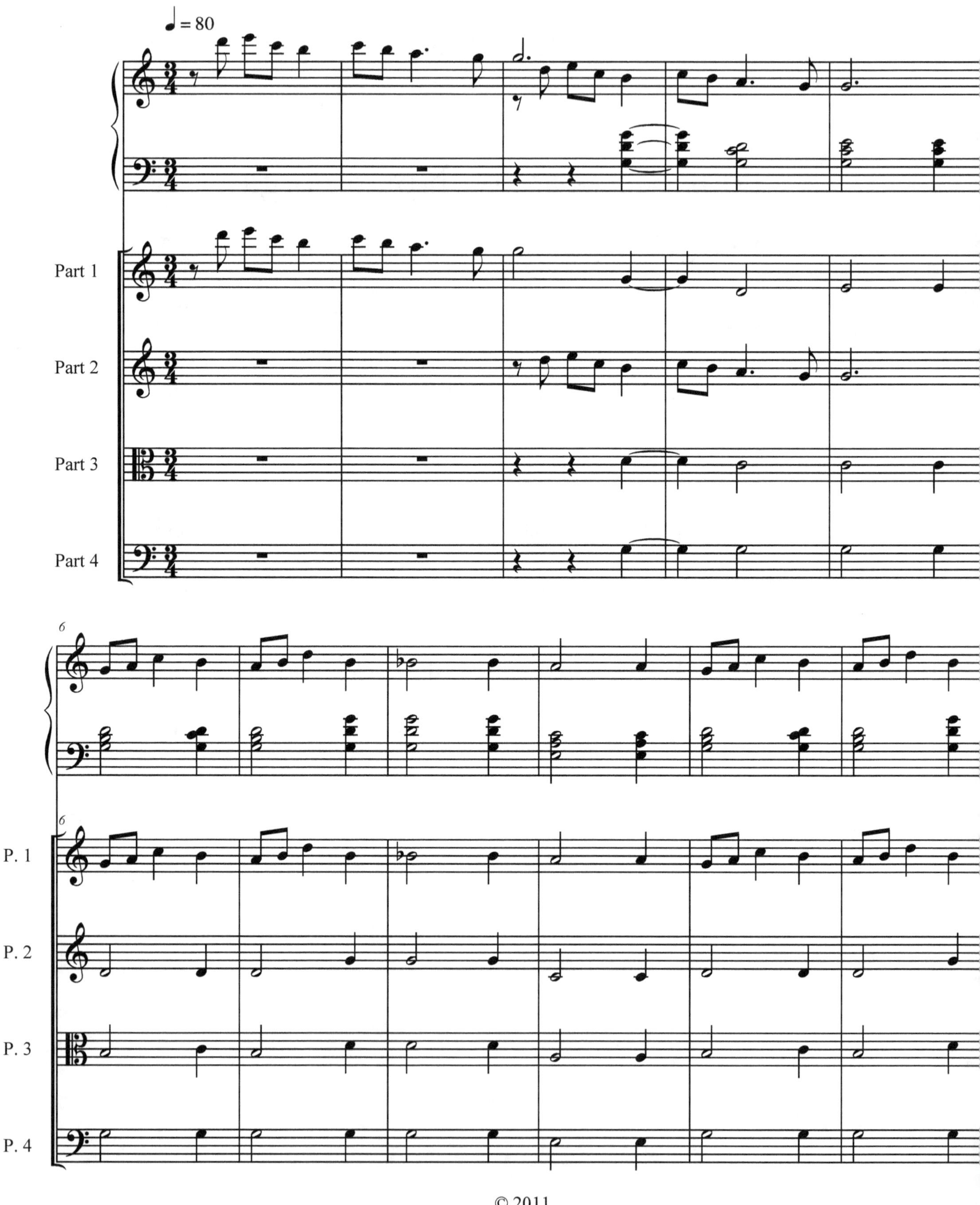

J

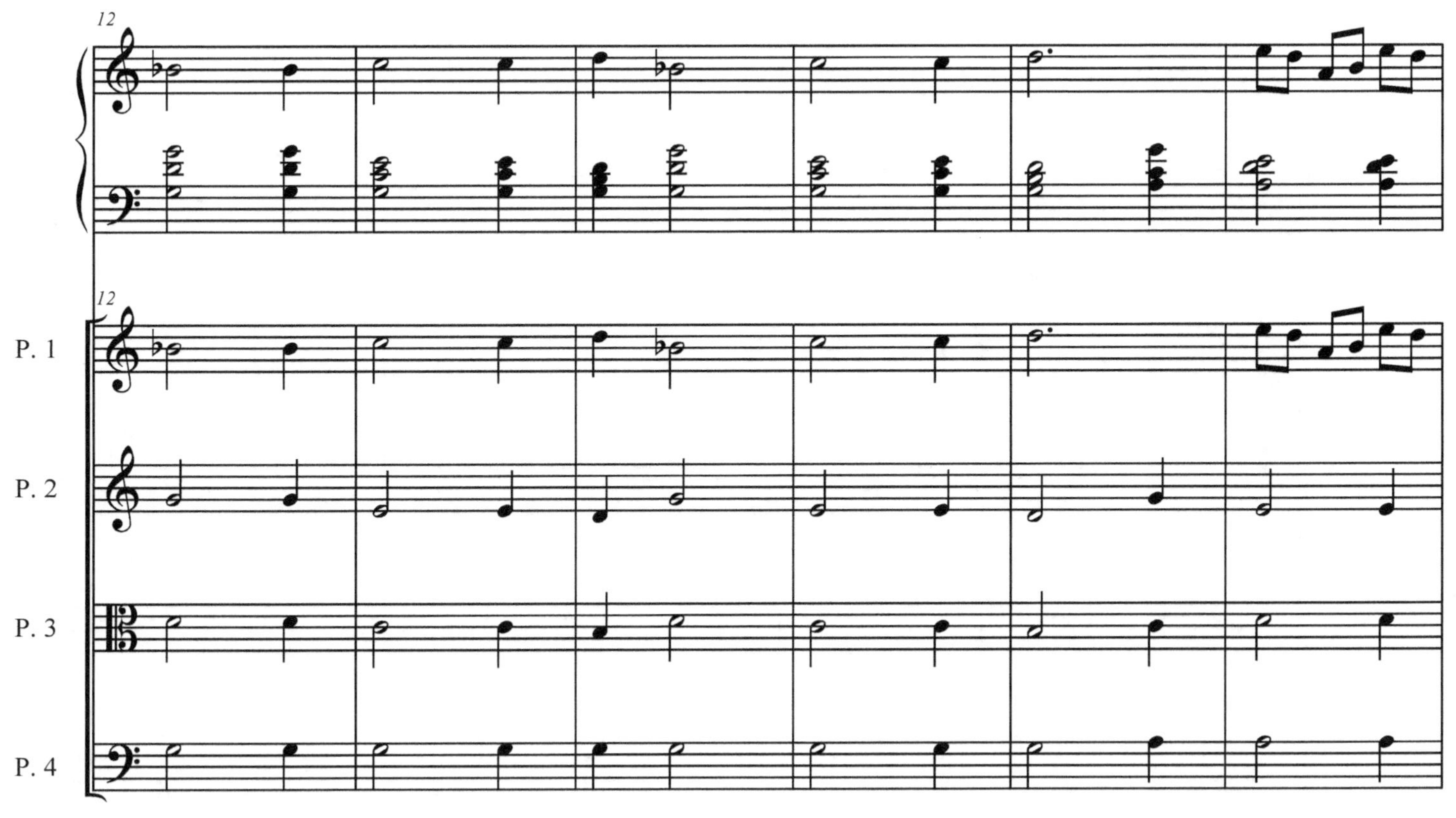

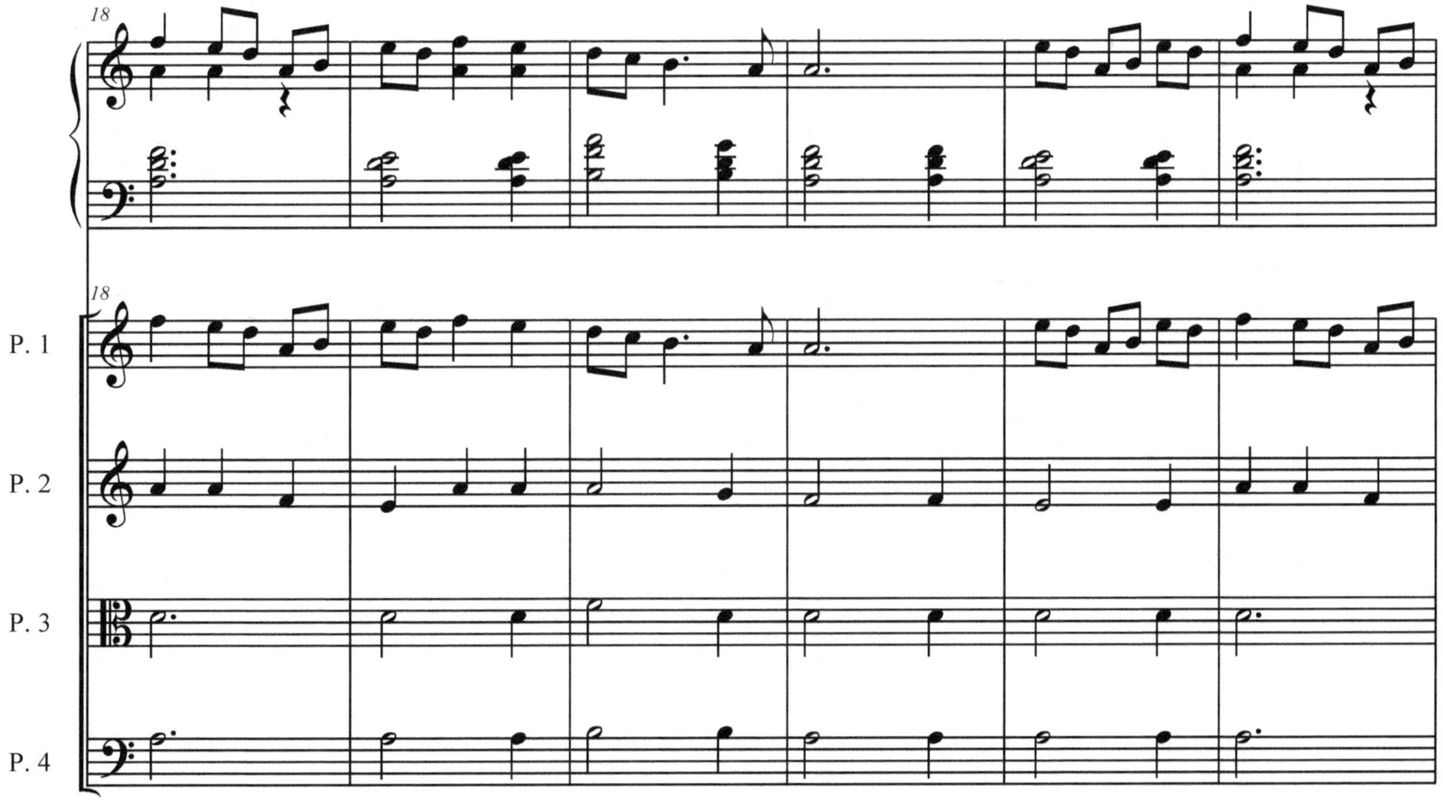

18

18

P. 1

P. 2

P. 3

P. 4

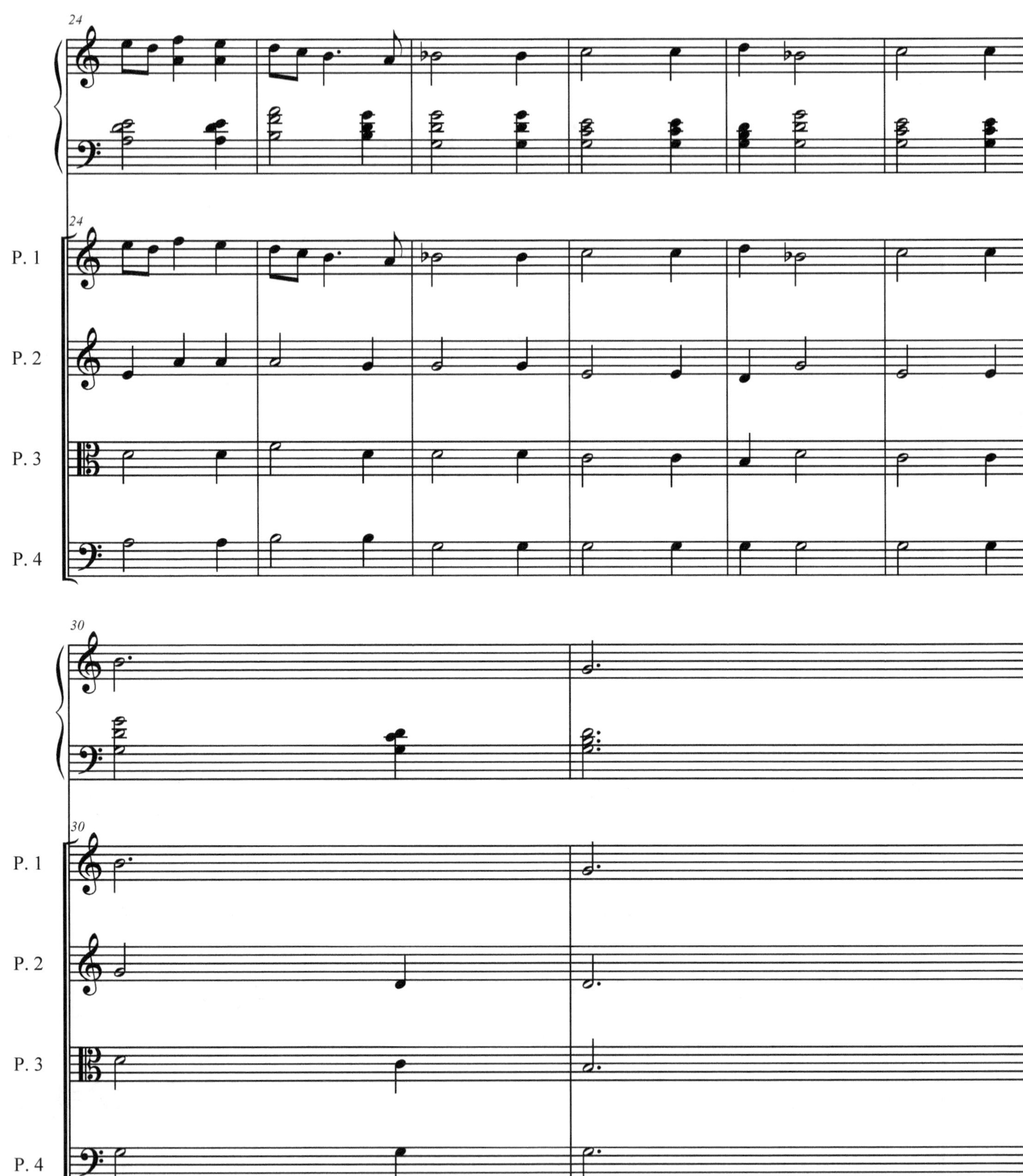

24
P. 1
P. 2
P. 3
P. 4
30

A

Joost de Groot

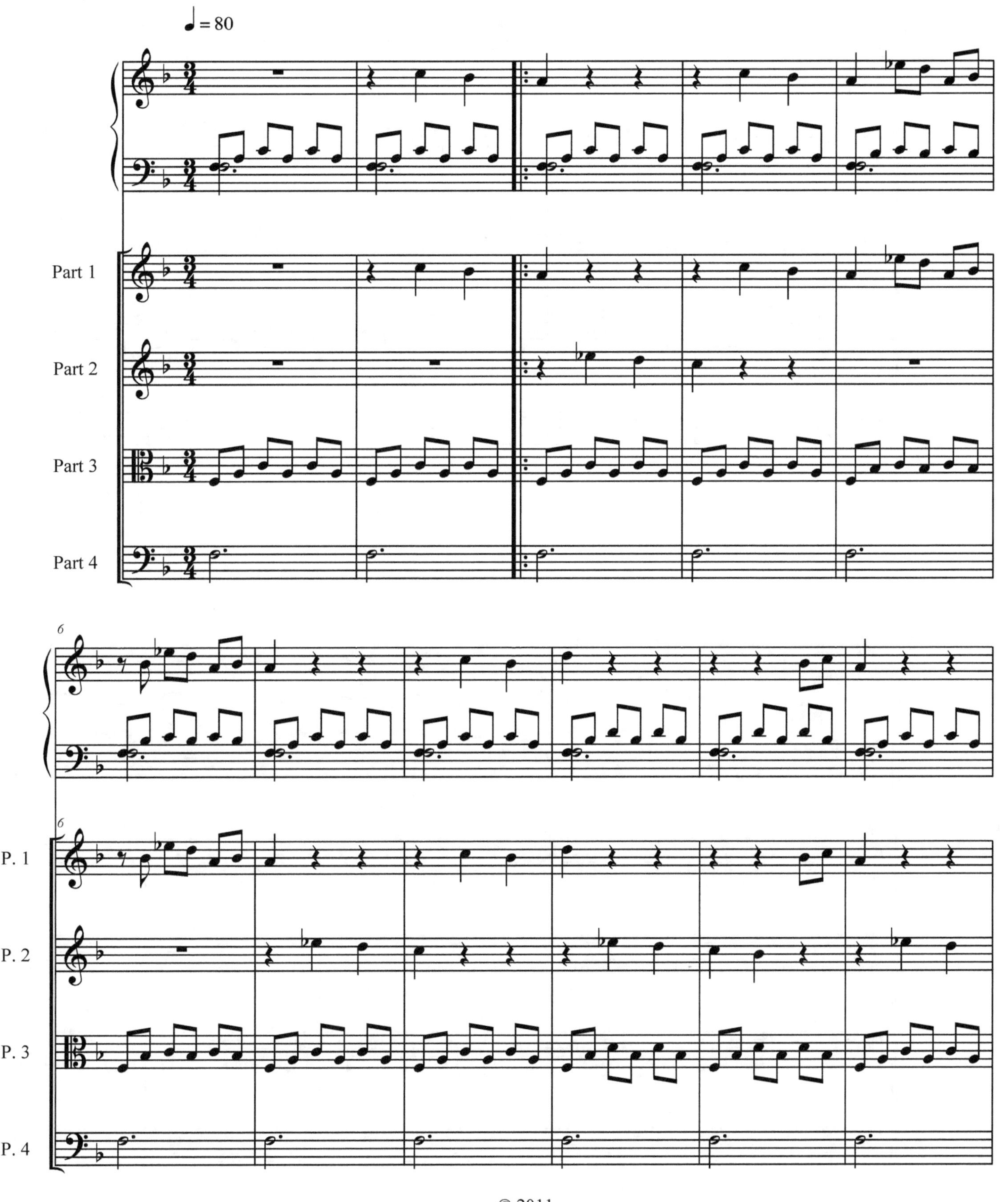

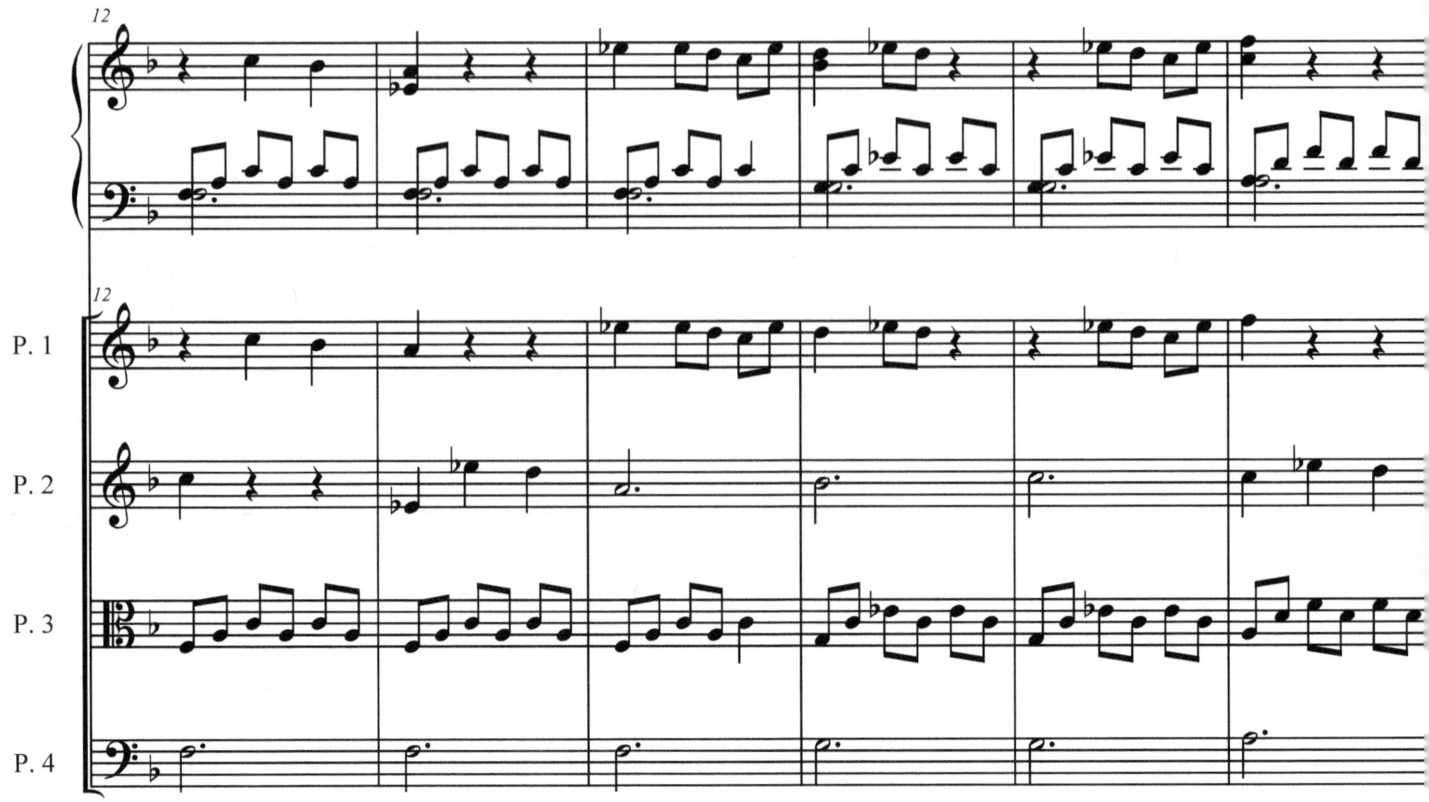
12
12
P. 1
P. 2
P. 3
P. 4

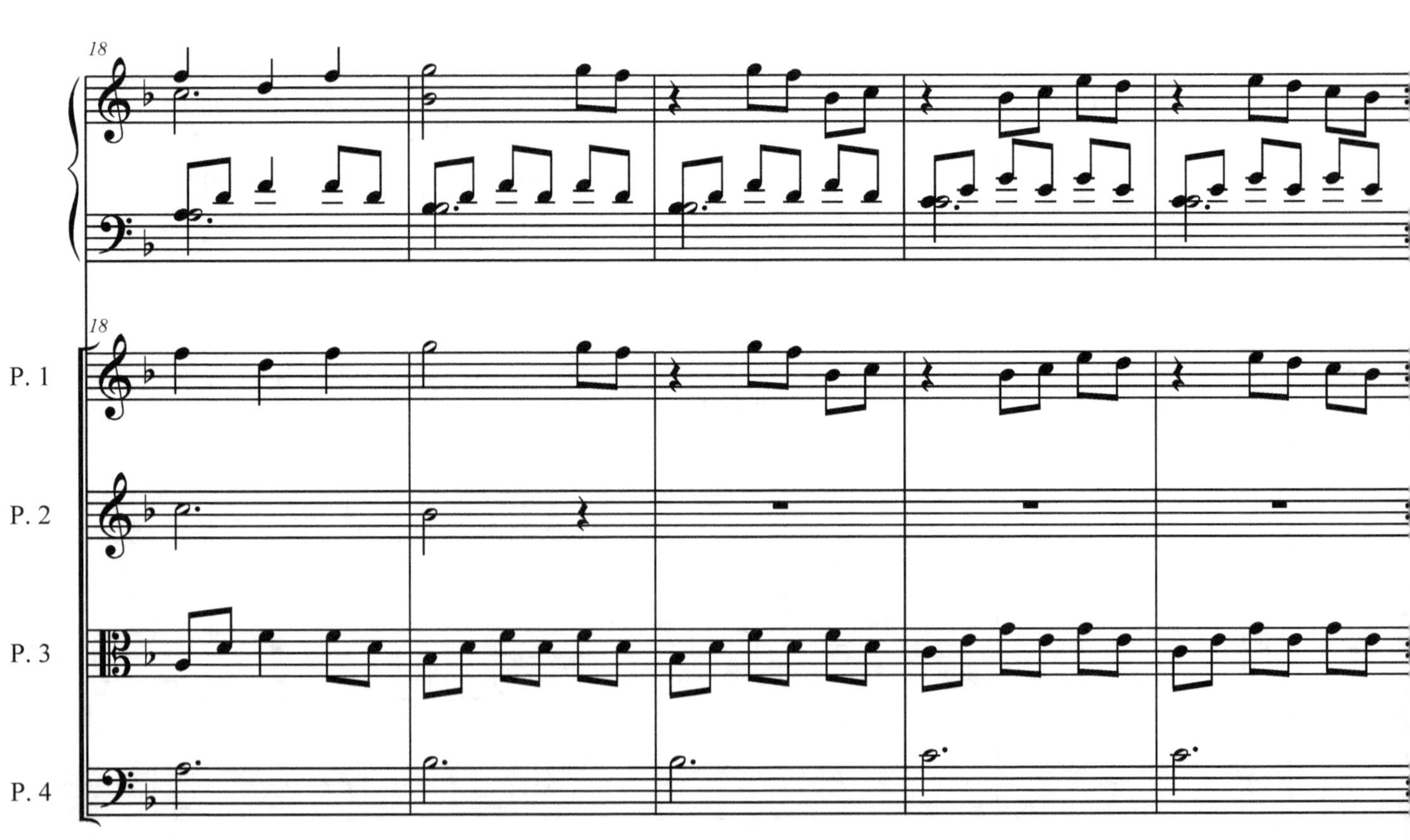
18
18
P. 1
P. 2
P. 3
P. 4

N

Joost de Groot

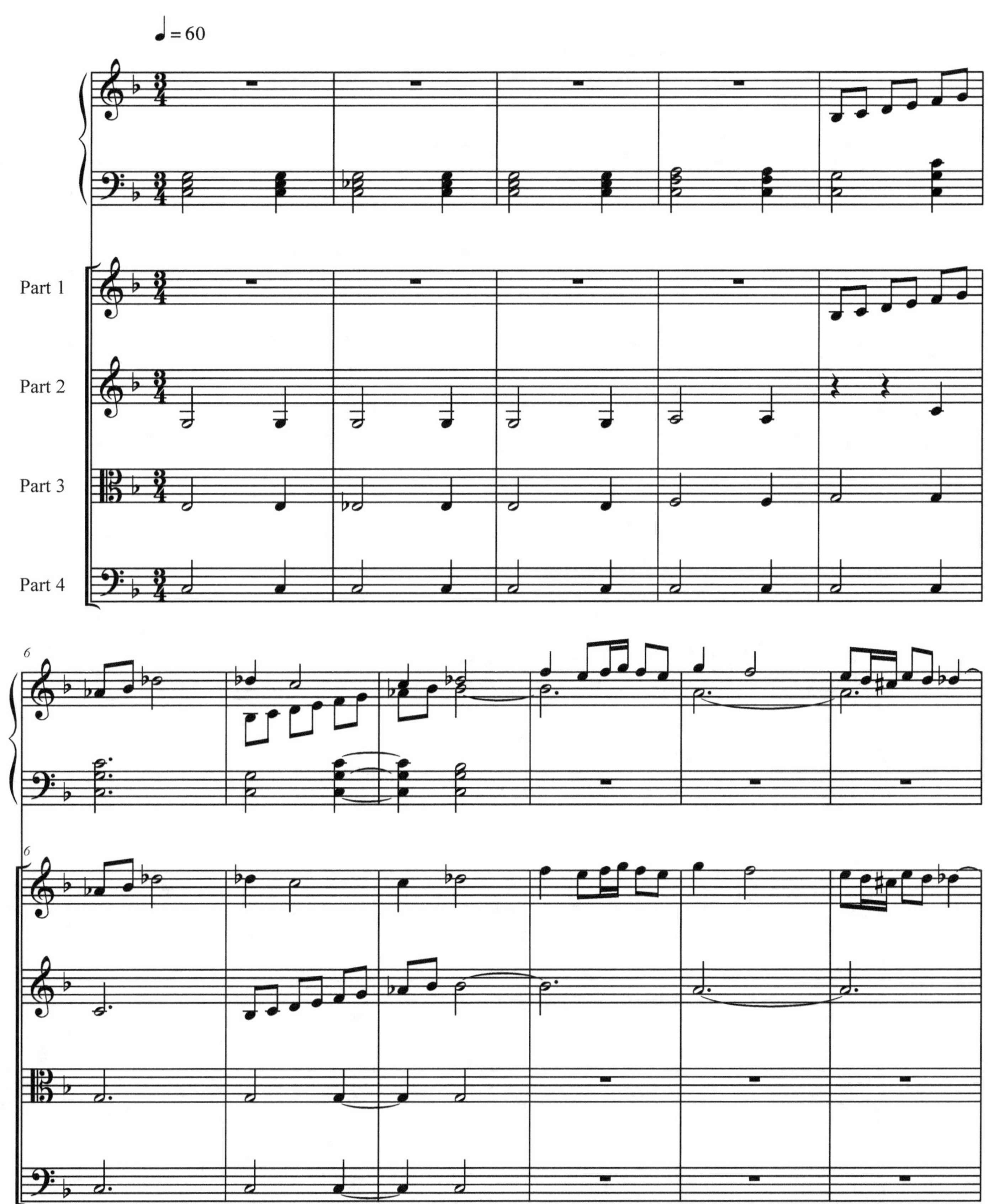

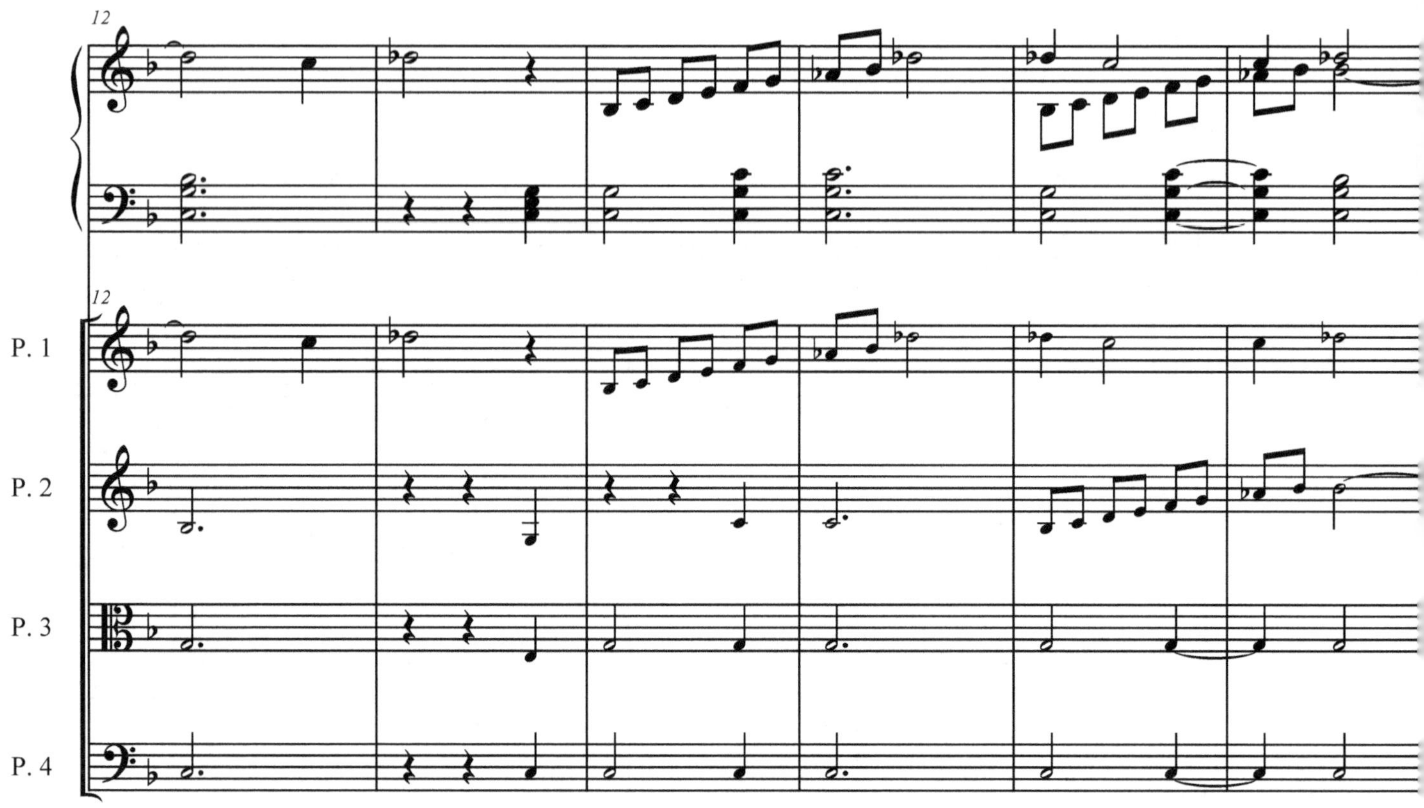
12
P. 1
P. 2
P. 3
P. 4

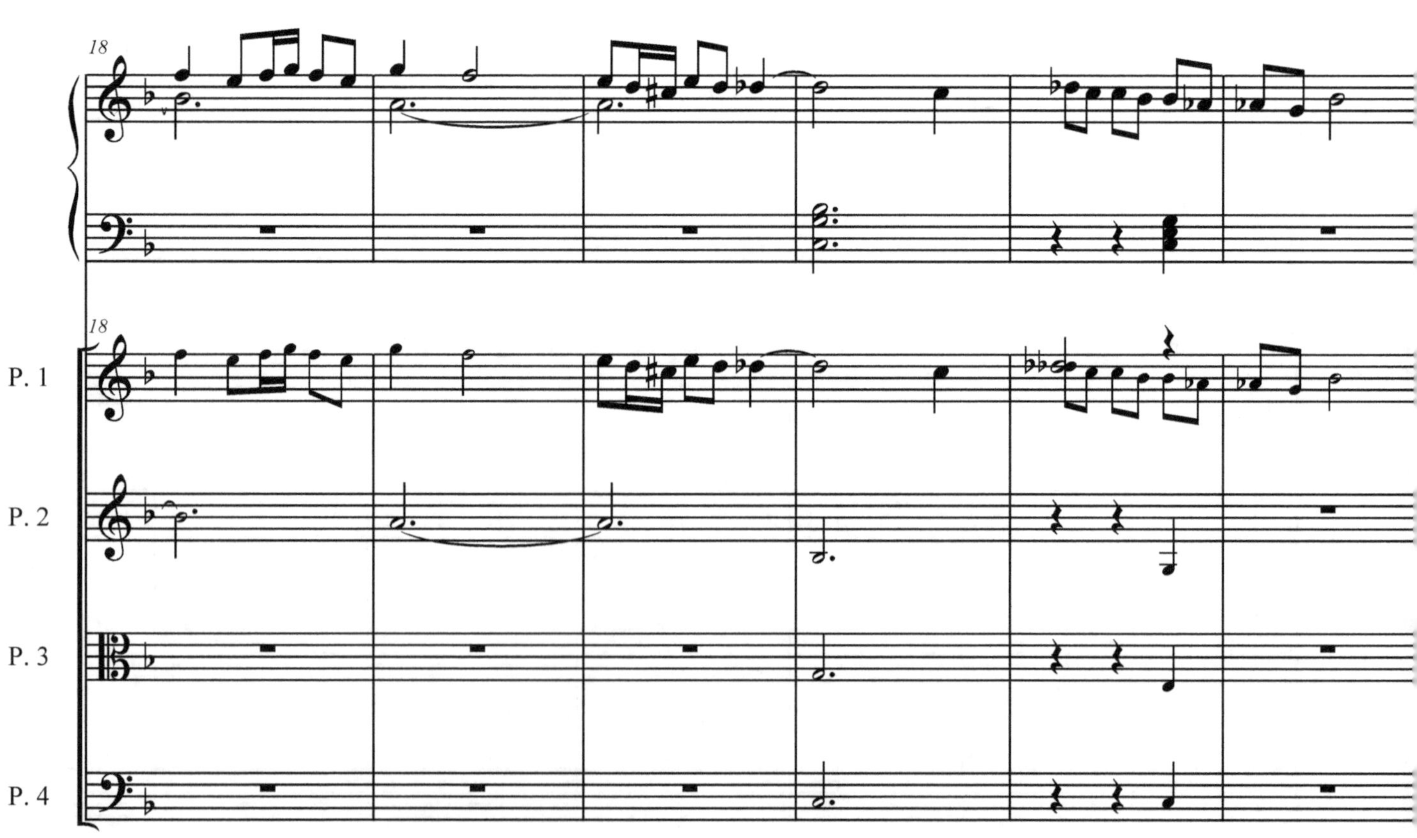
18
P. 1
P. 2
P. 3
P. 4

N

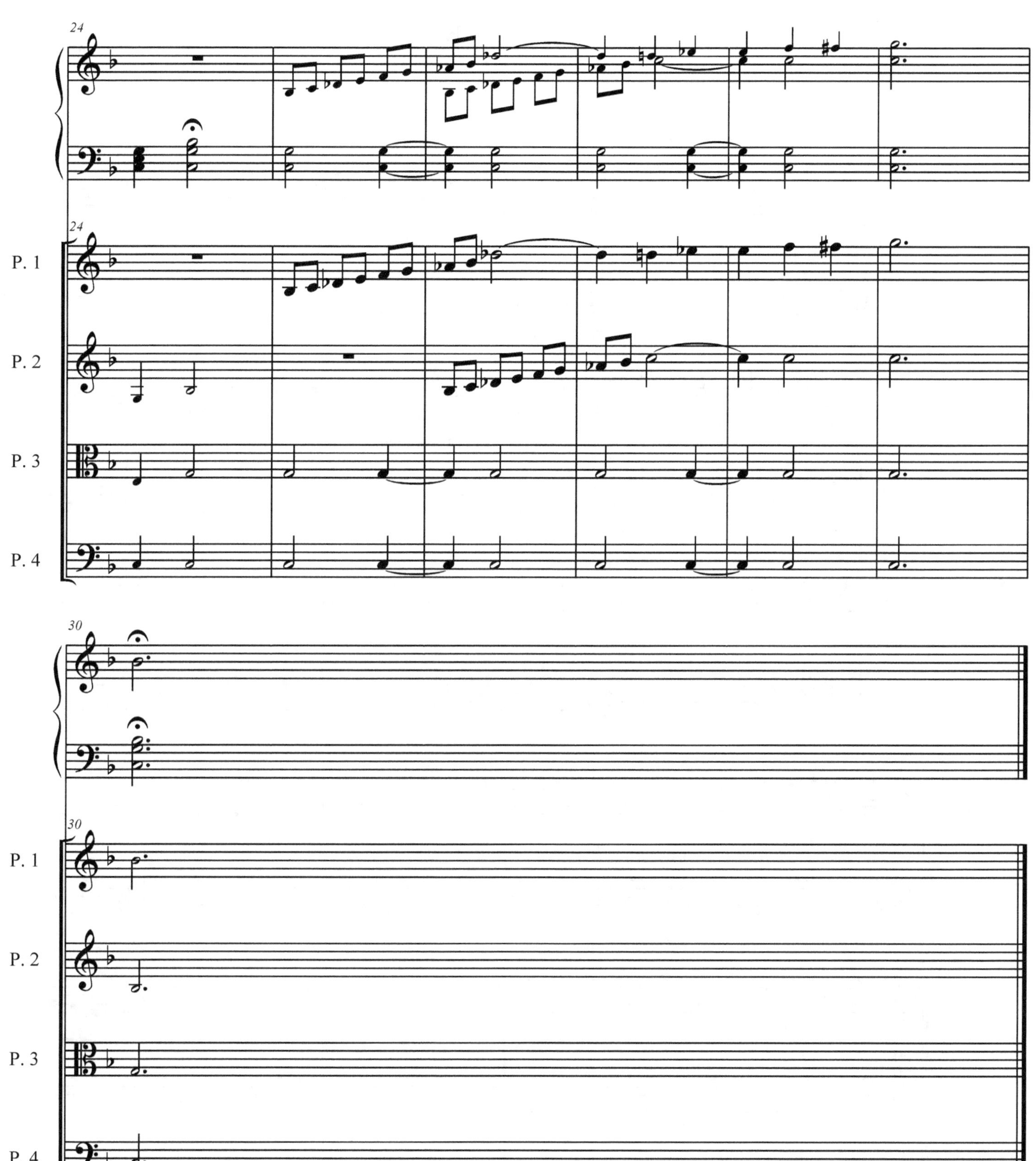

N

Joost de Groo

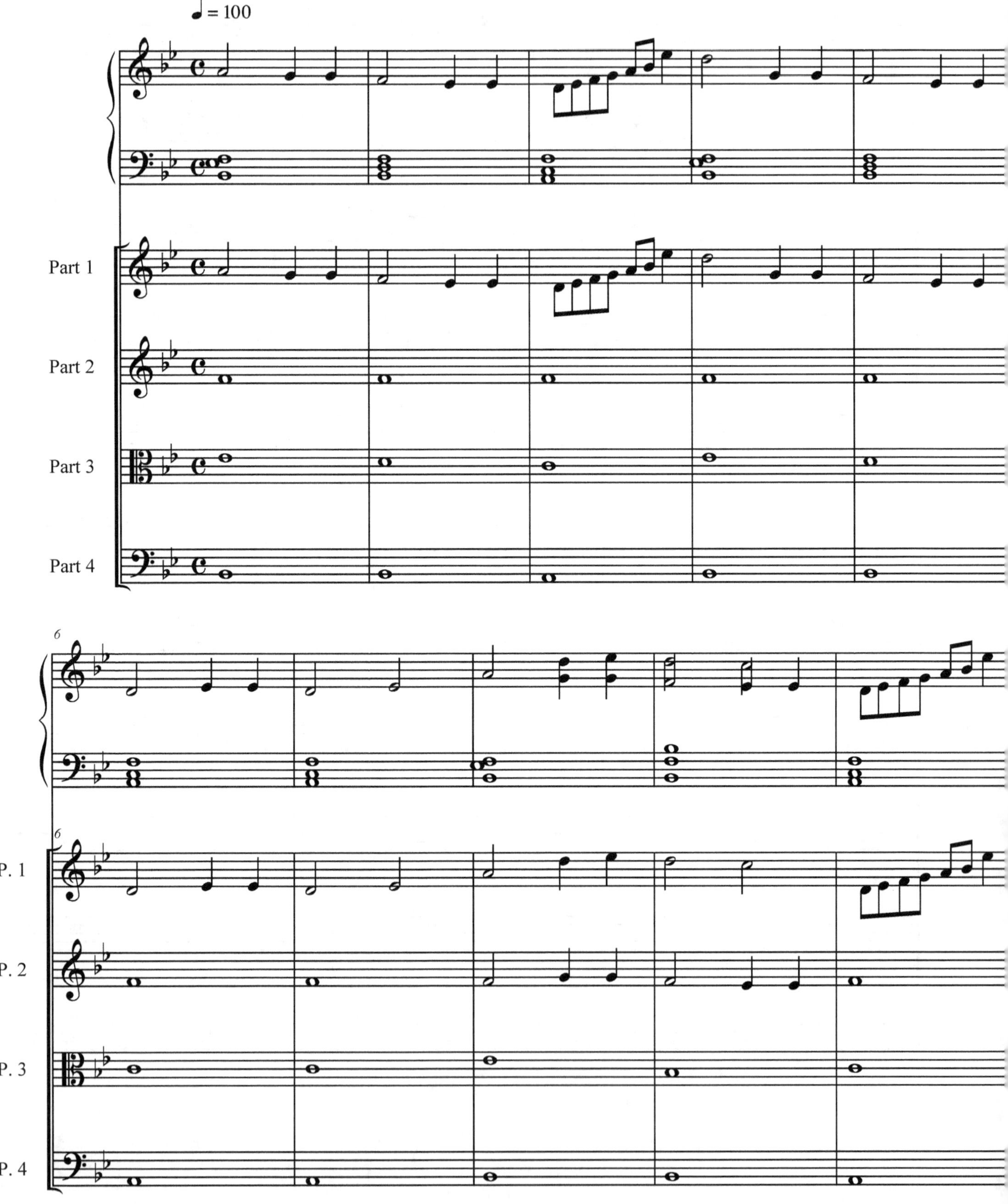

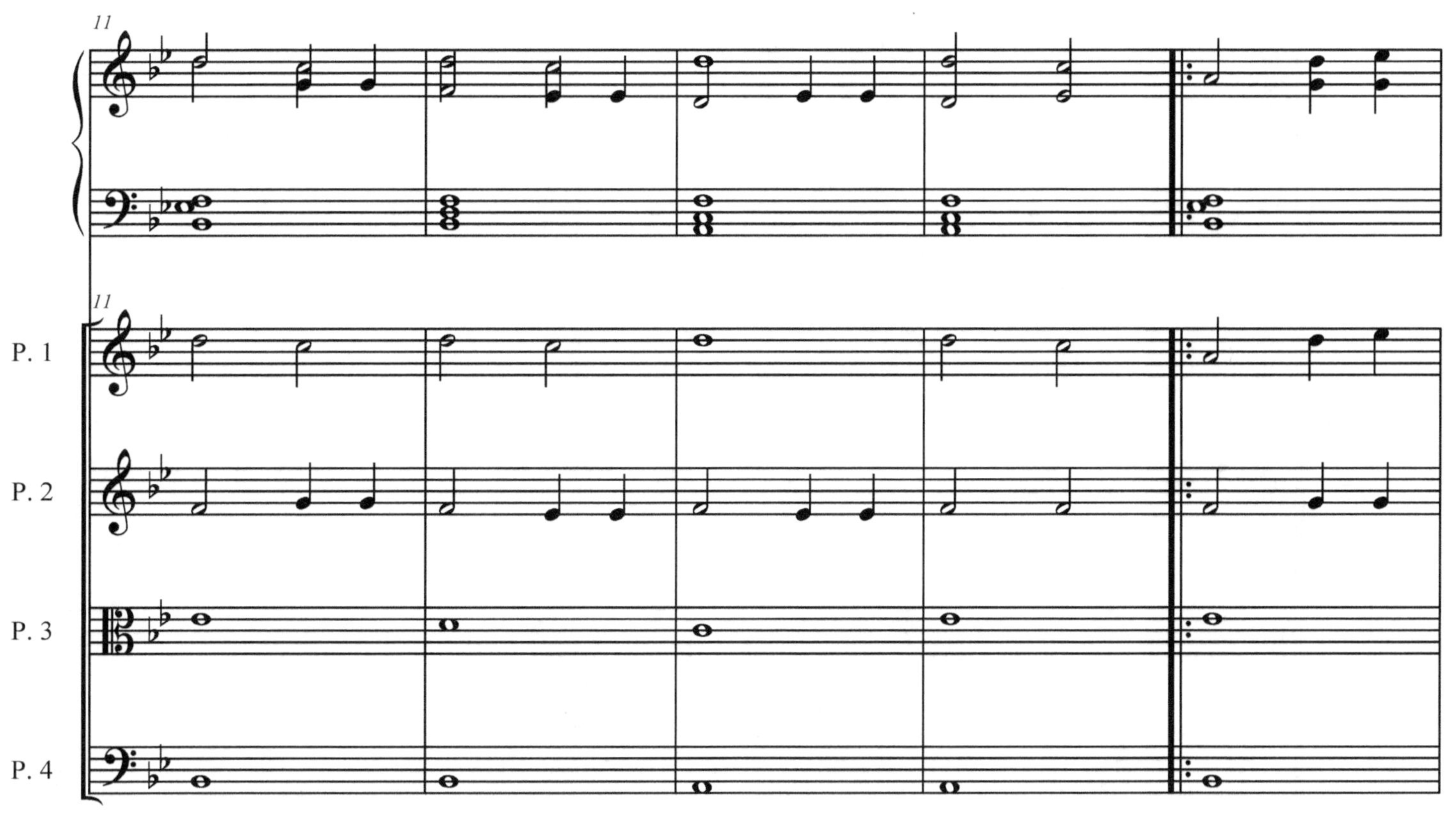
11
11
P. 1
P. 2
P. 3
P. 4

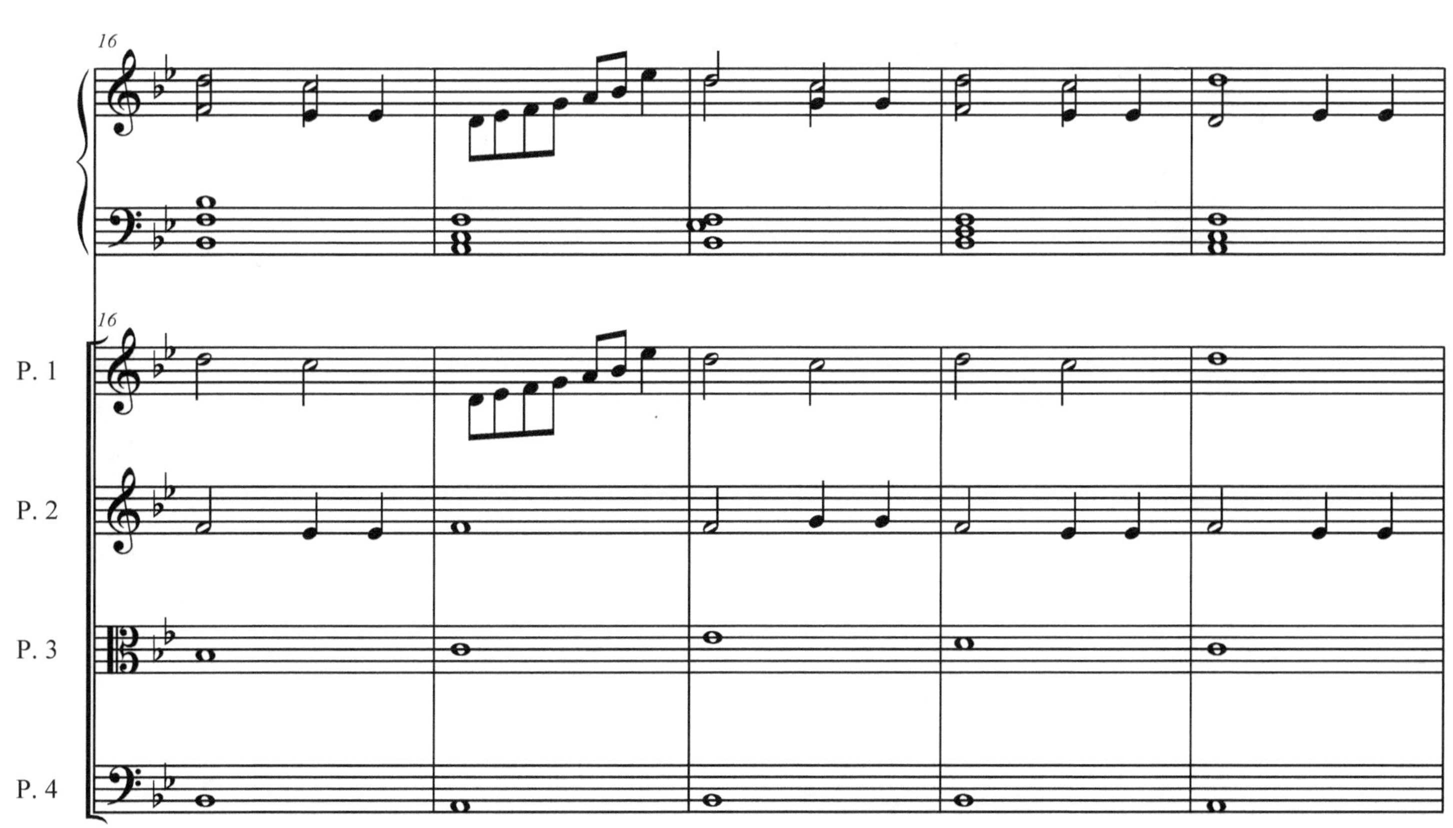
16
16
P. 1
P. 2
P. 3
P. 4

N

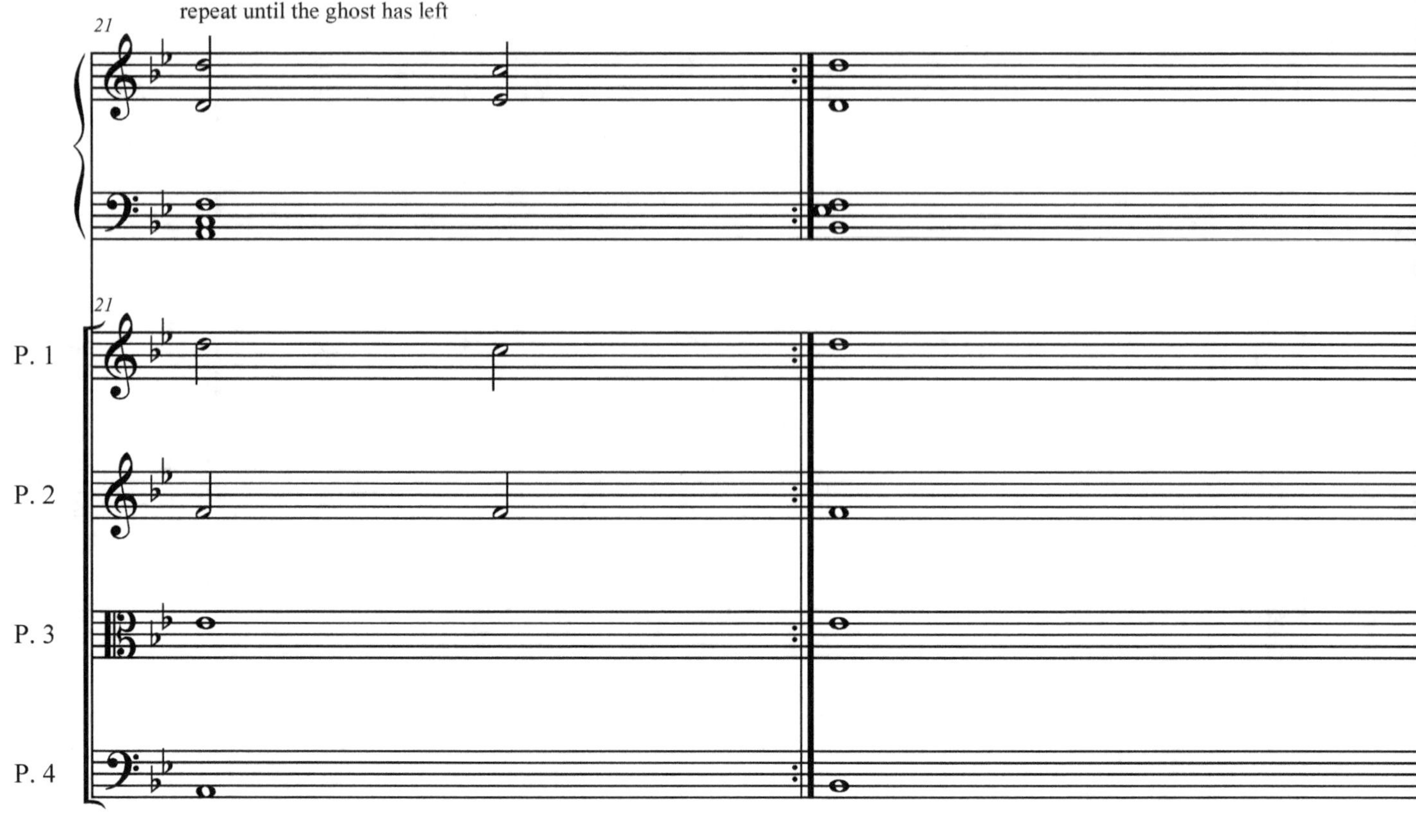

I

Joost de Groot

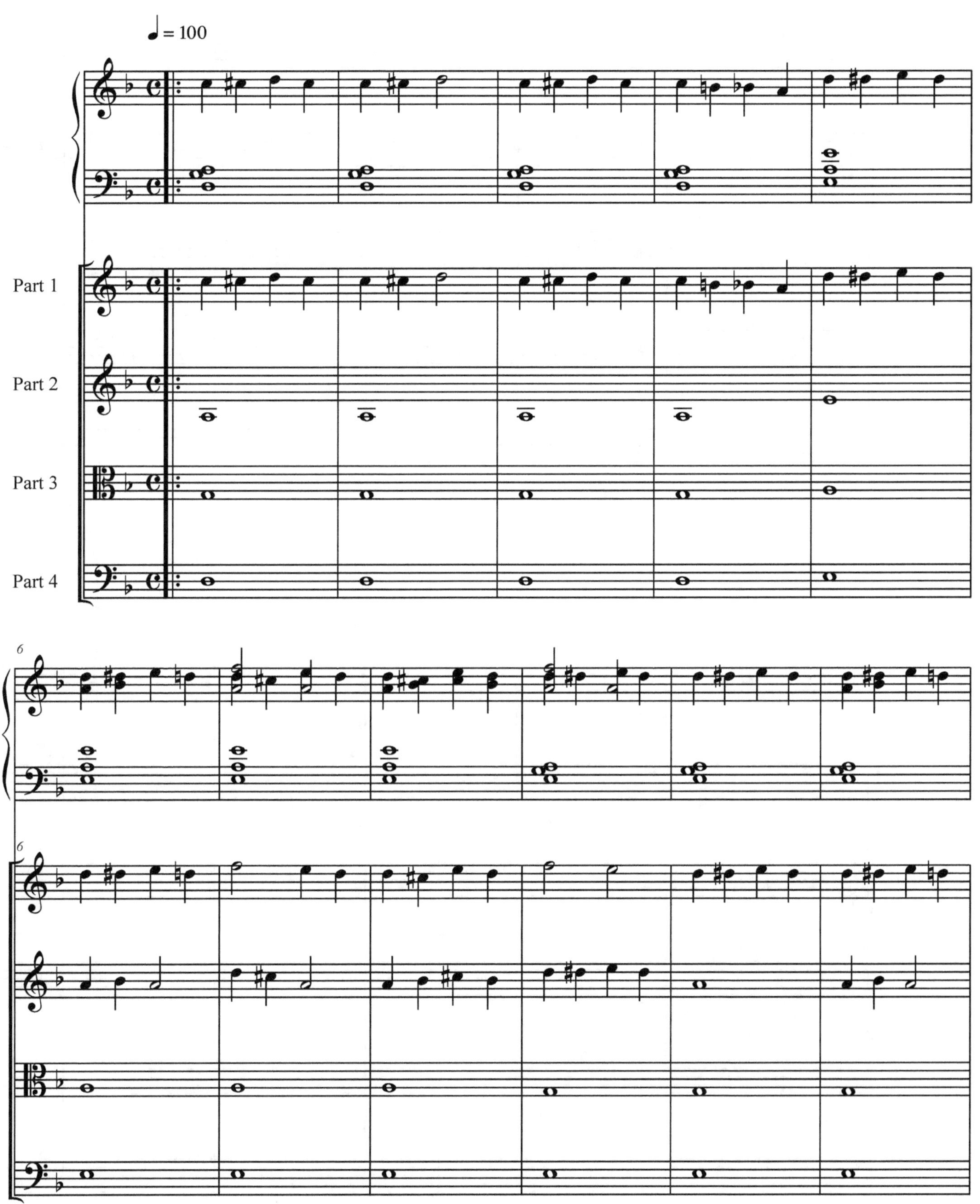

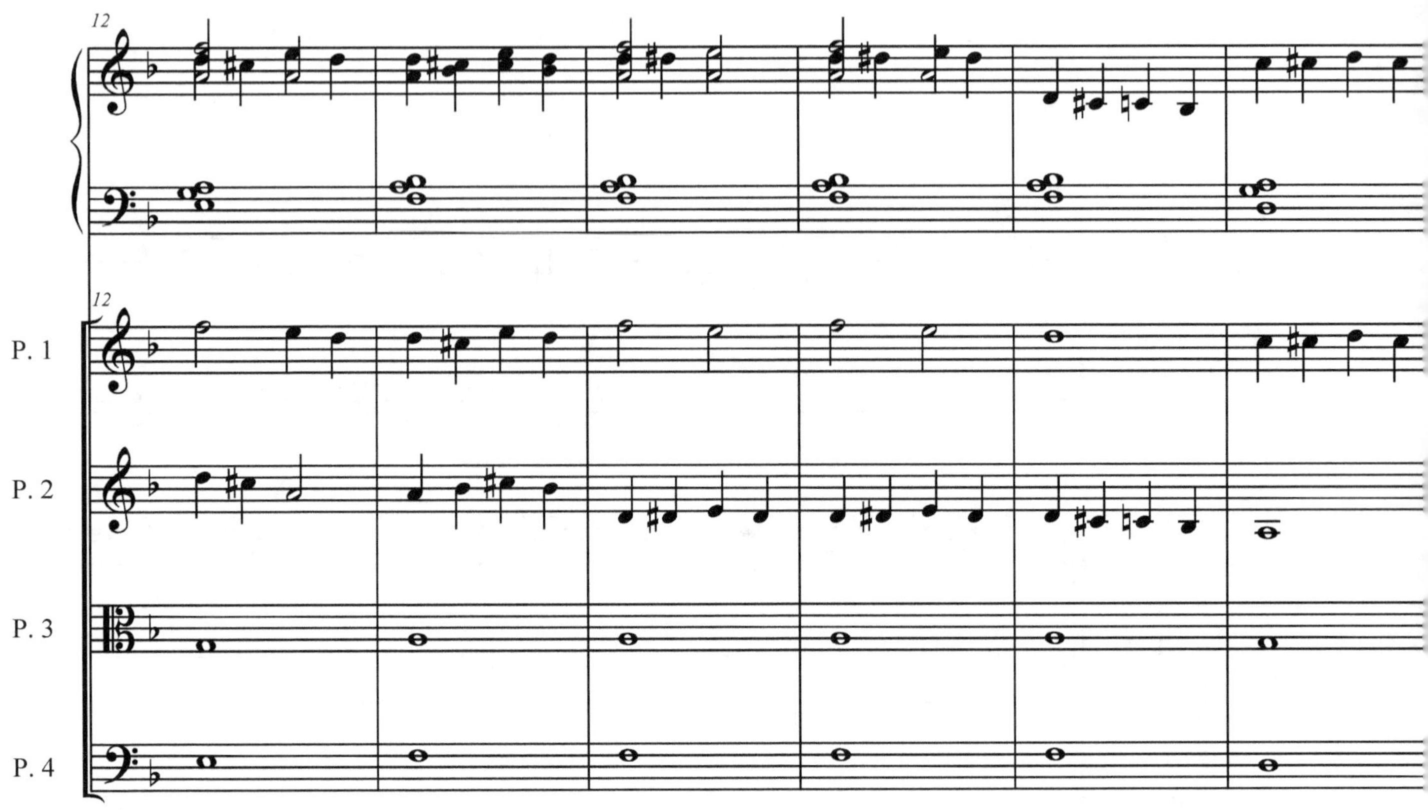
12
12
P. 1
P. 2
P. 3
P. 4

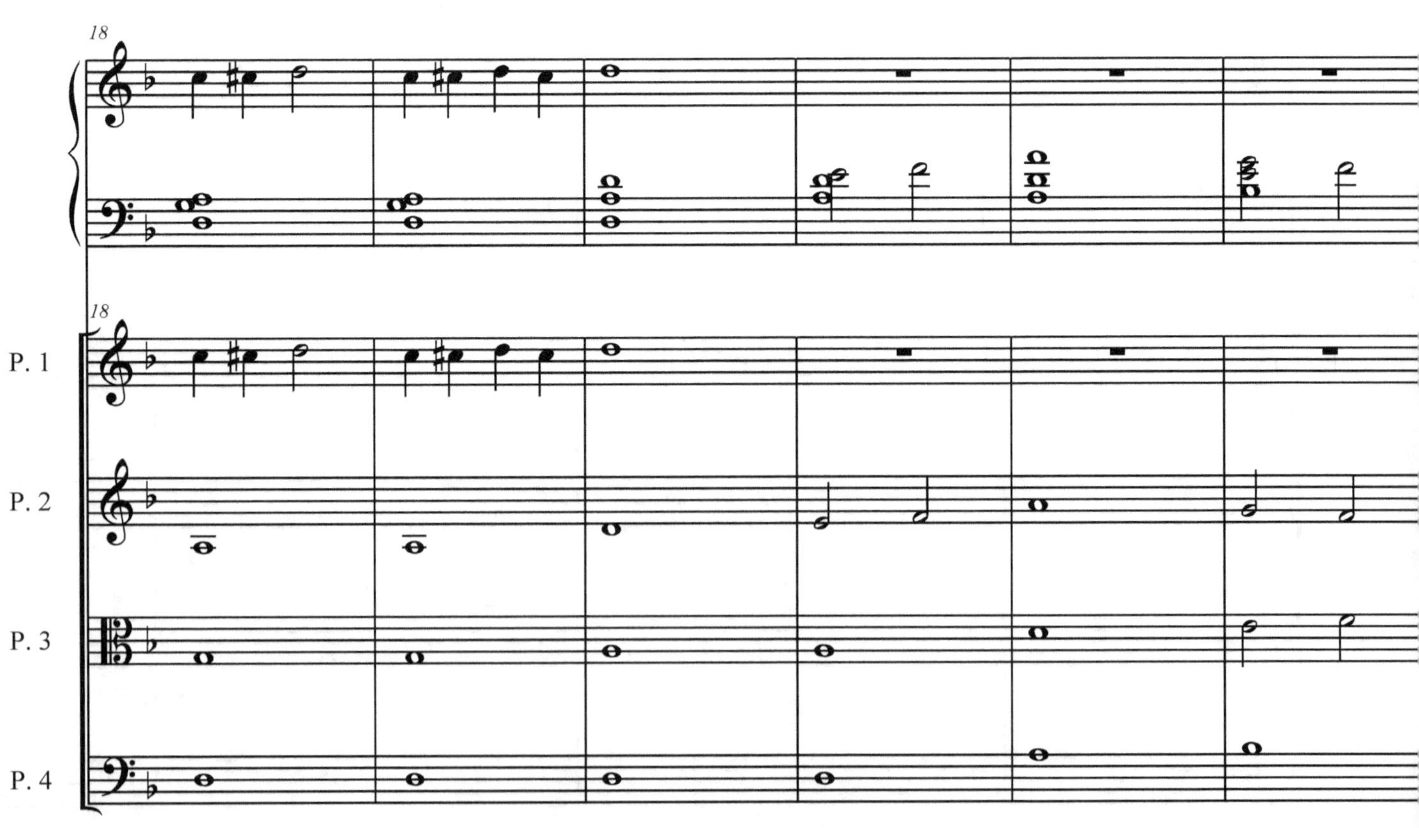
18
18
P. 1
P. 2
P. 3
P. 4

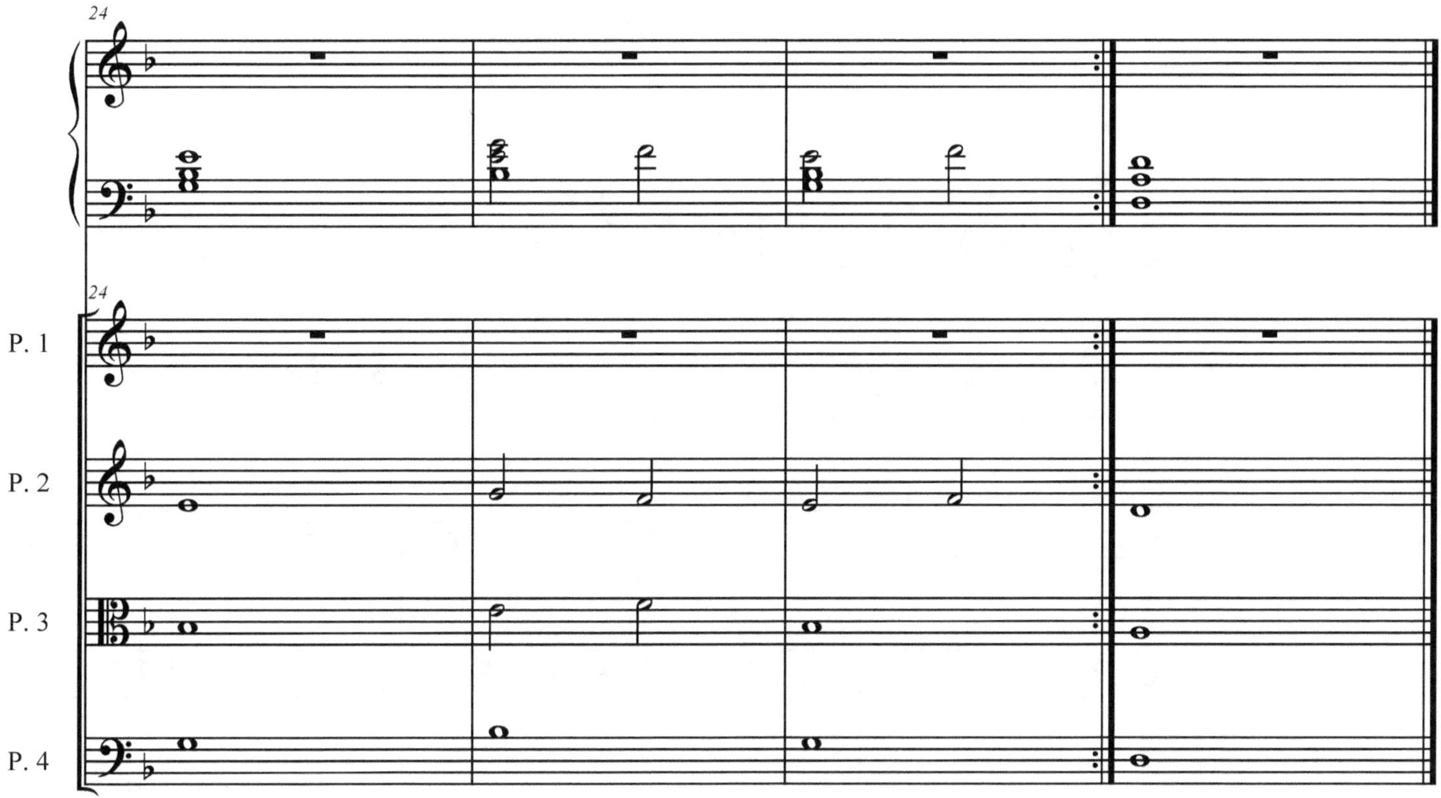
24
24
P. 1
P. 2
P. 3
P. 4

E

Joost de Gro

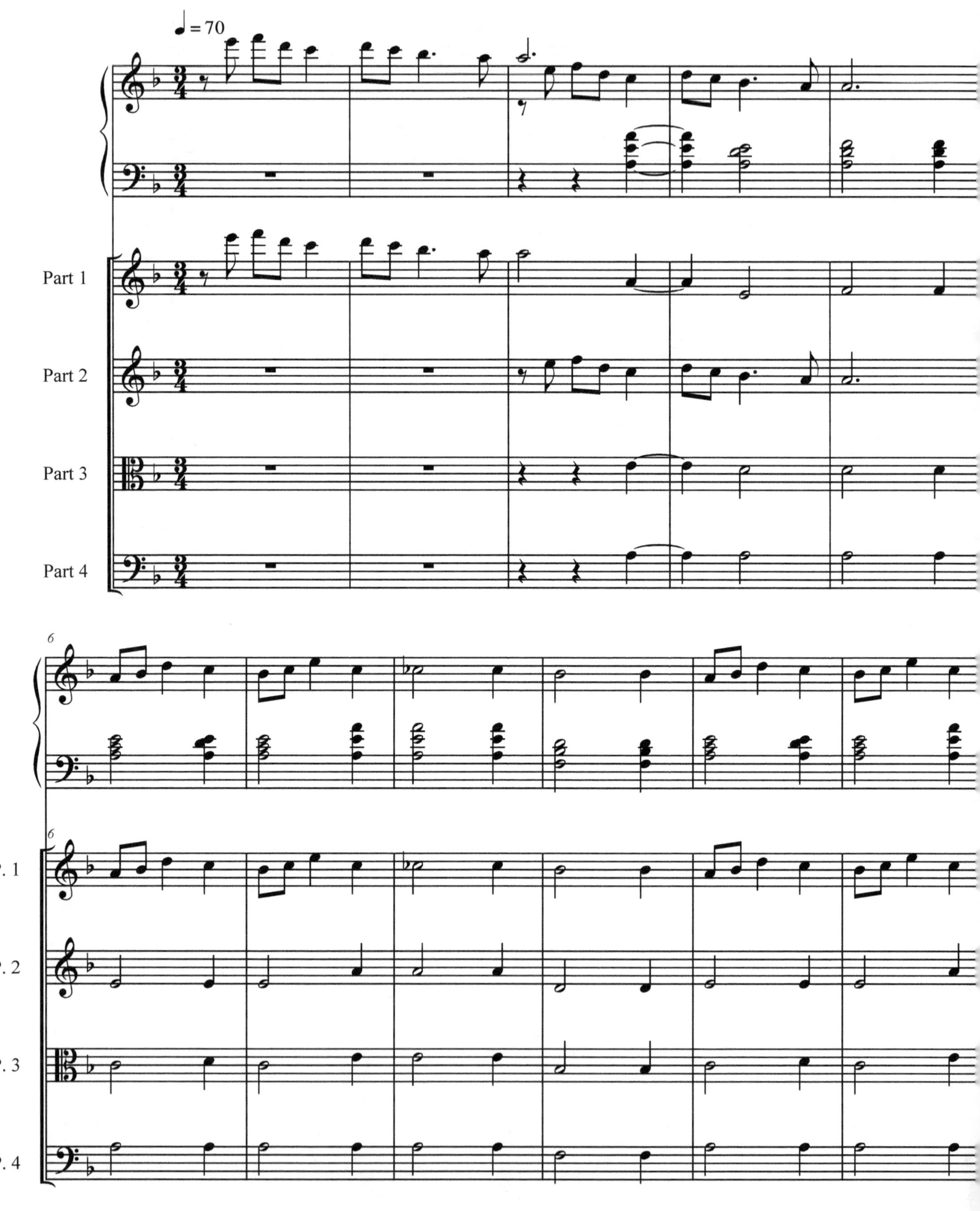

E

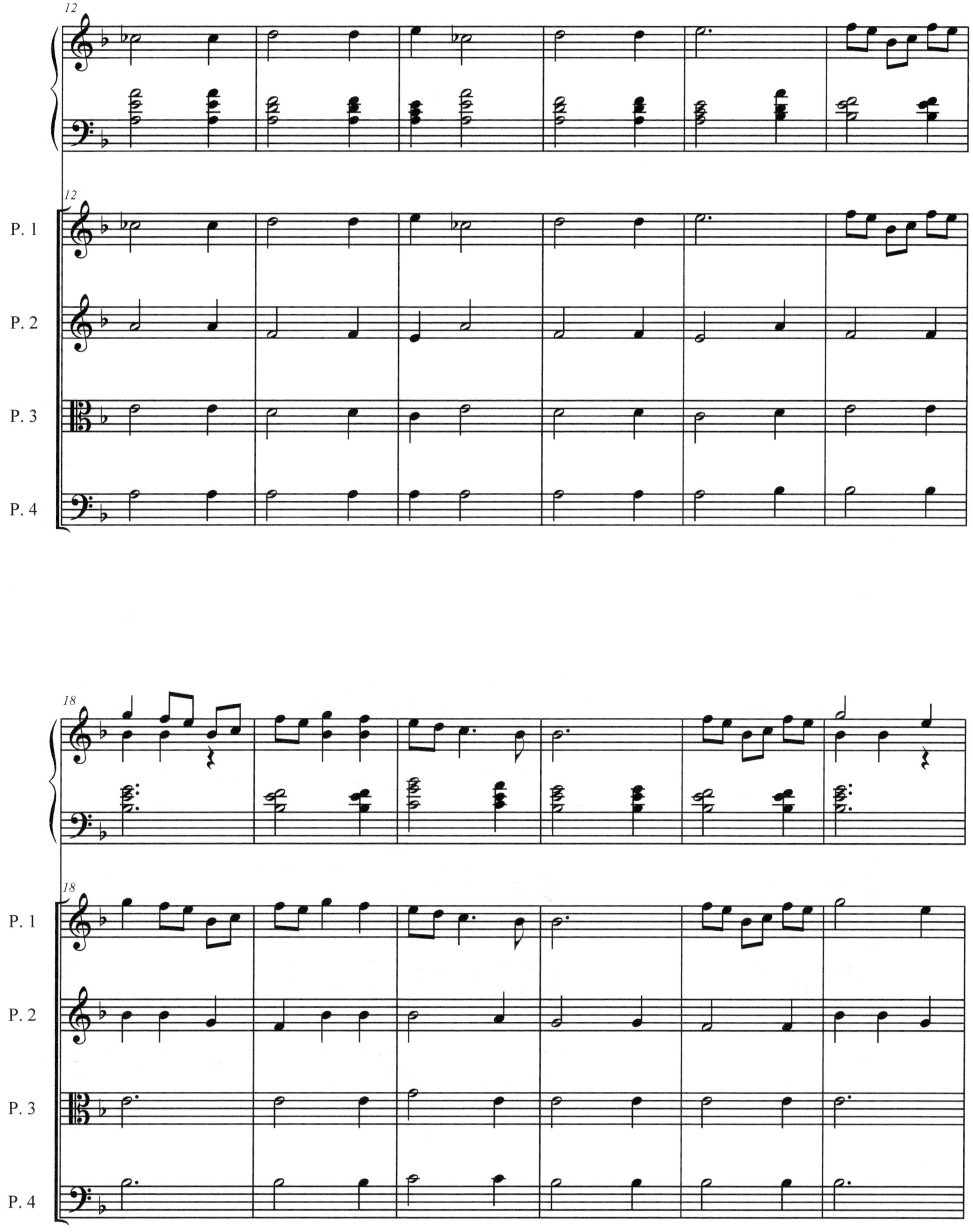

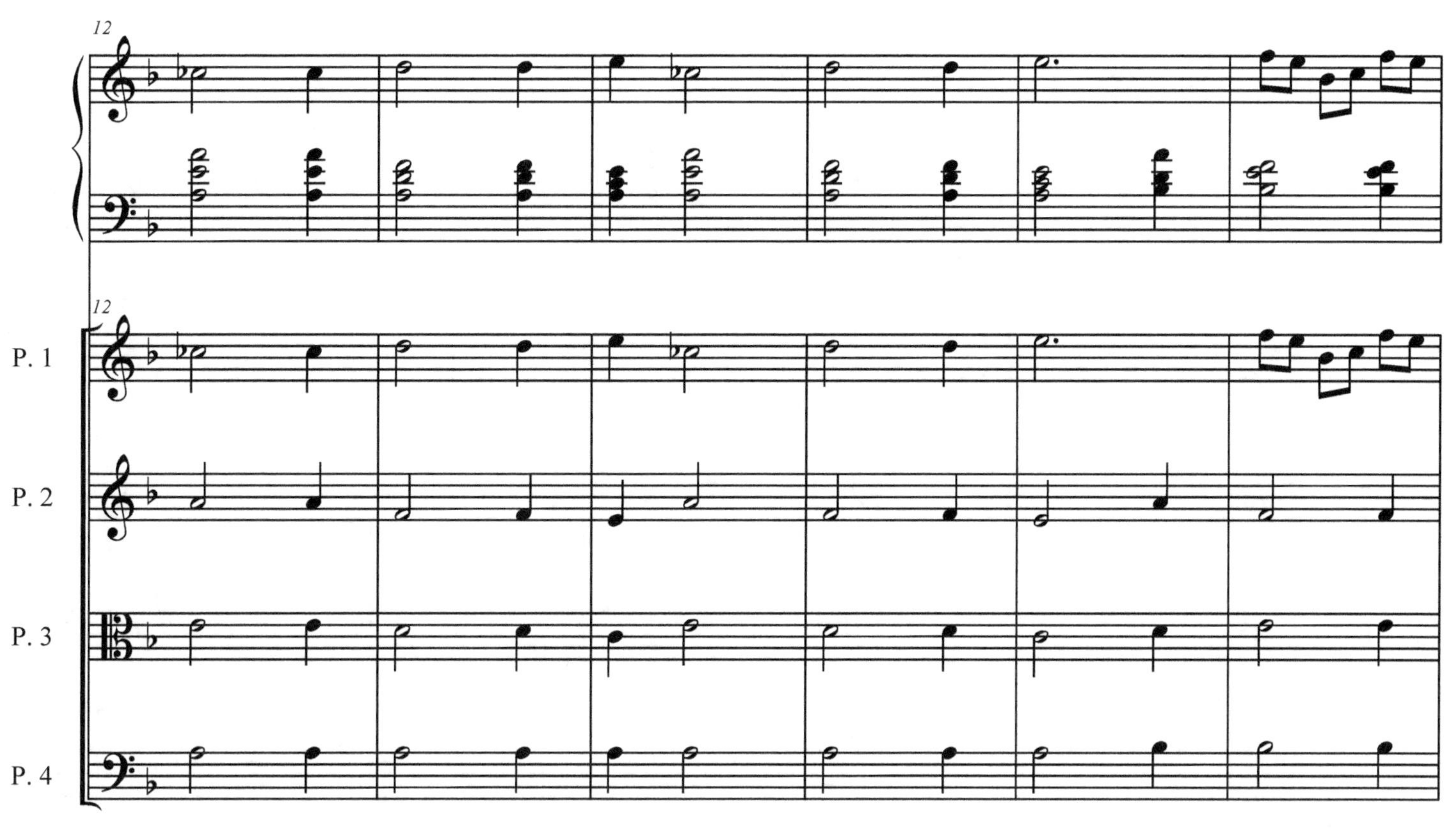

18

18

P. 1

P. 2

P. 3

P. 4

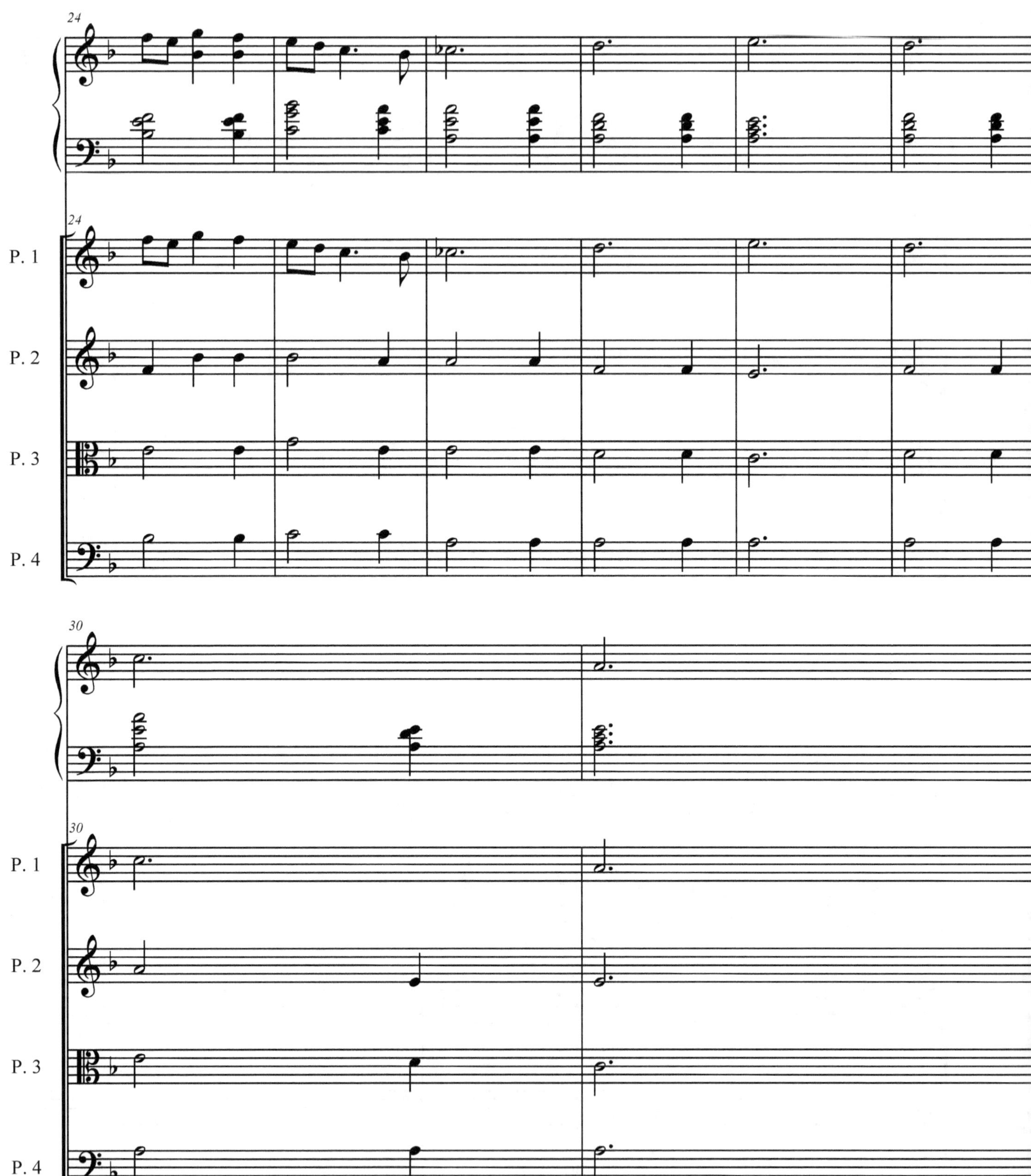
24
P. 1
P. 2
P. 3
P. 4
30

J

Piano/Organ

Joost de Groot

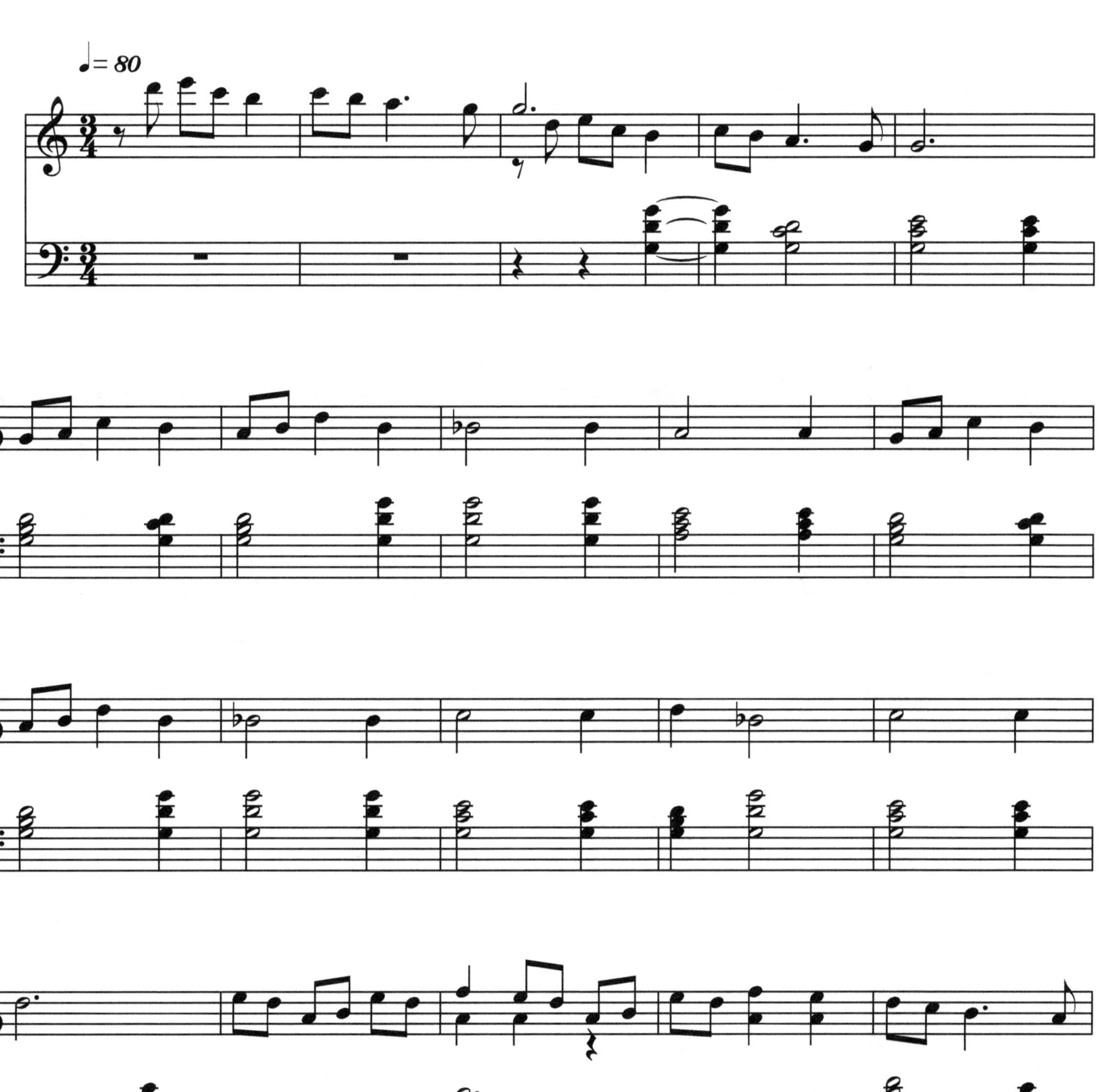

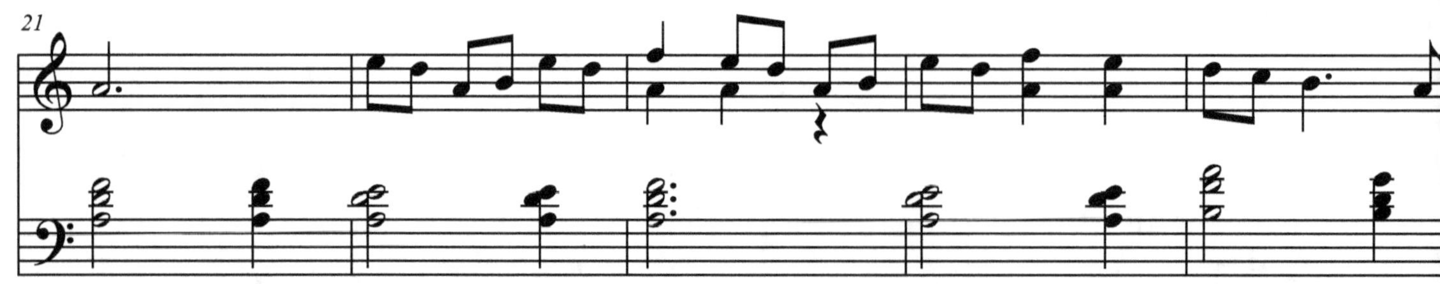
21

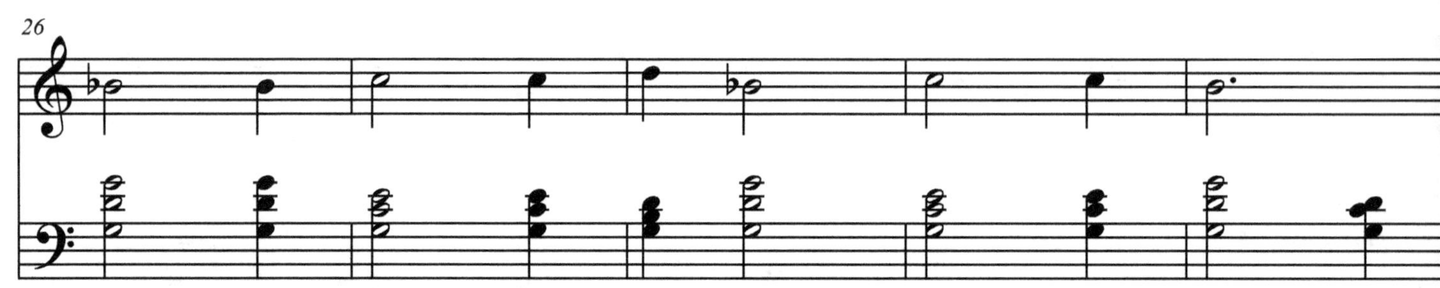
26

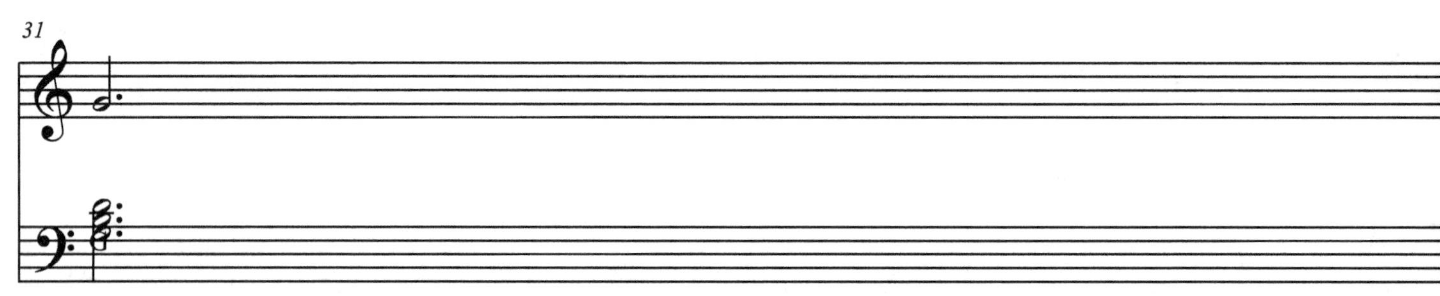
31

A

Piano/Organ

Joost de Groot

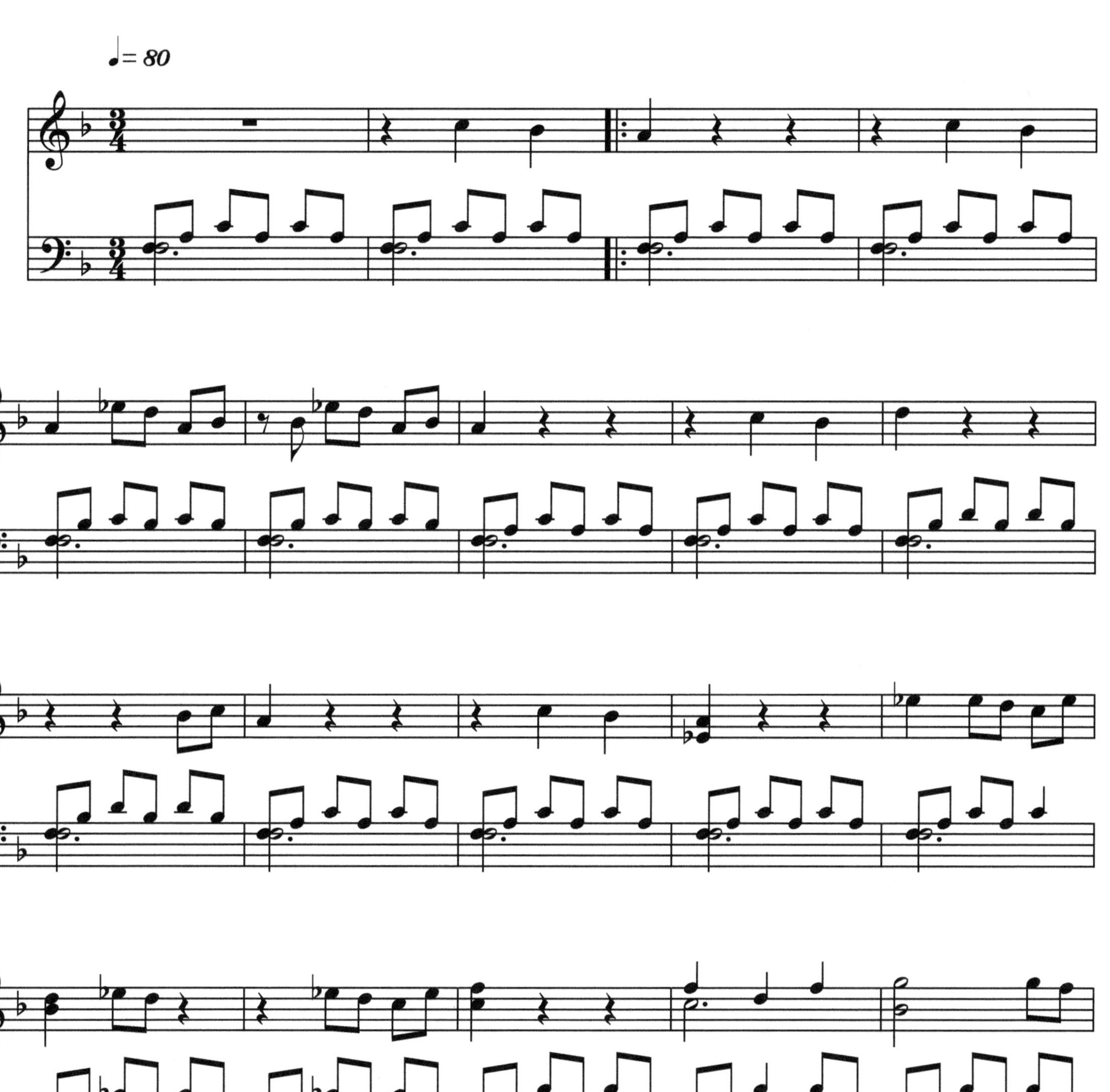

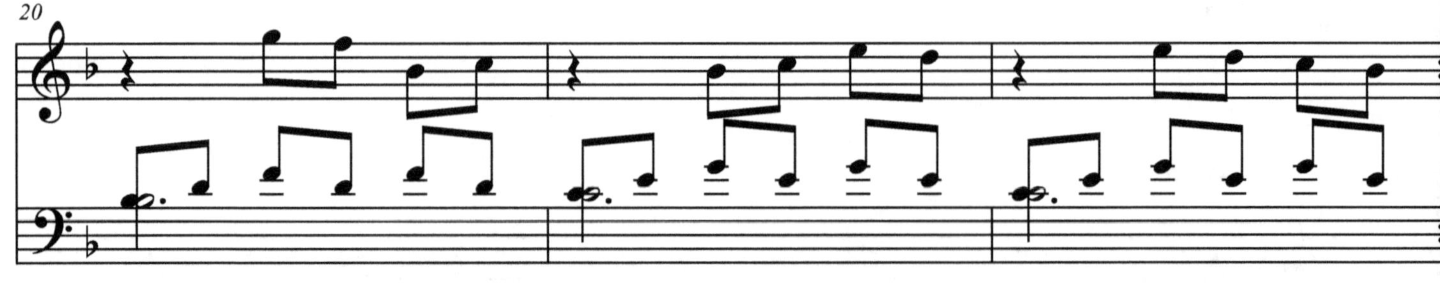
20

Piano/Organ

N

Joost de Groot

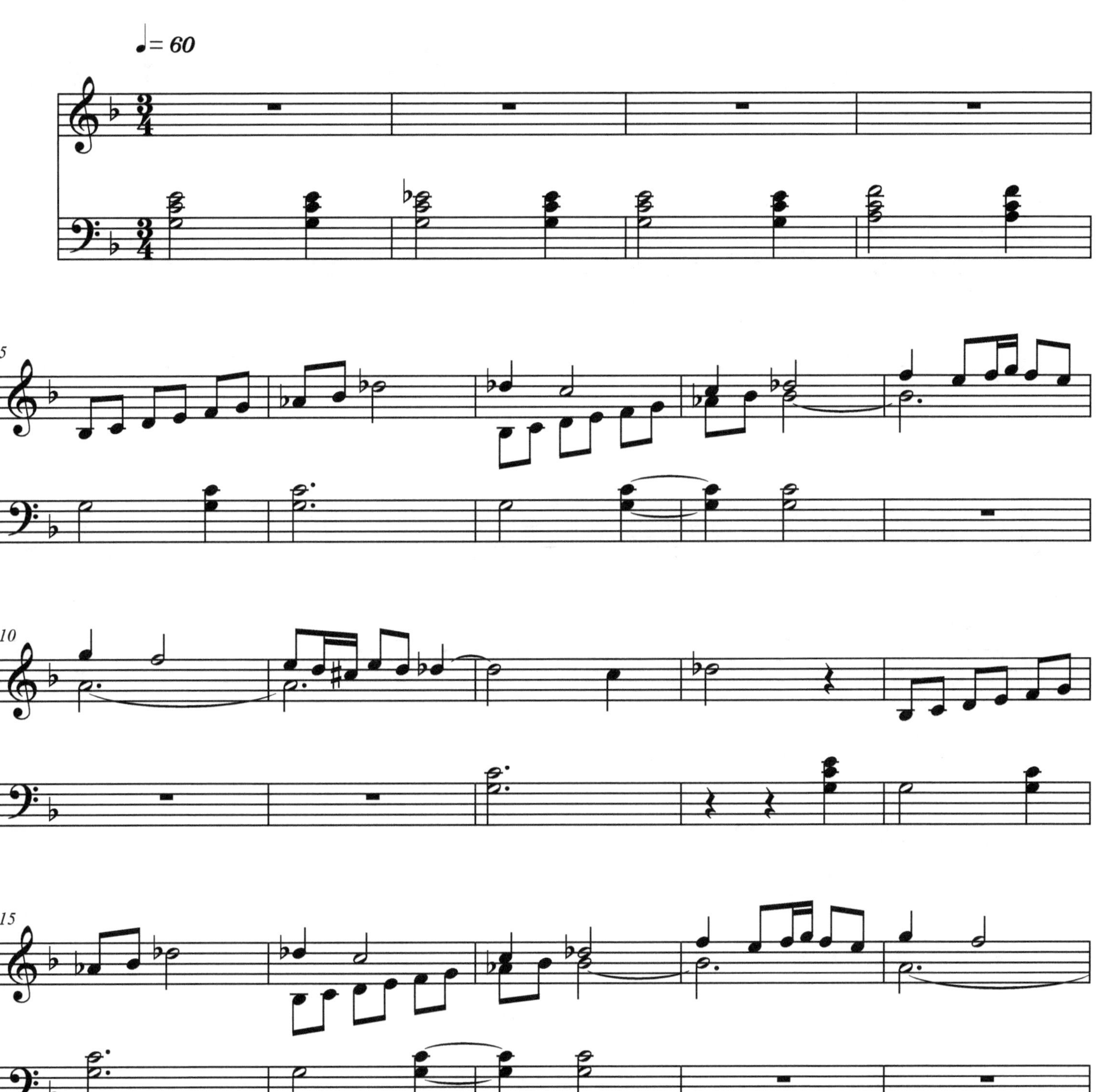

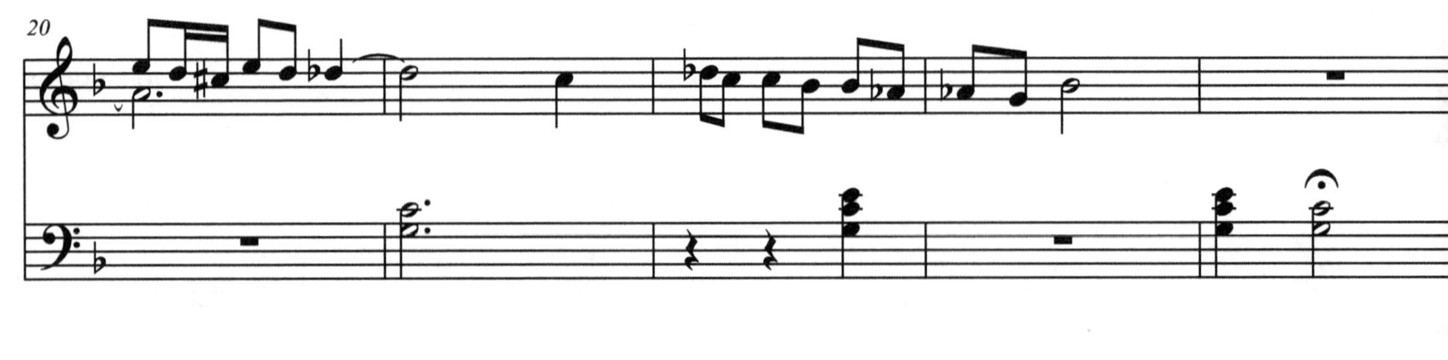
20

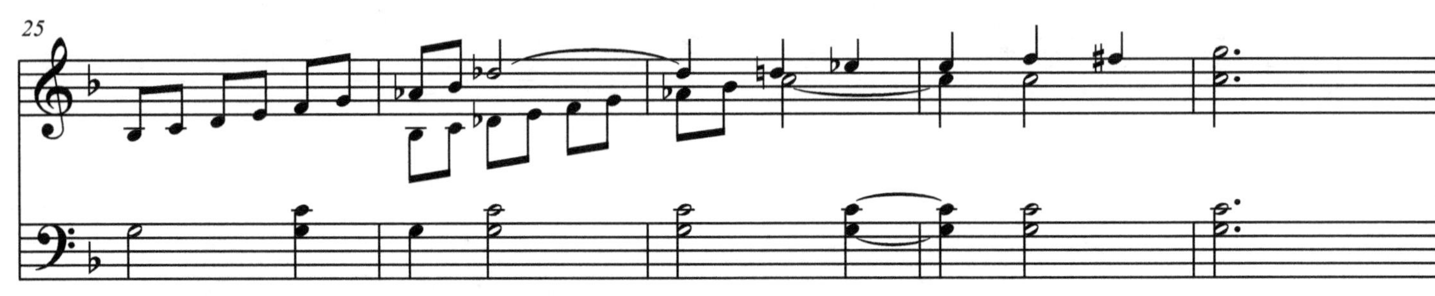
25

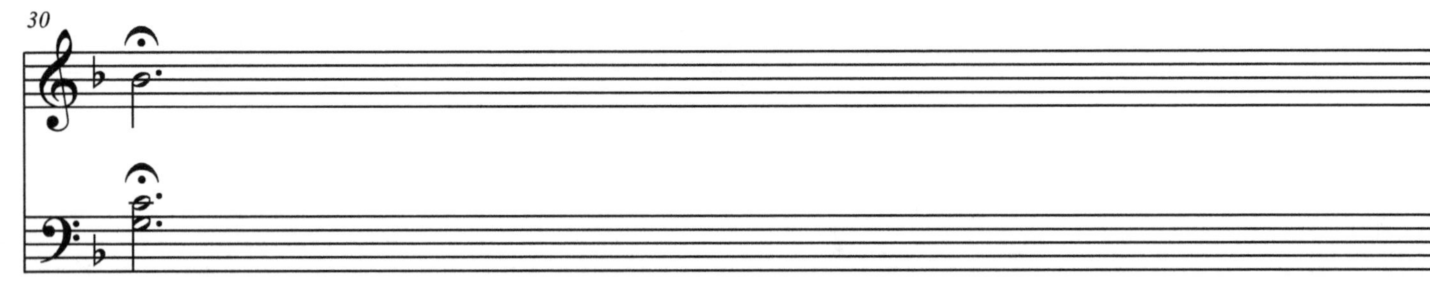
30

Piano/Organ

N

Joost de Groot

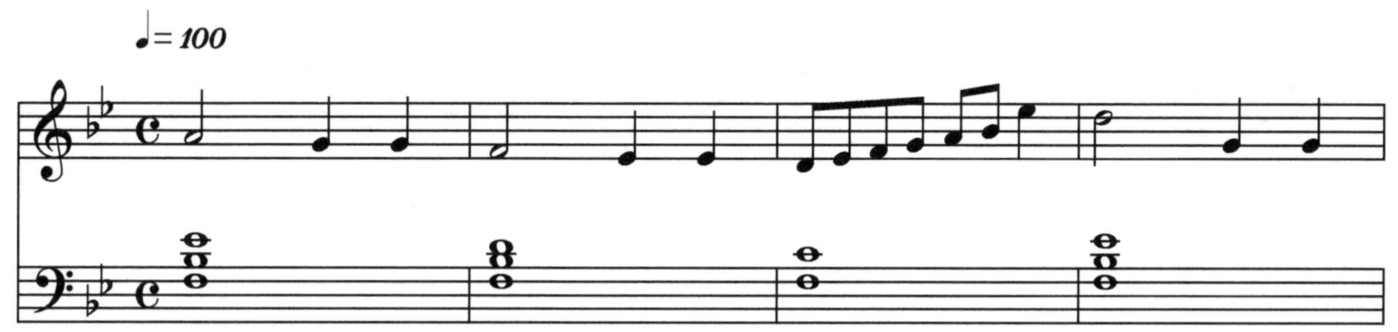

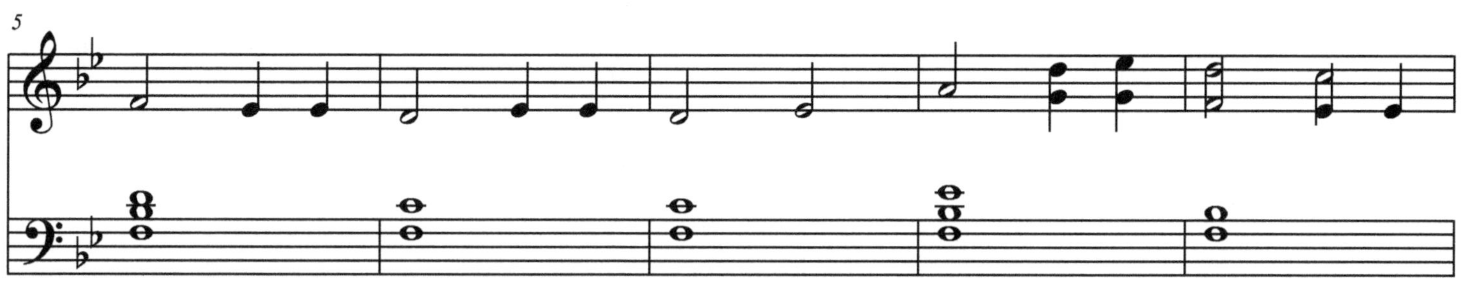

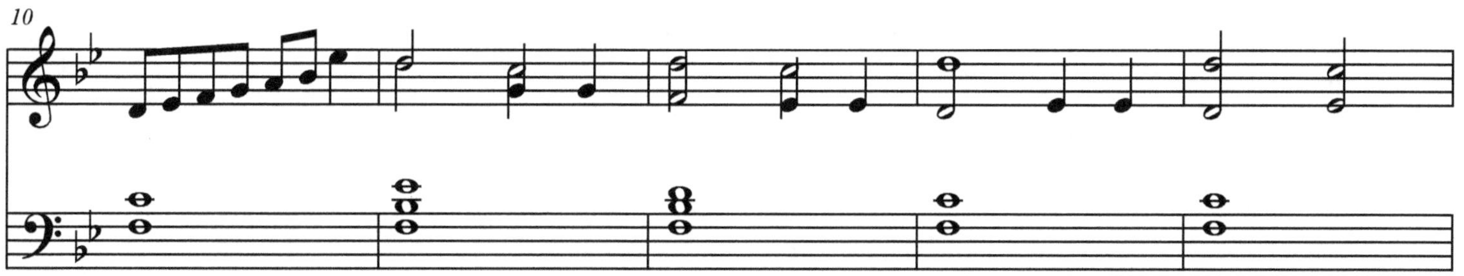

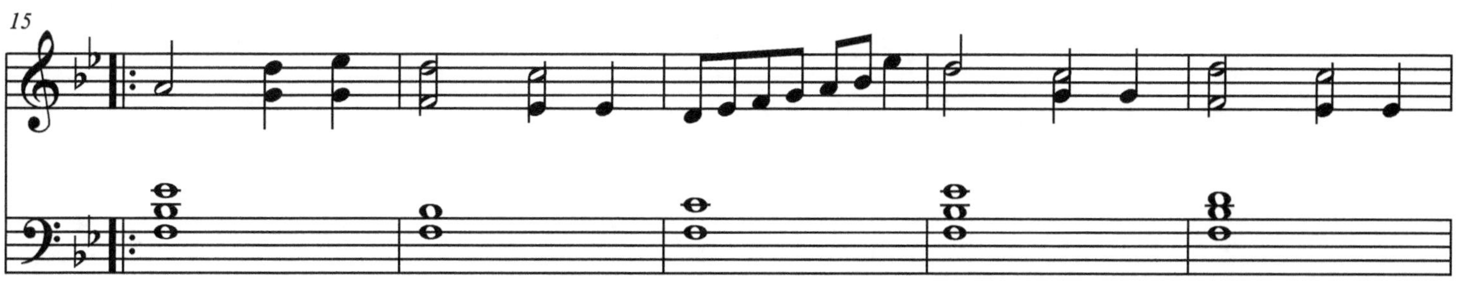

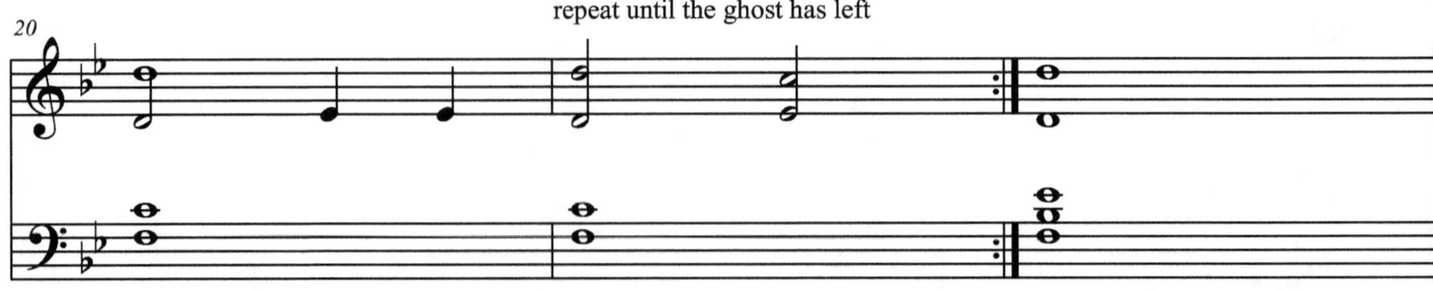
repeat until the ghost has left
20

I

Piano/Organ

Joost de Groot

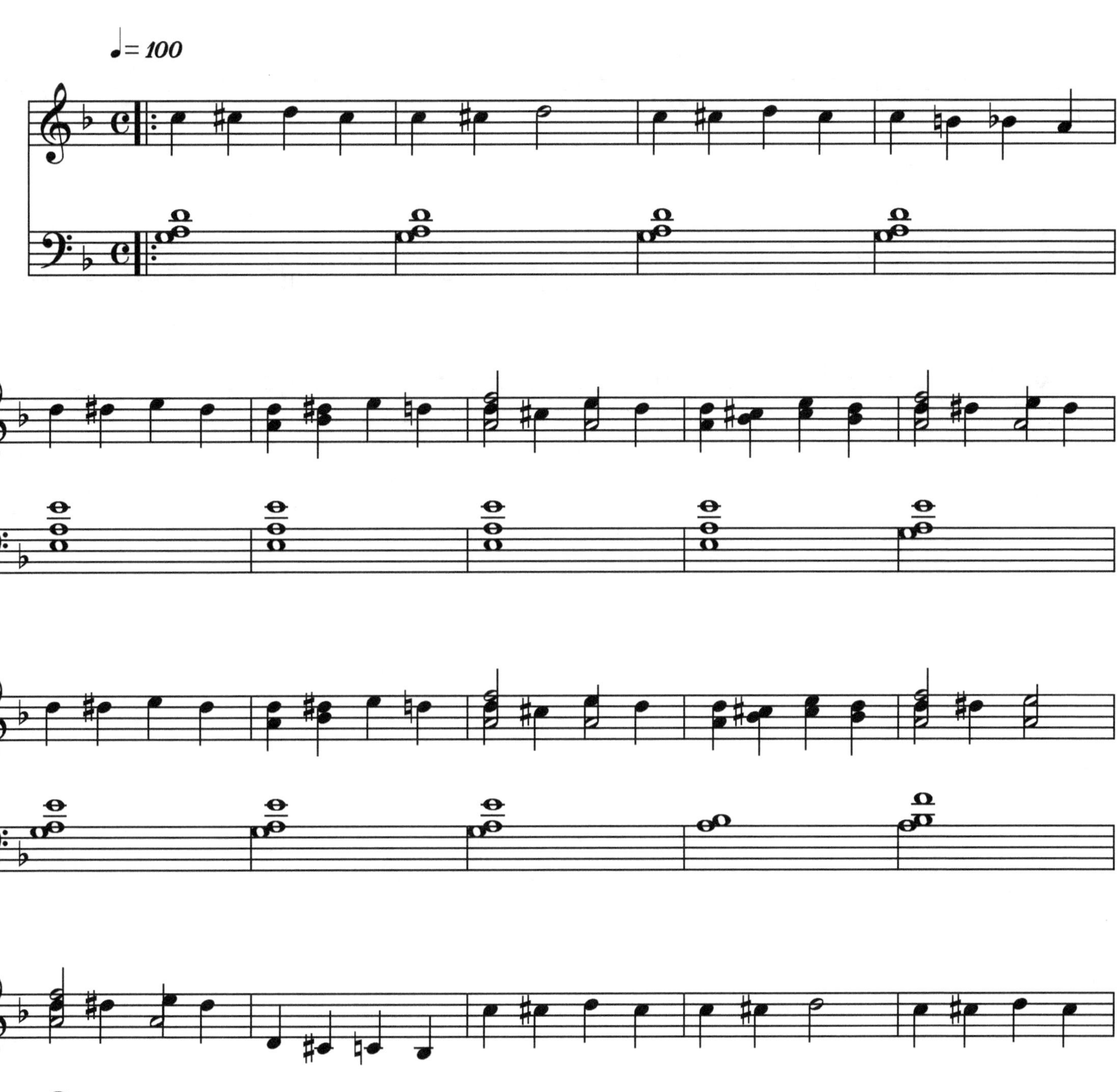

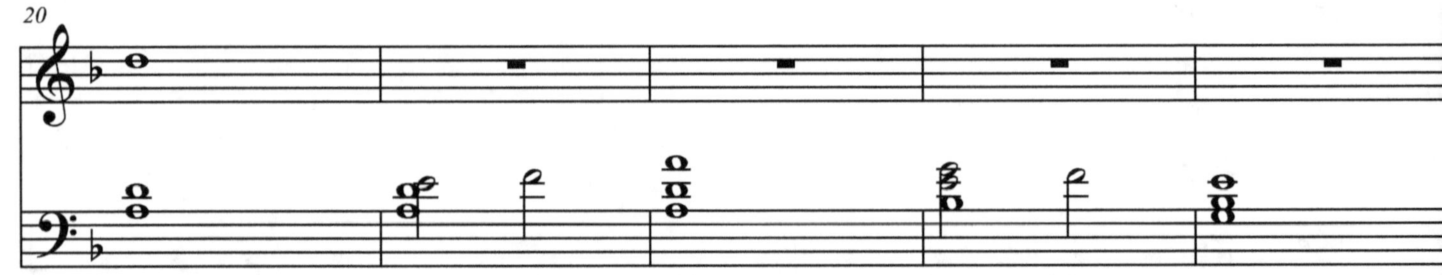
20

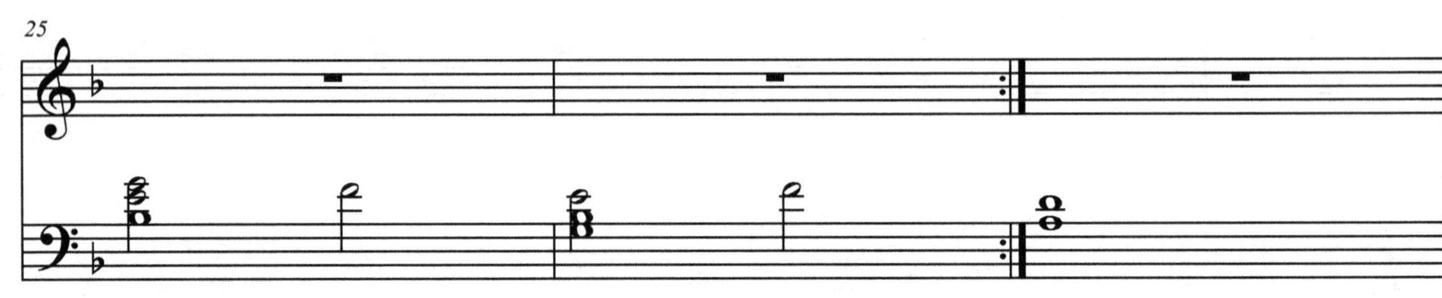
25

E

Piano/Organ

Joost de Groot

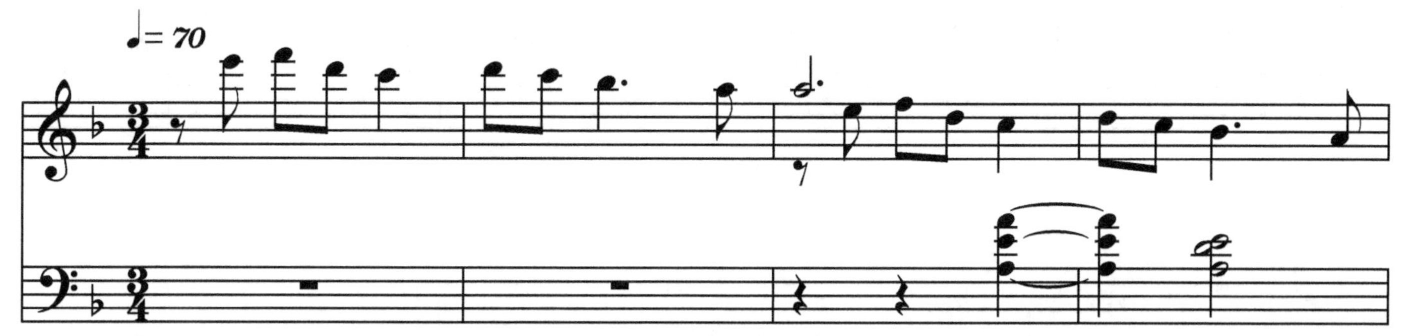

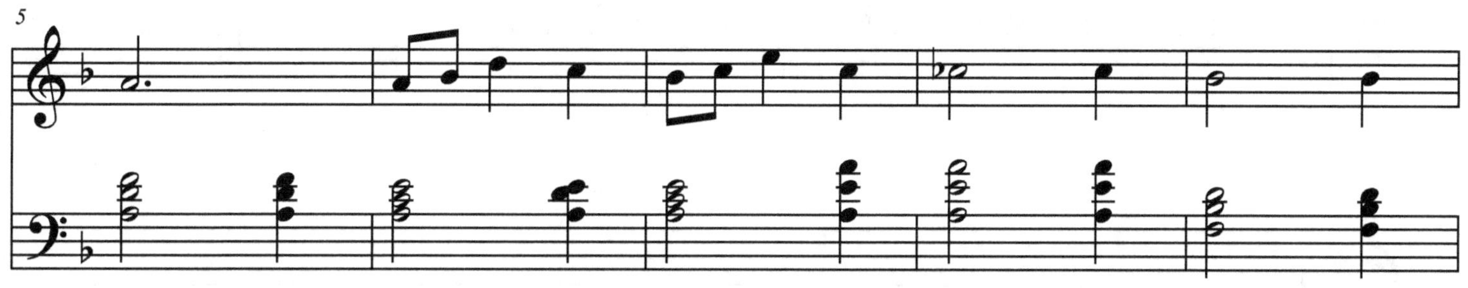

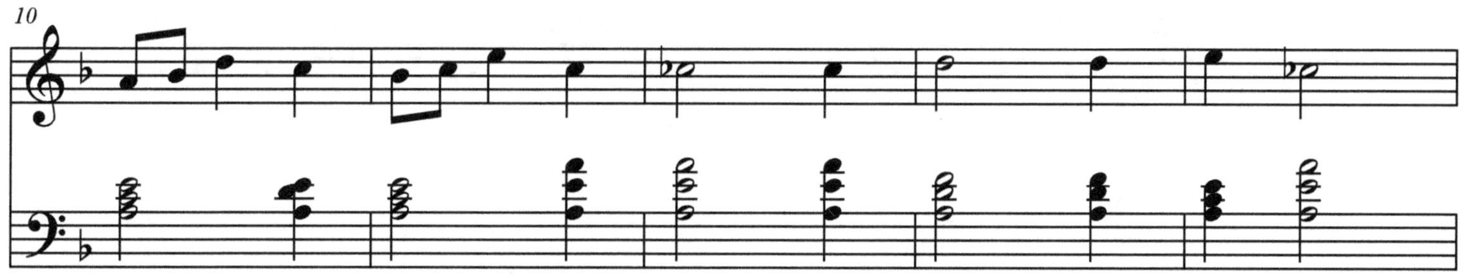

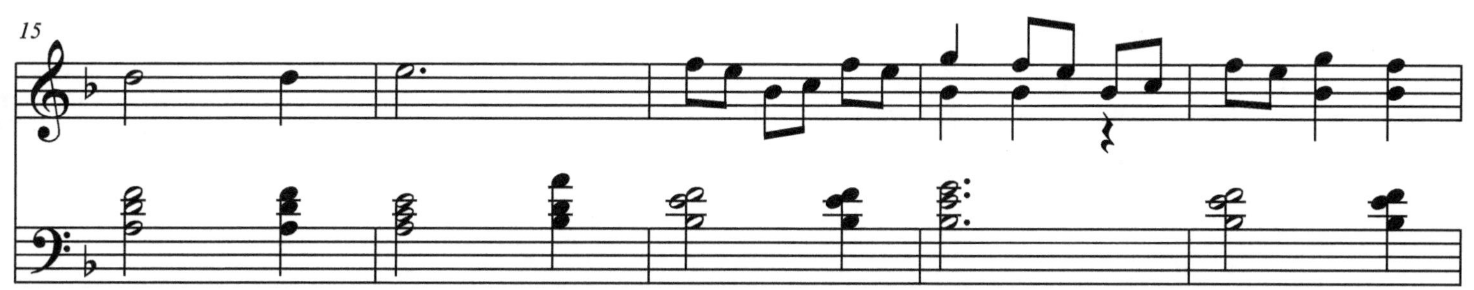

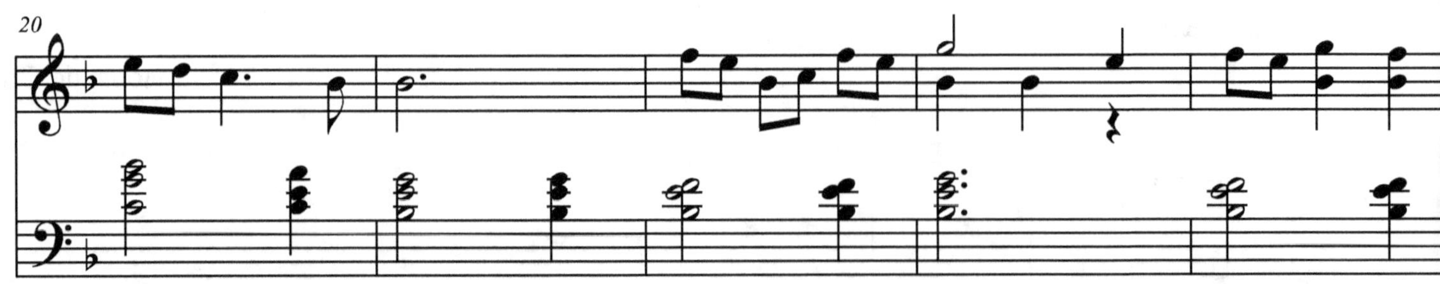
20

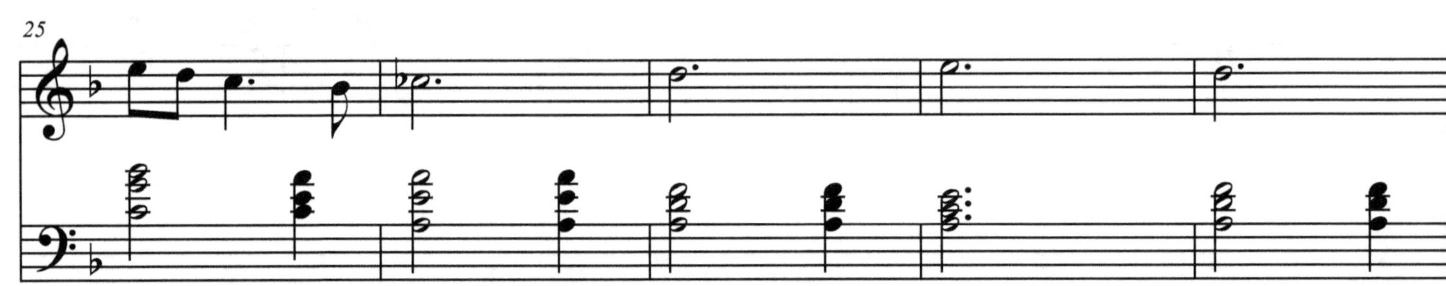
25

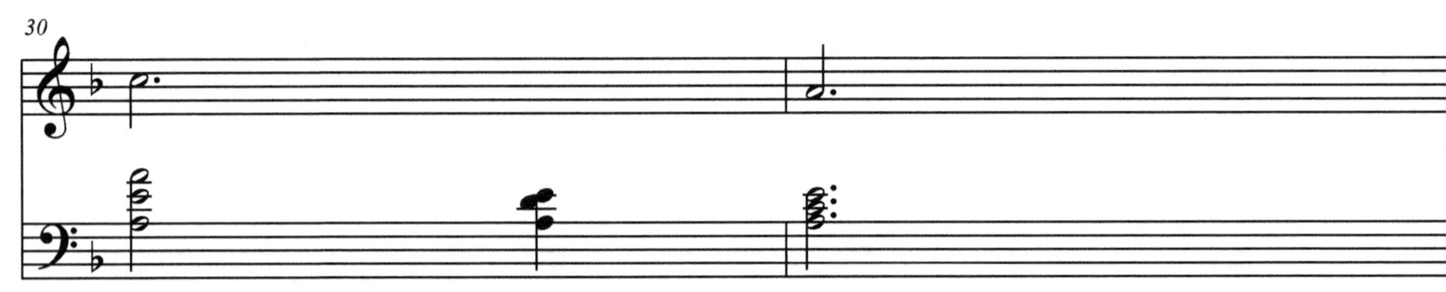
30

Guitar Duo

Part 1: Guitar 1

Part 2: Guitar 2

Guitar 1

J

Joost de Gro

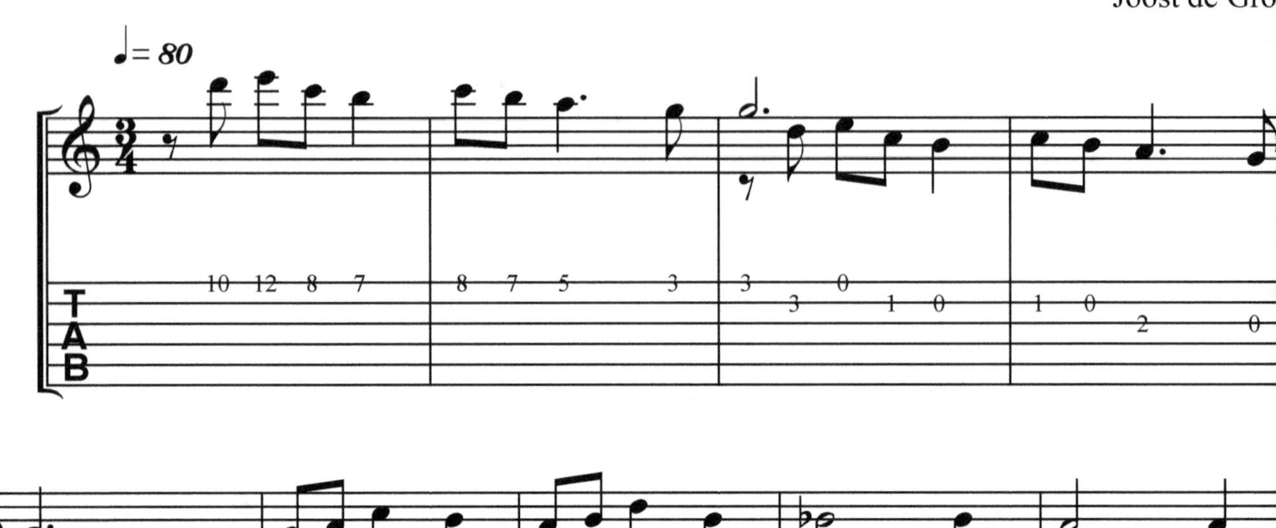

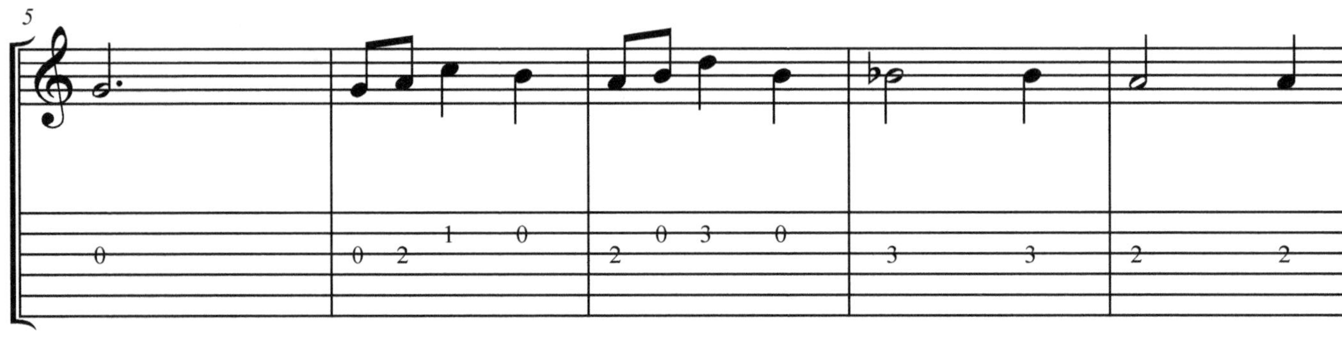

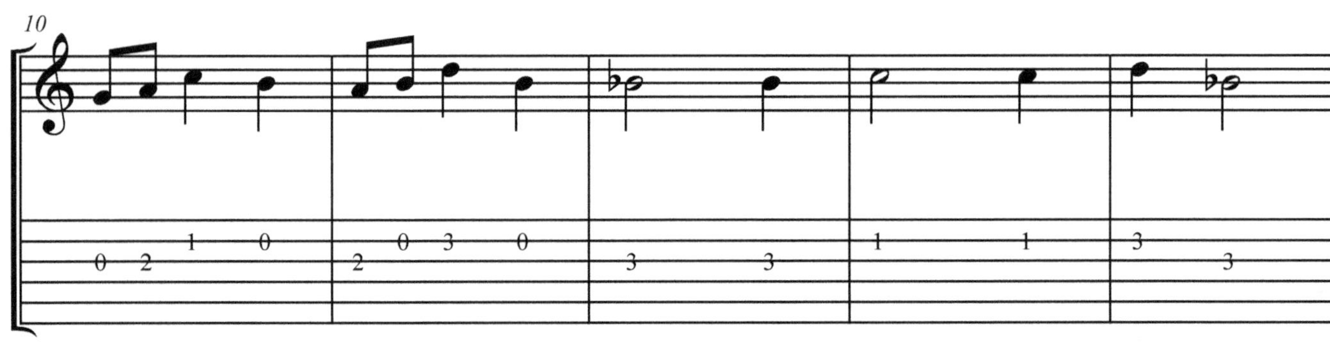

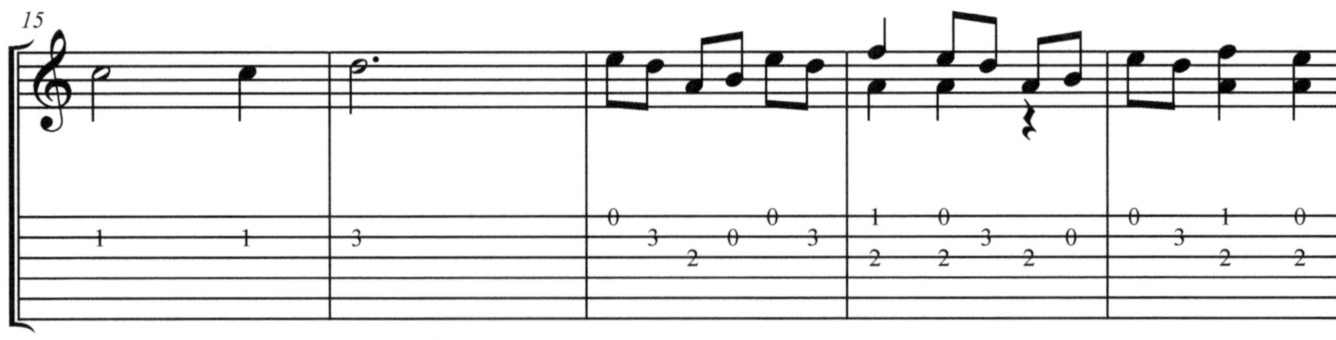

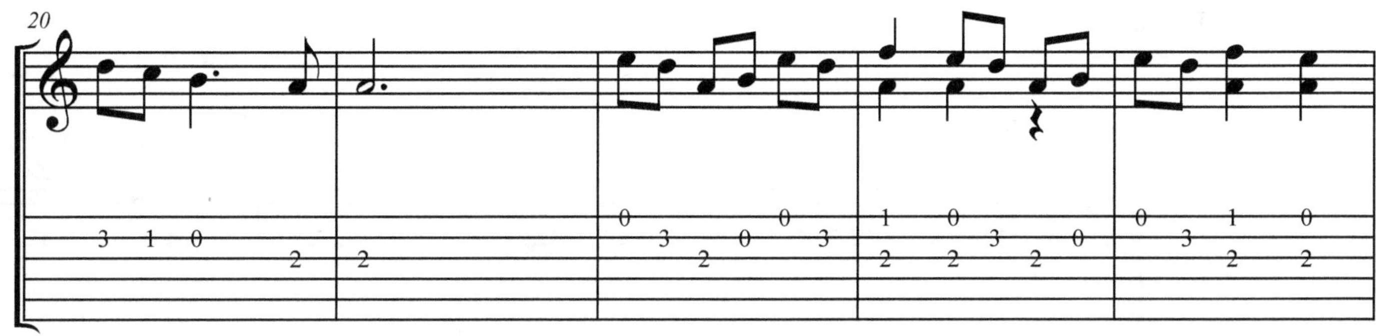
20
3 1 0 2
2
0 3 2 0 0 3
1 0 2 2 3 2 0
0 3 1 2 0 2

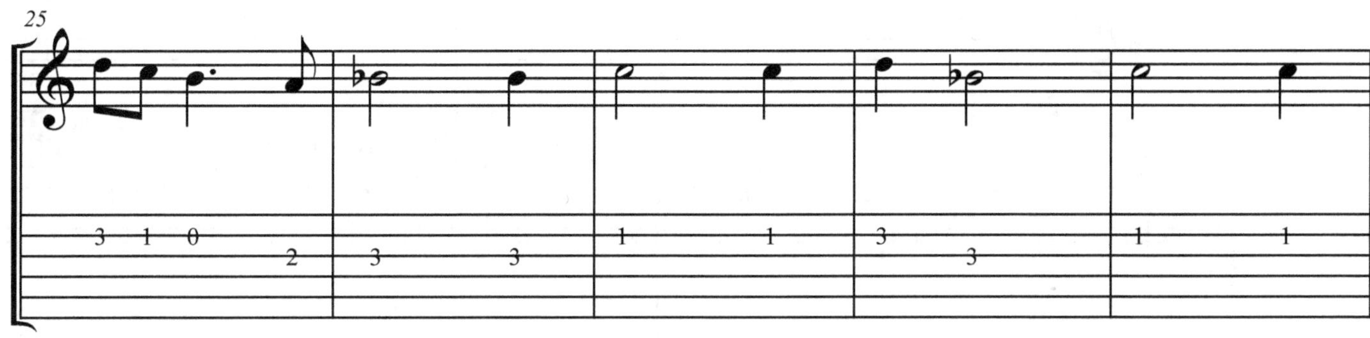
25
3 1 0 2
3 3
1 1
3 3
1 1

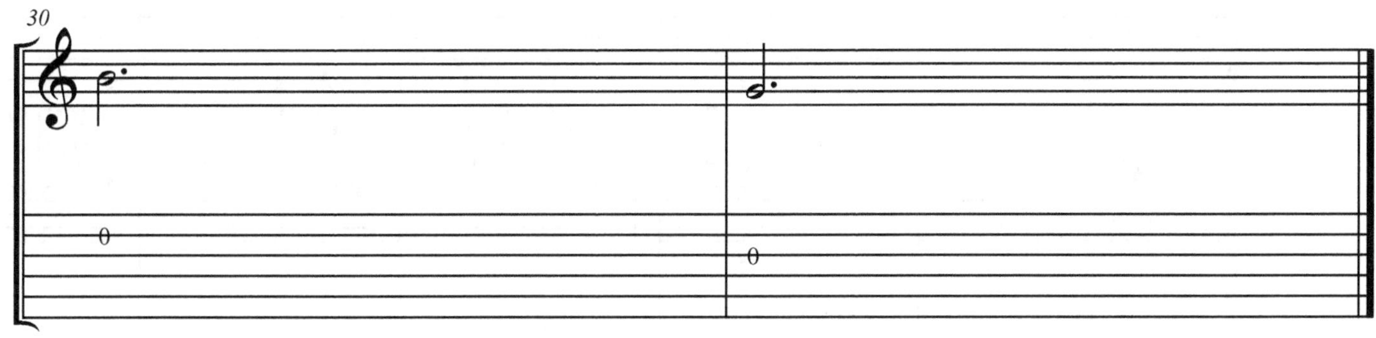
30
0
0

Guitar 2

J

Joost de Groo
♩= 80
G
G sus4
C/G
G
G sus4
G
G
G min
3fr.
A min
G
G sus4
G
G
G min
3fr.
C/G
G
G min
C/G
G
Am7
A sus4
D min/A
A sus4

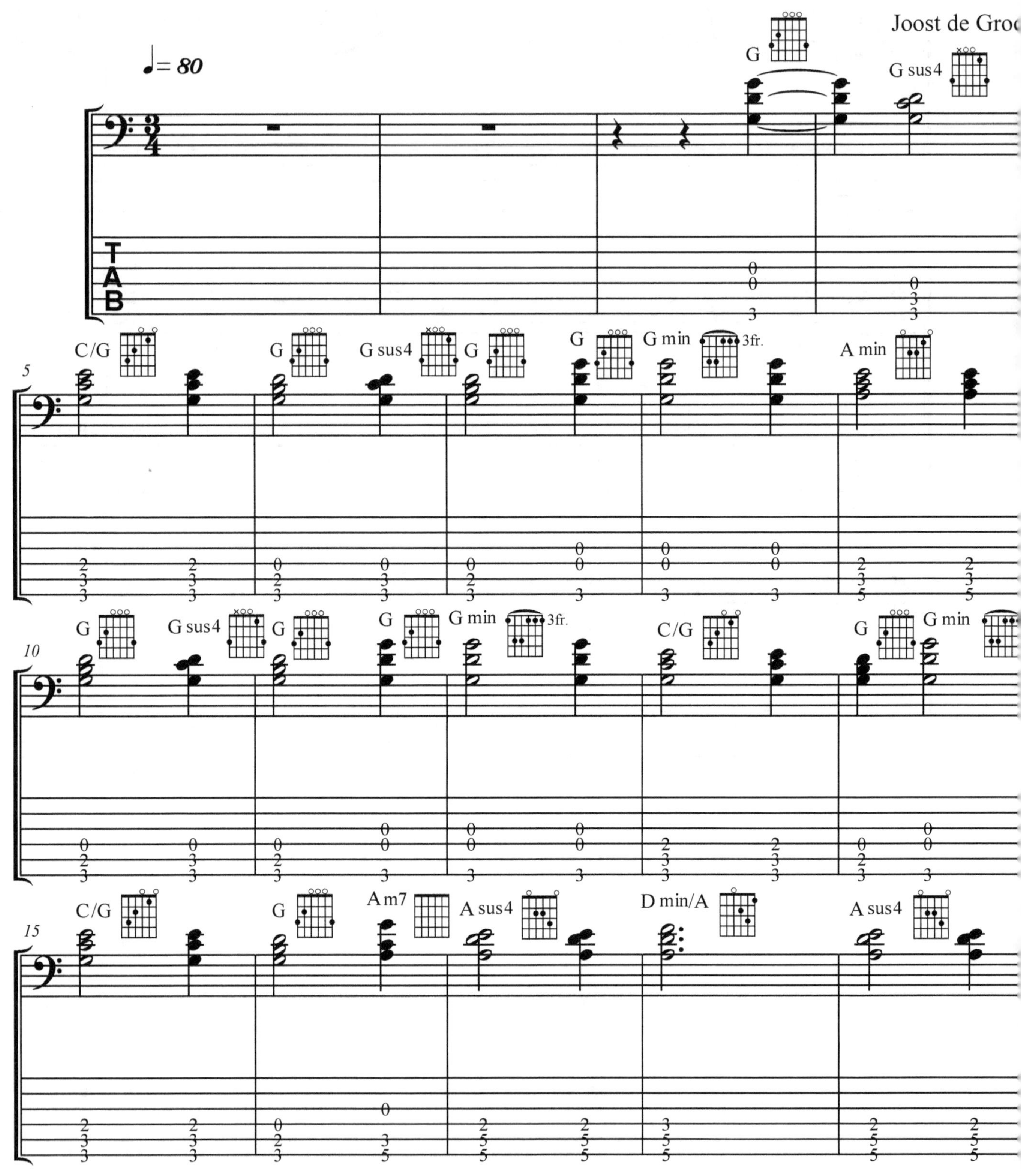

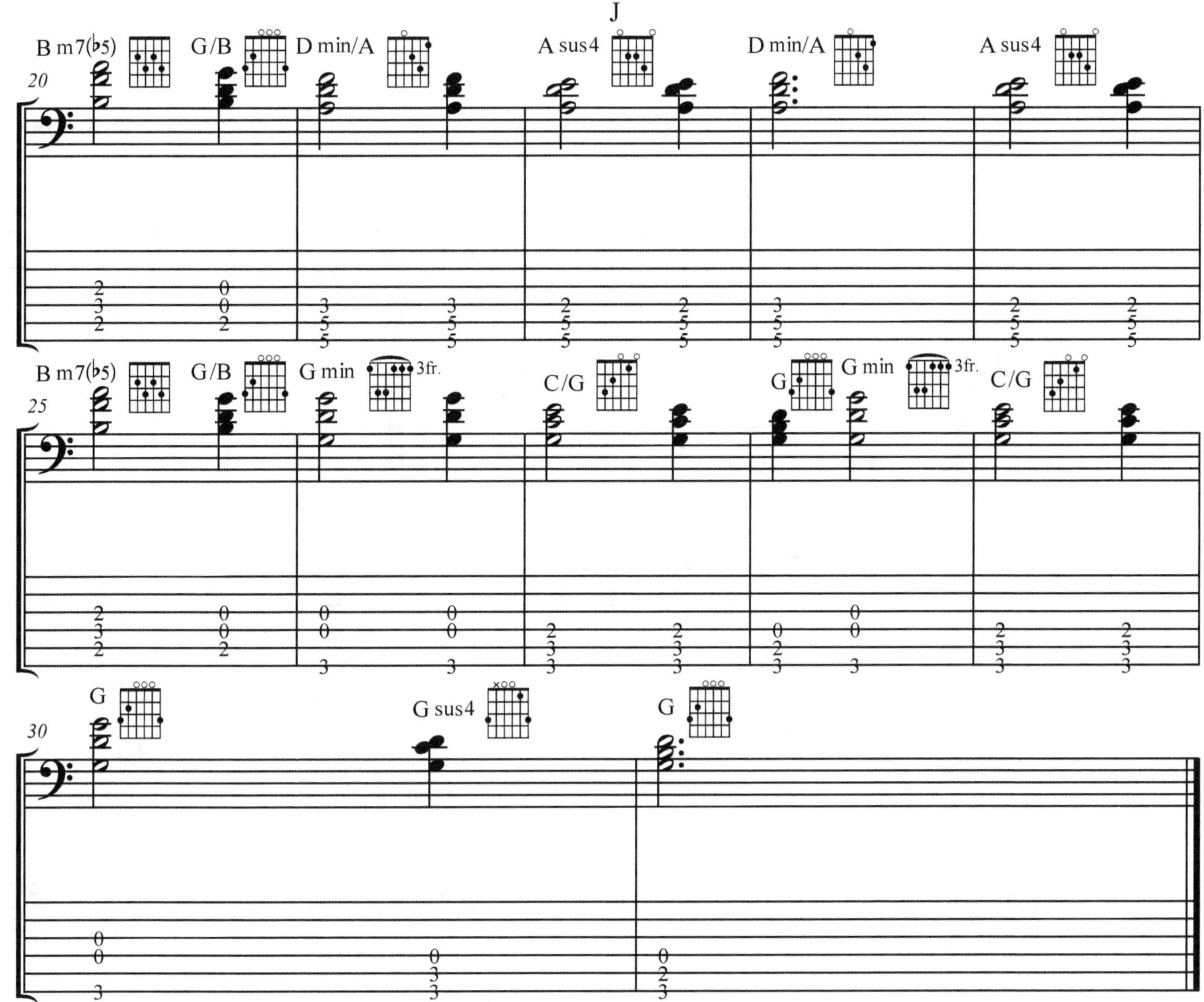
J
B m7(♭5)
G/B
D min/A
A sus4
D min/A
A sus4
B m7(♭5)
G/B
G min
3fr.
C/G
G
G min
3fr.
C/G
G
G sus4
G

Guitar 1

A

Joost de Gro

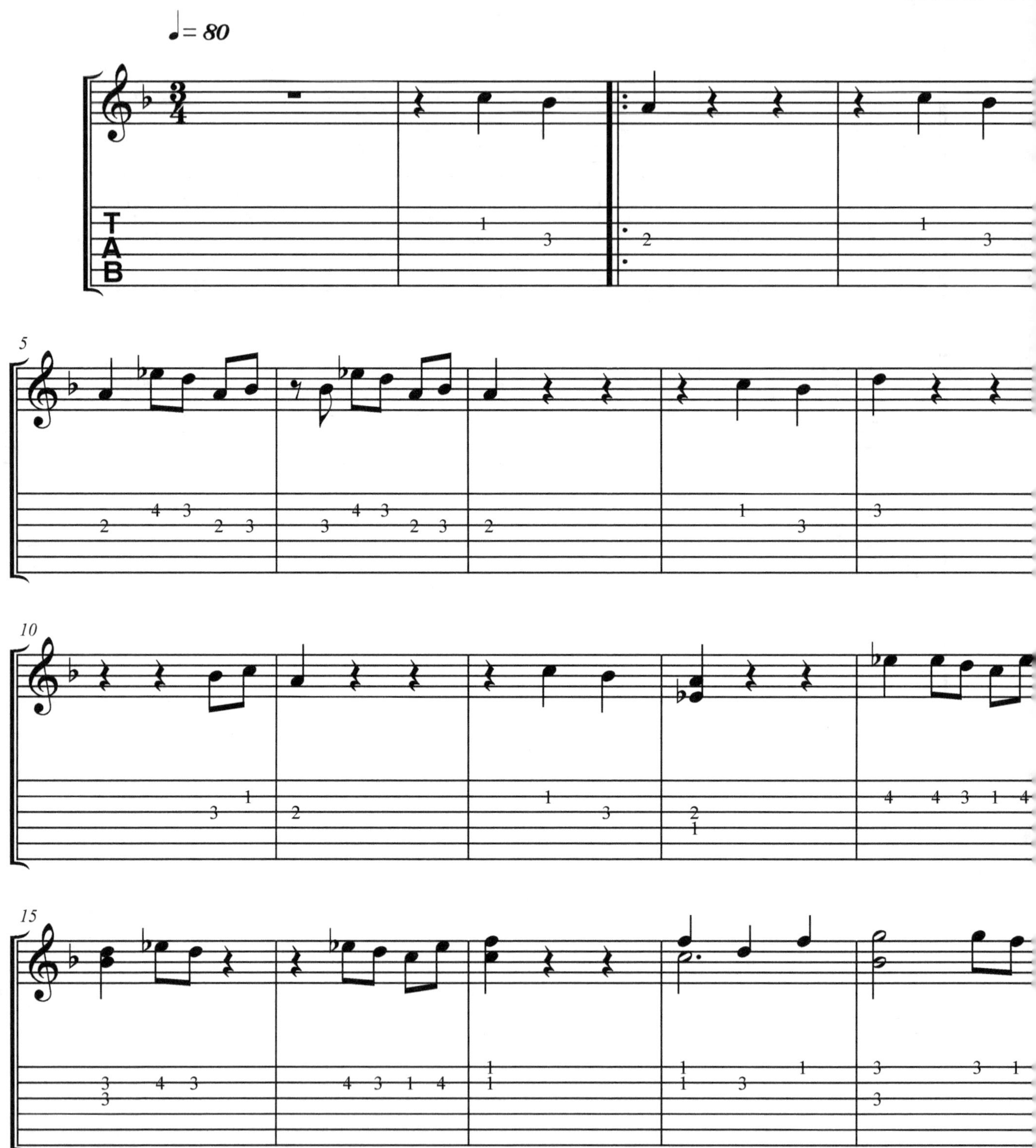

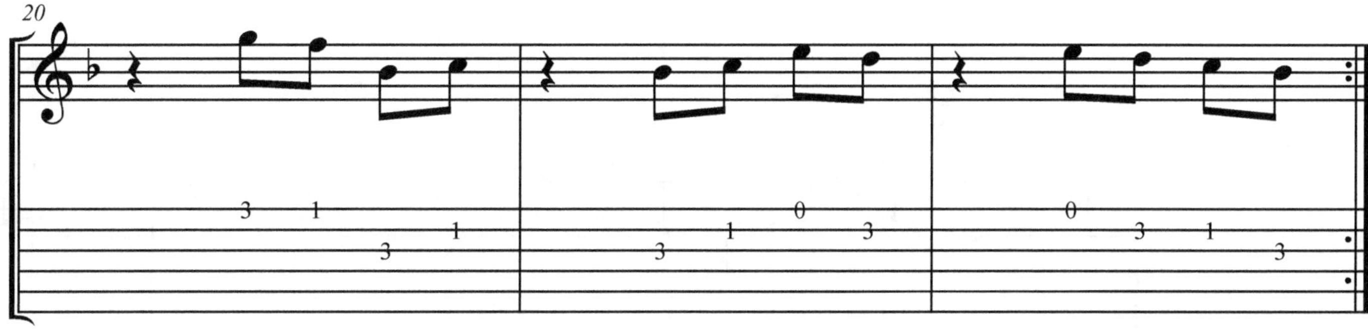
20
3 1
3 1
3 1 0 3
0 3 1 3

Guitar 2

A

Joost de Groo

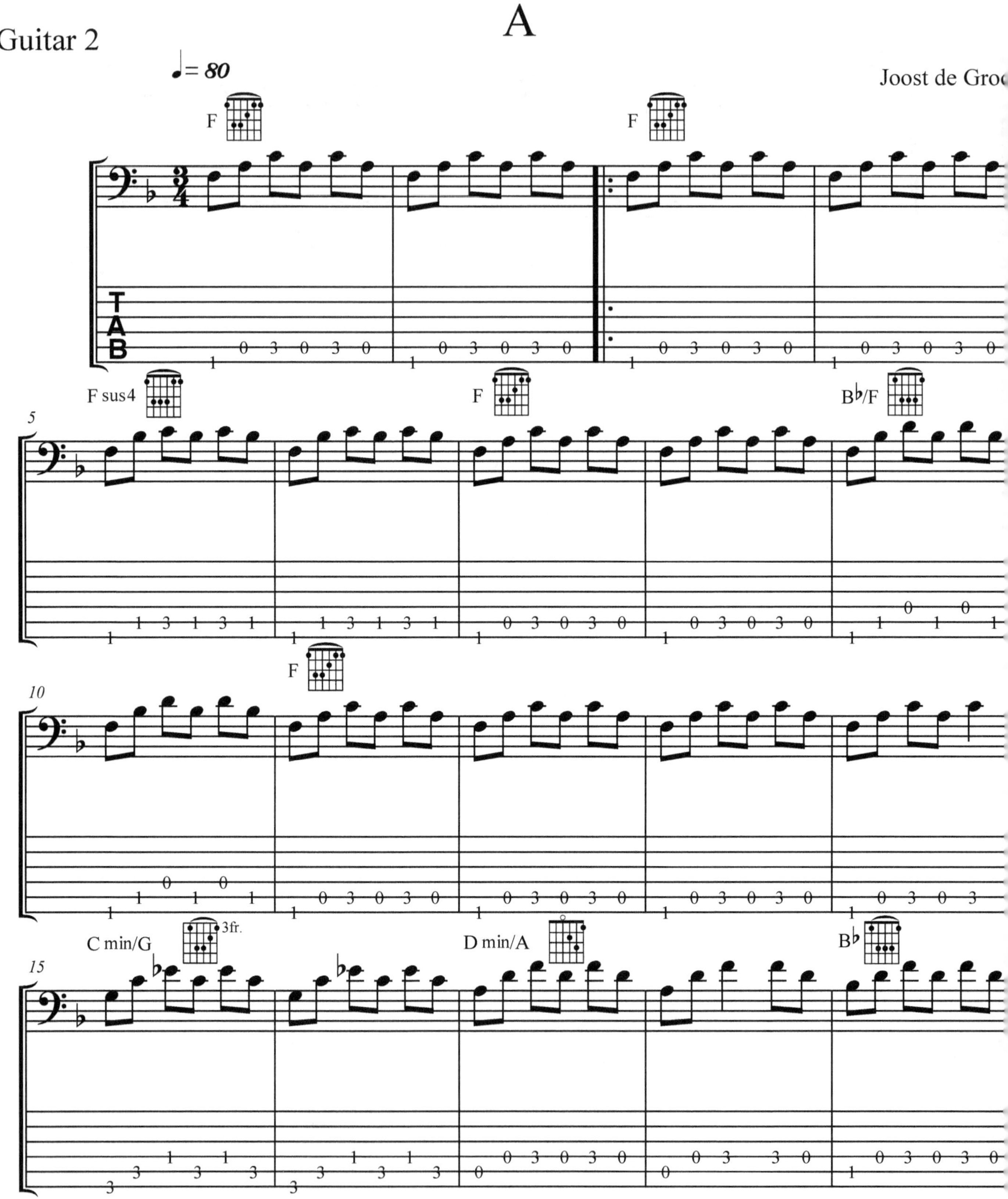

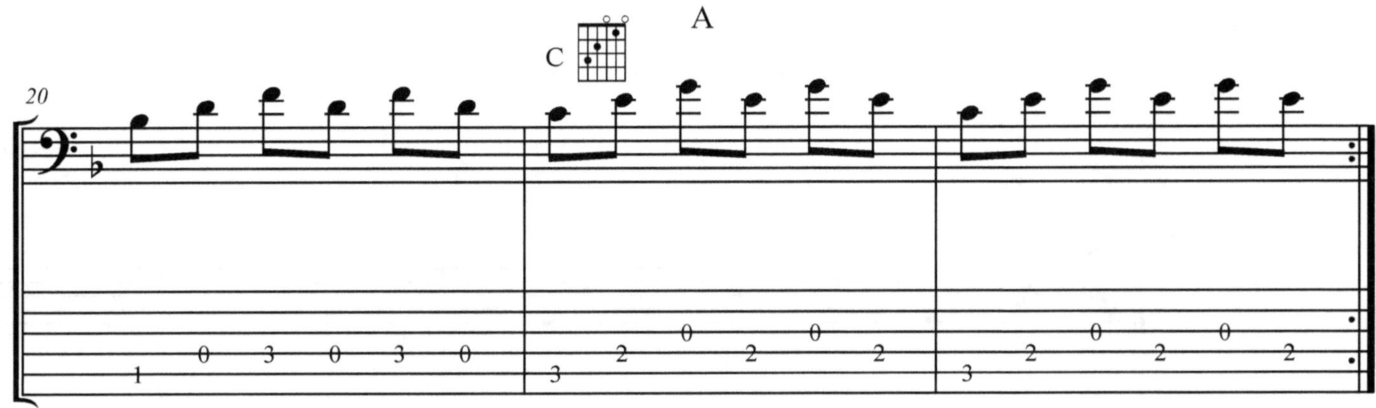

20
C
A
1
0
3
0
3
0
3
2
0
2
0
2
3
2
0
2
0
2

Guitar 1

N

Joost de Gro

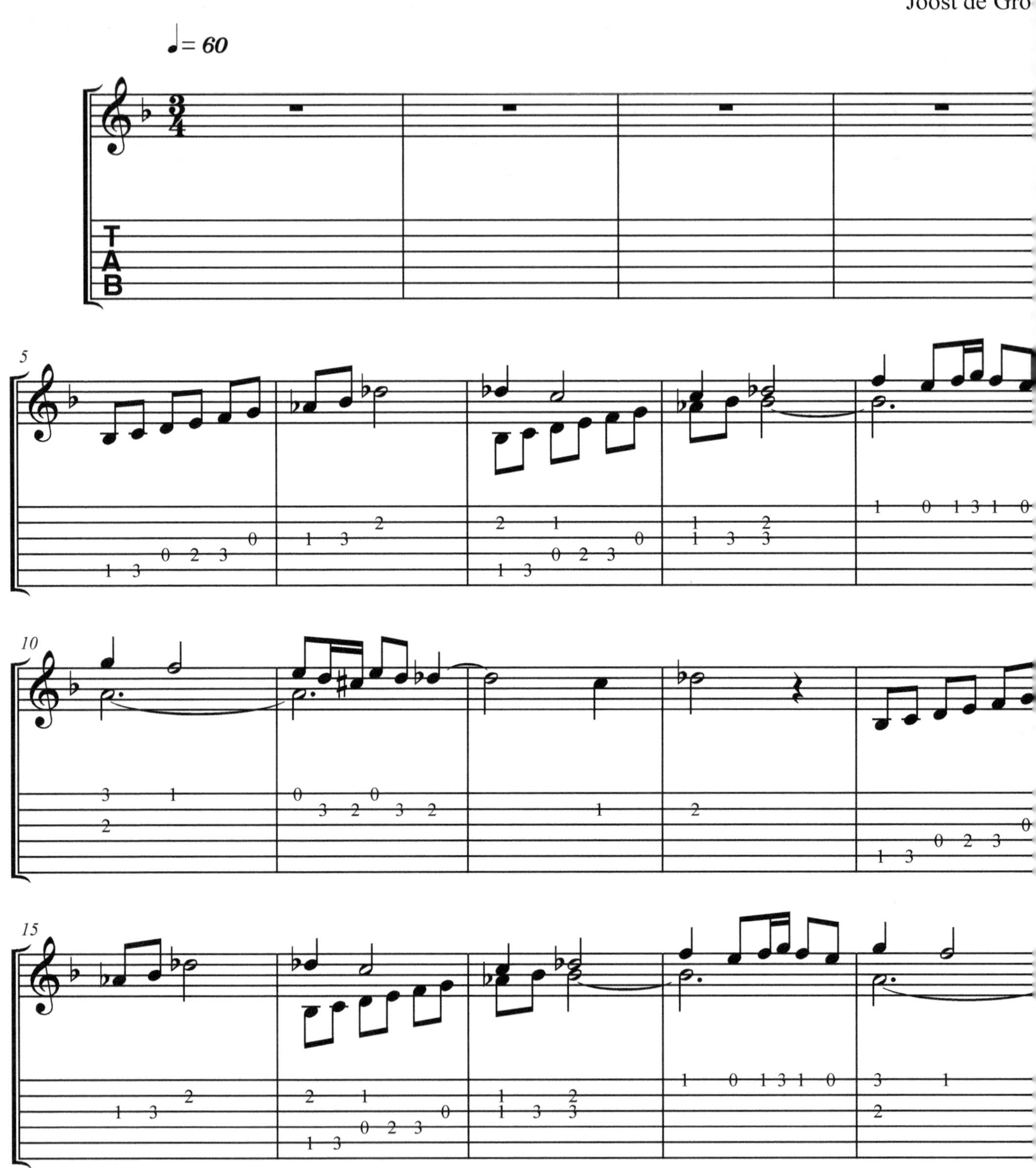

N

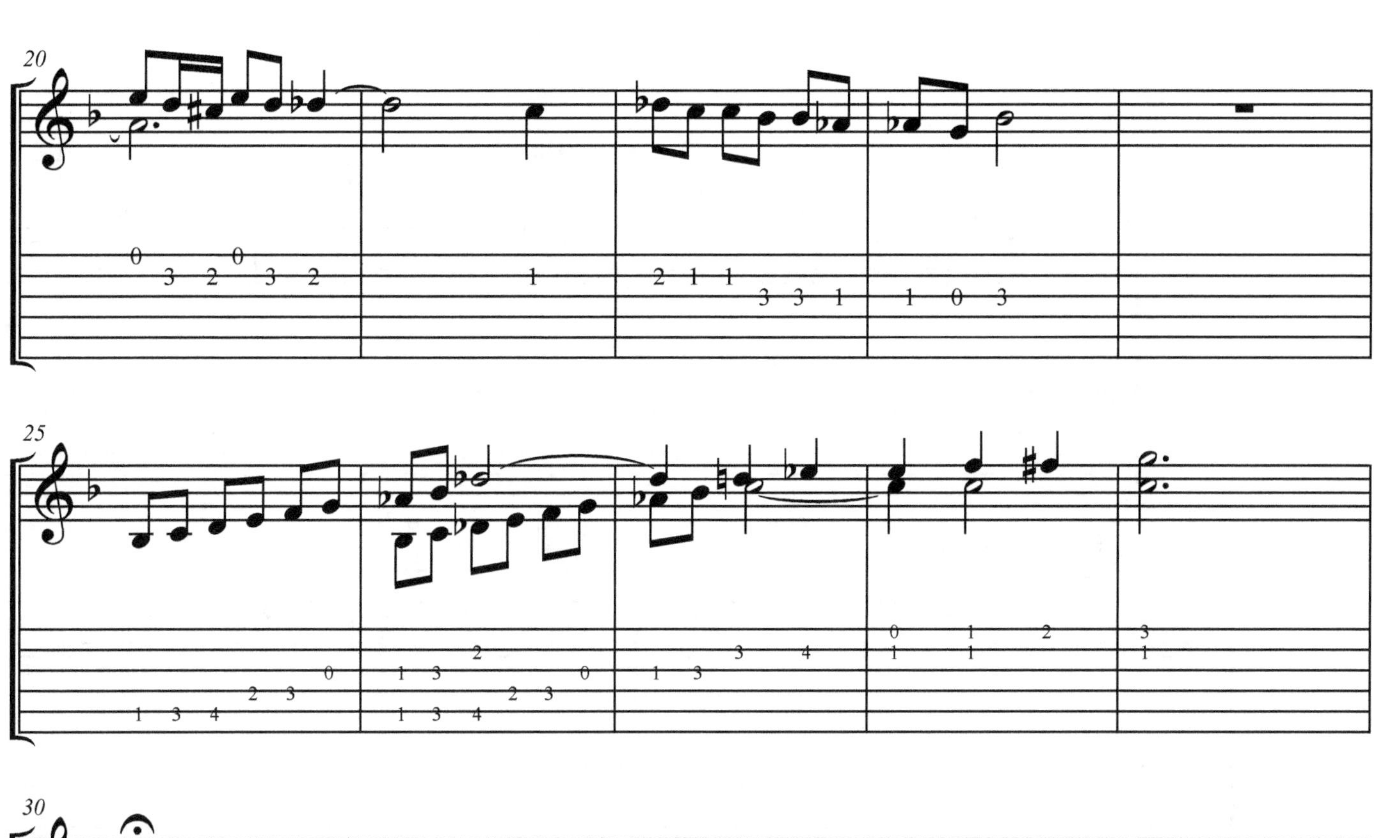

Guitar 2

N

♩= 60
Joost de Gro
C/G
C min/G
3fr.
C/G
F/A
C/G
C sus4/G
C/G
C/G
C sus4/G
C 7/G
C 7/G
C/G
C/G
C sus4/G
C/G
C/G
C sus4/G
C 7/G

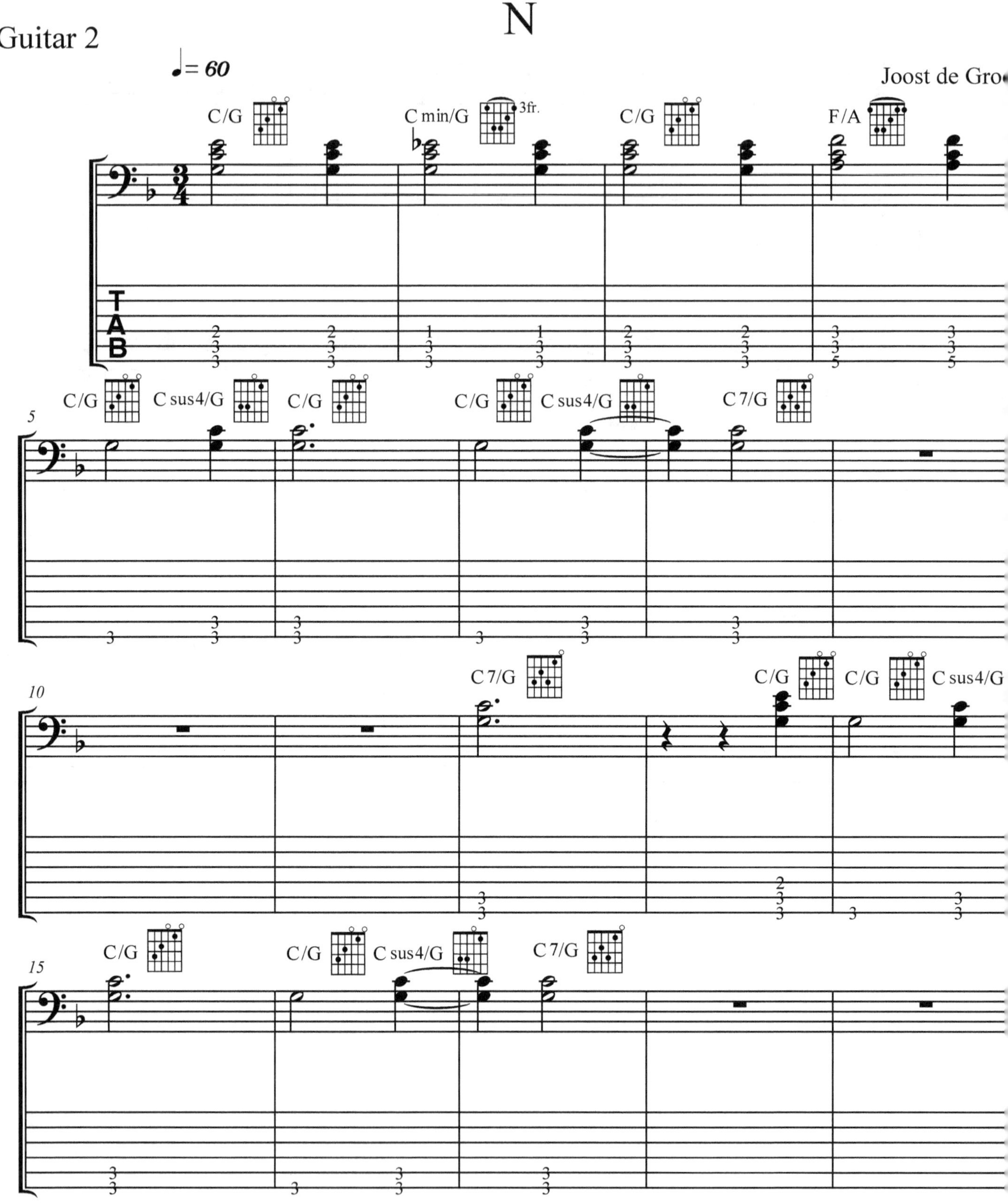

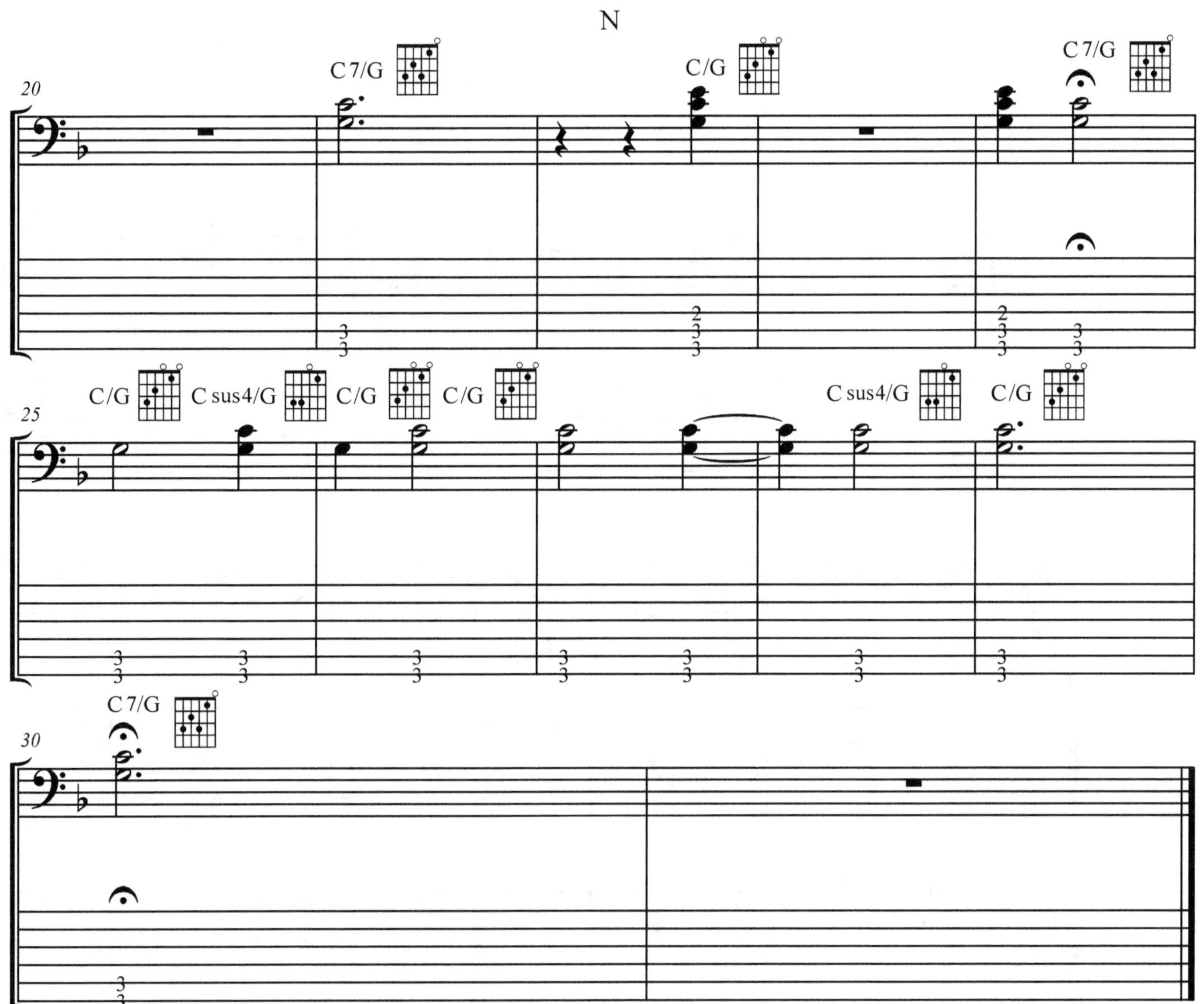
N
20
C 7/G
C/G
C 7/G
25
C/G
C sus4/G
C/G
C/G
C sus4/G
C/G
30
C 7/G

Guitar 1

N

Joost de Gro

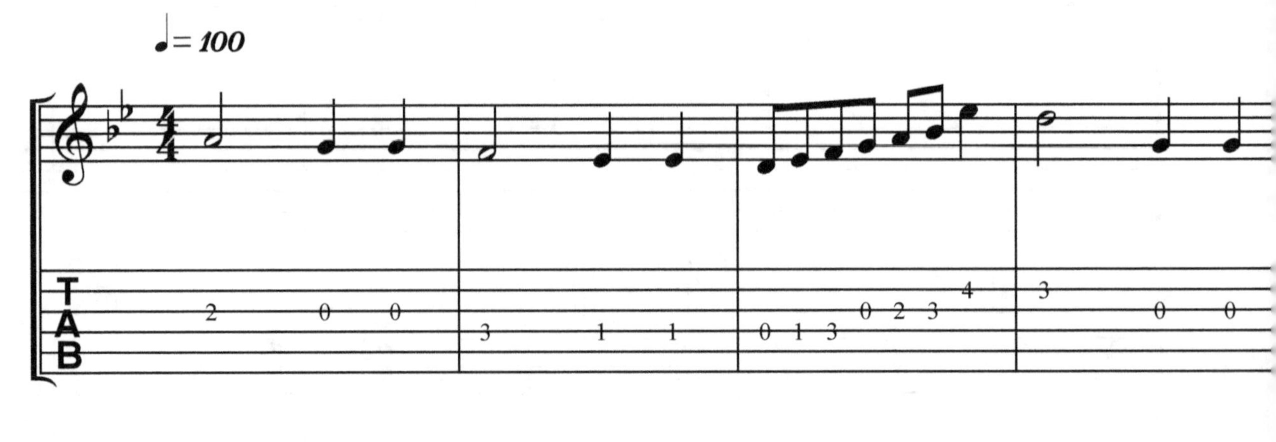

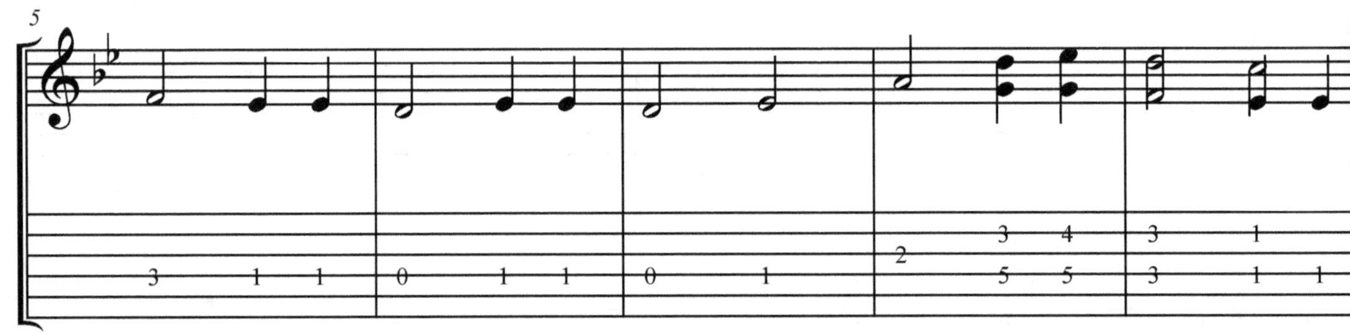

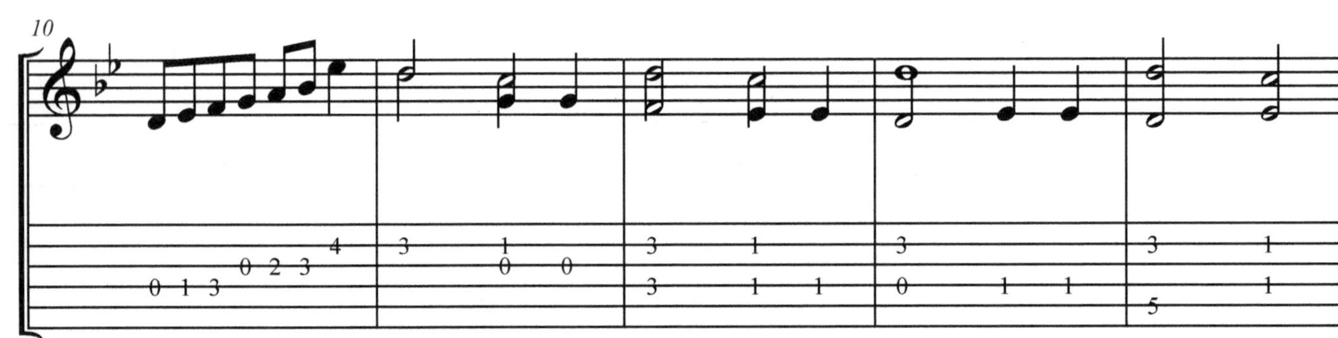

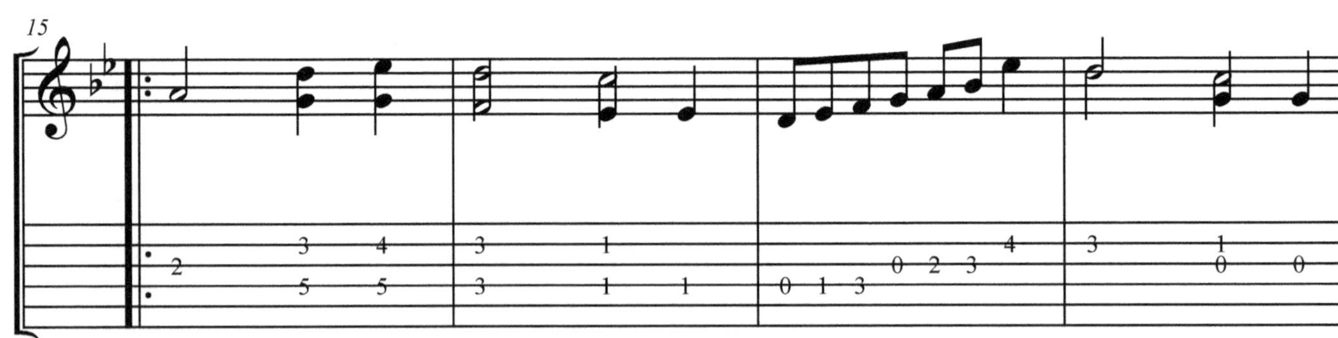

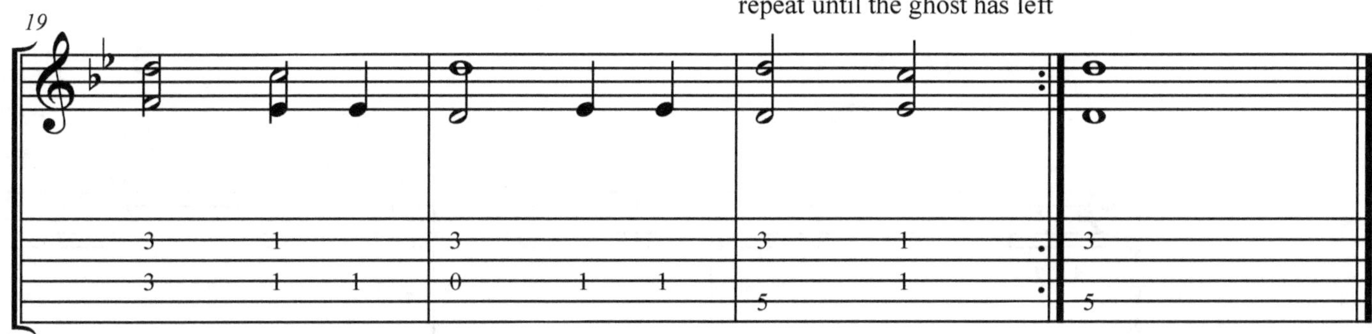
repeat until the ghost has left
19

Guitar 2

N

♩= 100

Joost de Gro

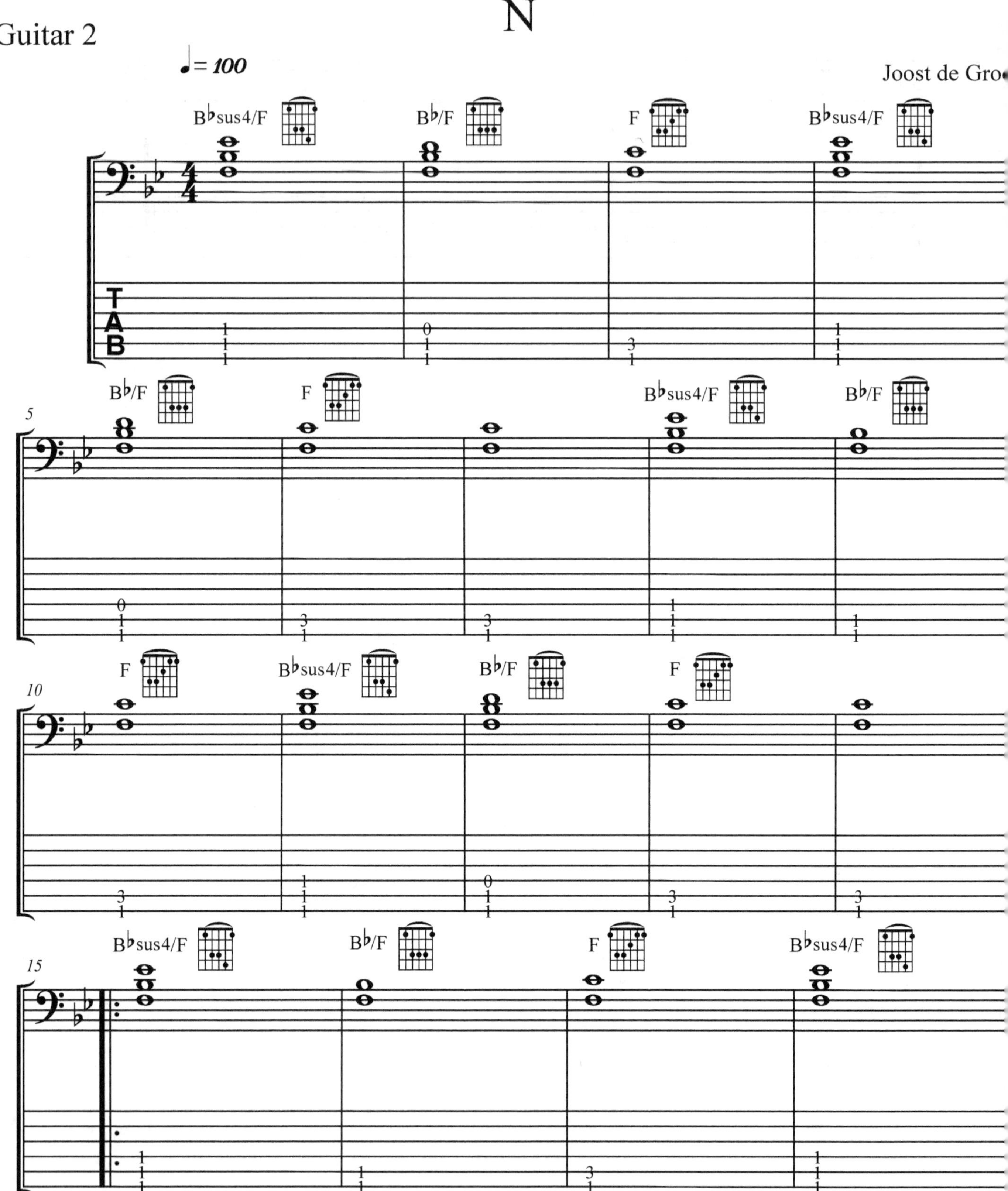

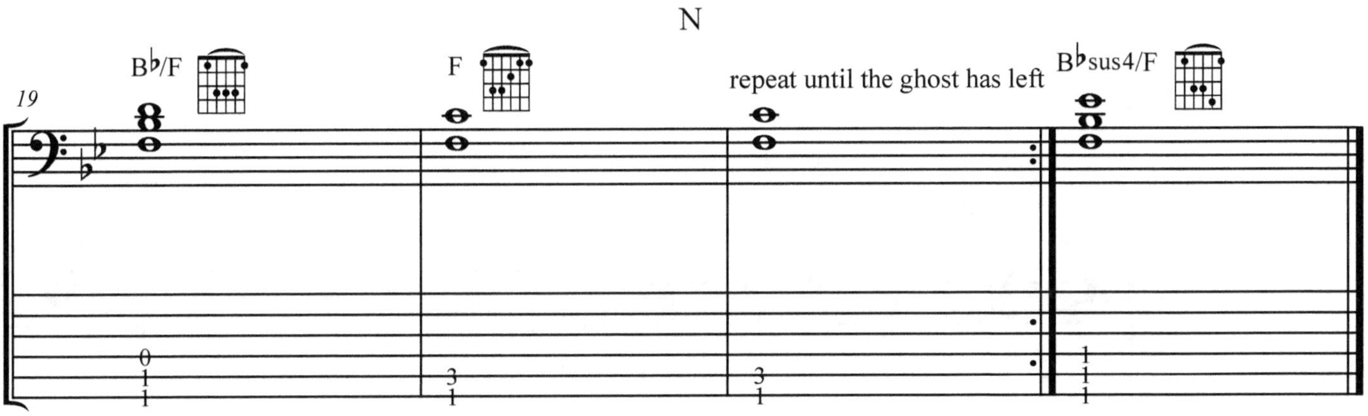

N

19

B♭/F

F

repeat until the ghost has left

B♭sus4/F

Guitar 1

I

Joost de Gro

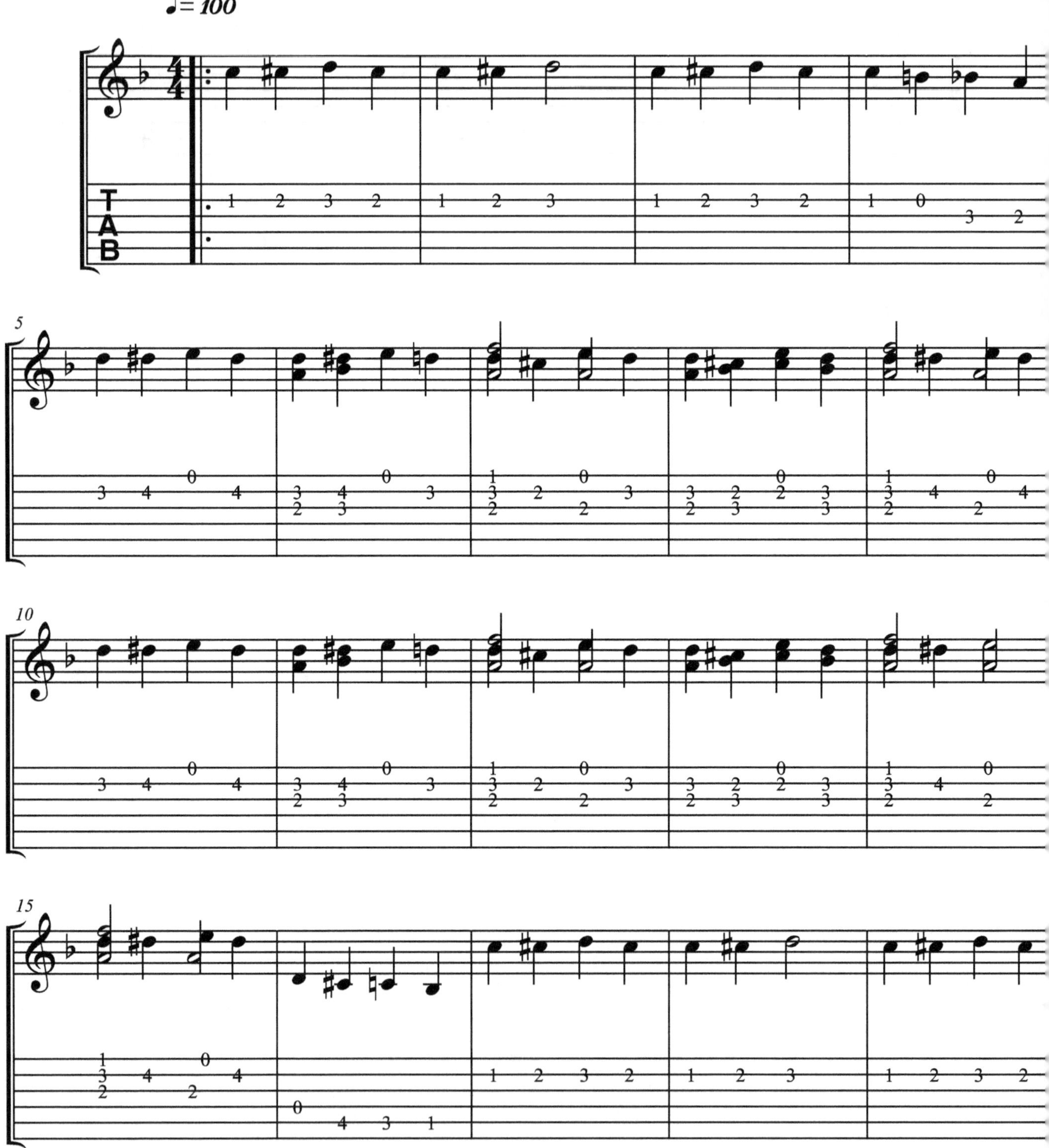

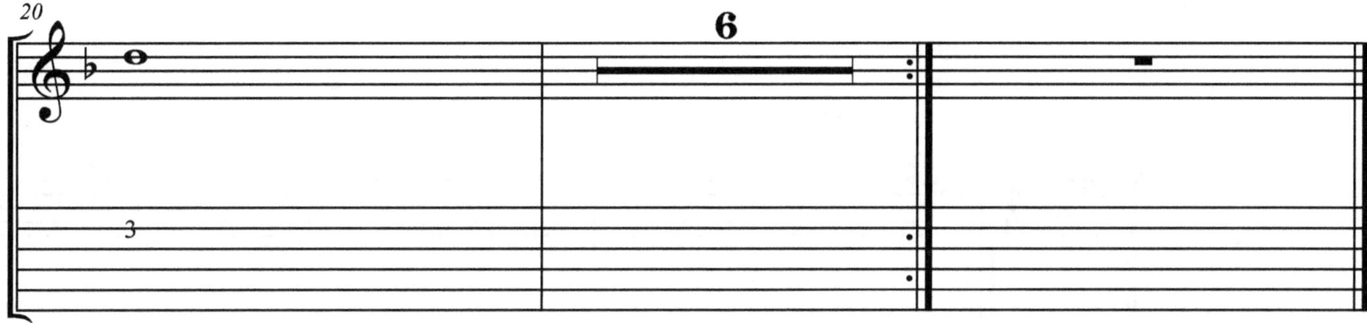
20
6
3

I

Guitar 2

Joost de Gro

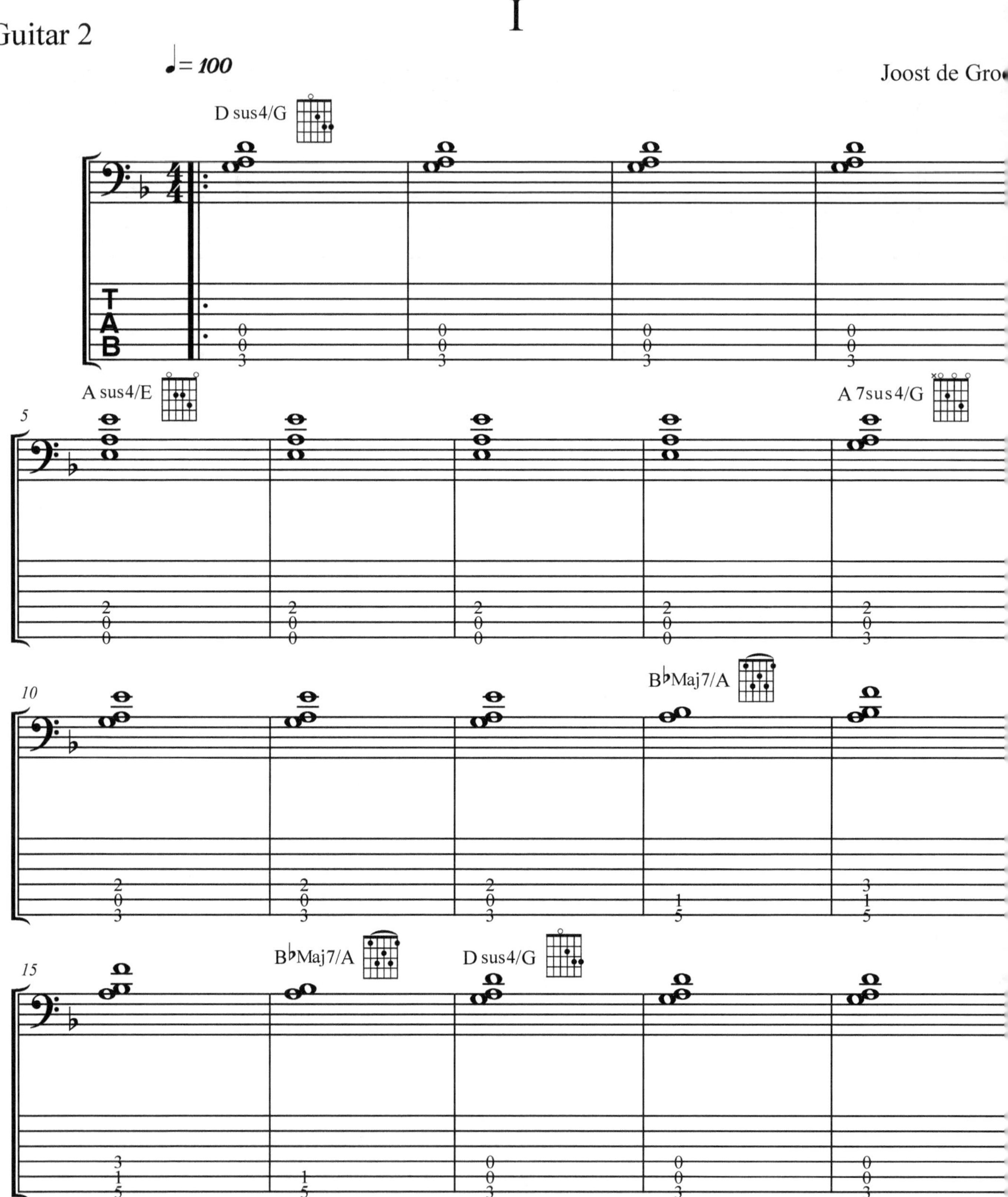

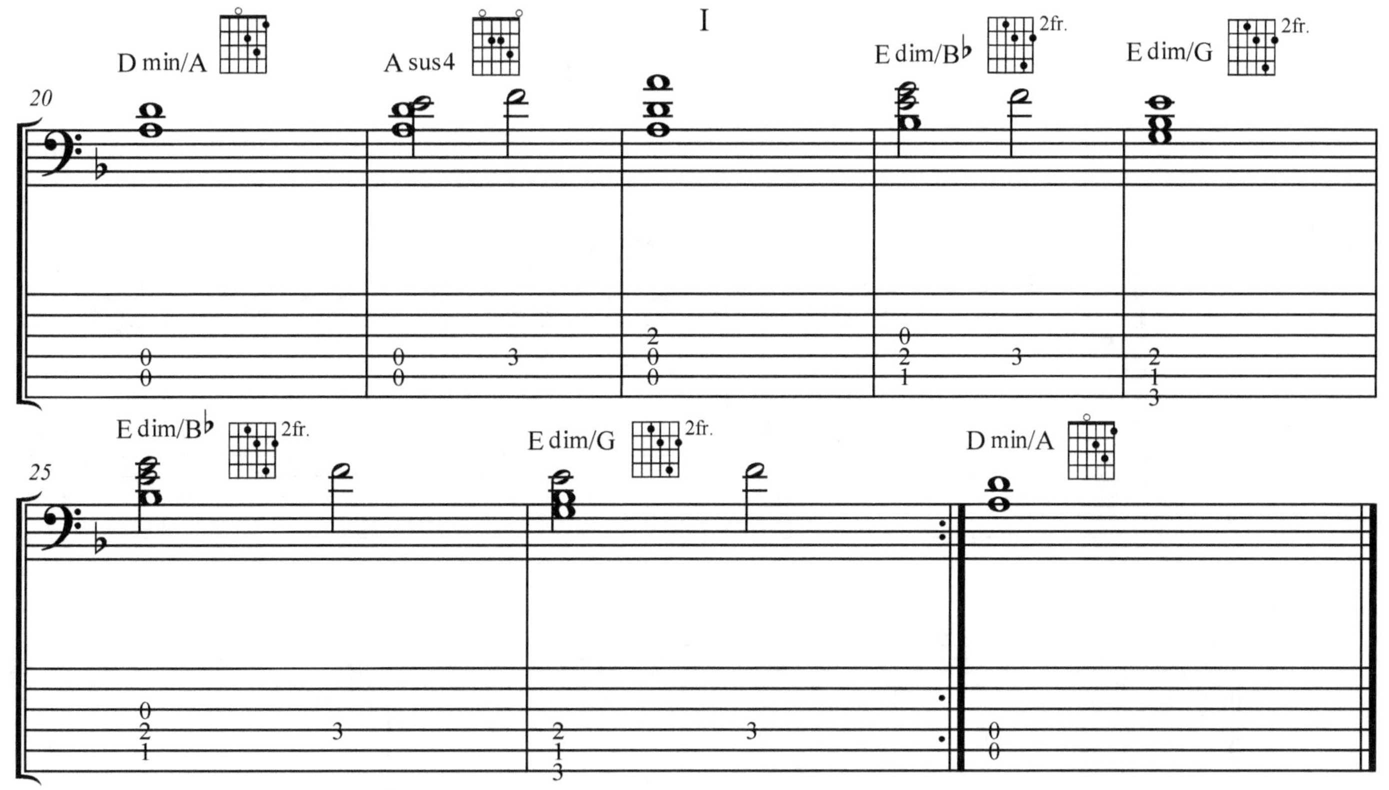
D min/A
A sus4
I
E dim/B♭
2fr.
E dim/G
2fr.
20
E dim/B♭
2fr.
E dim/G
2fr.
D min/A
25

Guitar 1

E

Joost de Gro

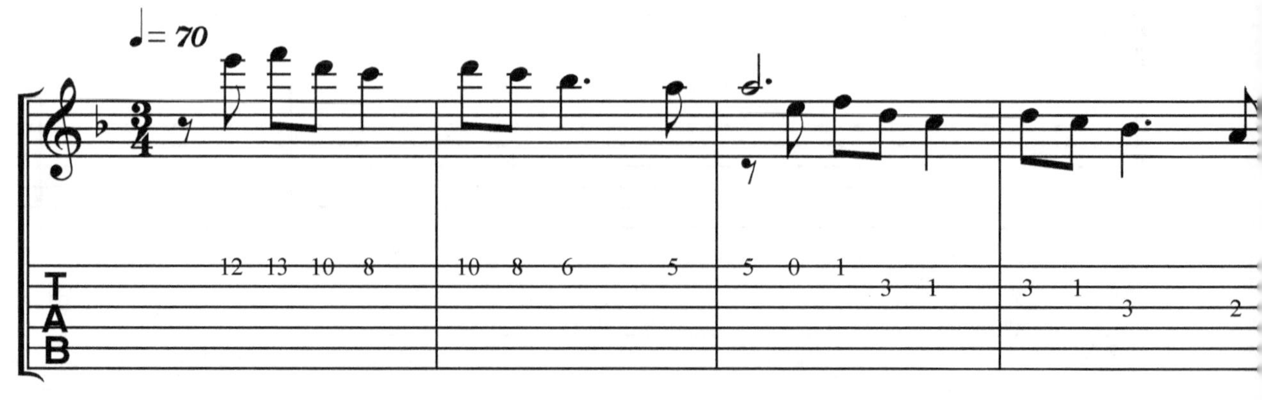

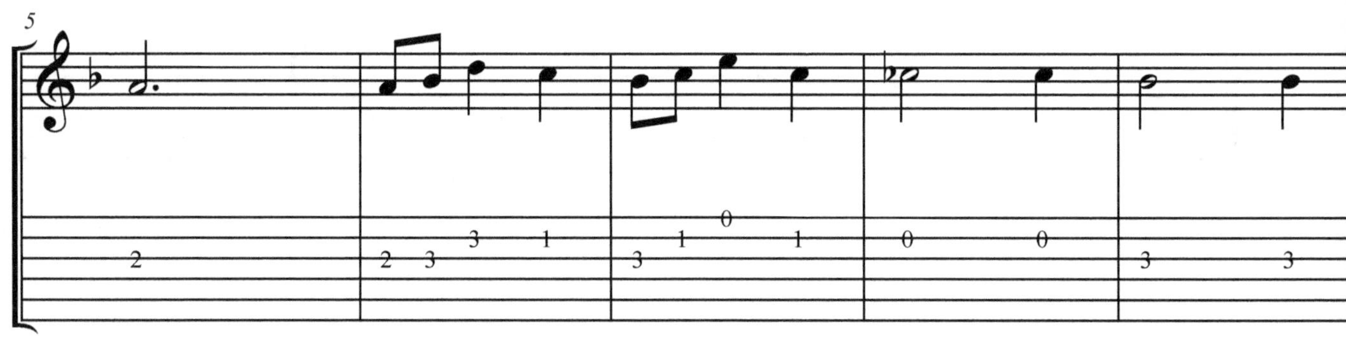

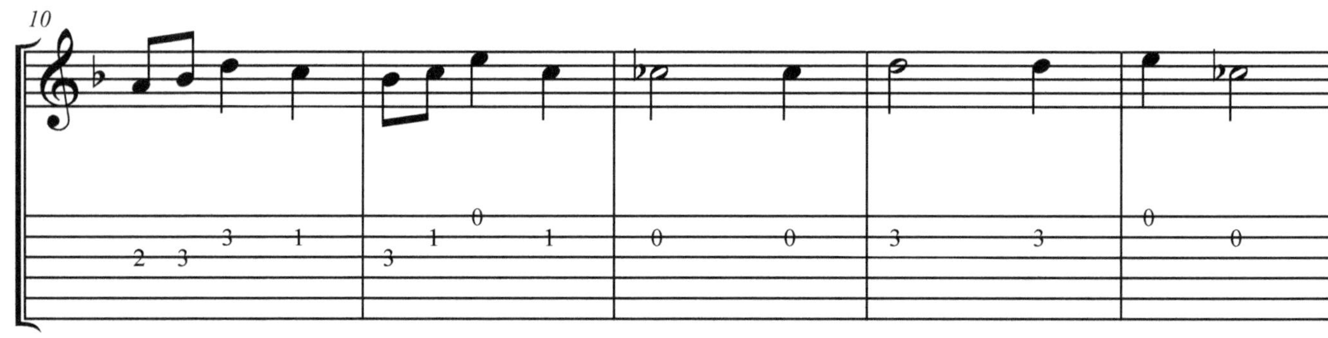

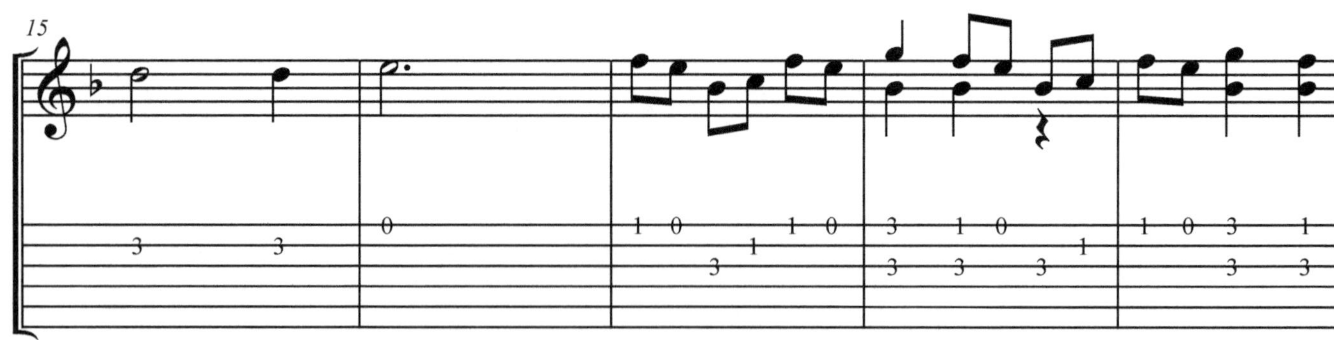

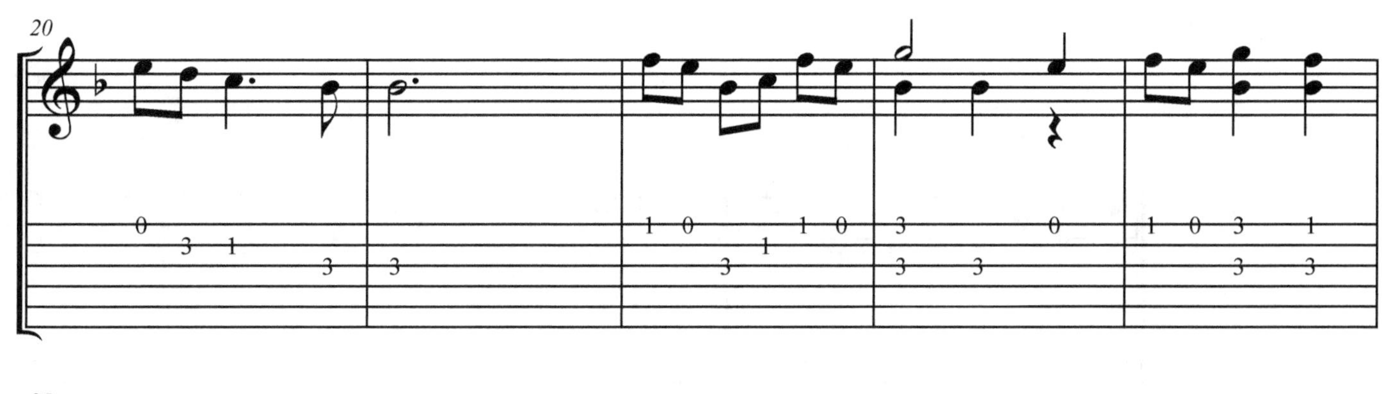

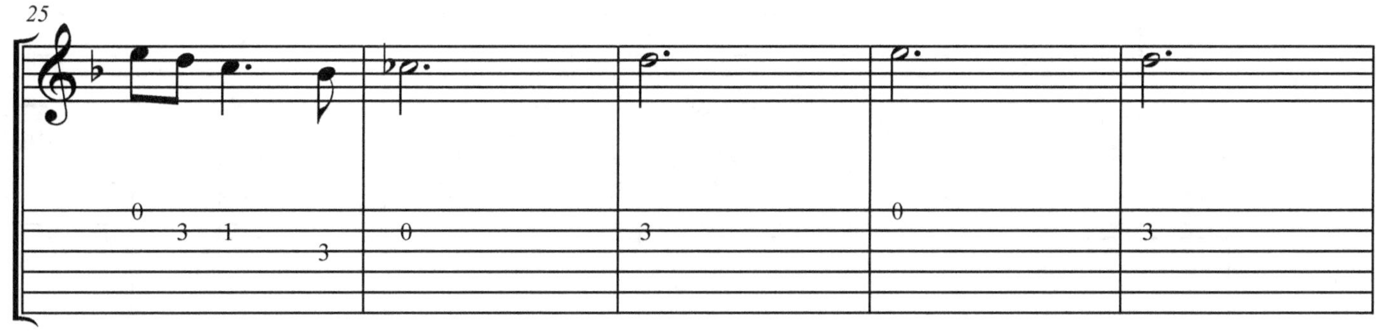

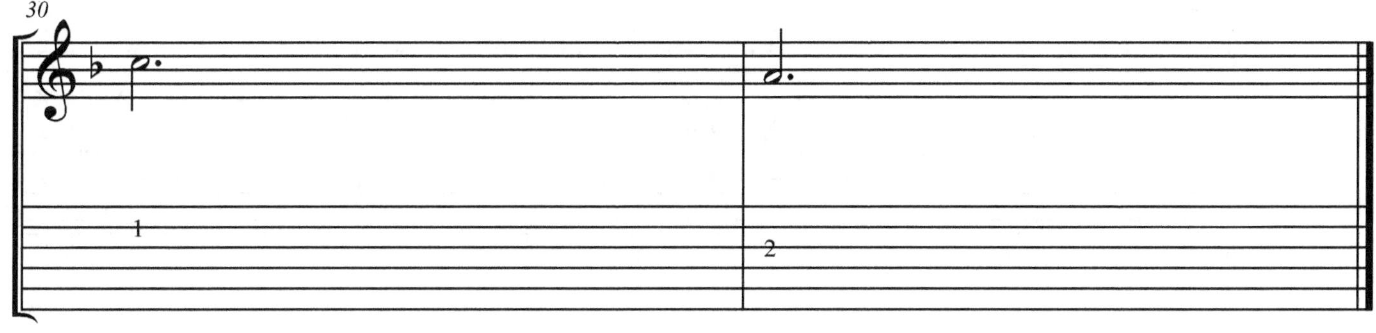

Guitar 2

E

Joost de Gro

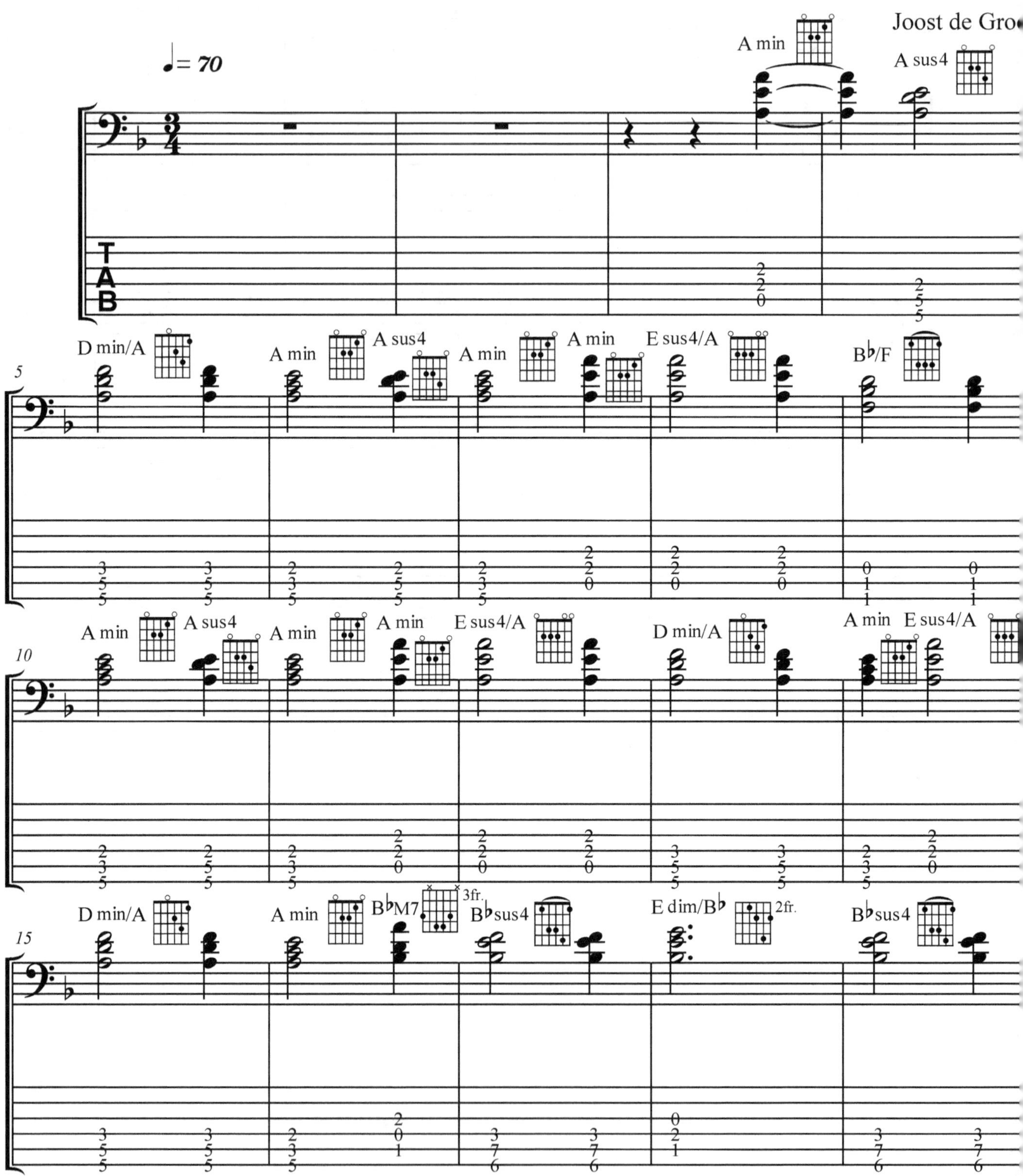

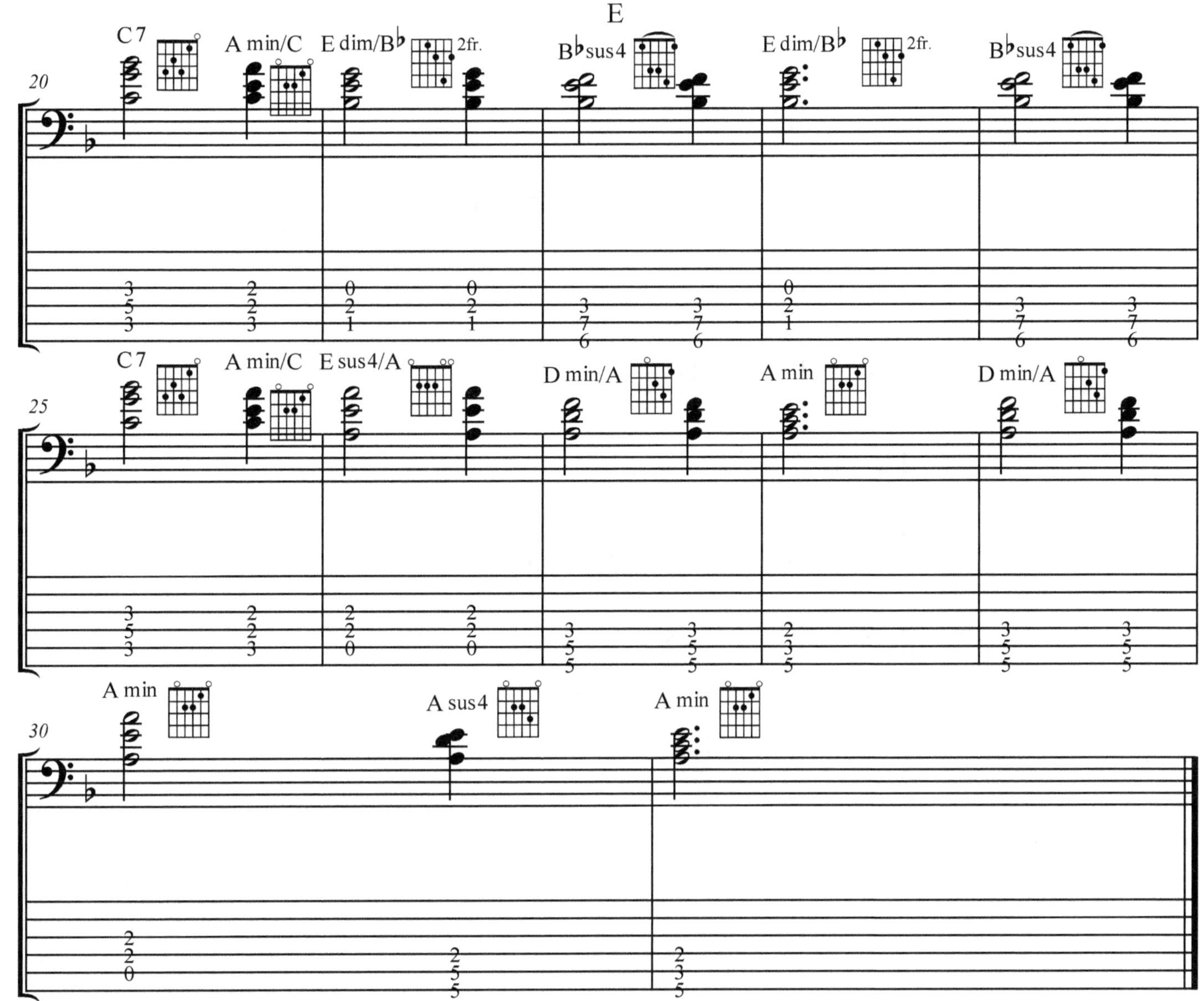
E
C7
A min/C
E dim/B♭
2fr.
B♭sus4
E dim/B♭
2fr.
B♭sus4
C7
A min/C
E sus4/A
D min/A
A min
D min/A
A min
A sus4
A min

Wood Wind Quartet

Part 1: C Flute

Part 2: C Oboe

Part 3: Bes Clarinet

Part 4: C Bassoon

Part 1: C Flute

J

Joost de Groot

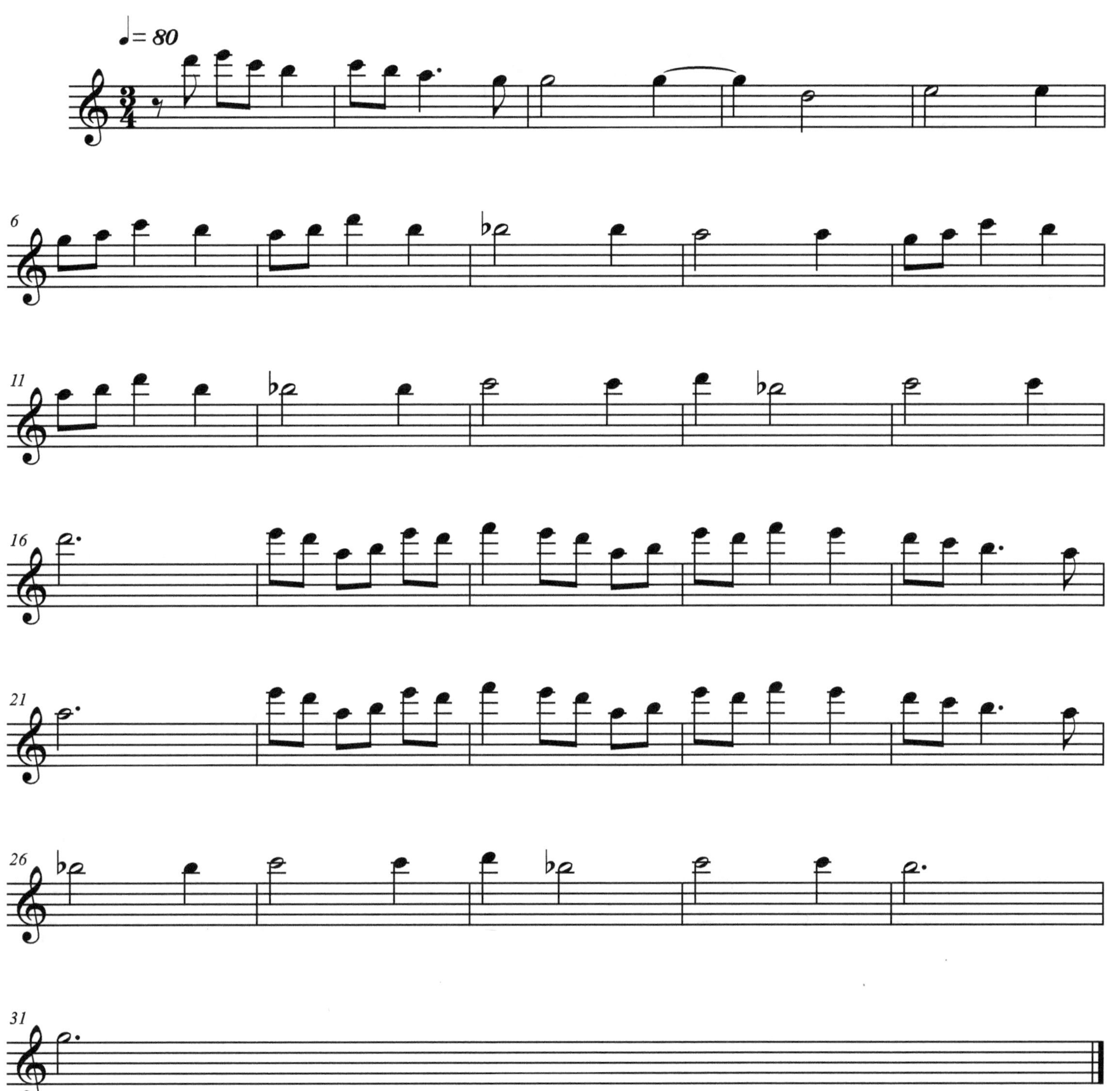

Part 2: C Oboe

J

Joost de Gro

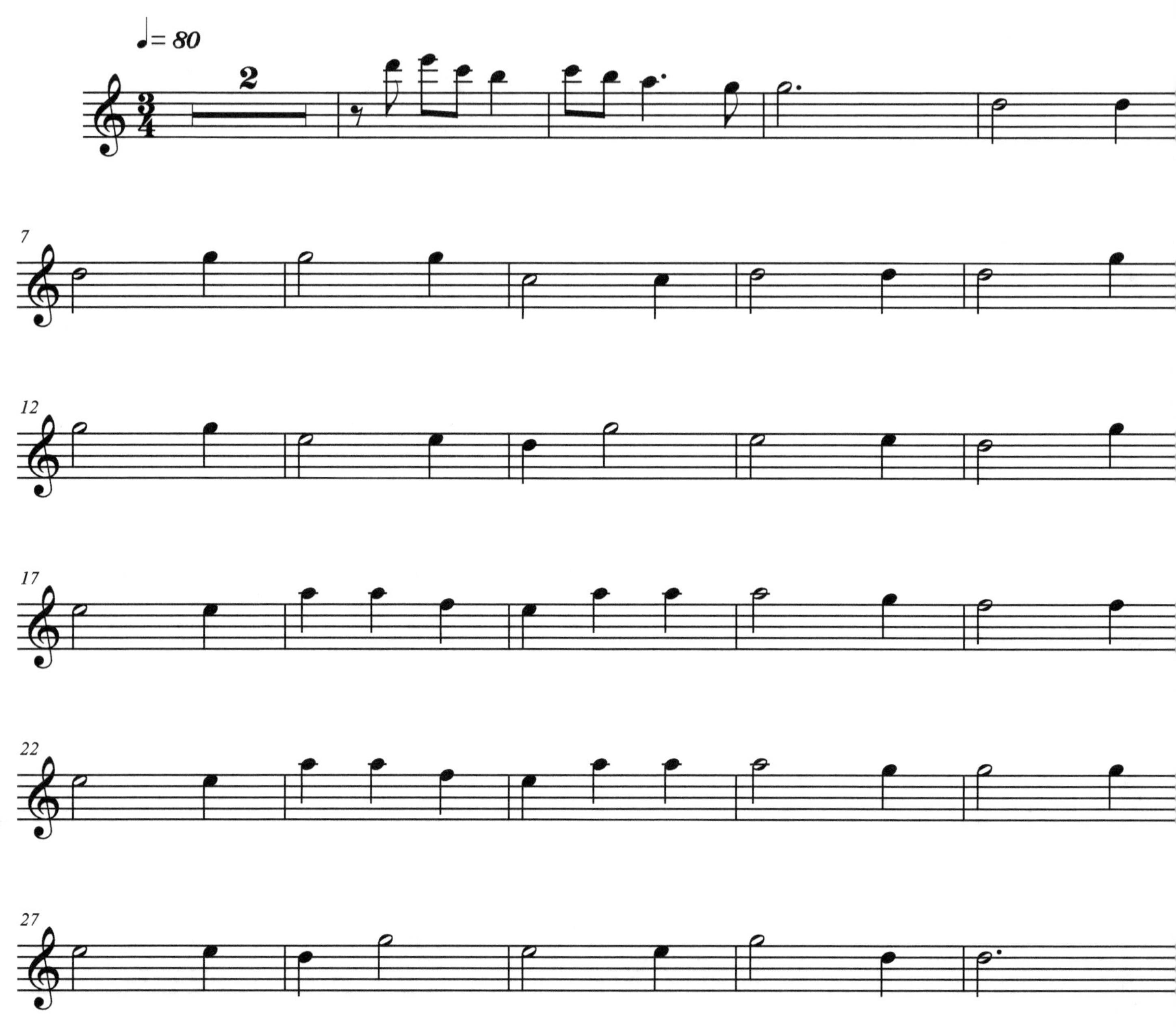

J

Part 3: Bes Clarinet

Joost de Groot

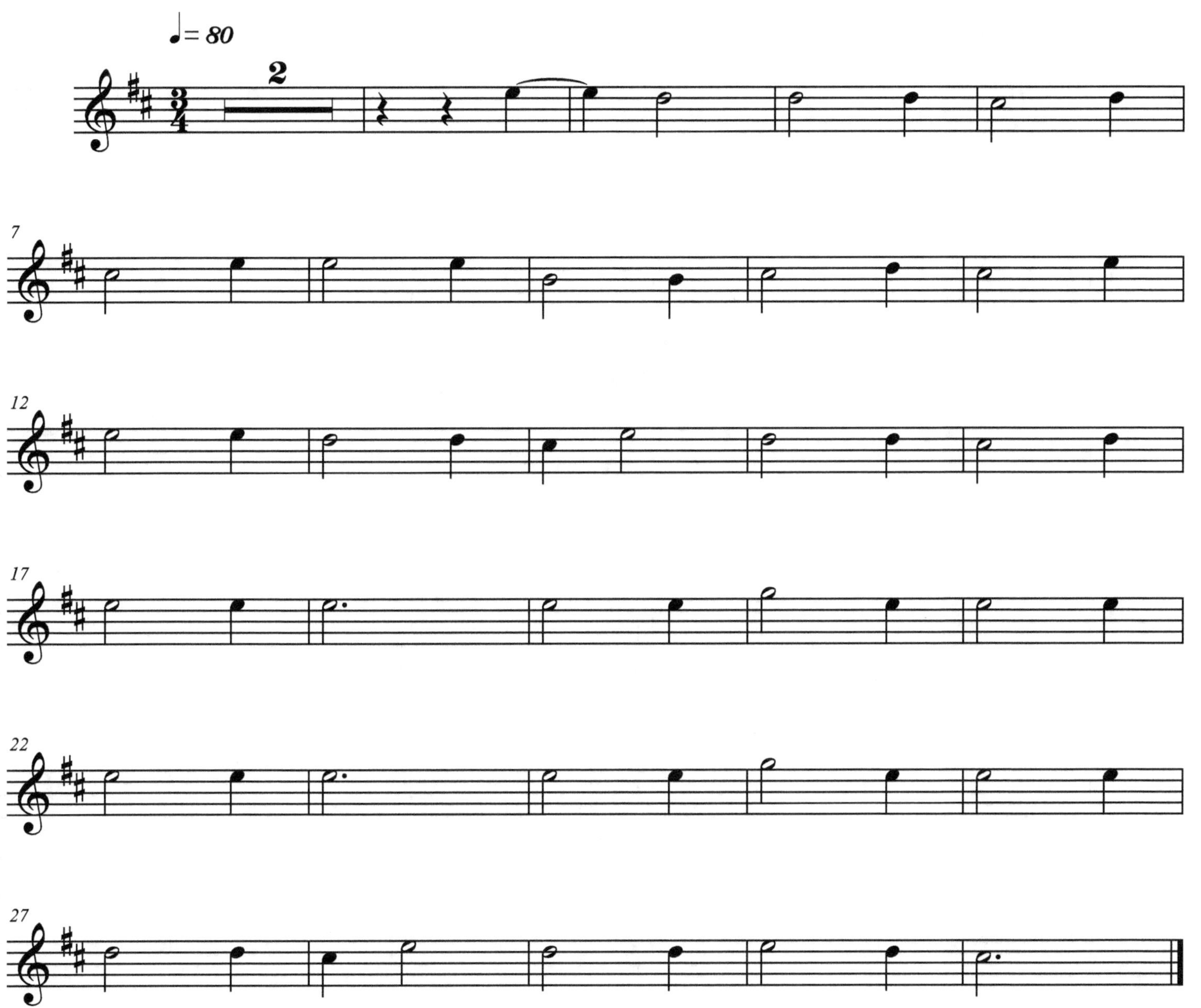

Part 4: C Bassoon

J

Joost de Gro

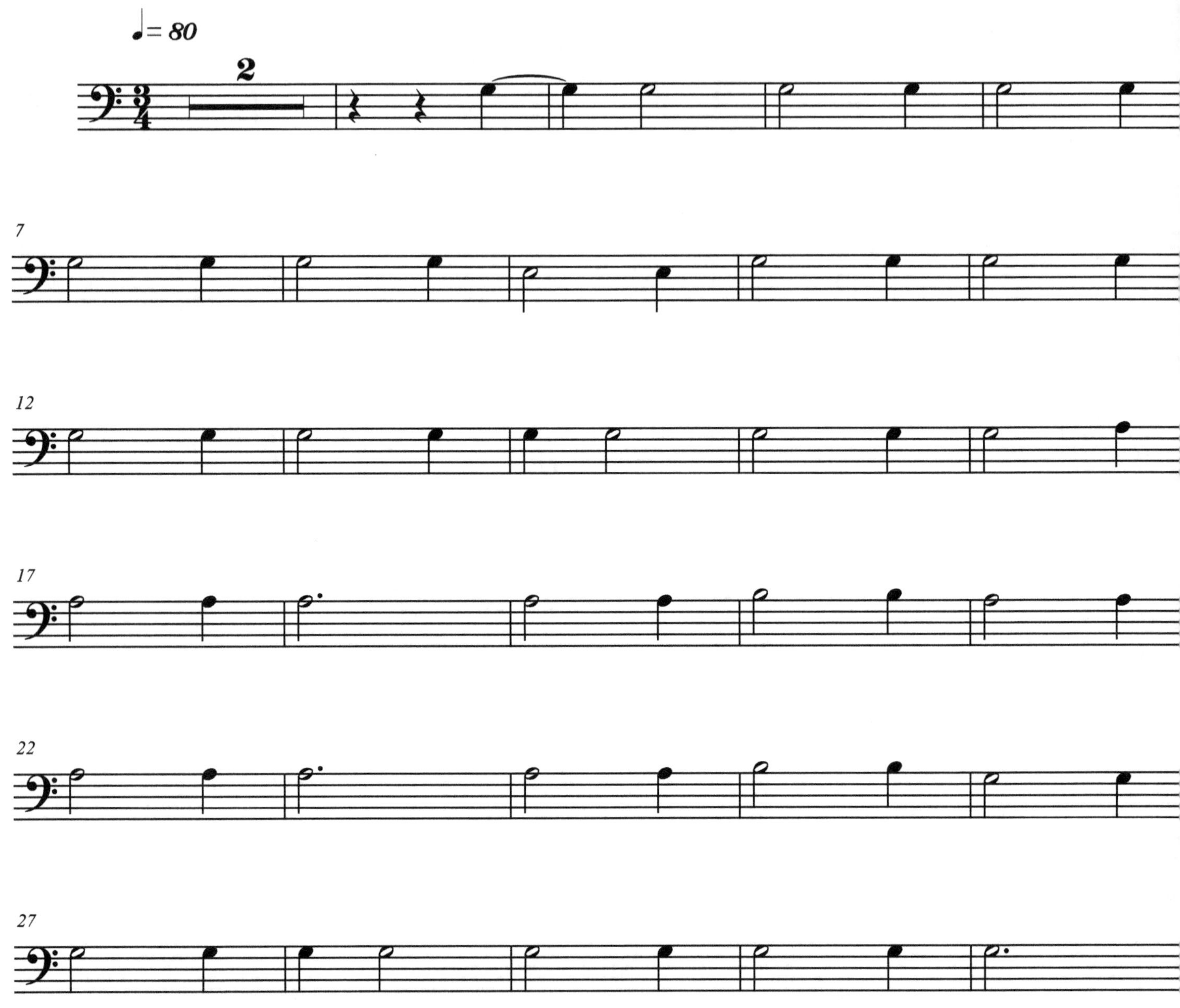

Part 1: C Flute

A

Joost de Groot

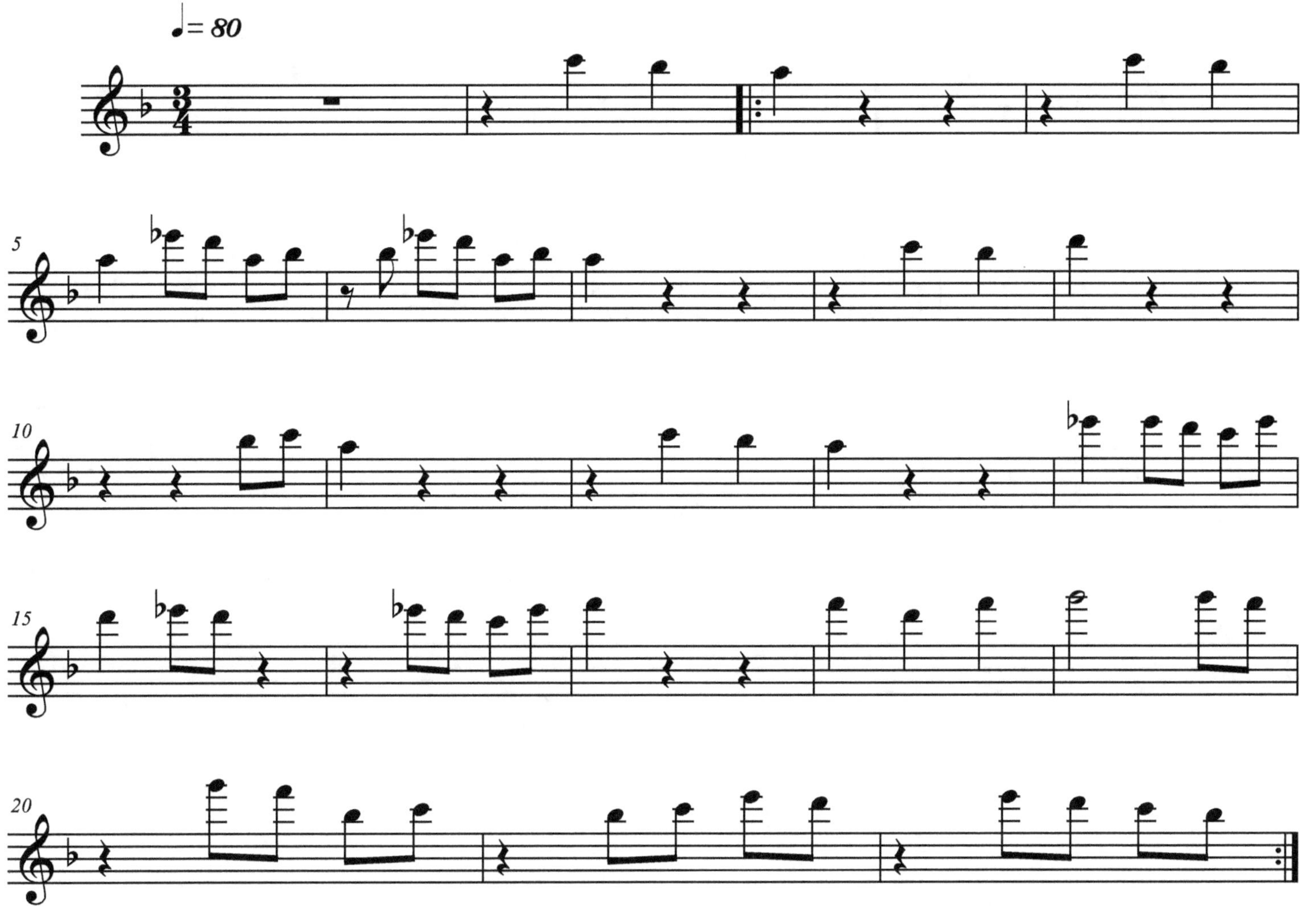

Part 2: C Oboe

A

Joost de Gro

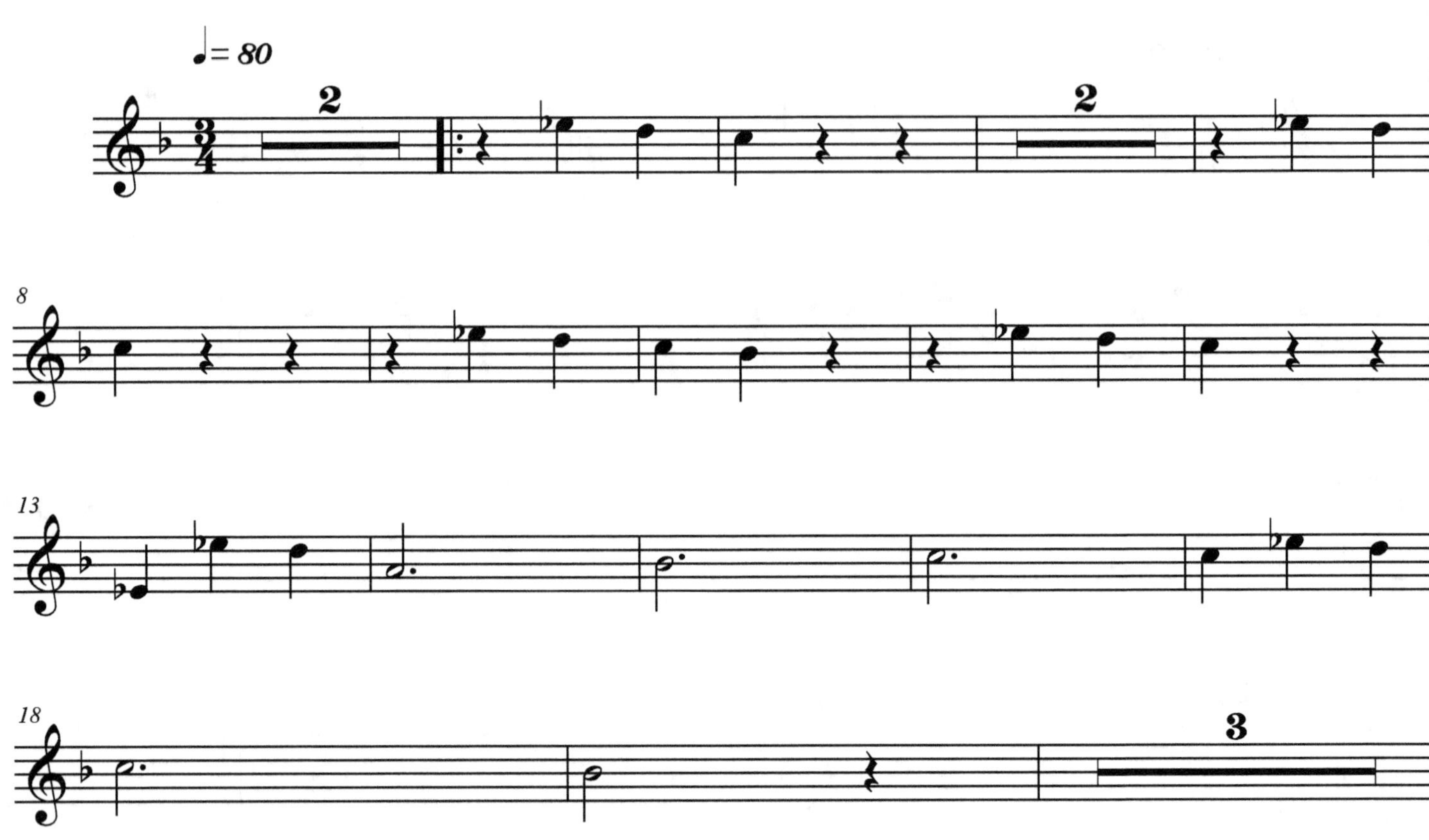

A

Part 3: Bes Clarinet

Joost de Groot

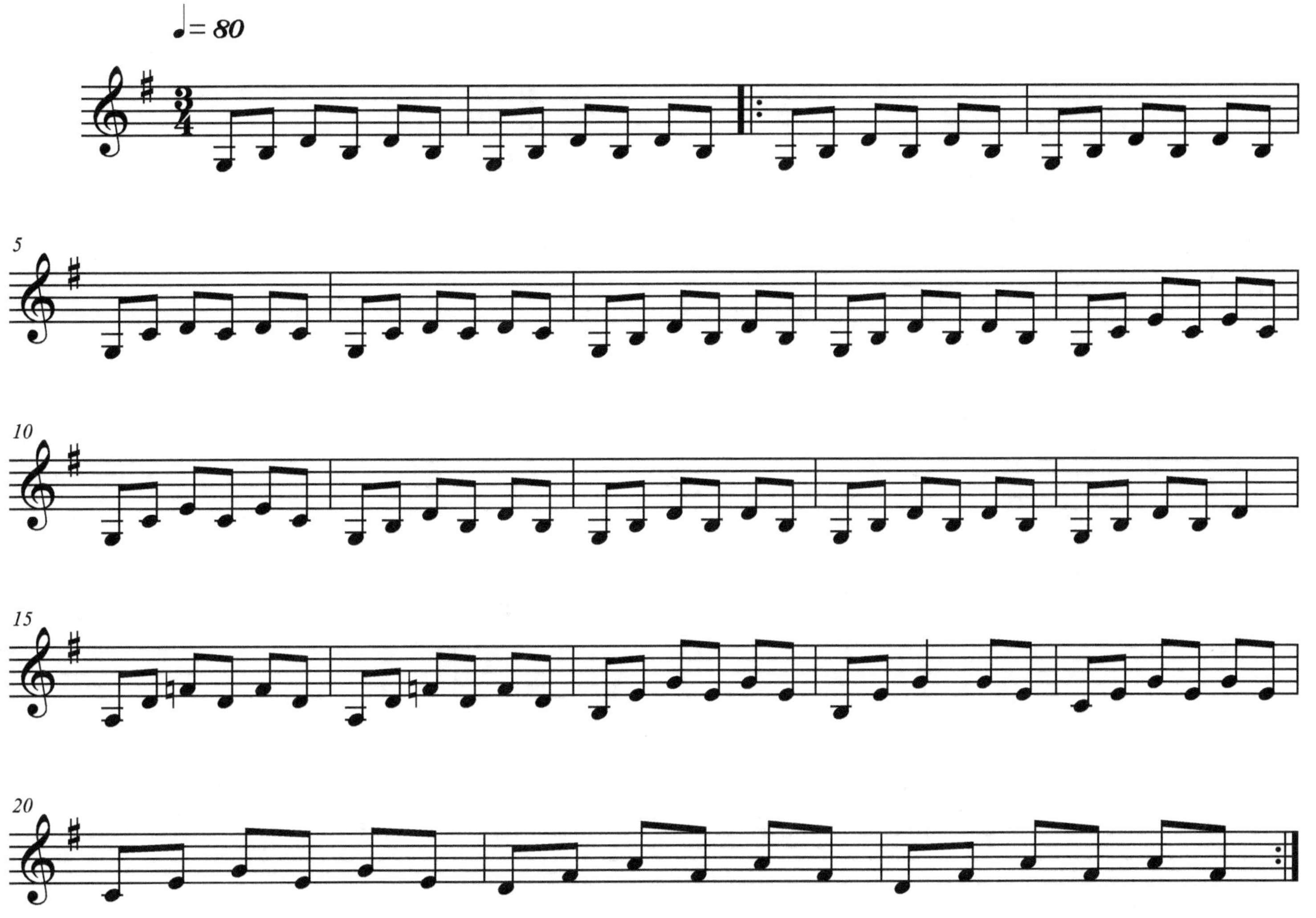

A

Part 4: C Bassoon

Joost de Gro

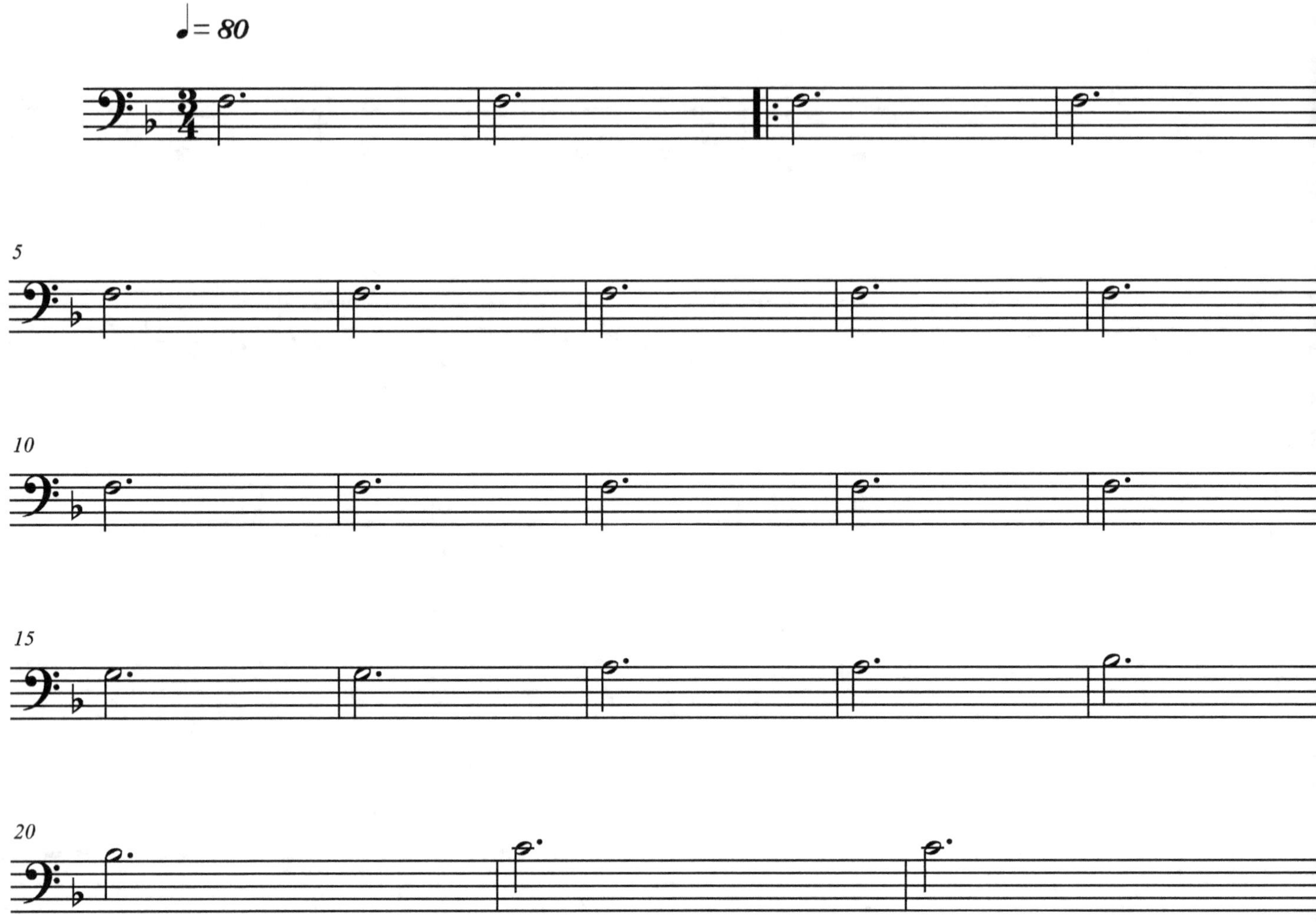

Part 1: C Flute

N

Joost de Groot

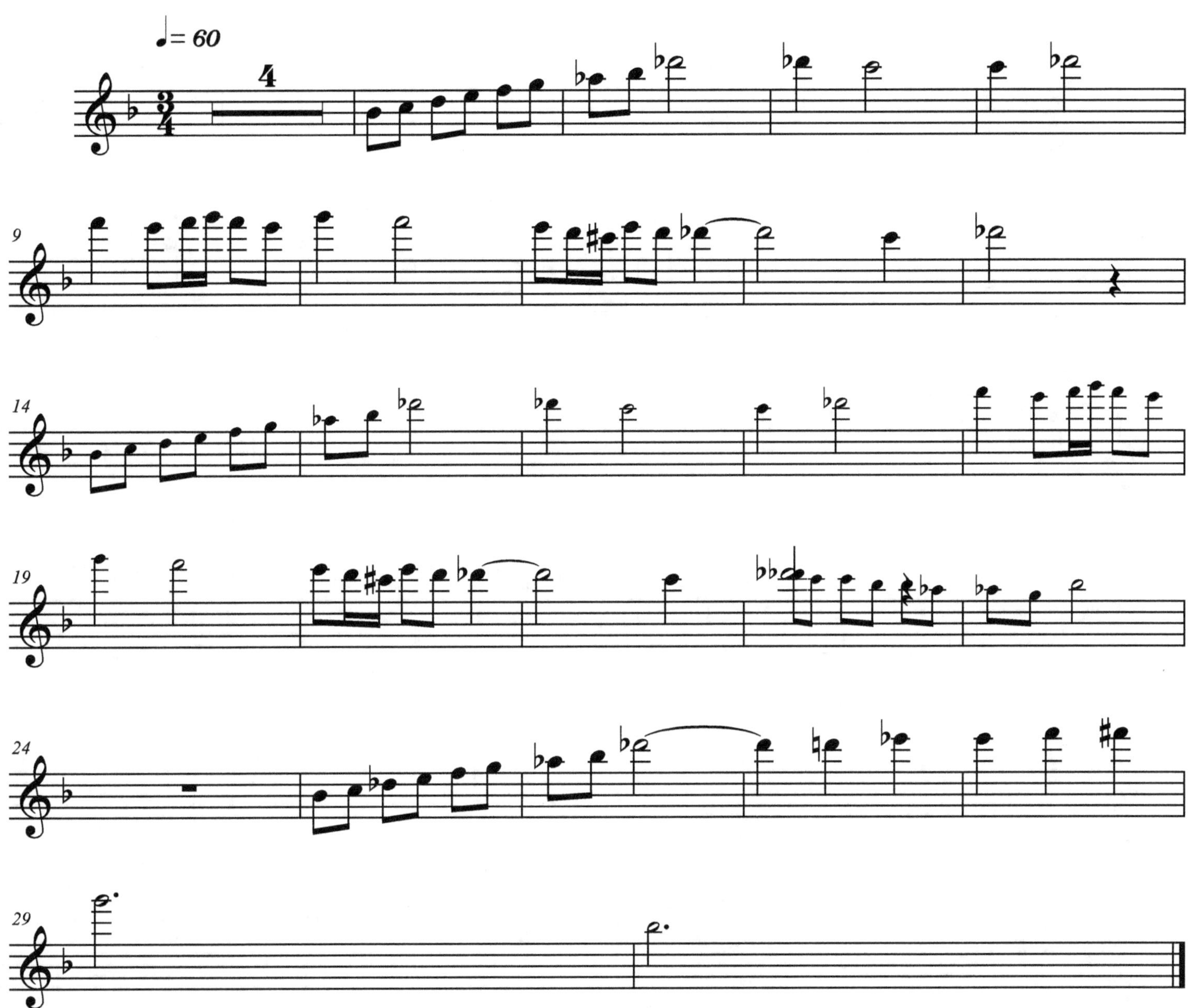

N

Part 2: C Oboe

Joost de Gro

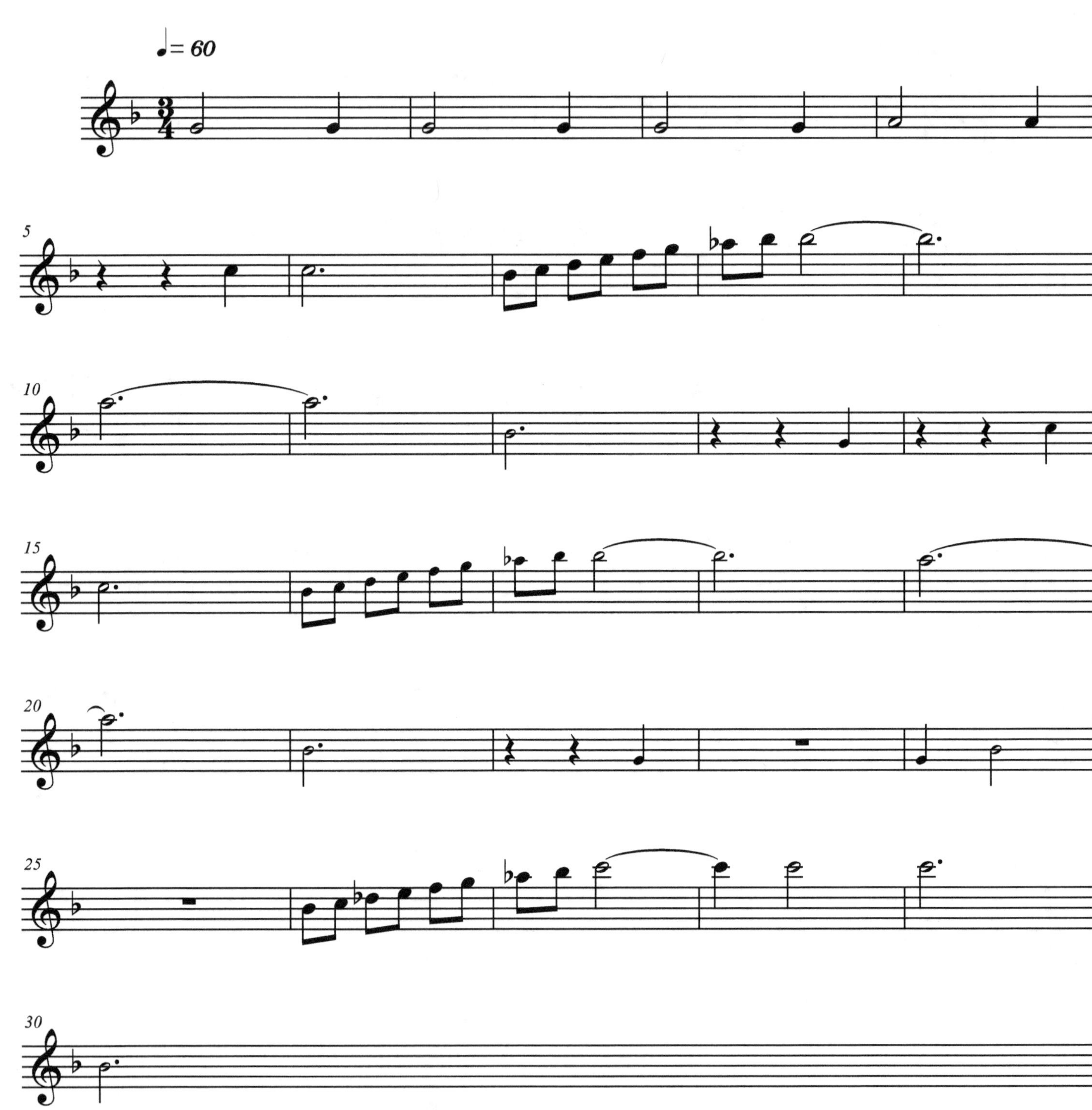

N

Part 3: Bes Clarinet

Joost de Groot

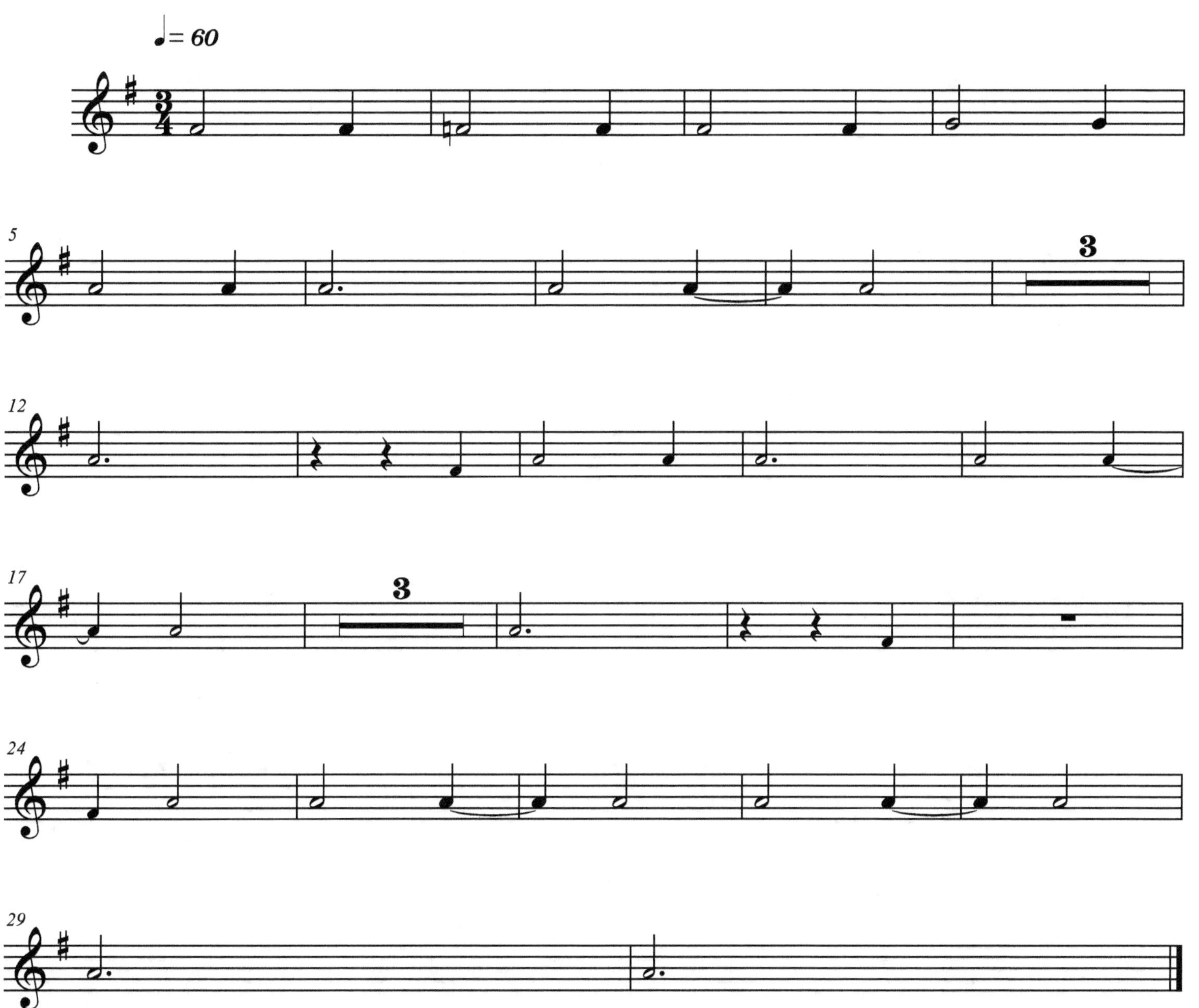

Part 4: C Bassoon

N

Joost de Gro

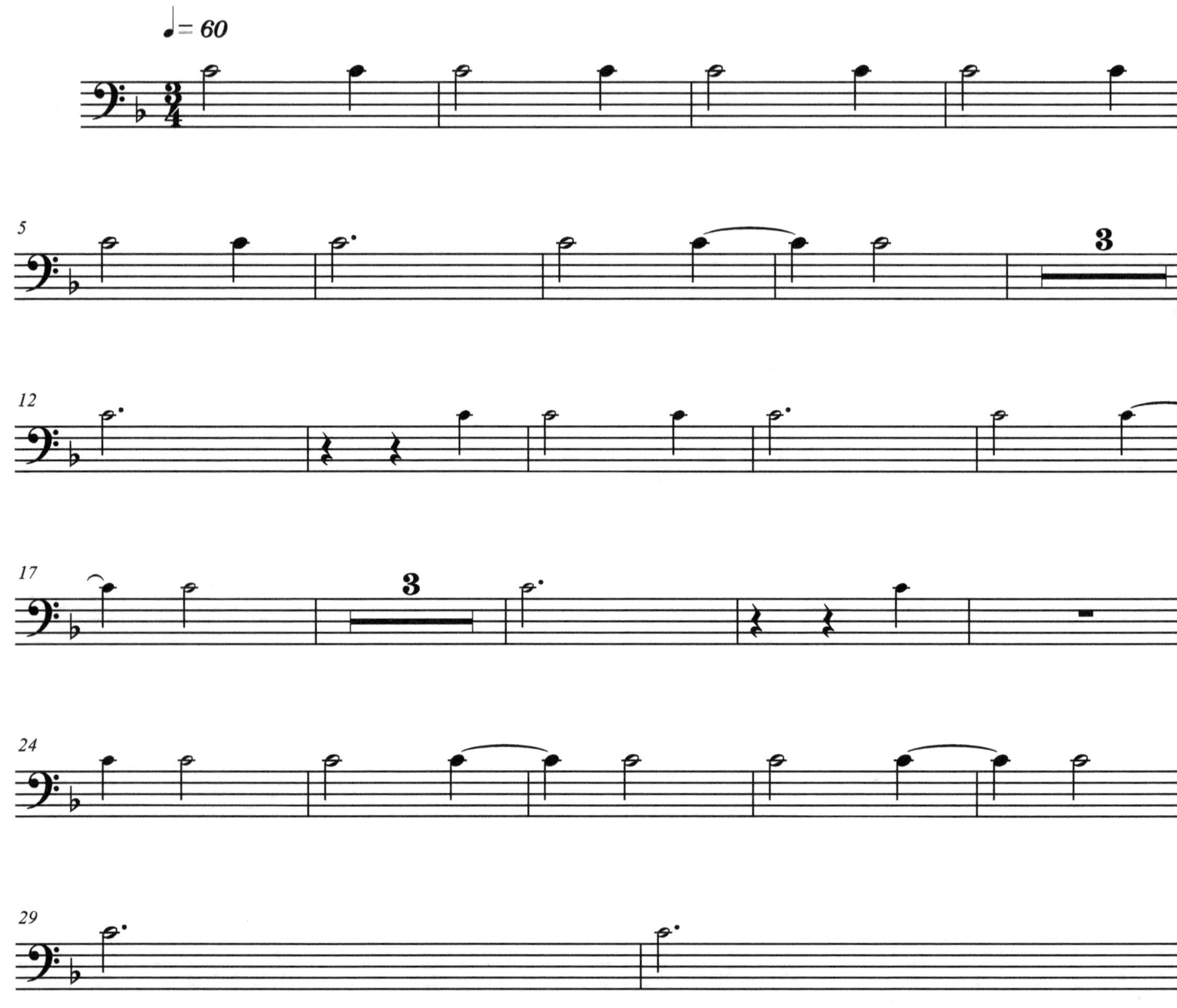

Part 1: C Flute

N

Joost de Groot

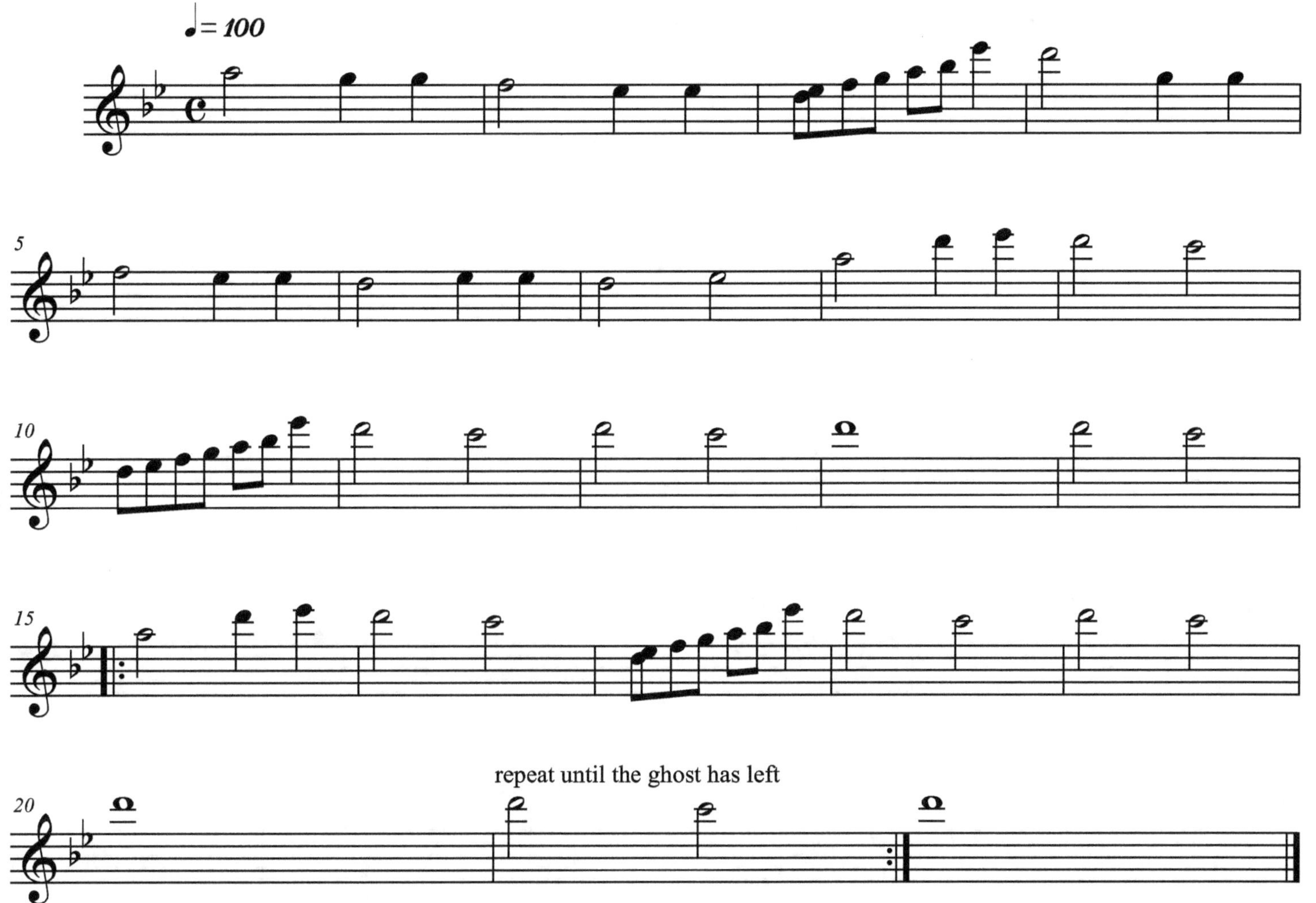

N

Part 2: C Oboe

Joost de Groo

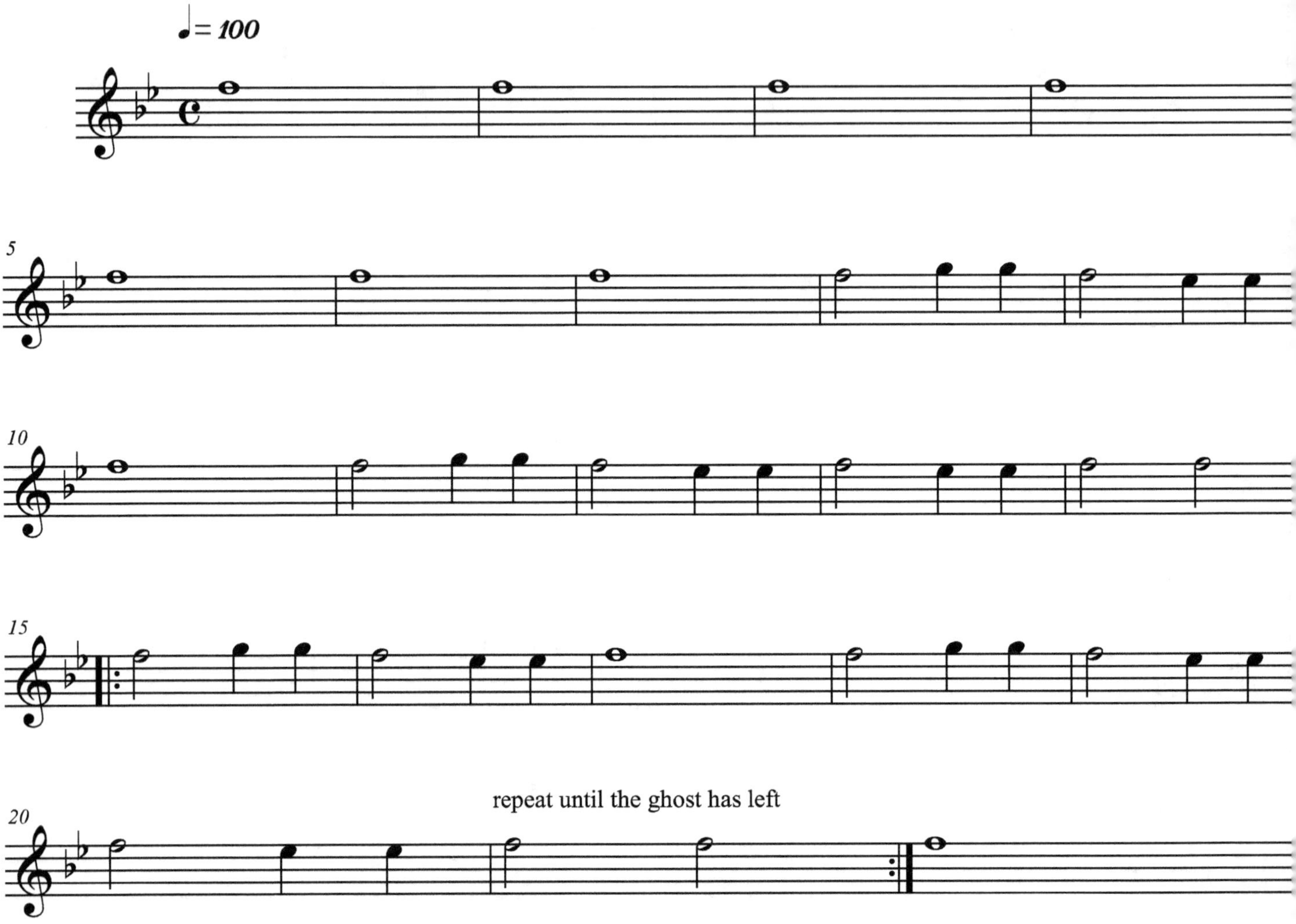

Part 3: Bes Clarinet

N

Joost de Groot

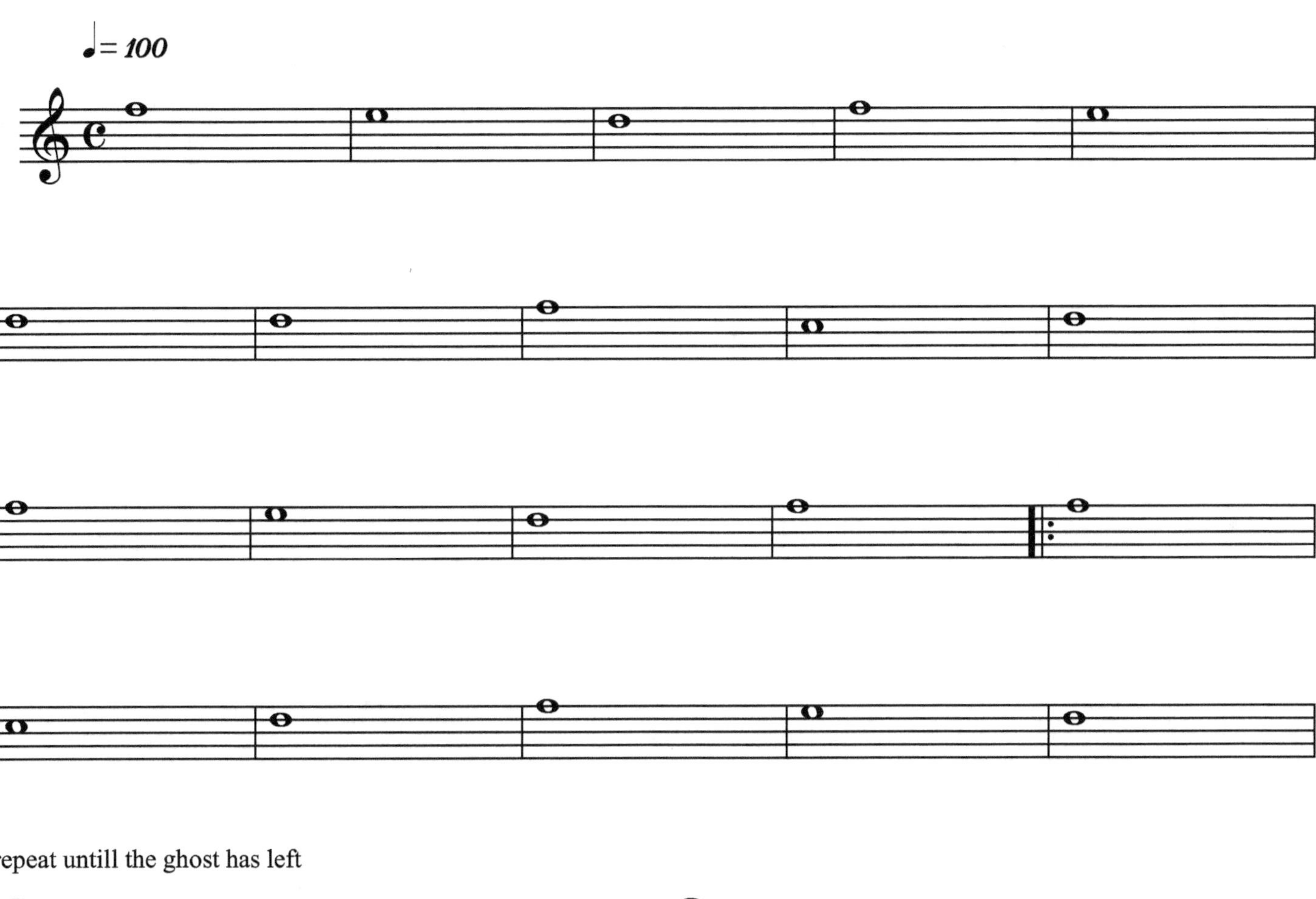

Part 4: C Bassoon

N

Joost de Gro

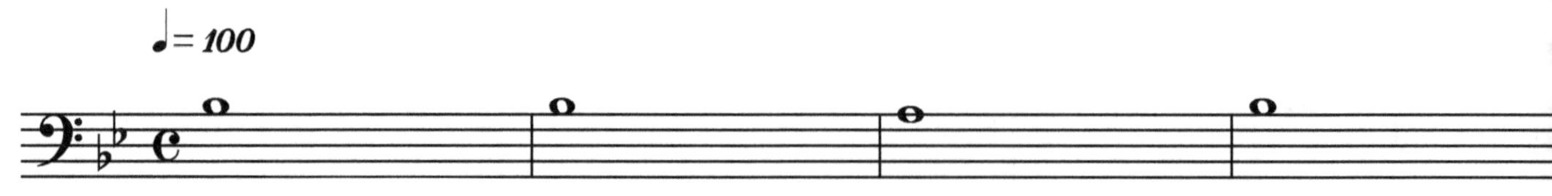

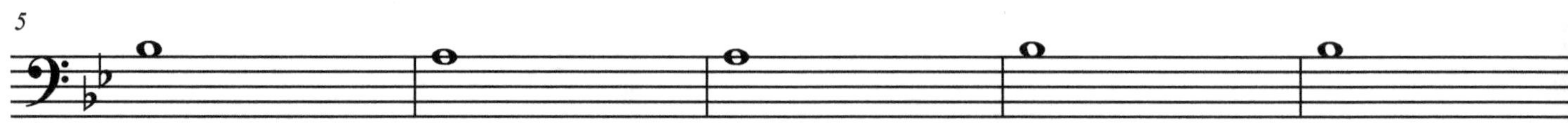

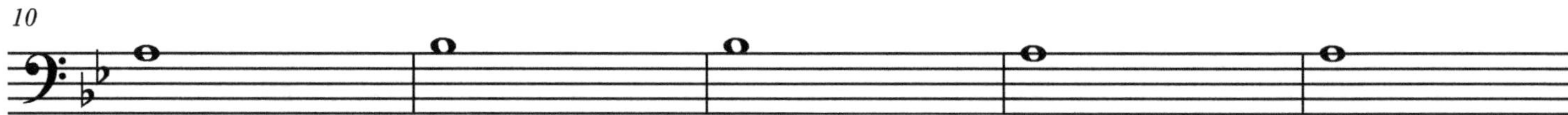

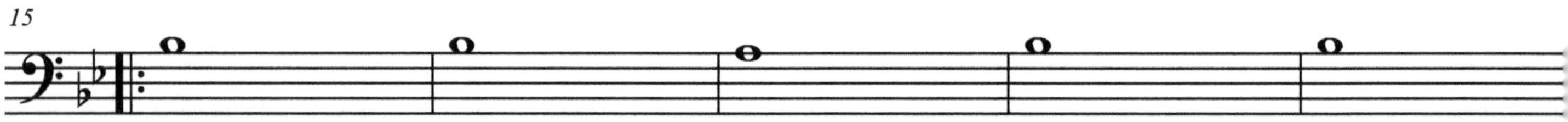

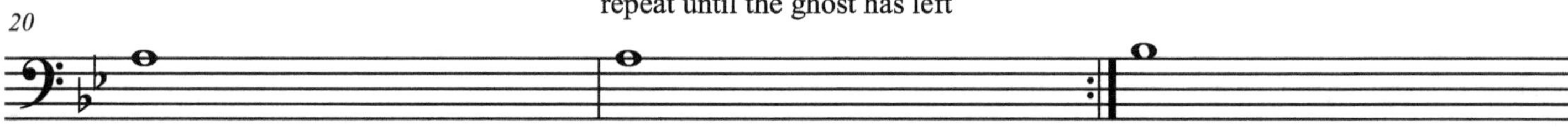

Part 1: C Flute

I

Joost de Groot

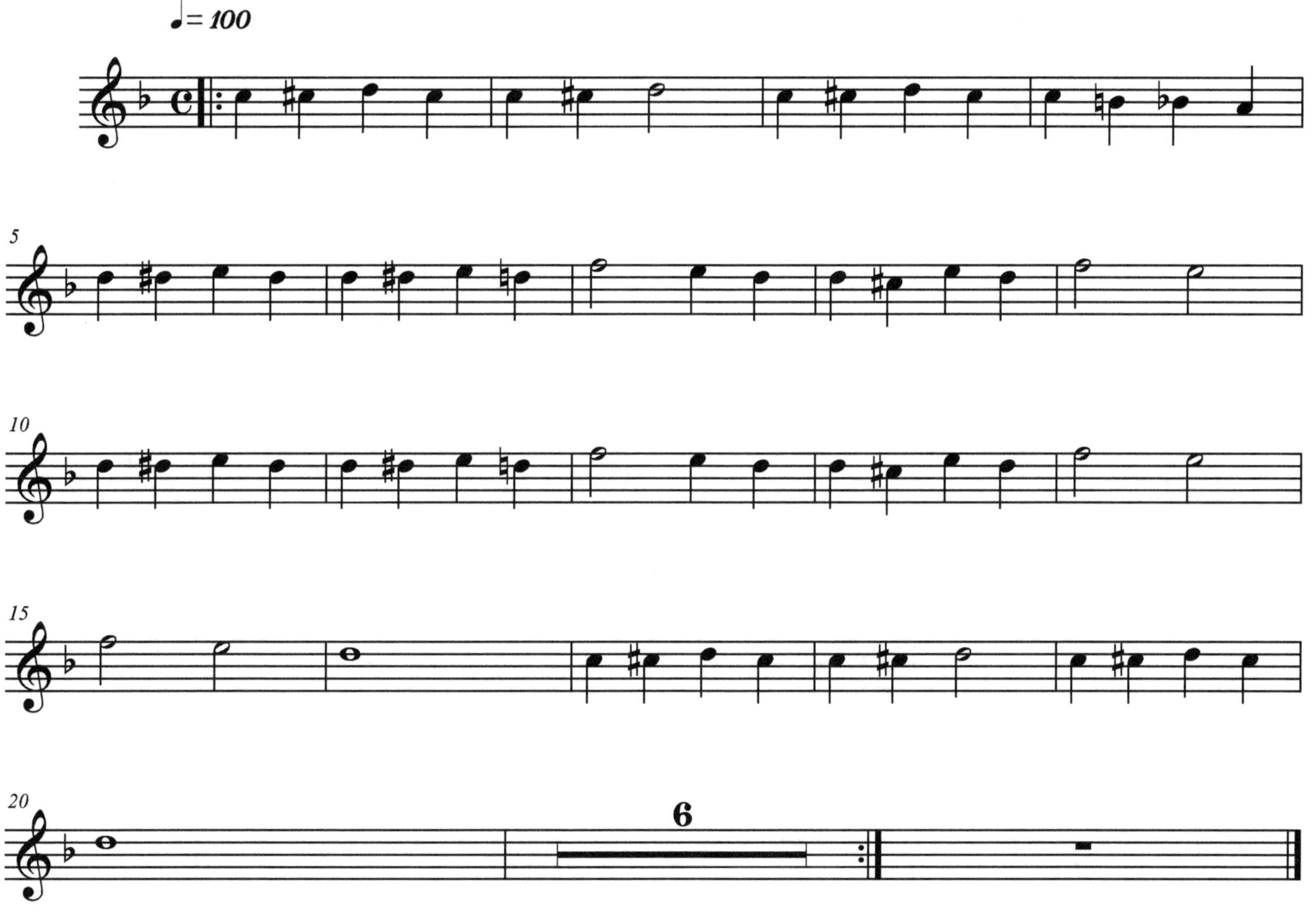

Part 2: C Oboe

I

Joost de Gro

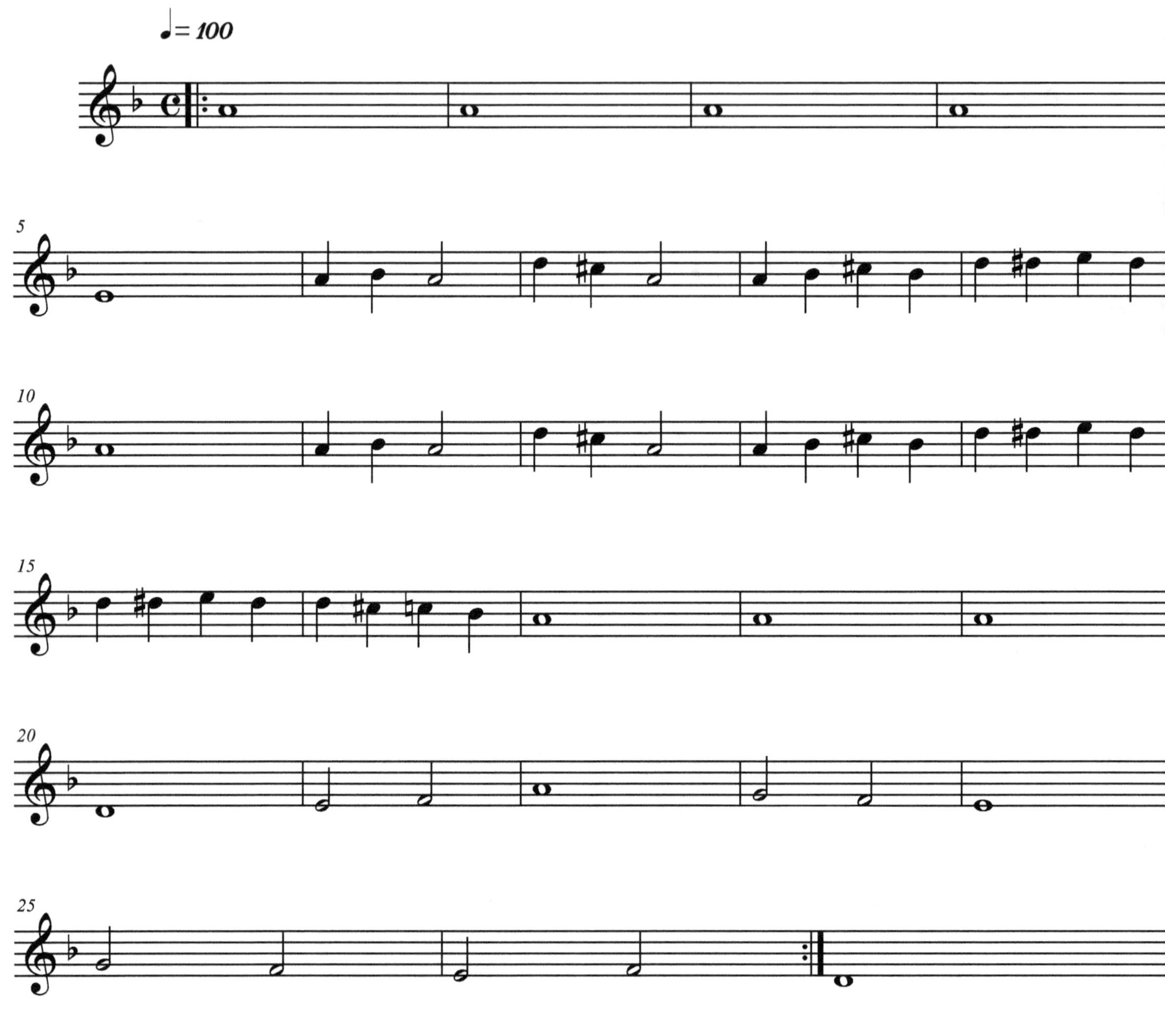

Part 3: Bes Clarinet

I

Joost de Groot

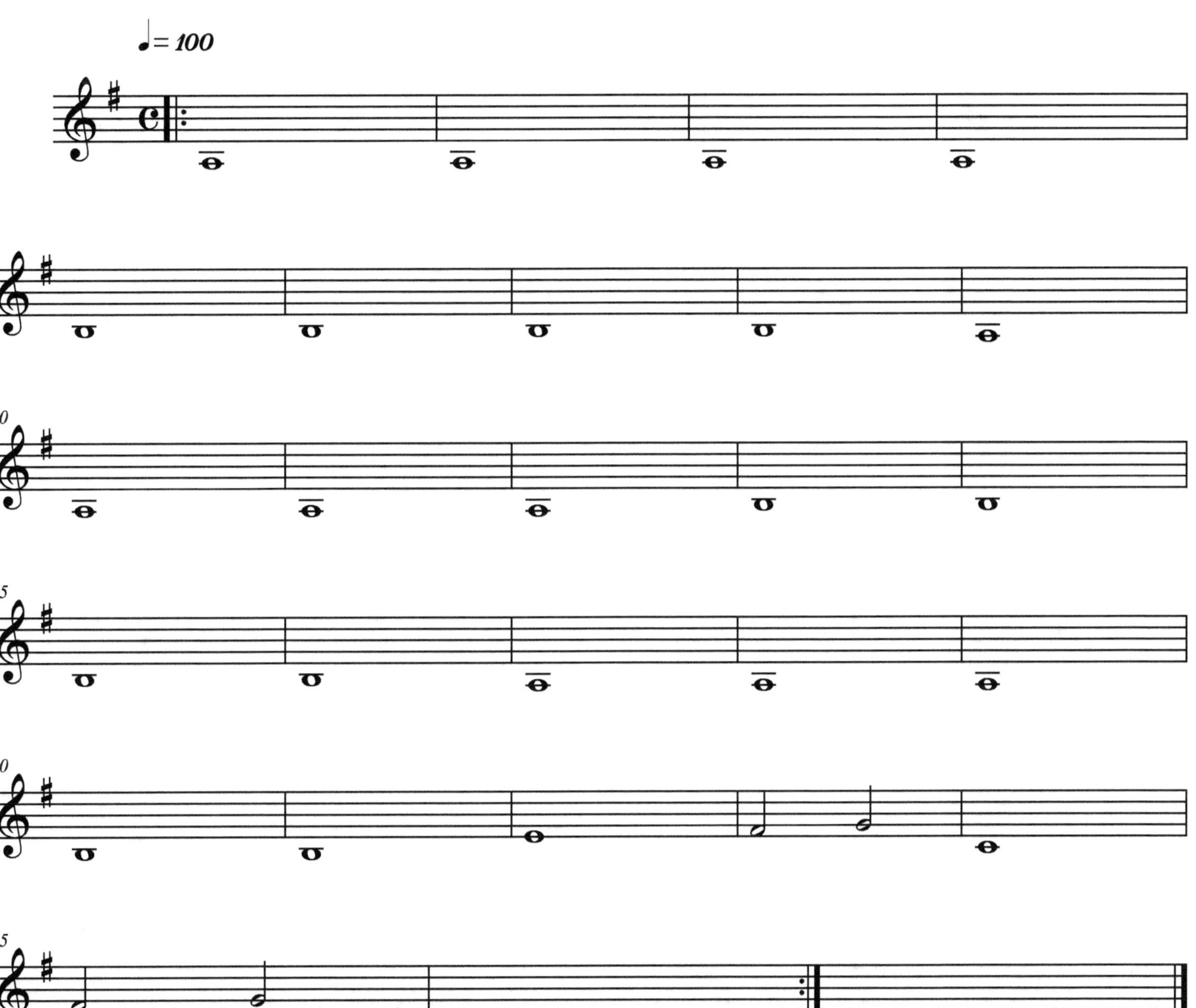

Part 4: C Bassoon

I

Joost de Gro

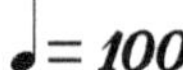

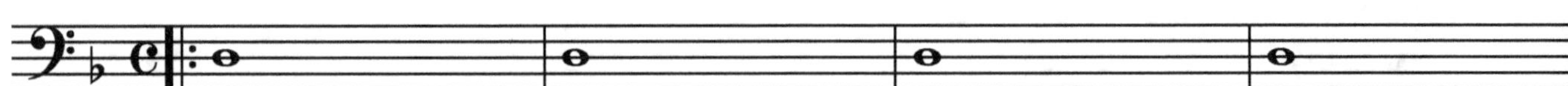

5

10

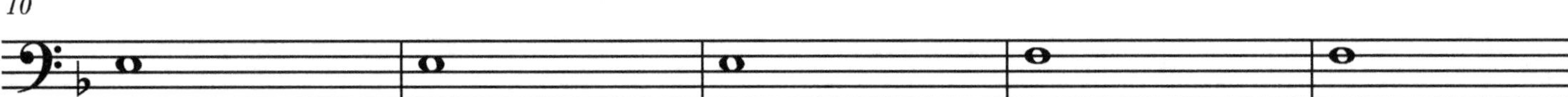

15

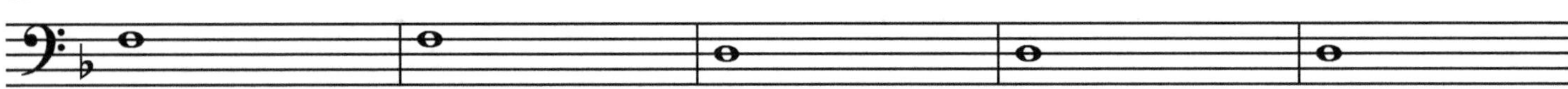

20

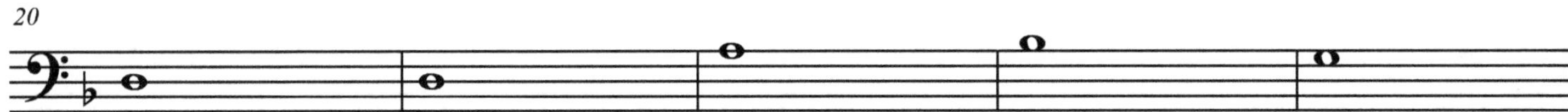

25

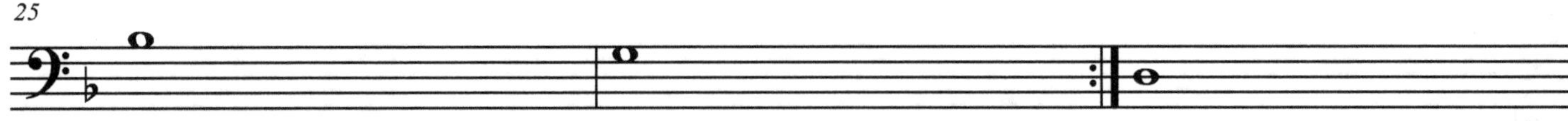

Part 1: C Flute

E

Joost de Groot

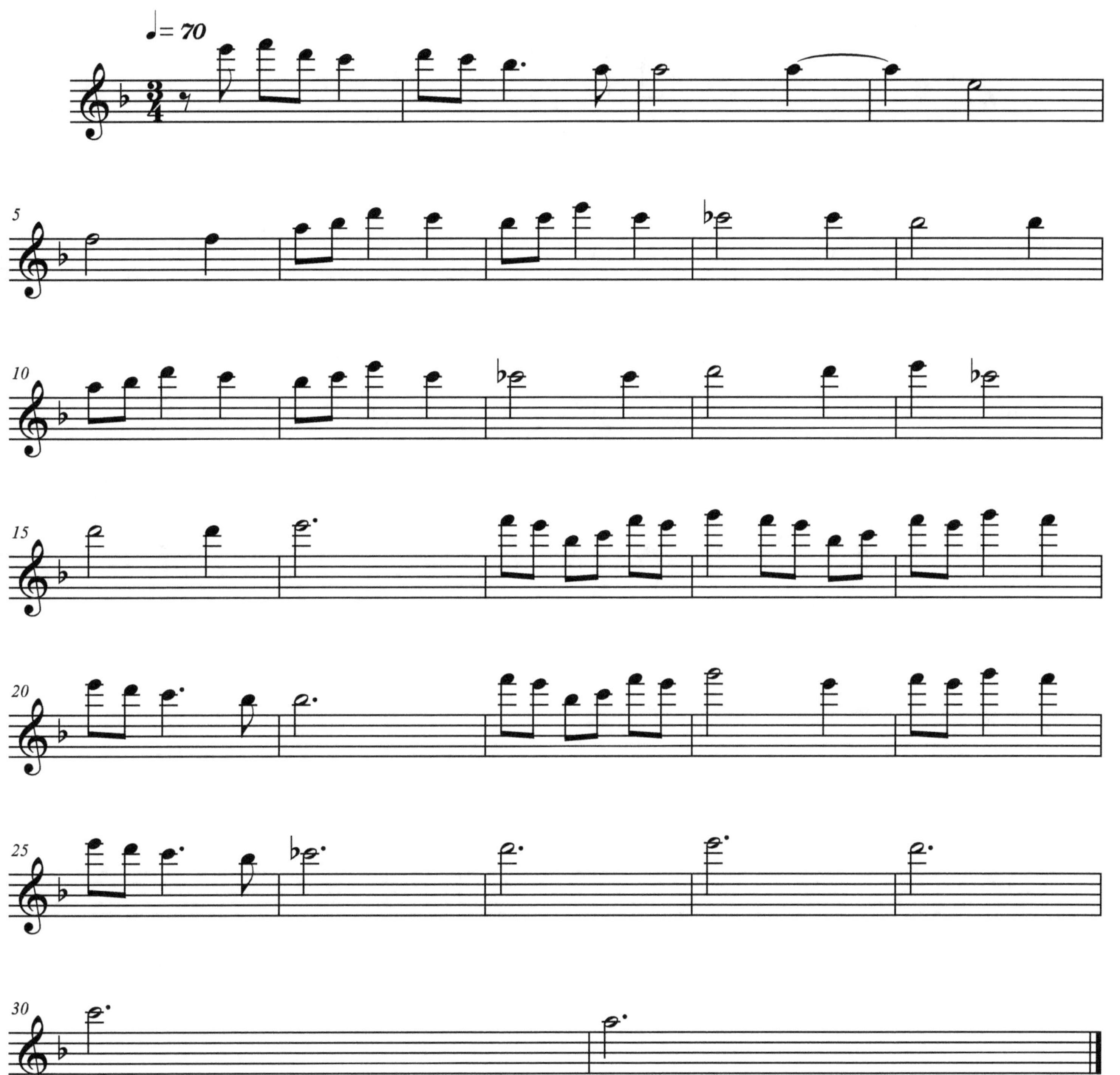

Part 2: C Oboe

E

Joost de Gro

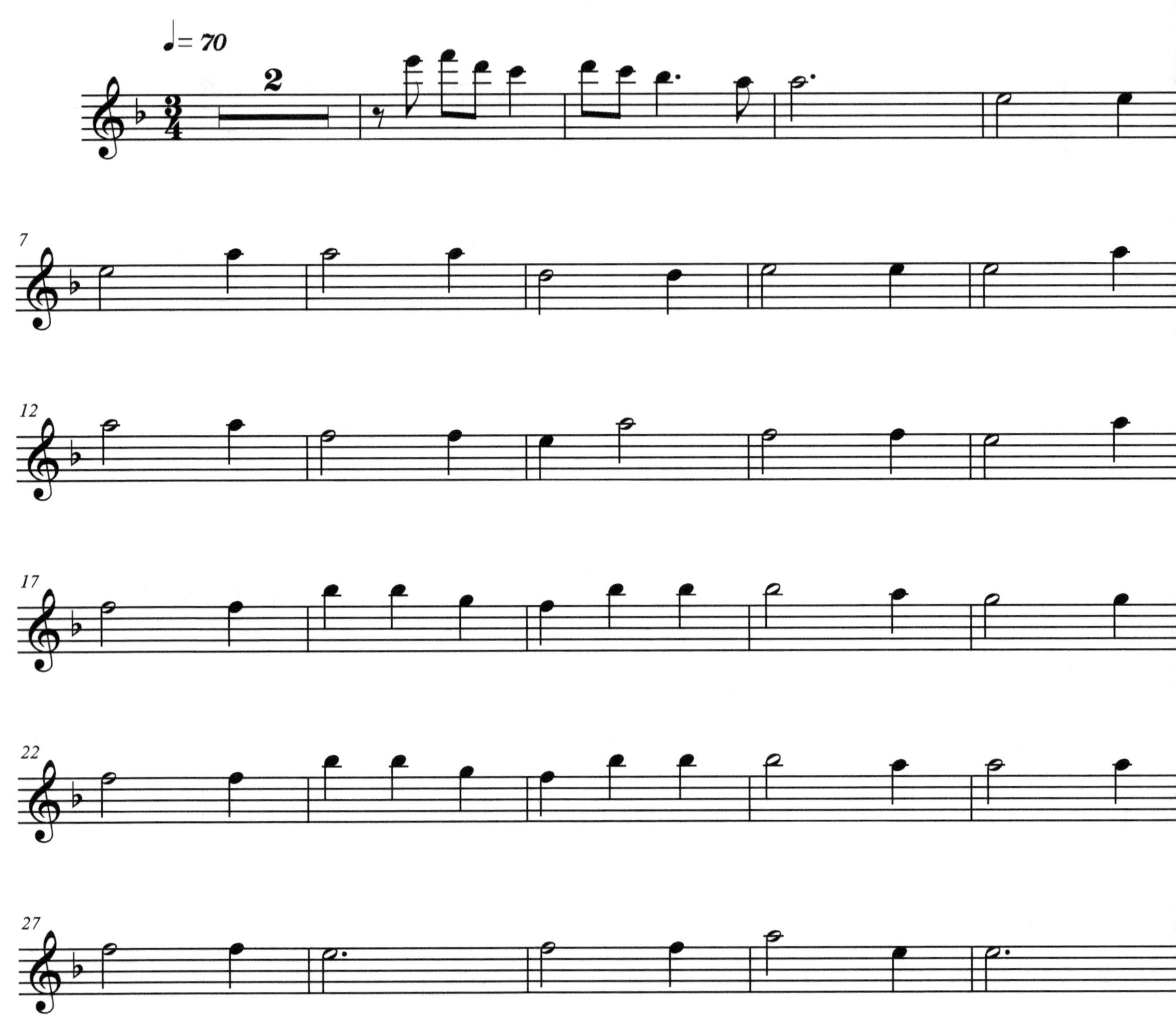

Part 3: Bes Clarinet

E

Joost de Groot

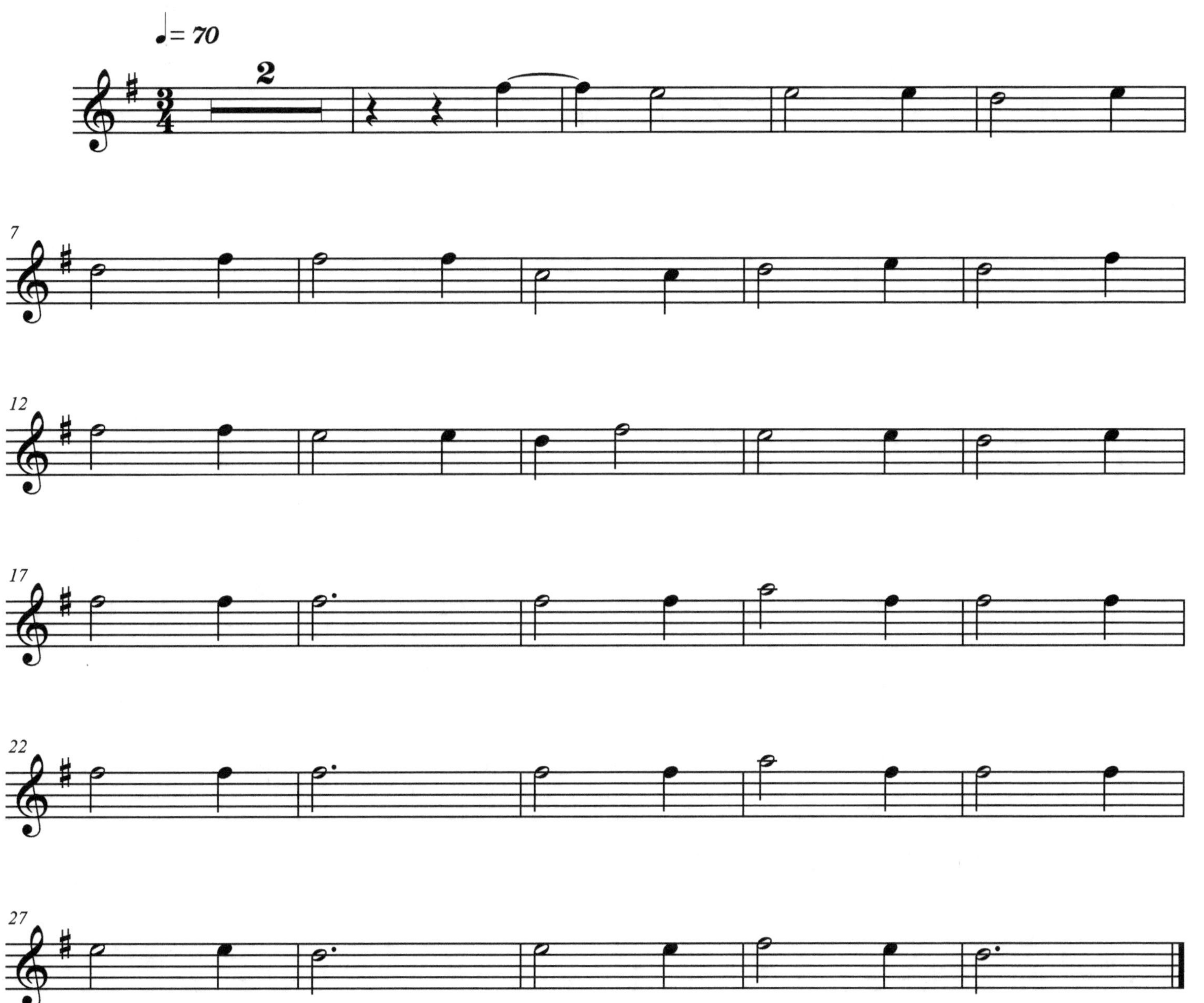

E

Part 4: C Bassoon

Joost de Gro

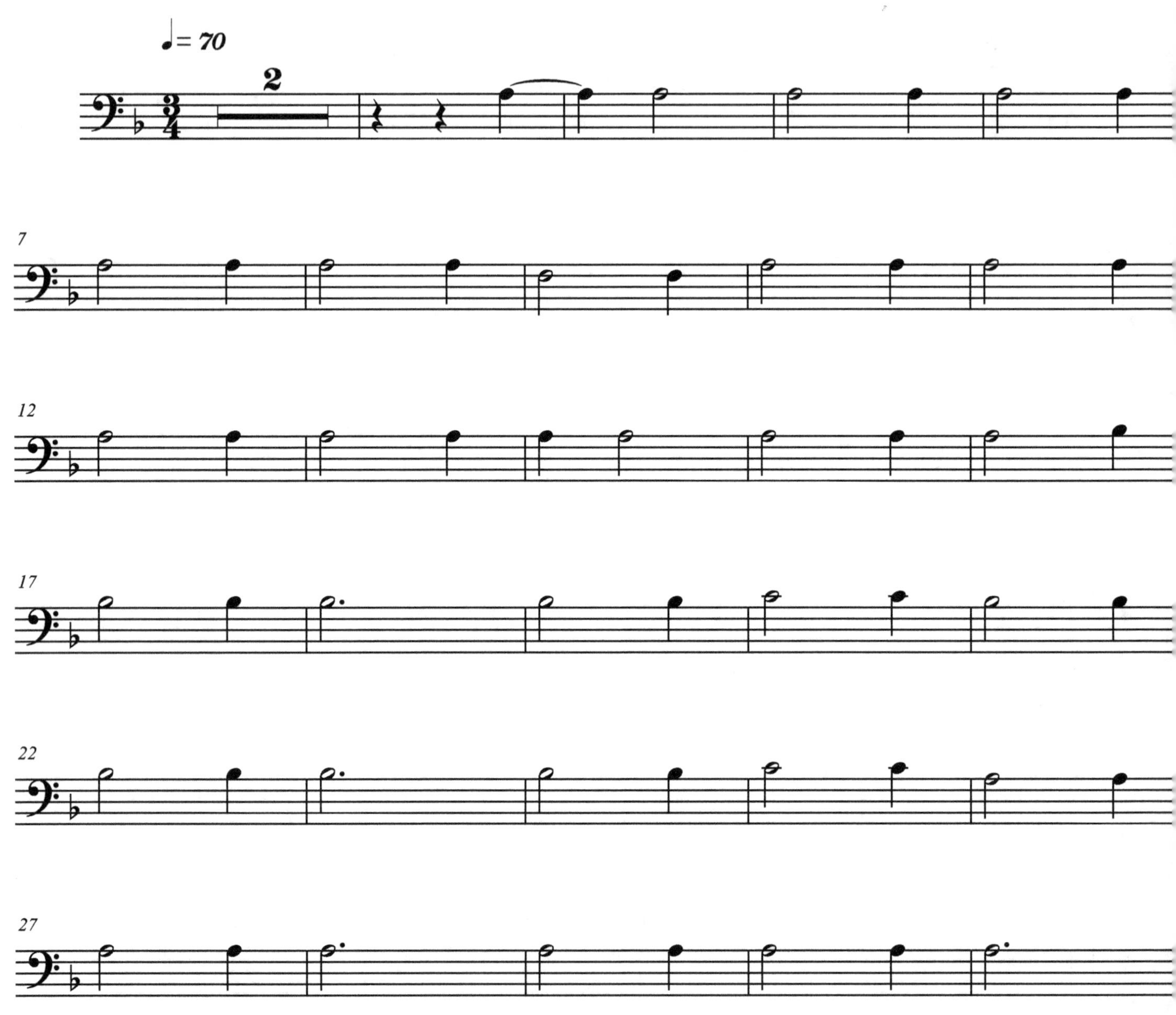

Clarinet Quartet

Part 1: Bes Clarinet 1

Part 2: Bes Clarinet 2

Part 3: Bes Clarinet 3/Es Alto Clarinet

Part 4: Bes Clarinet 4/Bes Bass Clarinet

J

Part 1: Bes Clarinet 1

Joost de Gro

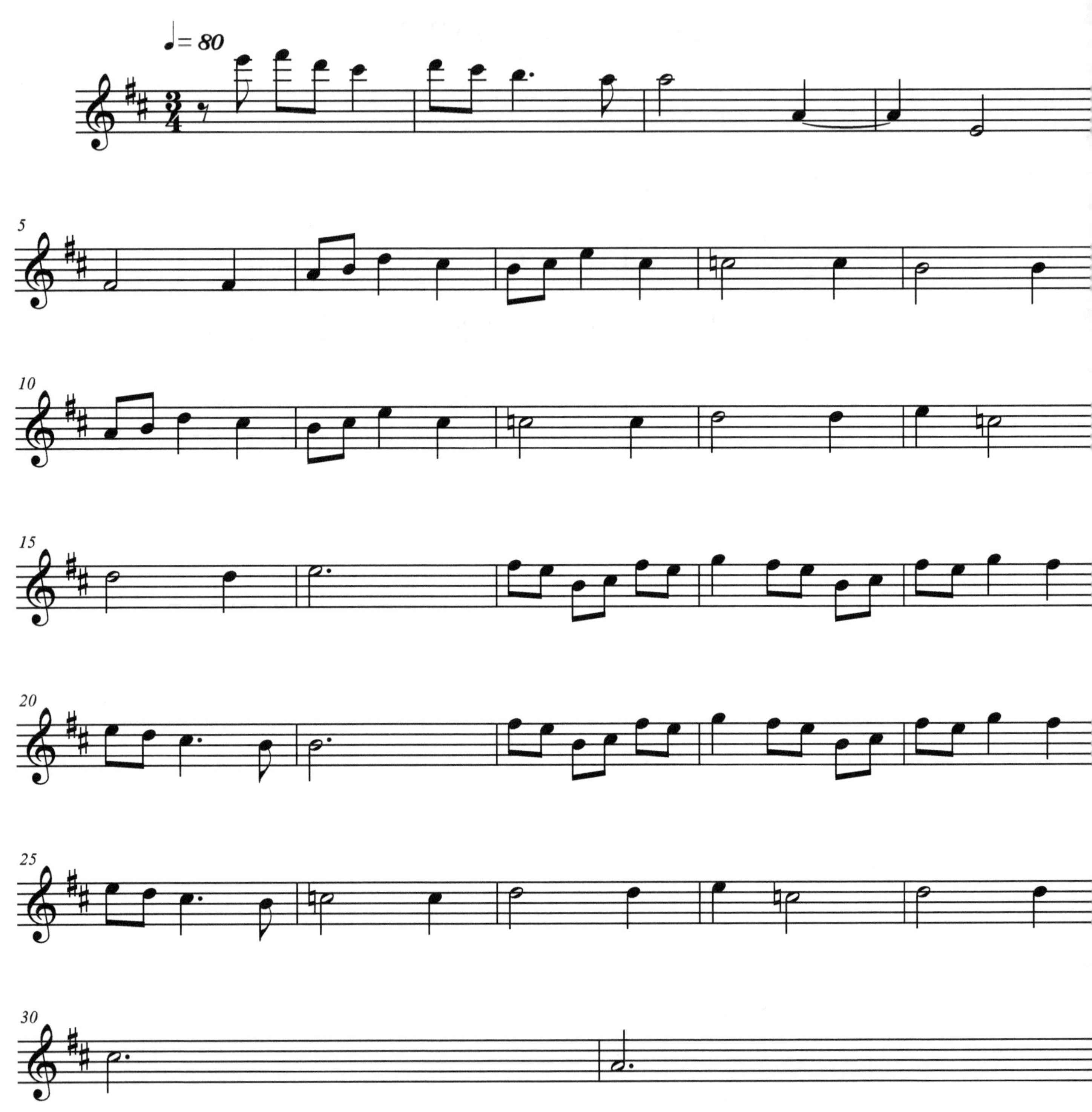

Part 2: Bes Clarinet 2

J

Joost de Groot

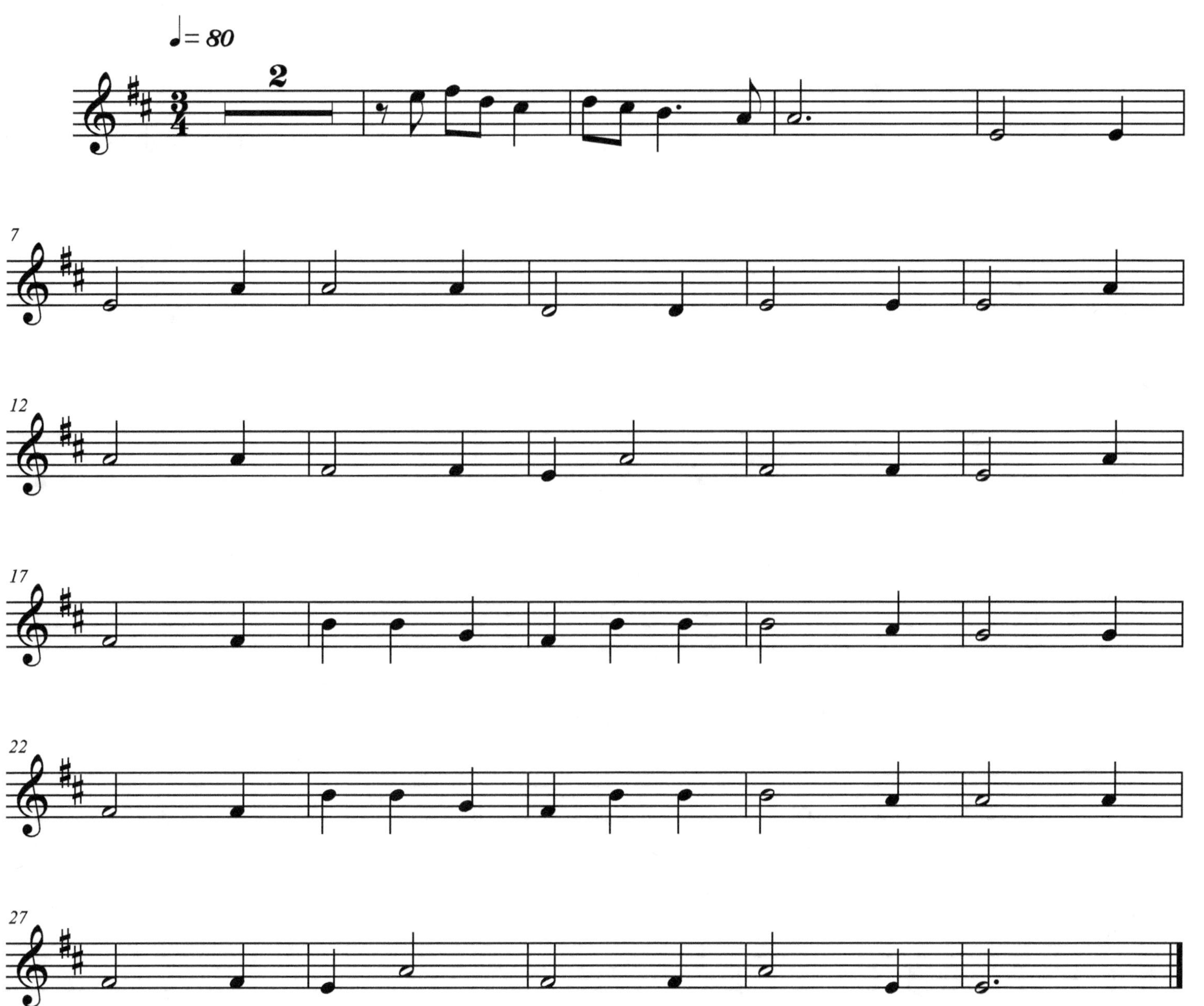

Part 3: Bes Clarinet 3

J

Joost de Gro

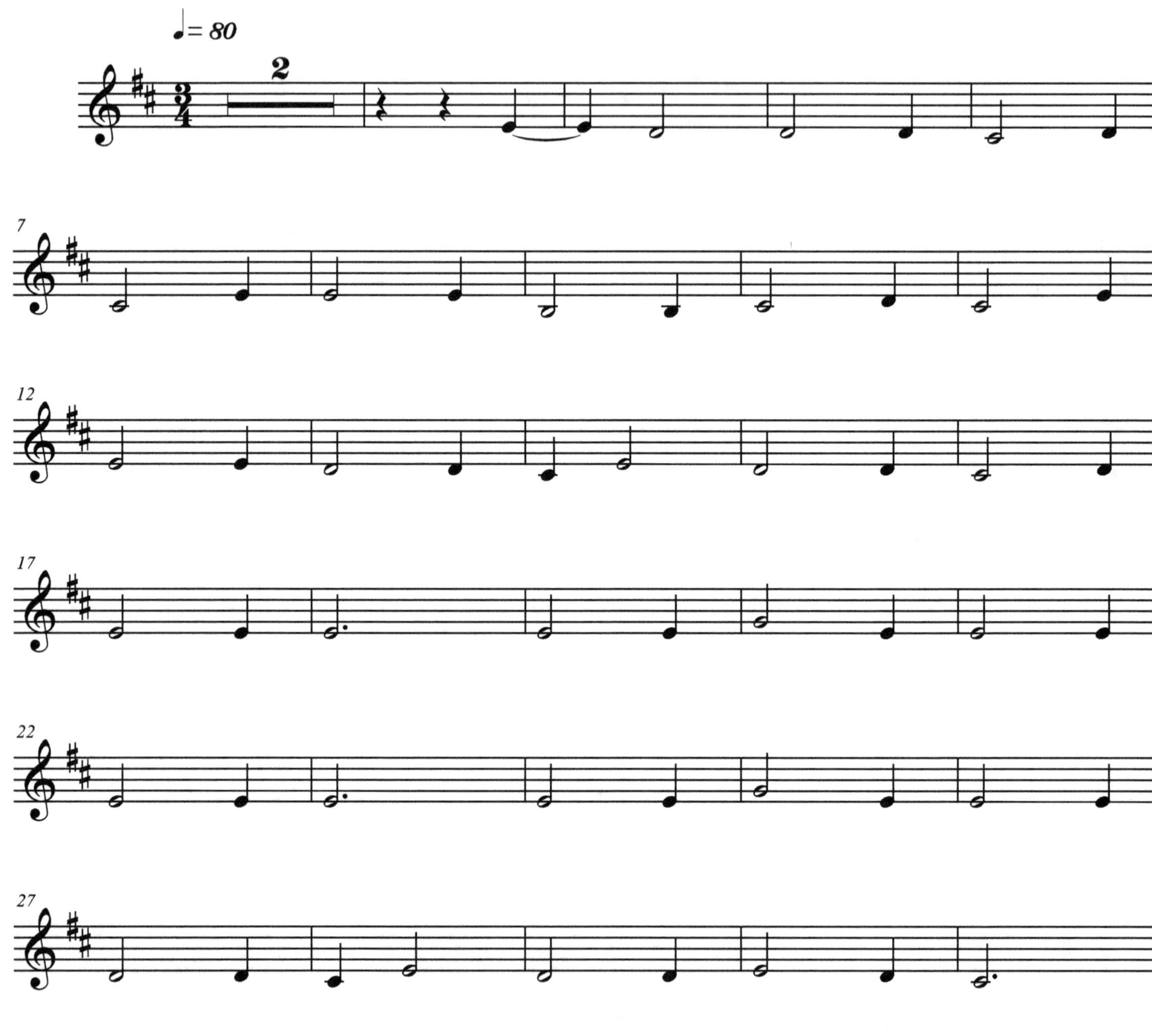

J

Part 3: Es Alto Clarinet

Joost de Groot

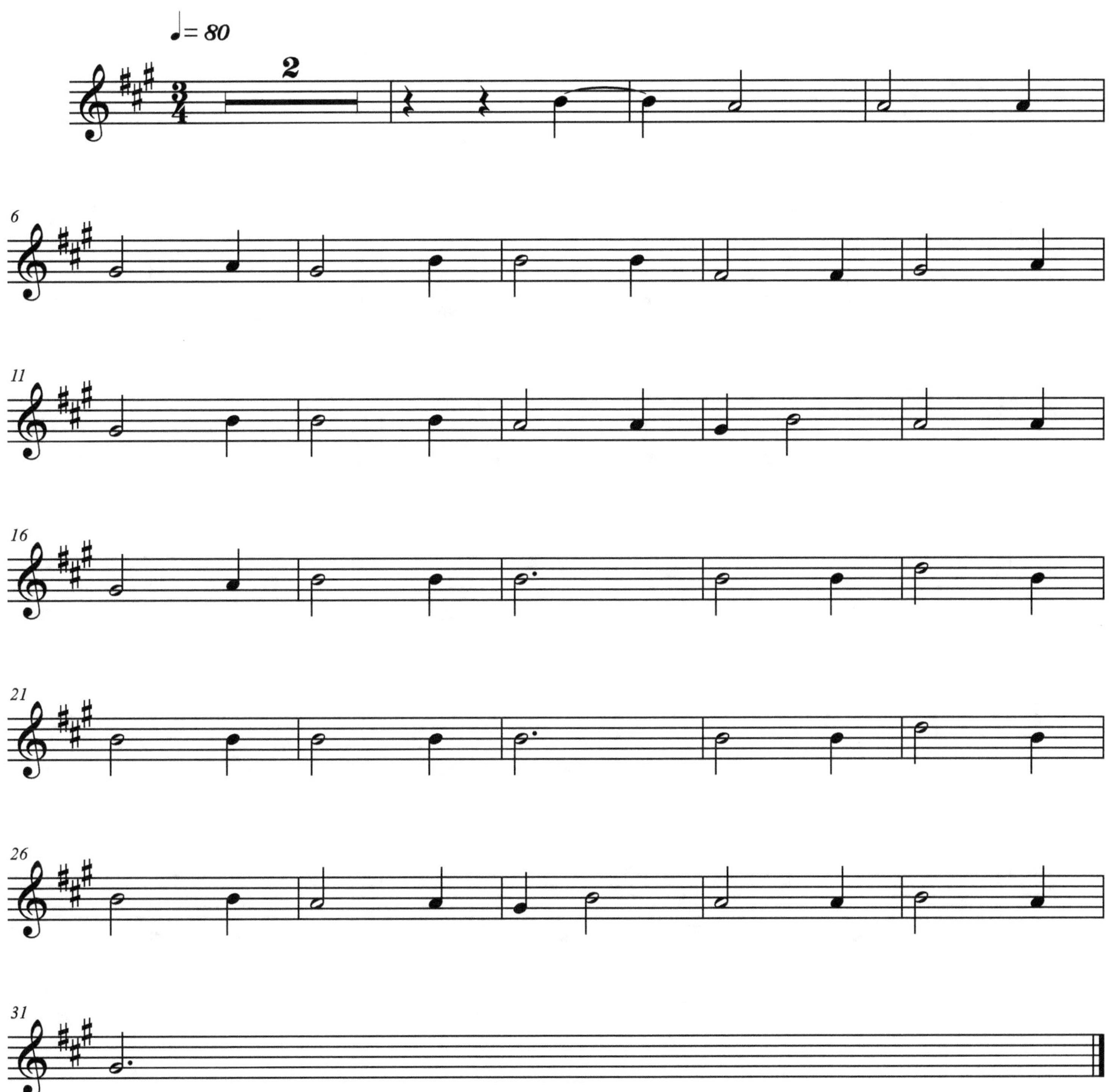

J

Part 4: Bes Clarinet 4

Joost de Gro

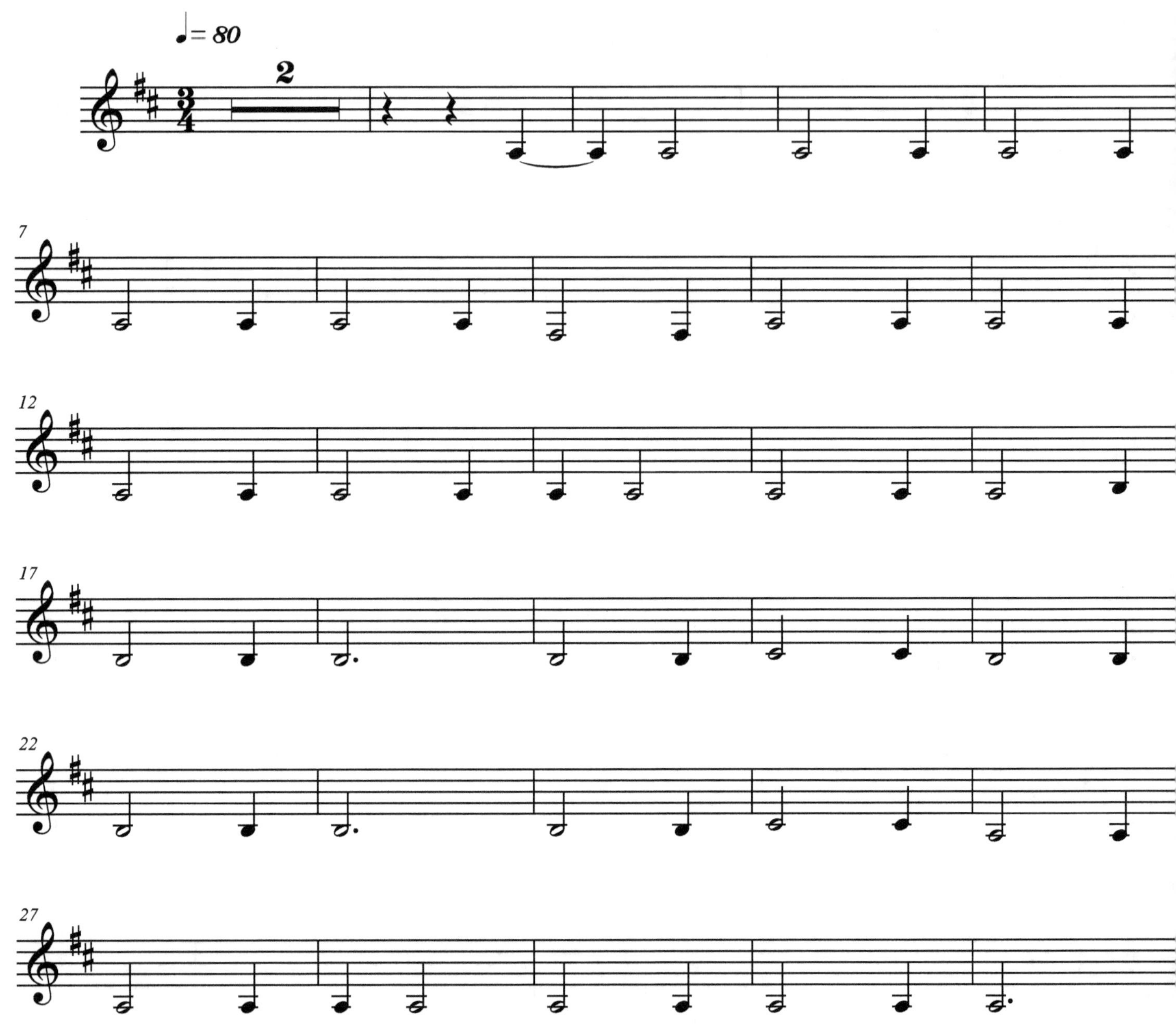

J

Part 4: Bes Bass Clarinet

Joost de Groot

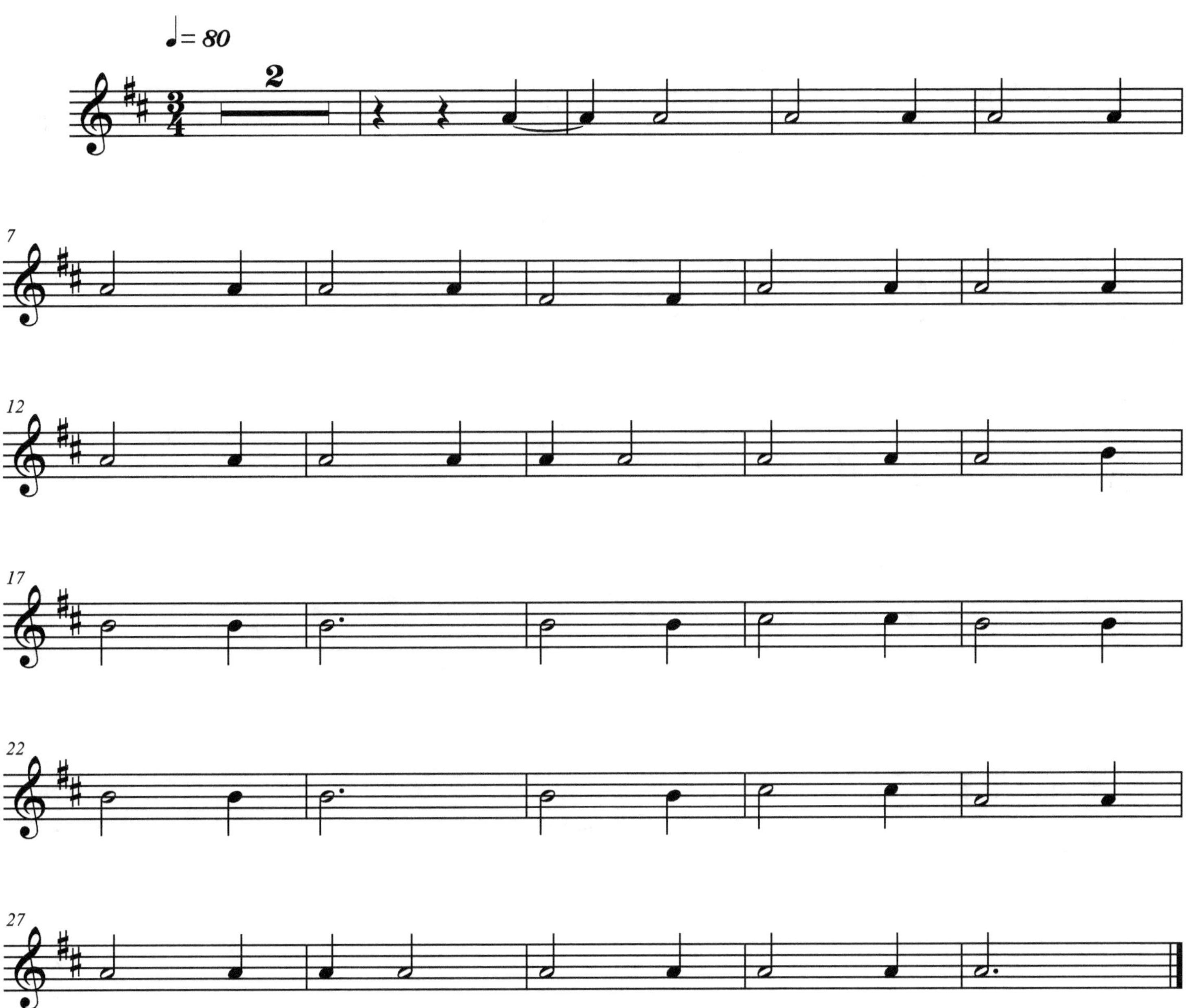

A

Part 1: Bes Clarinet 1

Joost de Gro

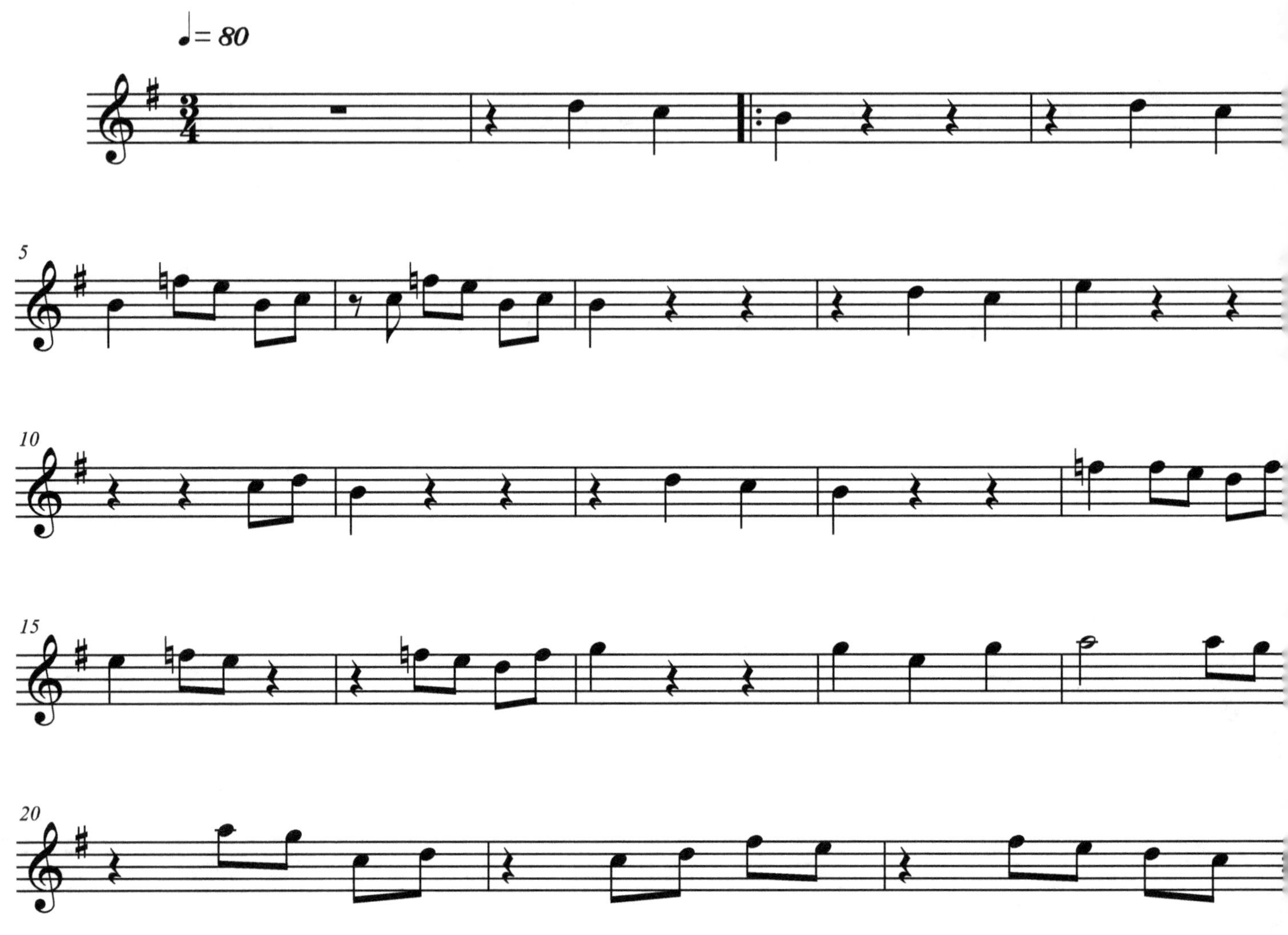

Part 2: Bes Clarinet 2

A

Joost de Groot

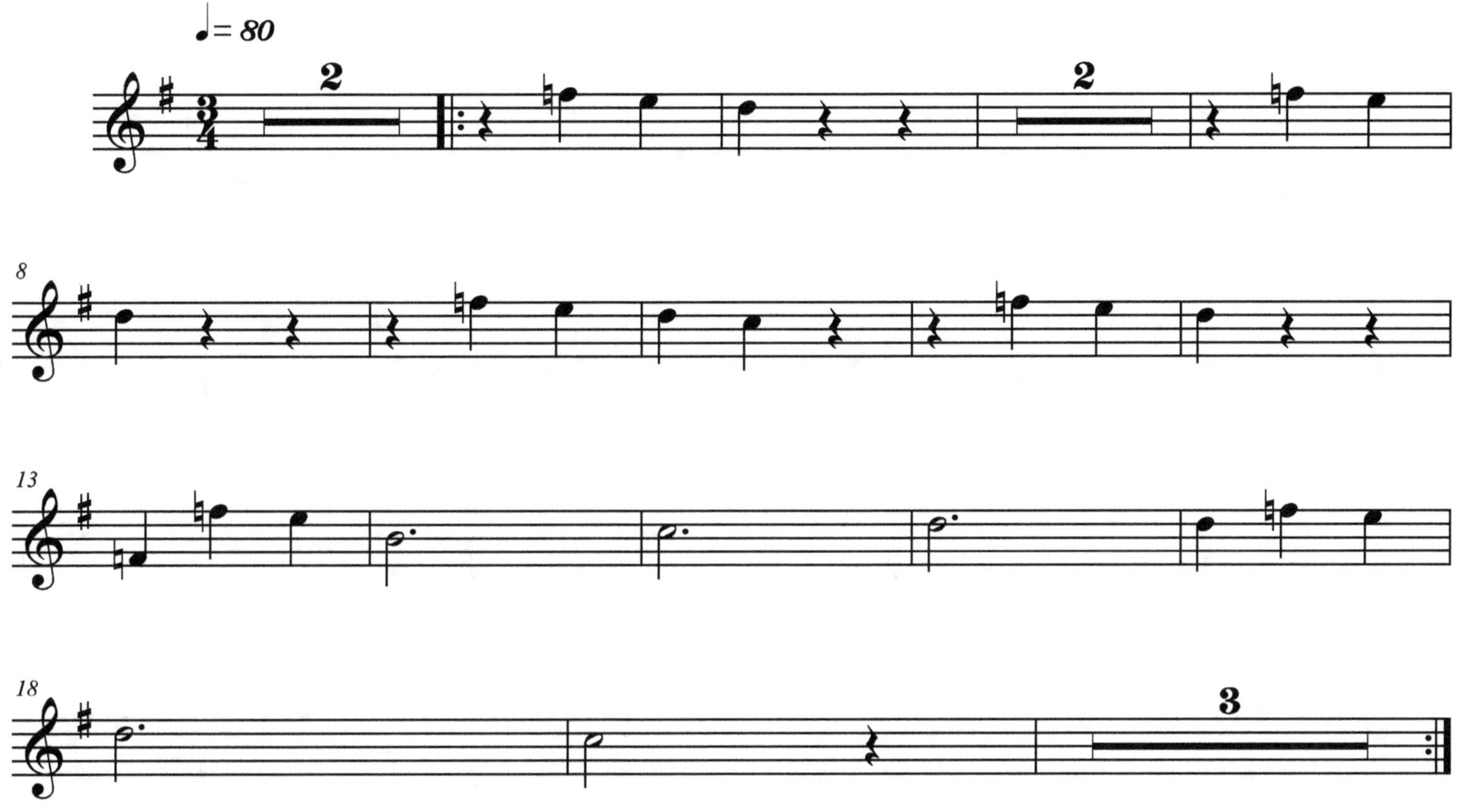

Part 3: Bes Clarinet 3

A

Joost de Gro

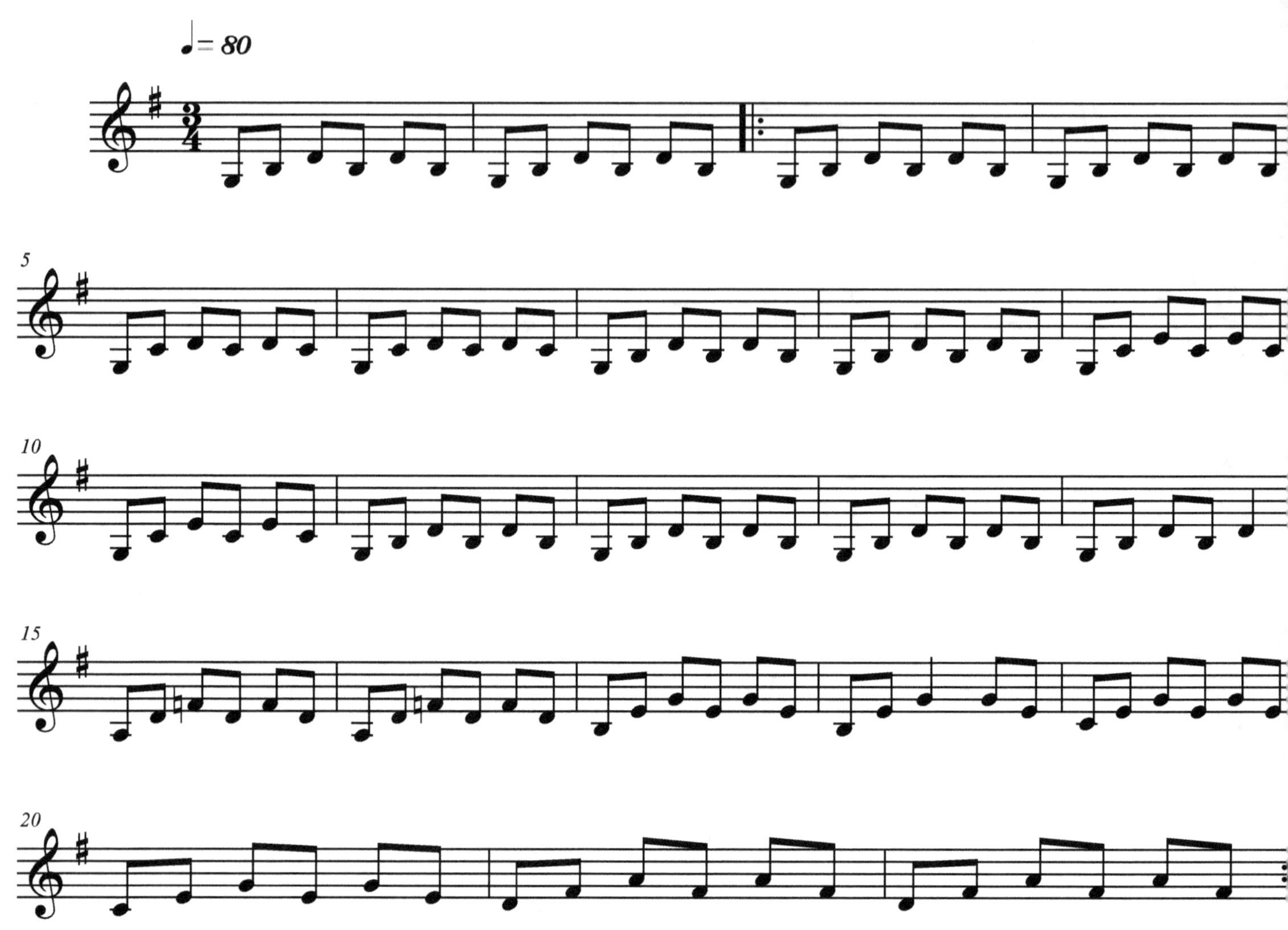

A

Part 3: Es Alto Clarinet

Joost de Groot

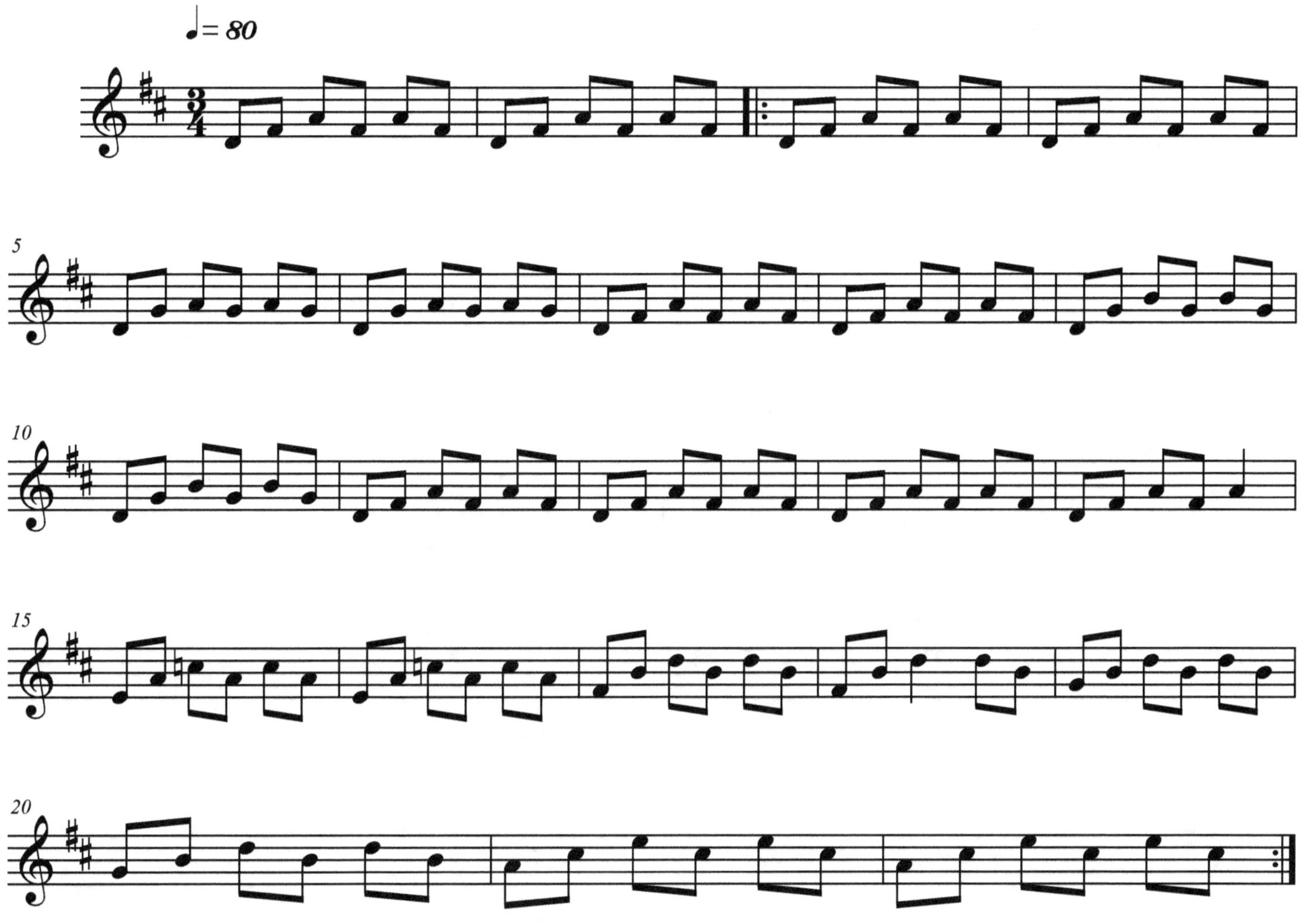

Part 4: Bes Clarinet 4

A

Joost de Gro

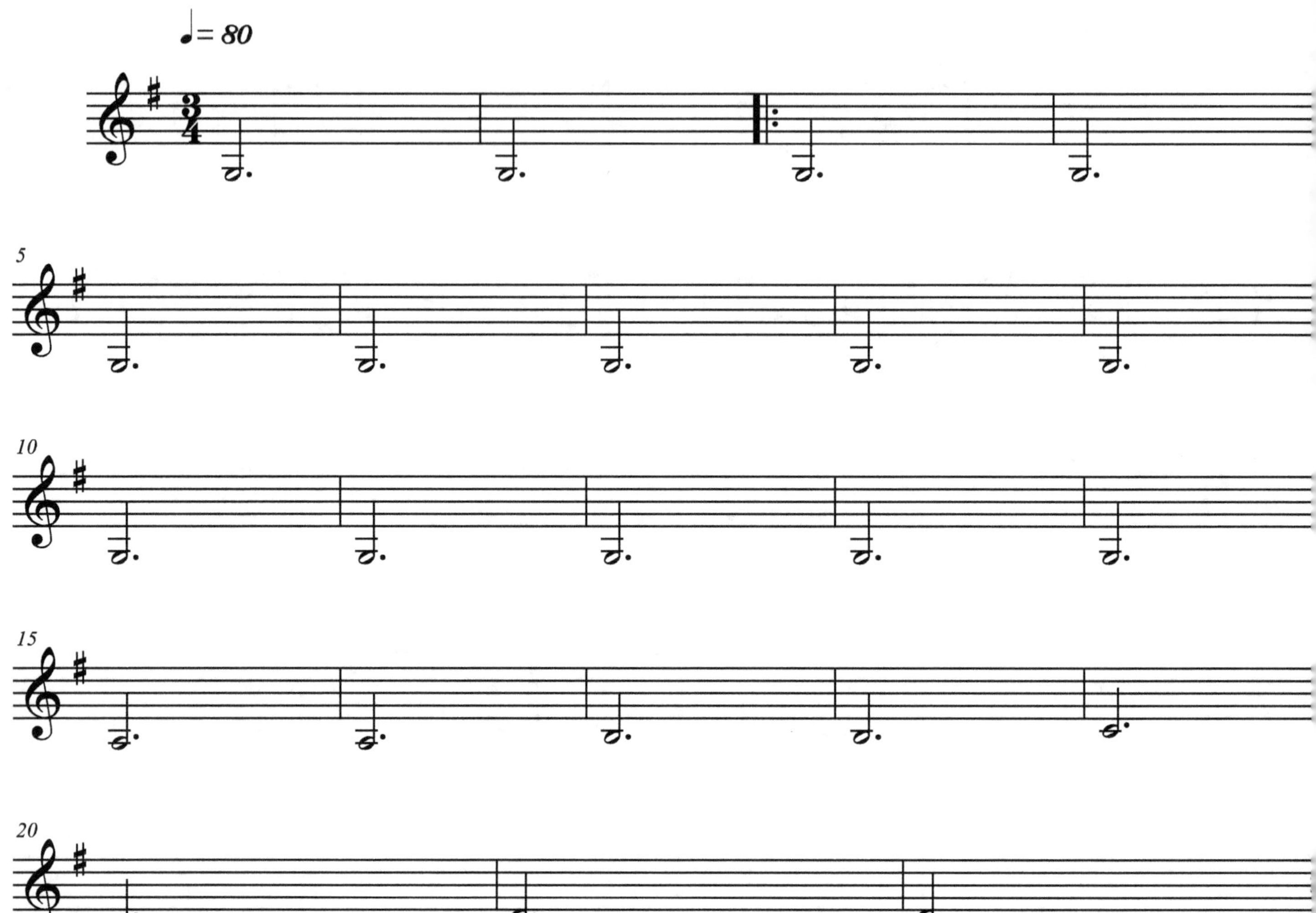

Part 4: Bes Bass Clarinet

A

Joost de Groot

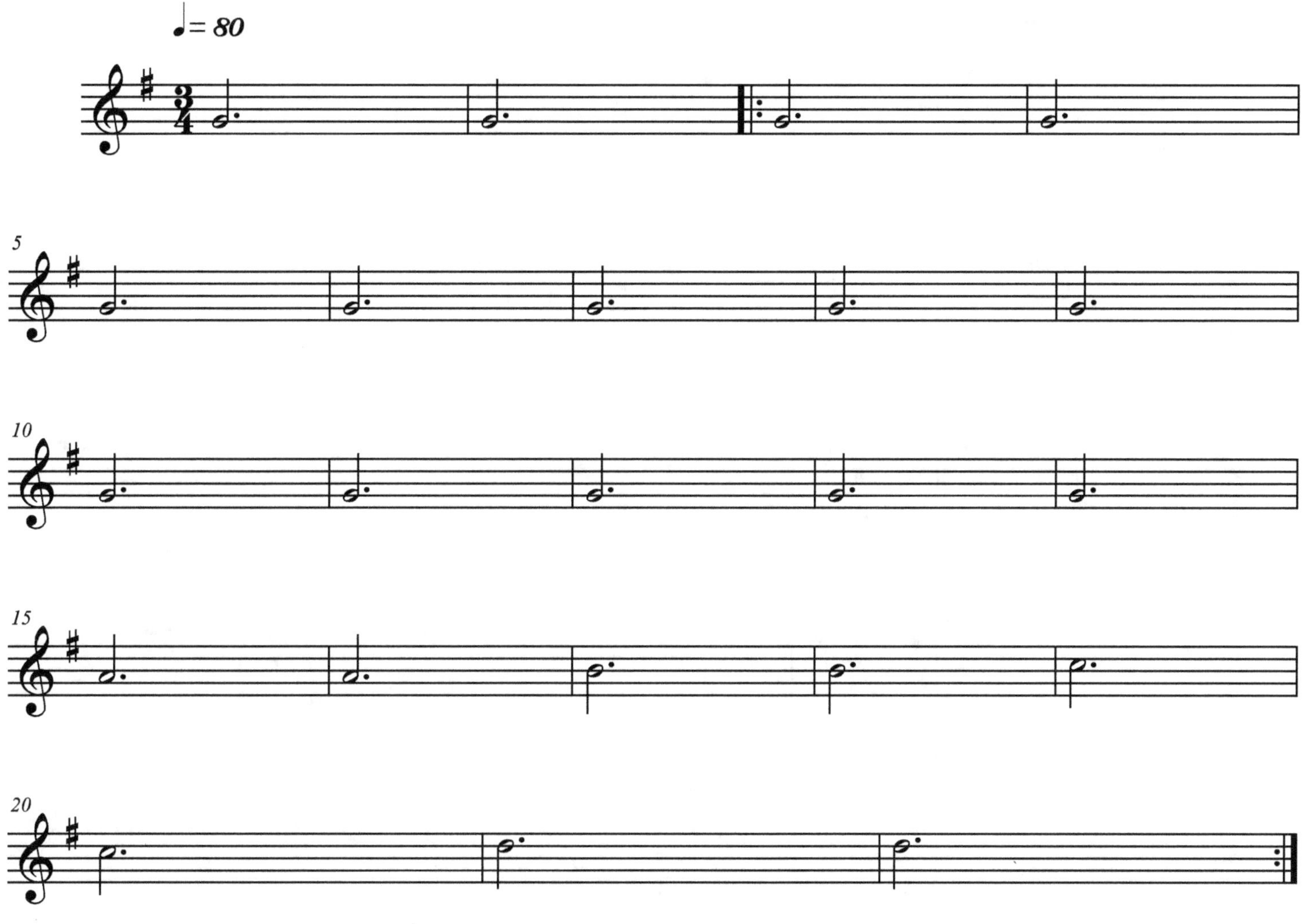

N

Part 1: Bes Clarinet 1

Joost de Gro

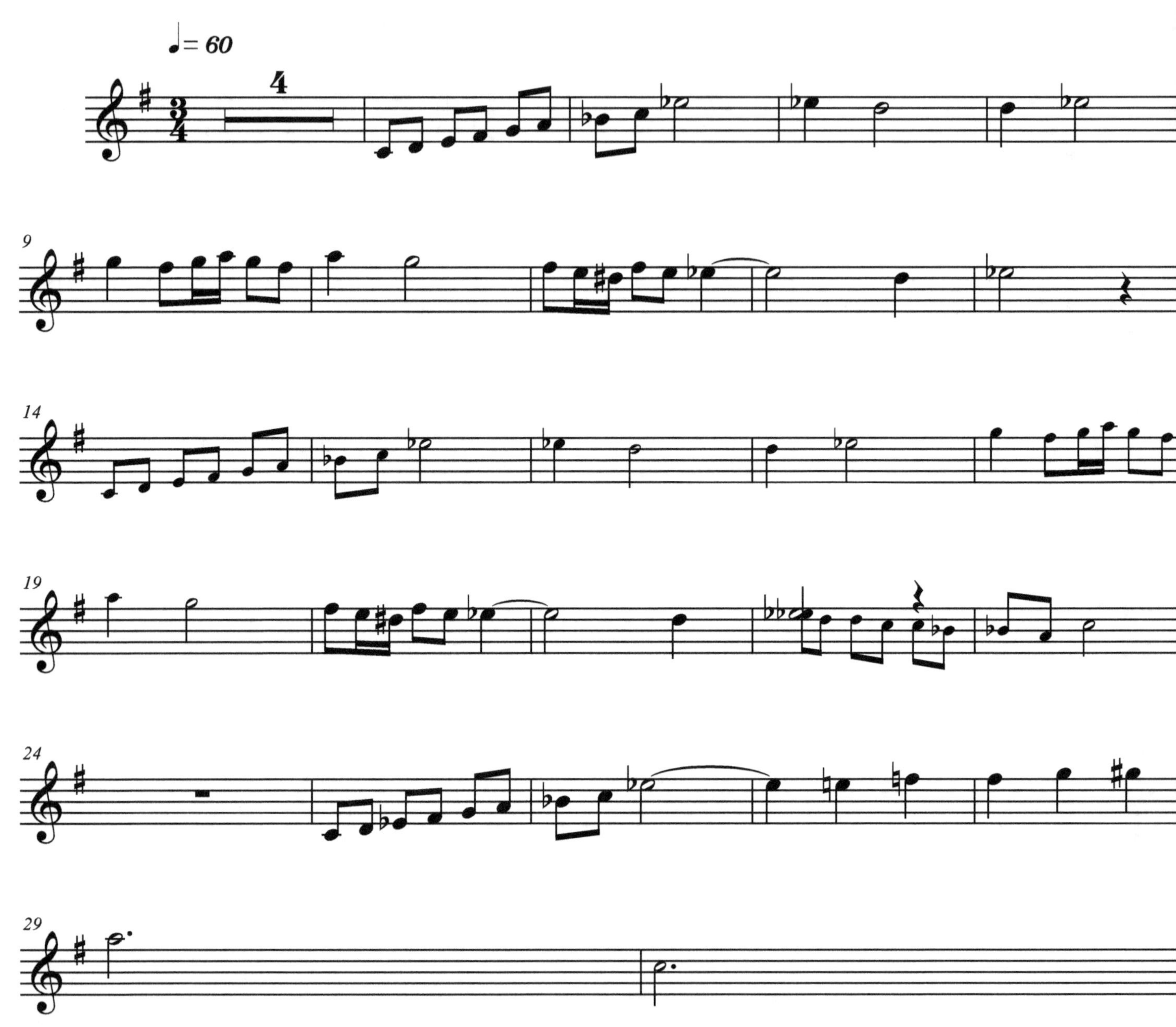

N

Part 2: Bes Clarinet 2

Joost de Groot

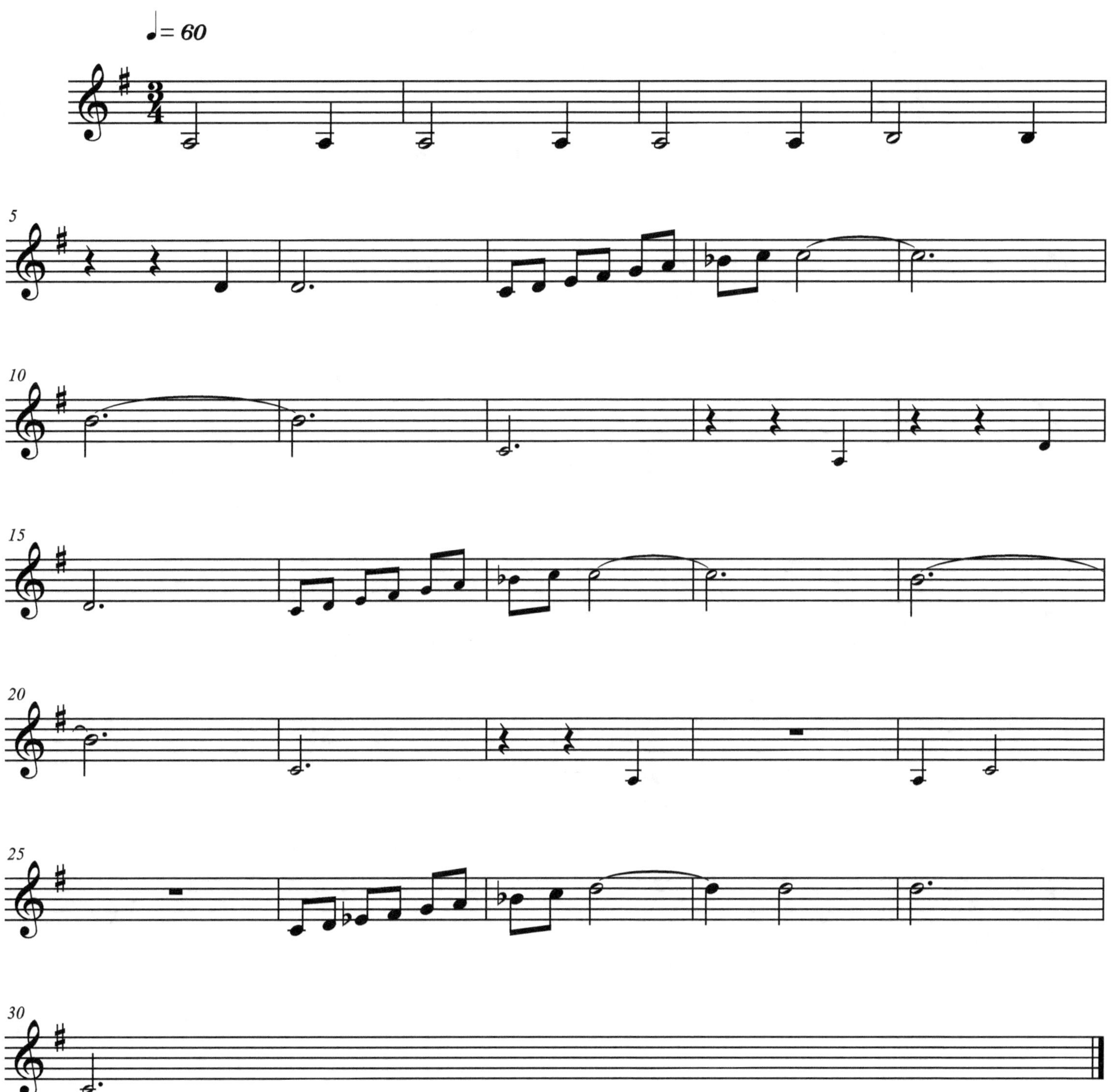

Part 3: Bes Clarinet 3

N

Joost de Gro

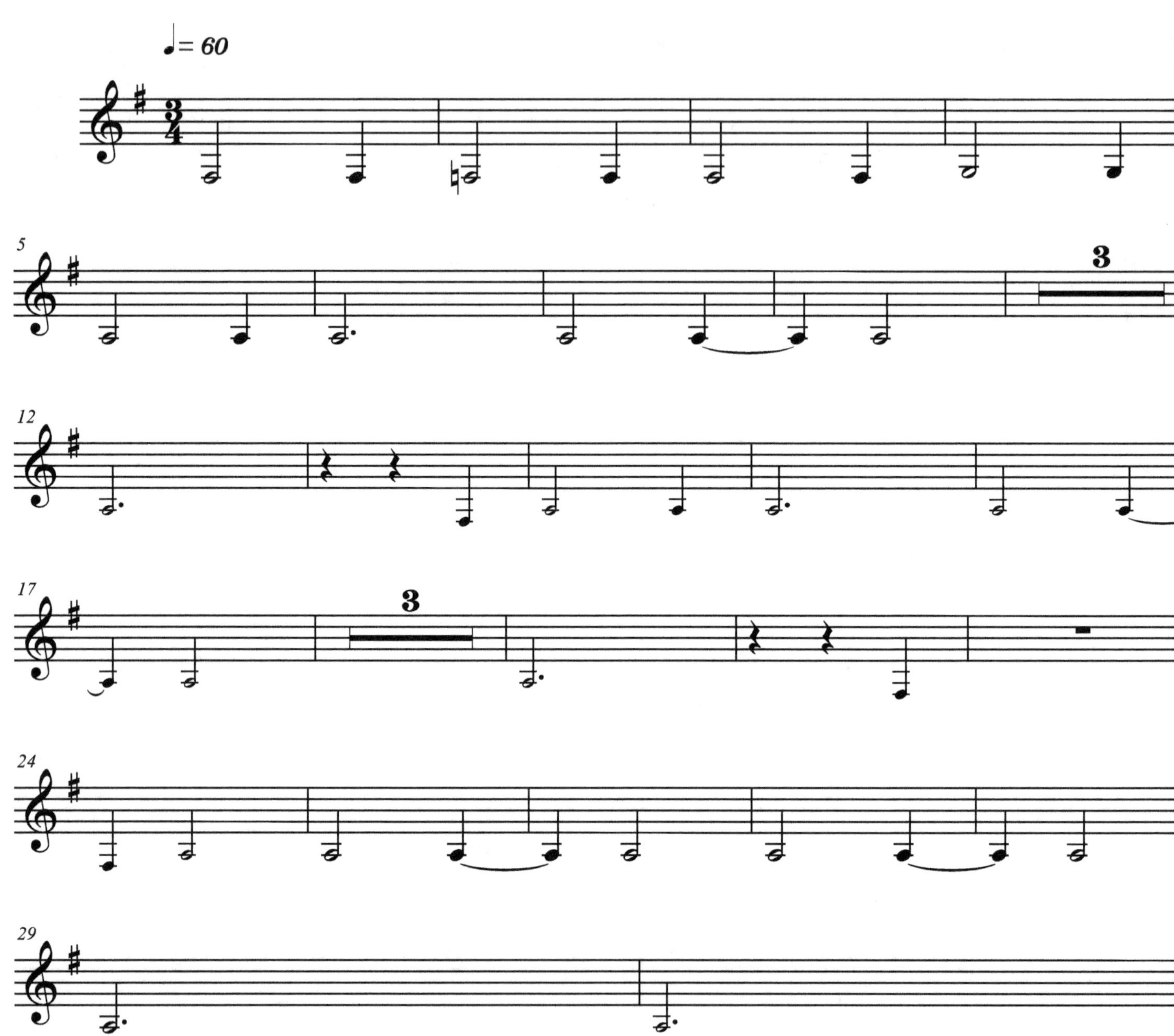

N

Part 3: Es Alto Clarinet

Joost de Groot

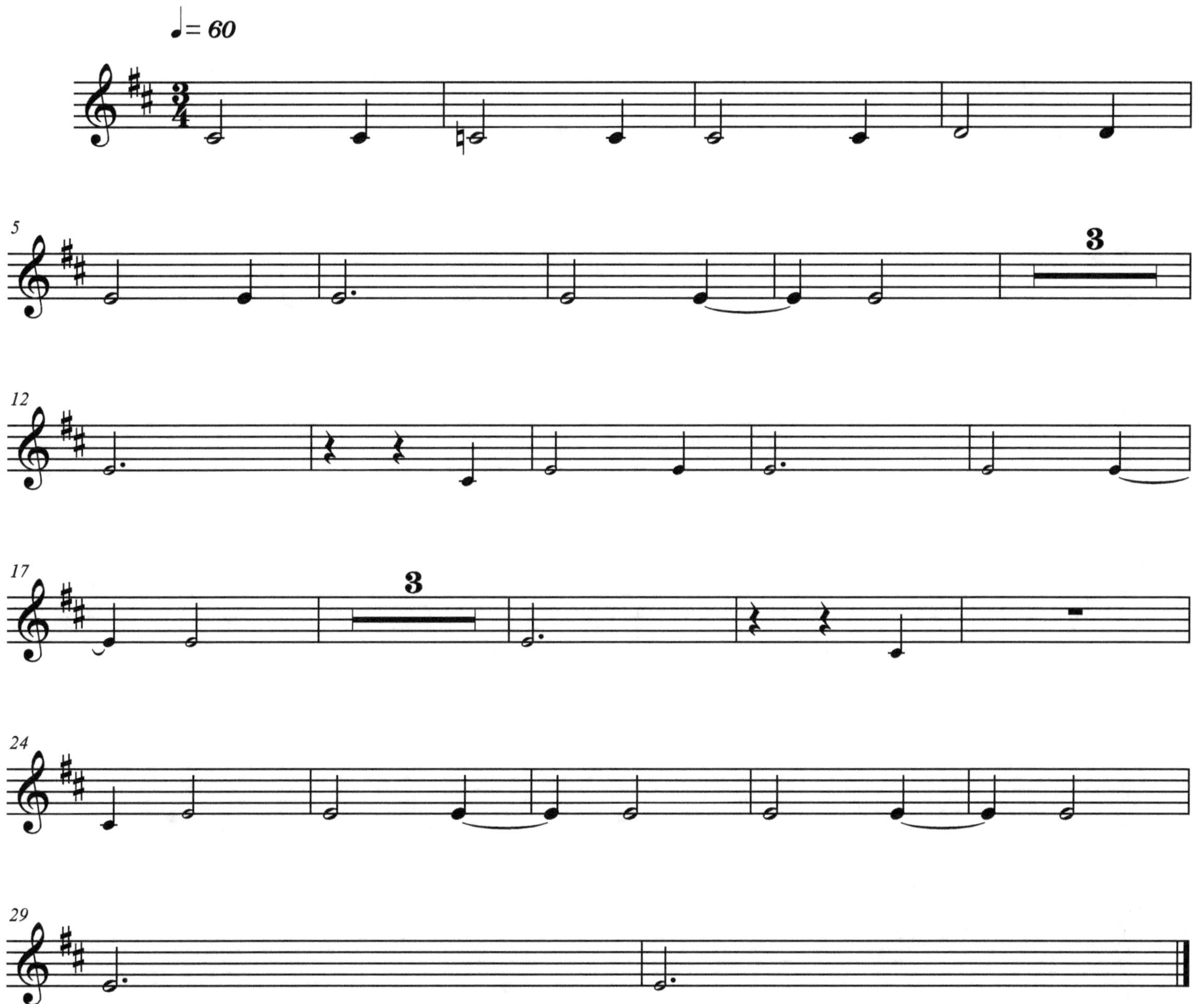

Part 4: Bes Bass Clarinet

N

Joost de Gro

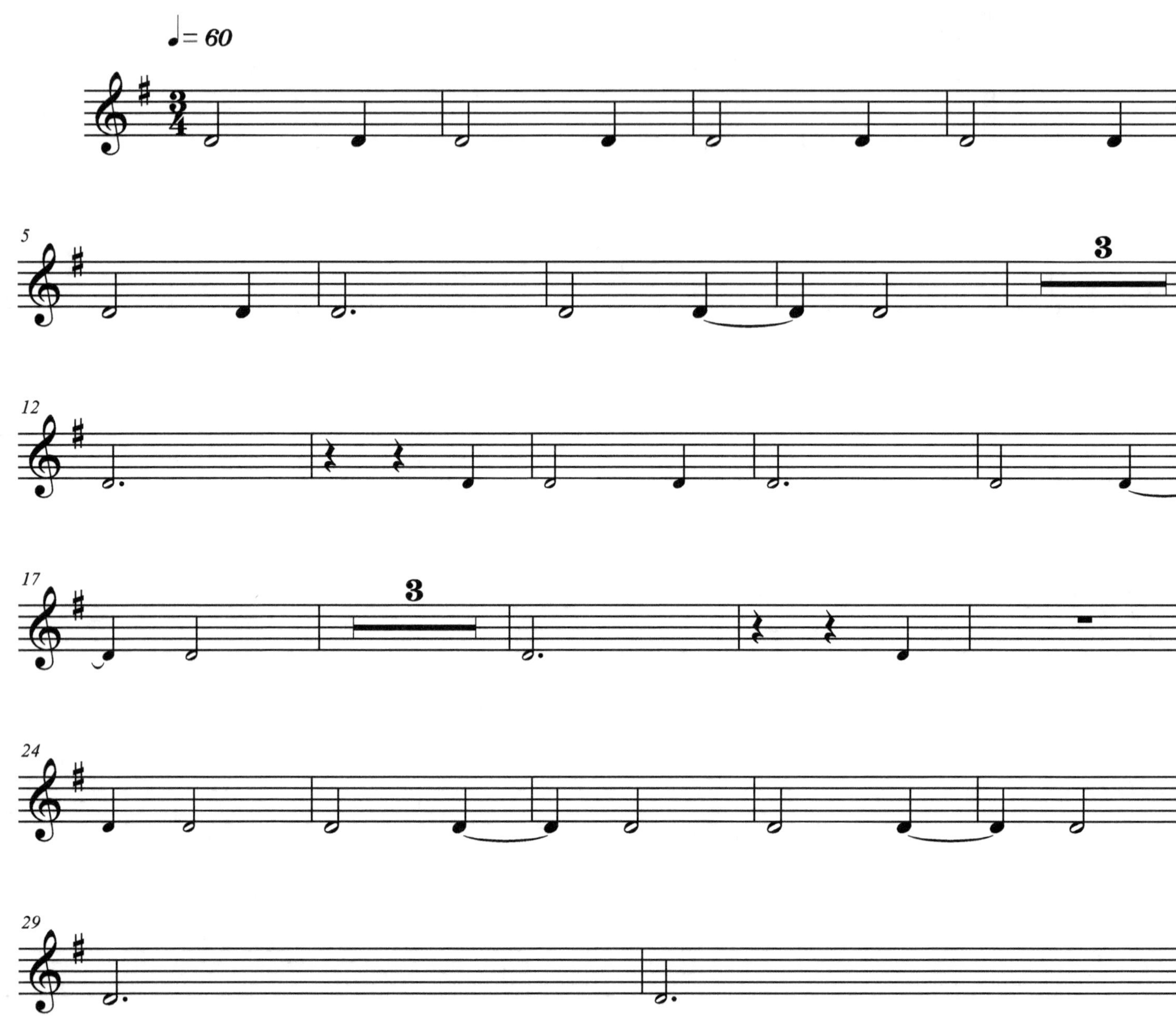

Part 1: Bes Clarinet 1

N

Joost de Groot

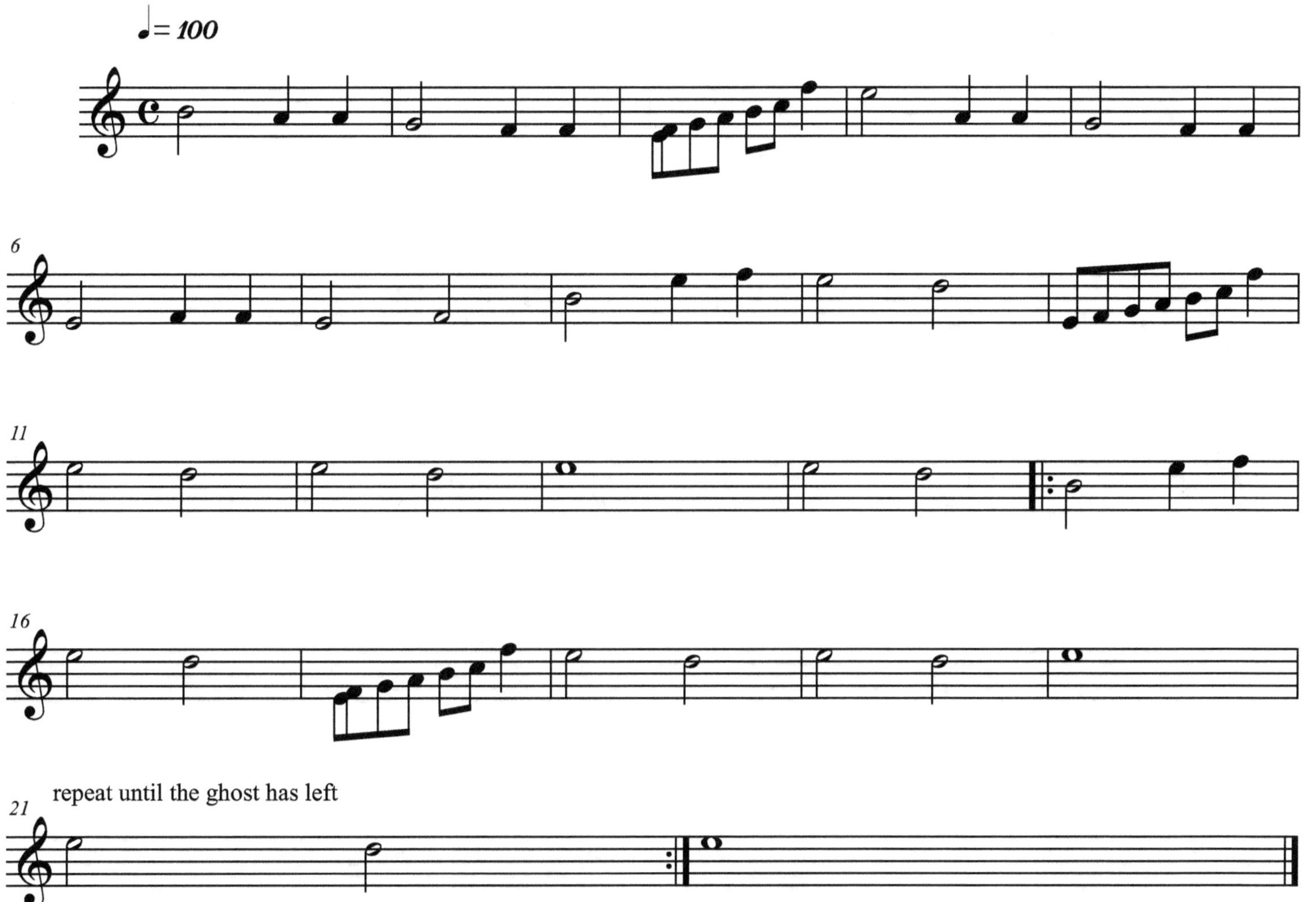

Part 2: Bes Clarinet 2

N

Joost de Gro

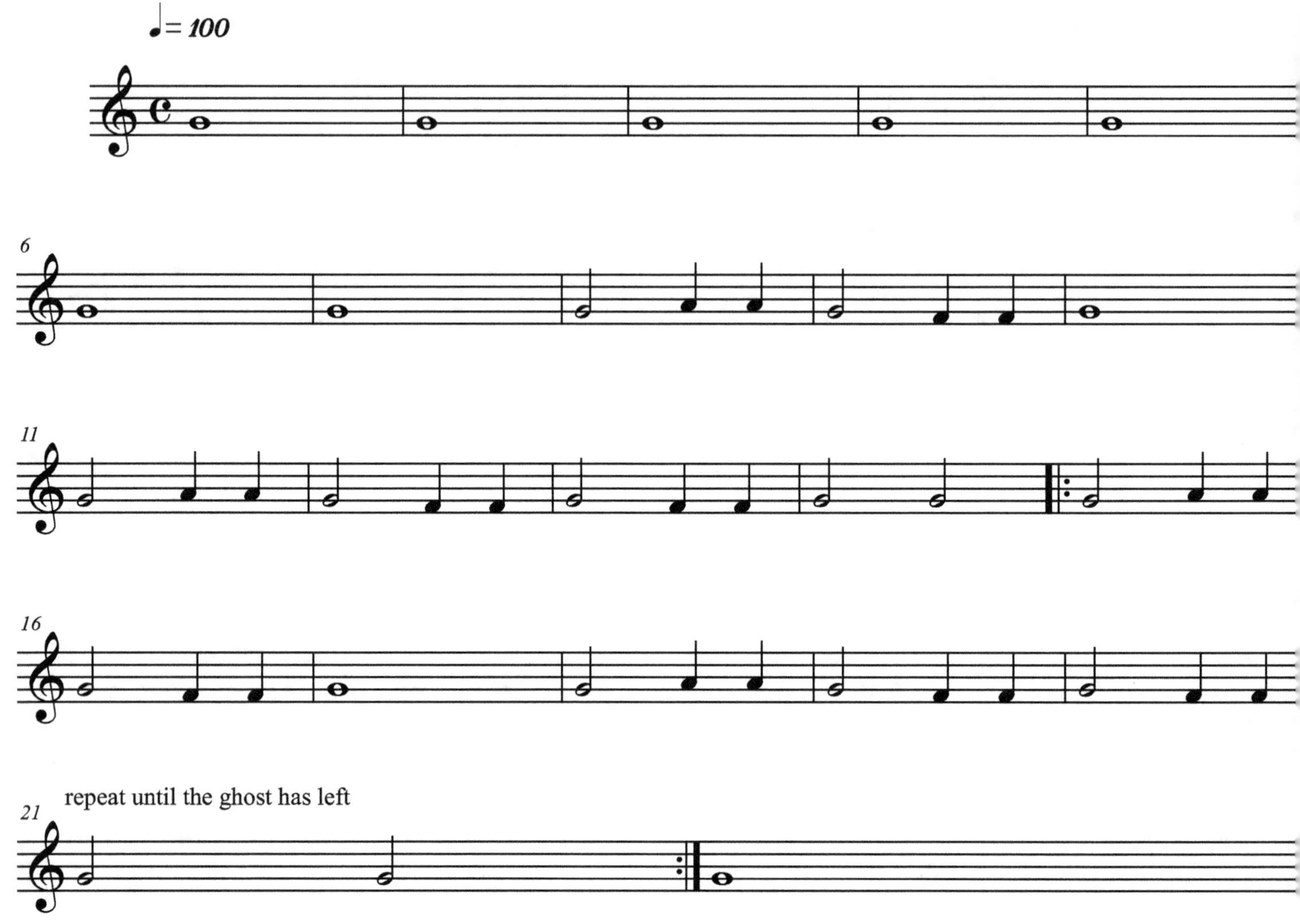

Part 3: Bes Clarinet 3

N

Joost de Groot

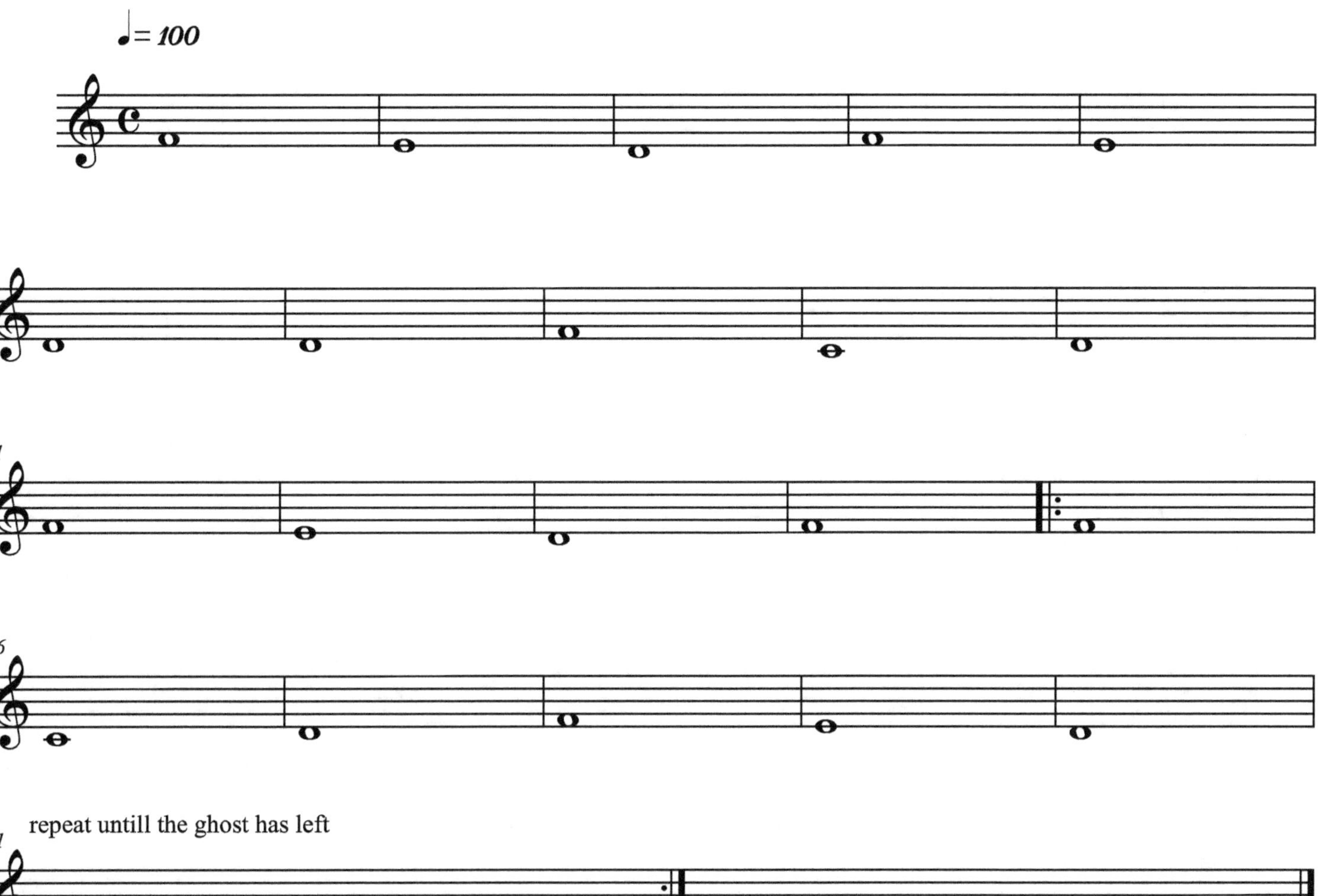

Part 3: Es Alto Clarinet

N

Joost de Gro

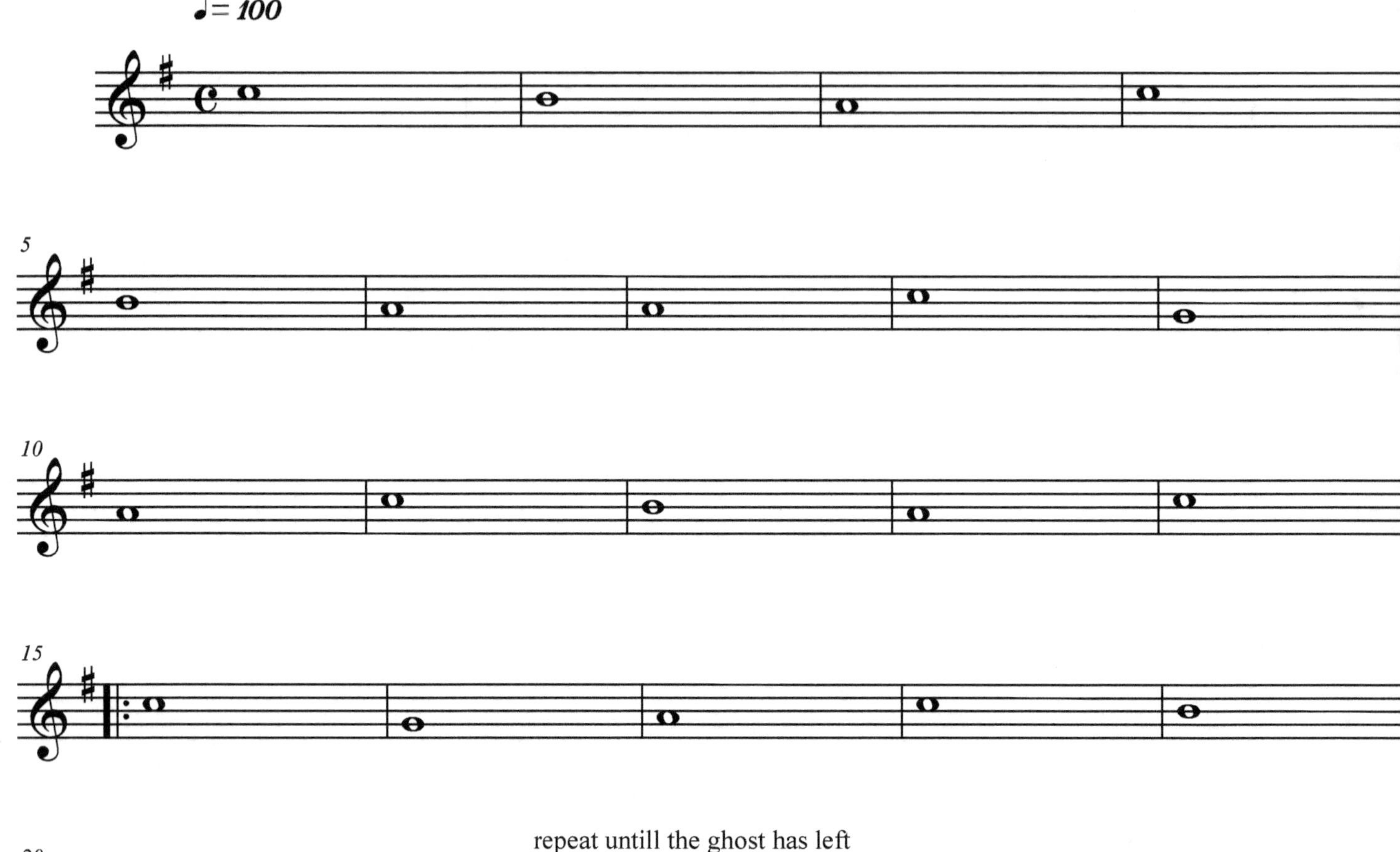

Part 4: Bes Bass Clarinet

N

Joost de Groot

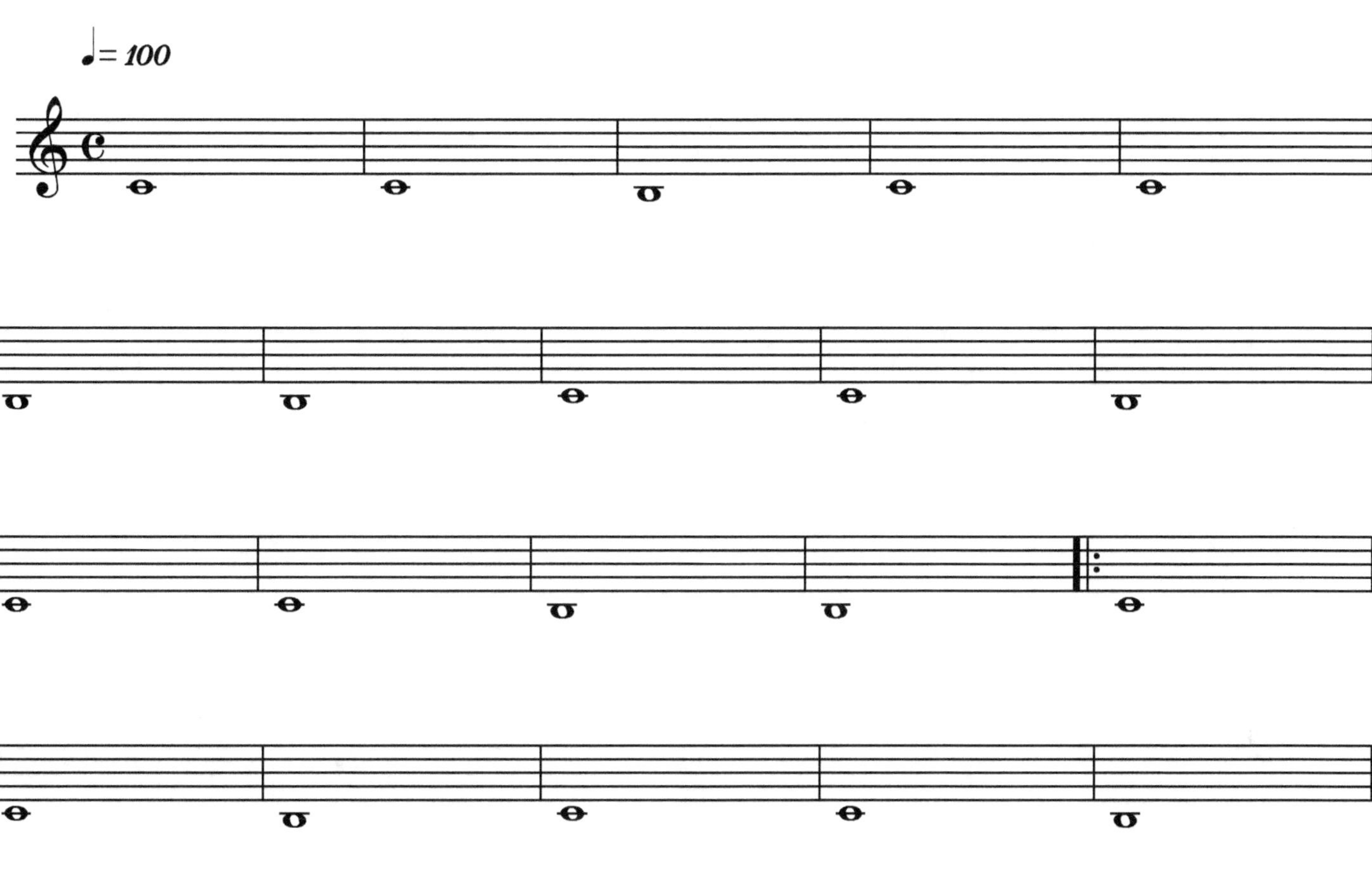

Part 1: Bes Clarinet 1

I

Joost de Gro

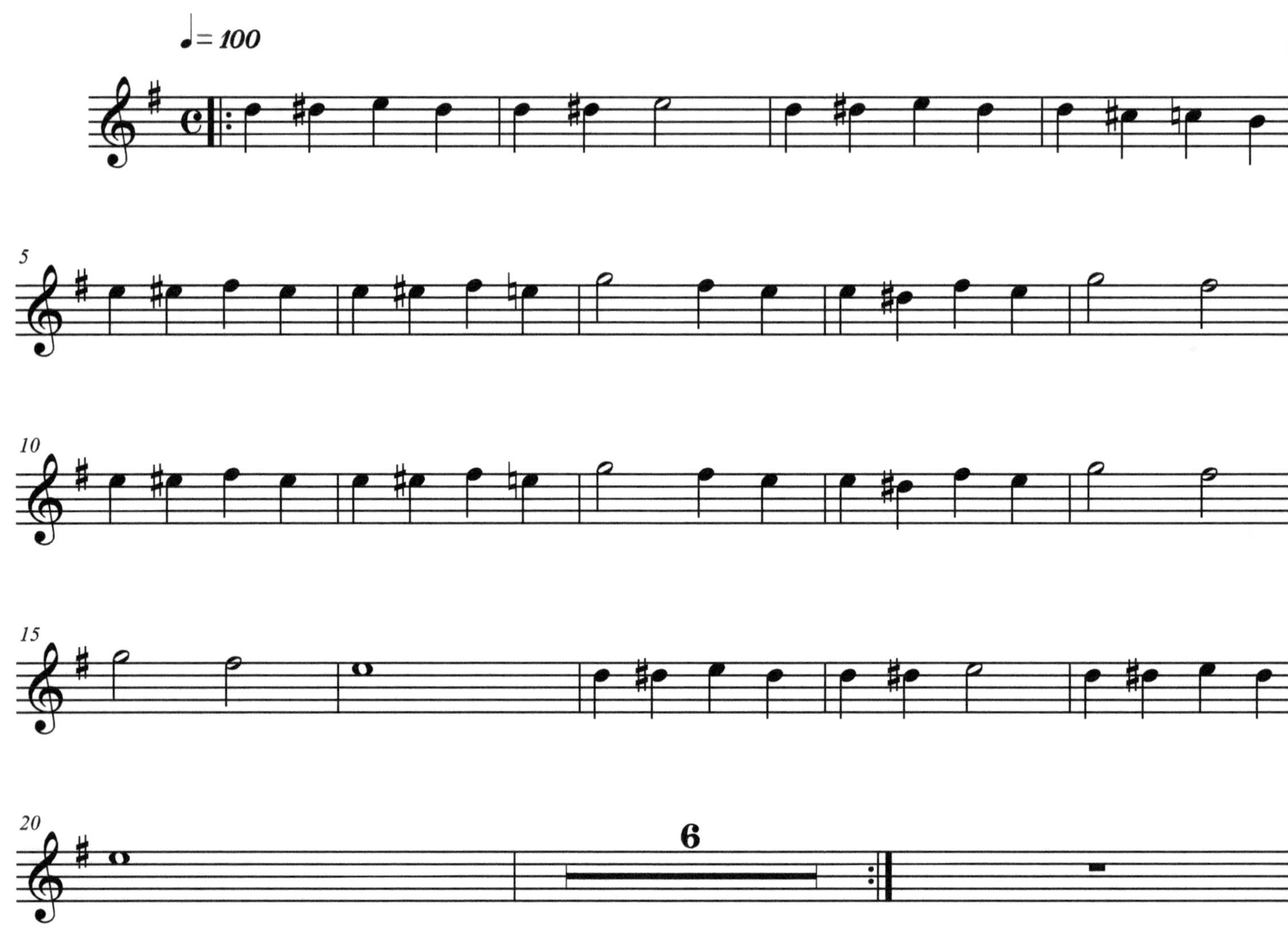

Part 2: Bes Clarinet 2

I

Joost de Groot

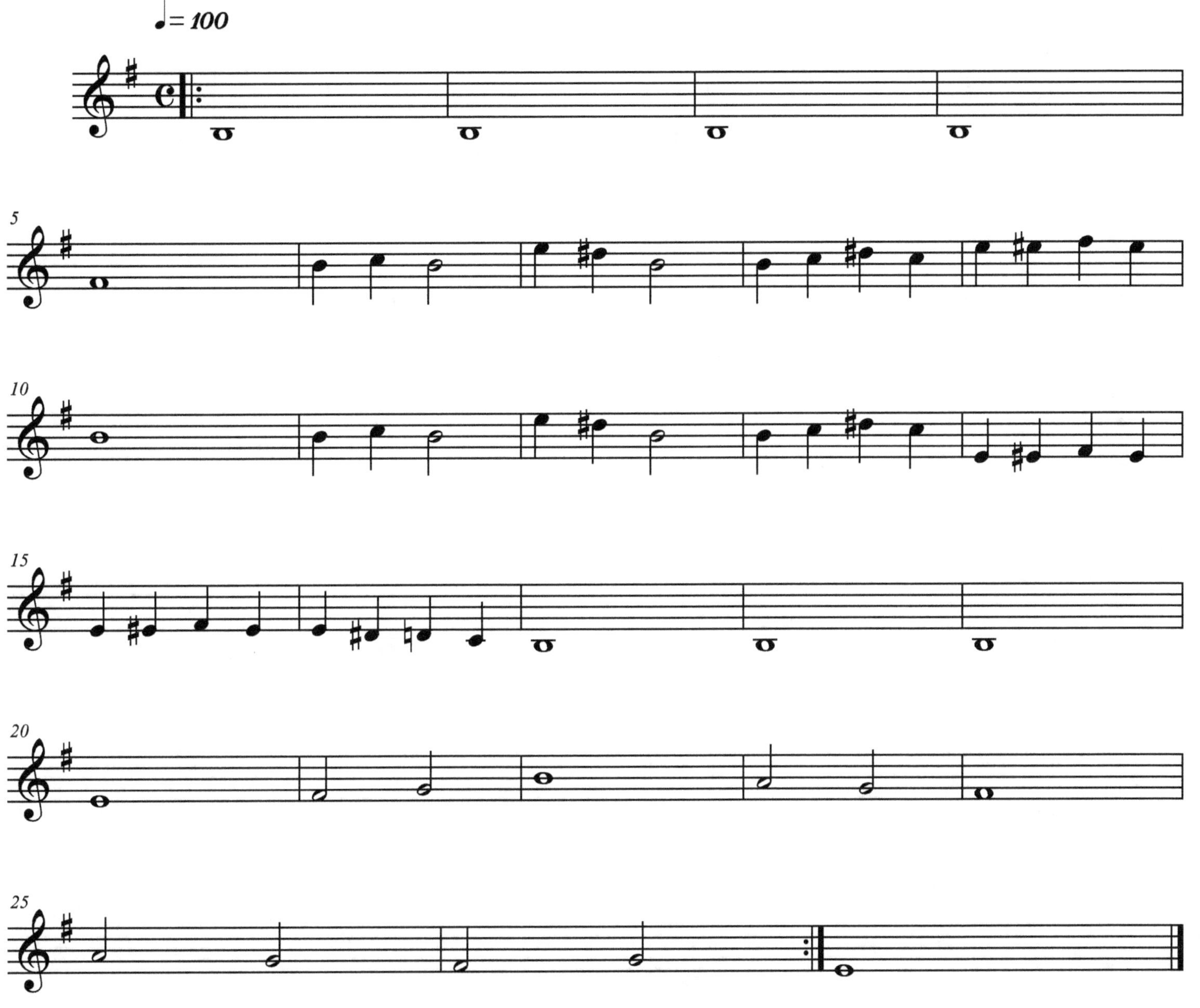

Part 3: Bes Clarinet 3

I

Joost de Gro

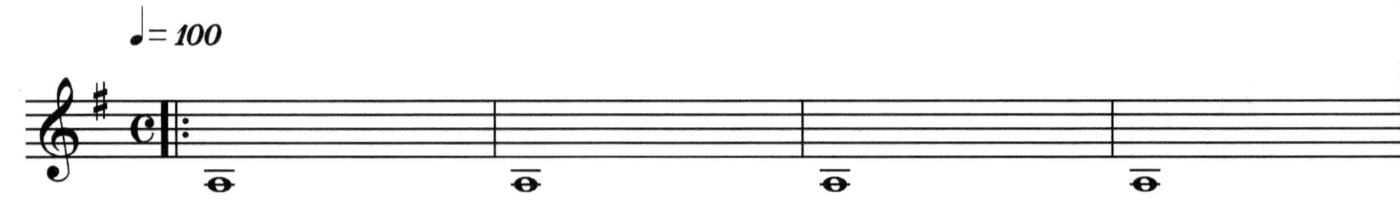

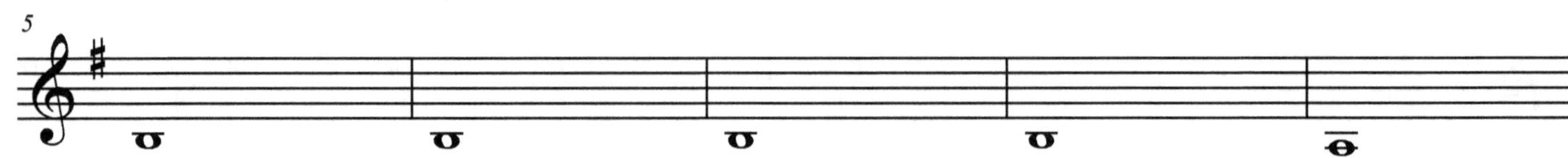

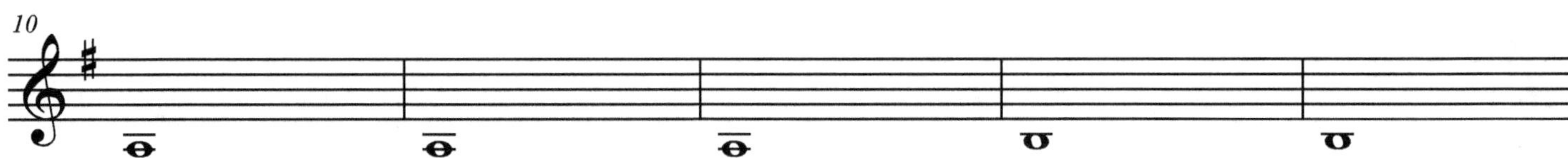

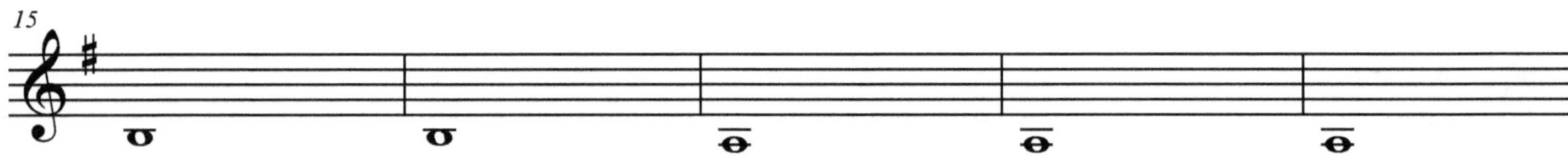

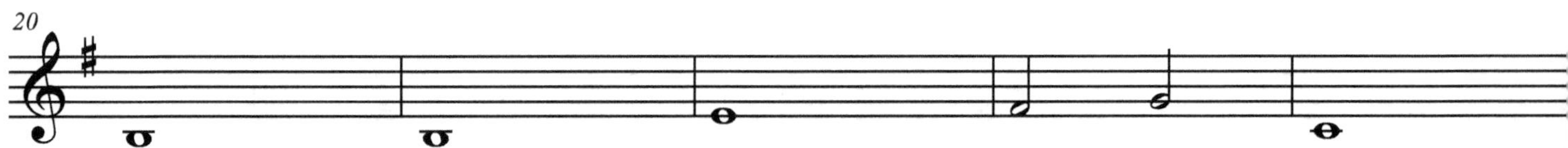

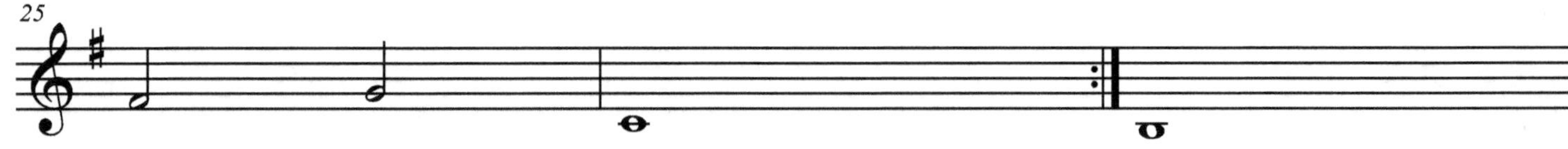

Part 3: Es Alto Clarinet

I

Joost de Groot

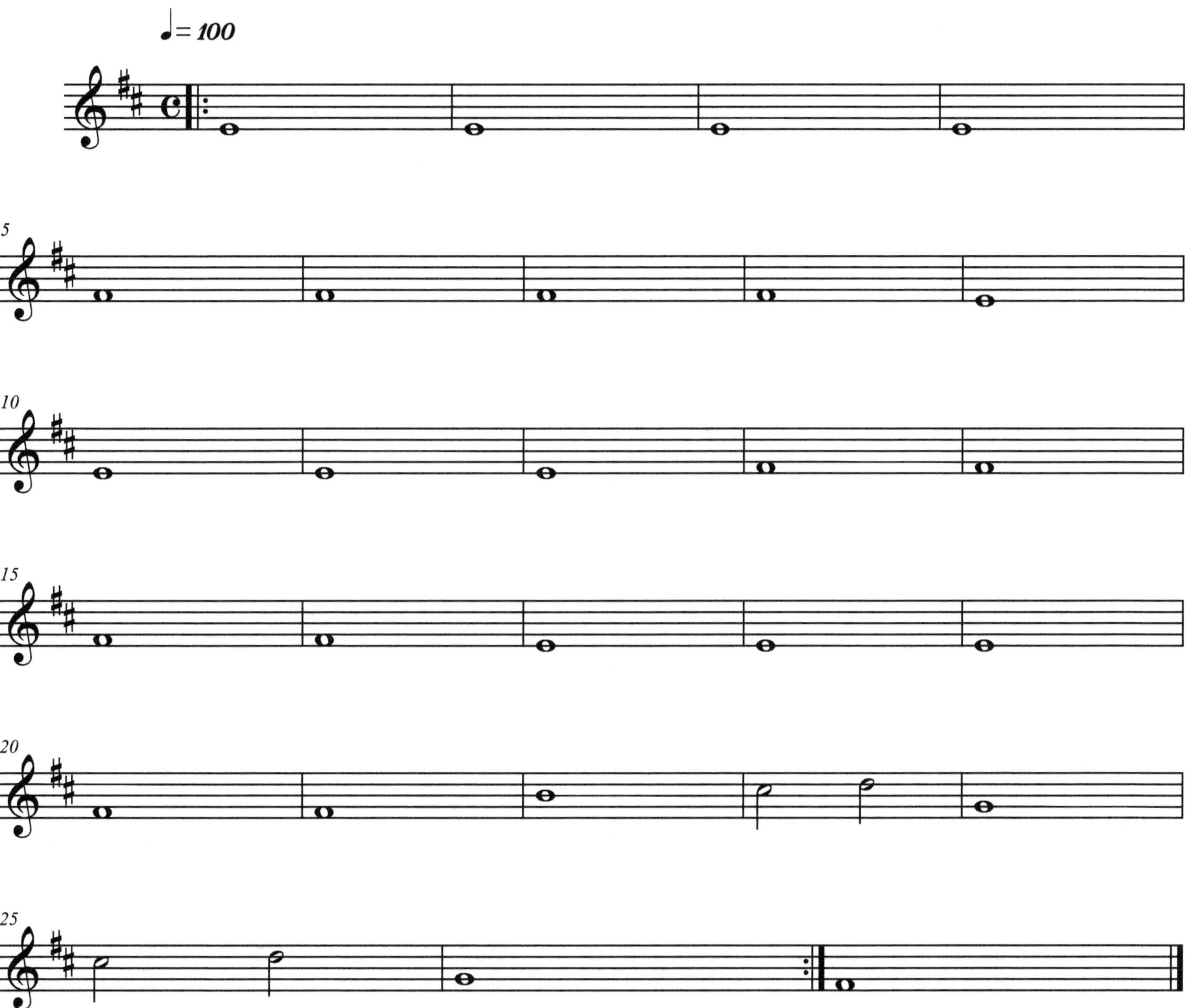

Part 4: Bes Clarinet 4

I

Joost de Gro

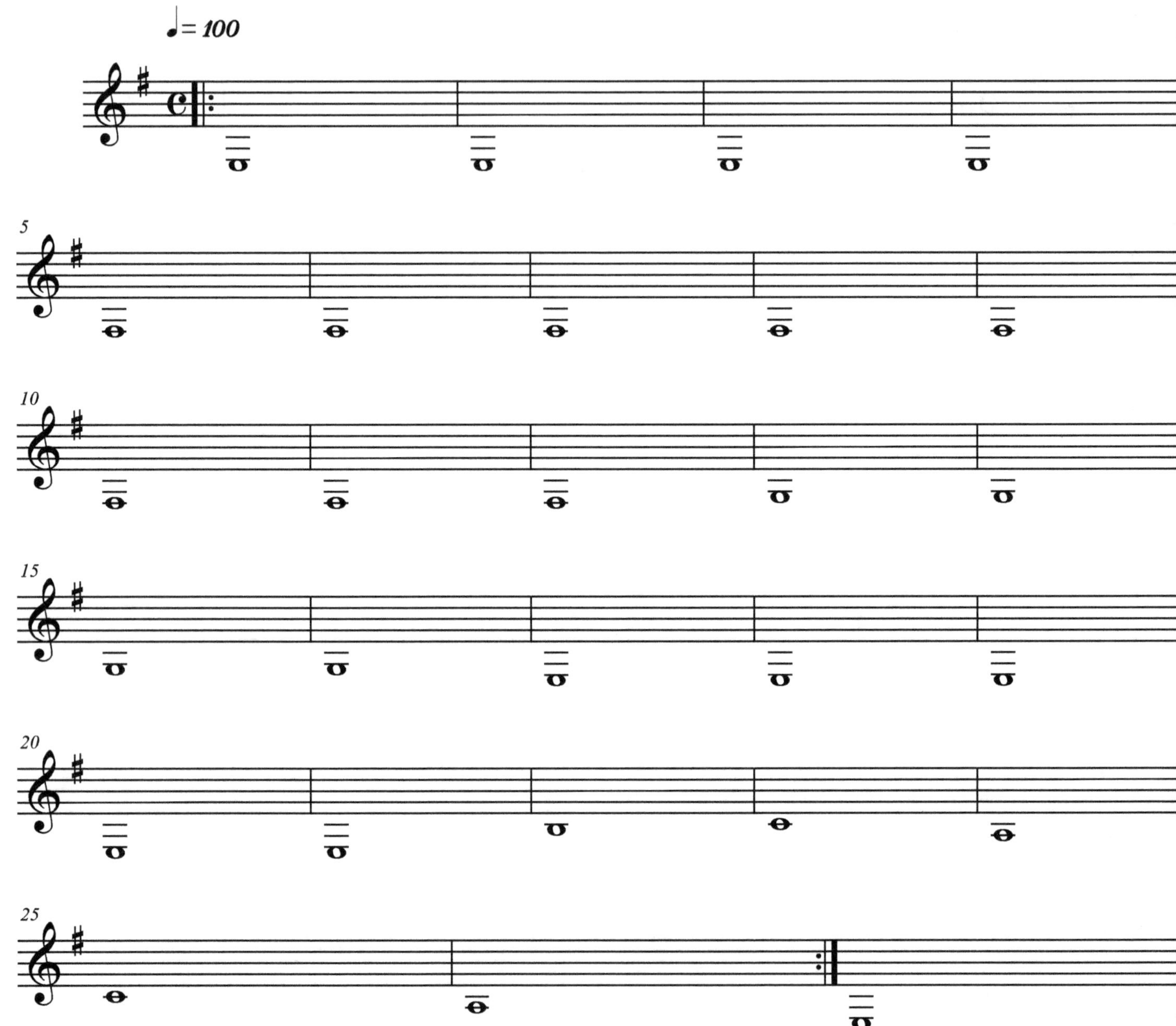

Part 4: Bes Bass Clarinet

I

Joost de Groot

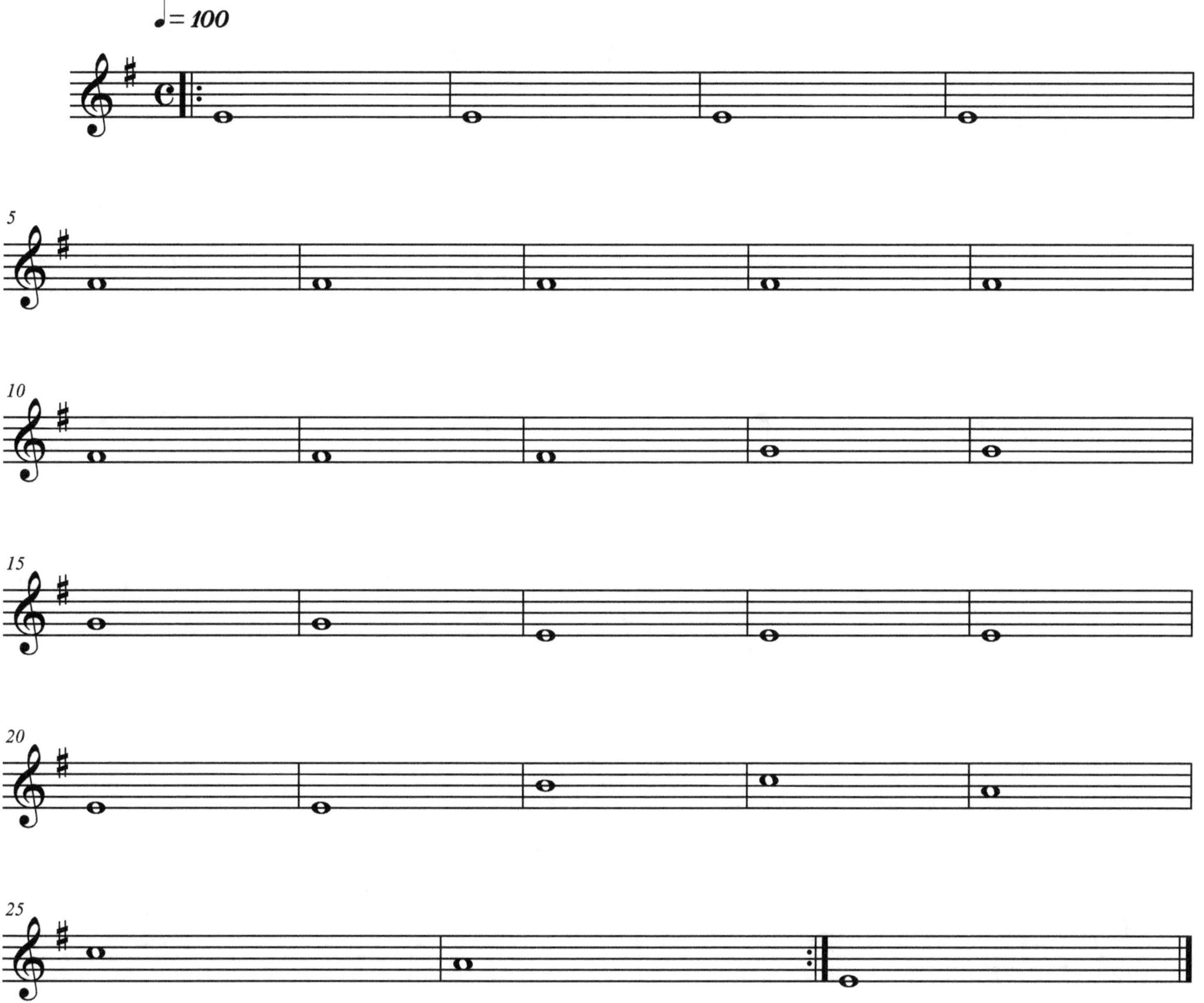

E

Part 1: Bes Clarinet 1

Joost de Gro

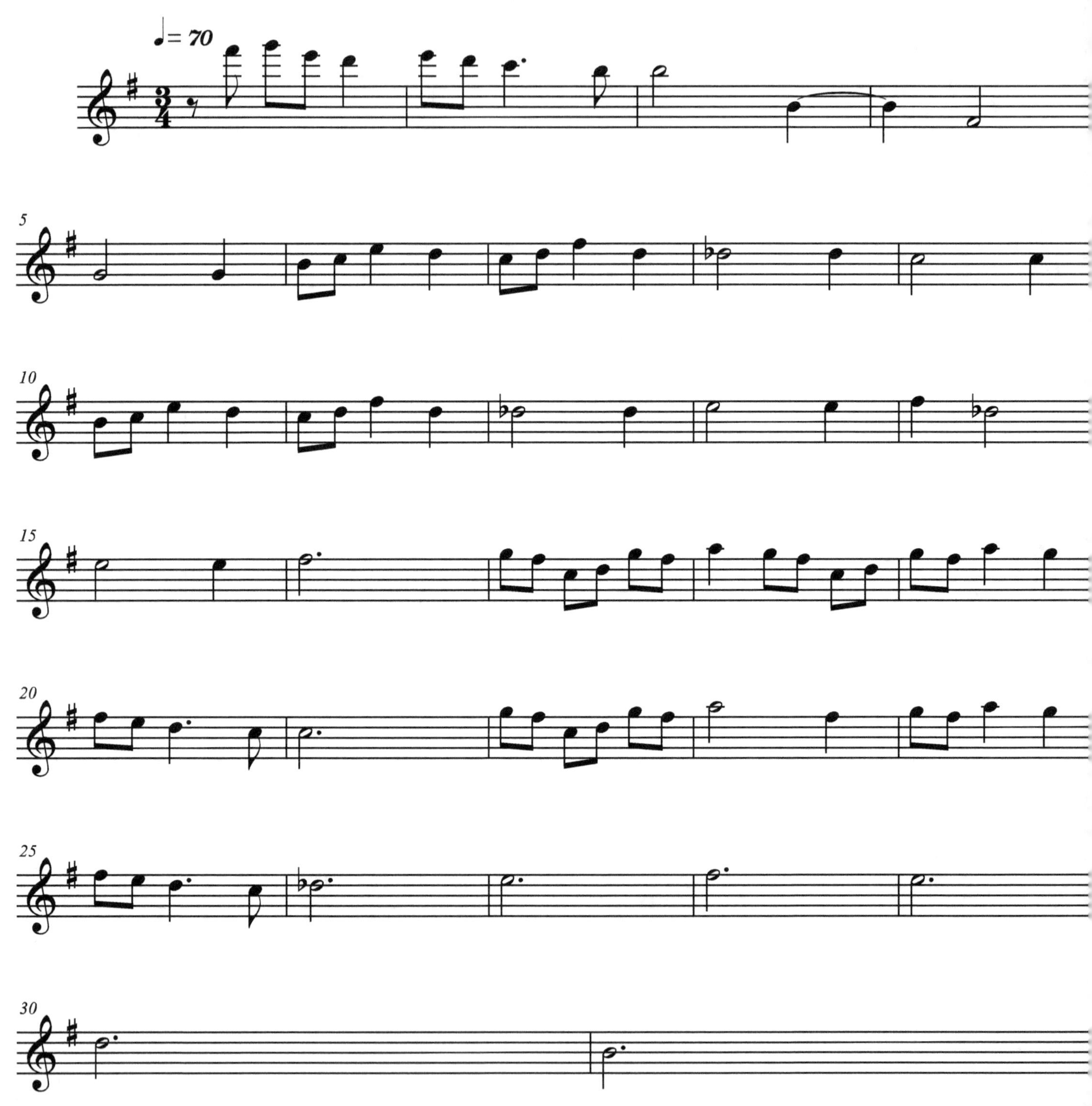

Part 2: Bes Clarinet 2

E

Joost de Groot

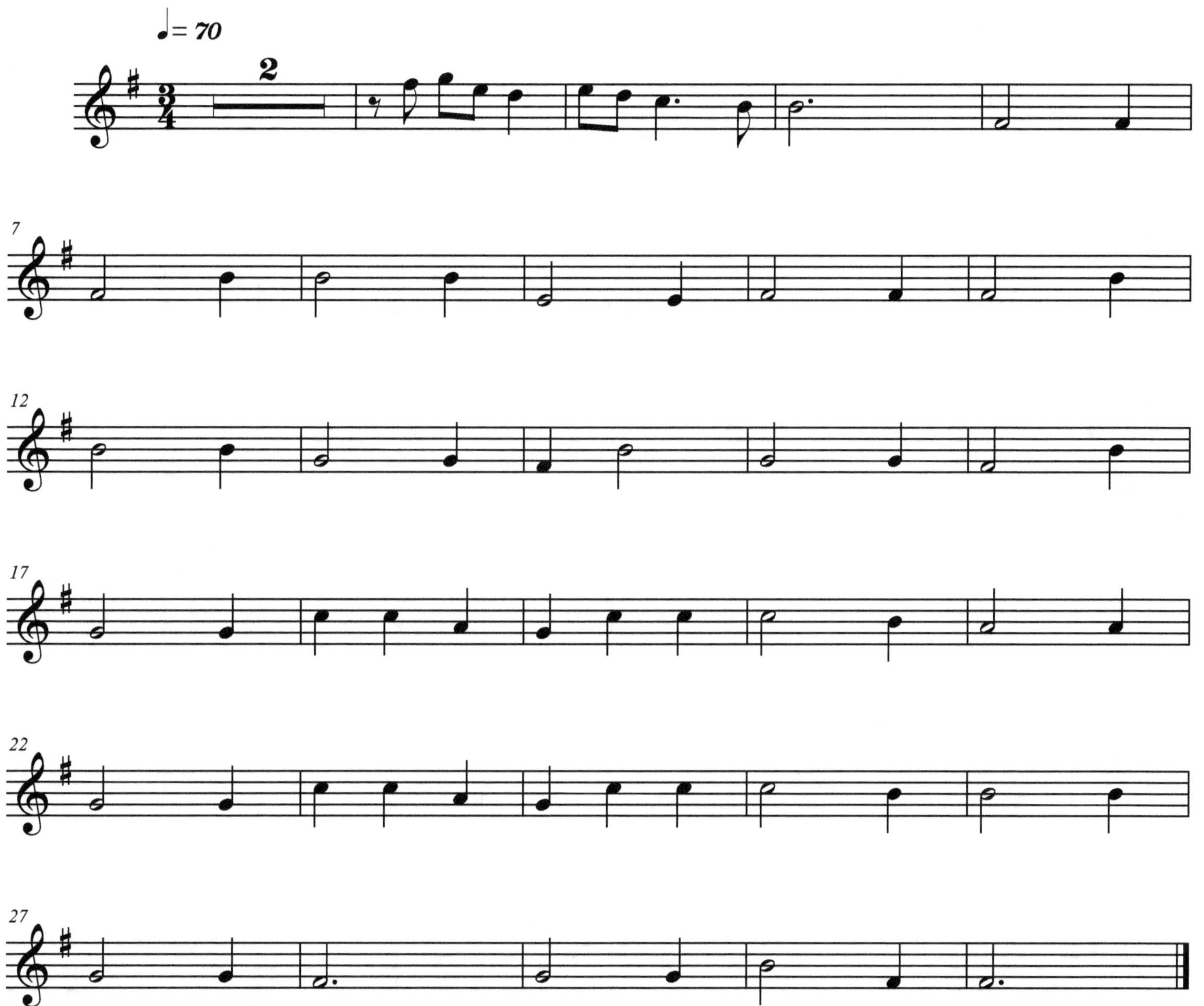

E

Part 3: Bes Clarinet 3

Joost de Gro

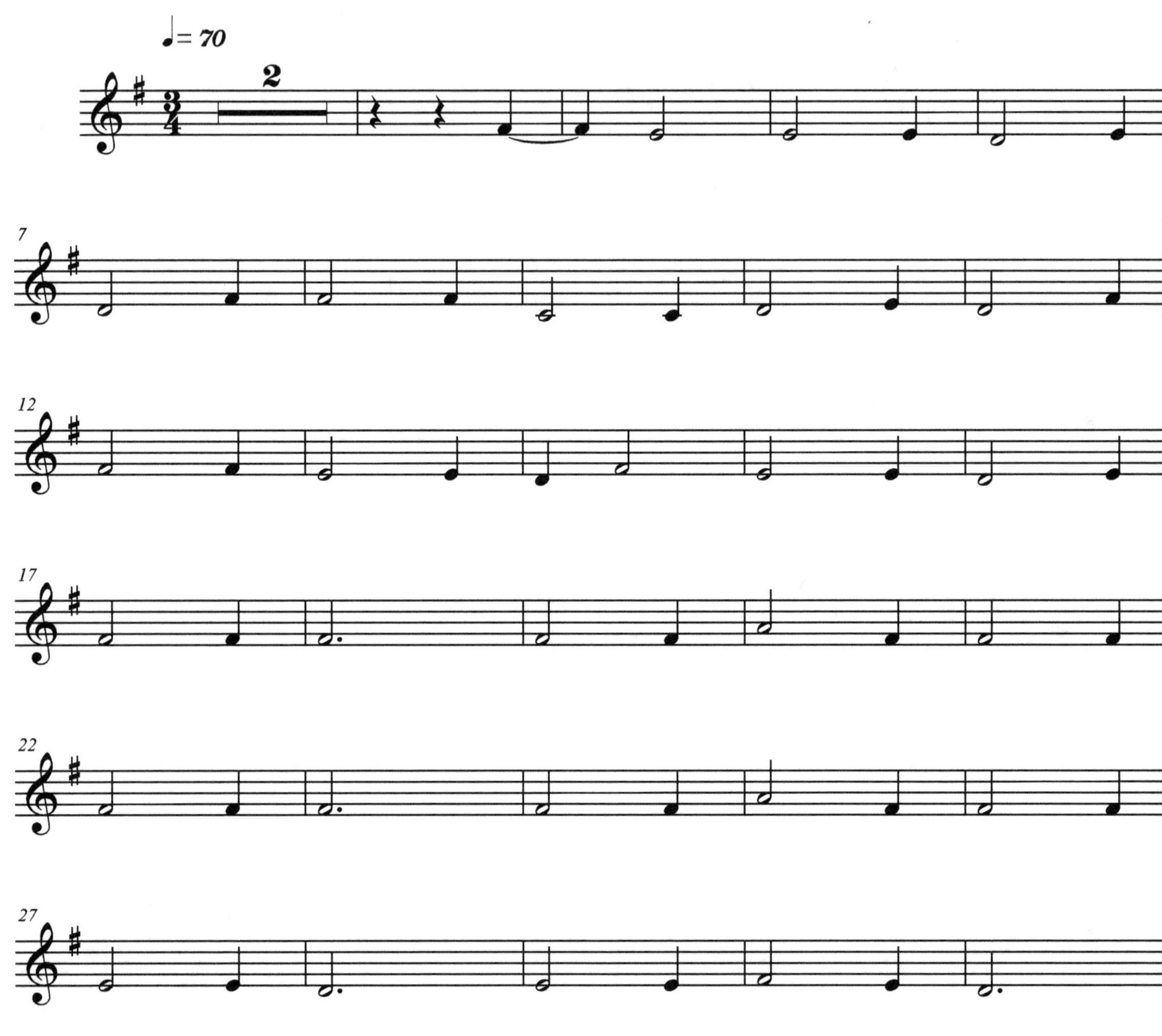

E

Part 3: Es Alto Clarinet

Joost de Groot

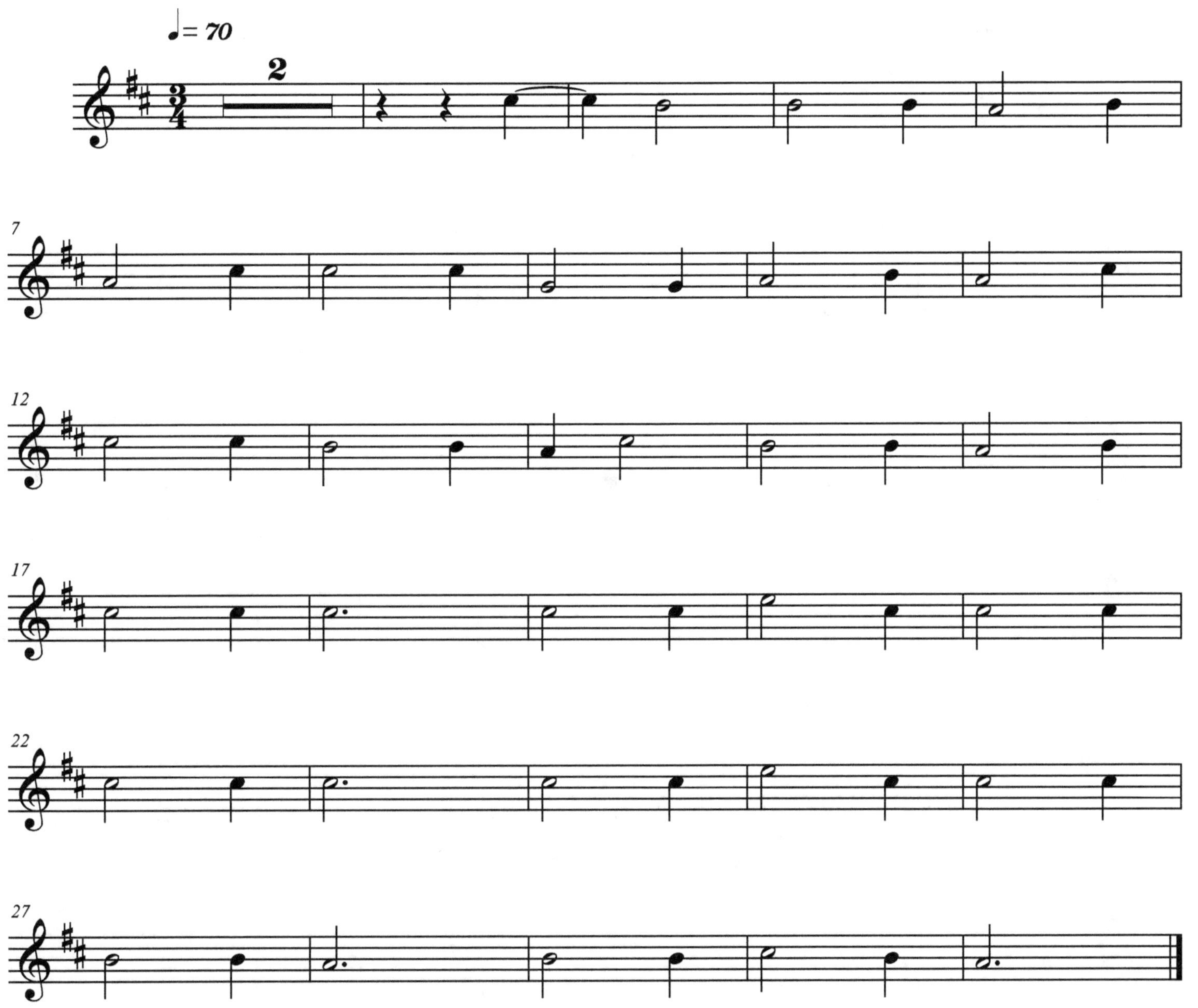

E

Part 4: Bes Clarinet 4

Joost de Gro

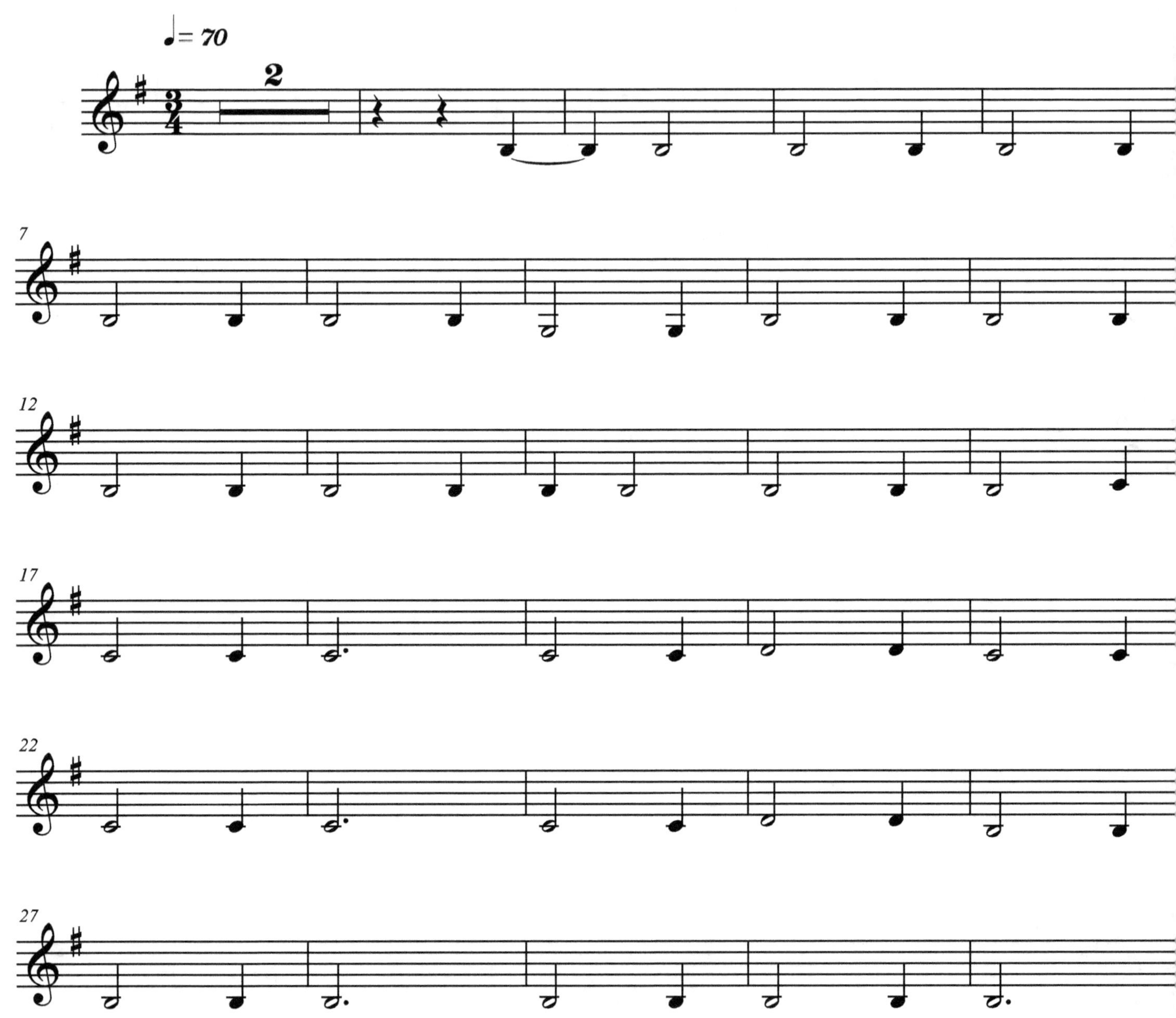

E

Part 4: Bes Bass Clarinet

Joost de Groot

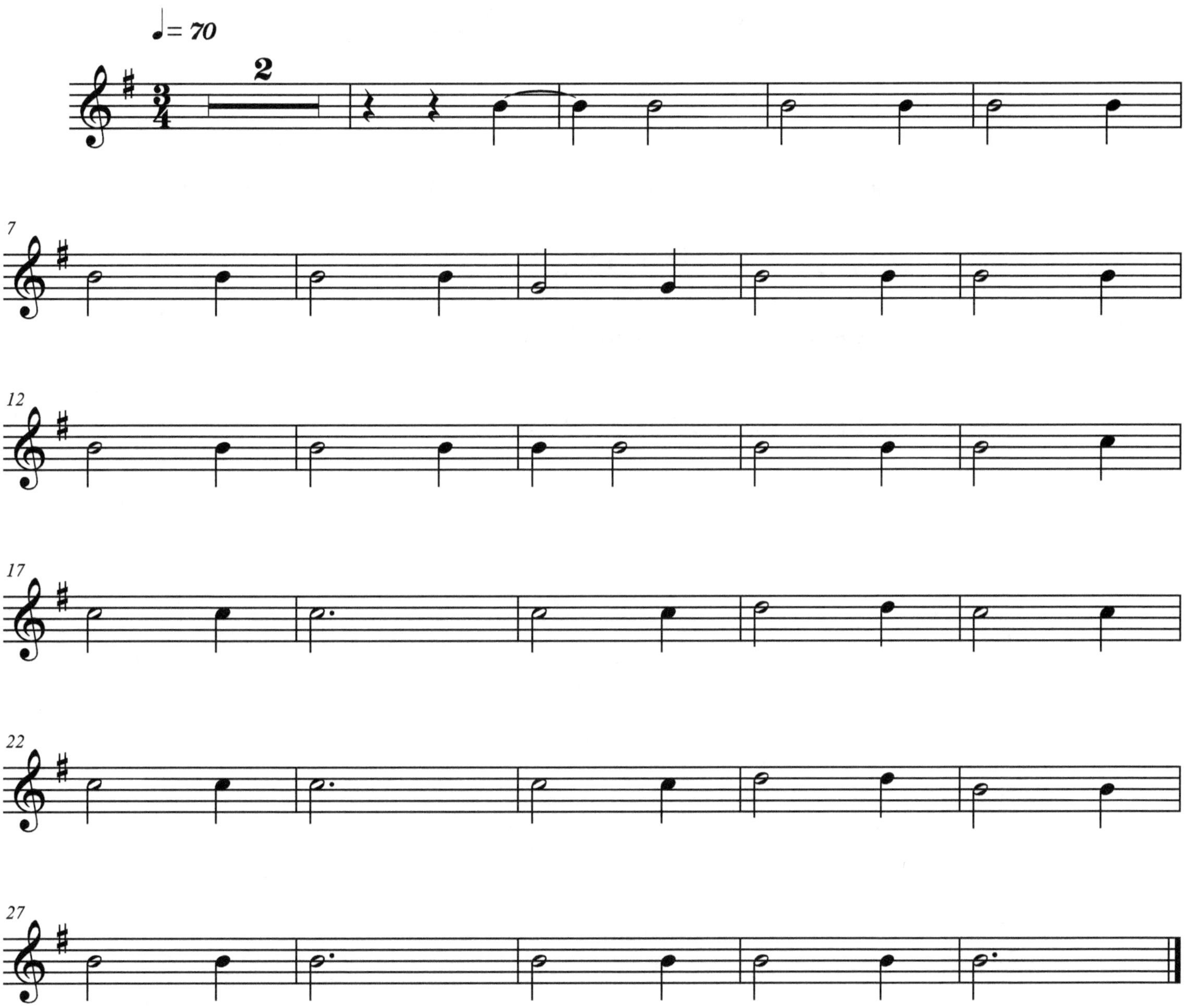

SAXOPHONE QUARTET

Part 1: Bes Soprano Sax./Es Alto Sax. 1

Part 2: Es Alto Sax. 2

Part 3: Bes Tenor Sax.

Part 4: Es Baritone Sax.

J

Part 1: Bes Soprano Sax.

Joost de Groot

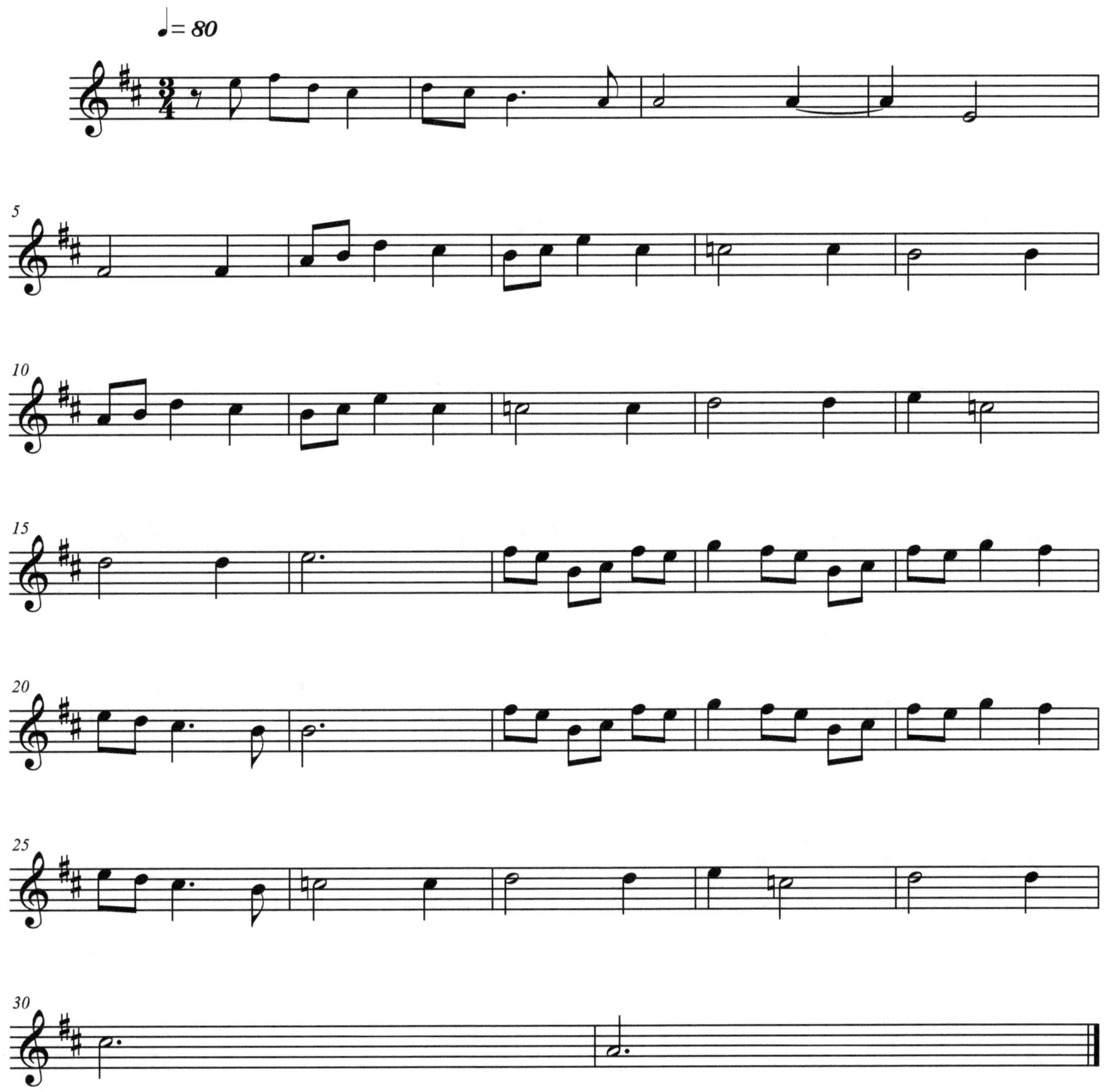

Part 1: Es Alto Sax. 1

J

Joost de Gro

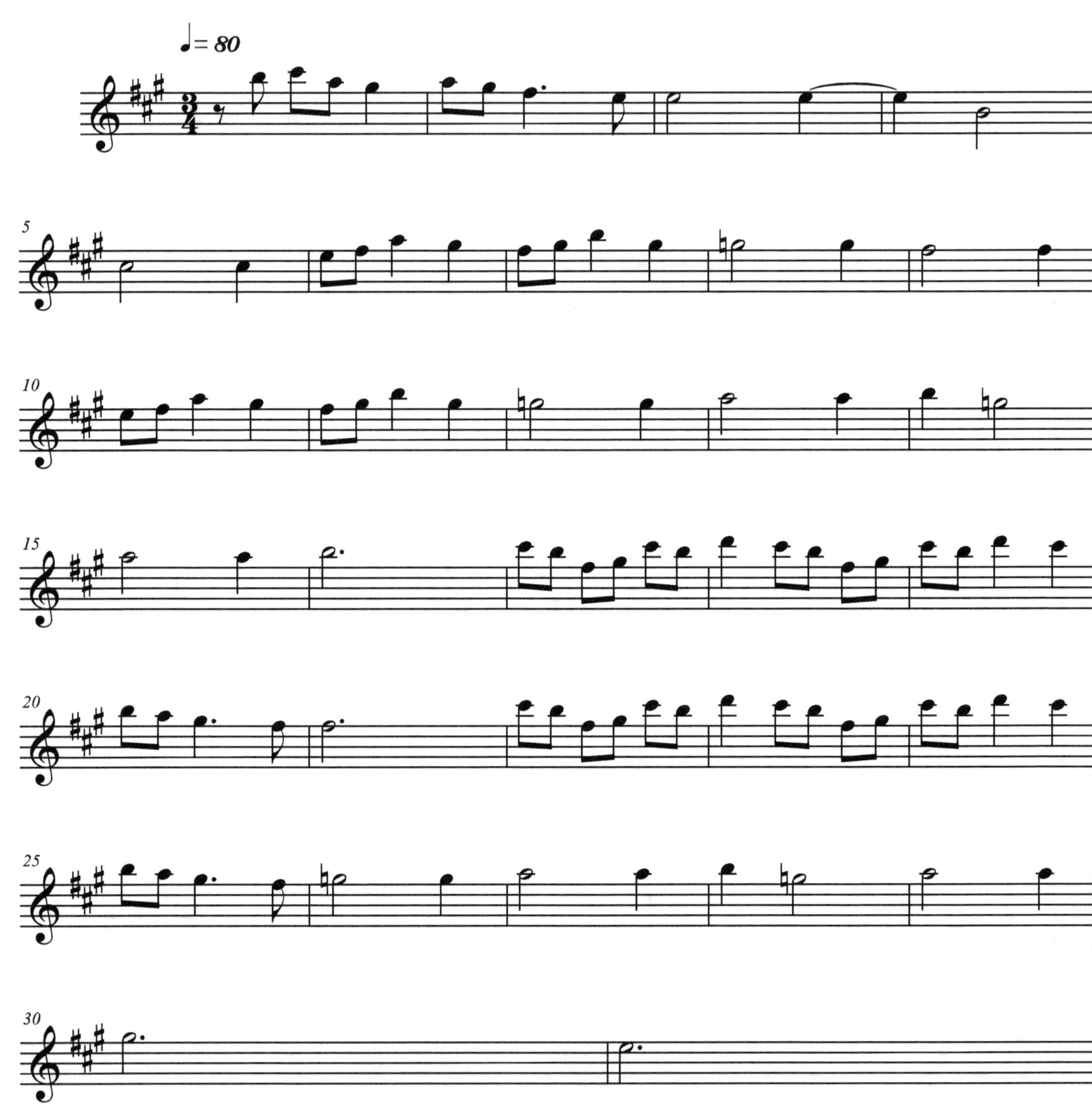

Part 2: Es Alto Sax. 2

J

Joost de Groot

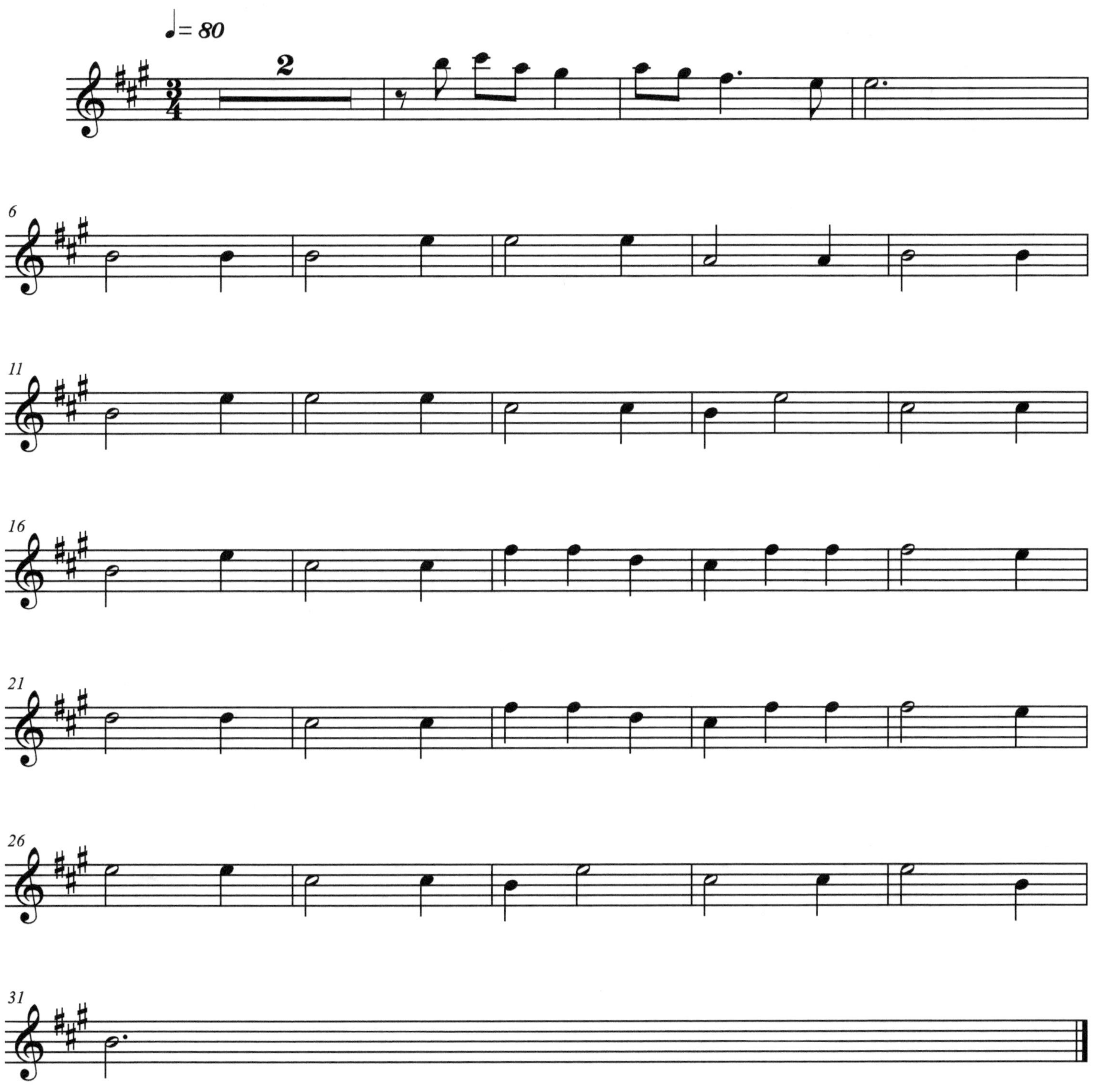

J

Part 3: Bes Tenor Sax.

Joost de Gro

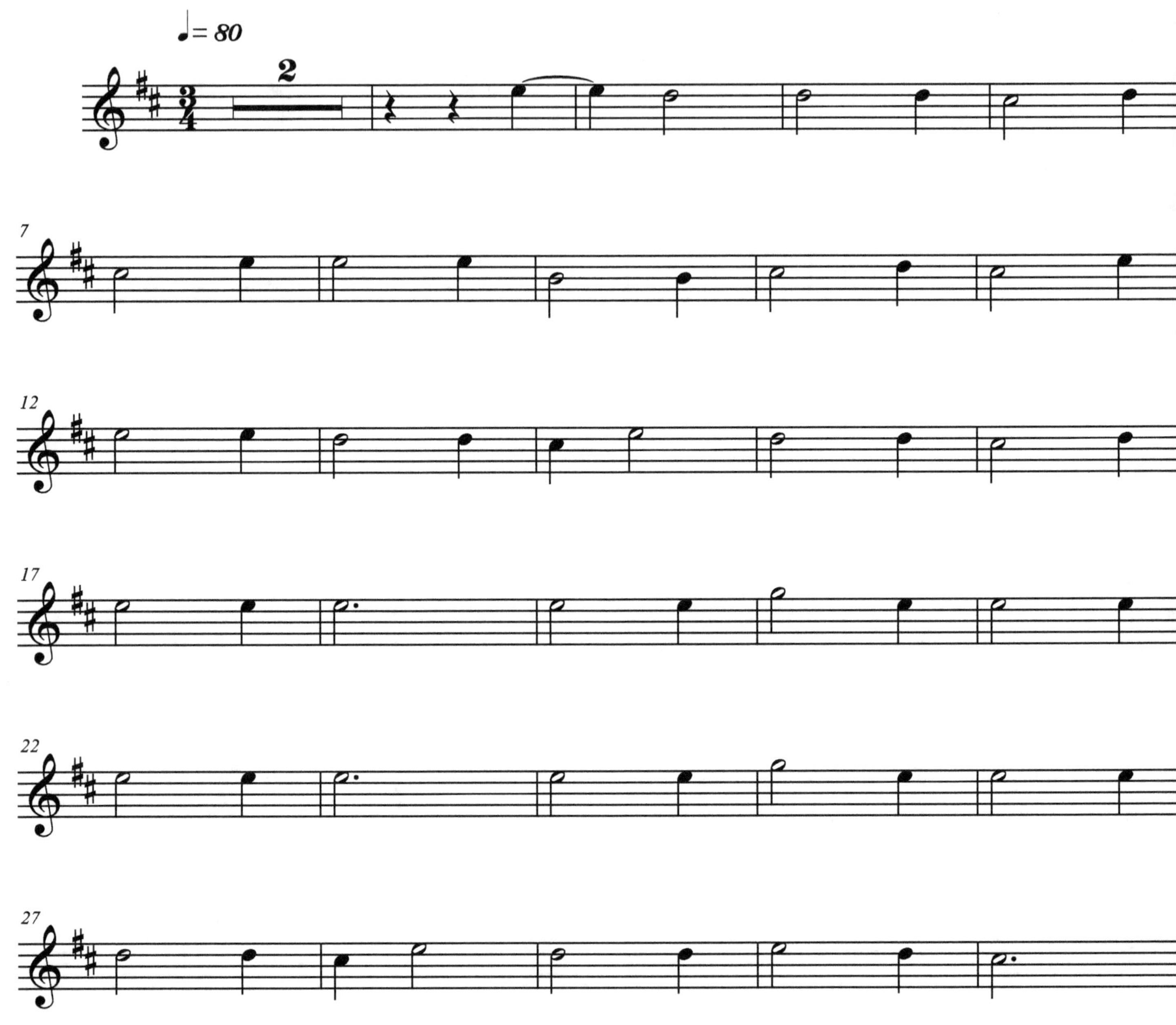

Part 4: Es Baritone Sax.

J

Joost de Groot

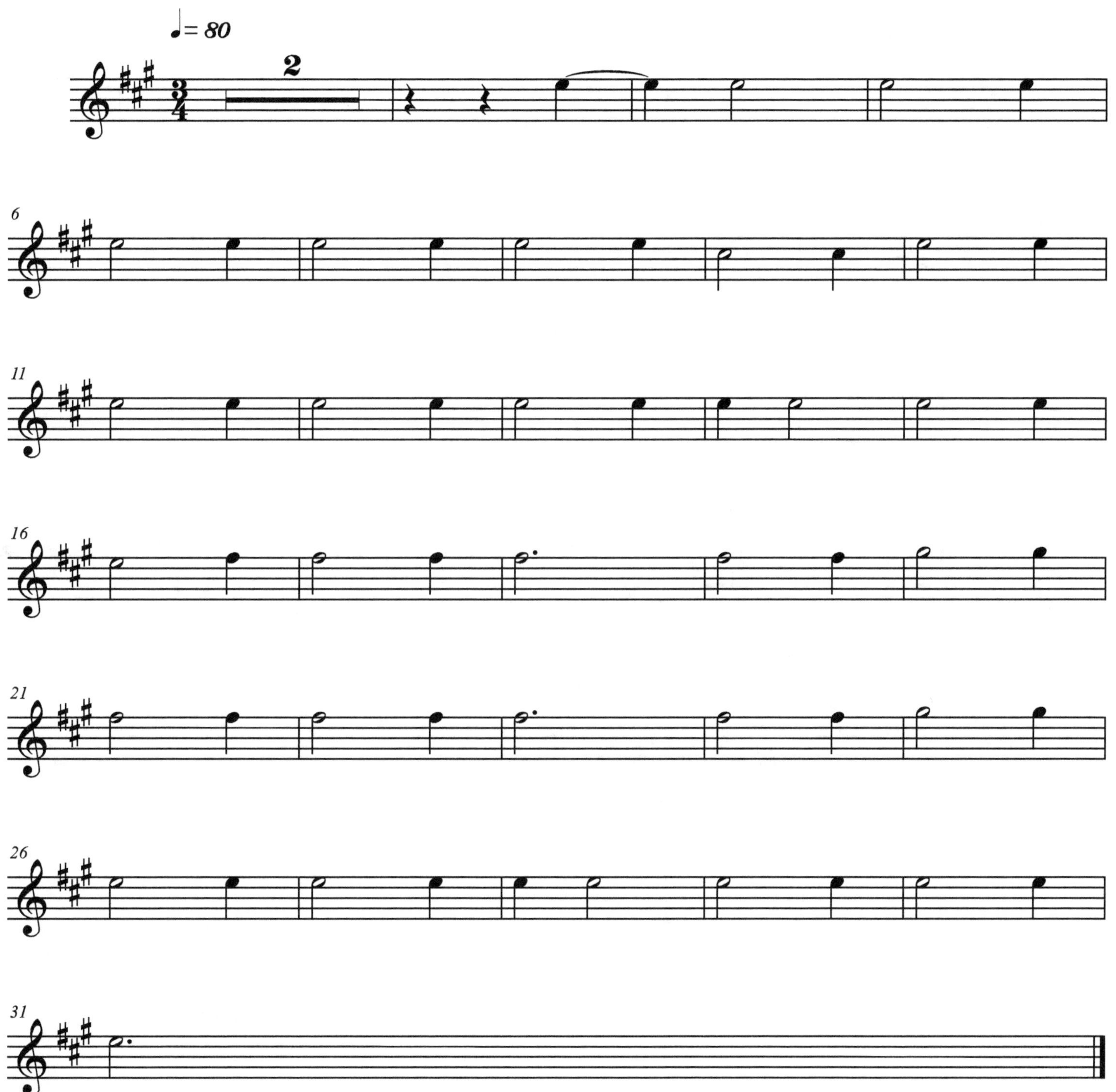

A

Part 1: Bes Soprano Sax.

Joost de Groo

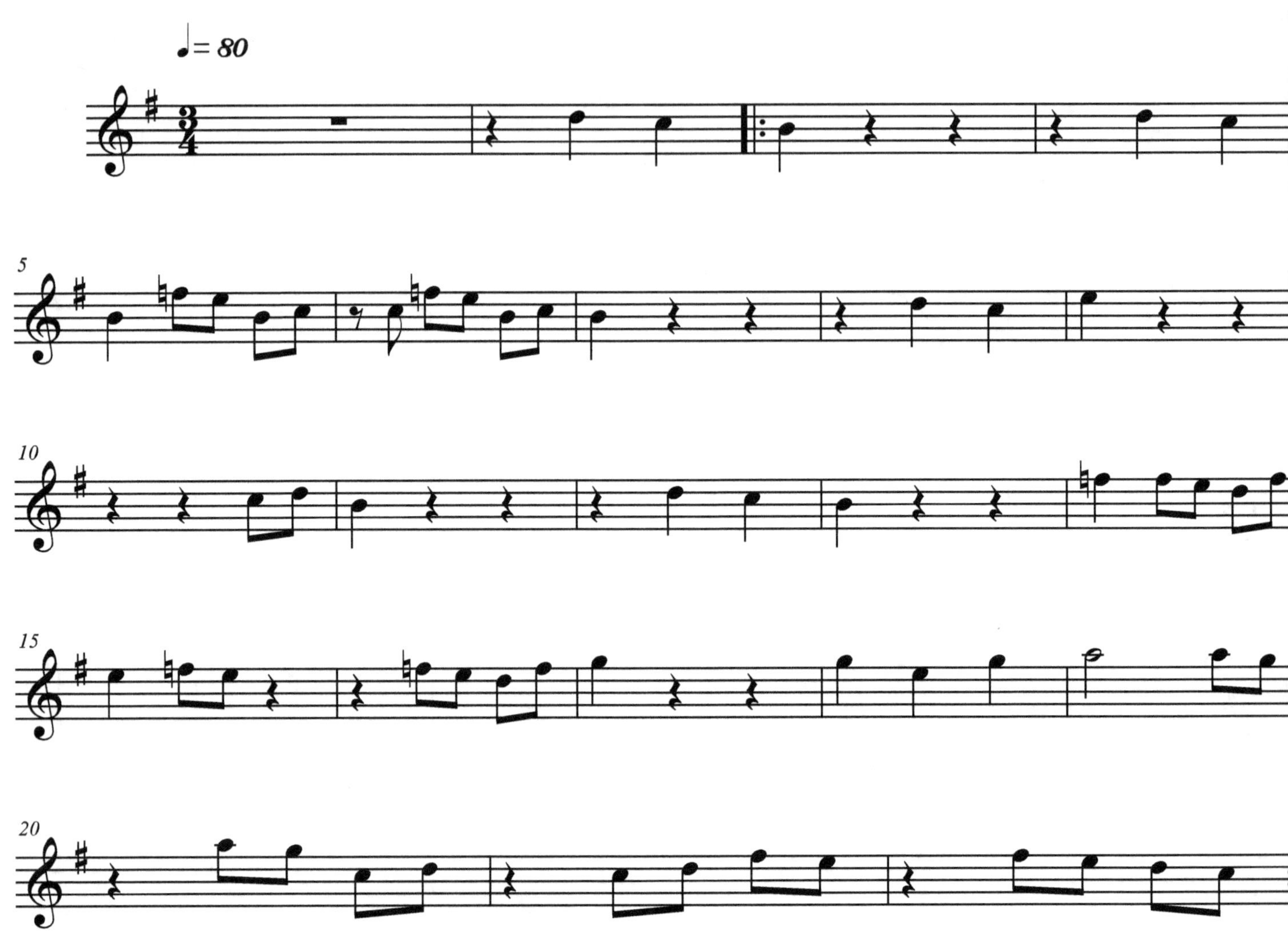

Part 1: Es Alto Sax. 1

A

Joost de Groot

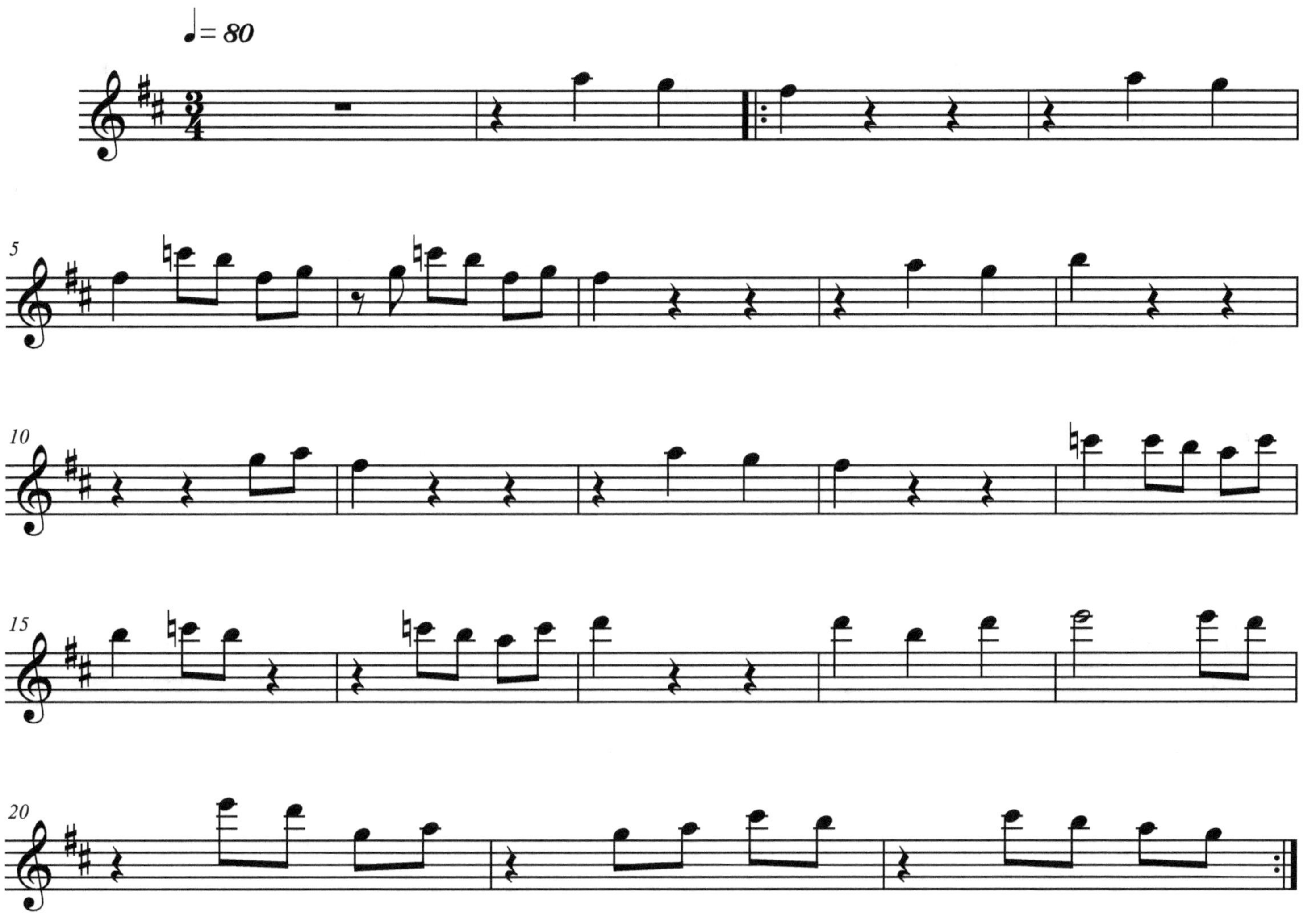

A

Part 2: Es Alto Sax. 2

Joost de Gro

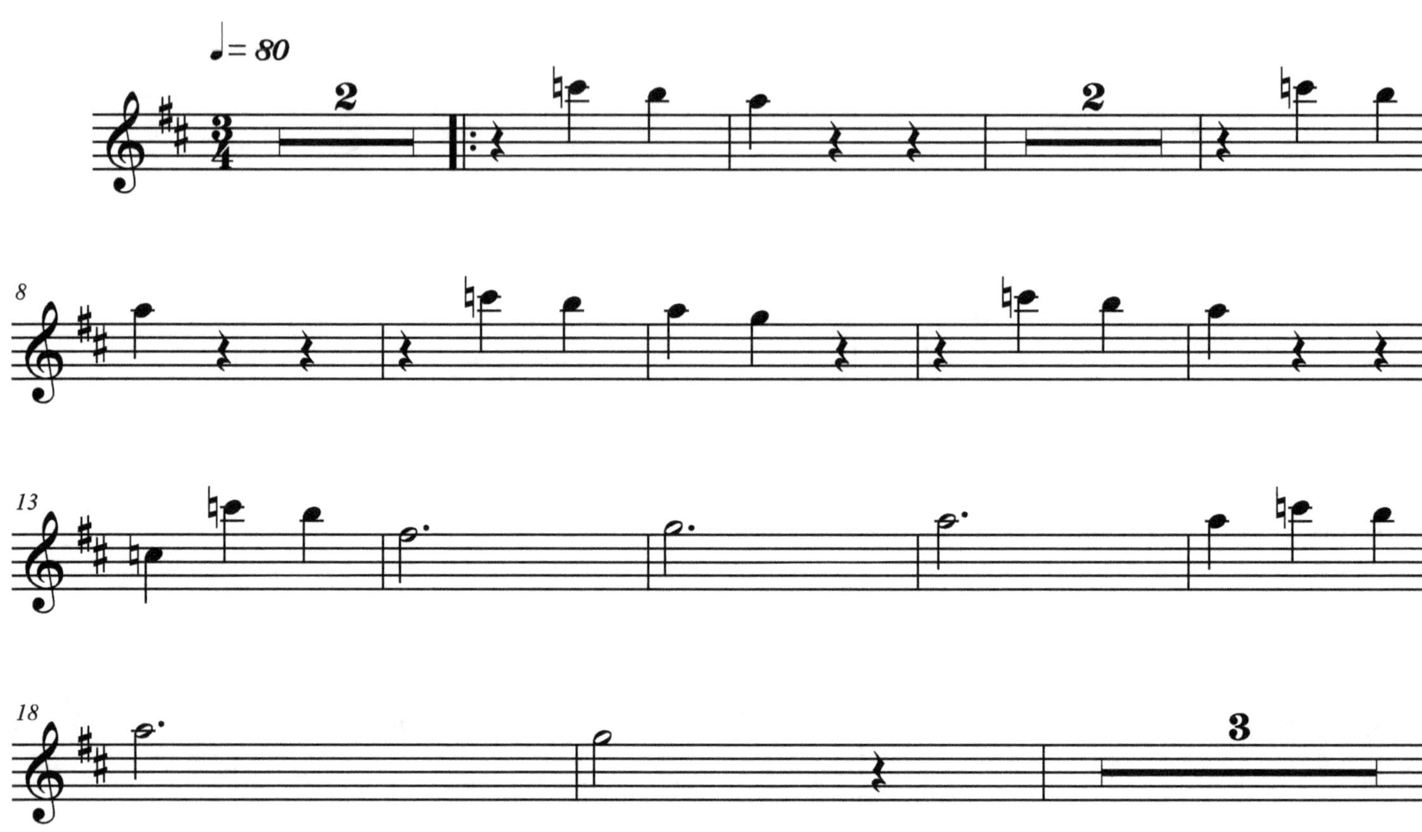

Part 3: Bes Tenor Sax.

A

Joost de Groot

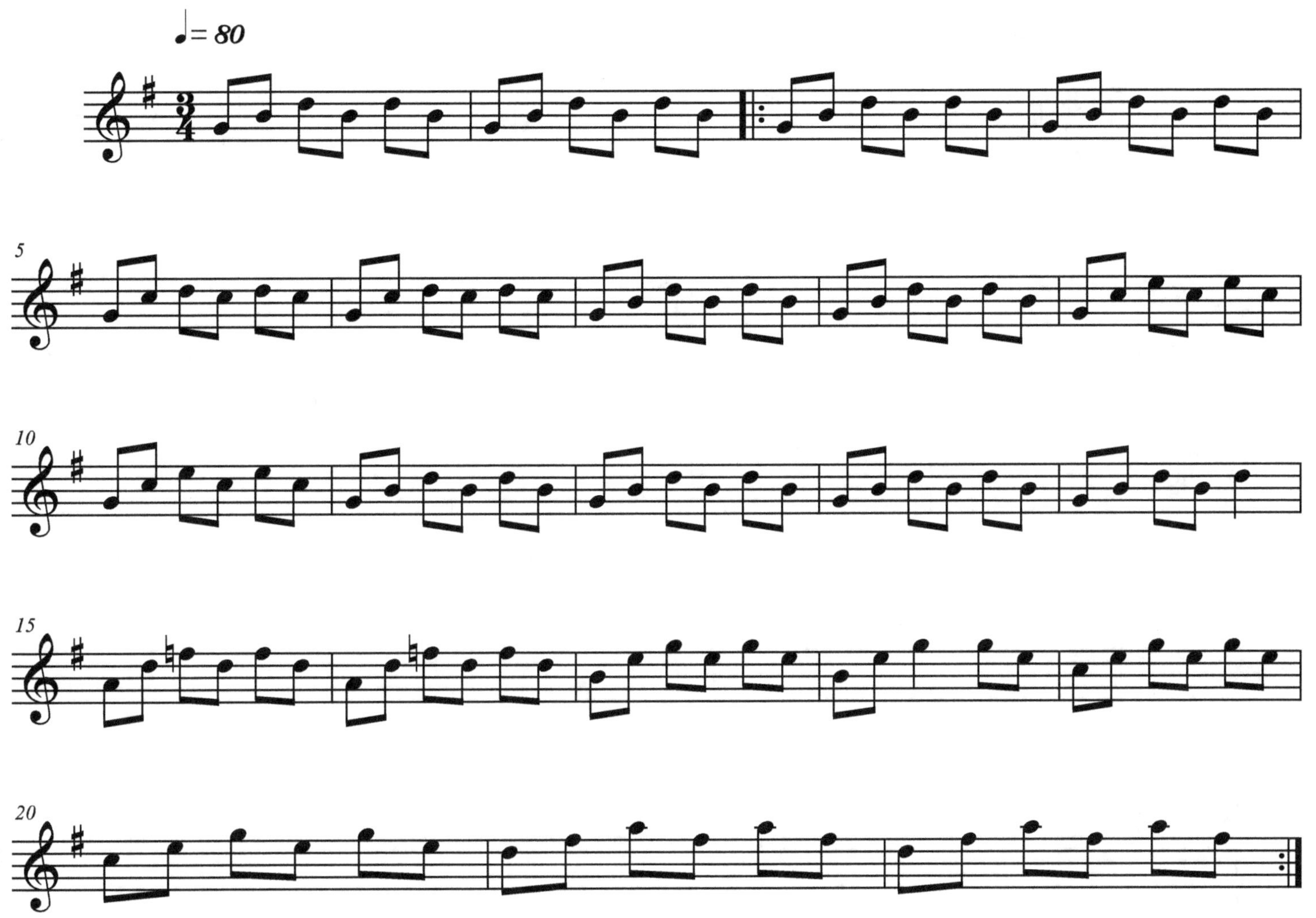

A

Part 4: Es Baritone Sax.

Joost de Gro

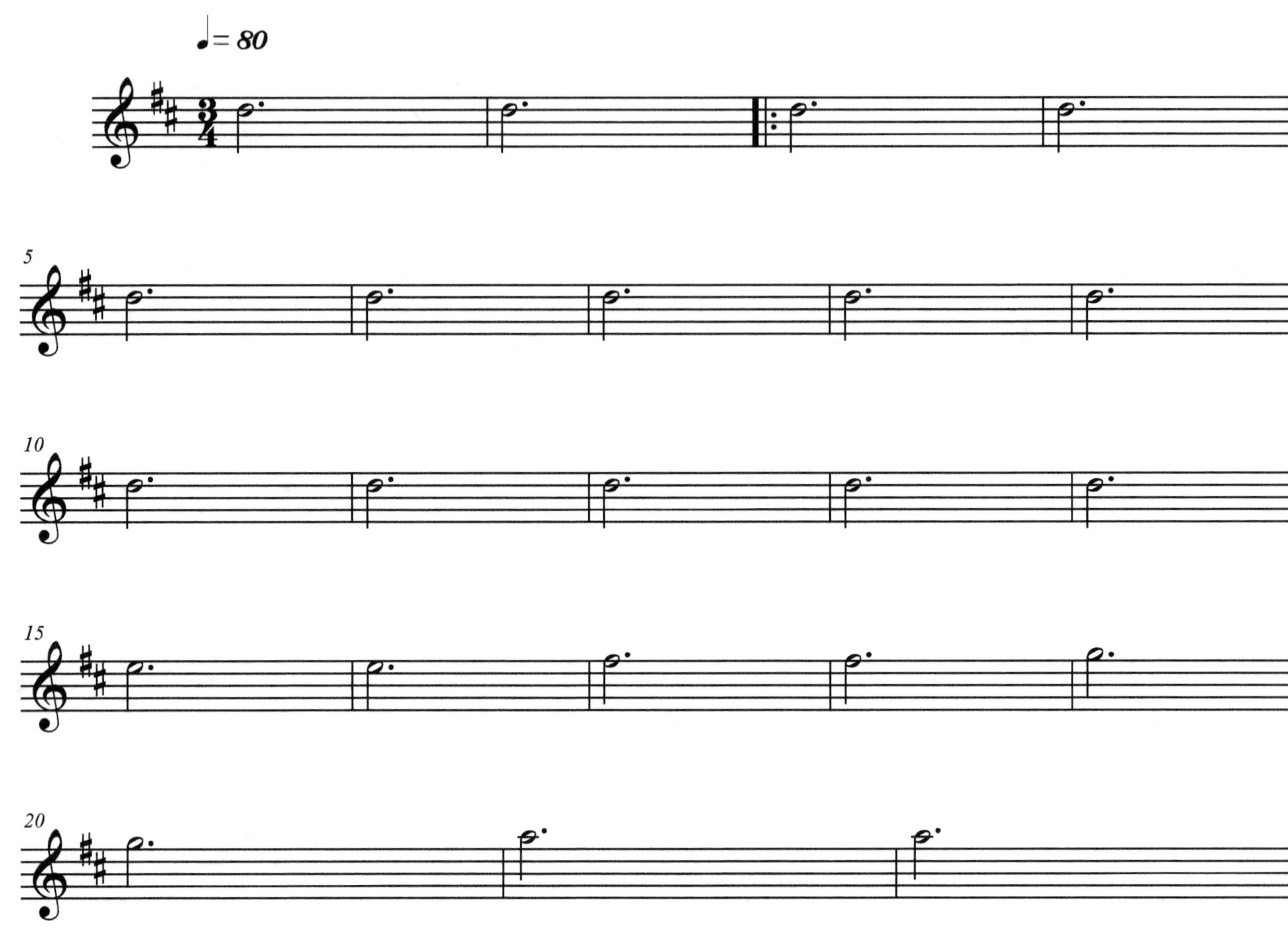

N

Part 1: Bes Soprano Sax.

Joost de Groot

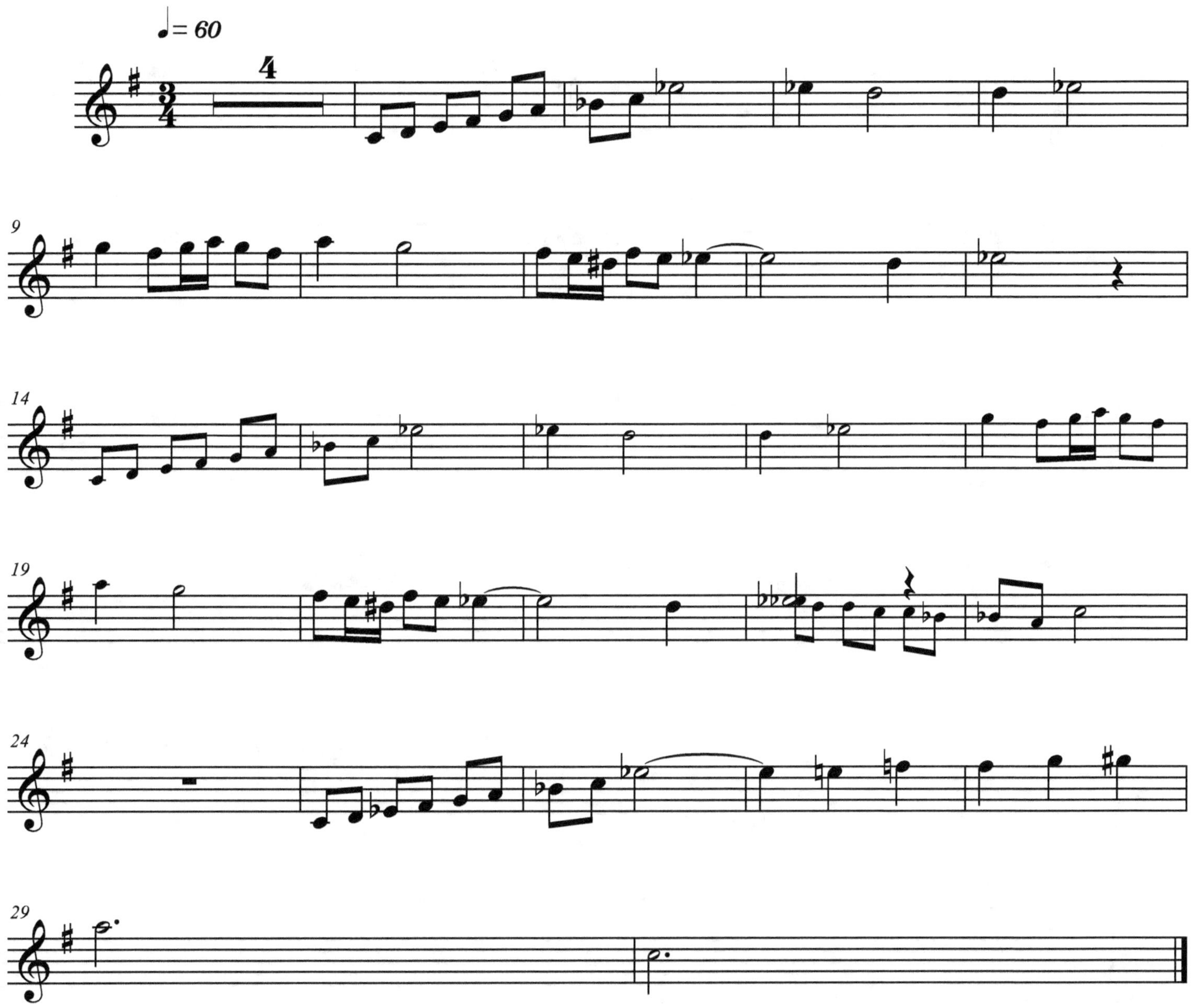

Part 1: Es Alto Sax. 1

N

Joost de Gro

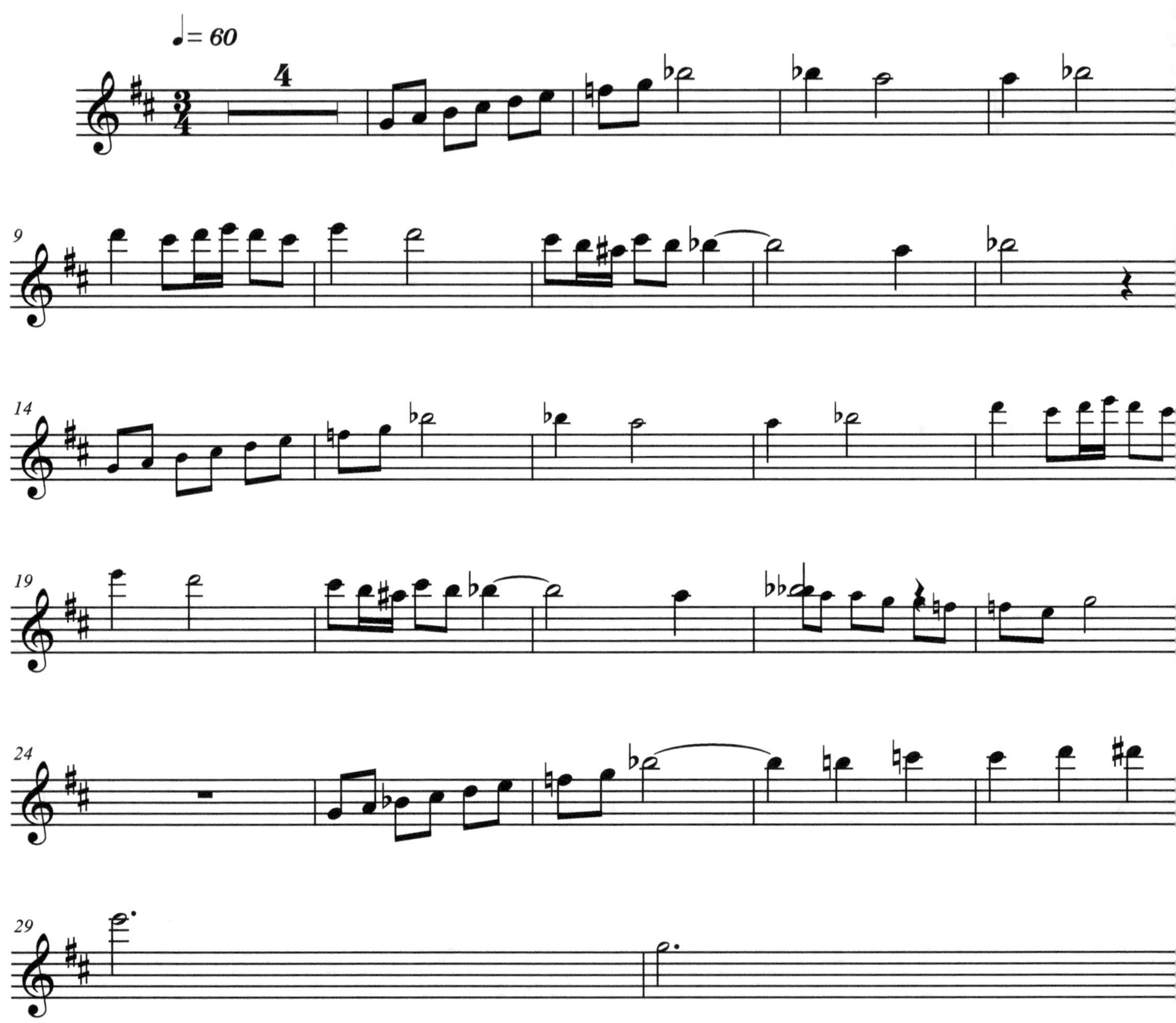

N

Part 2: Es Alto Sax. 2

Joost de Groot

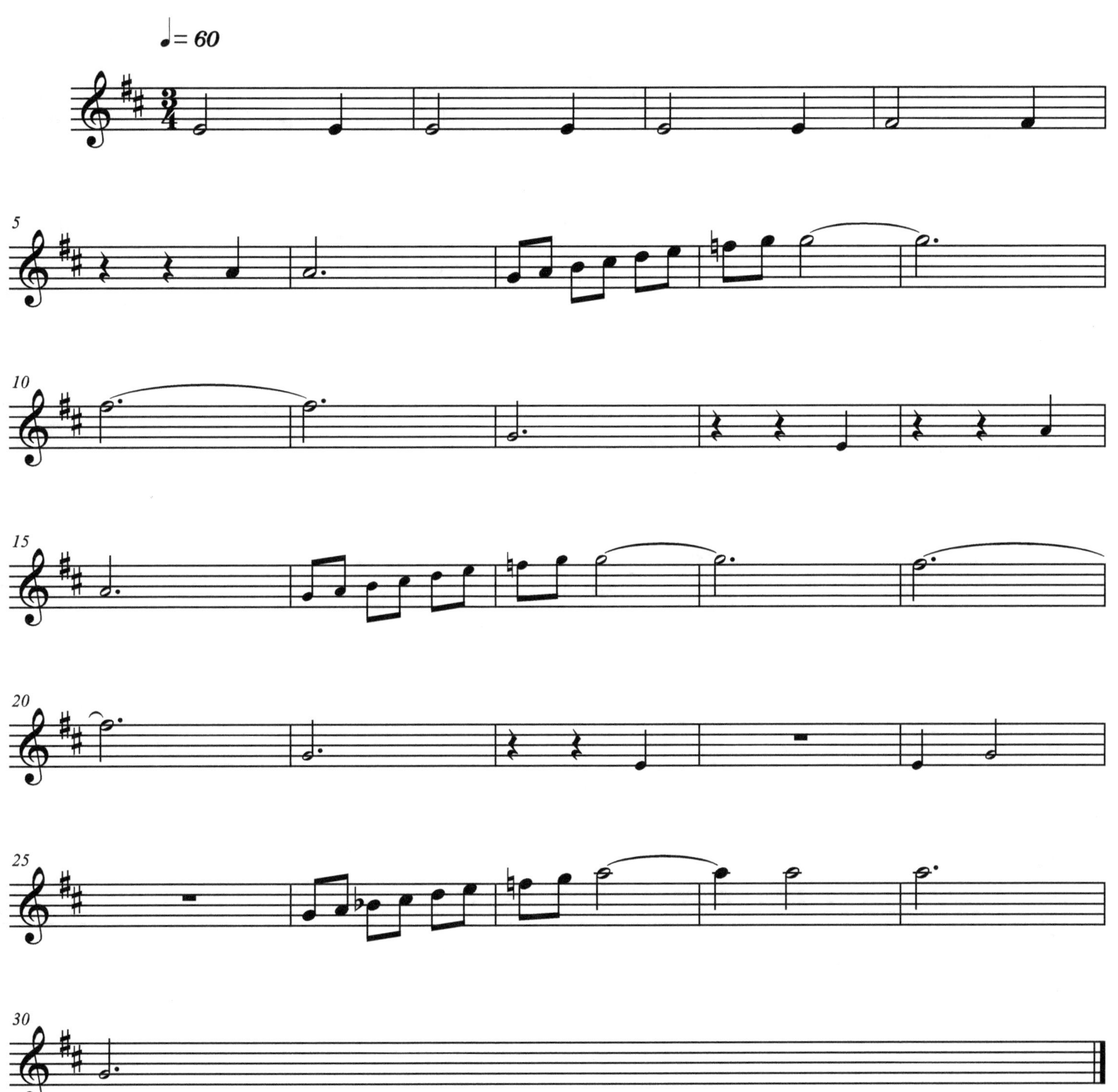

Part 3: Bes Tenor Sax.

N

Joost de Gro

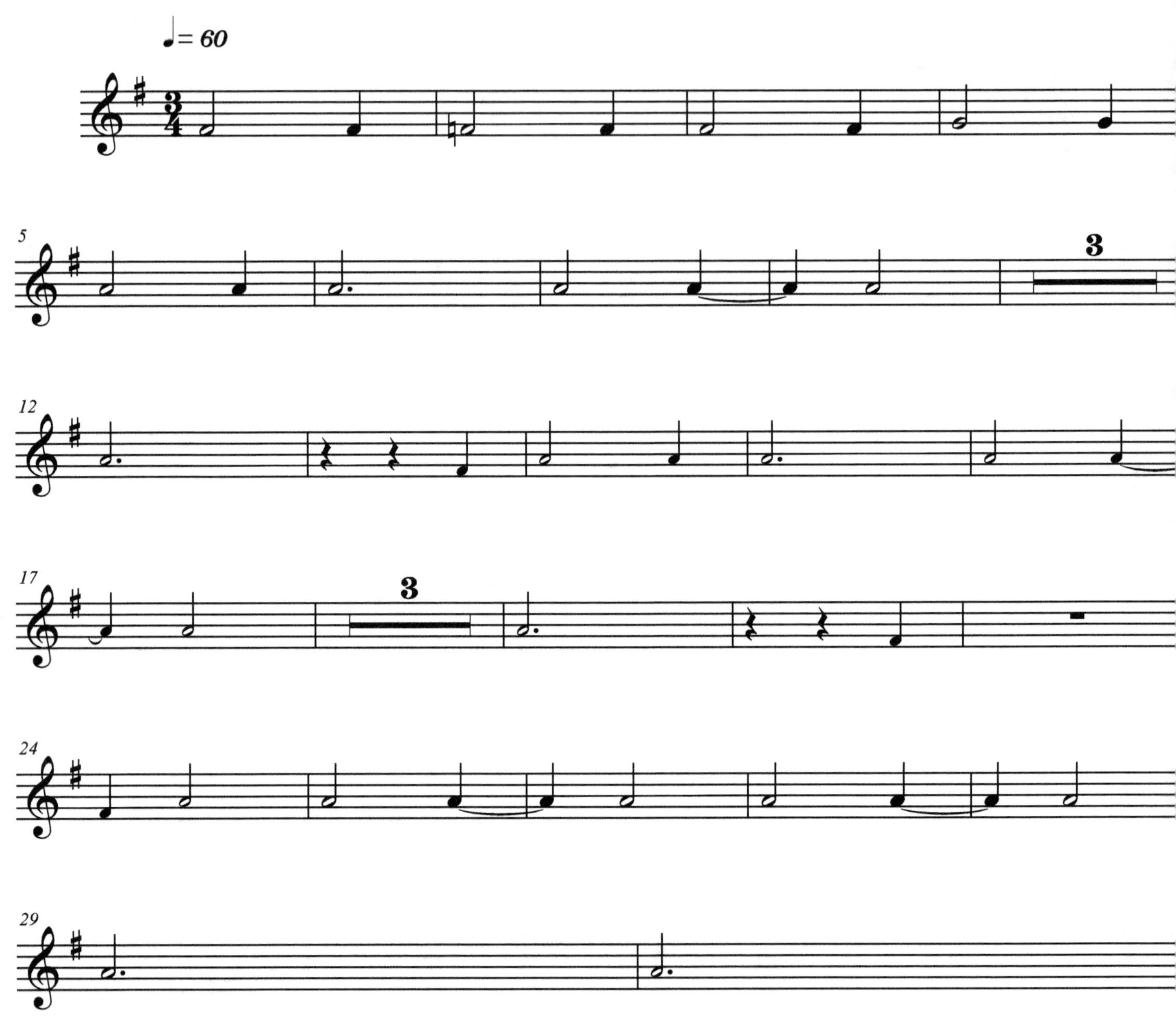

Part 4: Es Baritone Sax.

N

Joost de Groot

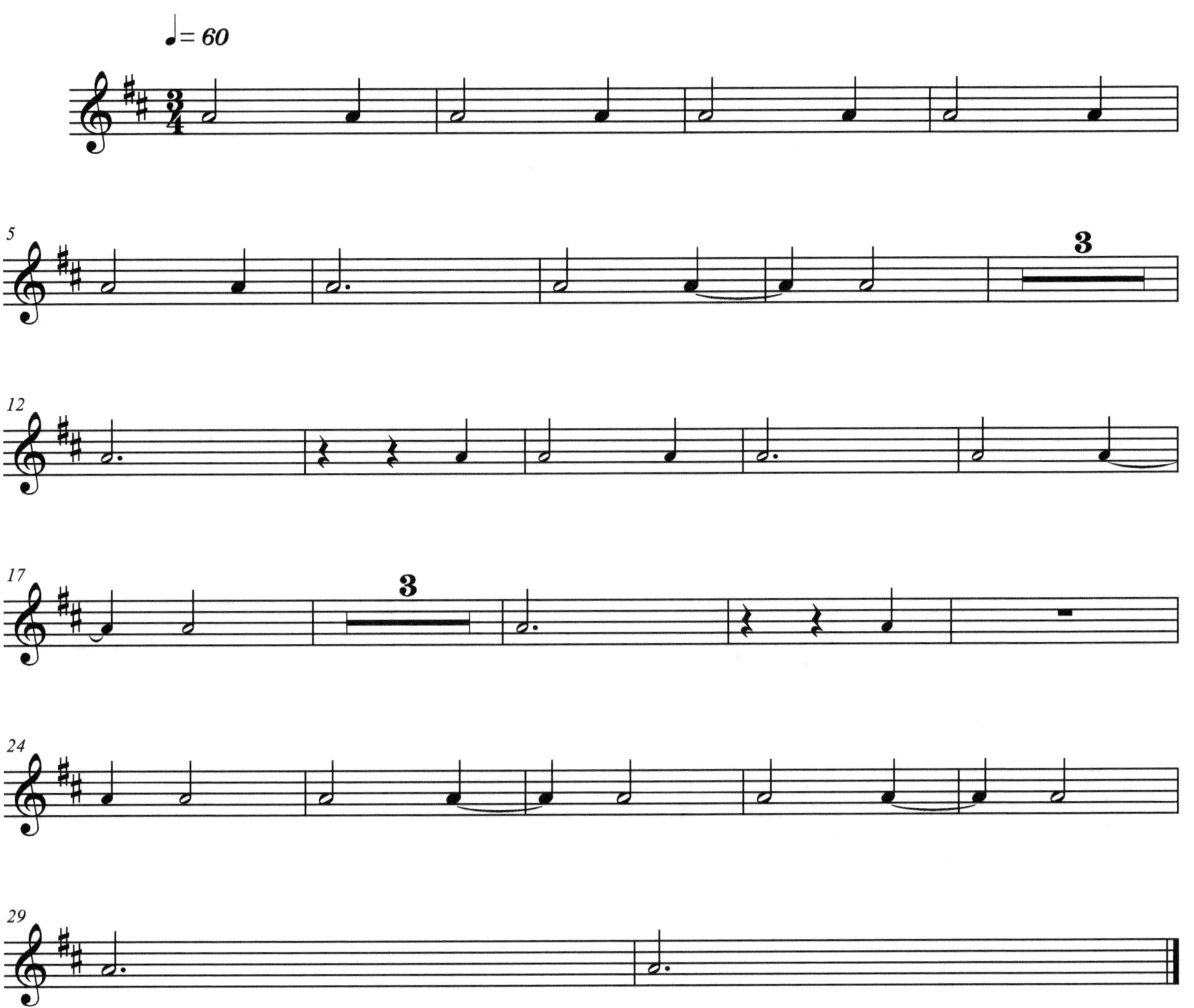

N

Part 1: Bes Soprano Sax.

Joost de Gro

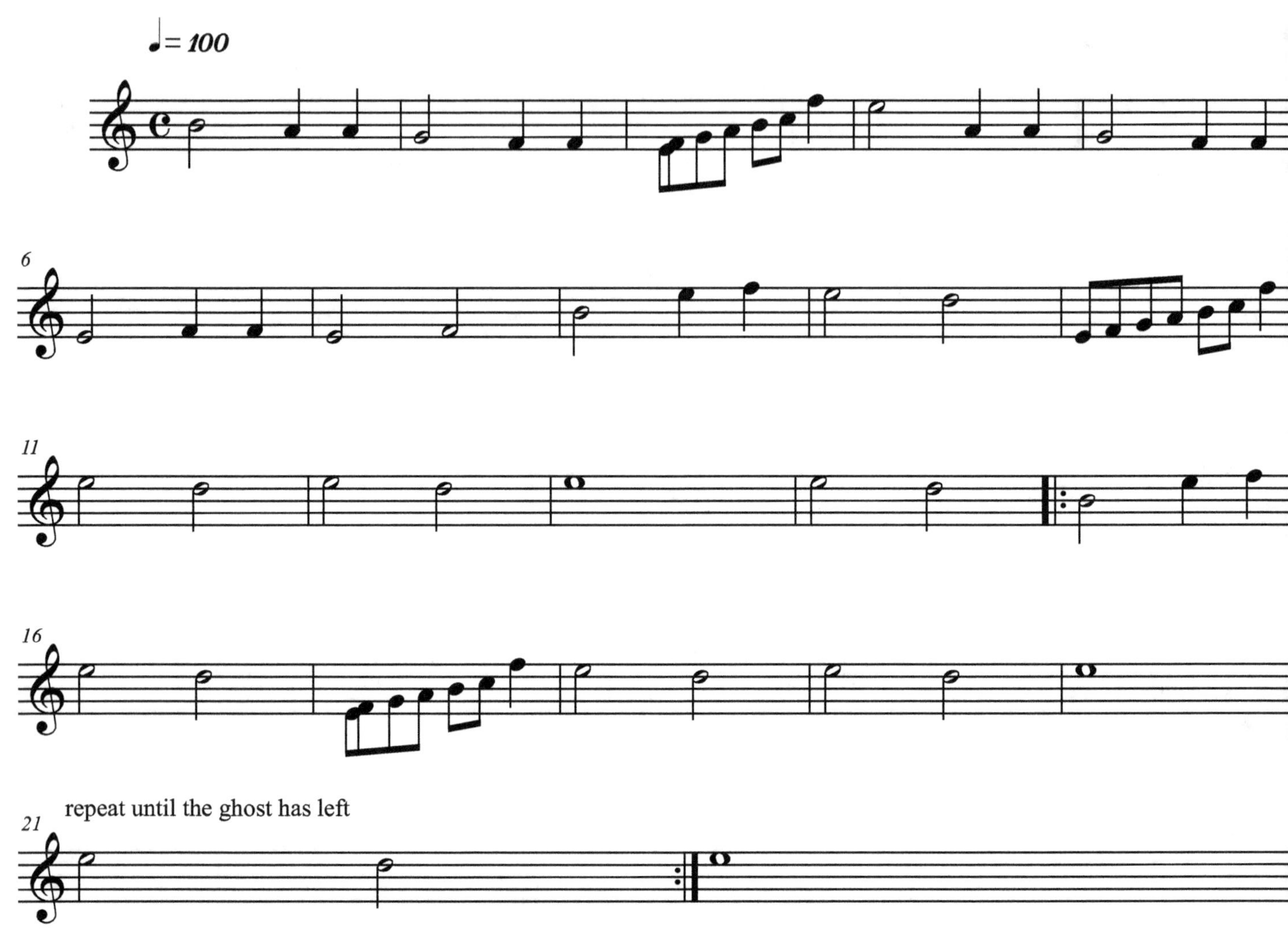

Part 1: Es Alto Sax. 1

N

Joost de Groot

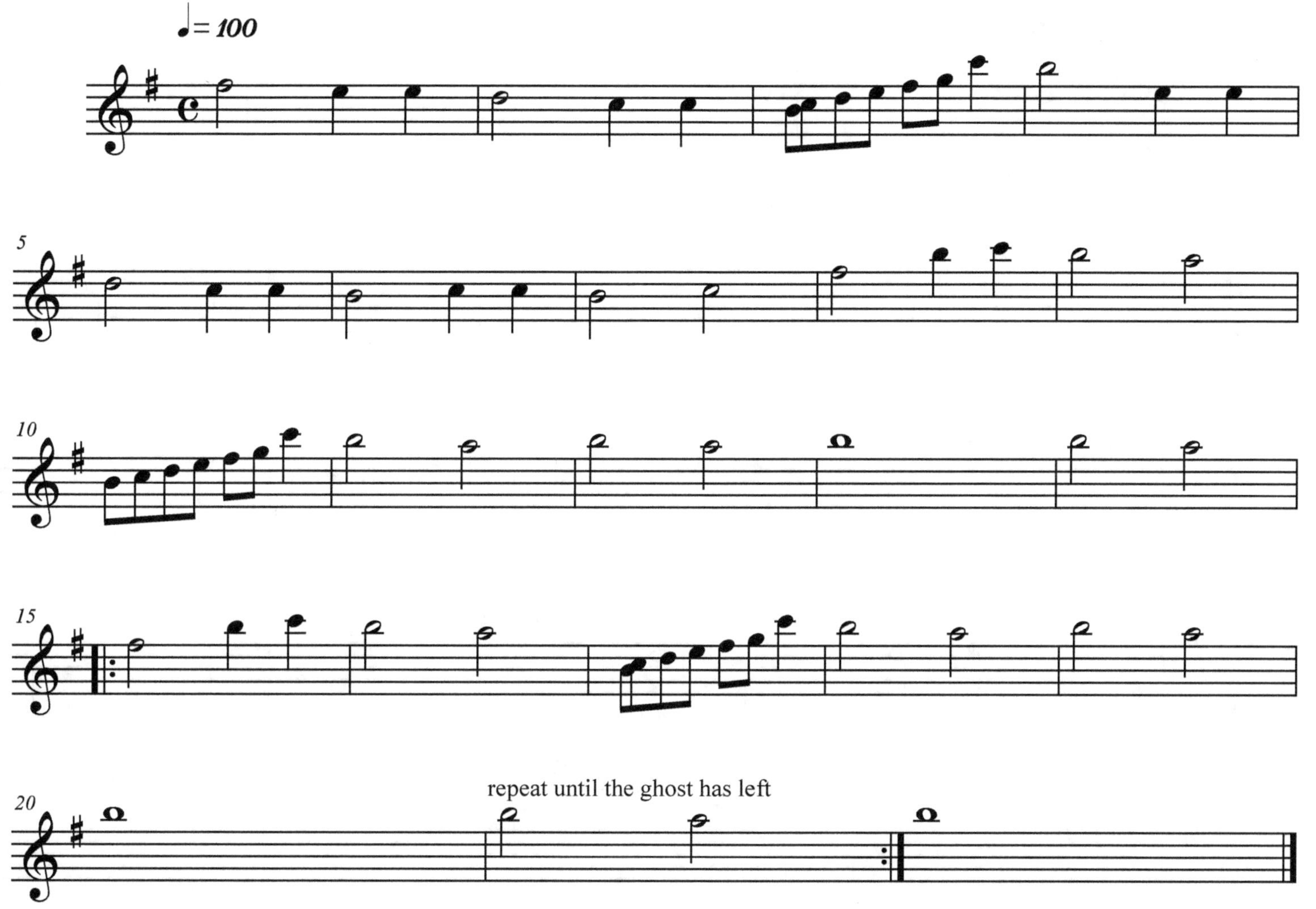

N

Part 2: Es Alto Sax. 2

Joost de Groo

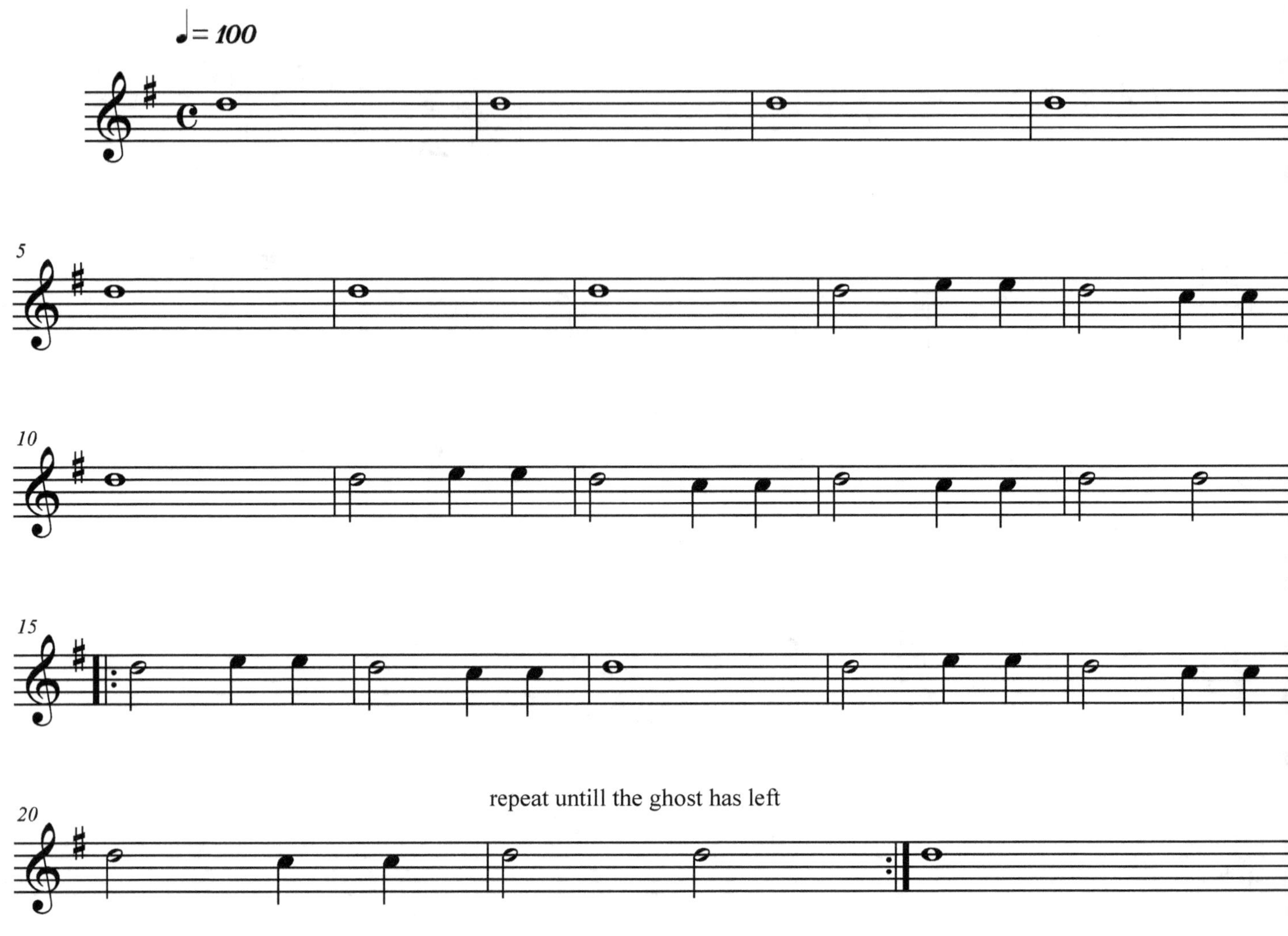

Part 3: Bes Tenor Sax.

N

Joost de Groot

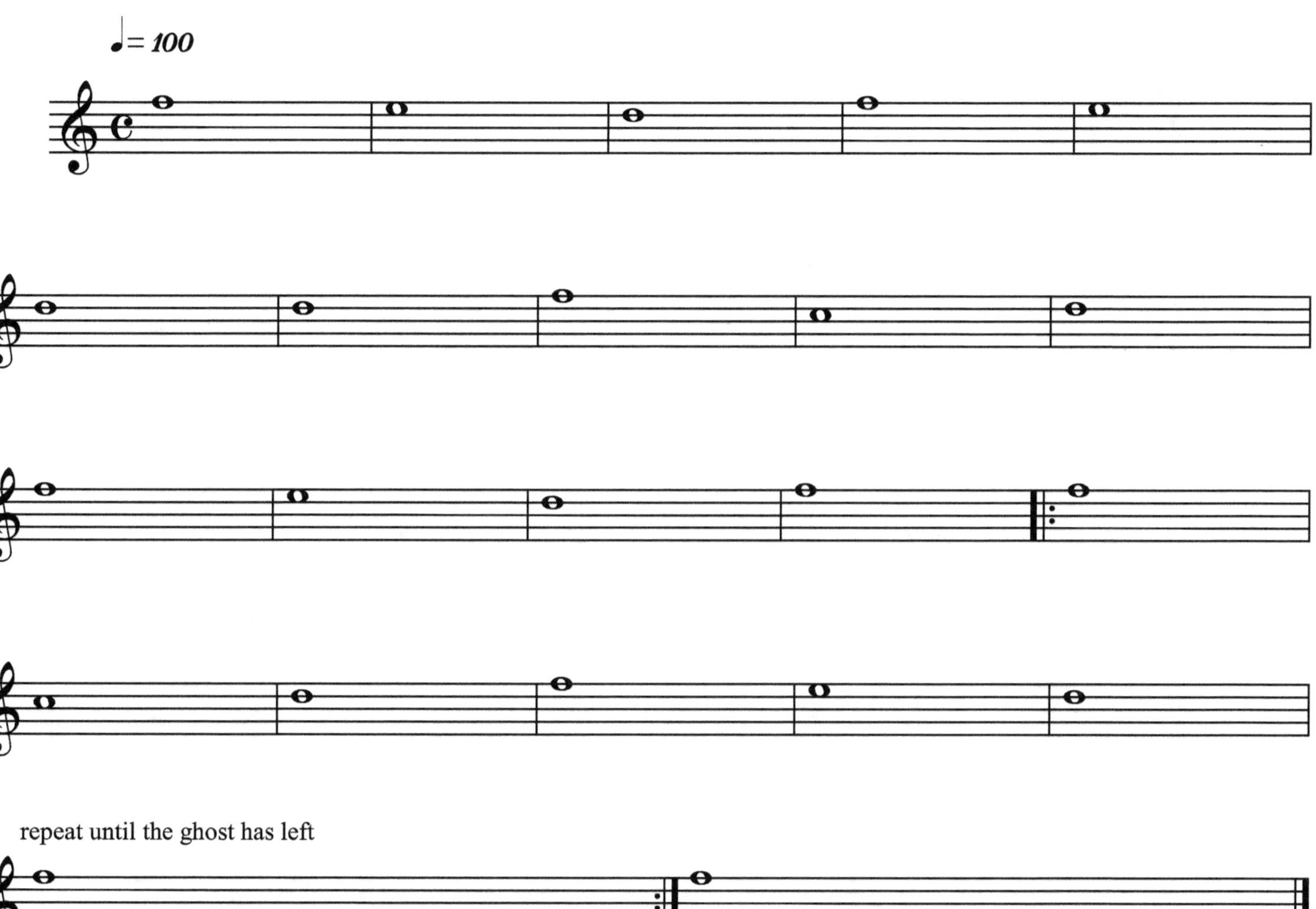

Part 4: Es Baritone Sax.

N

Joost de Gro

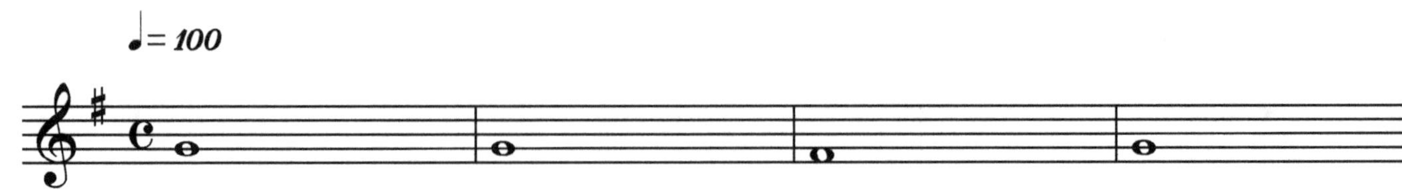

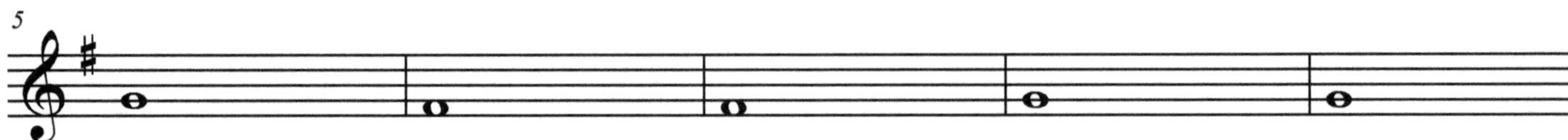

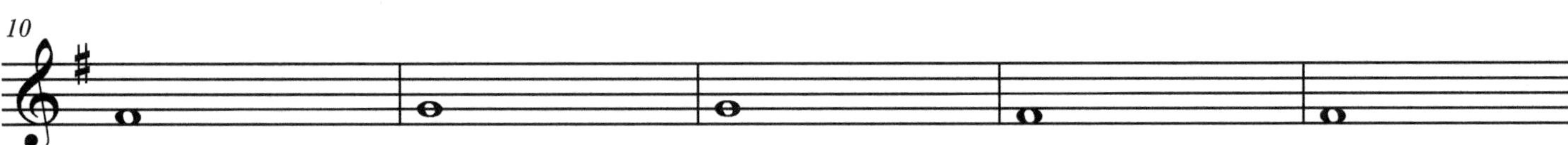

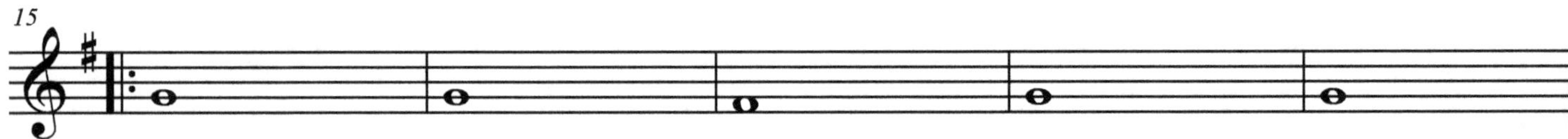

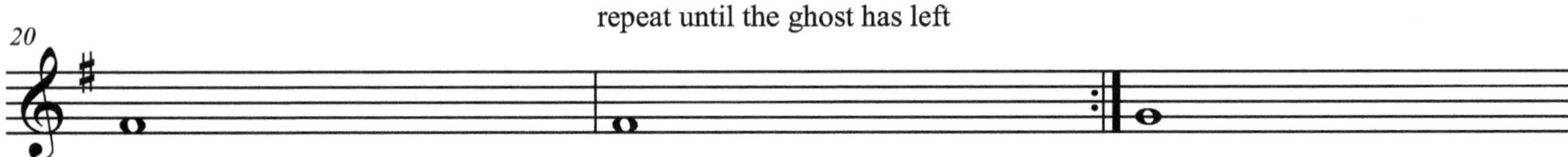

Part 1: Bes Soprano Sax.

I

Joost de Groot

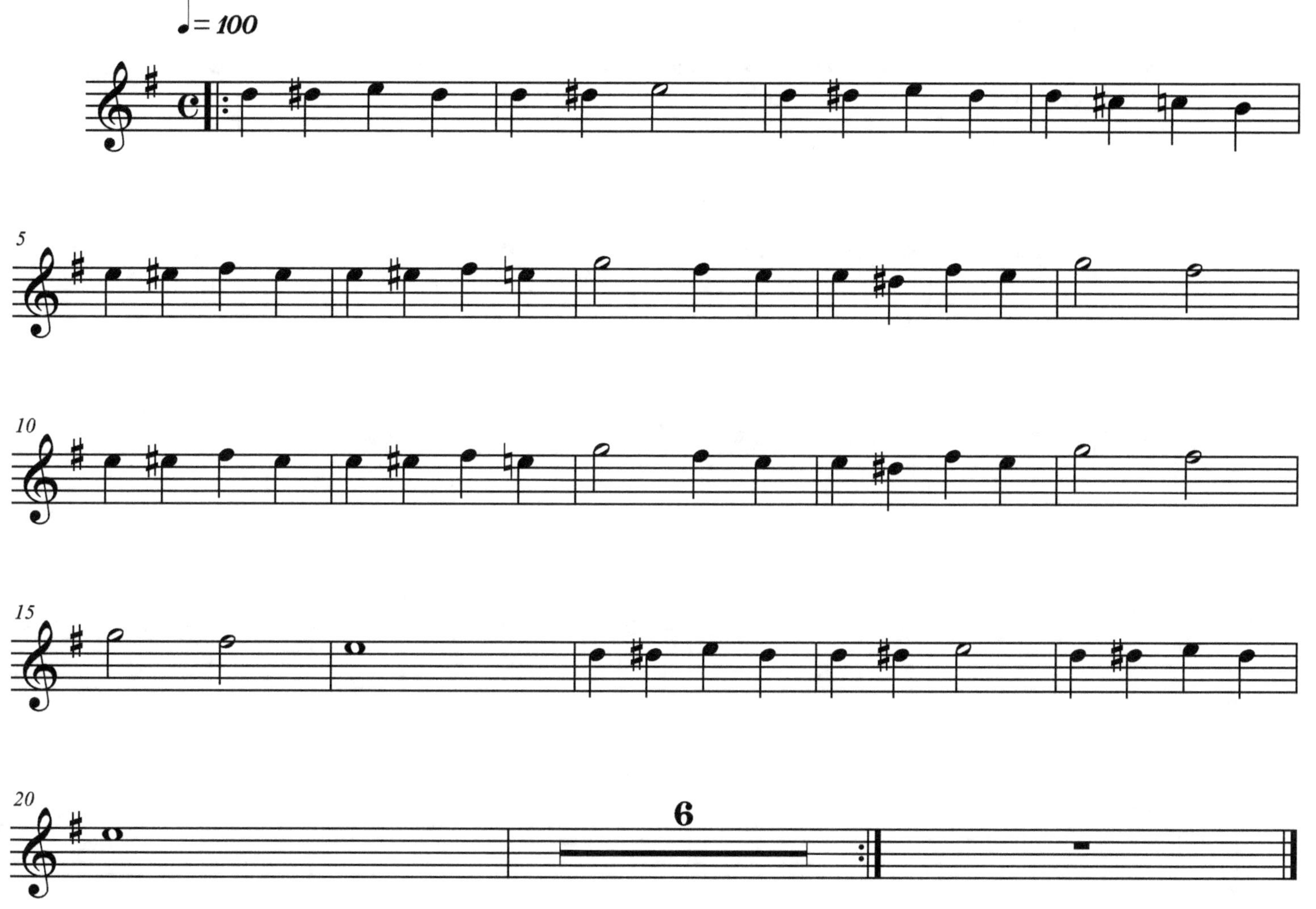

Part 1: Es Alto Sax. 1

I

Joost de Groo

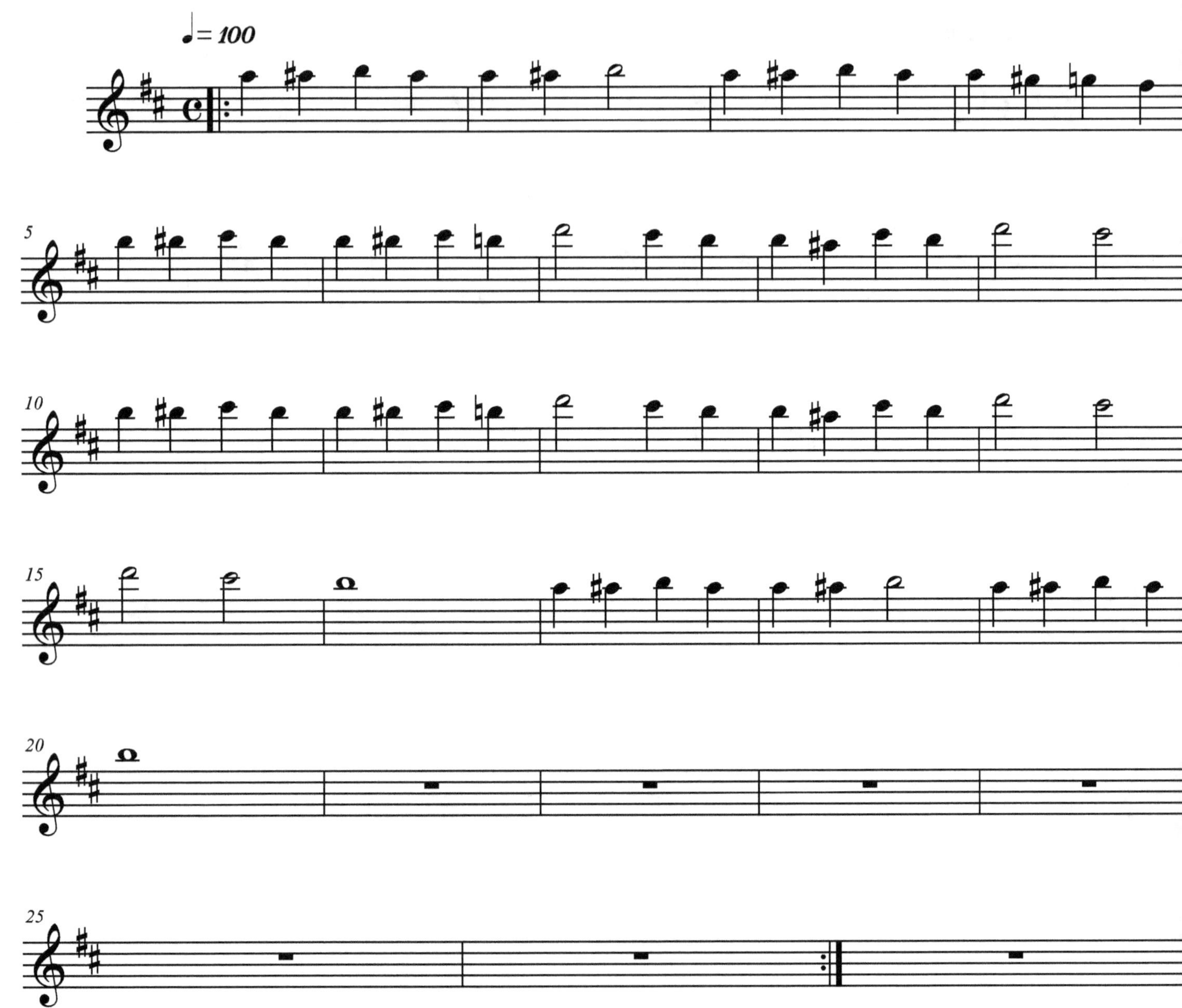

Part 2: Es Alto Sax. 2

I

Joost de Groot

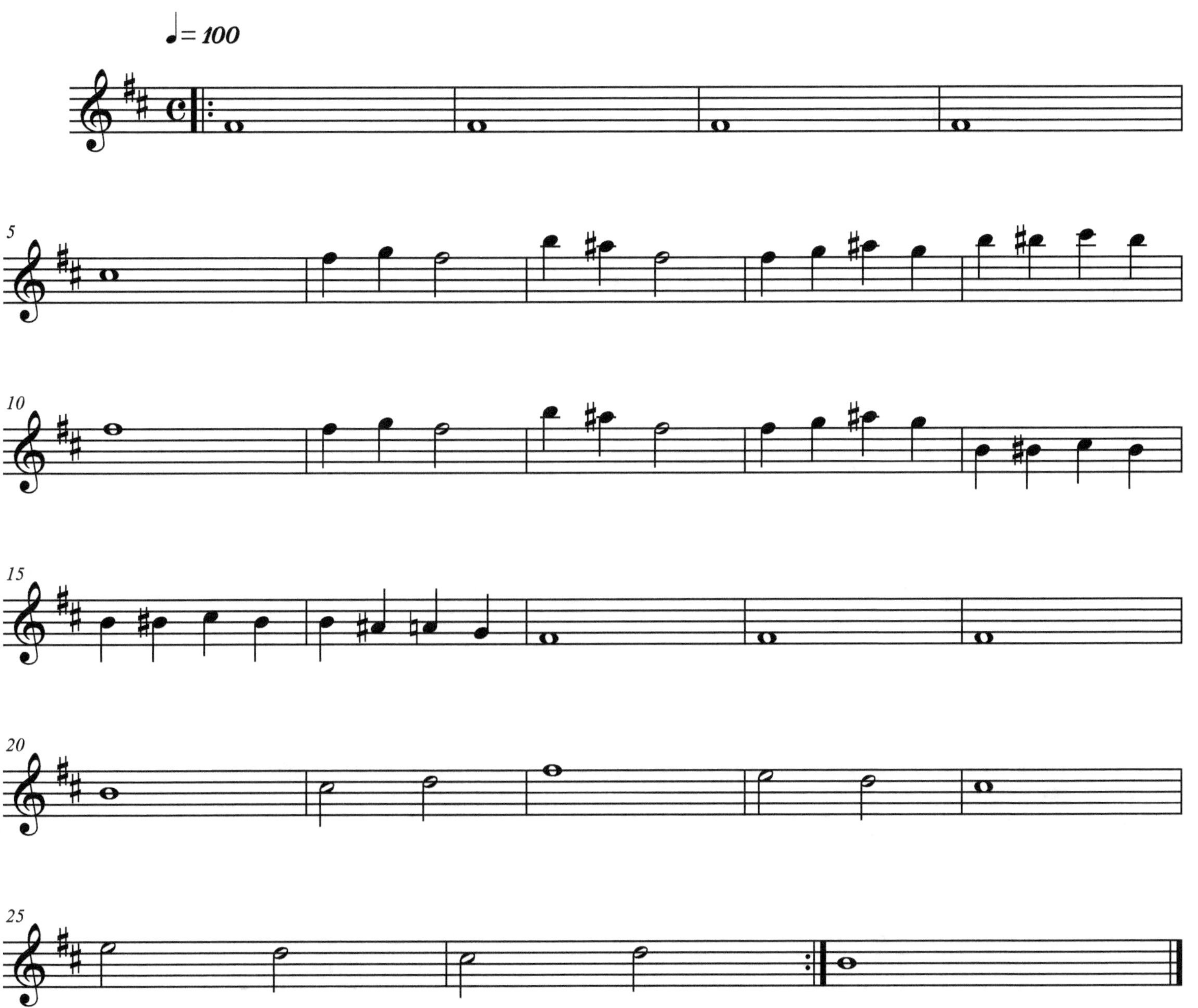

I

Part 3: Bes Tenor Sax.

Joost de Gro

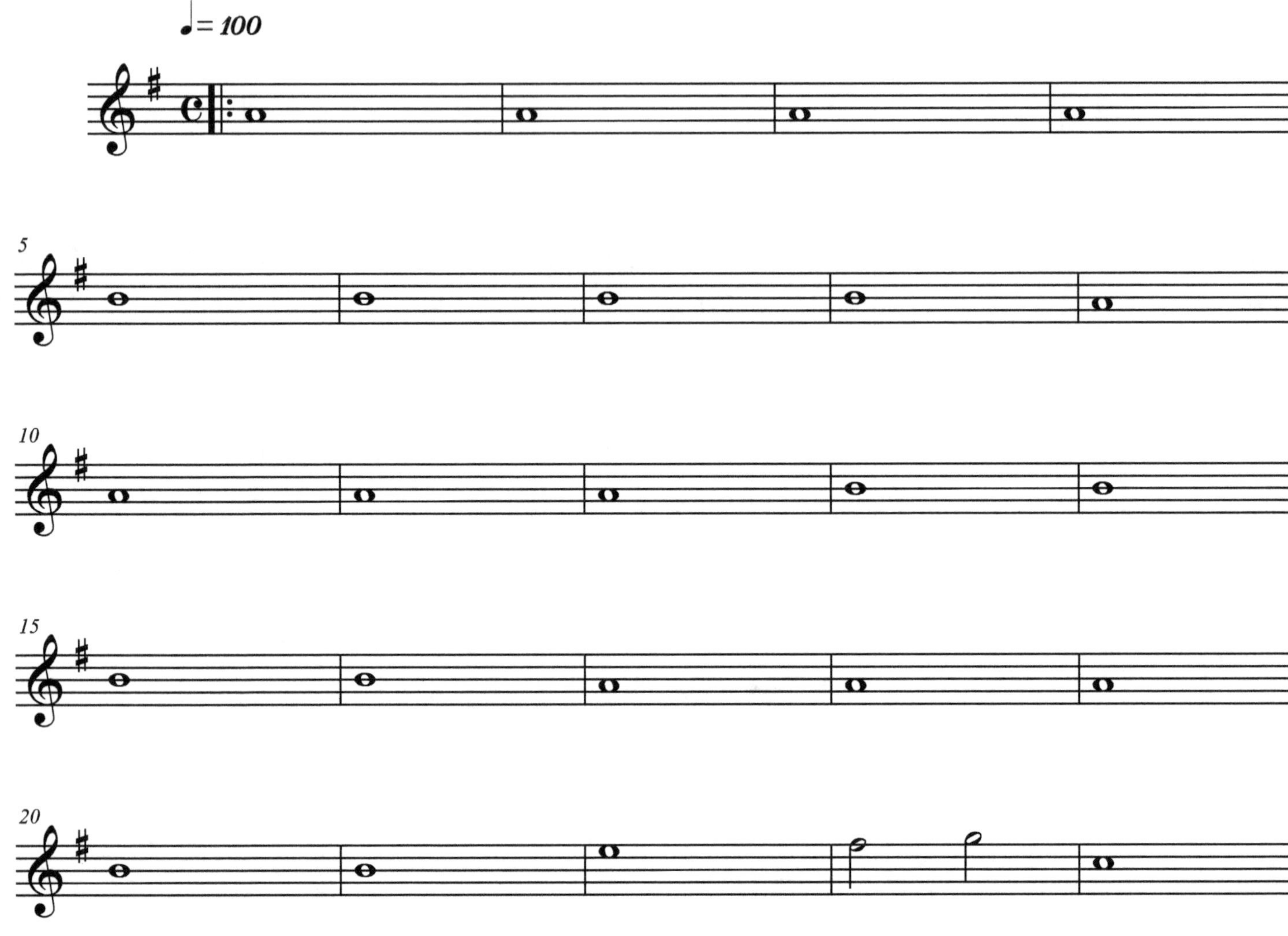

Part 4: Es Baritone Sax.

I

Joost de Groot

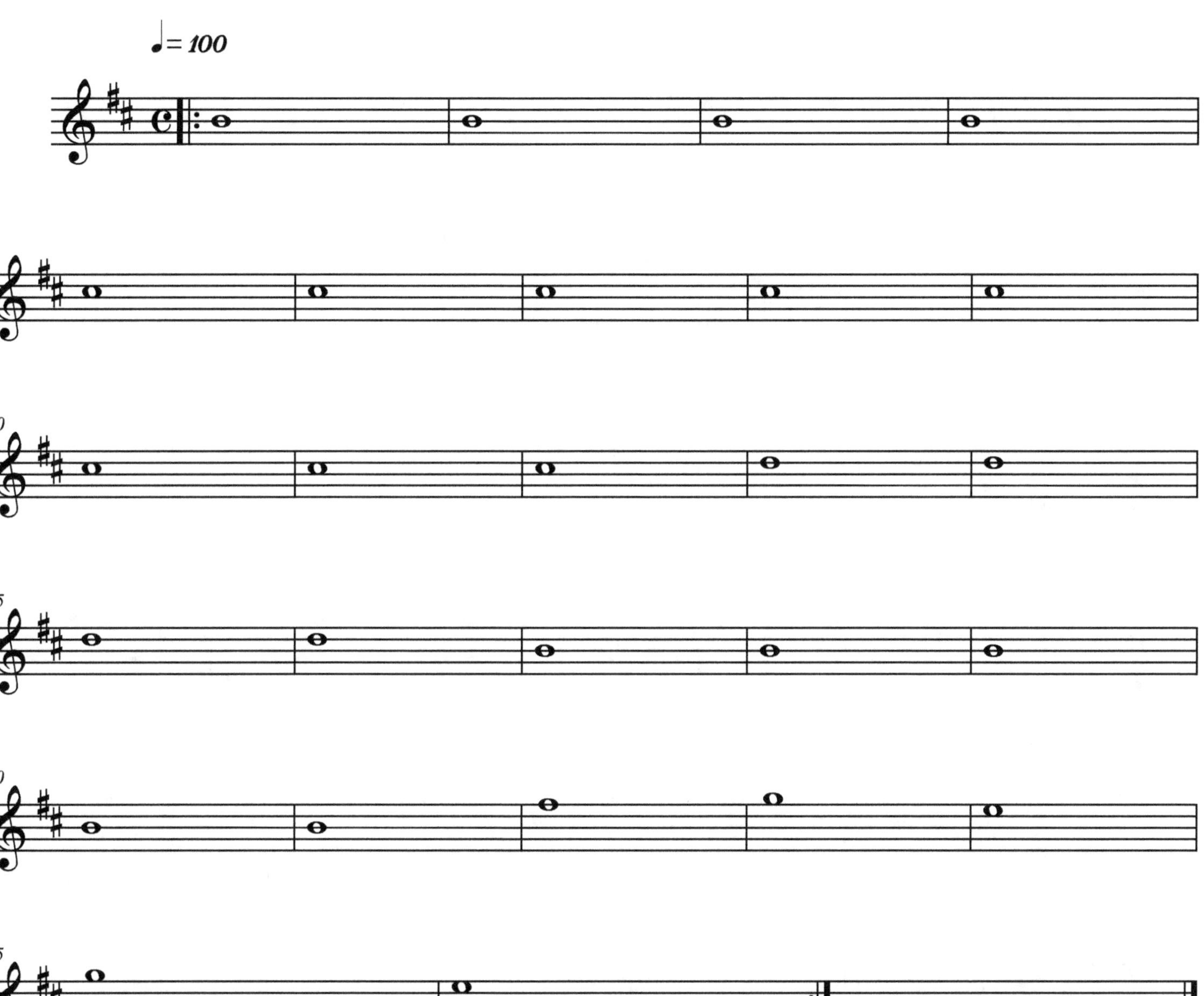

E

Part 1: Bes Soprano Sax.

Joost de Gro

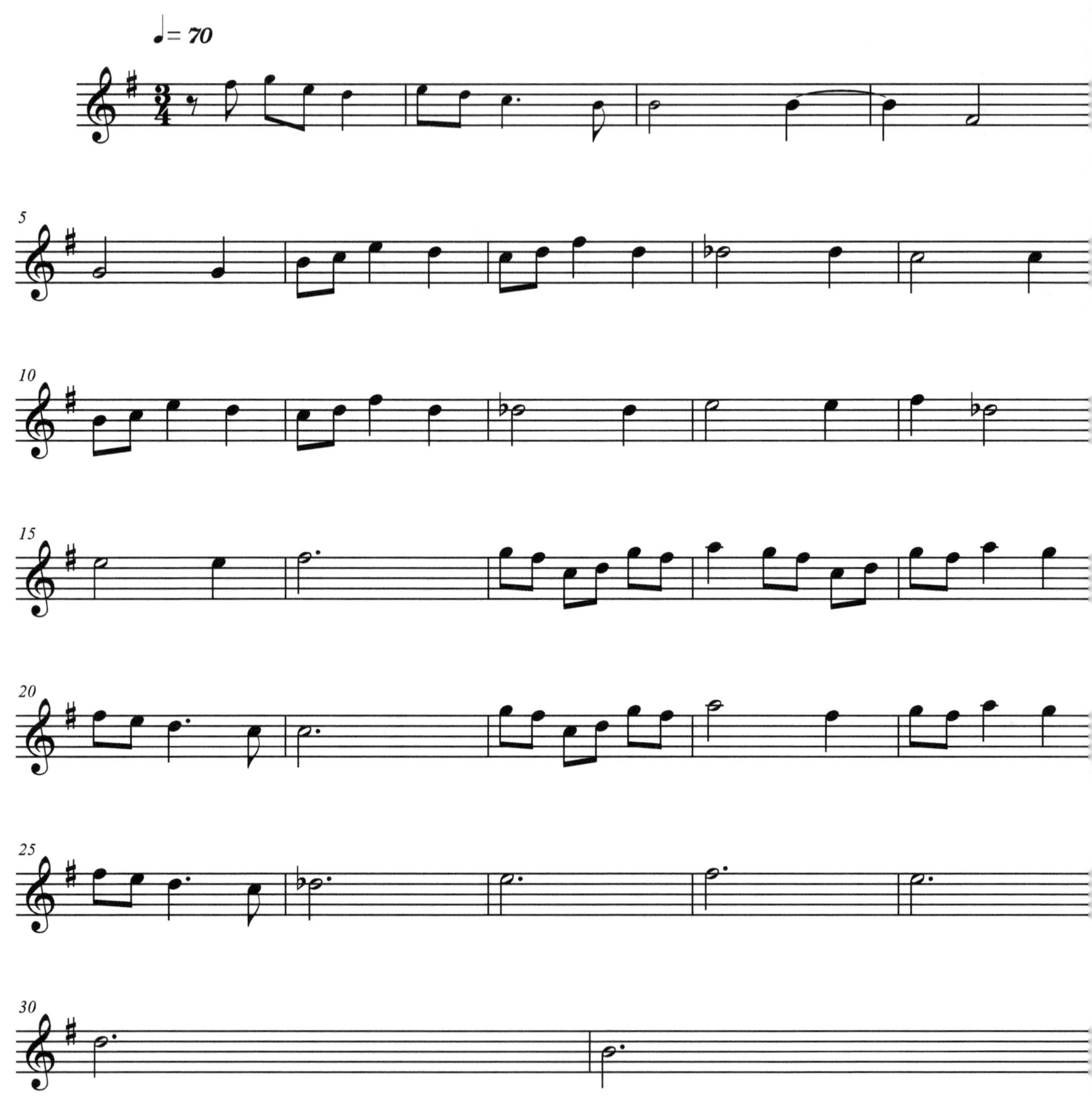

Part 1: Es Alto Sax. 1

E

Joost de Groot

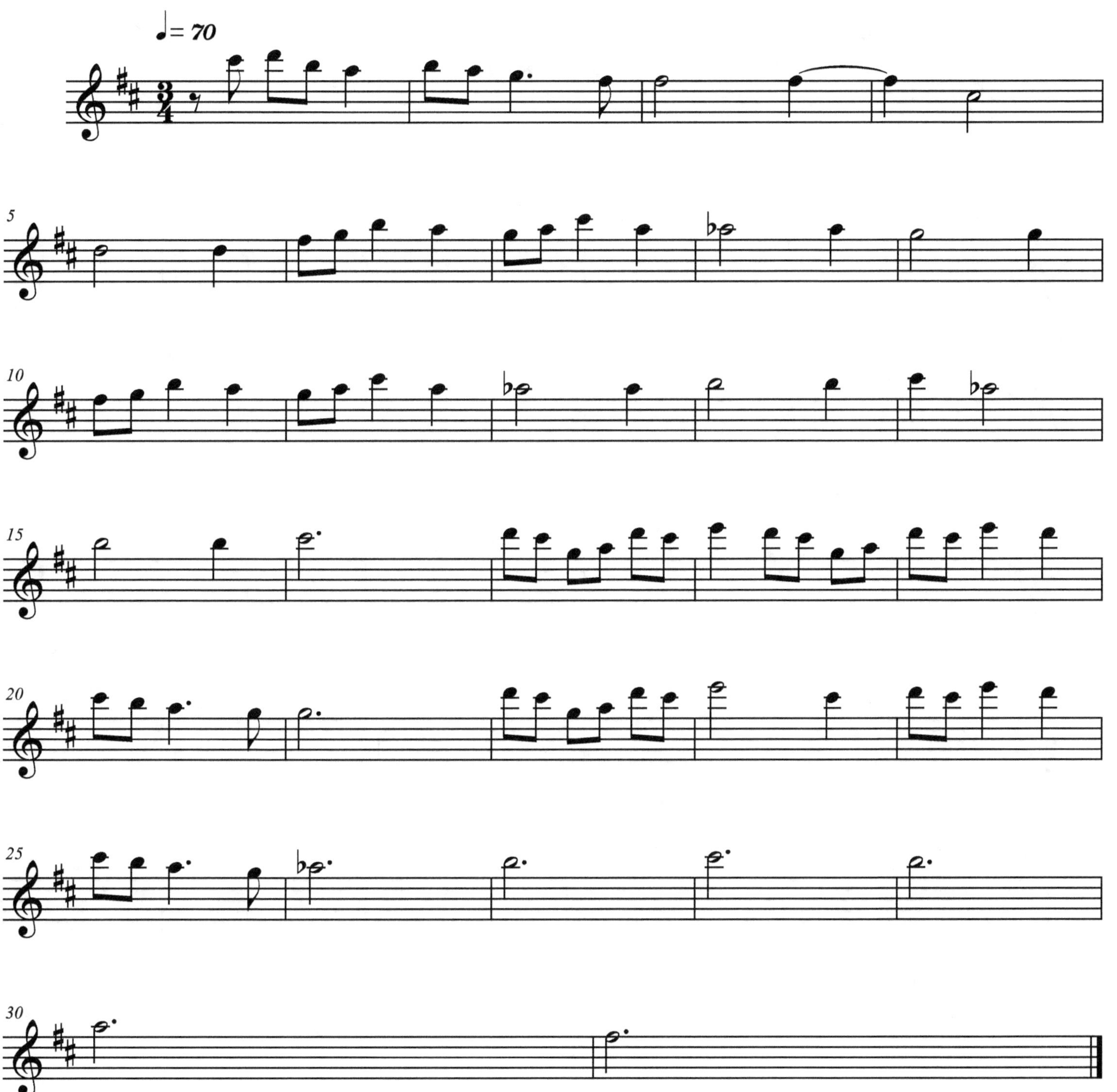

E

Part 2: Es Alto Sax. 2

Joost de Gro

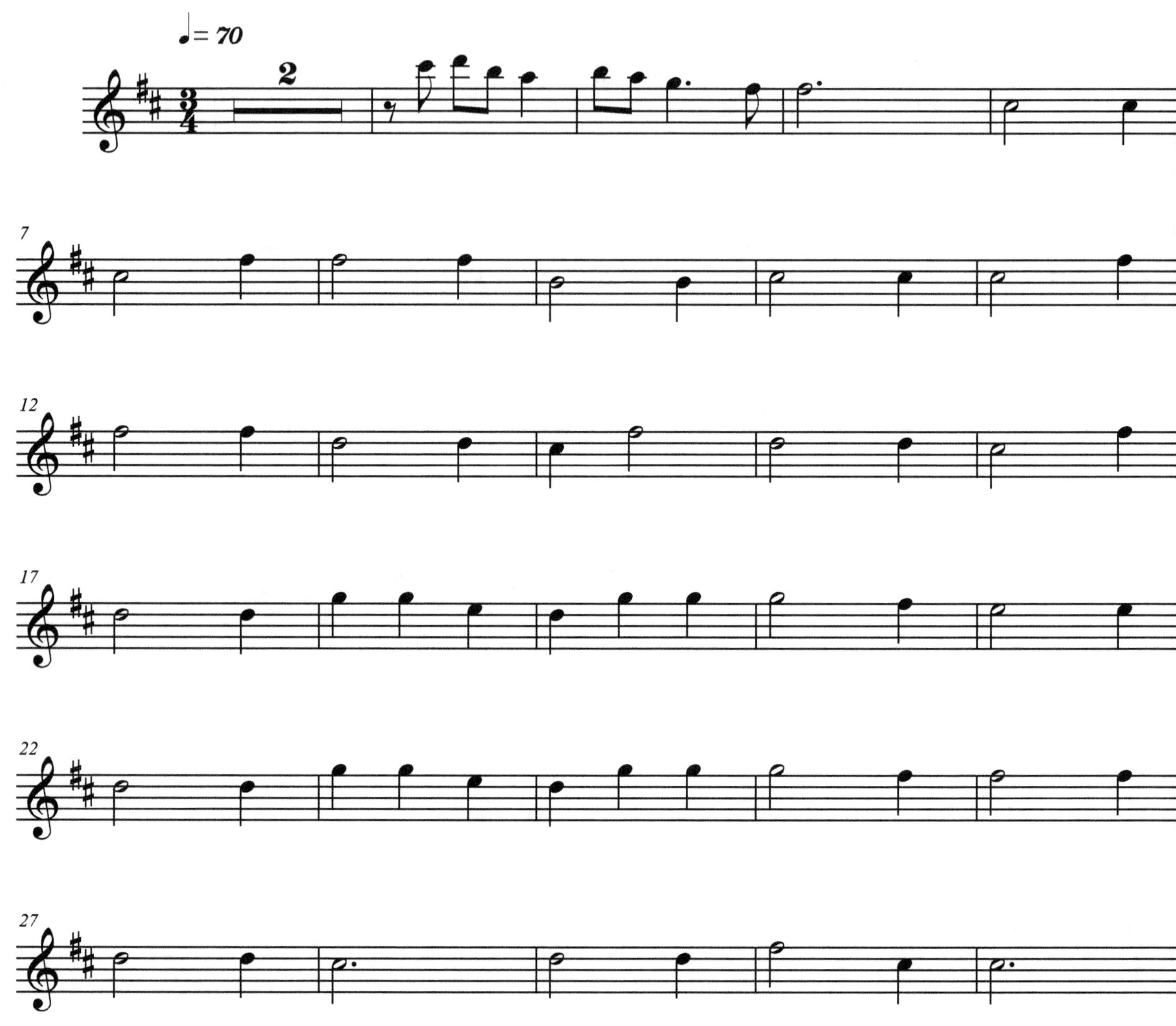

E

Part 3: Bes Tenor Sax.

Joost de Groot

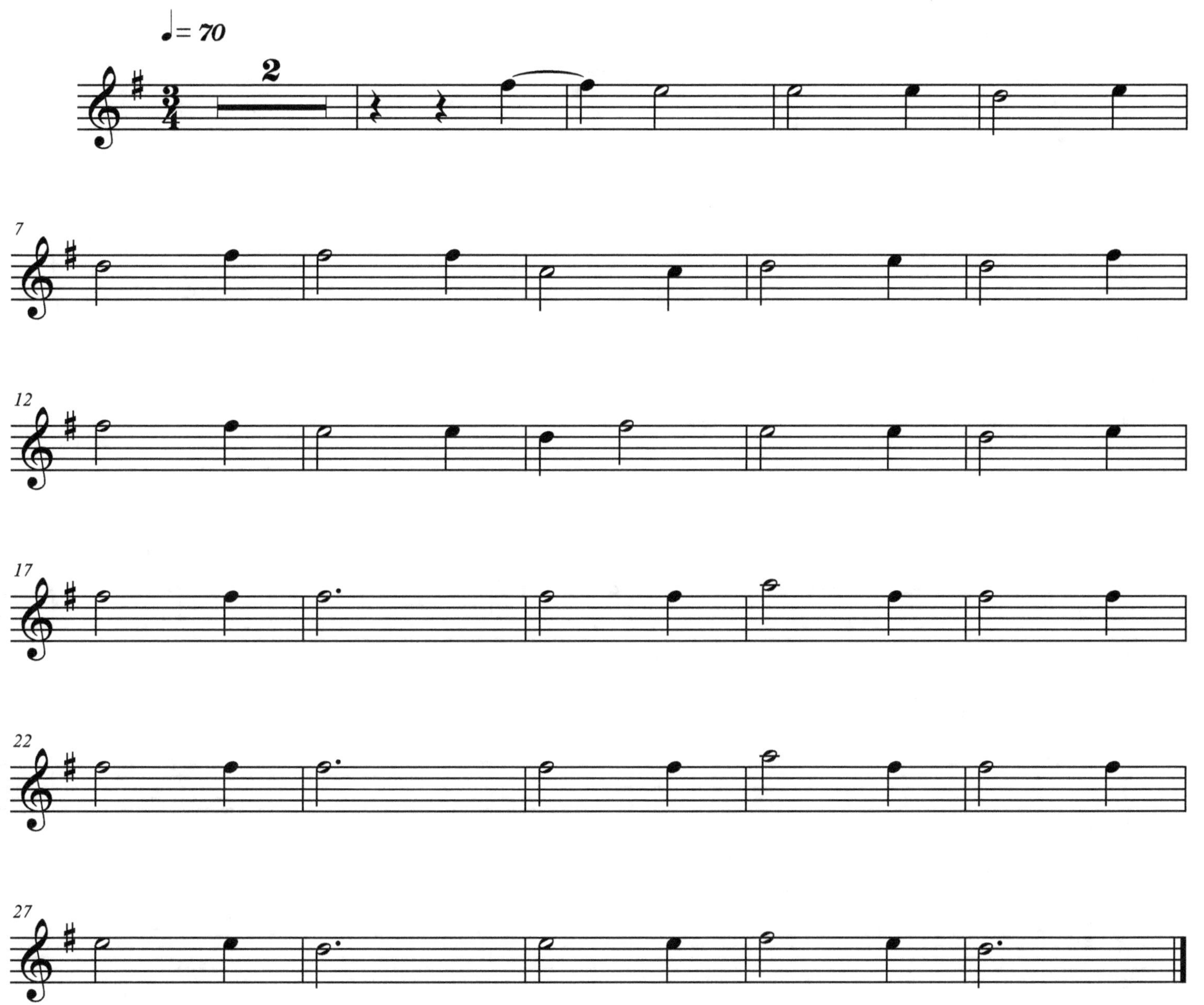

E

Part 4: Es Baritone Sax.

Joost de Gro

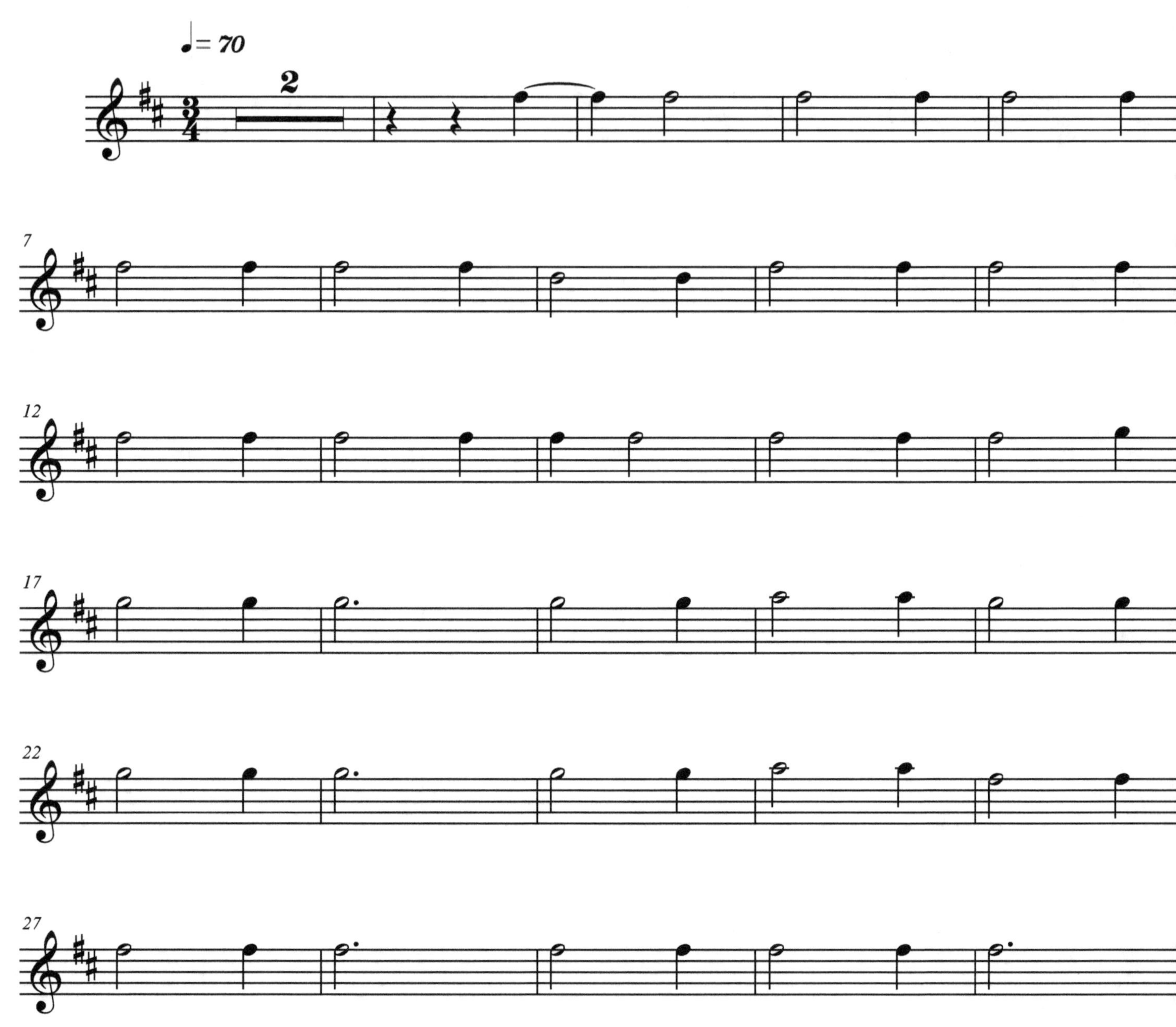

Brass Quartet

Part 1: Bes Trumpet 1

Part 2: Bes Trumpet 2

Part 3: F Horn

Part 4: C Trombone

Part 1: Bes Trumpet 1

J

Joost de Gro

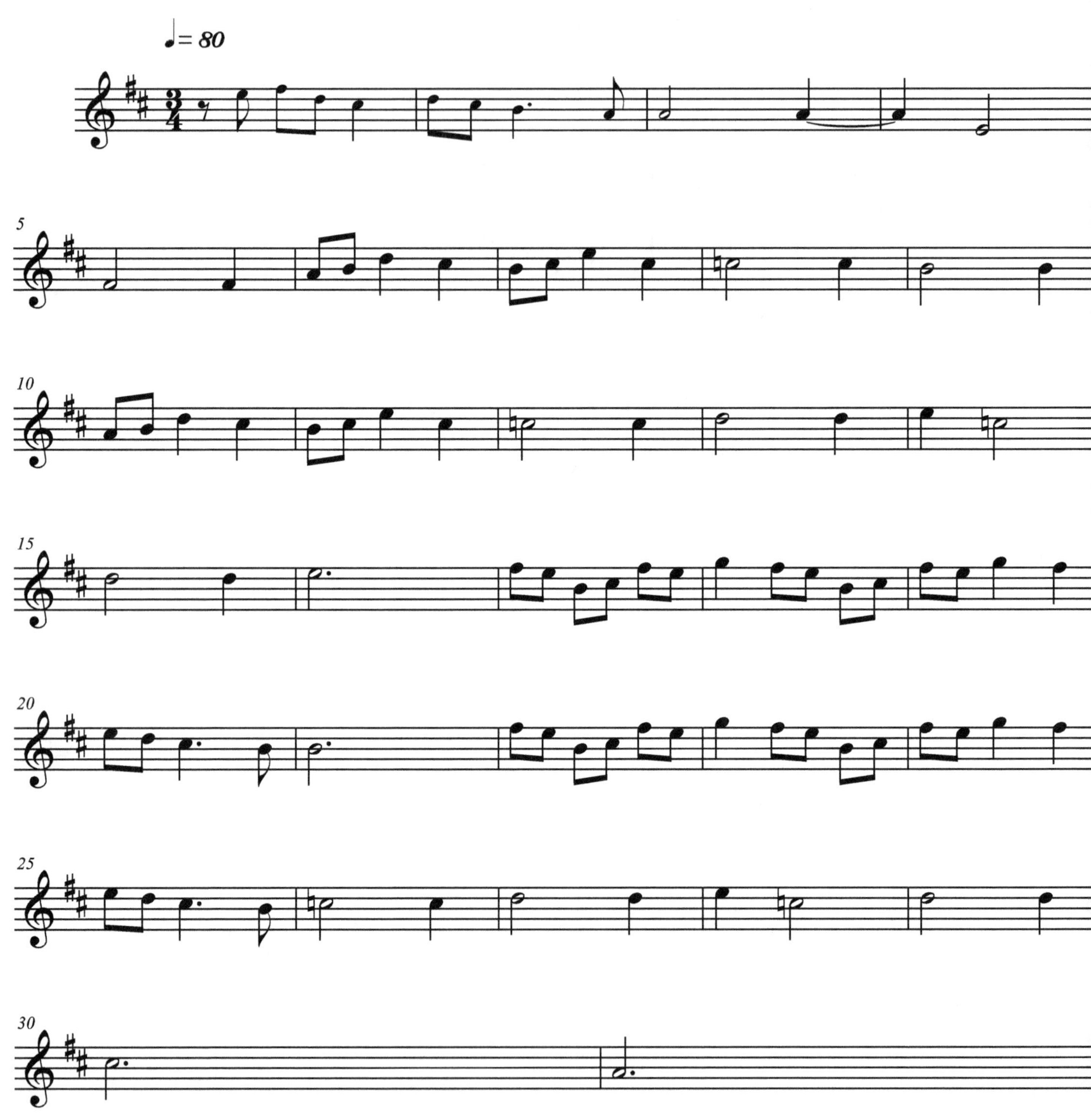

J

Part 2: Bes Trumpet 2

Joost de Groot

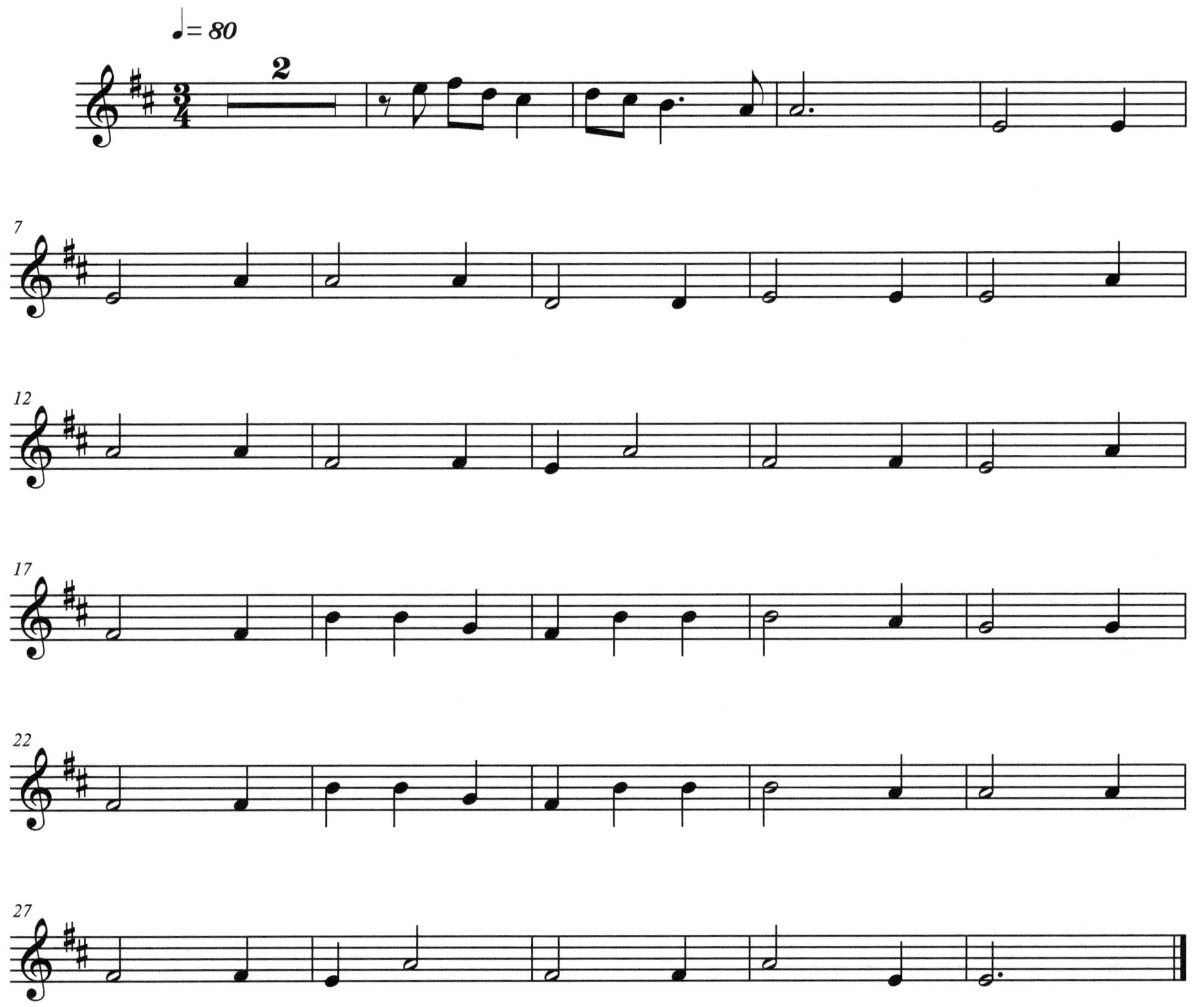

Part 3: F Horn

J

Joost de Groo

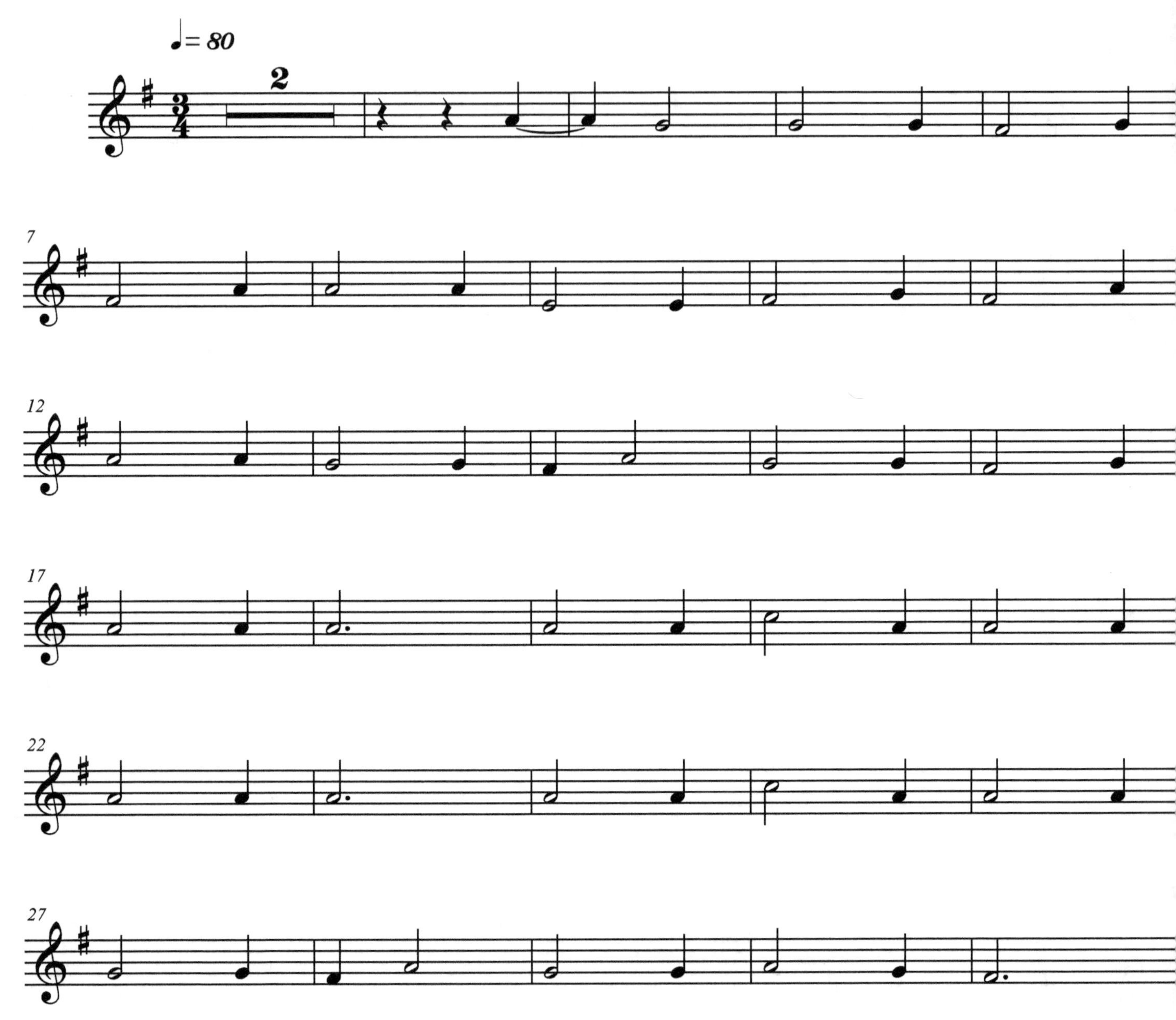

Part 4: C Trombone

J

Joost de Groot

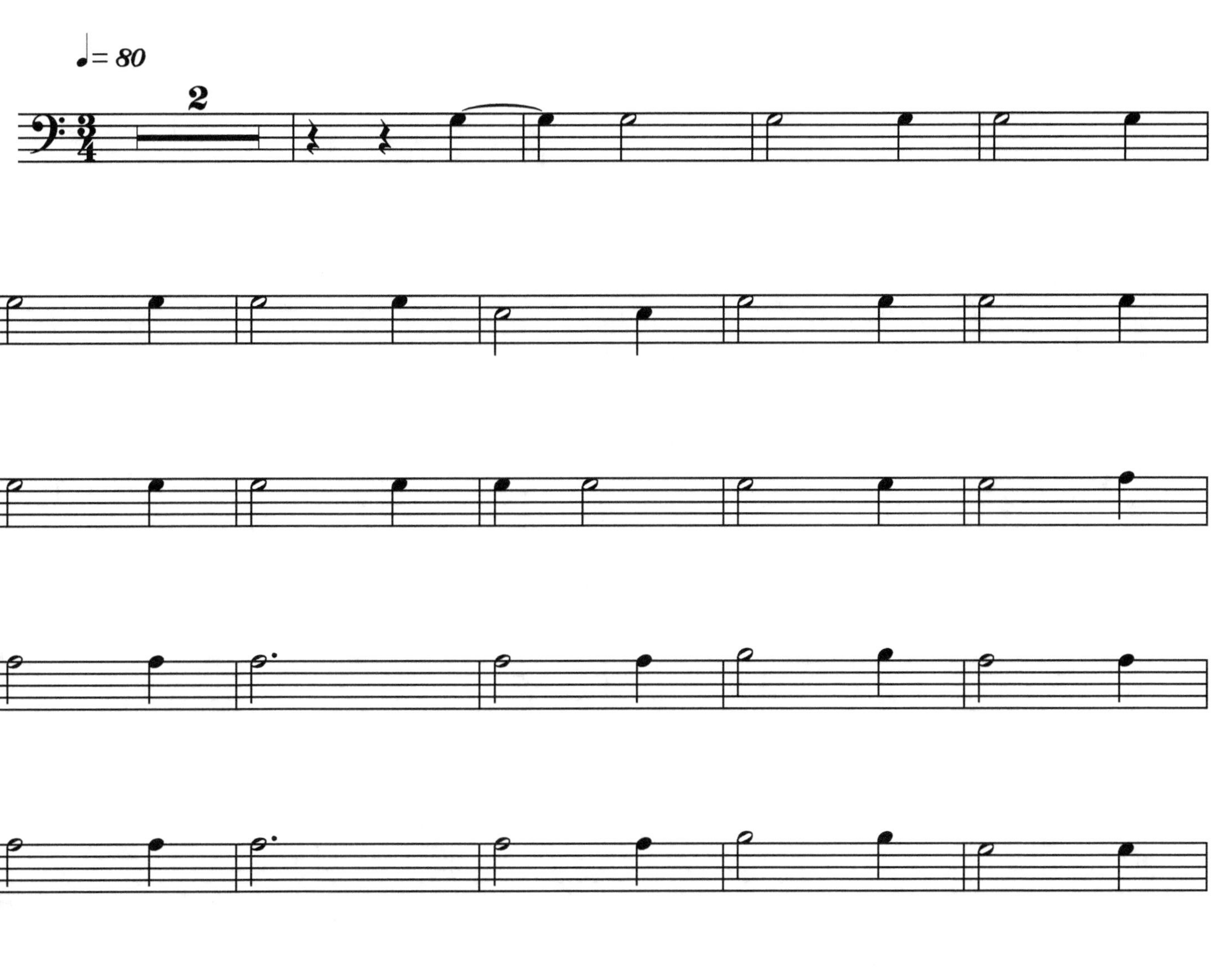

Part 1: Bes Trumpet 1

A

Joost de Gro

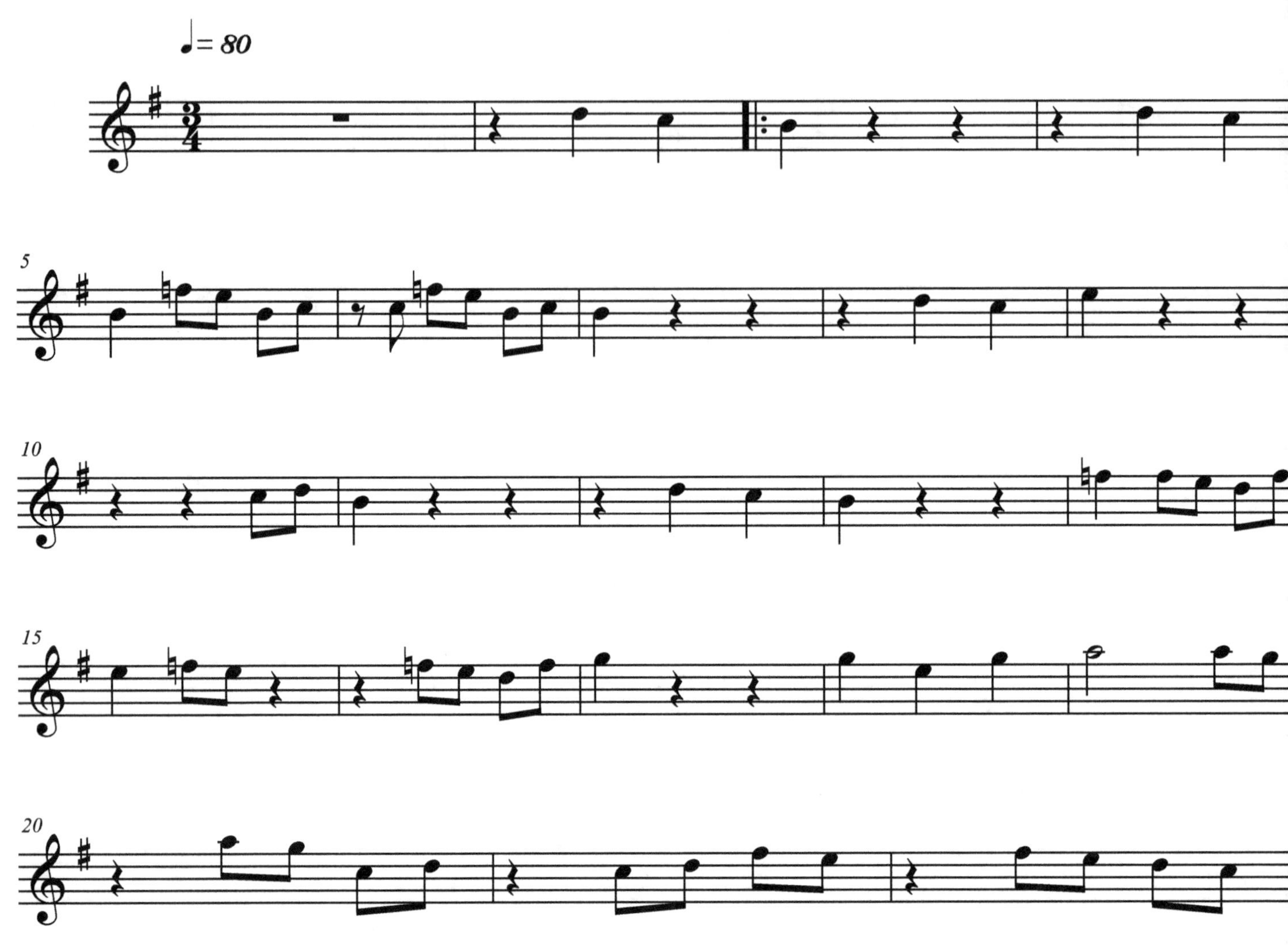

A

Part 2: Bes Trumpet 2

Joost de Groot

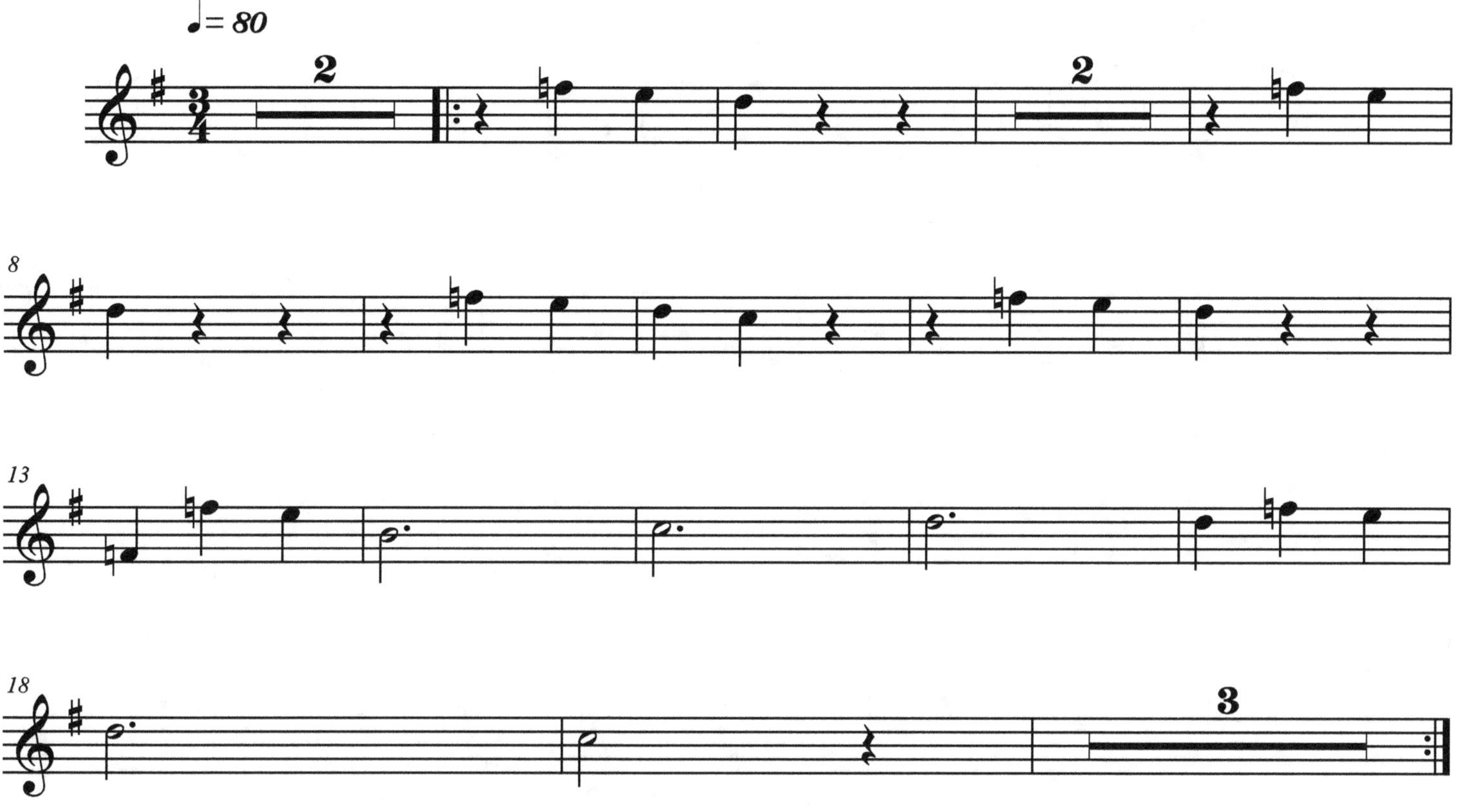

Part 3: F Horn

A

Joost de Groo

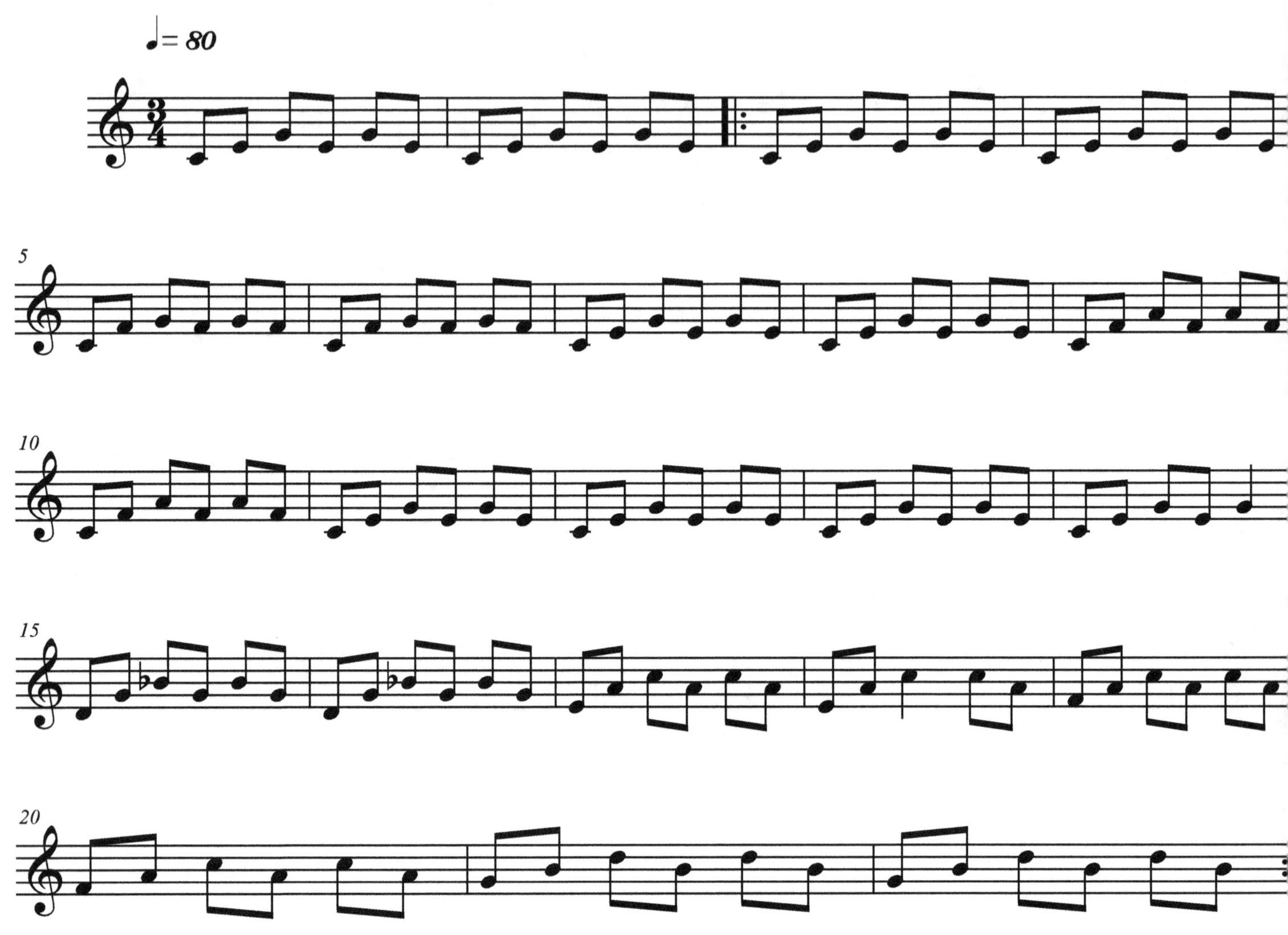

Part 4: C Trombone

A

Joost de Groot

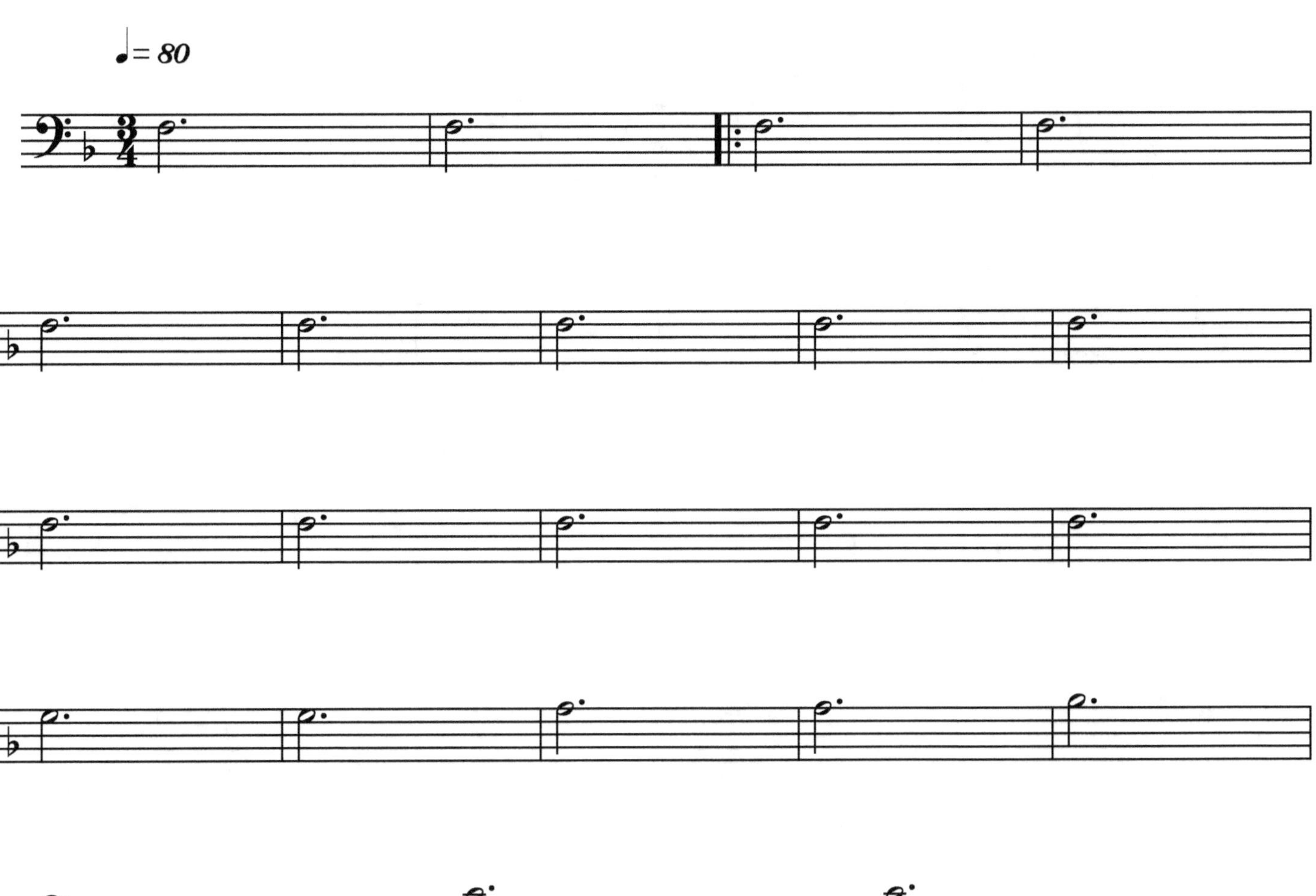

N

Part 1: Bes Trumpet 1

Joost de Gro

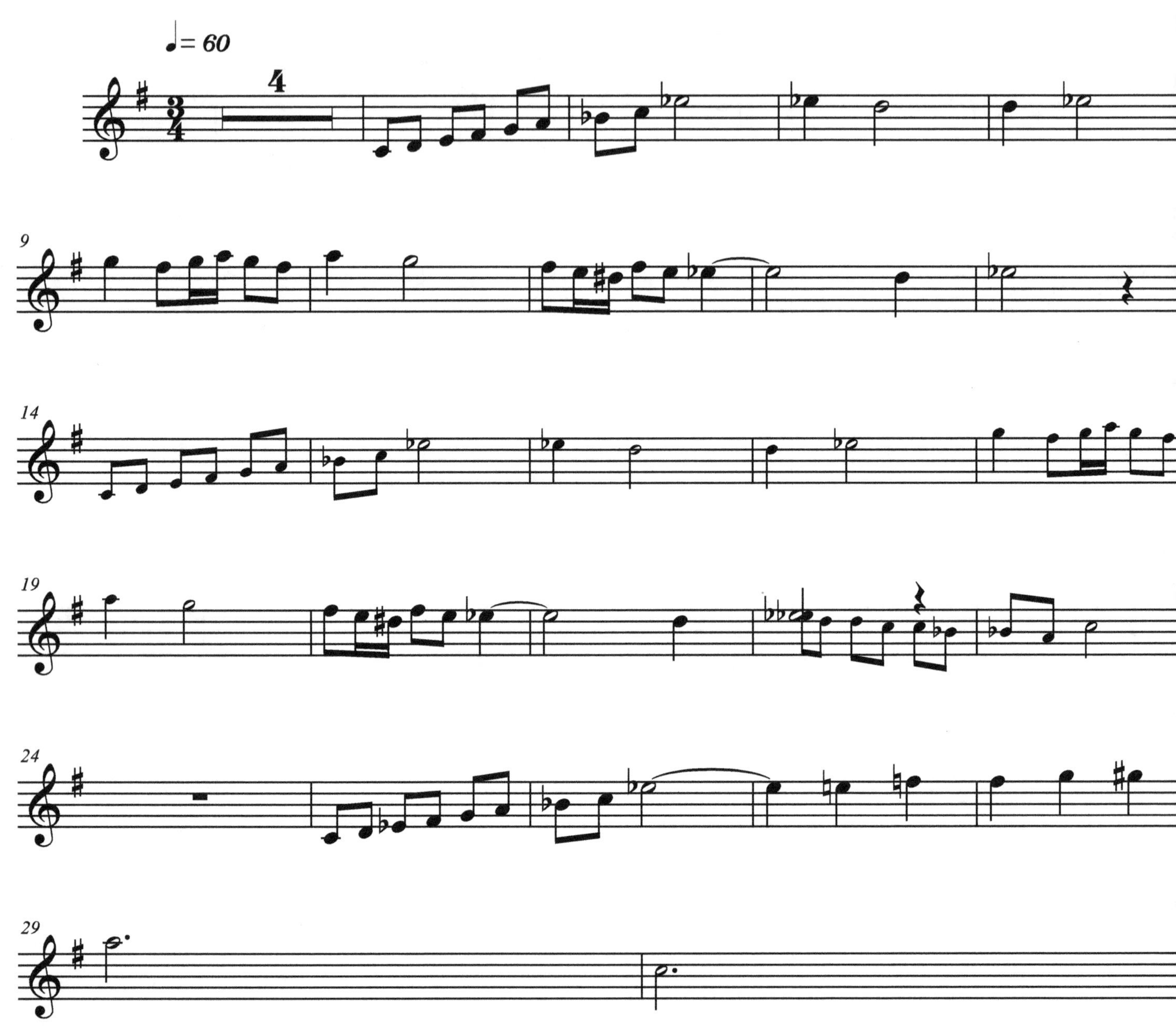

N

Part 2: Bes Trumpet 2

Joost de Groot

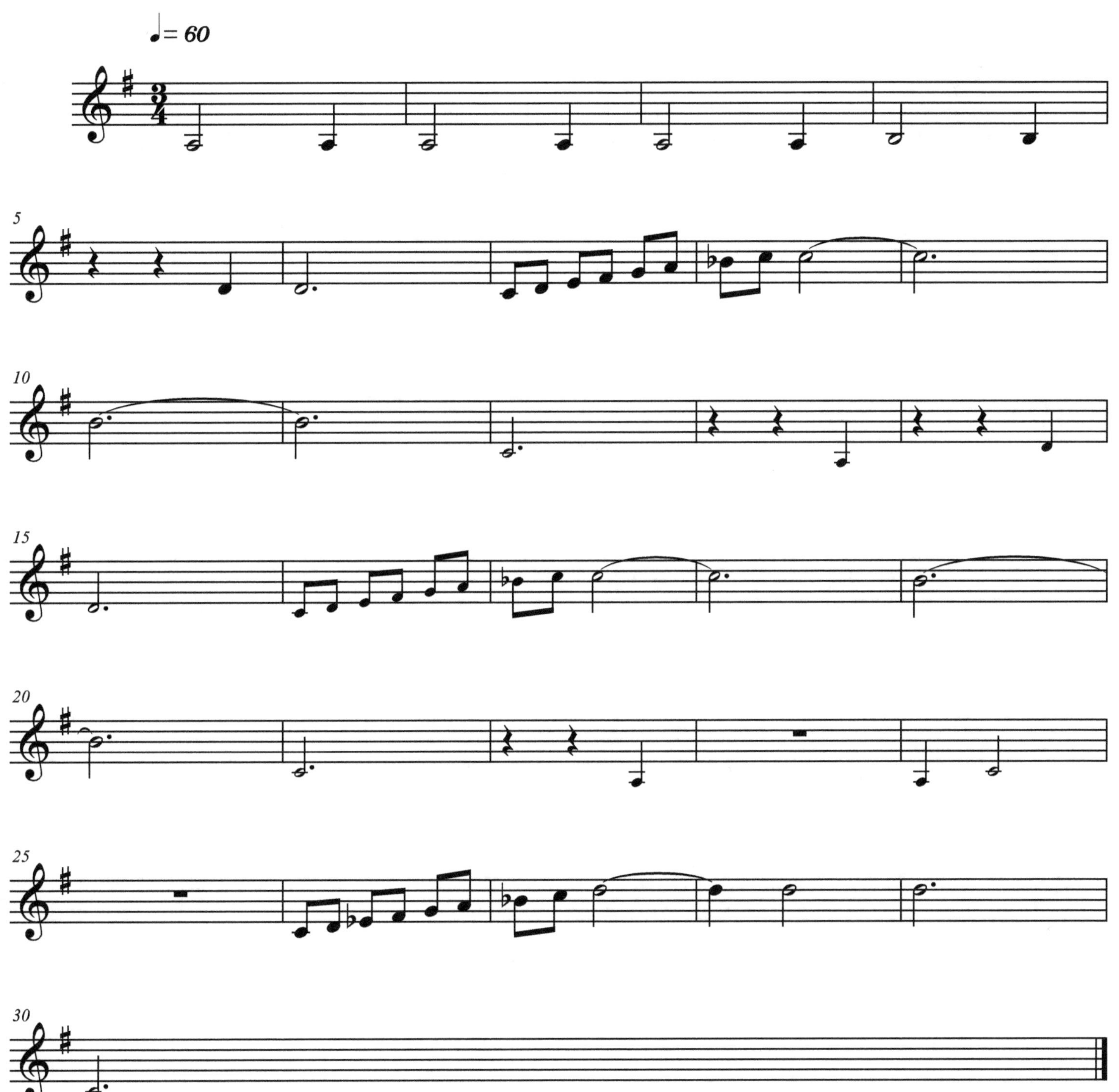

Part 3: F Horn

N

Joost de Groo

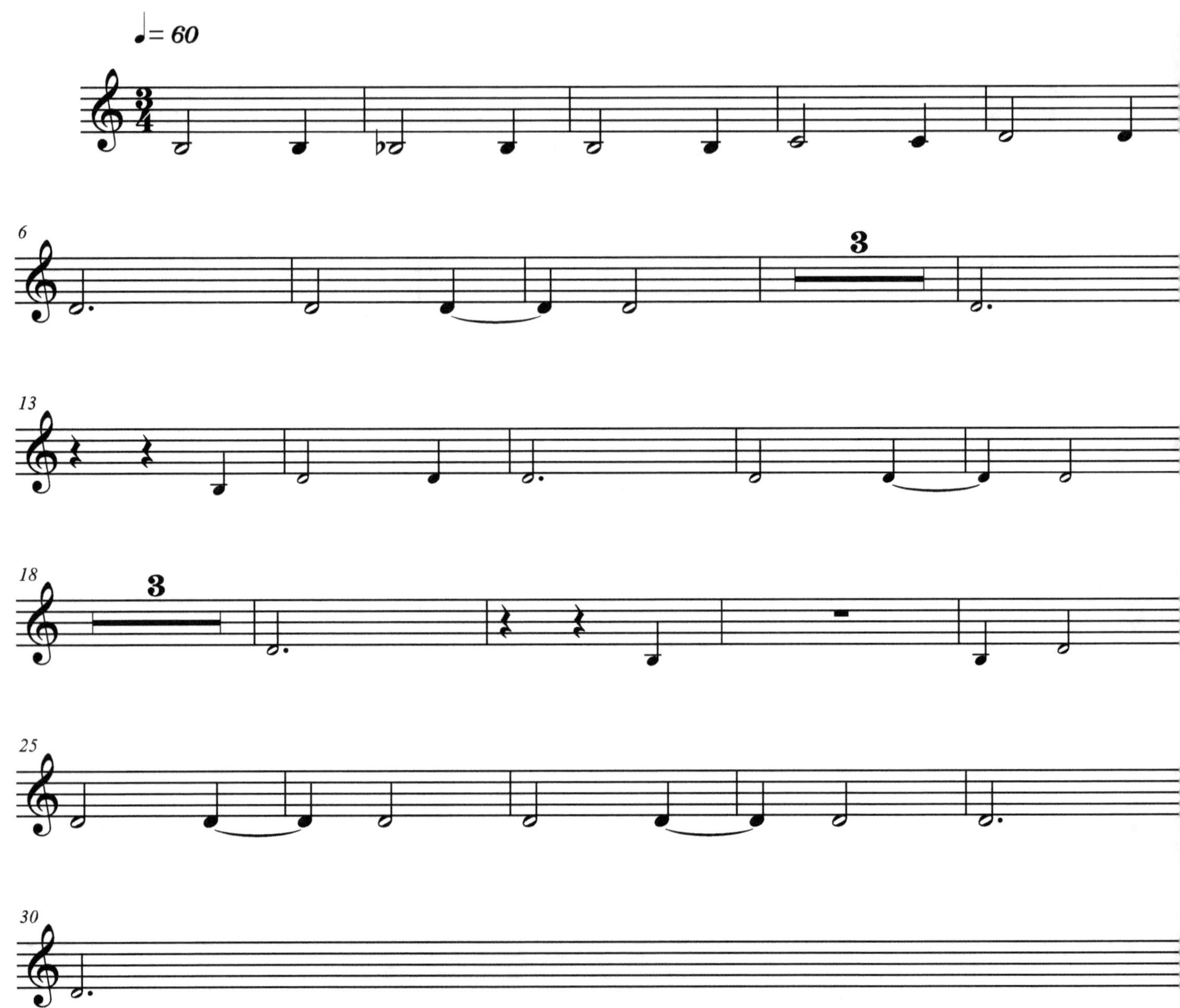

Part 4: C Trombone

N

Joost de Groot

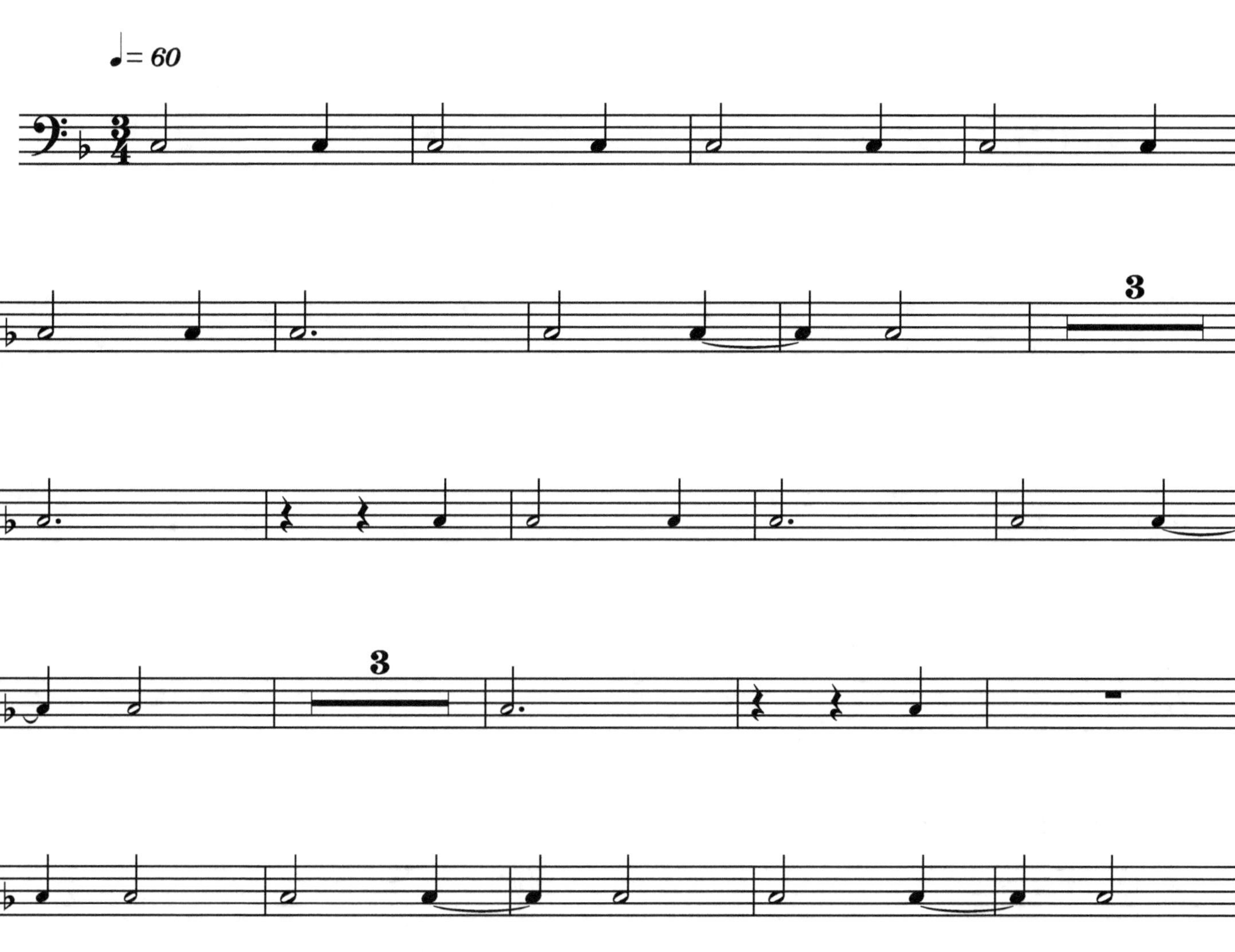

Part 1: Bes Trumpet 1

N

Joost de Gro

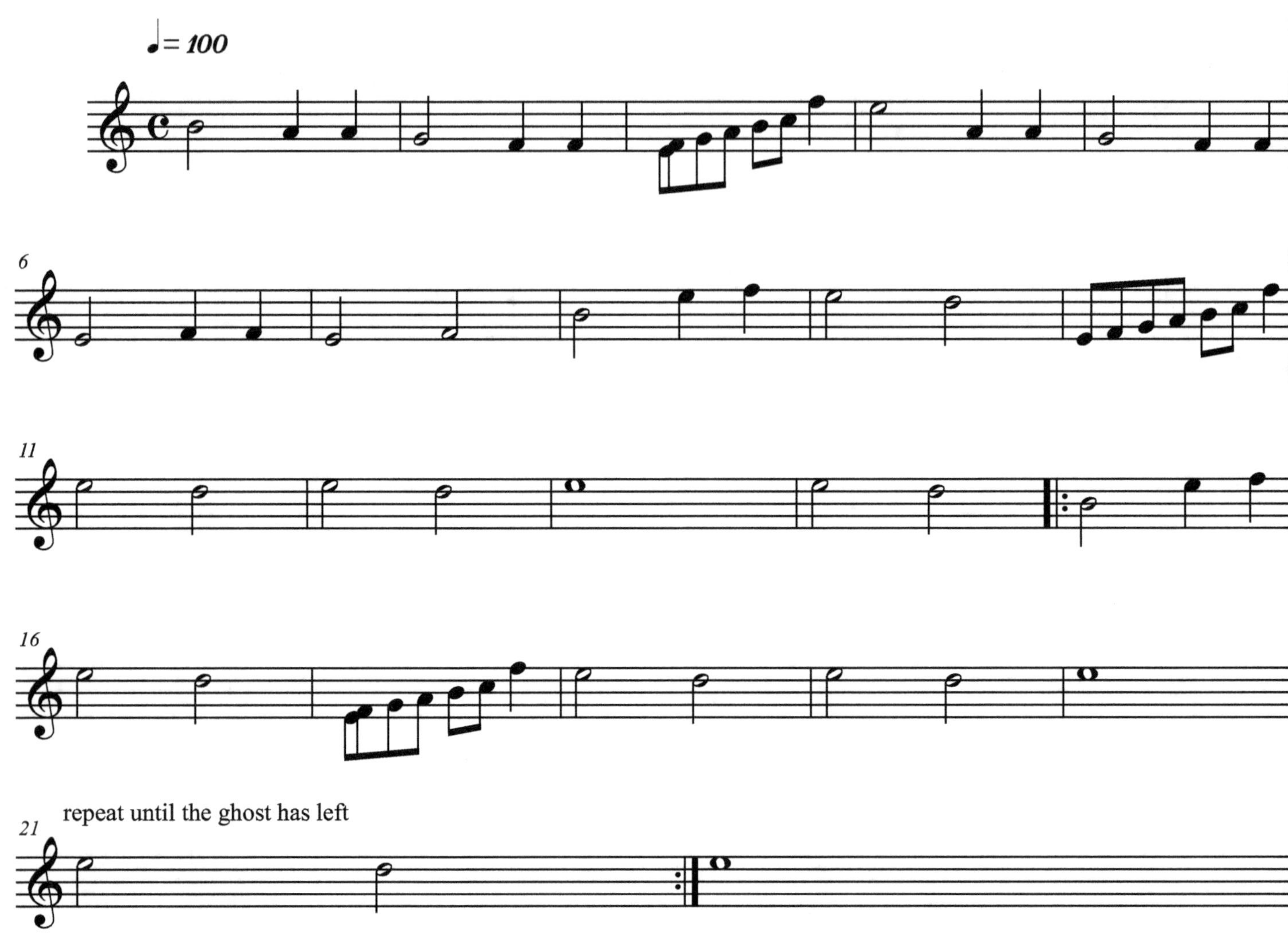

Part 2: Bes Trumpet 2

N

Joost de Groot

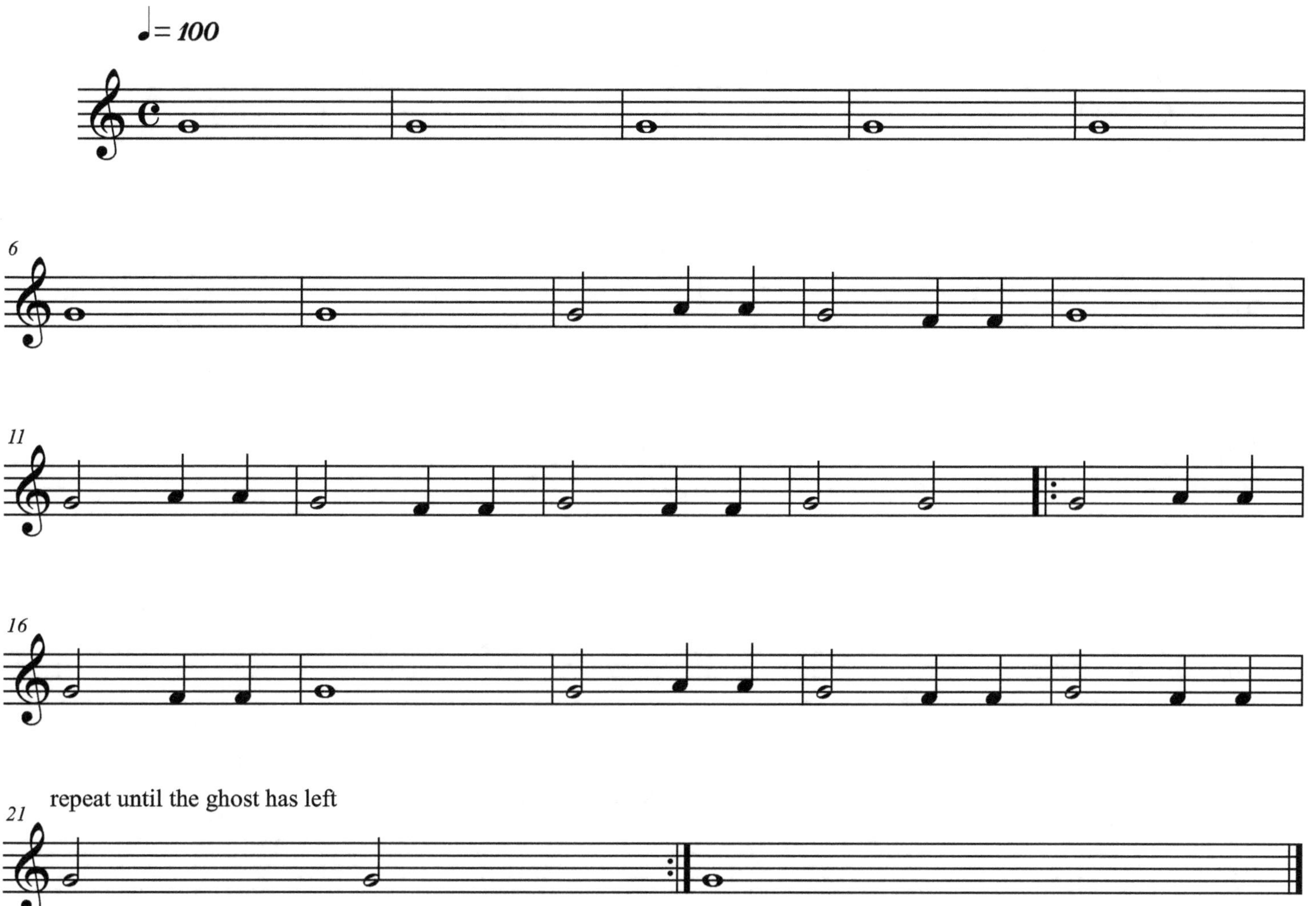

Part 3: F Horn

N

Joost de Gro

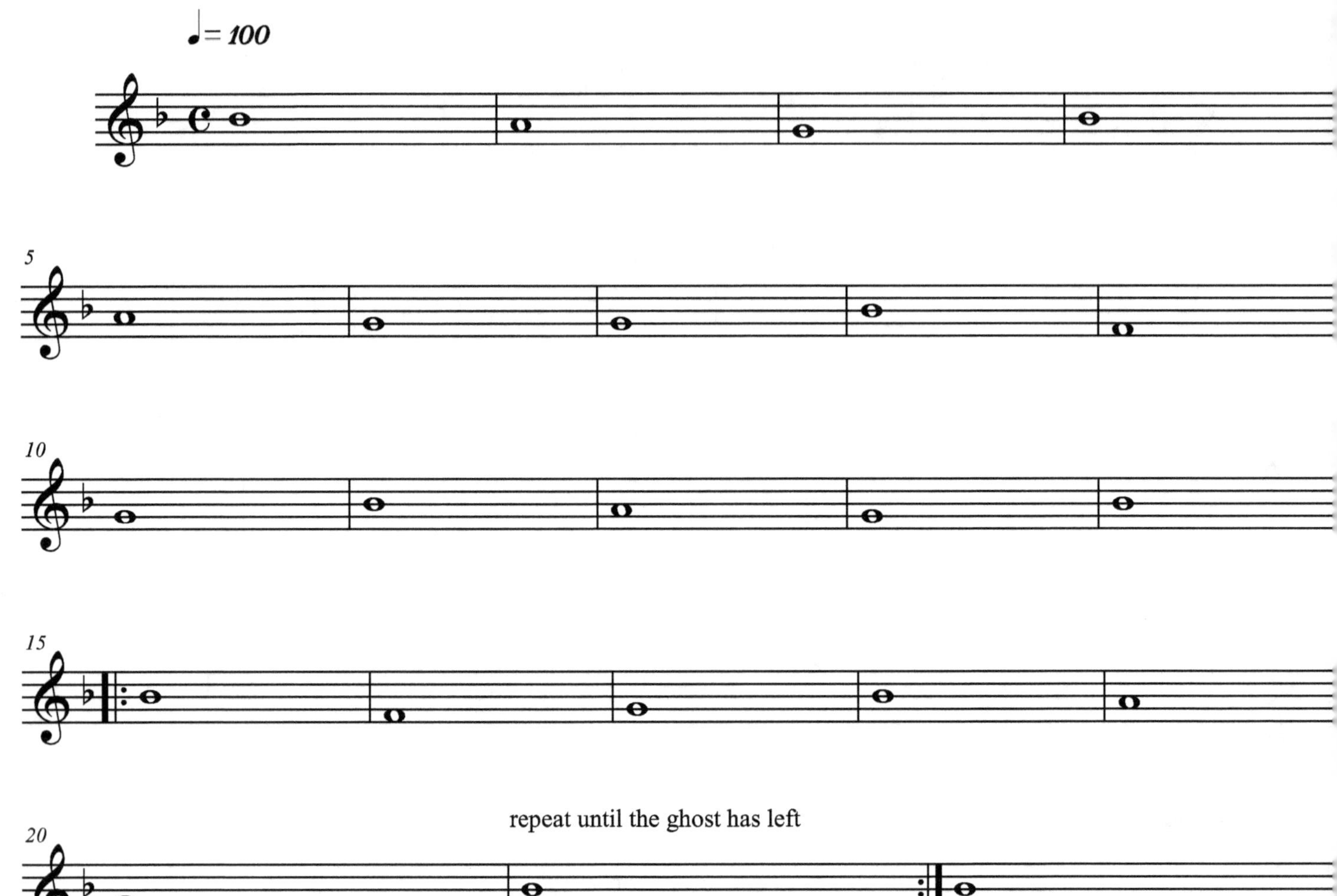

N

Part 4: C Trombone

Joost de Groot

♩= 100

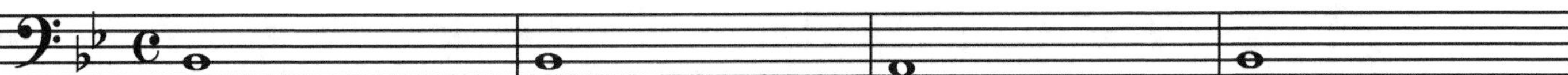

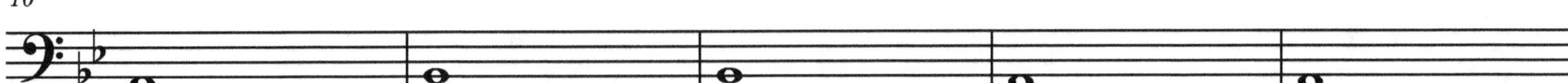

repeat until the ghost has left

I

Part 1: Bes Trumpet 1

Joost de Gro

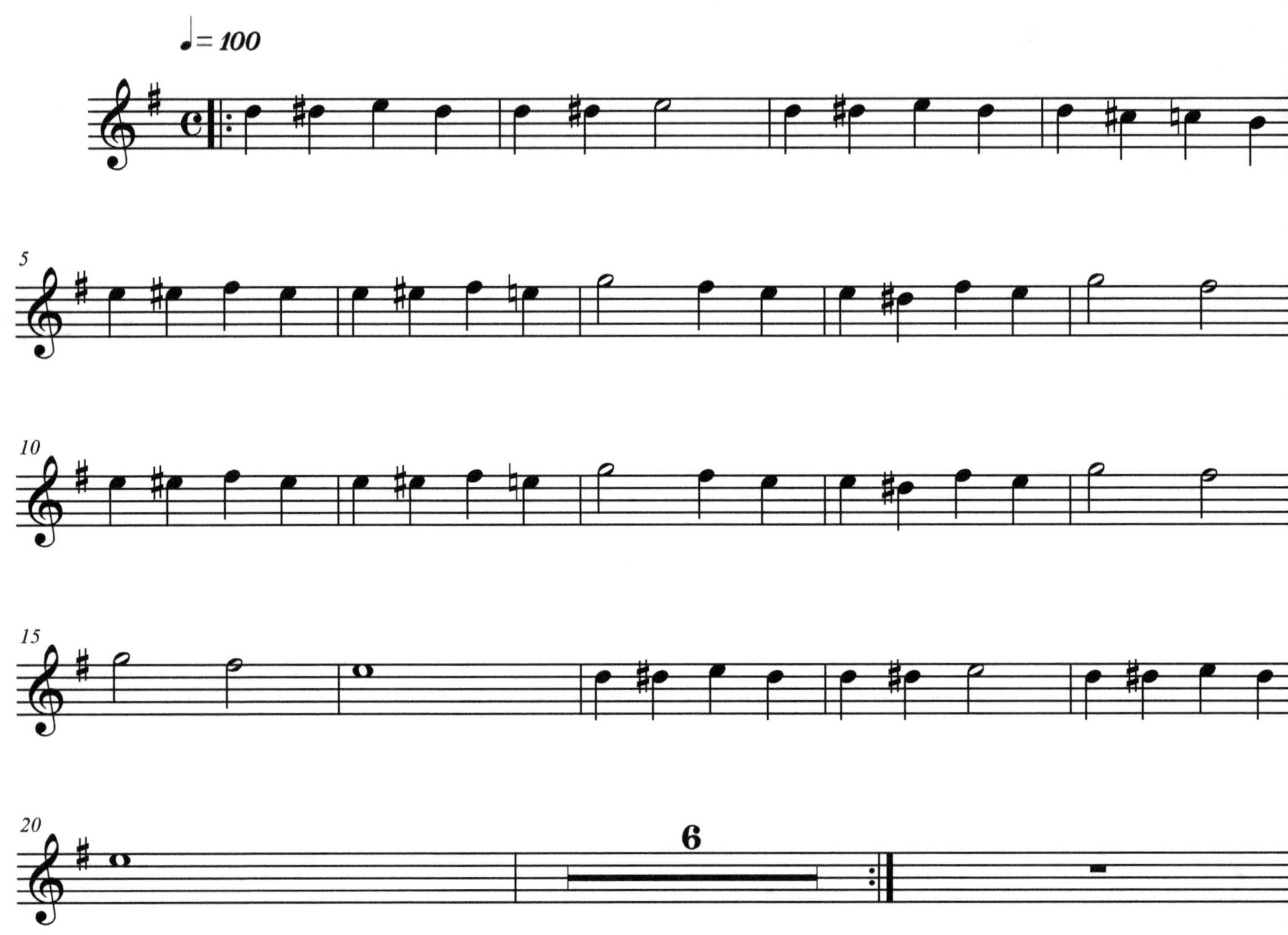

Part 2: Bes Trumpet 2

I

Joost de Groot

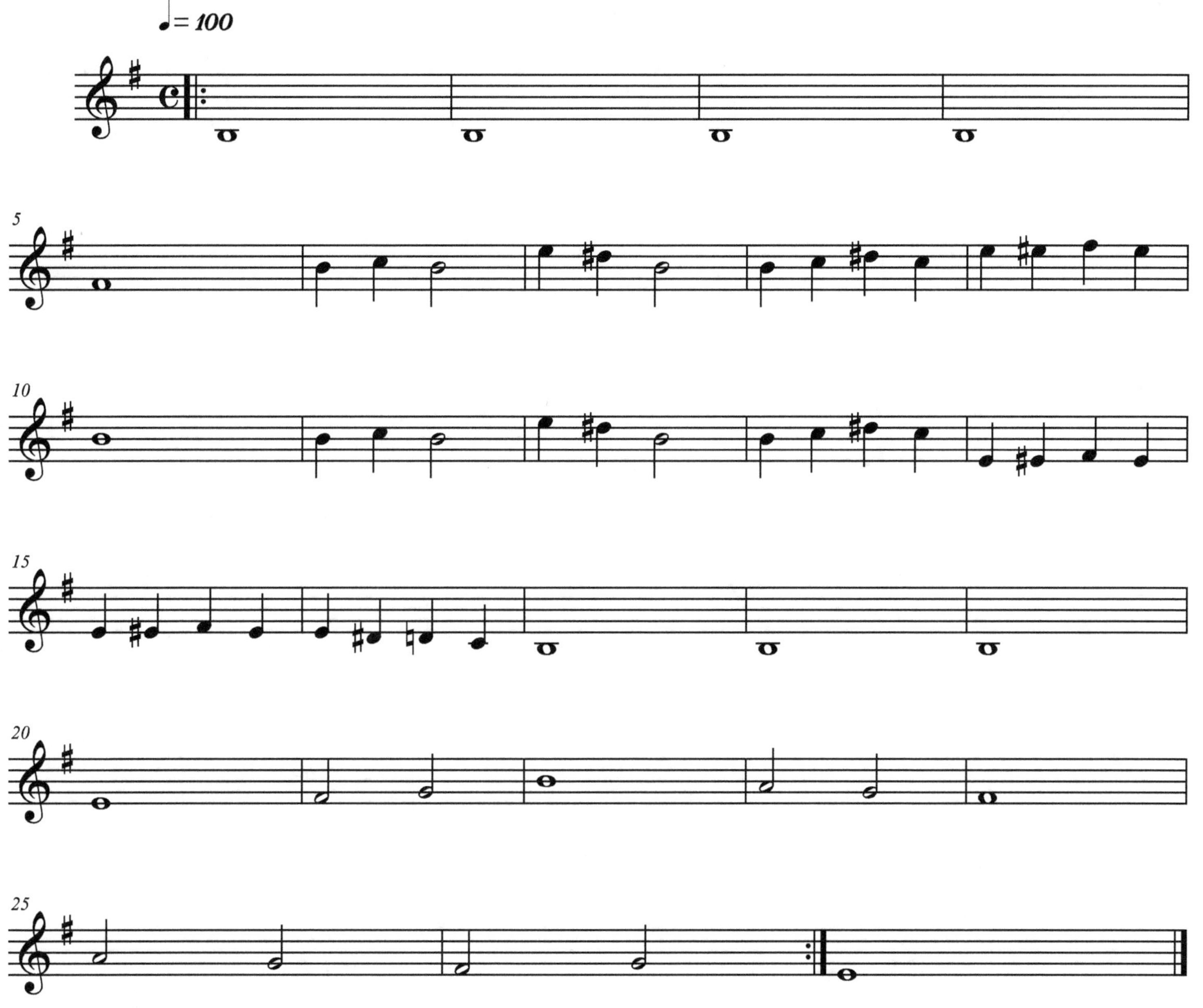

Part 3: F Horn

I

Joost de Gro

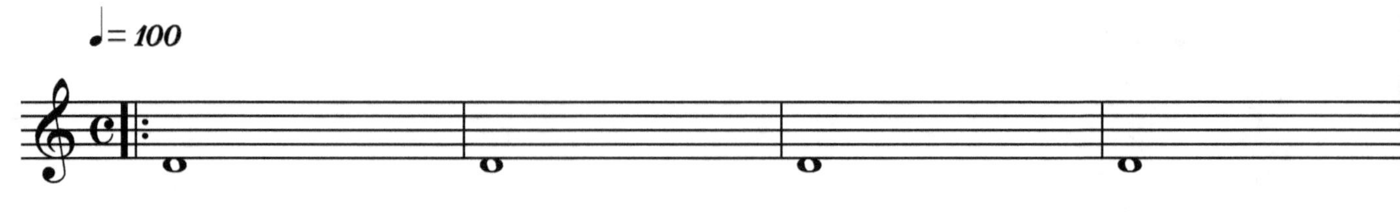

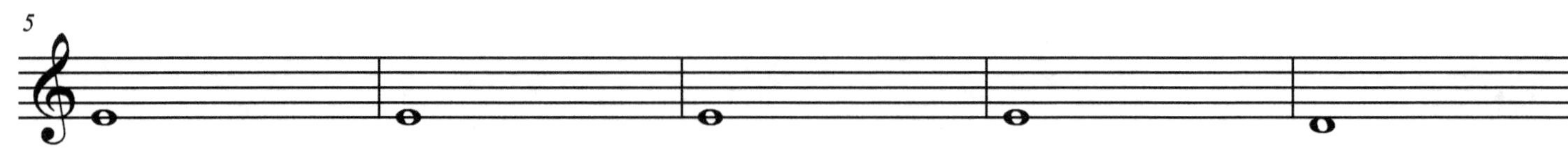

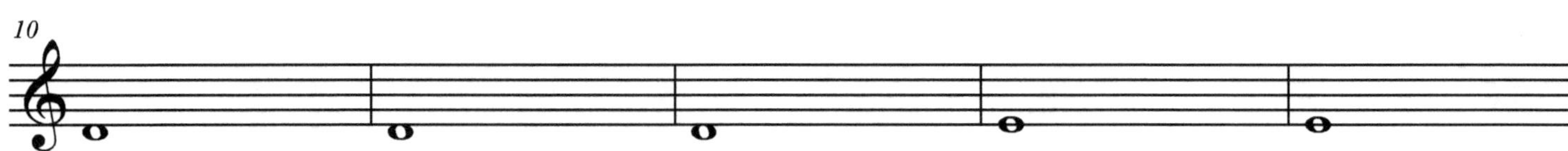

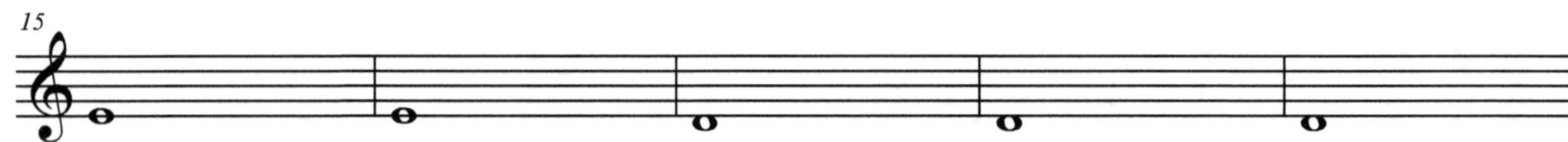

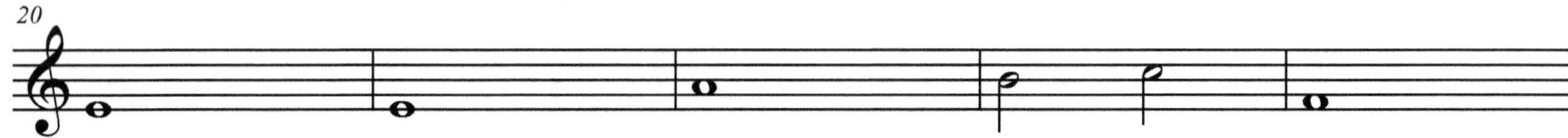

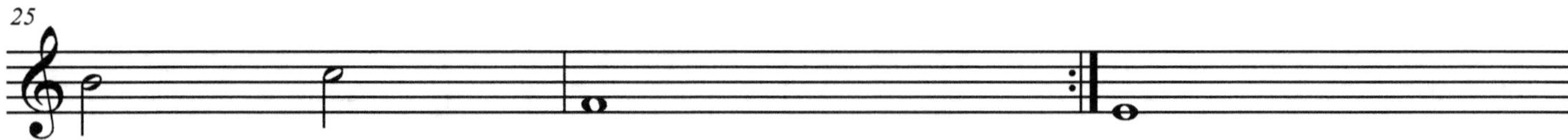

Part 4: C Trombone

I

Joost de Groot

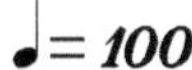

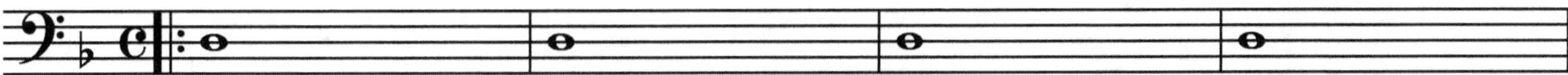

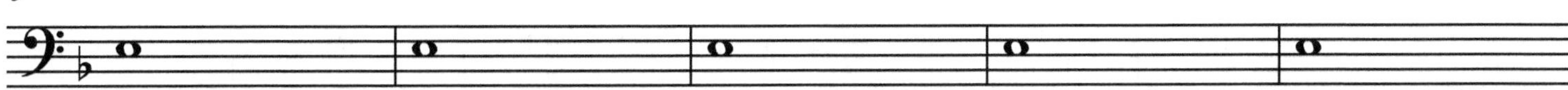

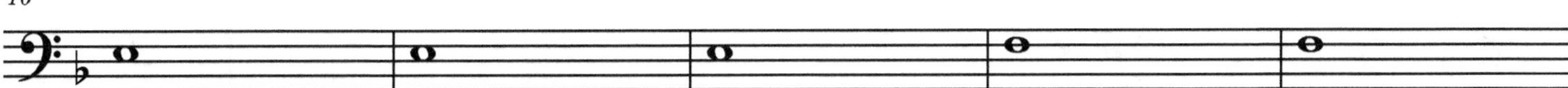

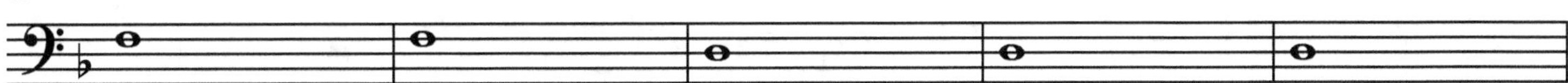

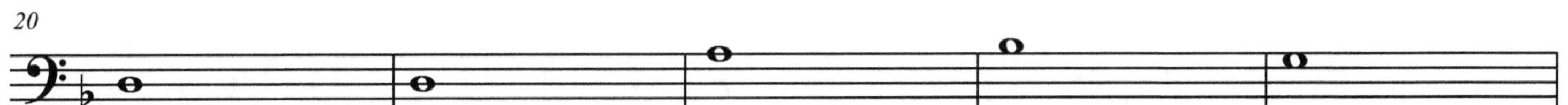

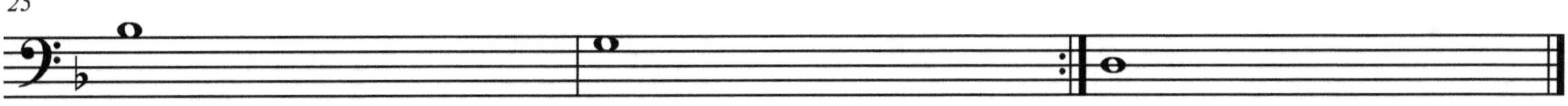

E

Part 1: Bes Trumpet 1

Joost de Gro

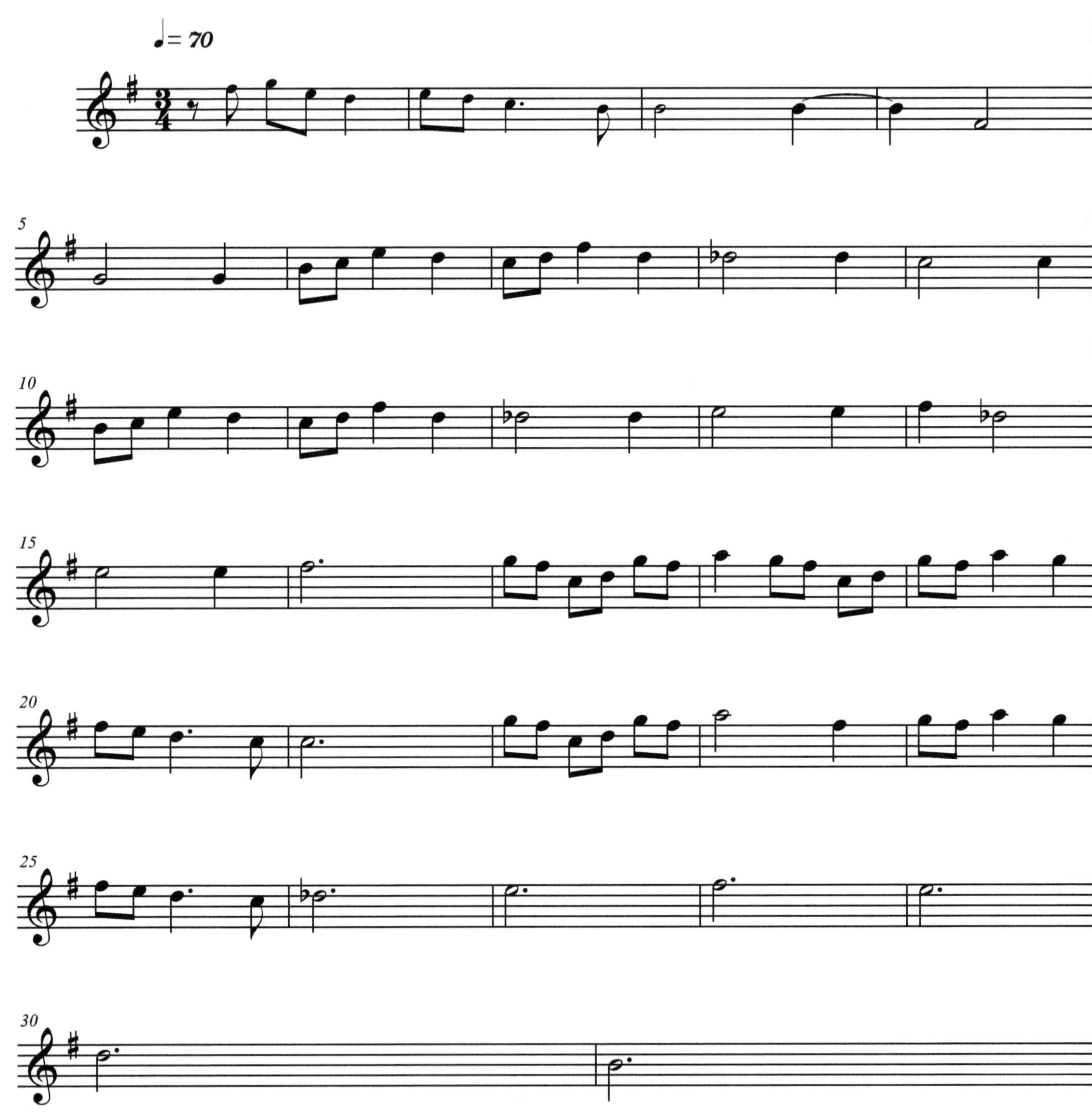

E

Part 2: Bes Trumpet 2

Joost de Groot

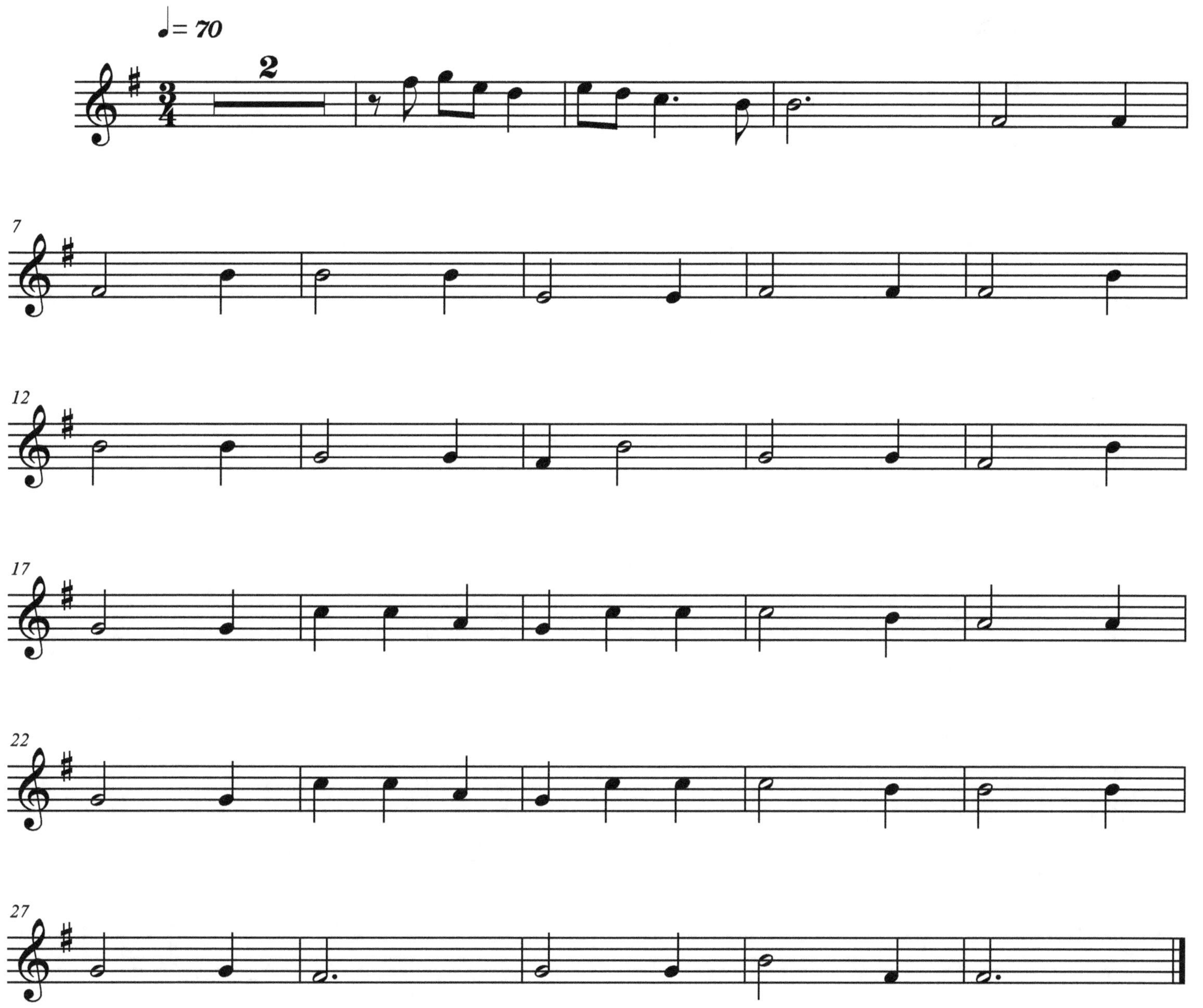

Part 3: F Horn

E

Joost de Gro

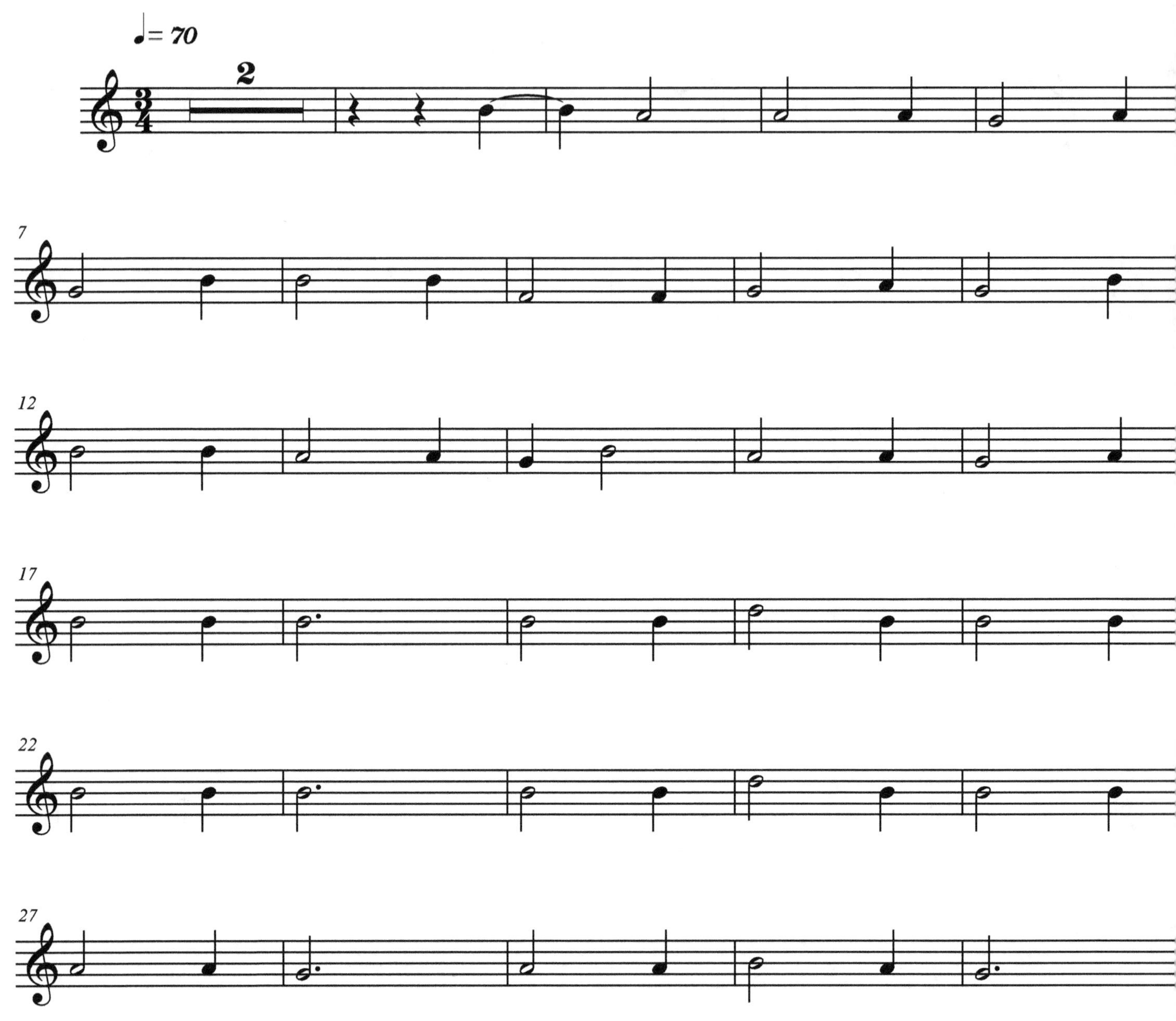

Part 4: C Tombone

E

Joost de Groot

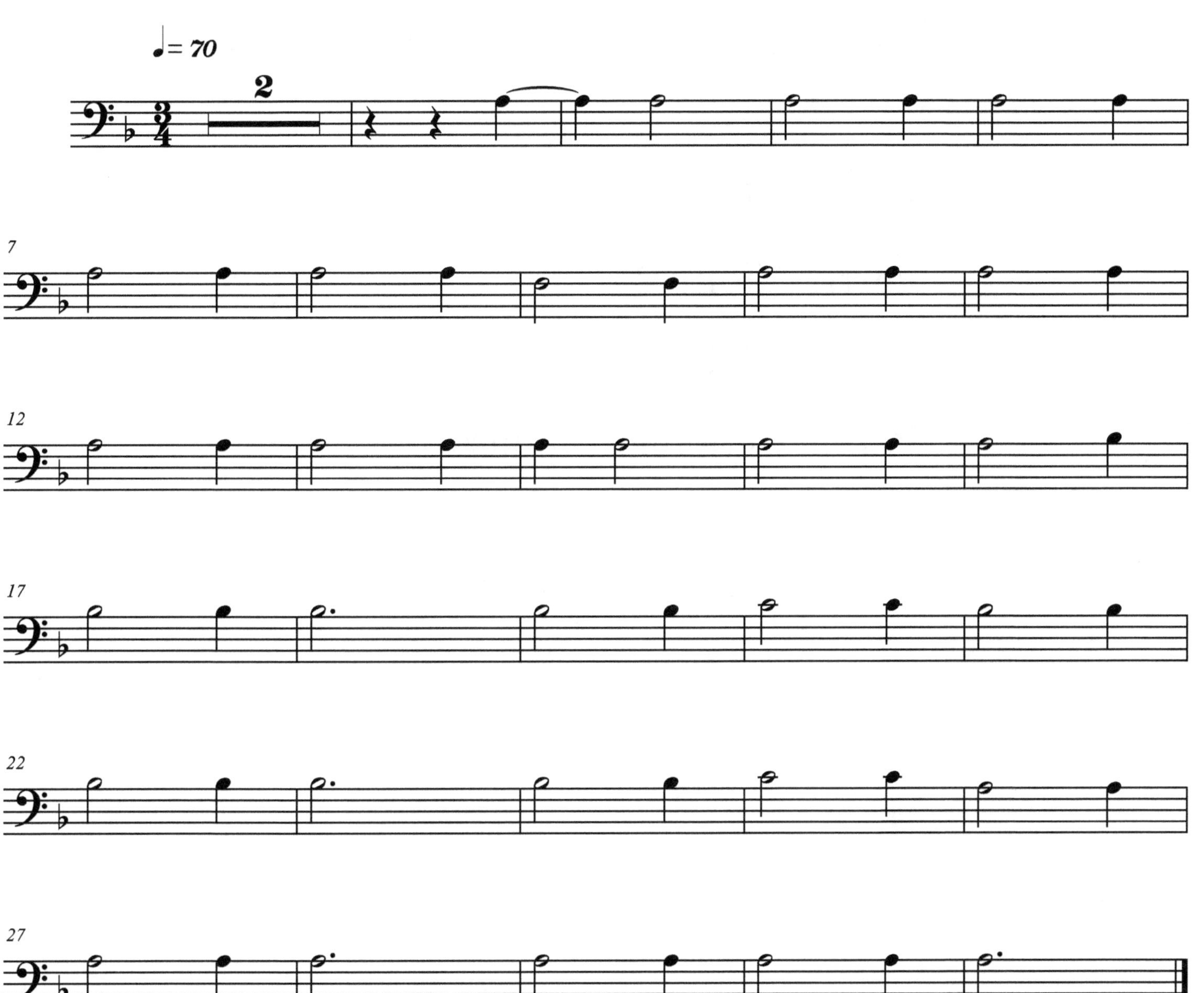

String Quartet/String Orchestra

Part 1: Violin 1

Part 2: Violin 2

Part 3: Viola

Part 4: Cello/Contrabass

Part 1: Violin 1

J

Joost de Groot

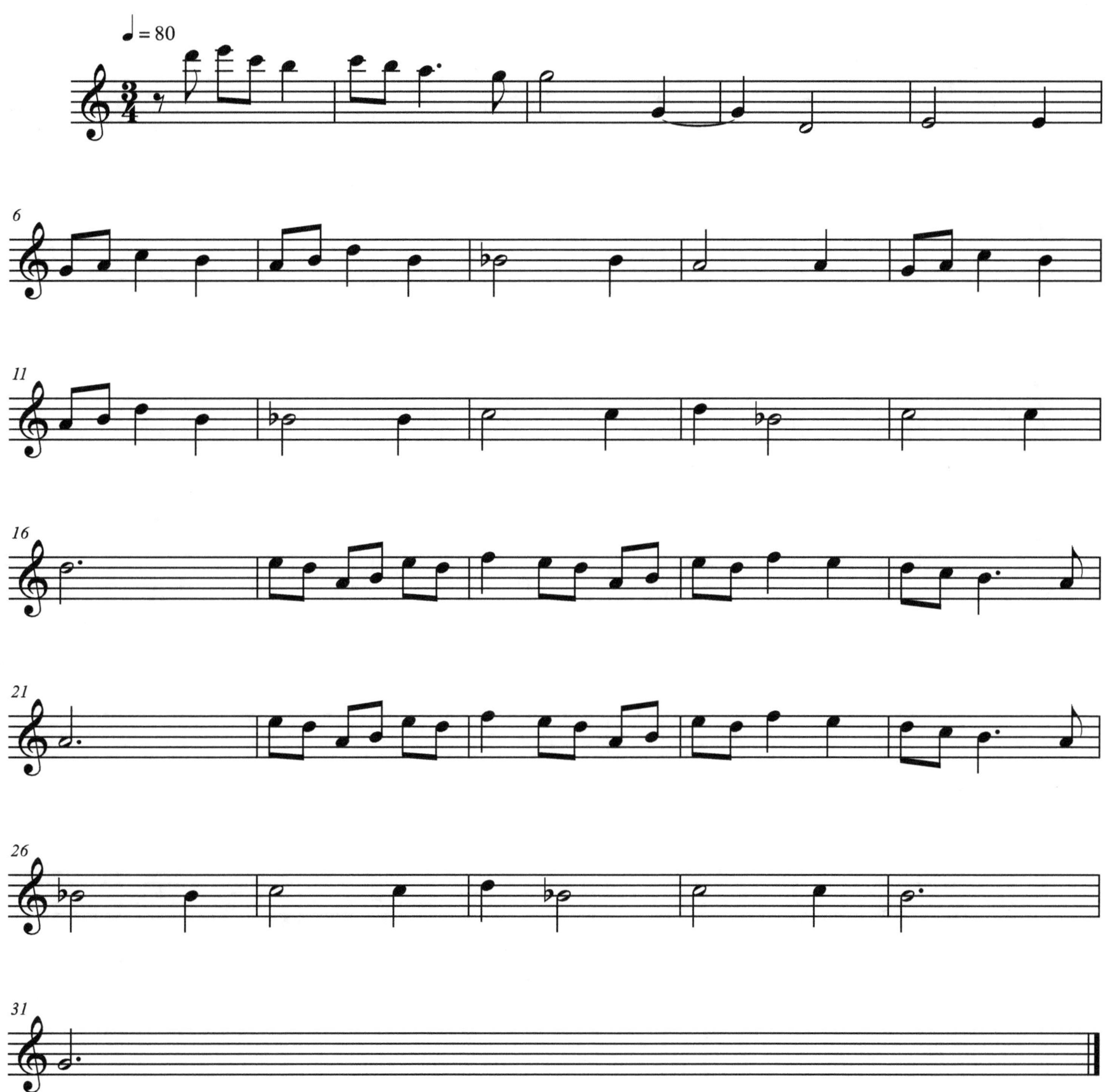

J

Part 2: Violin 2

Joost de Gro

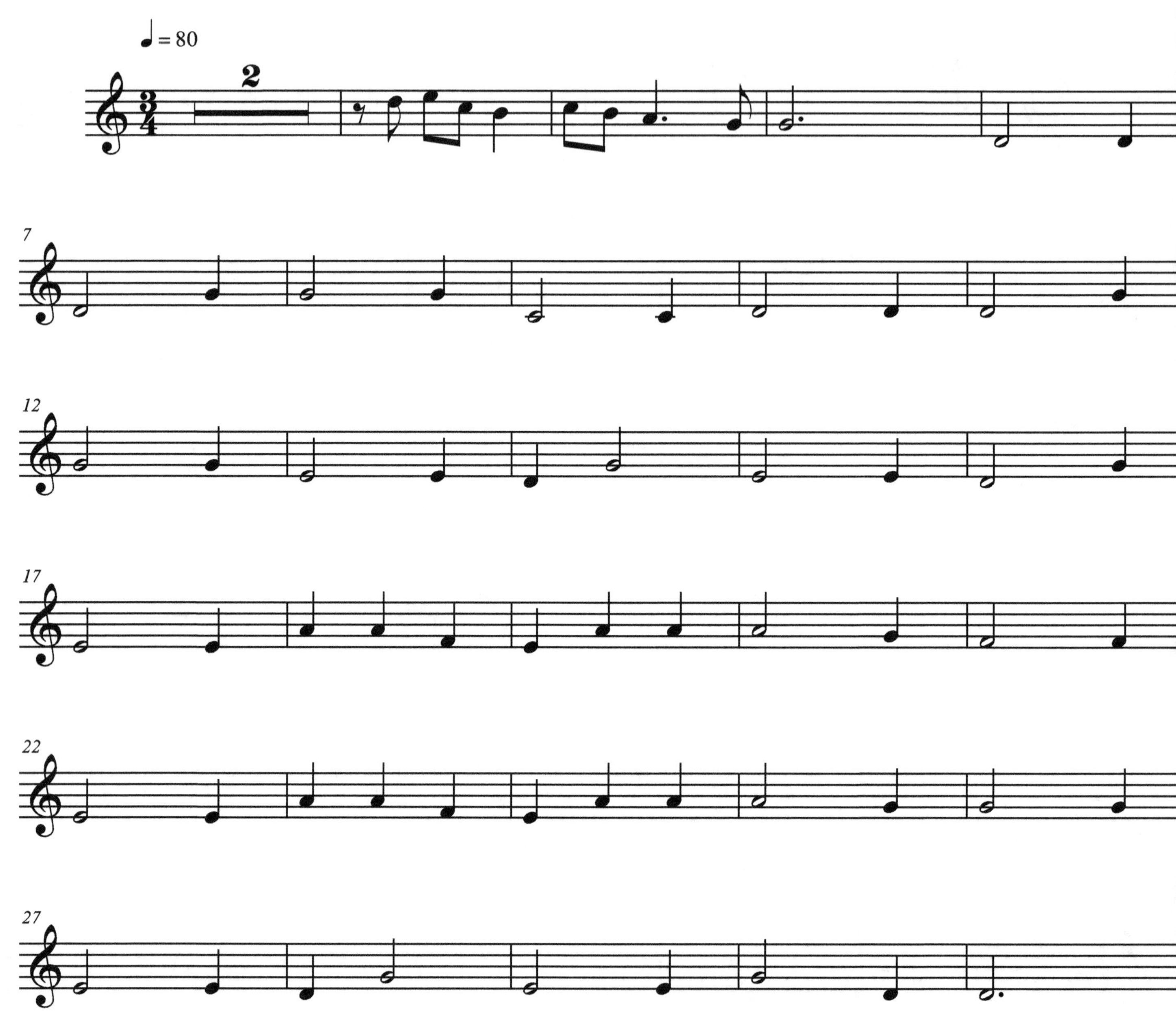

Part 3: Viola

J

Joost de Groot

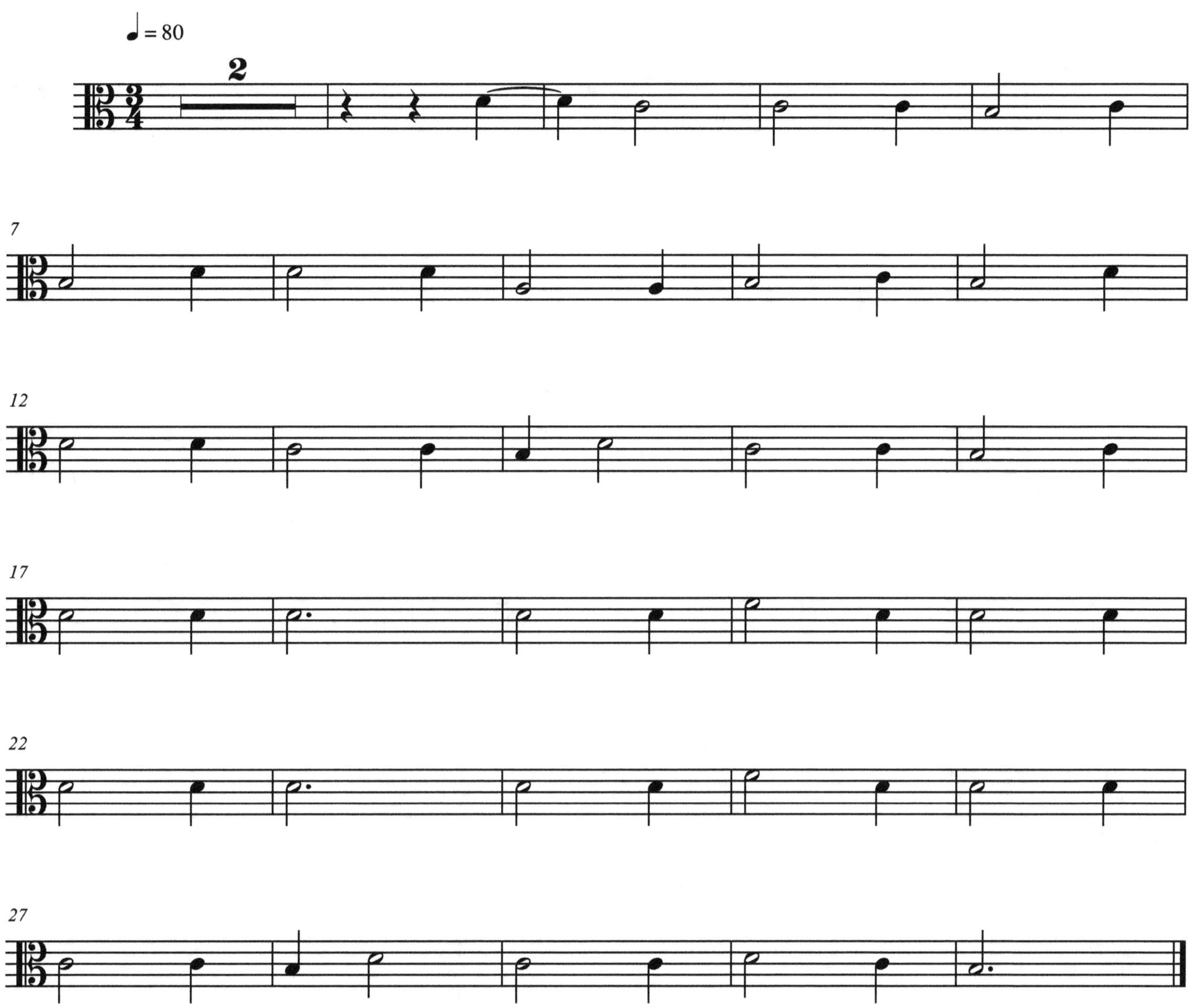

Part 4: Cello/Contrabass

J

Joost de Gro

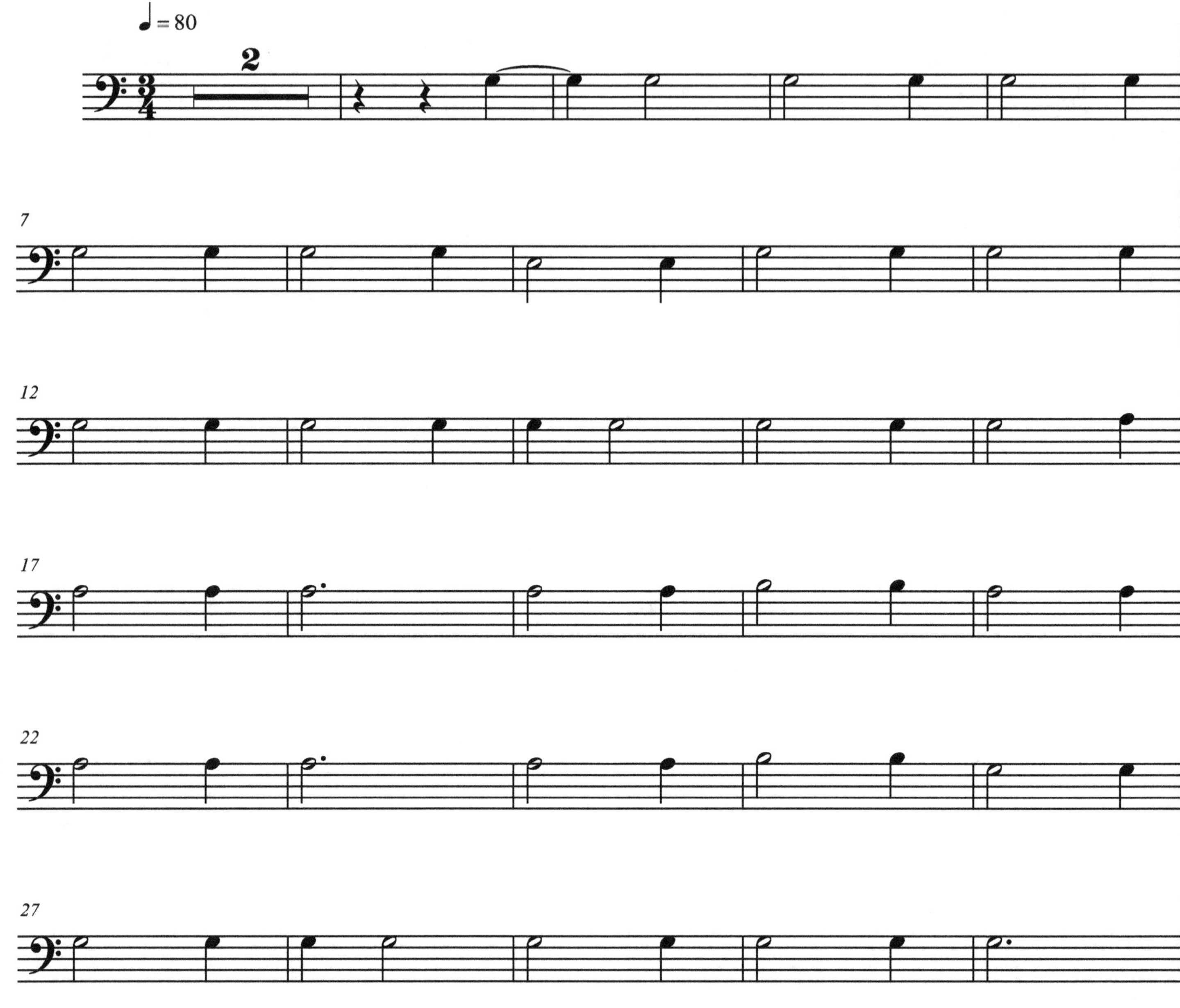

Part 1: Violin 1

A

Joost de Groot

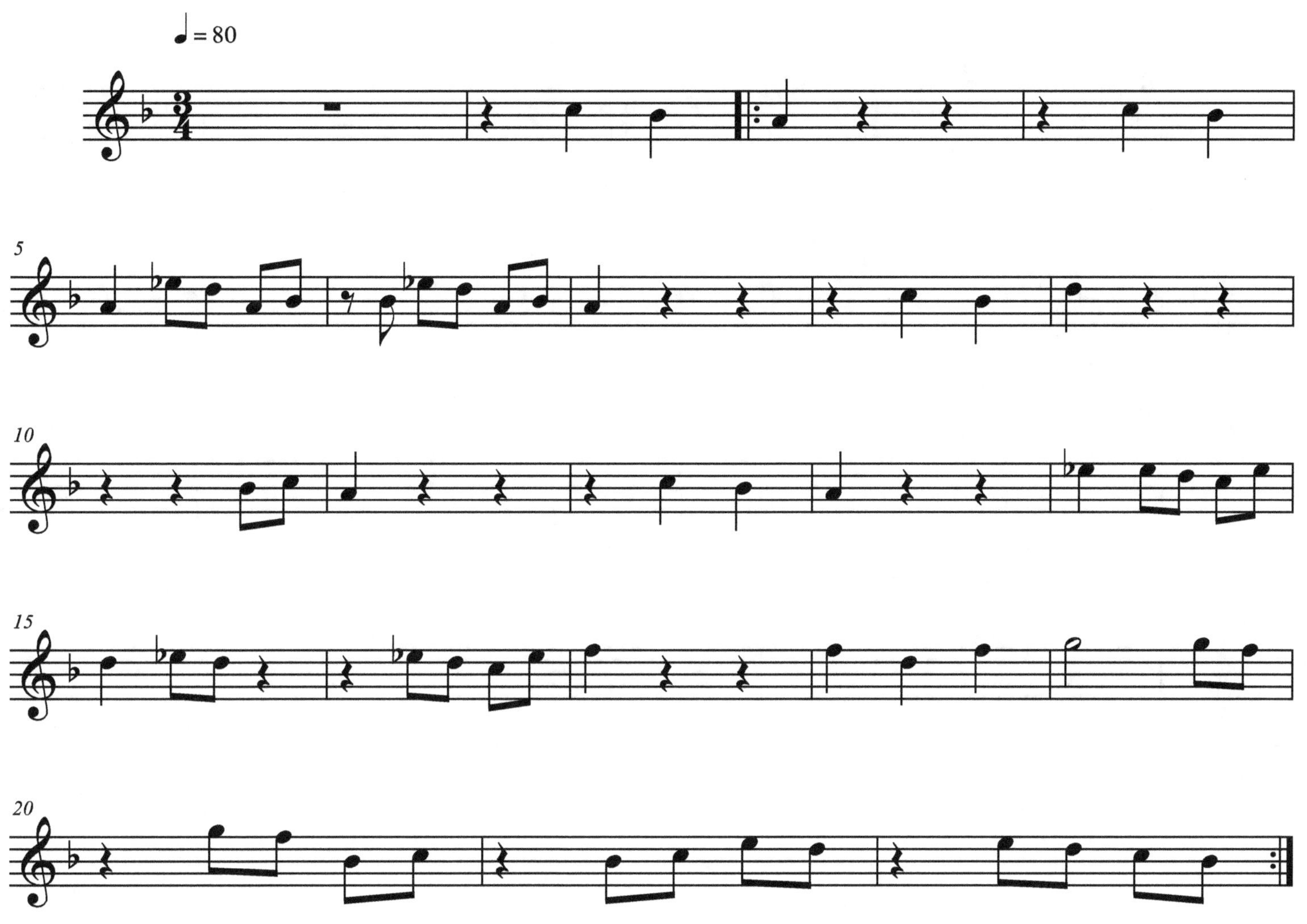

Part 2: Violin 2

A

Joost de Groo

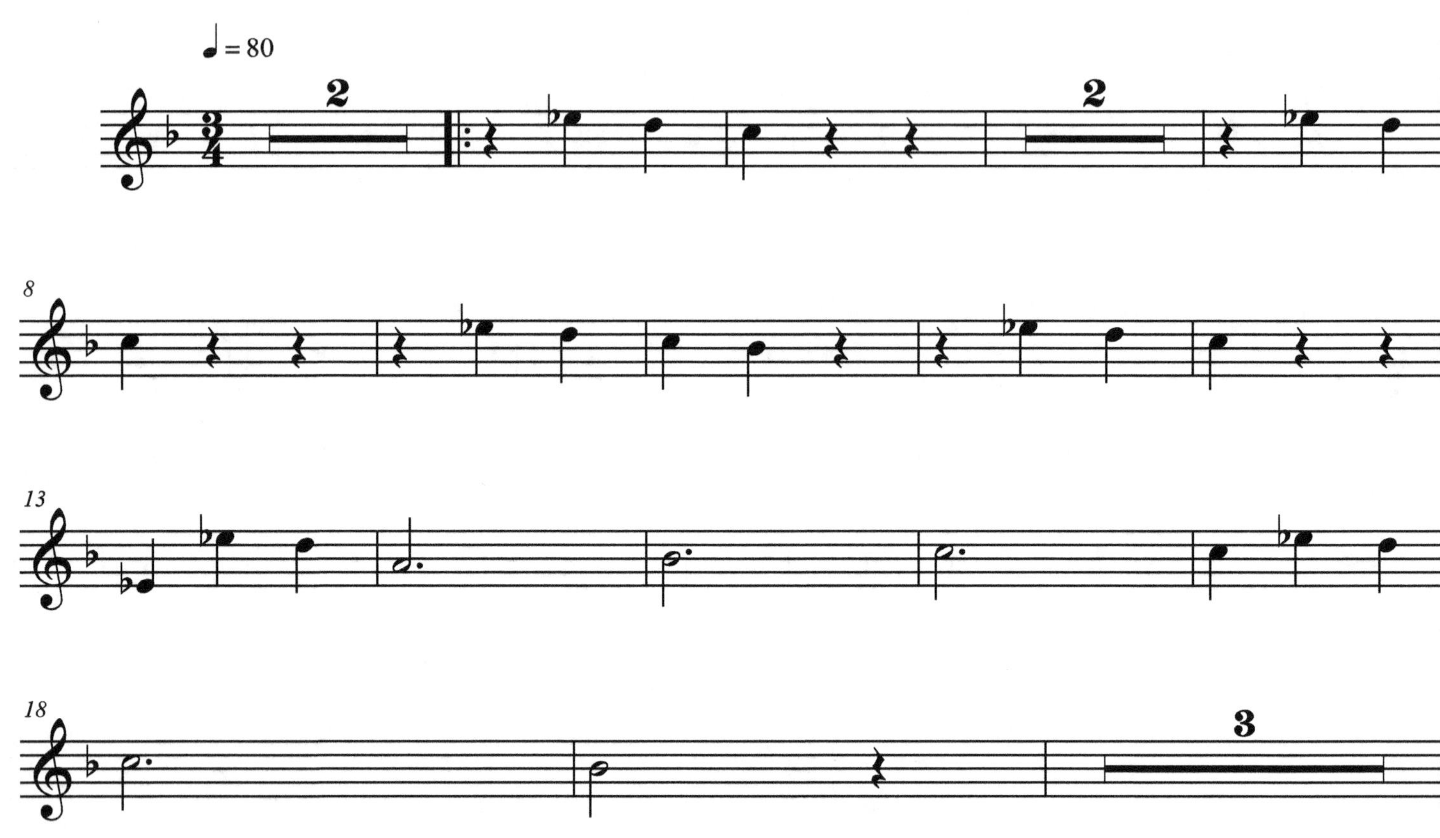

Part 3: Viola

A

Joost de Groot

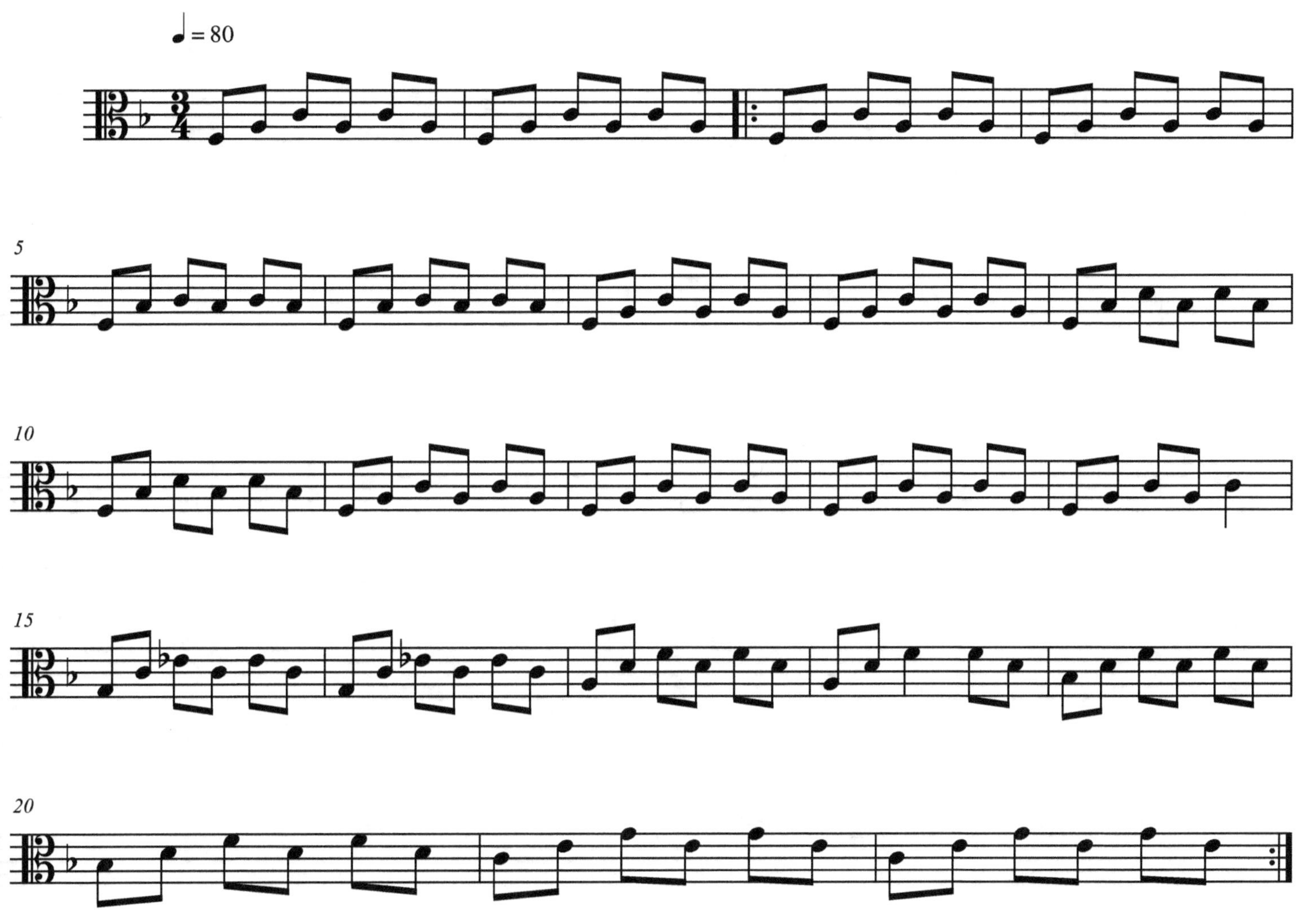

Part 4: Cello/Contrabass

A

Joost de Gro

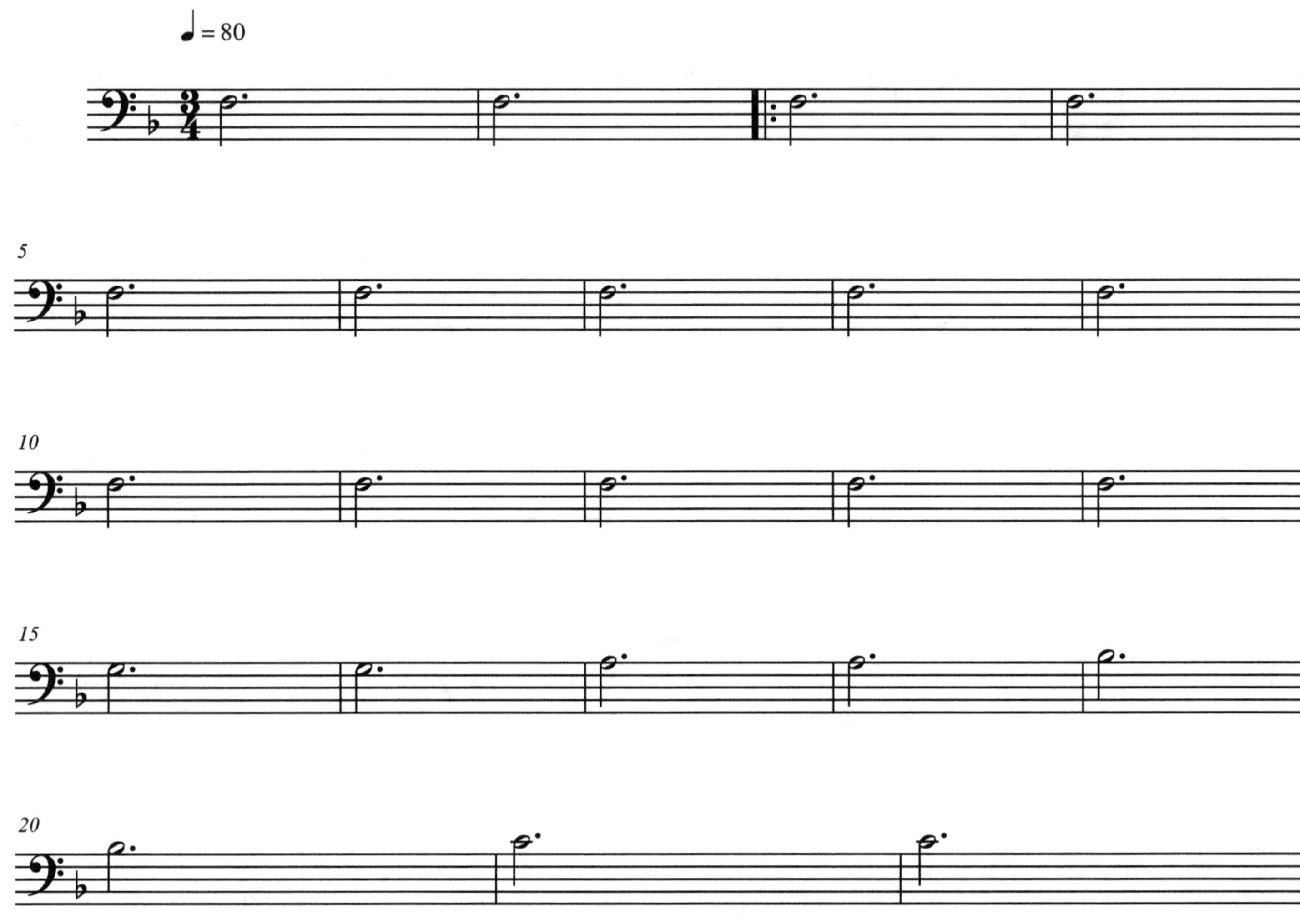

Part 1: Violin 1

N

Joost de Groot

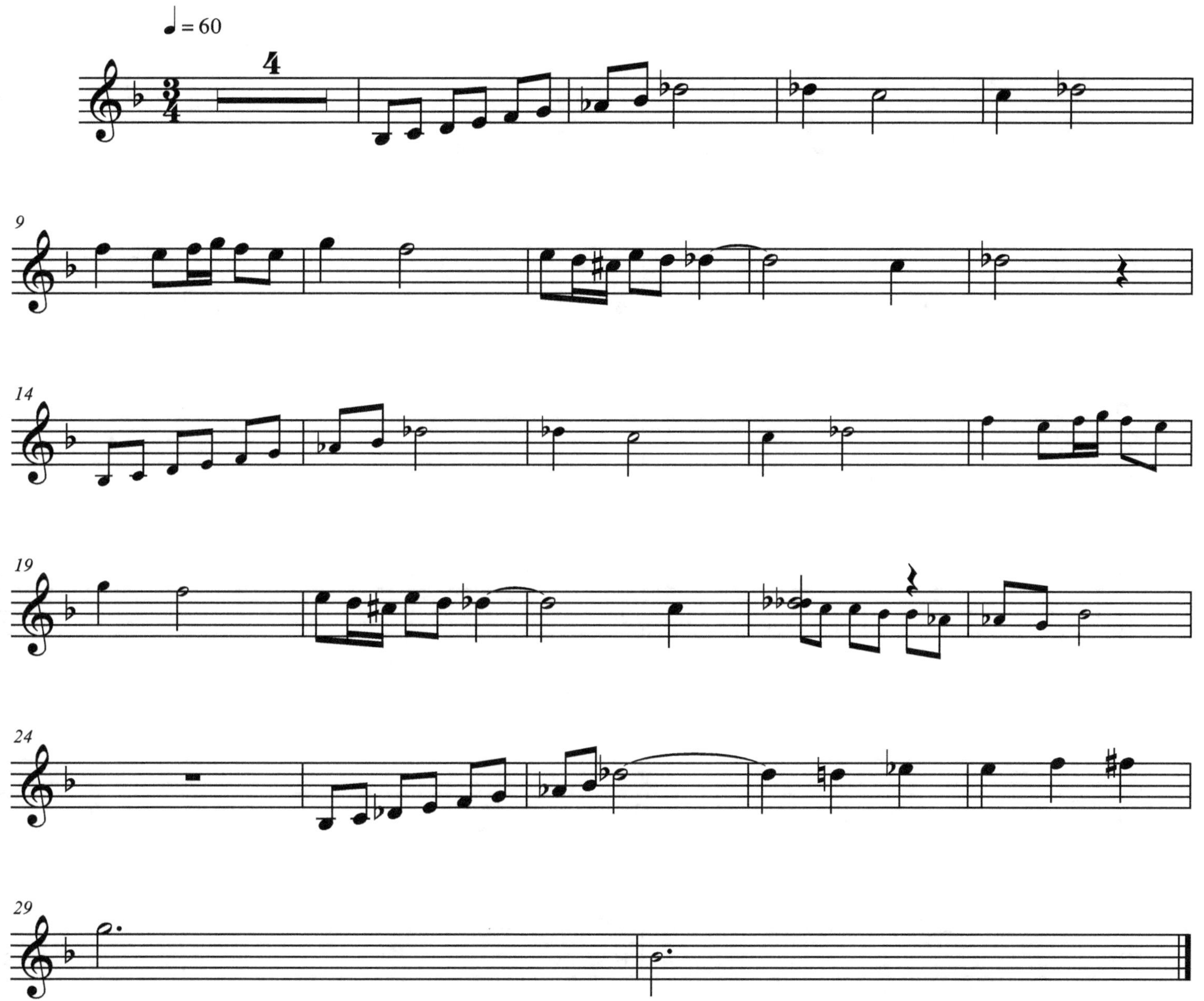

Part 2: Violin 2

N

Joost de Gro[illegible]

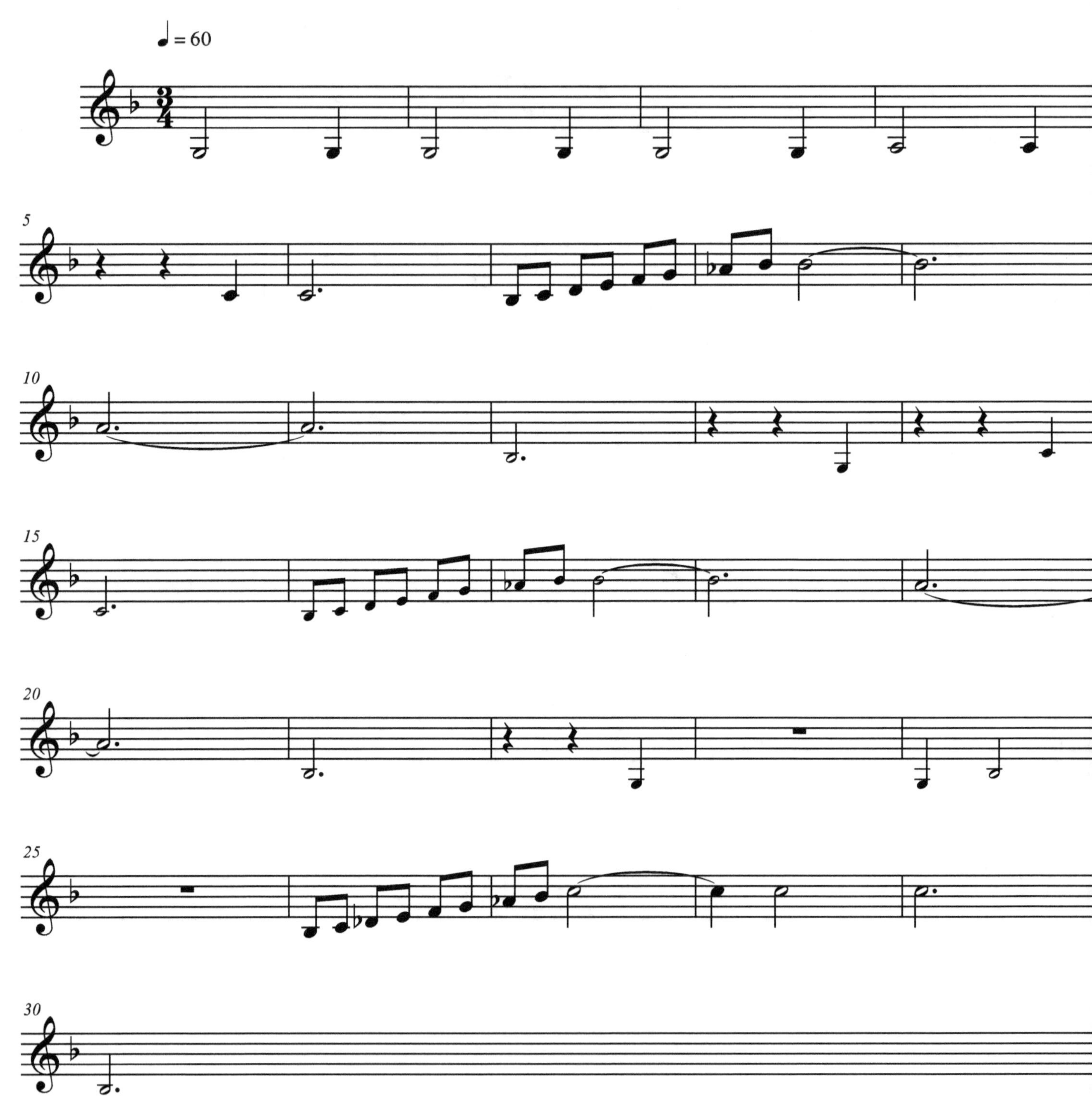

N

Part 3: Viola

Joost de Groot

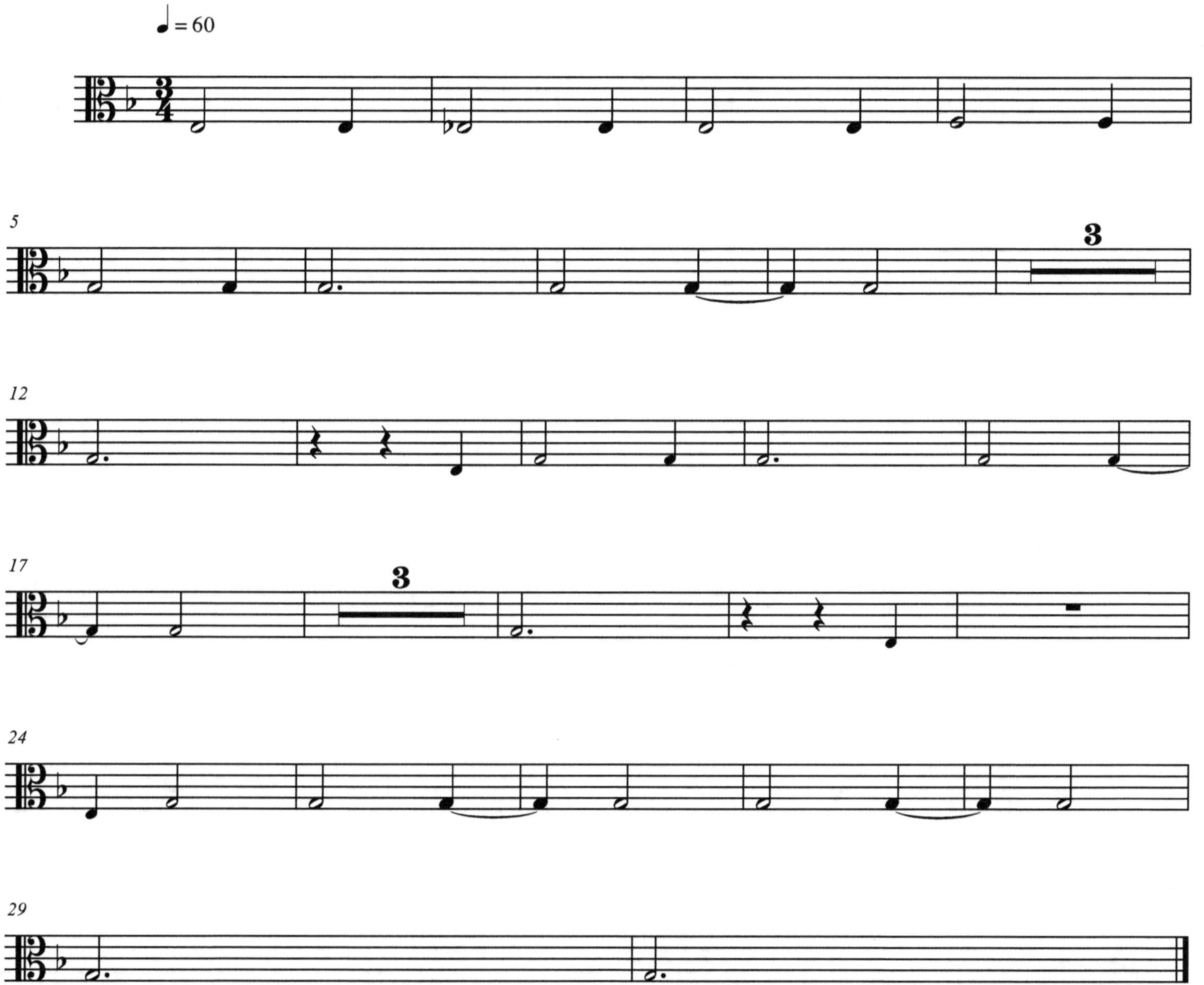

N

Part 4: Cello/Contrabass

Joost de Gro

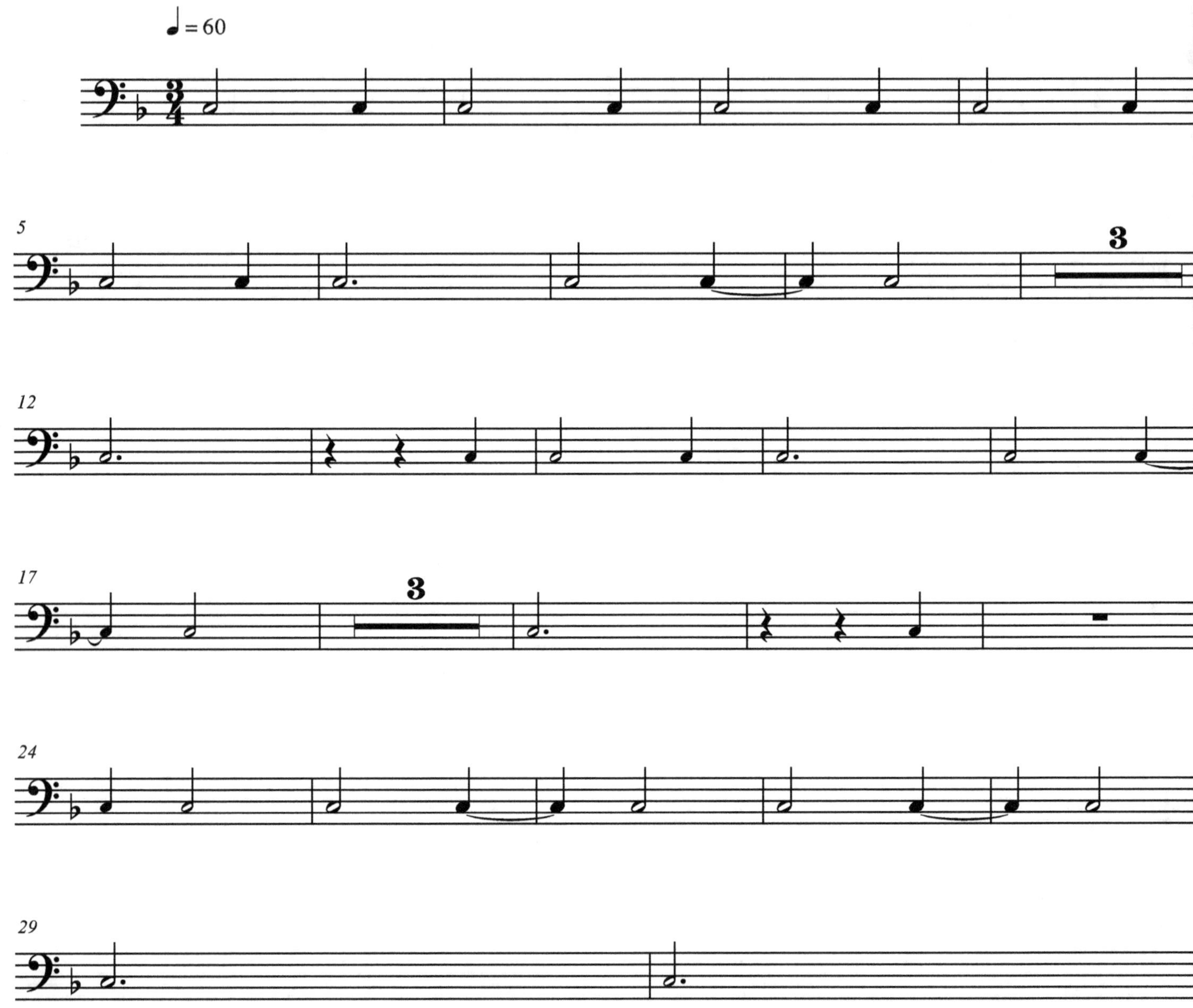

Part 1: Violin 1

N

Joost de Groot

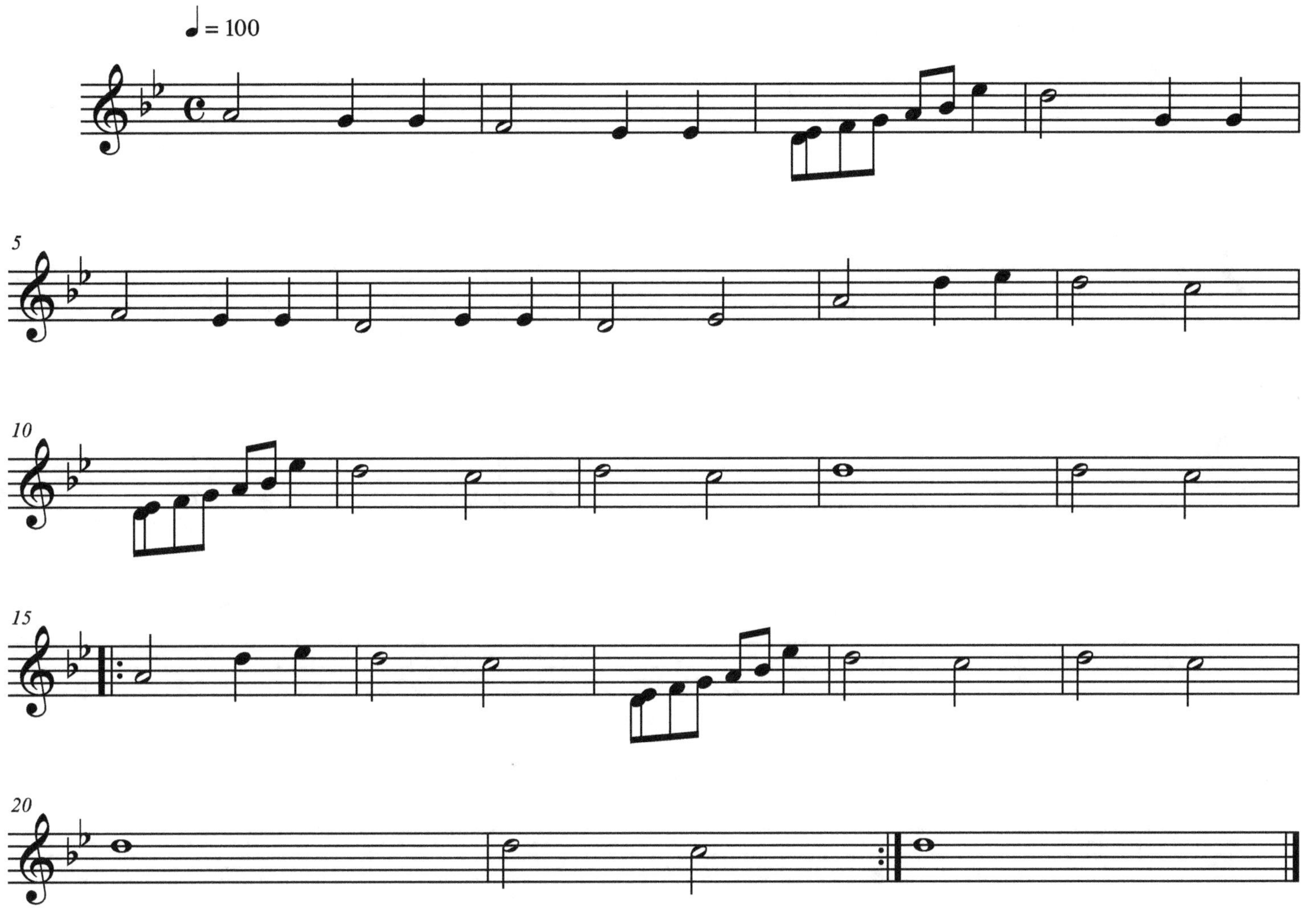

N

Part 2: Violin 2

Joost de Groo

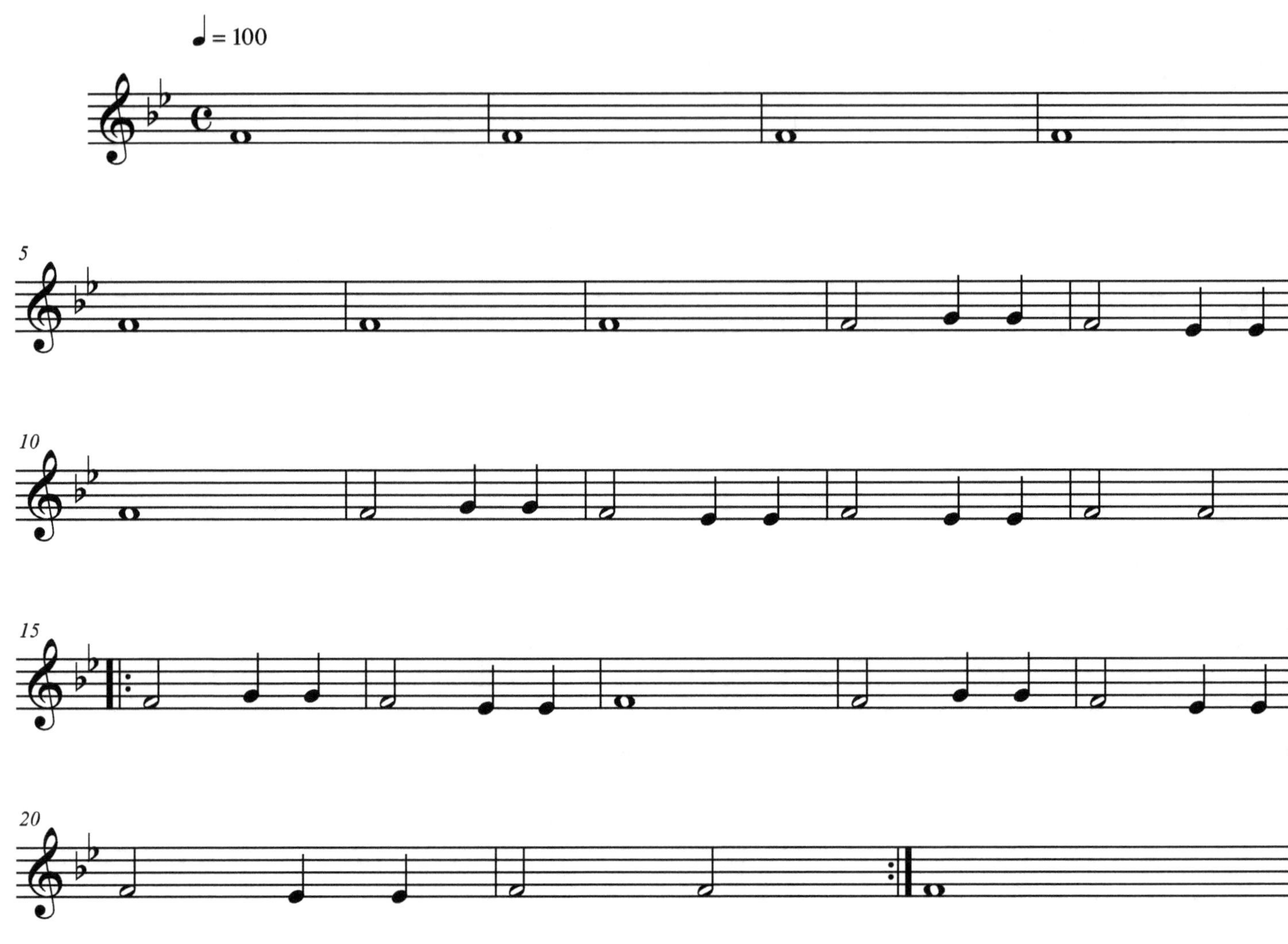

Part 3: Viola

N

Joost de Groot

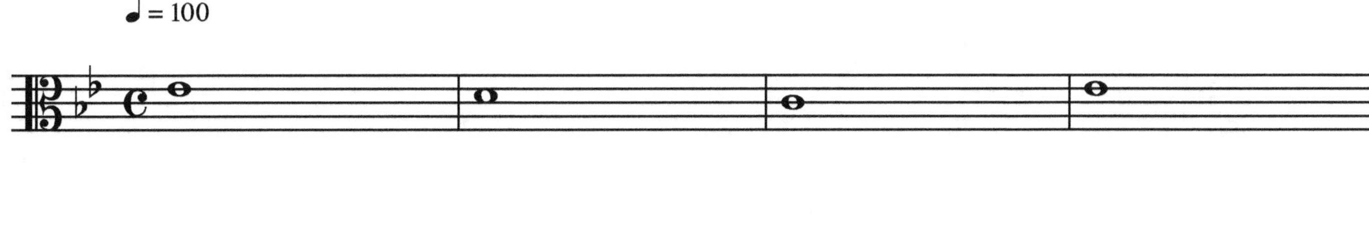

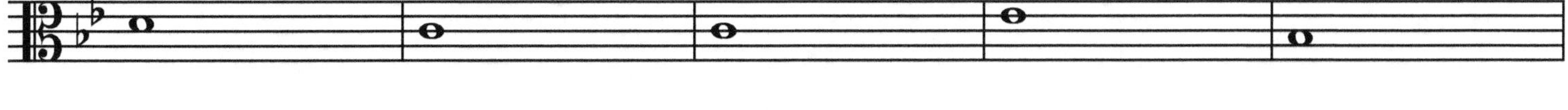

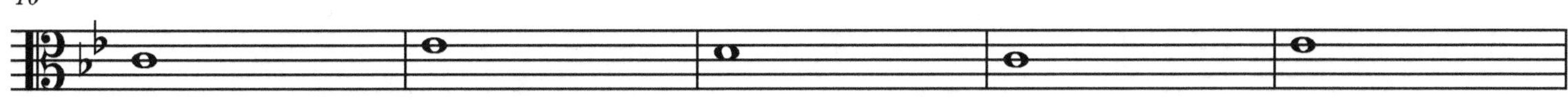

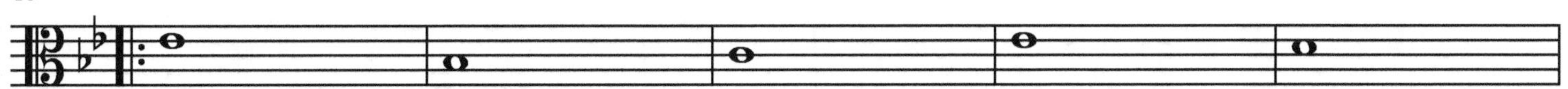

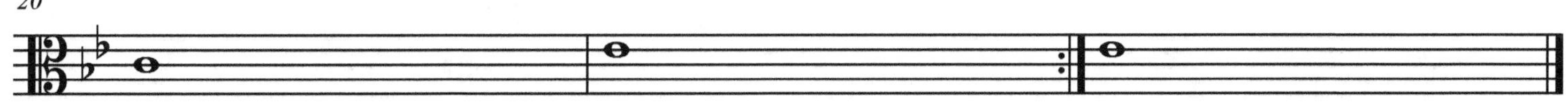

N

Part 4: Cello/Contrabass

Joost de Gro

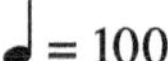

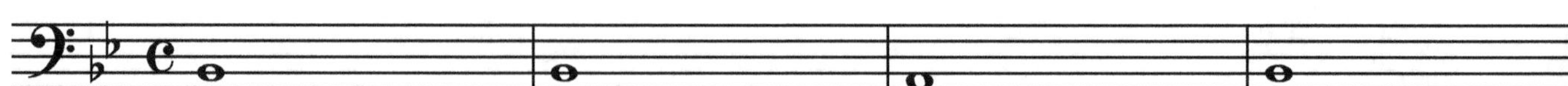

5

10

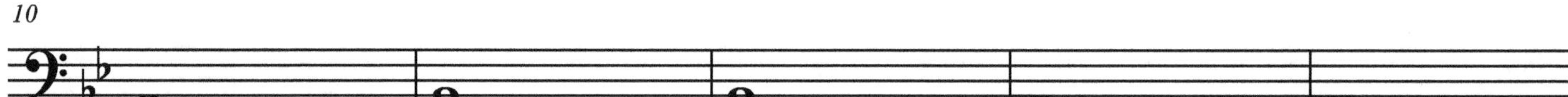

15

20

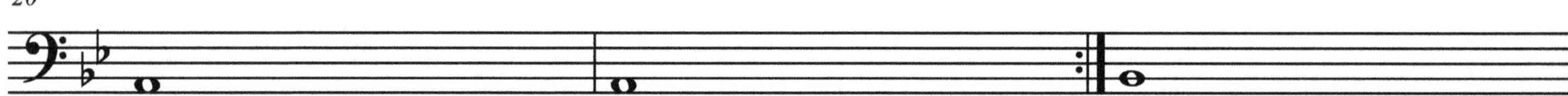

Part 1: Violin 1

I

Joost de Groot

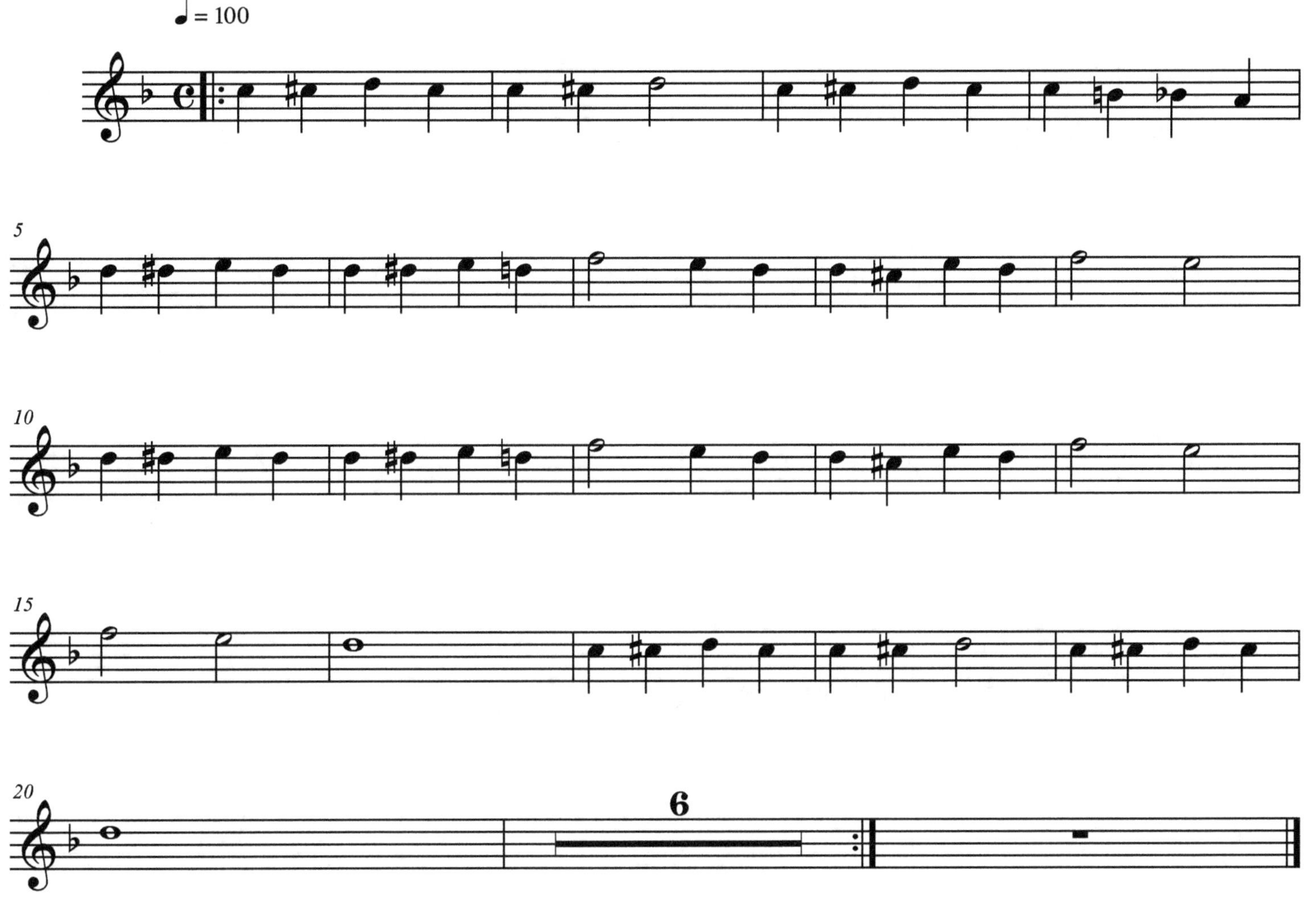

Part 2: Violin 2

I

Joost de Groo

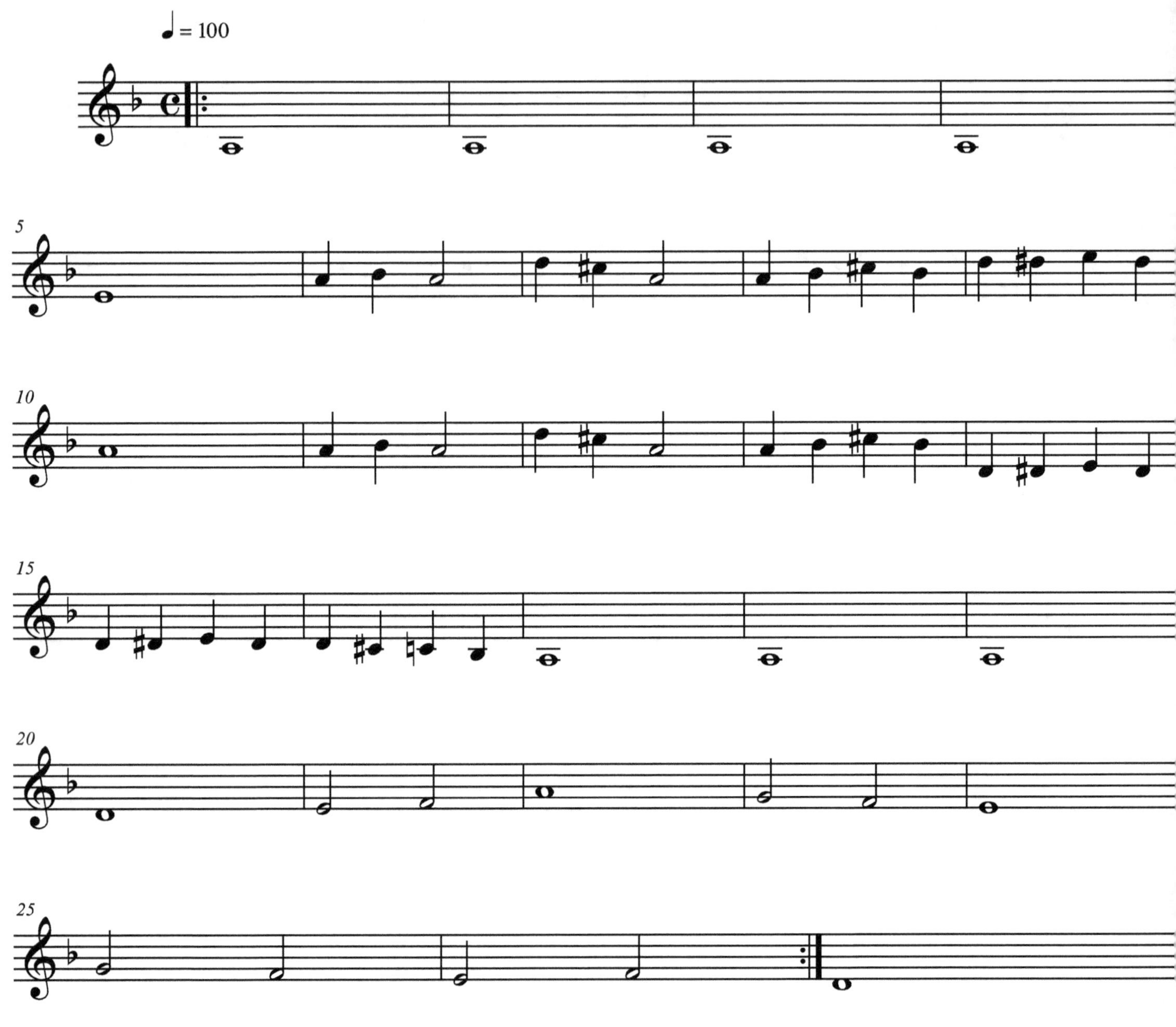

I

Part 3: Viola

Joost de Groot

♩ = 100

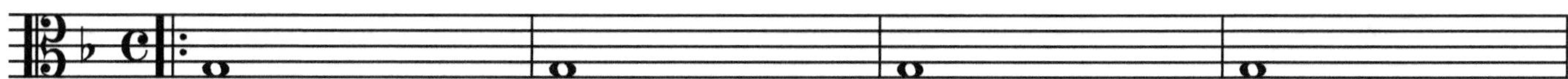

Part 4: Cello/Contrabass

I

Joost de Gro

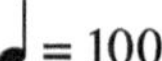

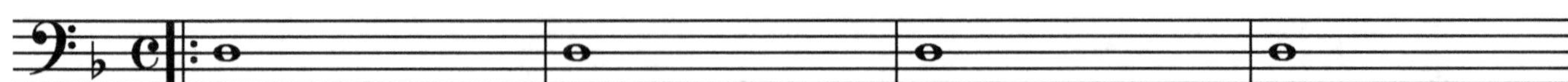

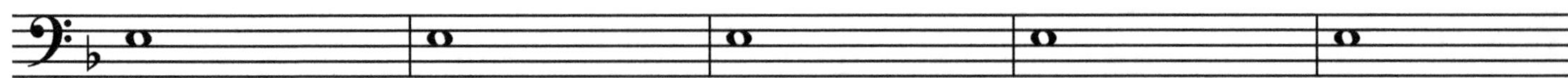

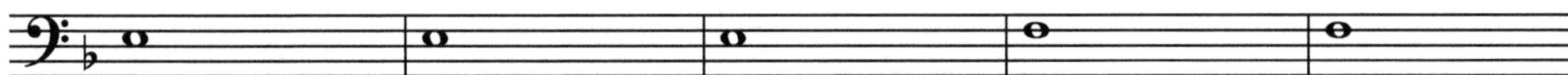

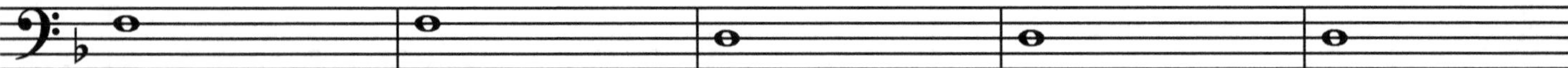

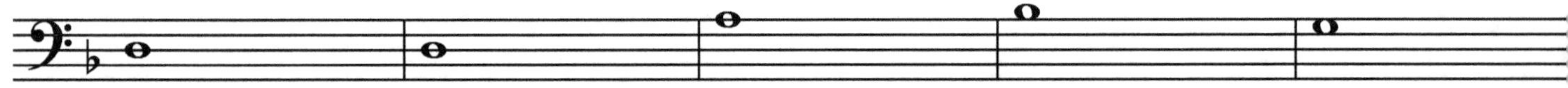

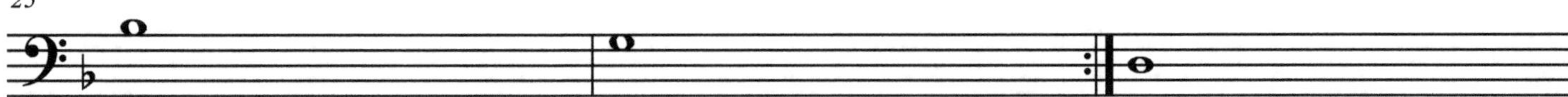

Part 1: Violin 1

E

Joost de Groot

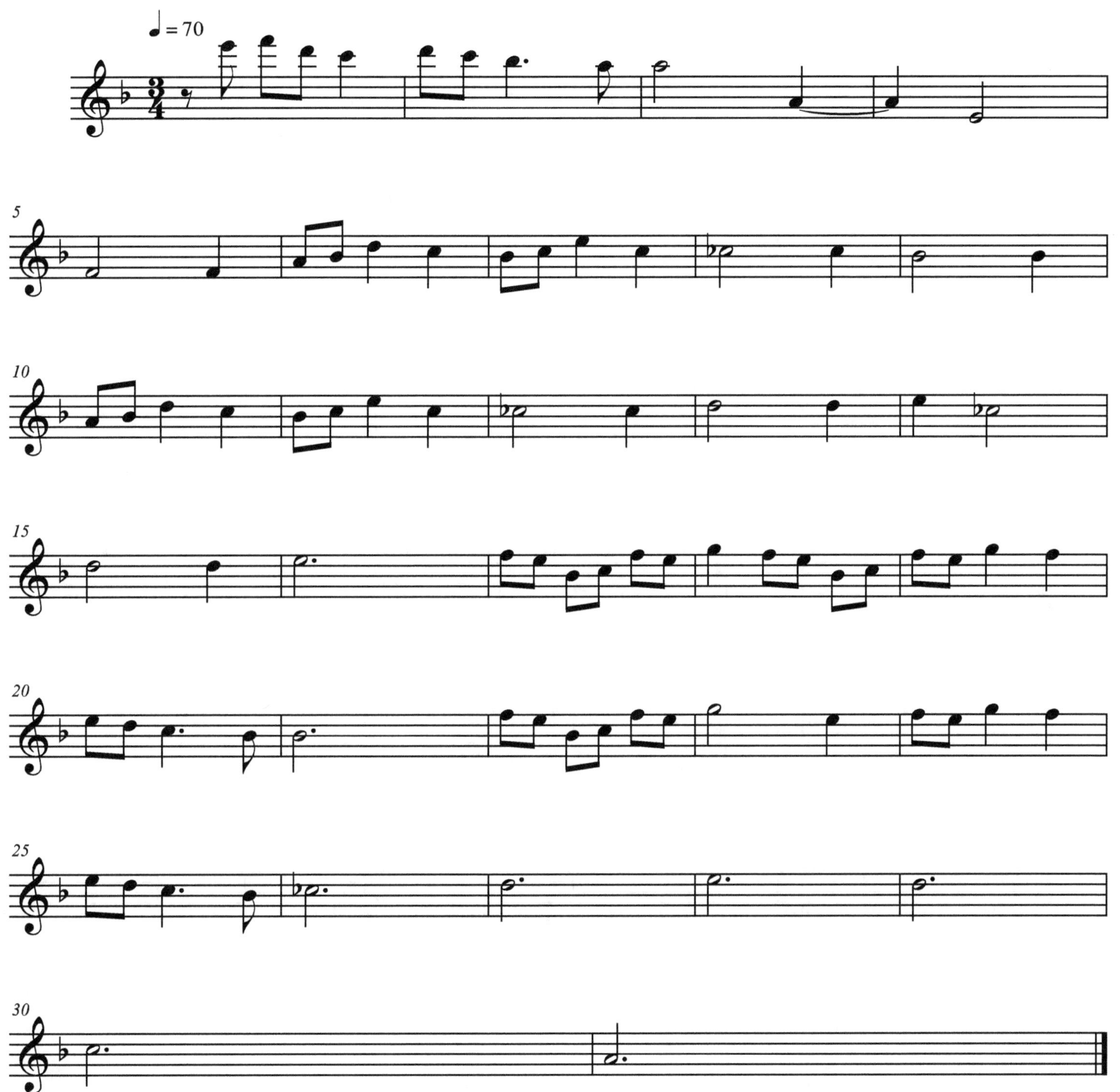

Part 2: Violin 2

E

Joost de Groo

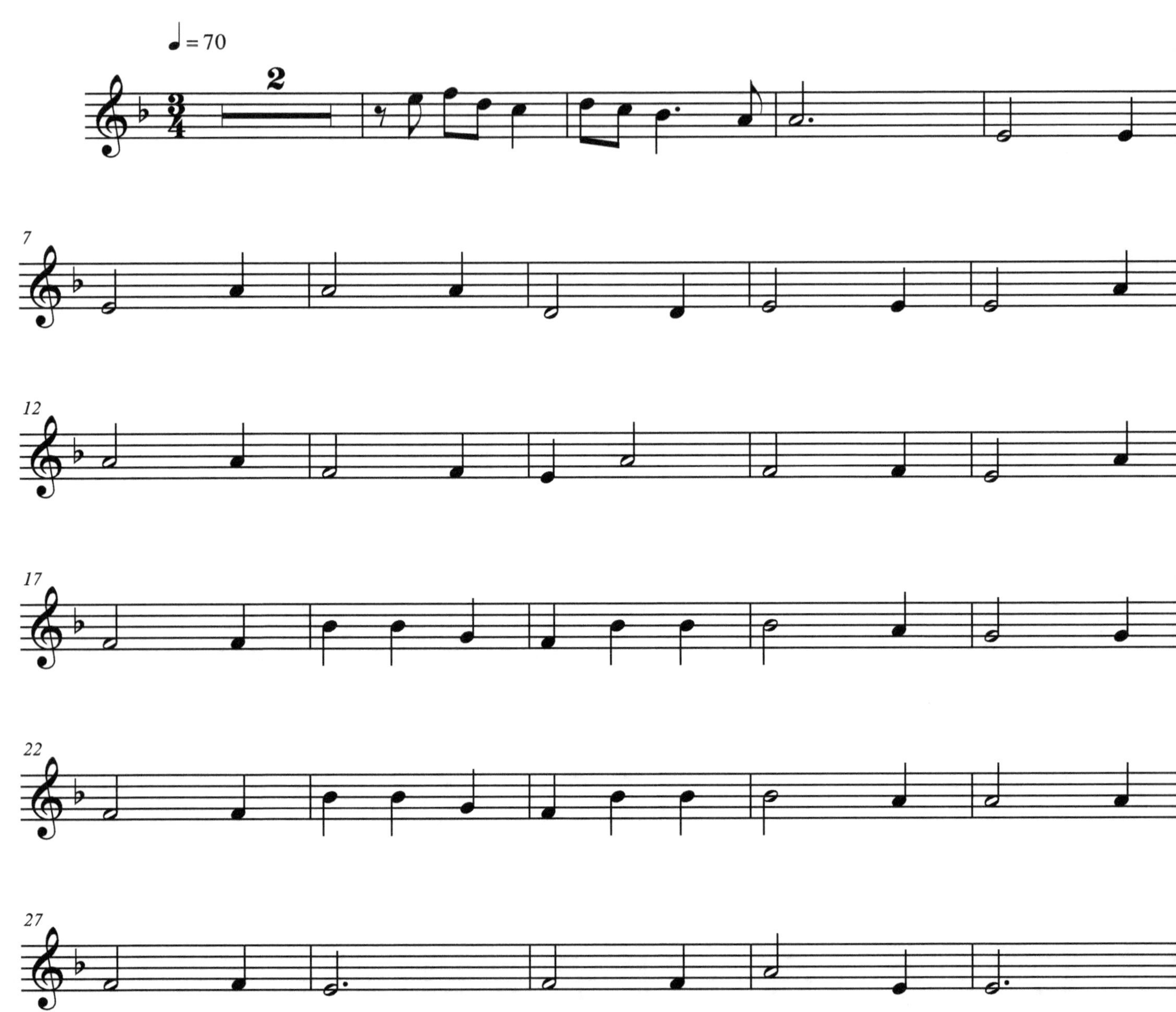

Part 3: Viola

E

Joost de Groot

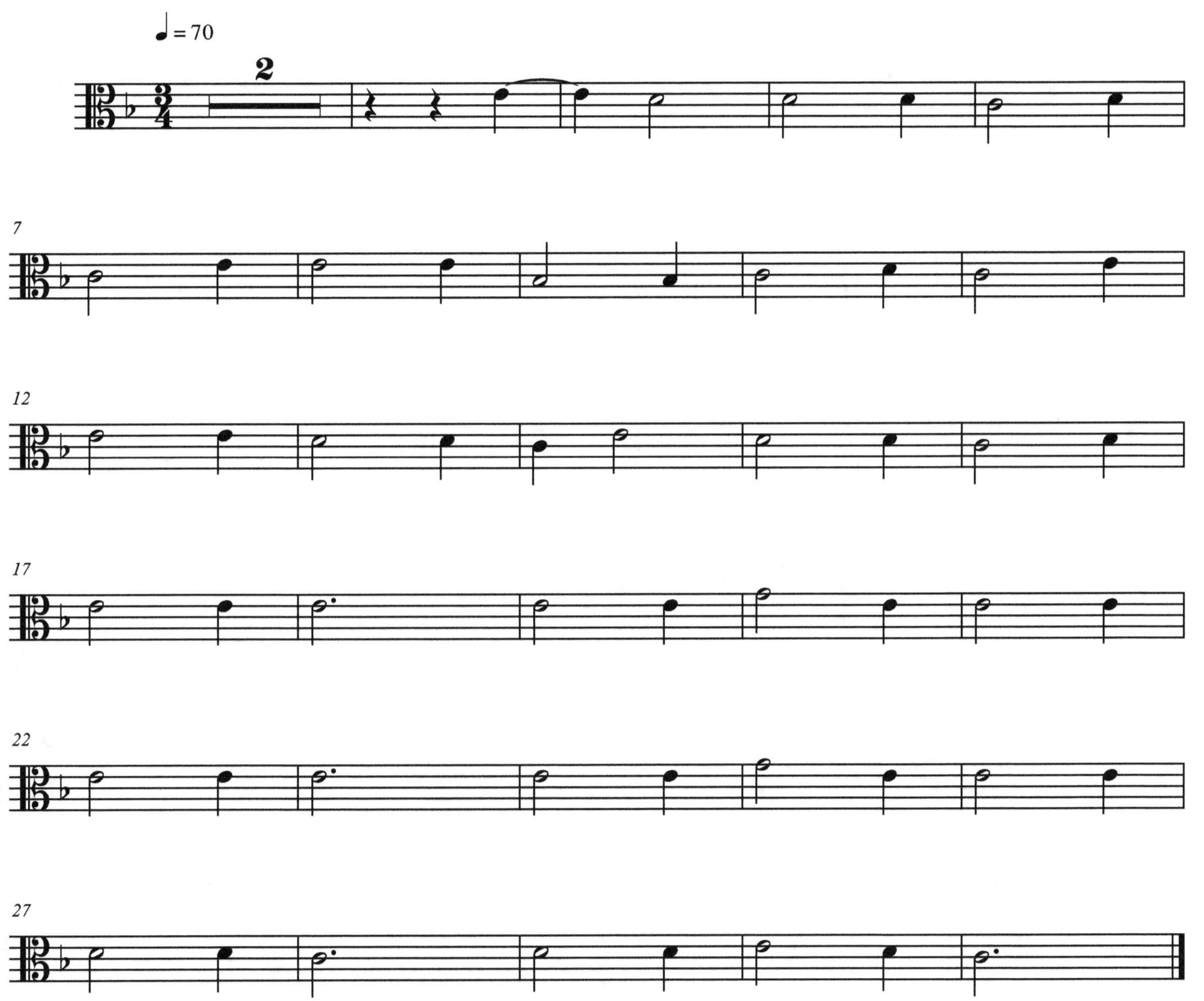

Part 4: Cello/Contrabass

E

Joost de Gro

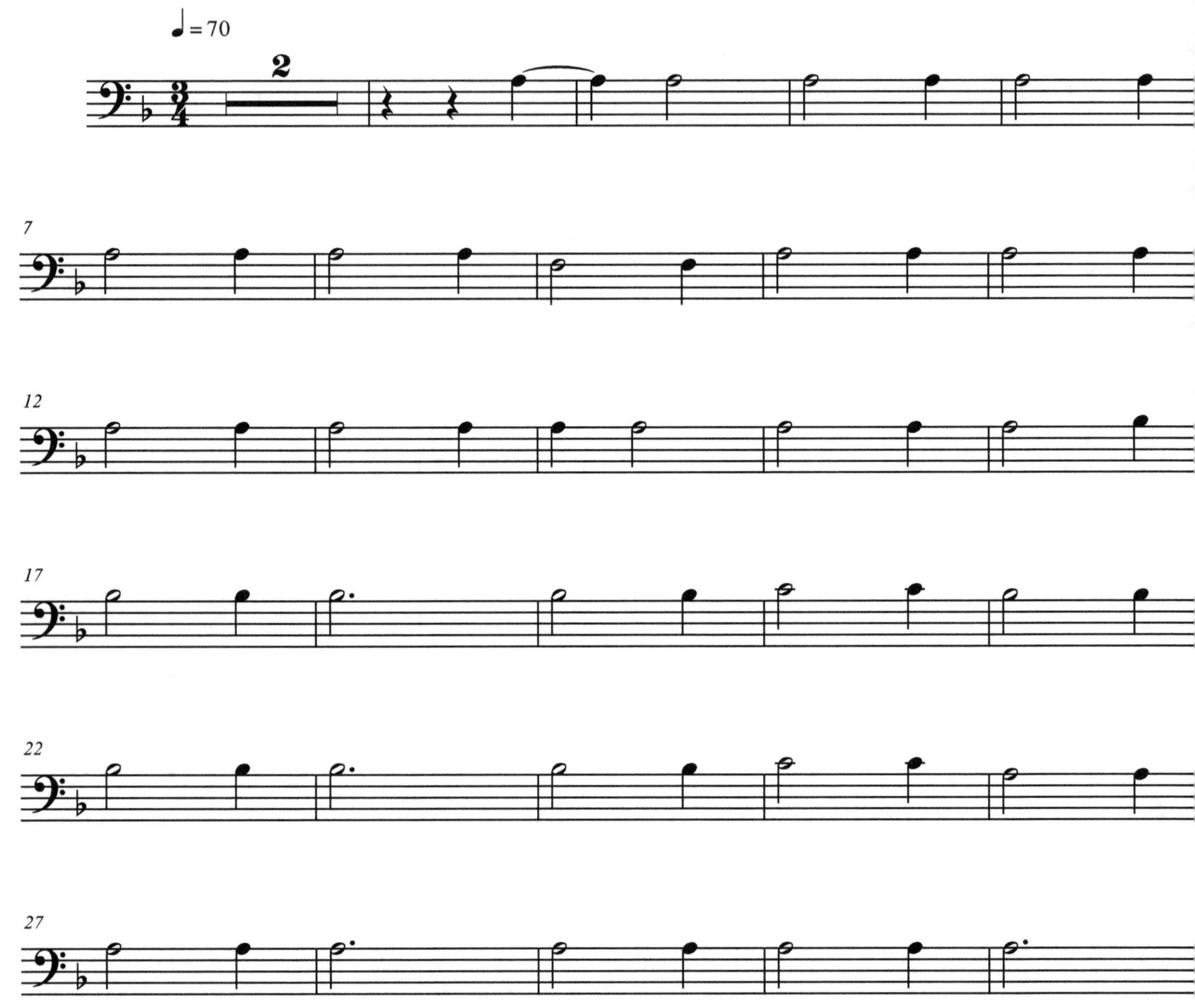

Concert Band

Part 1: C Flute, C Oboe, Bes Clarinet 1, Bes Trumpet 1

Part 2: Bes Clarinet 2 + 3, Es Alto Sax., F Horn 1 + 2,
Bes Trumpet 2 + 3

Part 3: Es Alto Clarinet, Bes Tenor Sax., F Horn 3 + 4,
C Trombone 1 + 2, C/Bes Baritone

Part 4: C Bassoon, Bes Bass Clarinet, Es Baritone Sax.,
C Bass Trombone, C/Bes/Es Bass Tuba

J

Joost de Gro

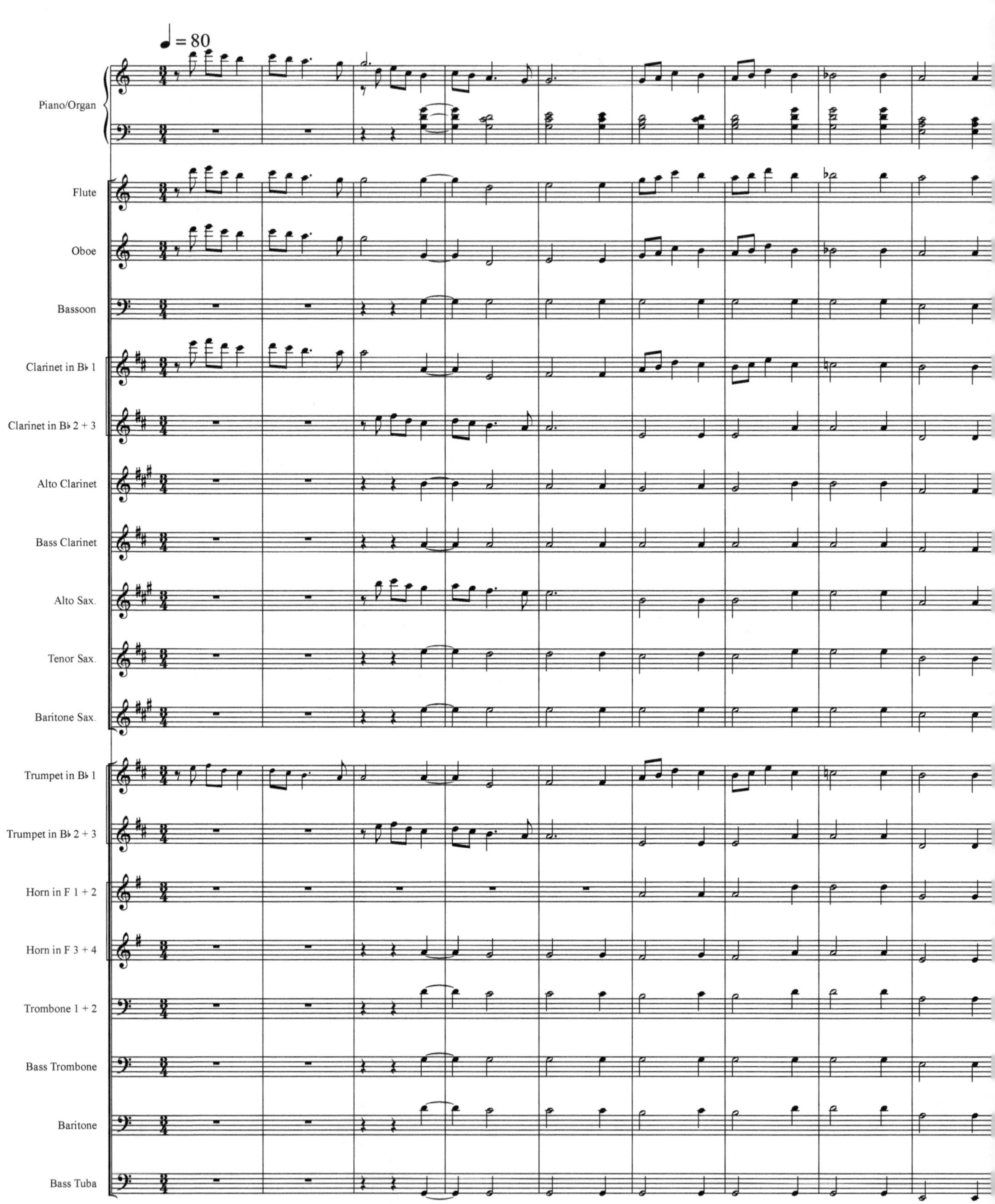

J

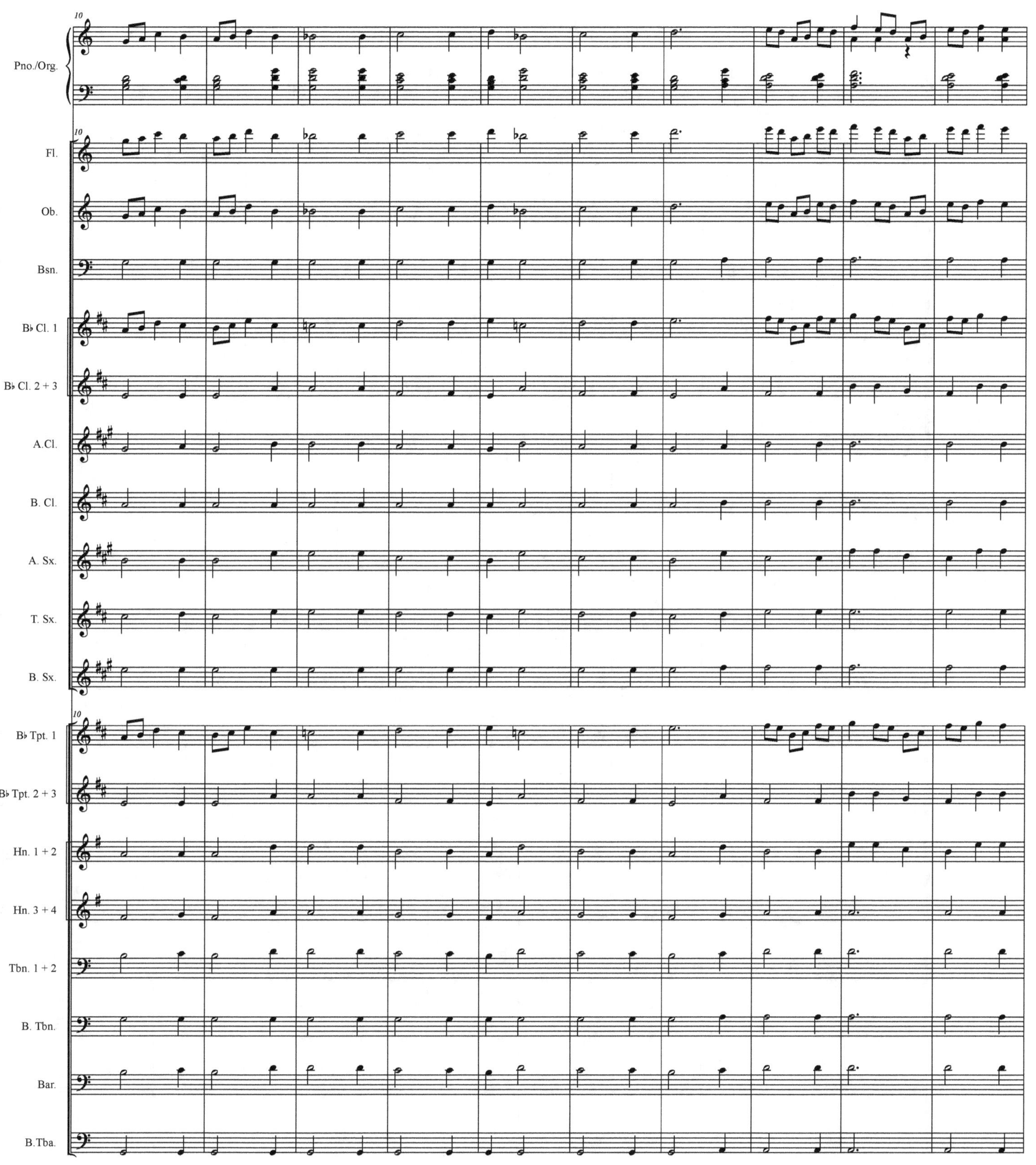

J

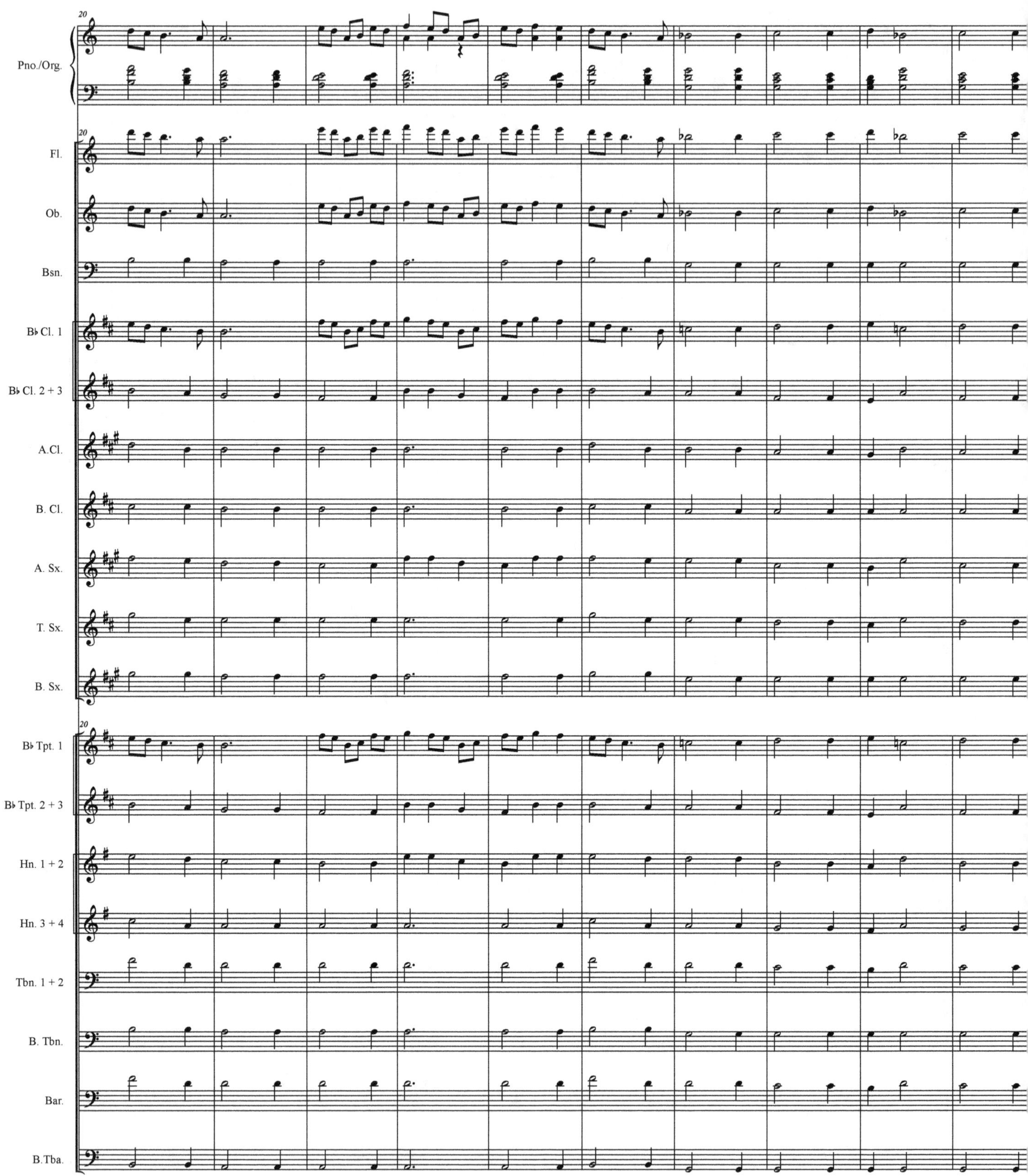

J

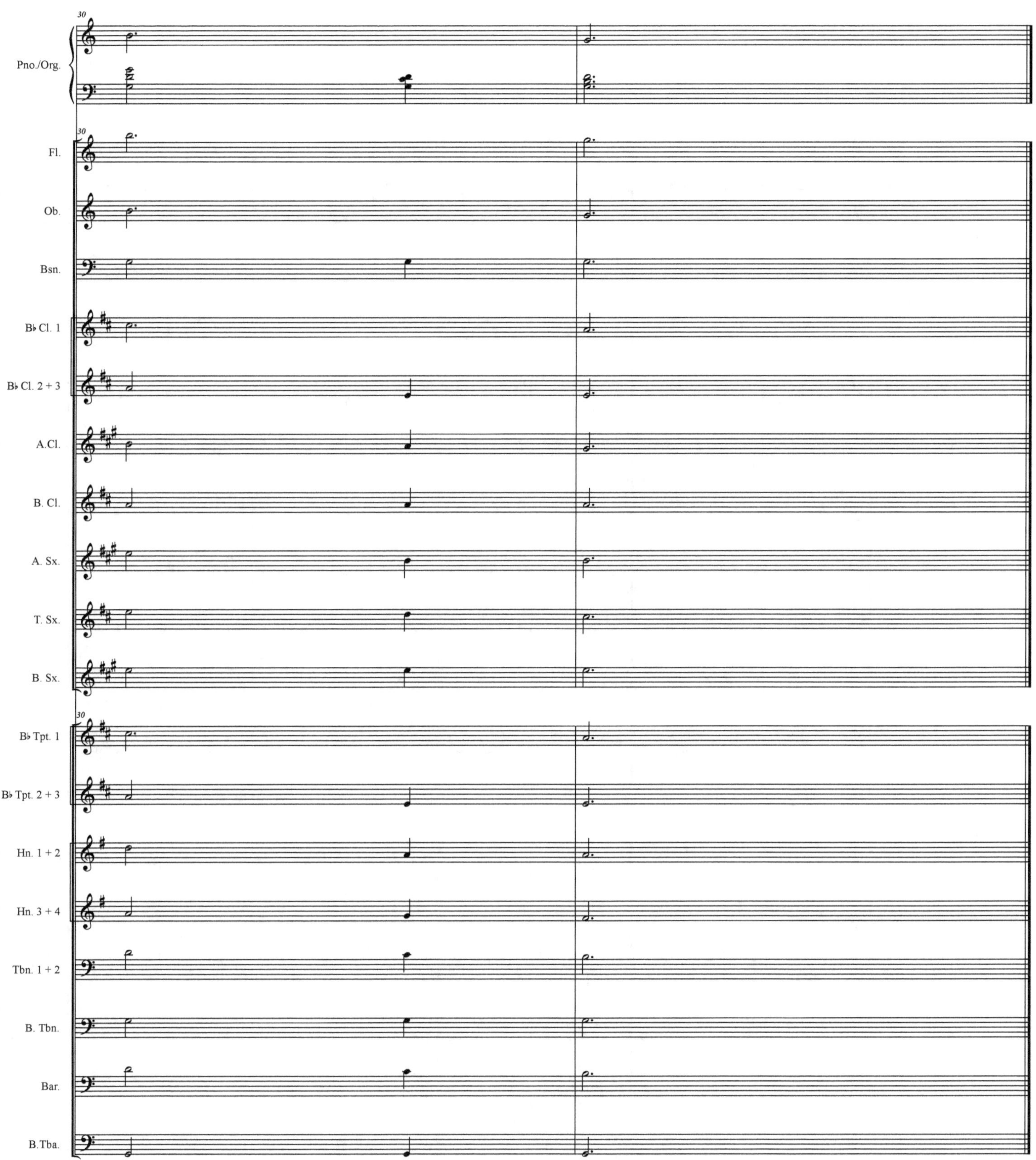

A

Joost de Gro

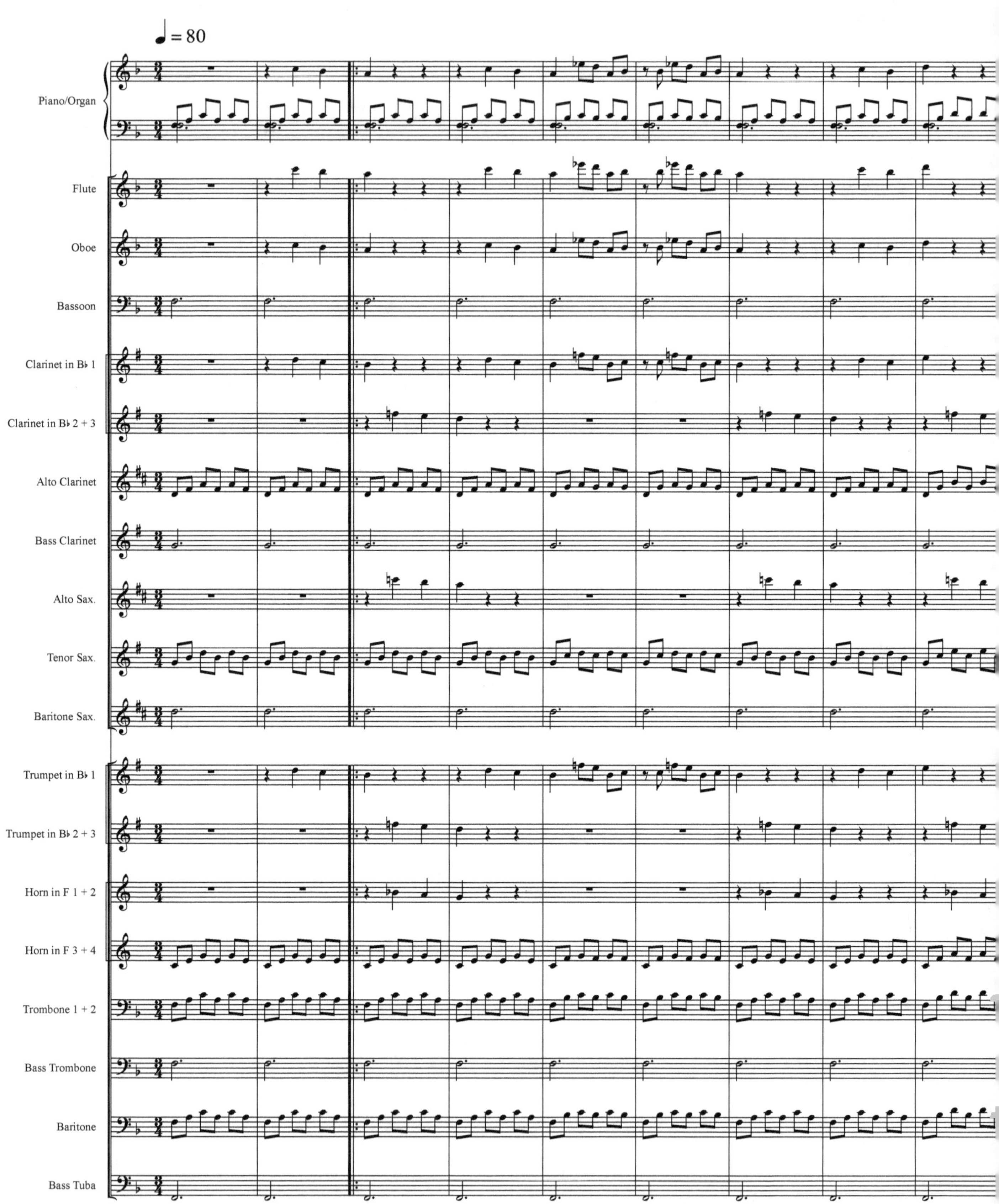

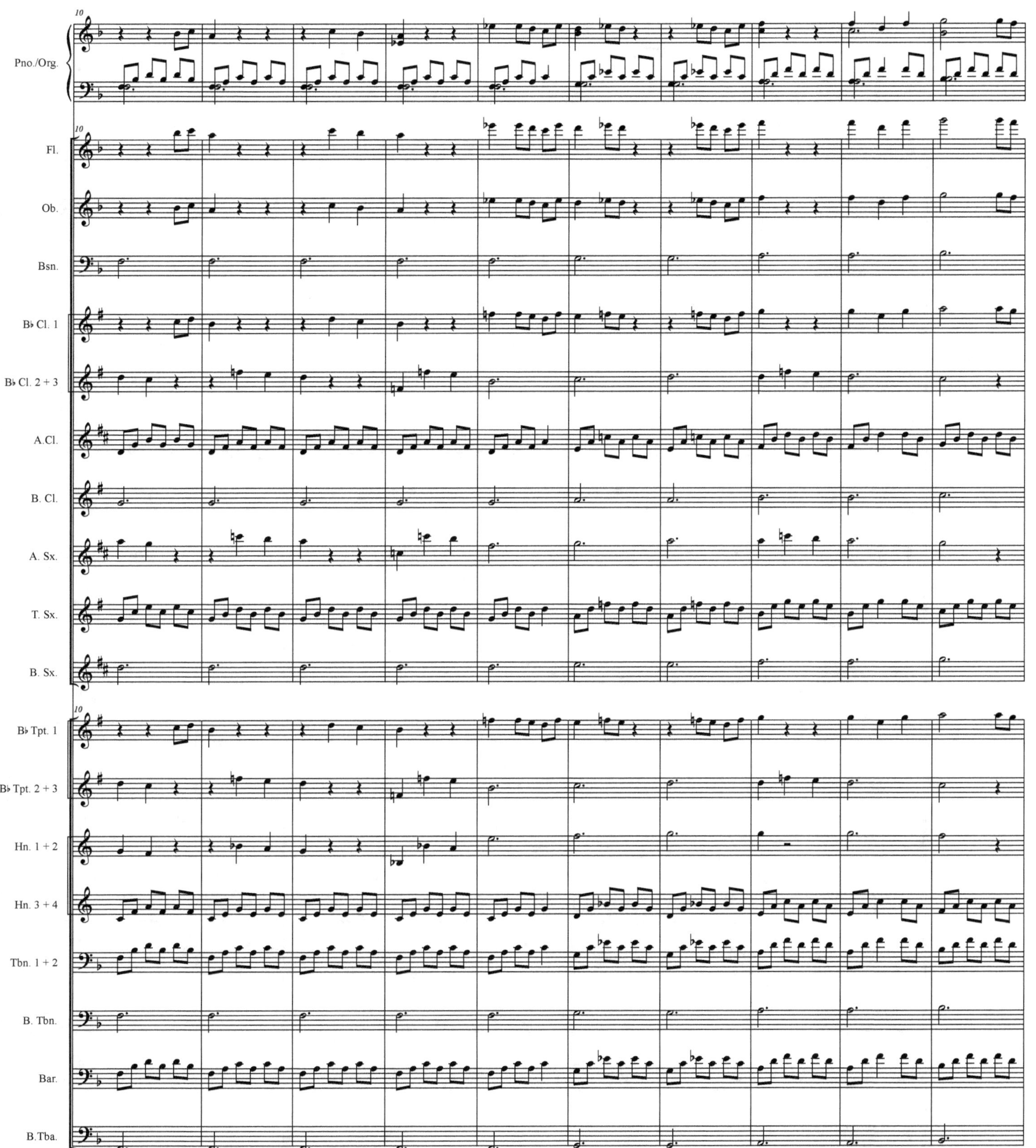
10
Pno./Org.
Fl.
Ob.
Bsn.
B♭ Cl. 1
B♭ Cl. 2 + 3
A.Cl.
B. Cl.
A. Sx.
T. Sx.
B. Sx.
B♭ Tpt. 1
B♭ Tpt. 2 + 3
Hn. 1 + 2
Hn. 3 + 4
Tbn. 1 + 2
B. Tbn.
Bar.
B.Tba.

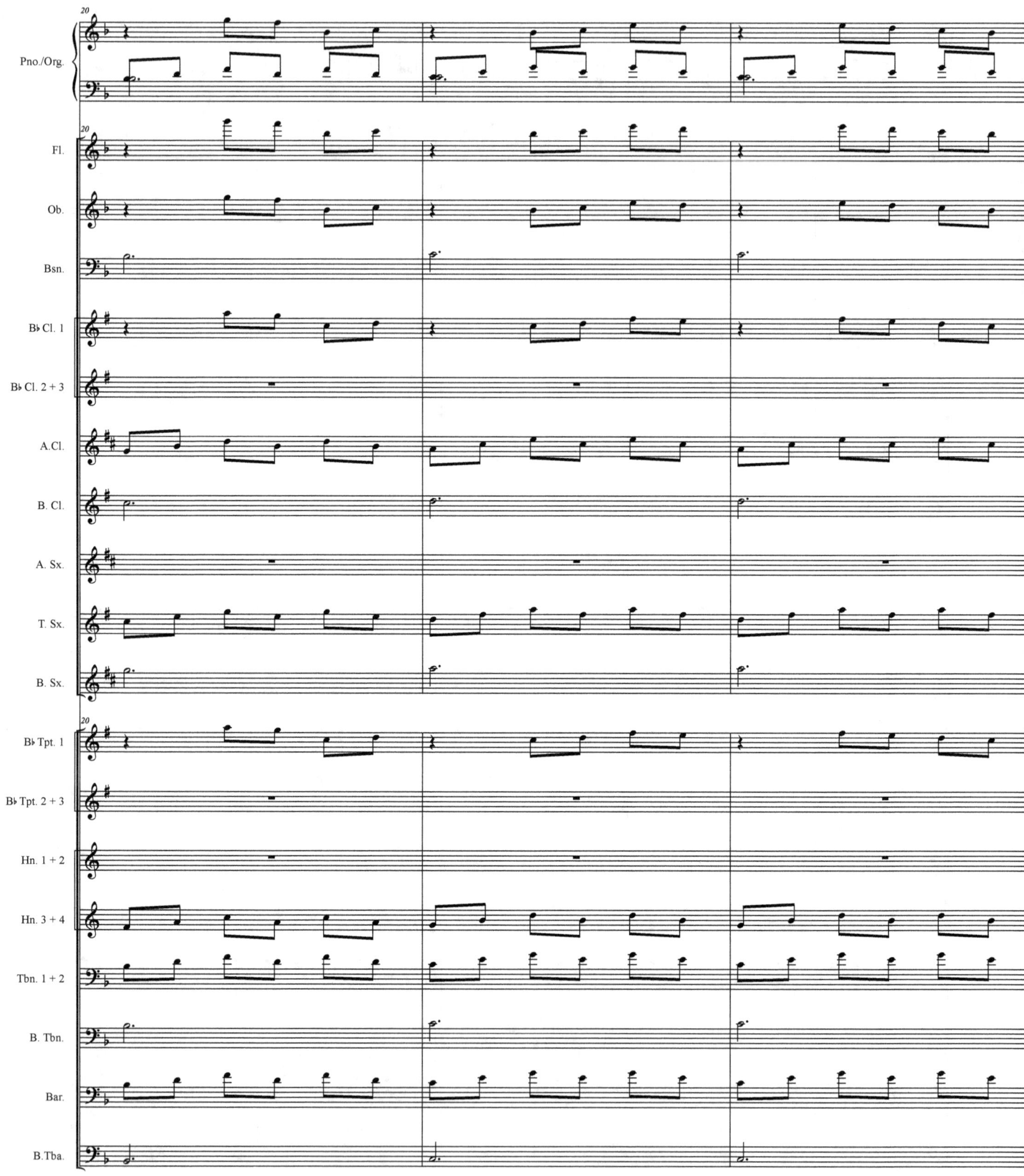
20
Pno./Org.
Fl.
Ob.
Bsn.
B♭ Cl. 1
B♭ Cl. 2 + 3
A.Cl.
B. Cl.
A. Sx.
T. Sx.
B. Sx.
B♭ Tpt. 1
B♭ Tpt. 2 + 3
Hn. 1 + 2
Hn. 3 + 4
Tbn. 1 + 2
B. Tbn.
Bar.
B.Tba.

N

Joost de Groot

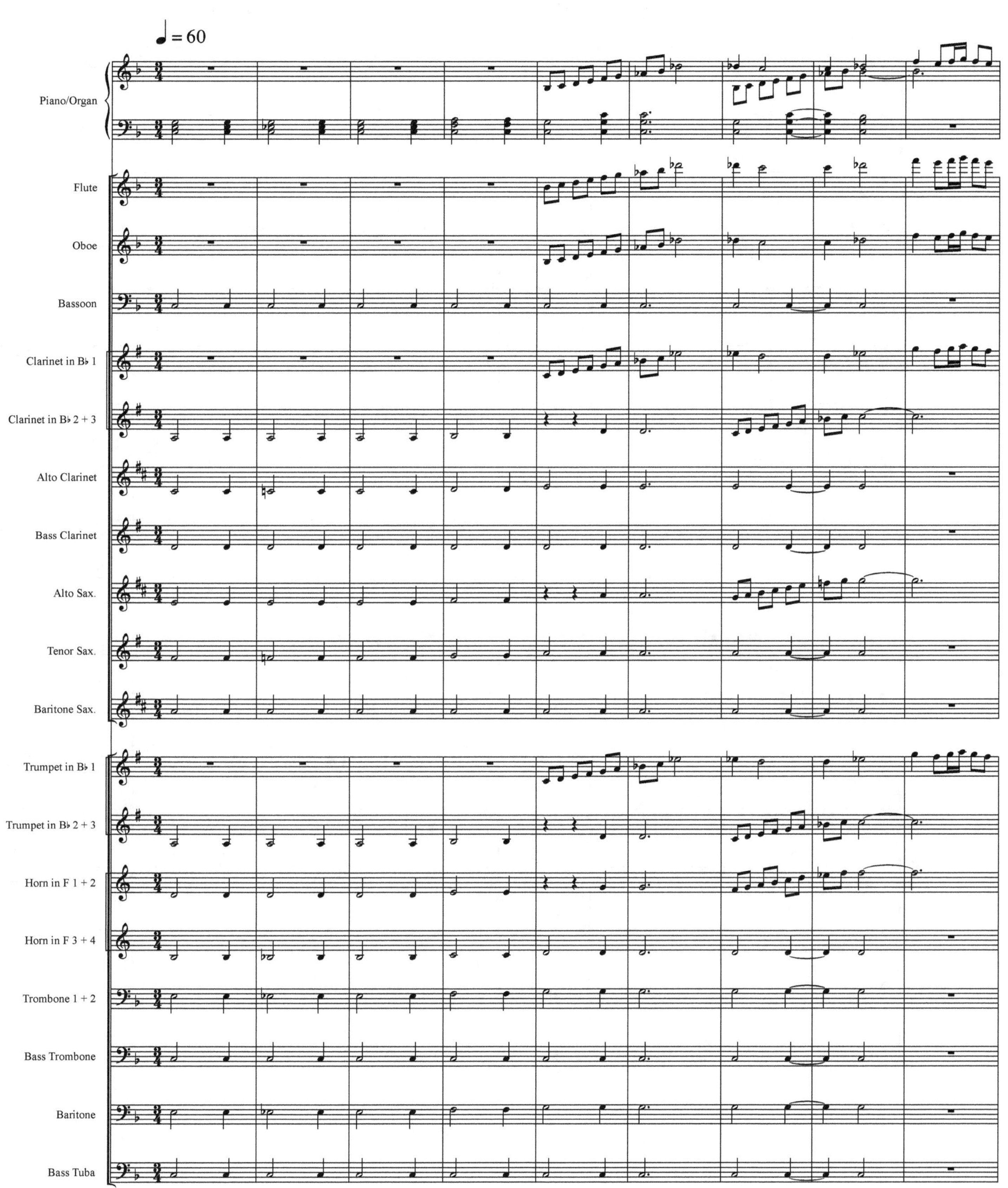

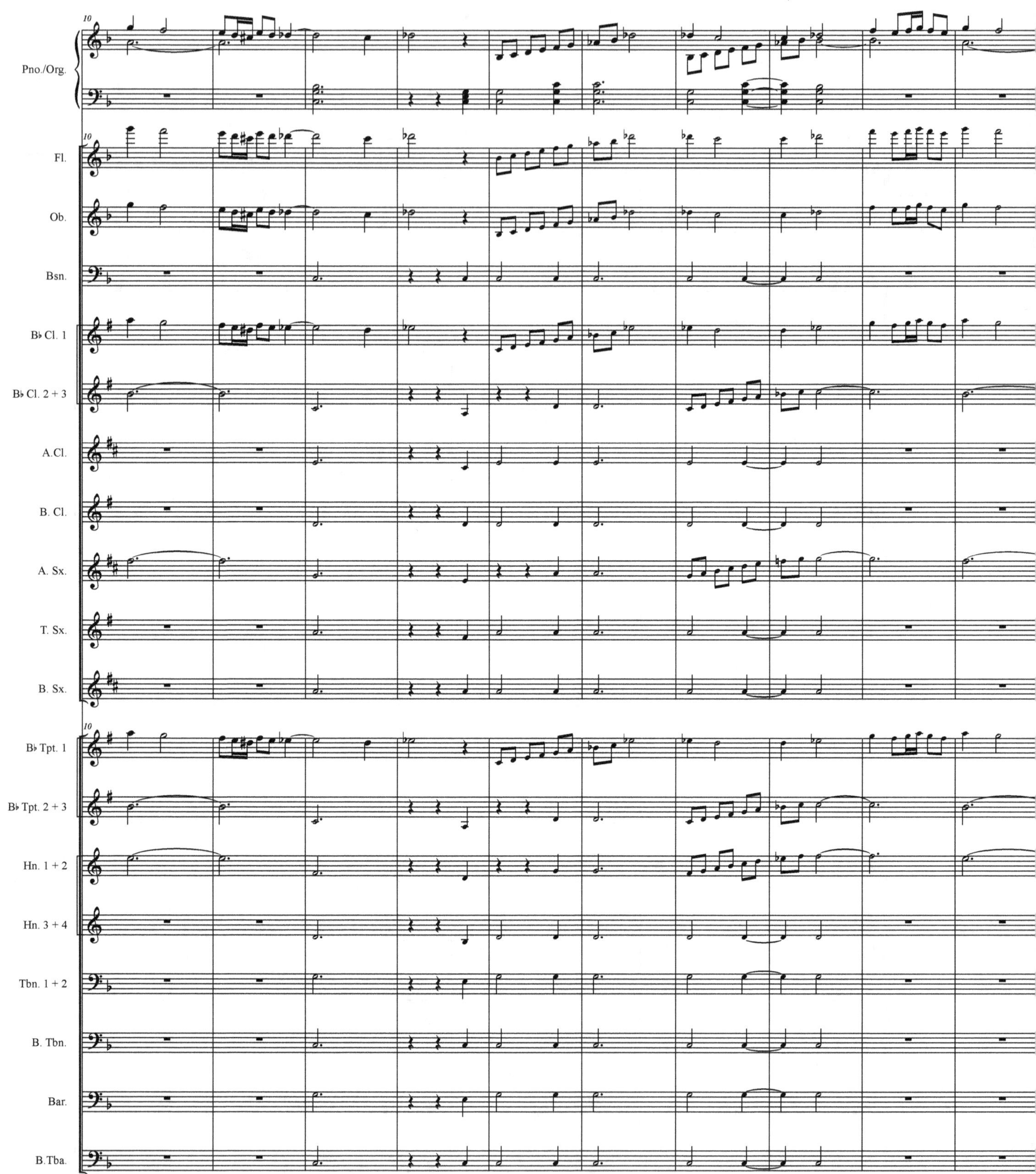
10
Pno./Org.
Fl.
Ob.
Bsn.
B♭ Cl. 1
B♭ Cl. 2 + 3
A.Cl.
B. Cl.
A. Sx.
T. Sx.
B. Sx.
B♭ Tpt. 1
B♭ Tpt. 2 + 3
Hn. 1 + 2
Hn. 3 + 4
Tbn. 1 + 2
B. Tbn.
Bar.
B.Tba.

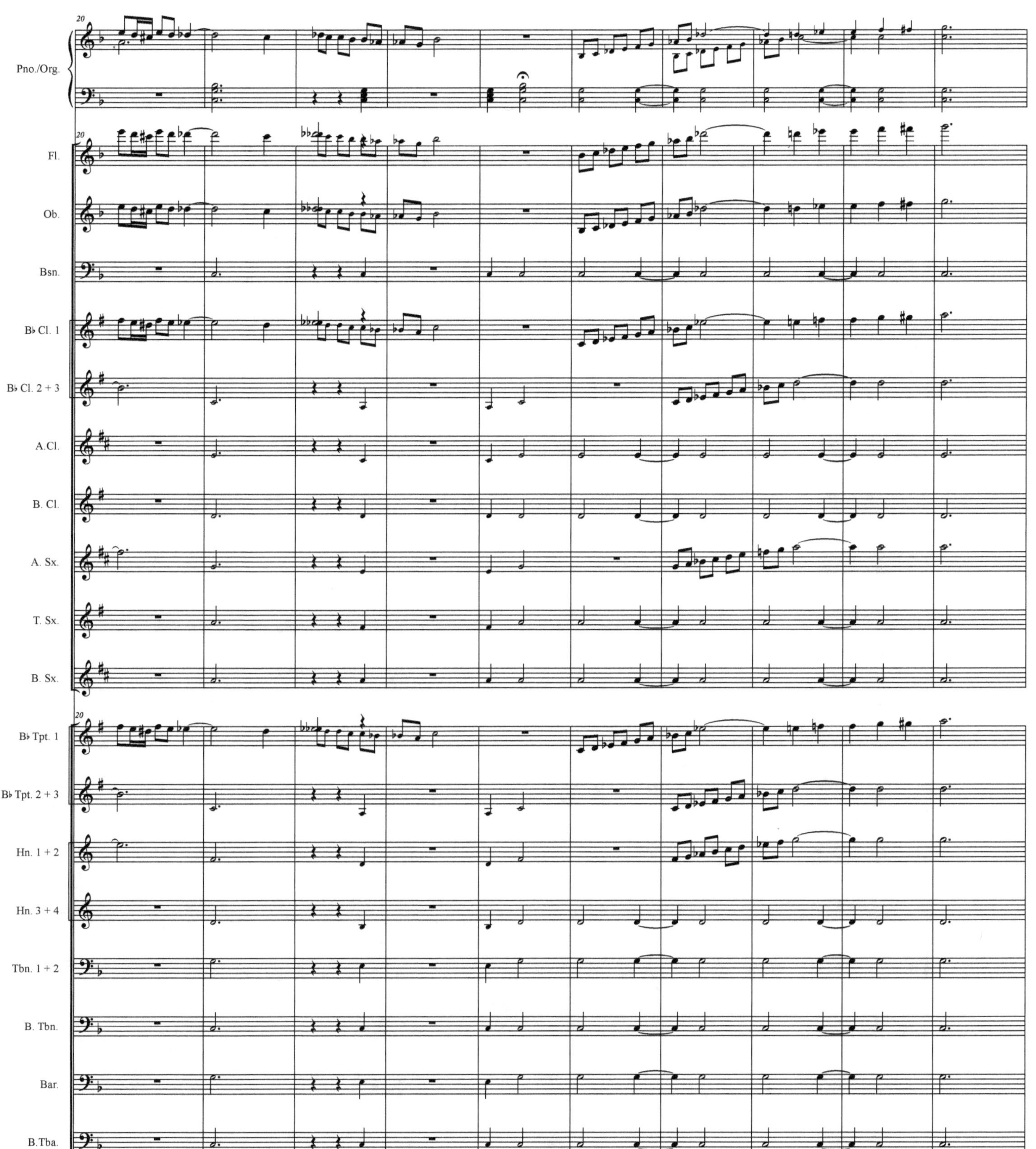
20
Pno./Org.
20
Fl.
Ob.
Bsn.
B♭ Cl. 1
B♭ Cl. 2 + 3
A.Cl.
B. Cl.
A. Sx.
T. Sx.
B. Sx.
20
B♭ Tpt. 1
B♭ Tpt. 2 + 3
Hn. 1 + 2
Hn. 3 + 4
Tbn. 1 + 2
B. Tbn.
Bar.
B.Tba.

N

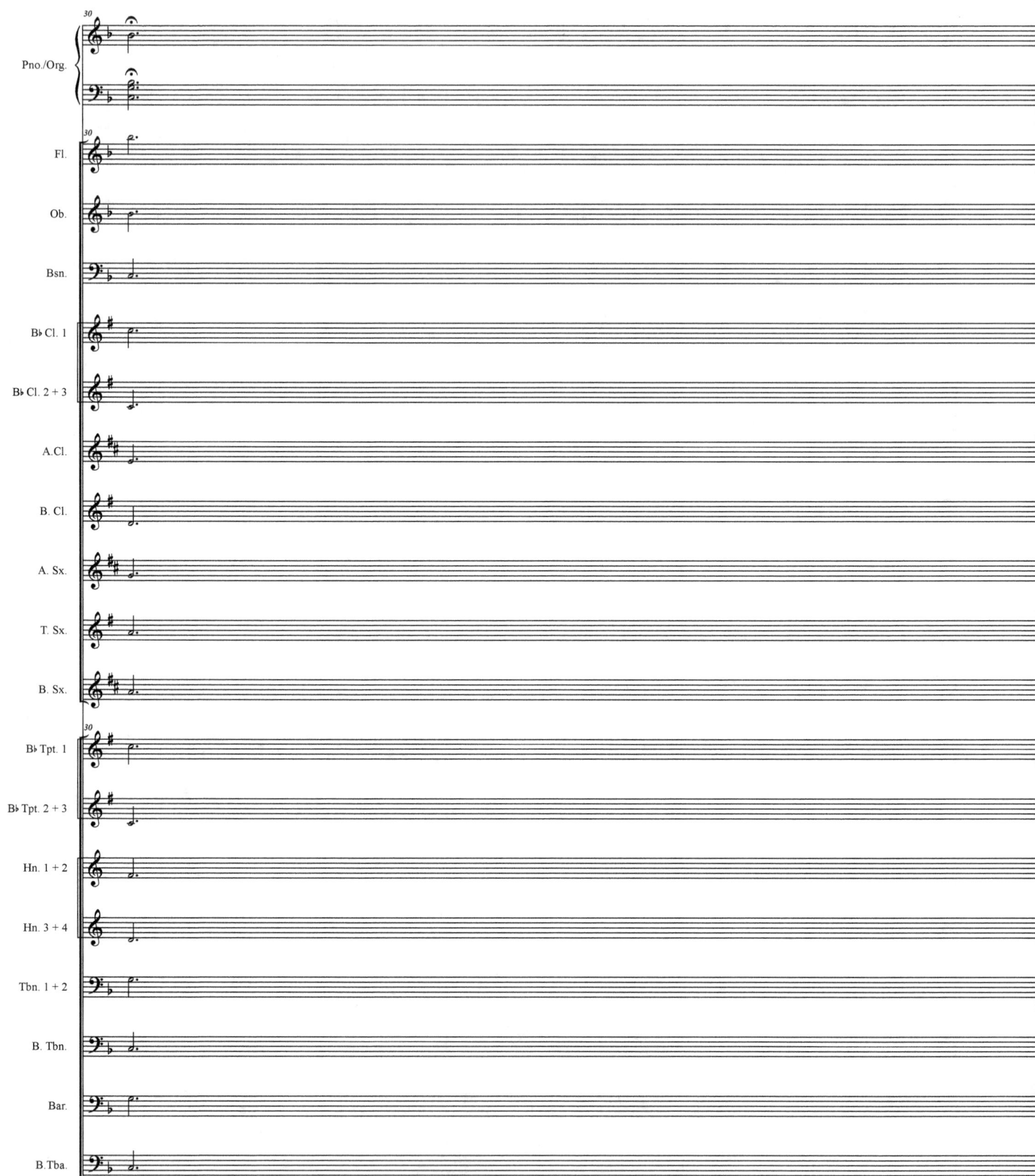

N

Joost de Groot

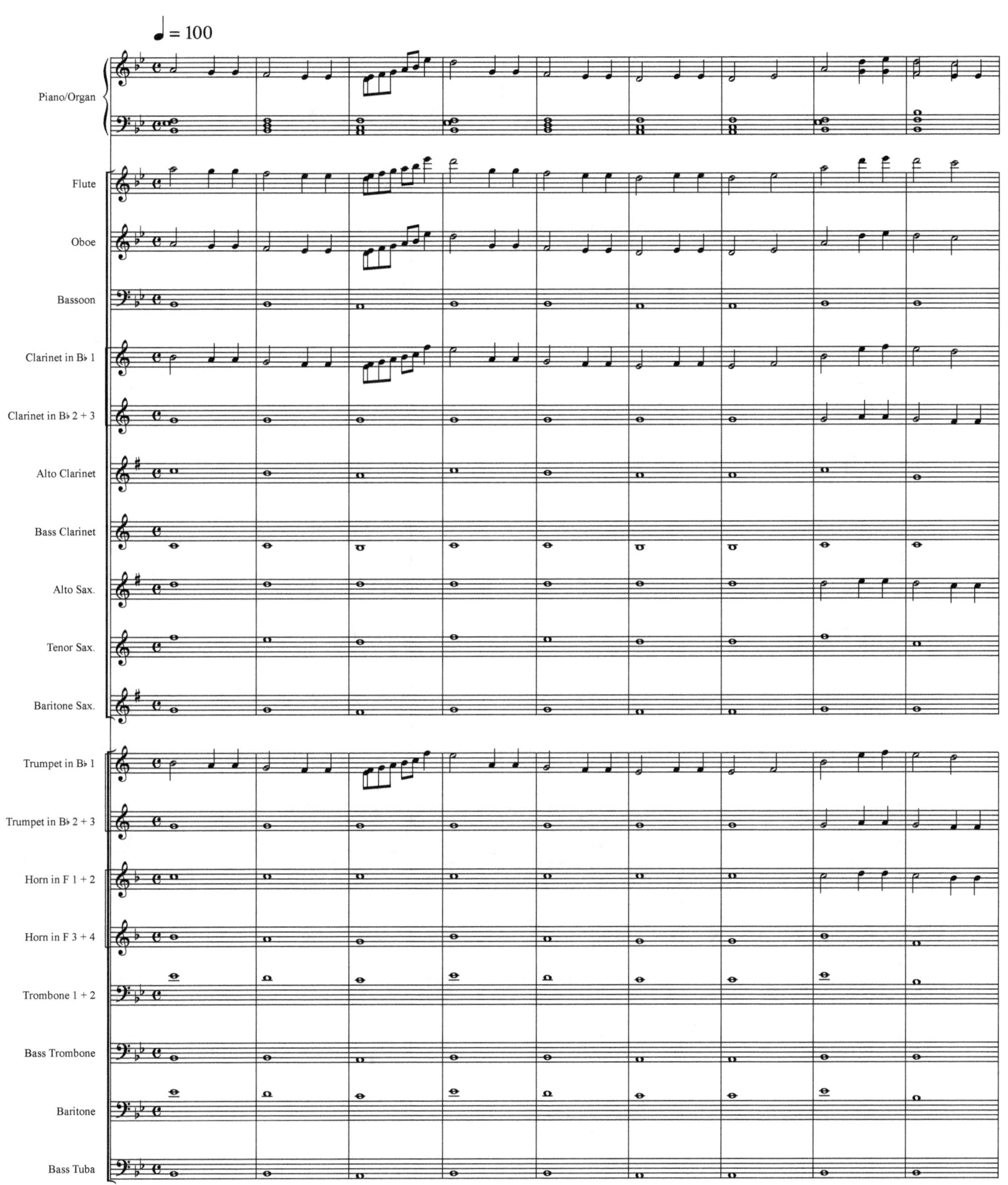

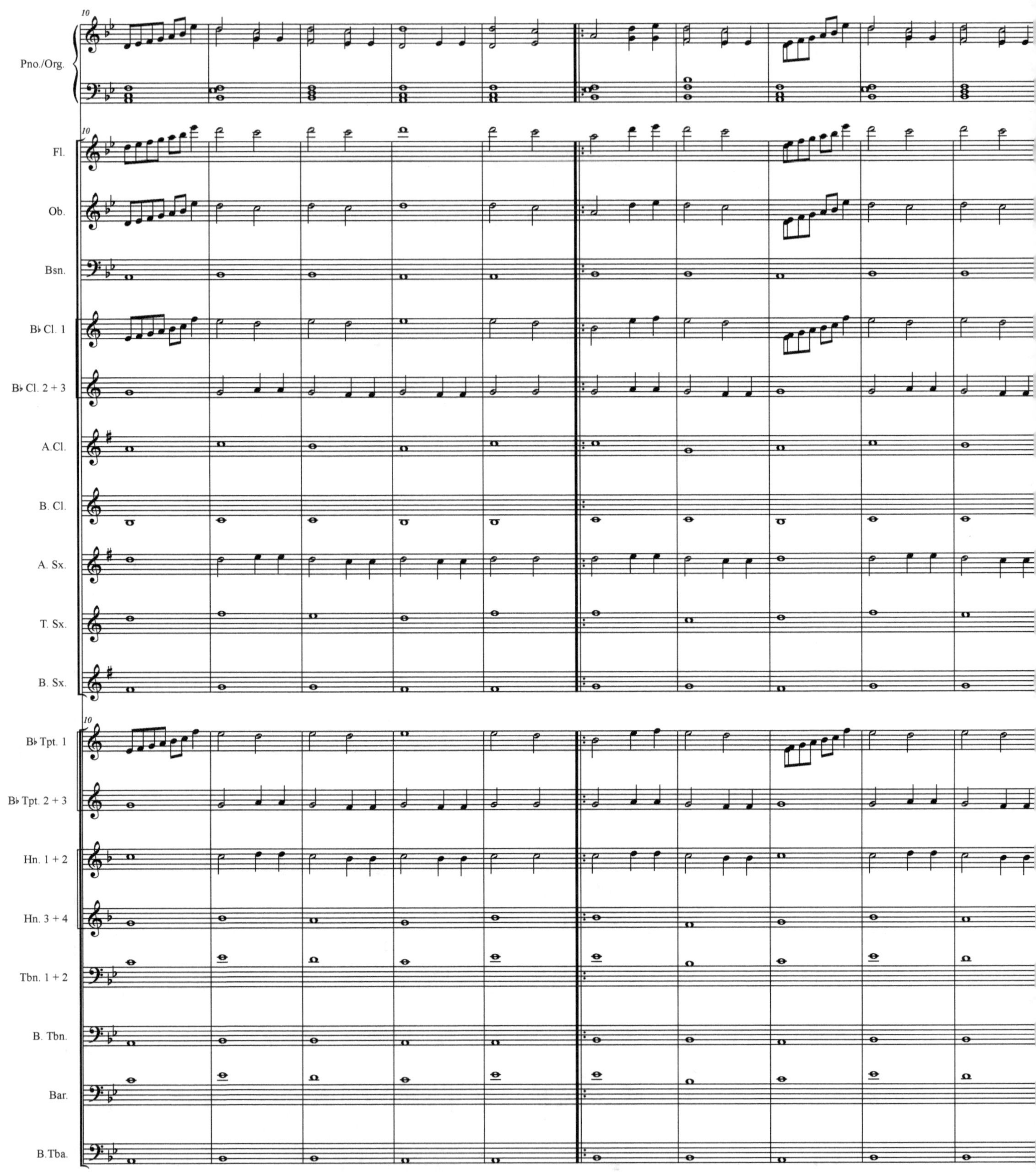
Pno./Org.
Fl.
Ob.
Bsn.
B♭ Cl. 1
B♭ Cl. 2 + 3
A.Cl.
B. Cl.
A. Sx.
T. Sx.
B. Sx.
B♭ Tpt. 1
B♭ Tpt. 2 + 3
Hn. 1 + 2
Hn. 3 + 4
Tbn. 1 + 2
B. Tbn.
Bar.
B.Tba.

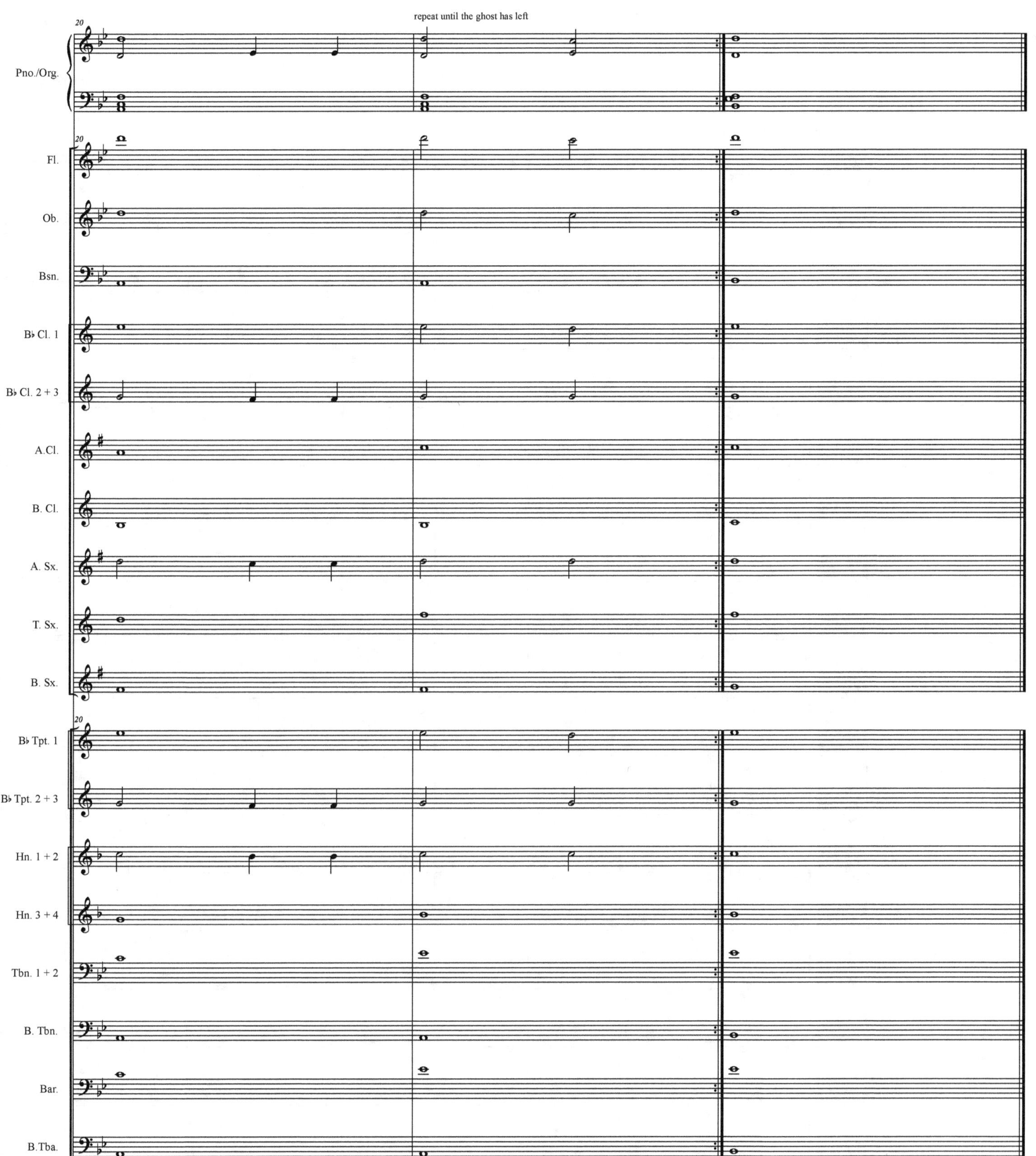
repeat until the ghost has left
20
Pno./Org.
Fl.
Ob.
Bsn.
B♭ Cl. 1
B♭ Cl. 2 + 3
A.Cl.
B. Cl.
A. Sx.
T. Sx.
B. Sx.
B♭ Tpt. 1
B♭ Tpt. 2 + 3
Hn. 1 + 2
Hn. 3 + 4
Tbn. 1 + 2
B. Tbn.
Bar.
B.Tba.

I

Joost de Gro

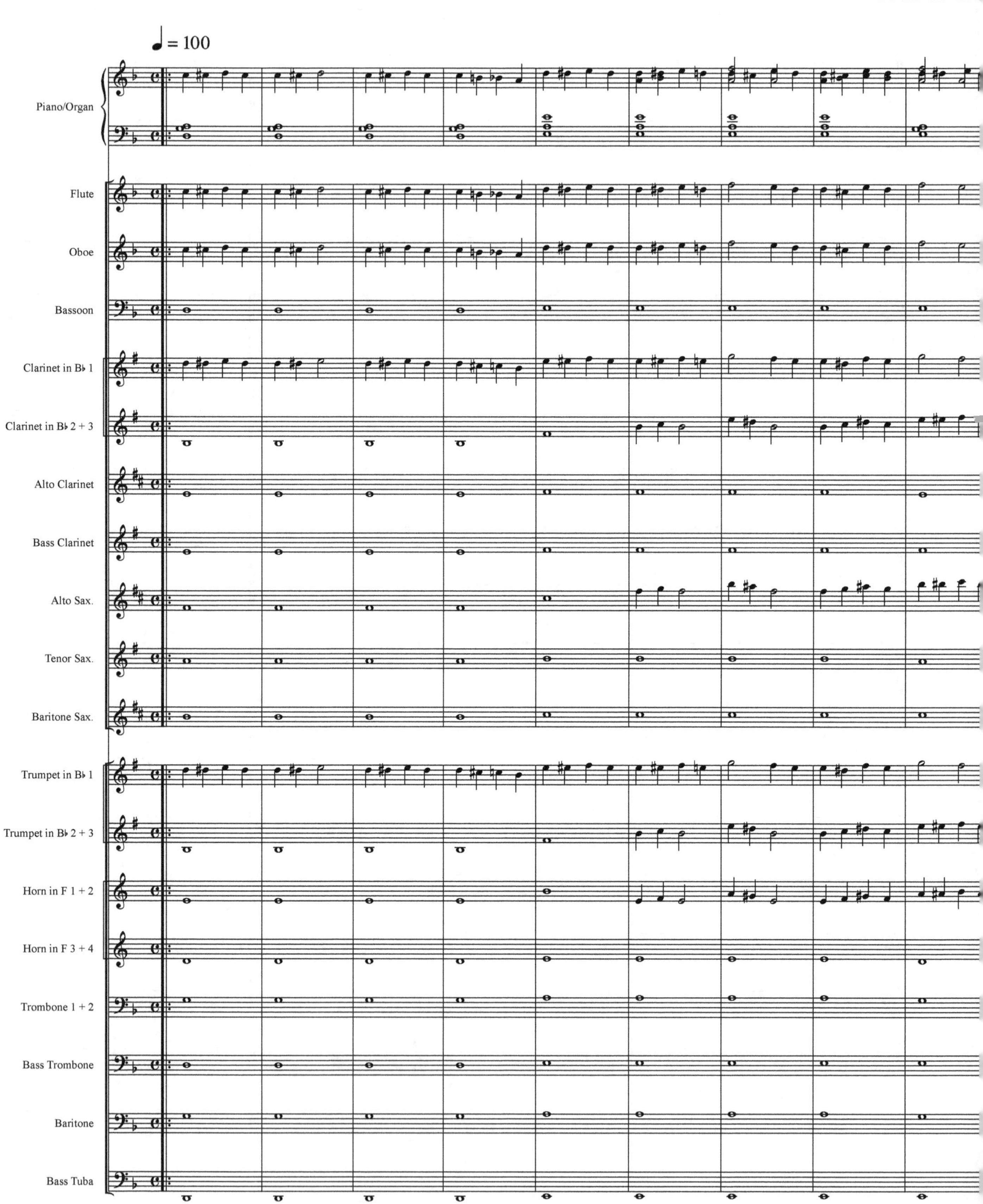

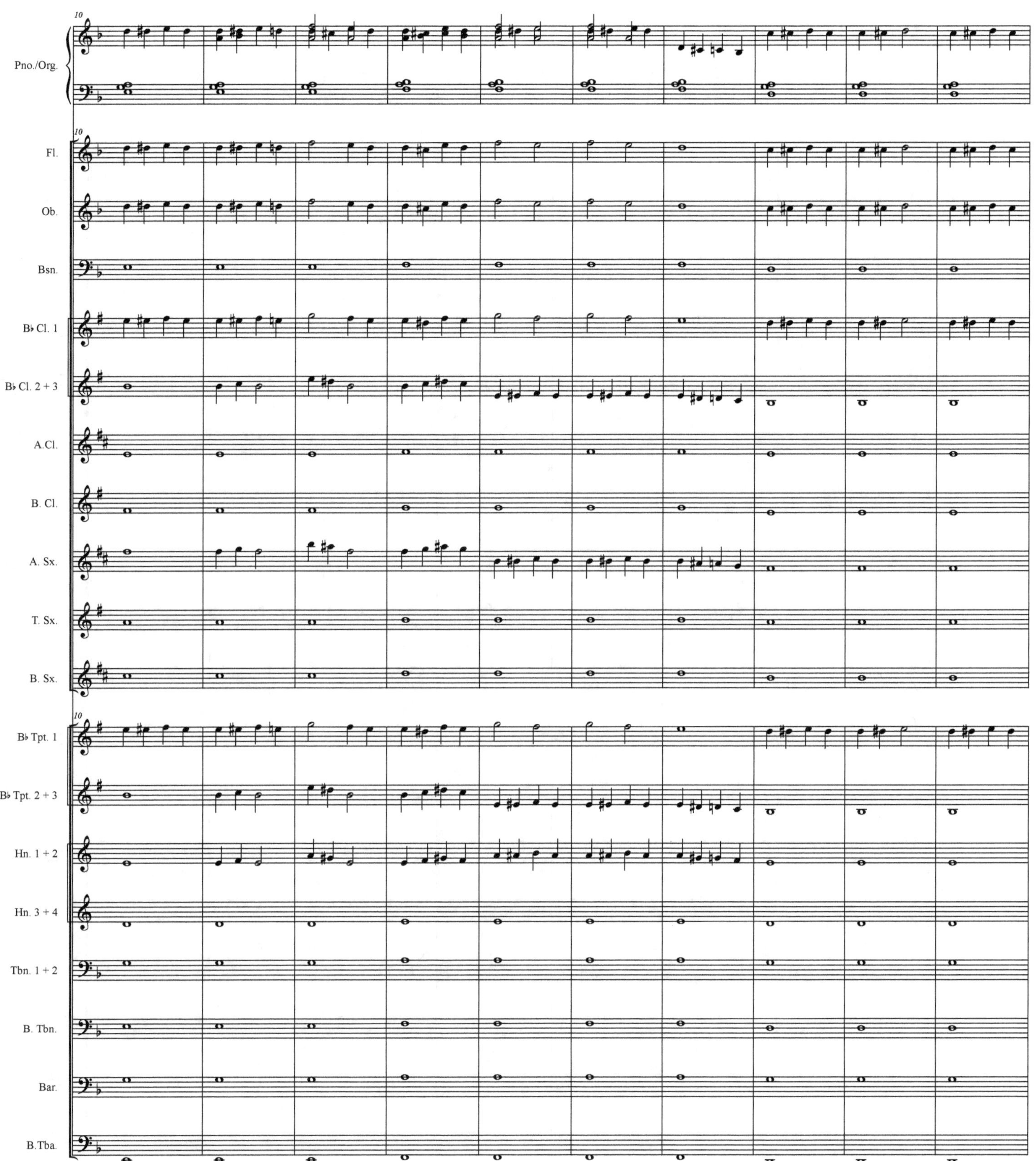
10
Pno./Org.
Fl.
Ob.
Bsn.
B♭ Cl. 1
B♭ Cl. 2 + 3
A.Cl.
B. Cl.
A. Sx.
T. Sx.
B. Sx.
B♭ Tpt. 1
B♭ Tpt. 2 + 3
Hn. 1 + 2
Hn. 3 + 4
Tbn. 1 + 2
B. Tbn.
Bar.
B.Tba.

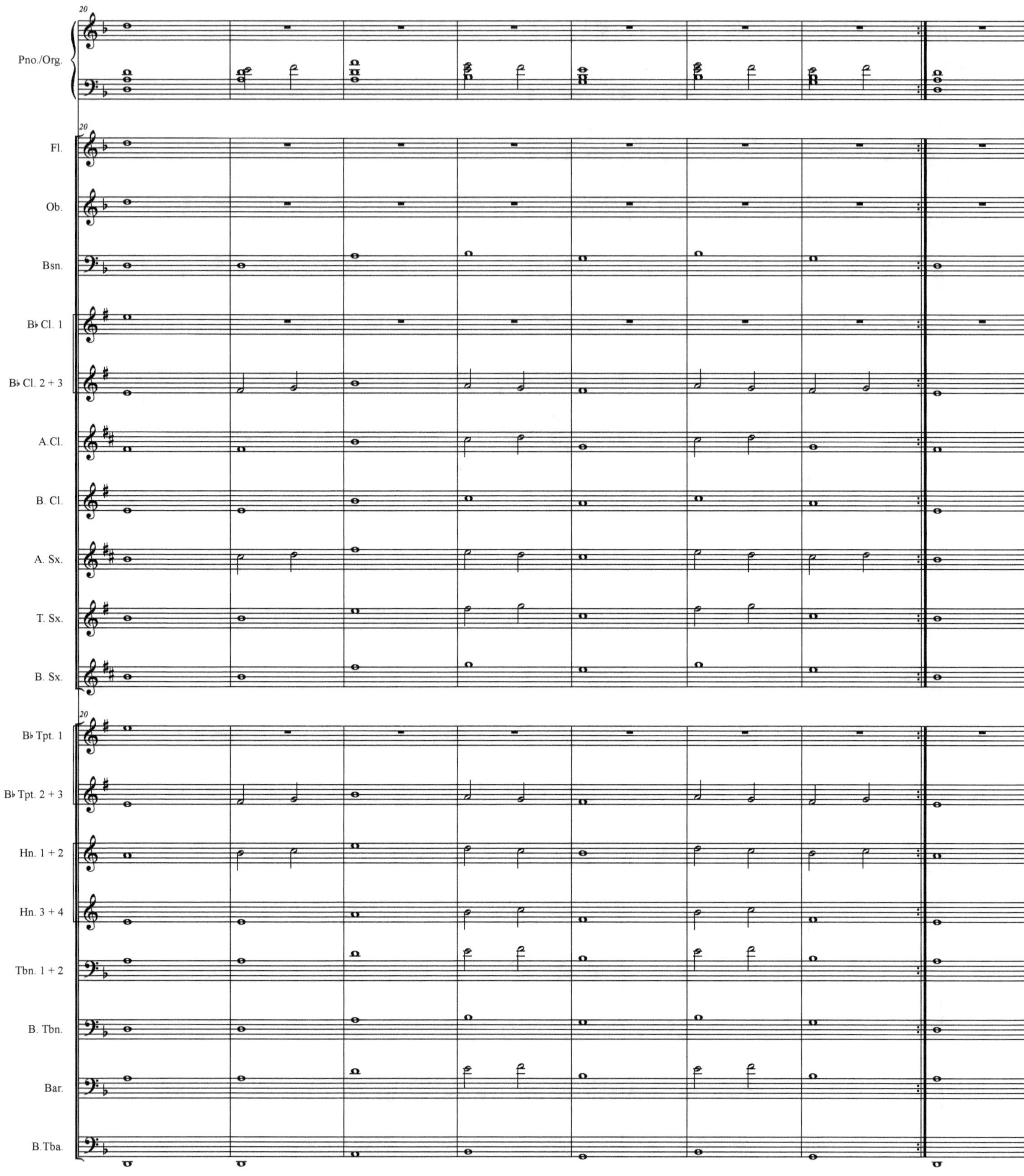
20
Pno./Org.
20
Fl.
Ob.
Bsn.
B♭ Cl. 1
B♭ Cl. 2 + 3
A.Cl.
B. Cl.
A. Sx.
T. Sx.
B. Sx.
20
B♭ Tpt. 1
B♭ Tpt. 2 + 3
Hn. 1 + 2
Hn. 3 + 4
Tbn. 1 + 2
B. Tbn.
Bar.
B.Tba.

E

Joost de Groot

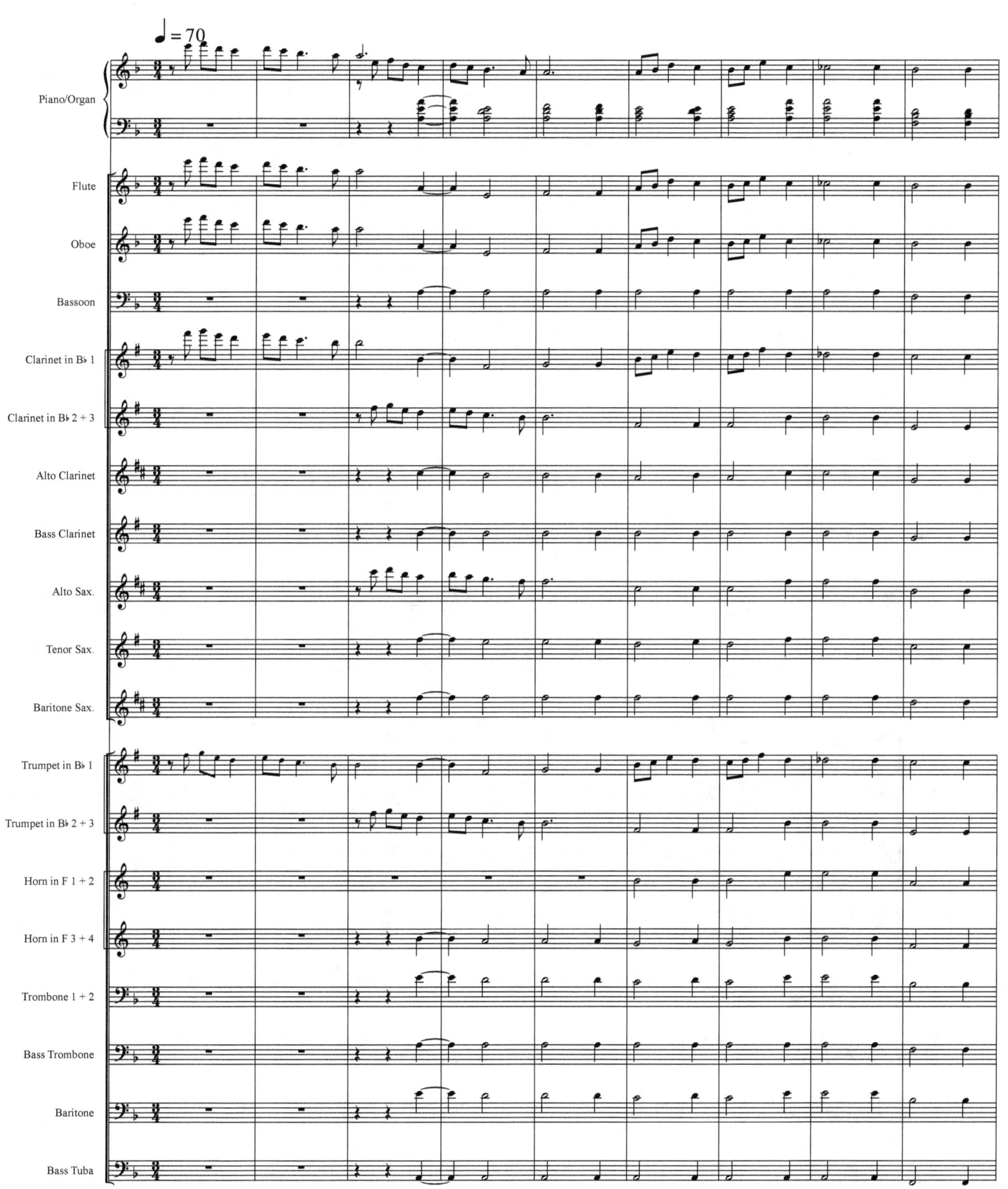

E

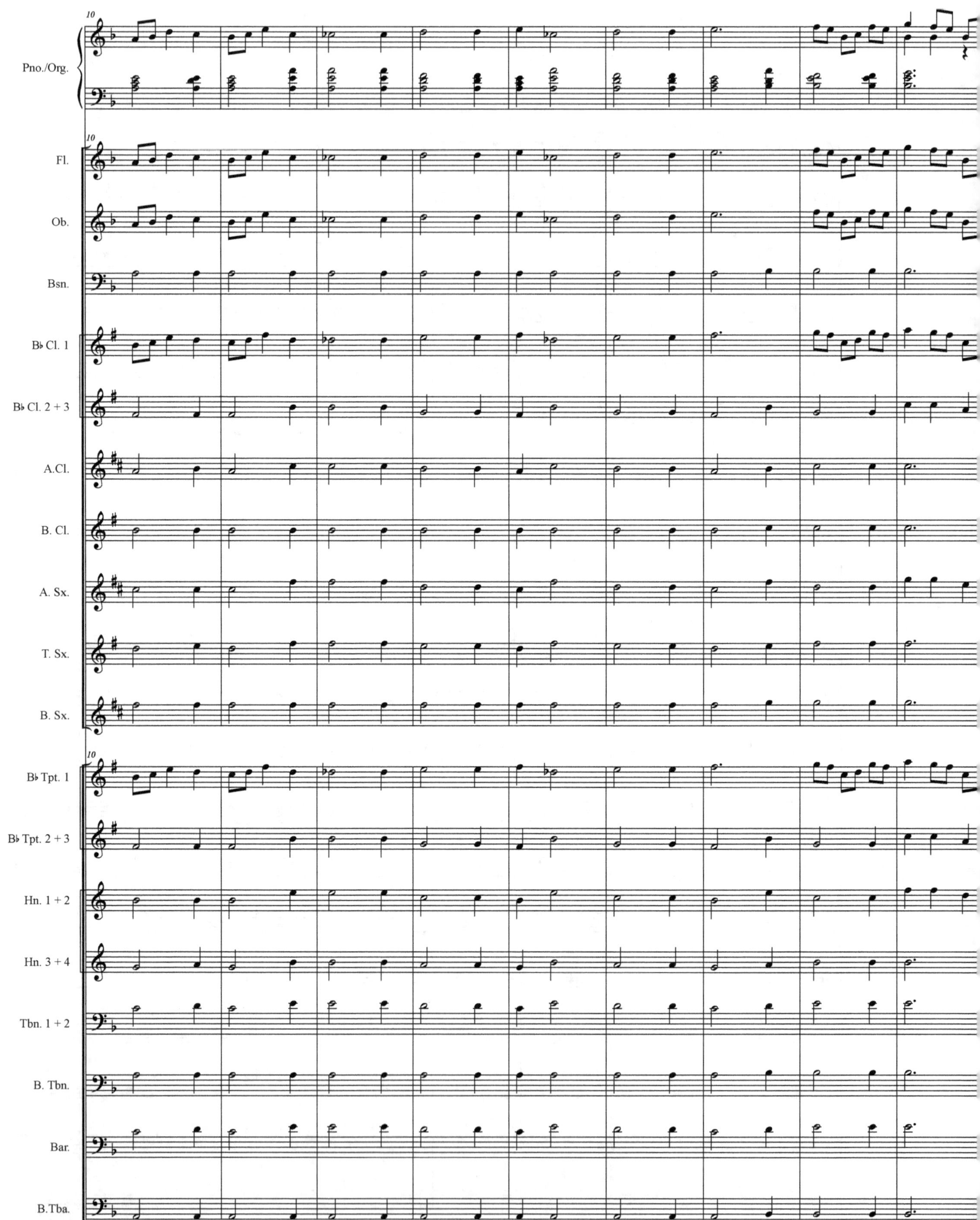

E

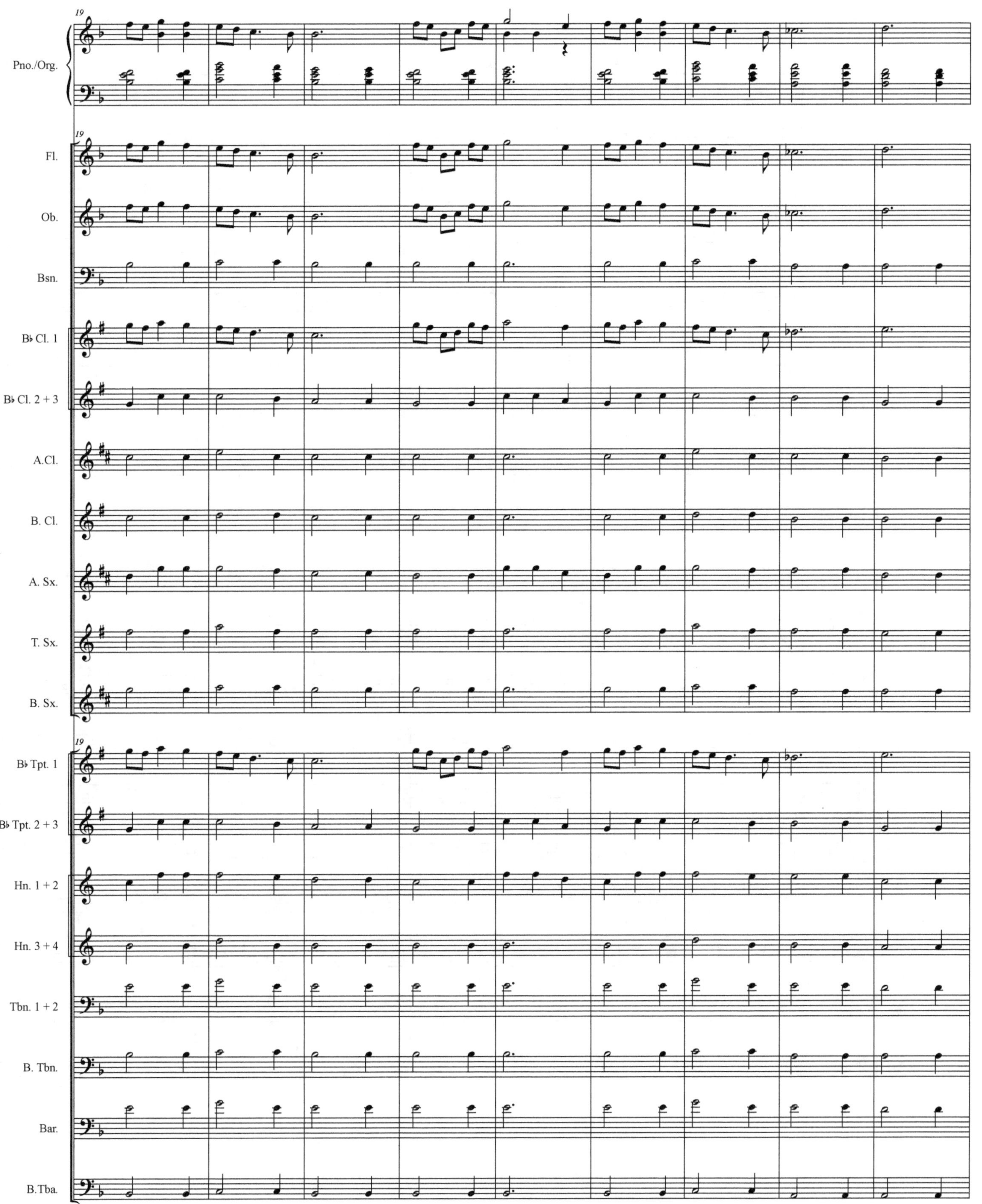

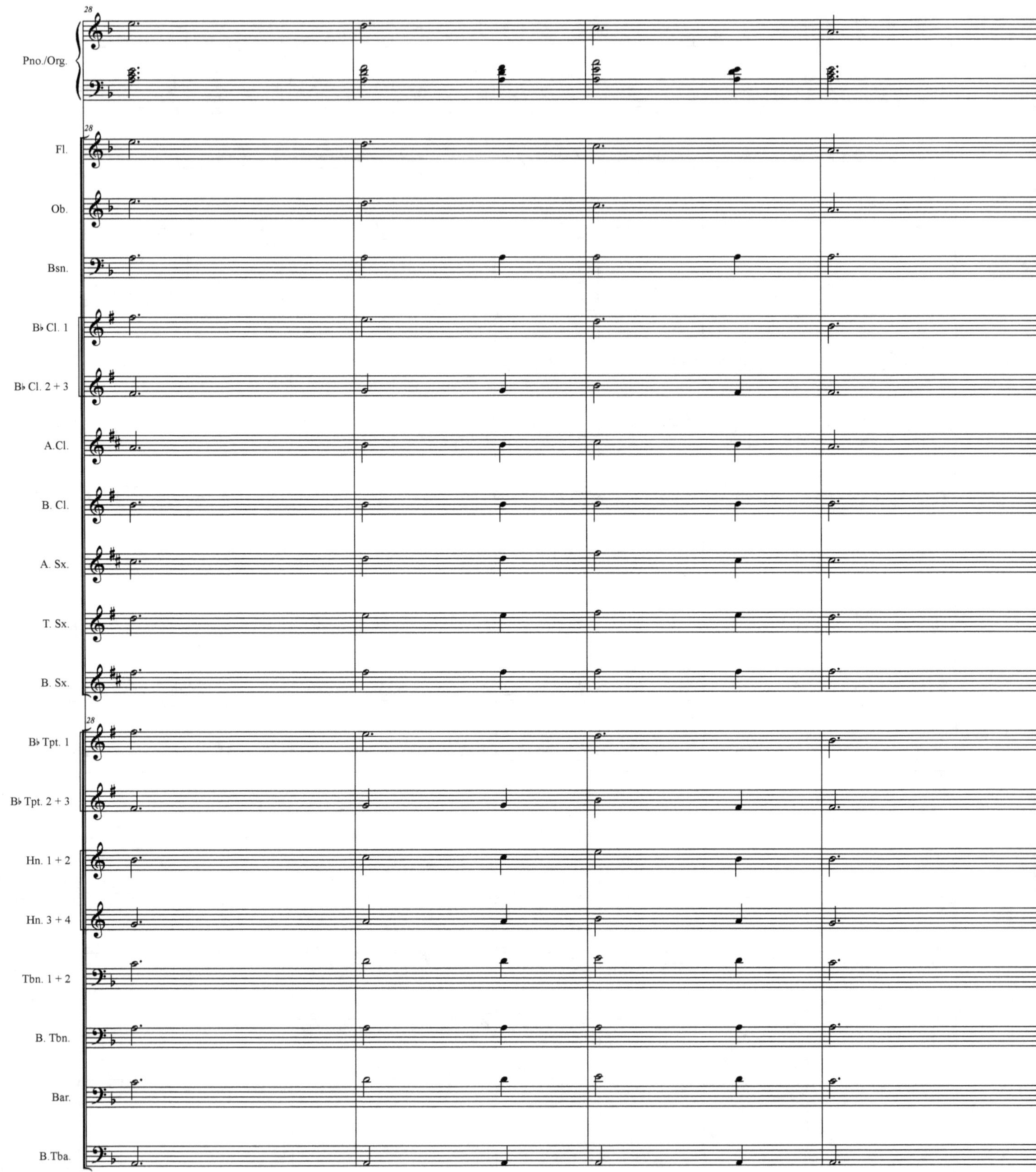
28
Pno./Org.
Fl.
Ob.
Bsn.
B♭ Cl. 1
B♭ Cl. 2 + 3
A.Cl.
B. Cl.
A. Sx.
T. Sx.
B. Sx.
B♭ Tpt. 1
B♭ Tpt. 2 + 3
Hn. 1 + 2
Hn. 3 + 4
Tbn. 1 + 2
B. Tbn.
Bar.
B.Tba.

Part 1: C Flute

J

Joost de Groot

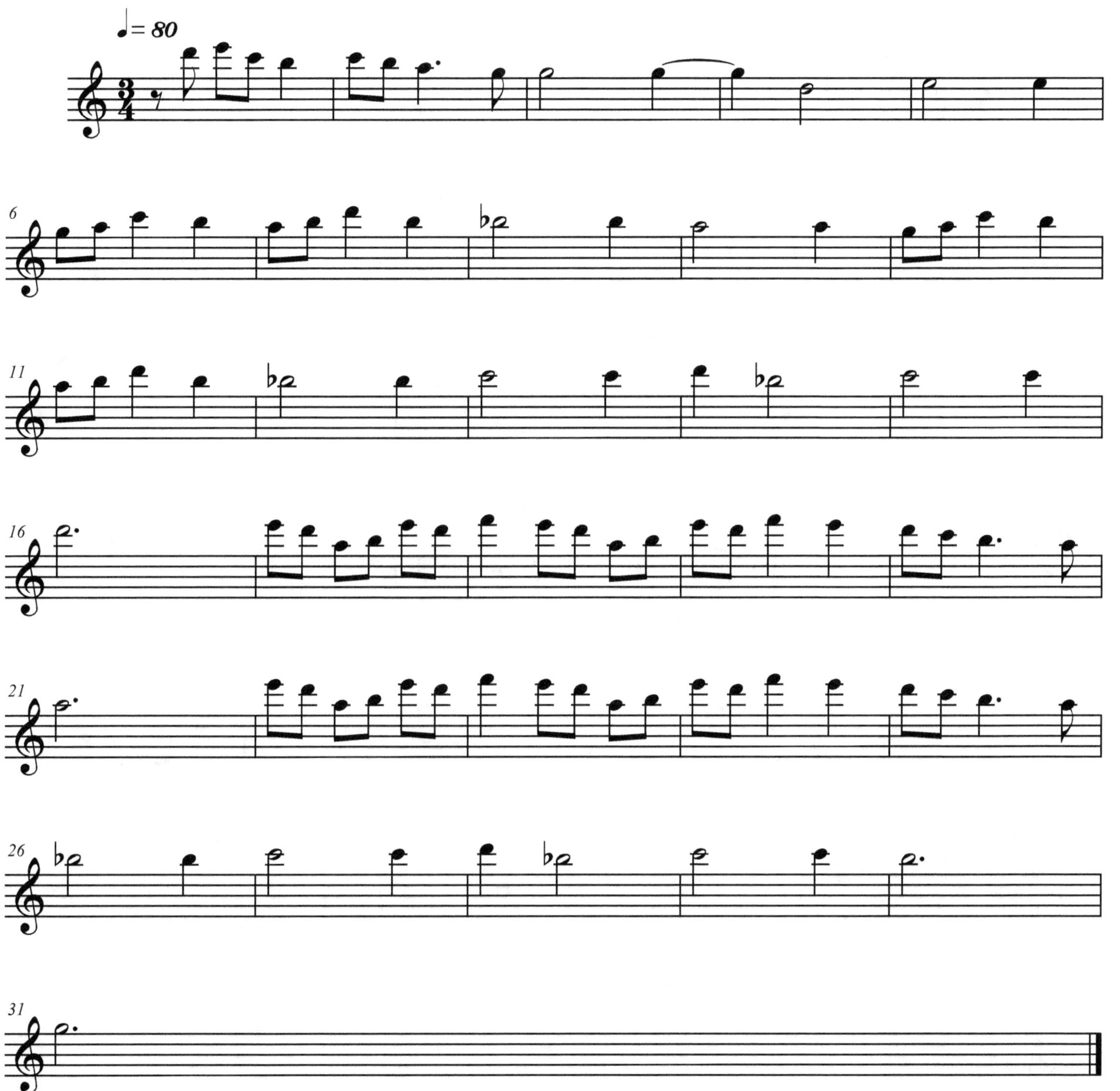

Part 1: C Oboe

J

Joost de Gro

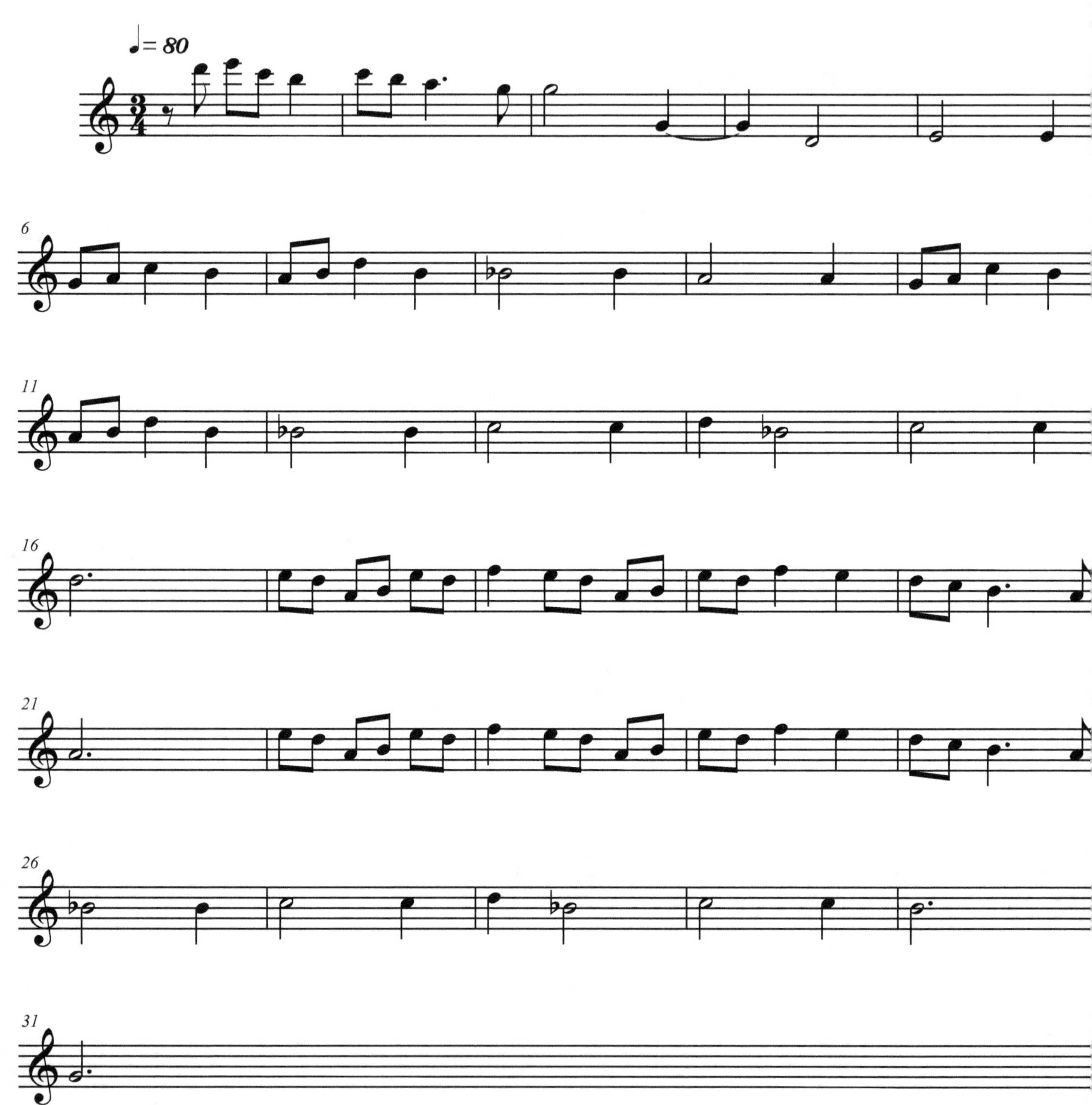

Part 4: C Bassoon

J

Joost de Groot

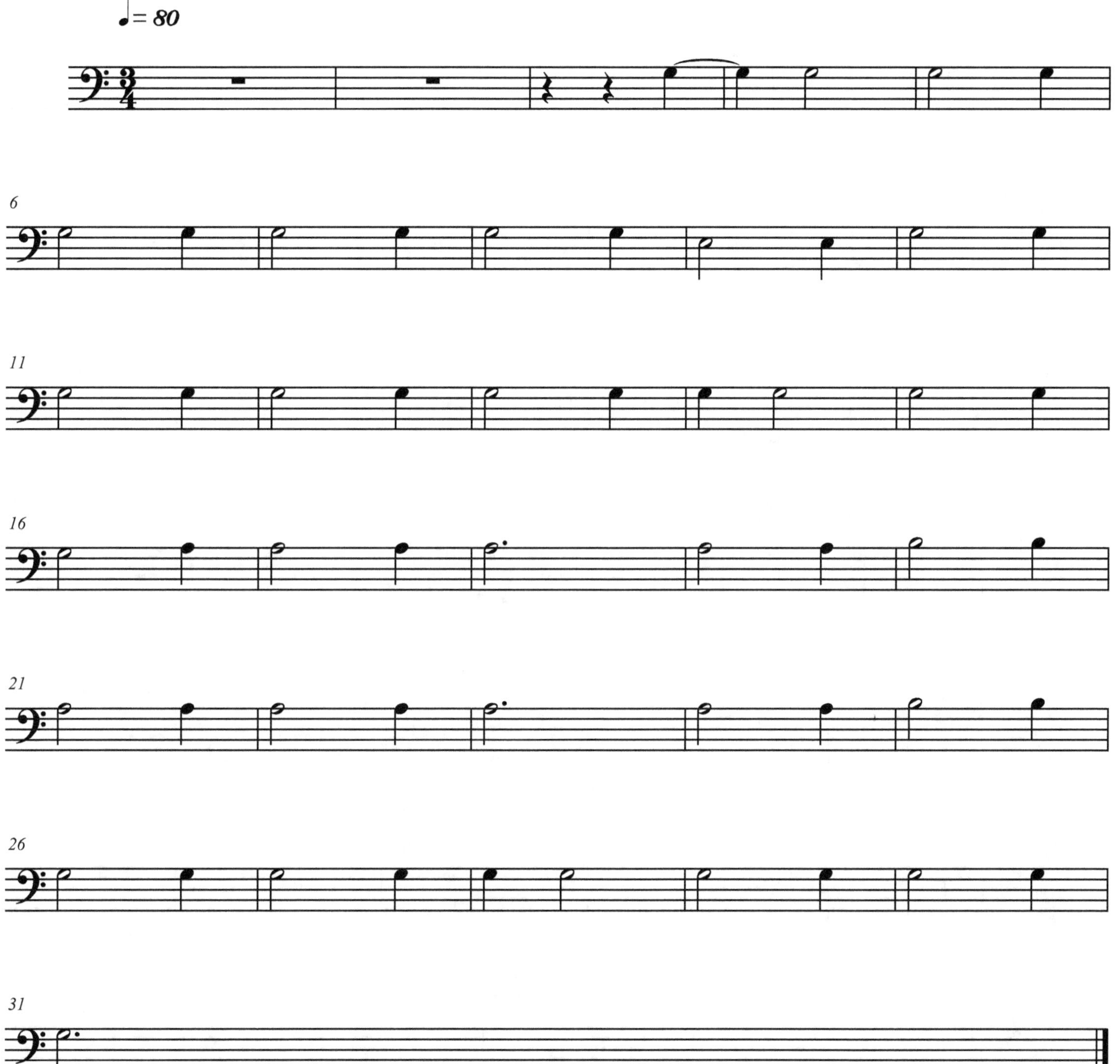

Part 1: Bes Clarinet 1

J

Joost de Gro

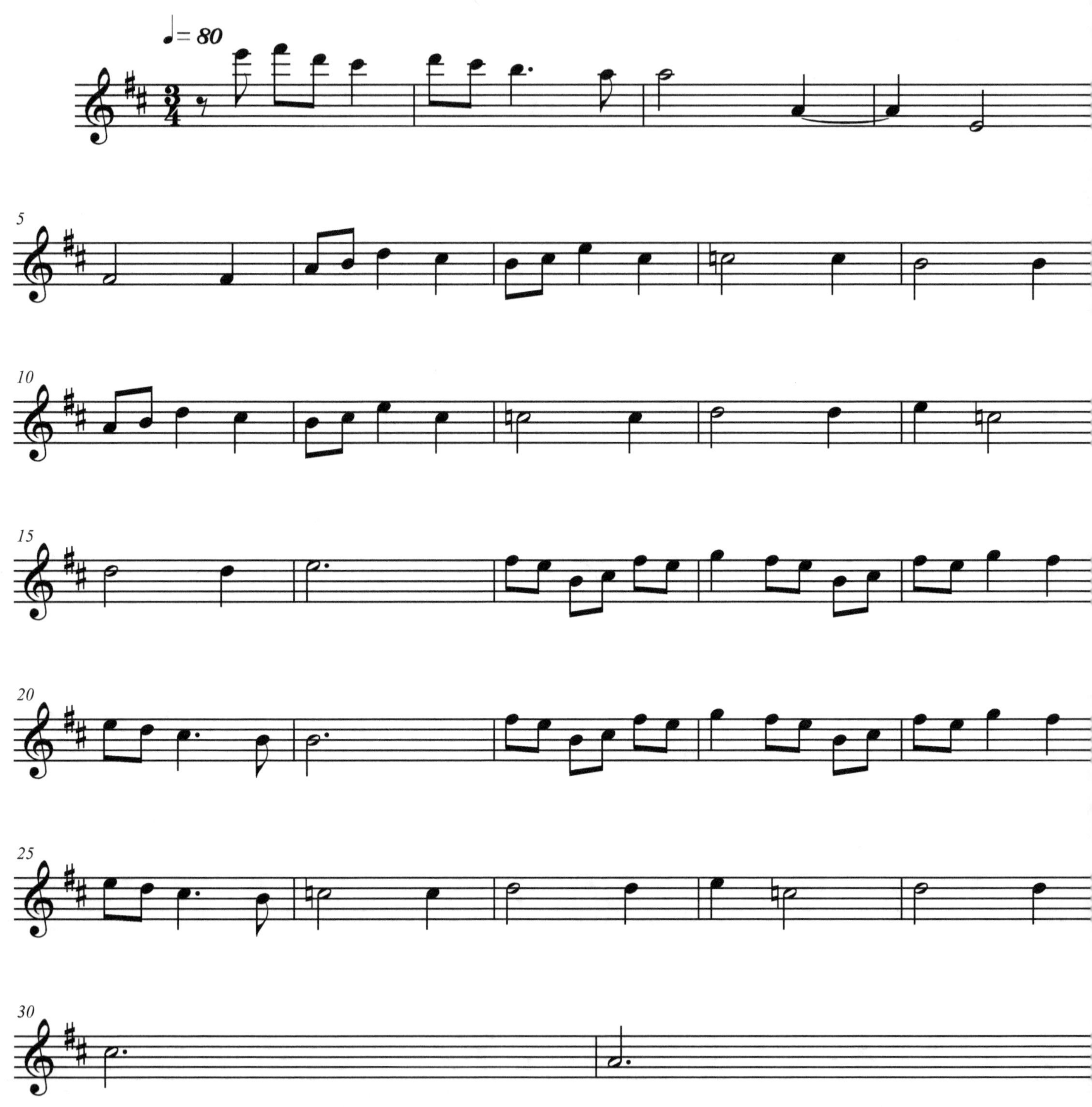

Part 2: Bes Clarinet 2 + 3

J

Joost de Groot

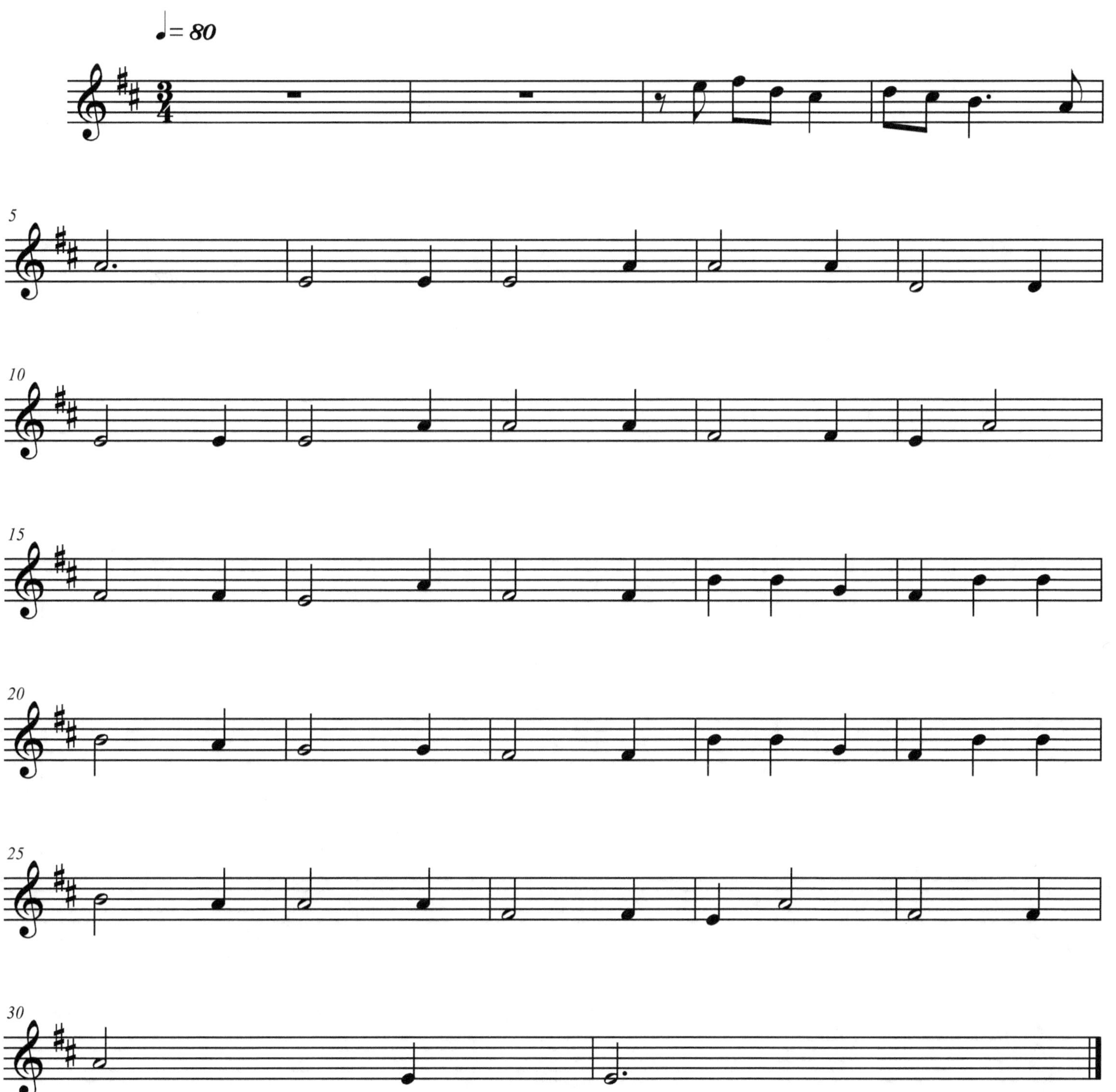

Part 3: Es Alto Clarinet

J

Joost de Gro

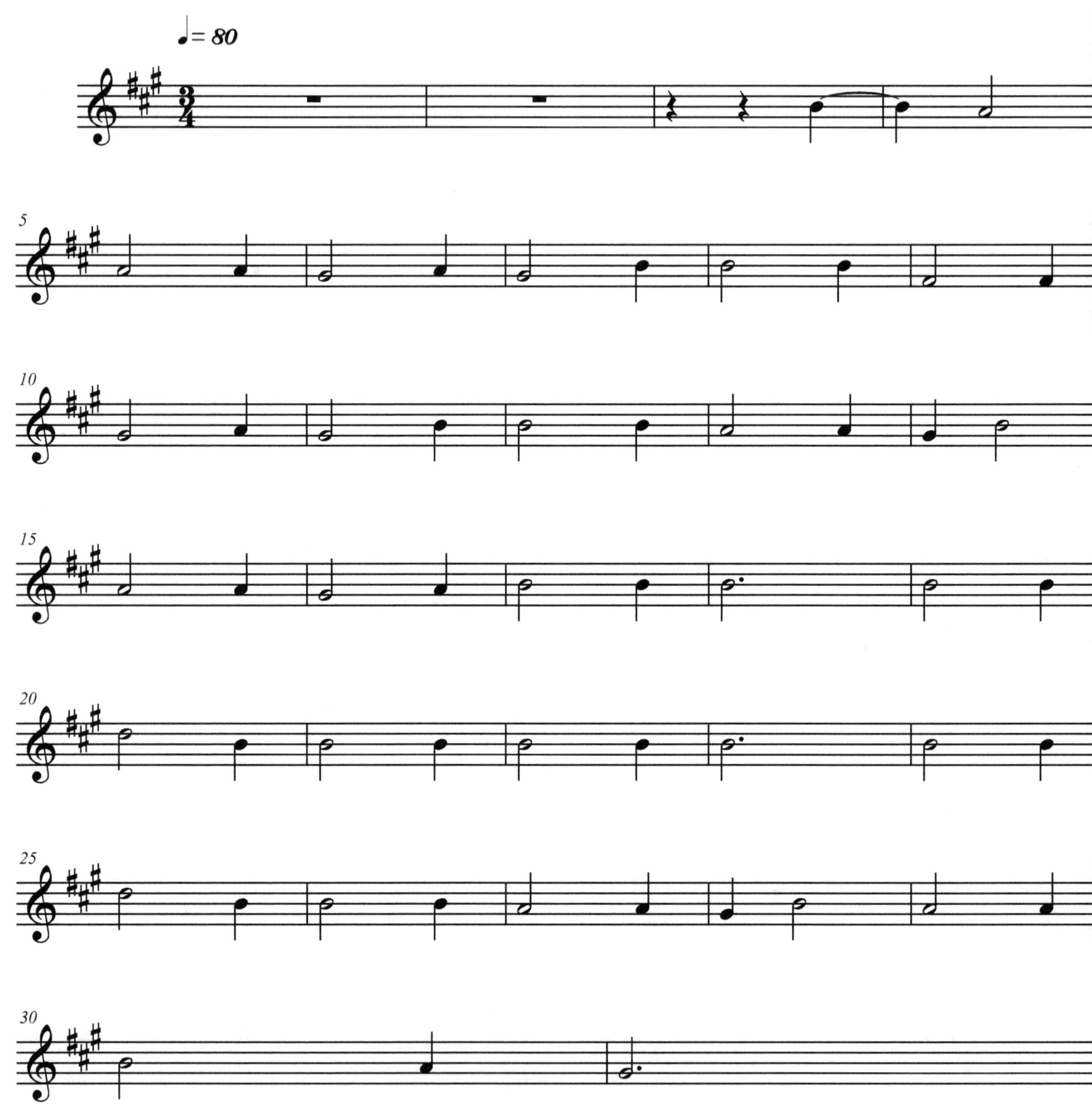

Part 4: Bes Bass Clarinet

J

Joost de Groot

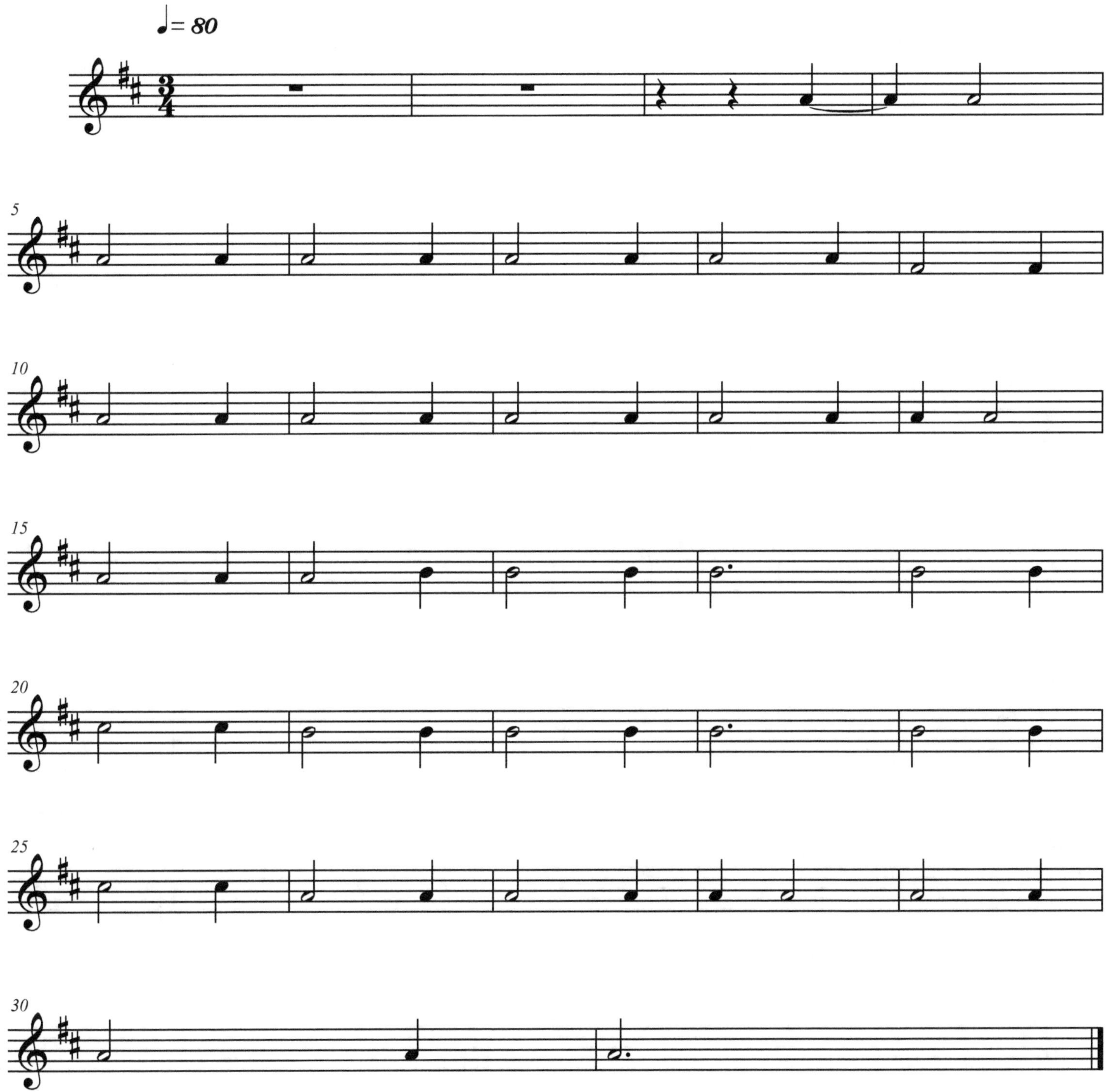

J

Part 2: Es Alto Sax.

Joost de Gro

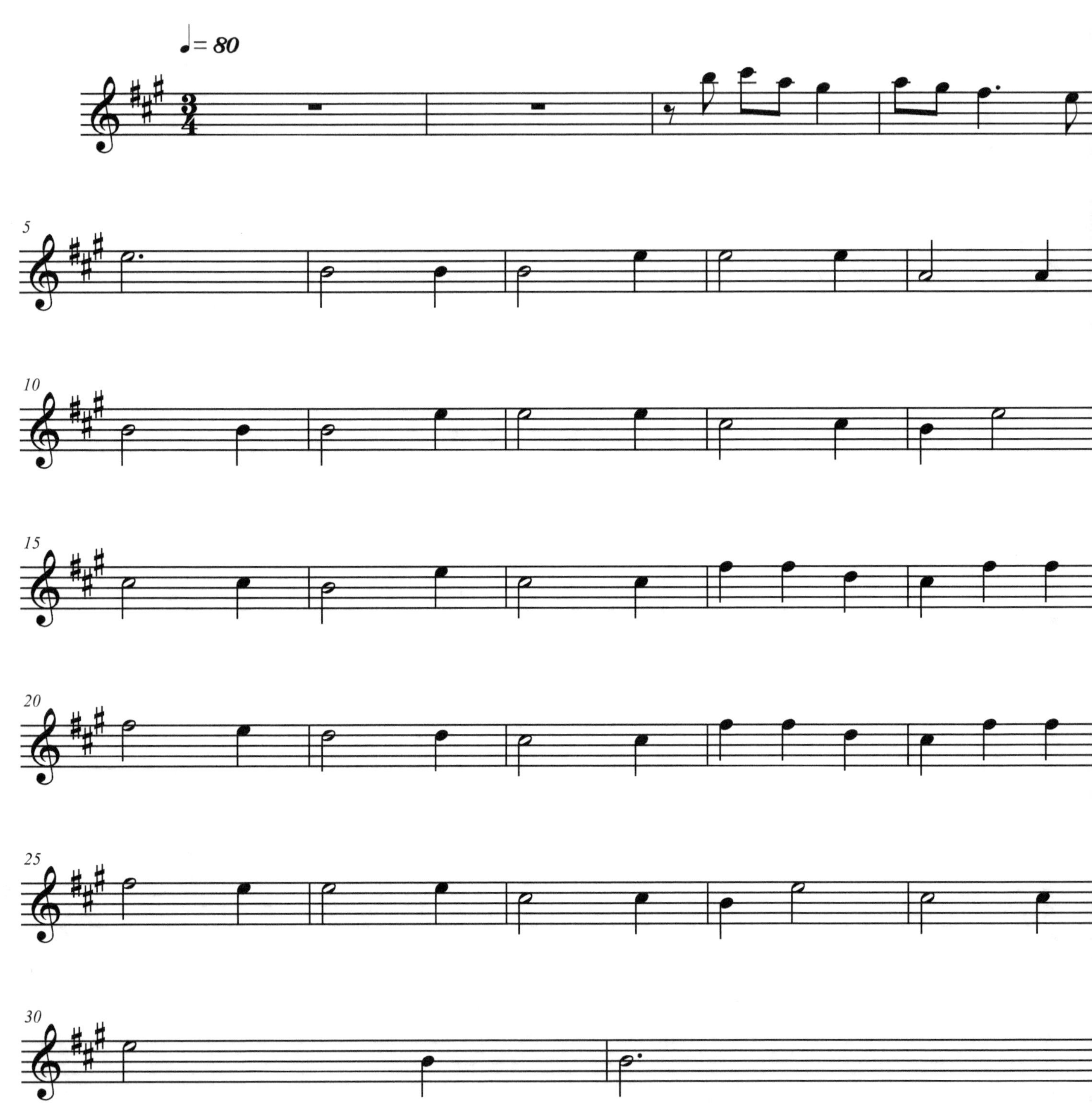

Part 3: Bes Tenor Sax.

J

Joost de Groot

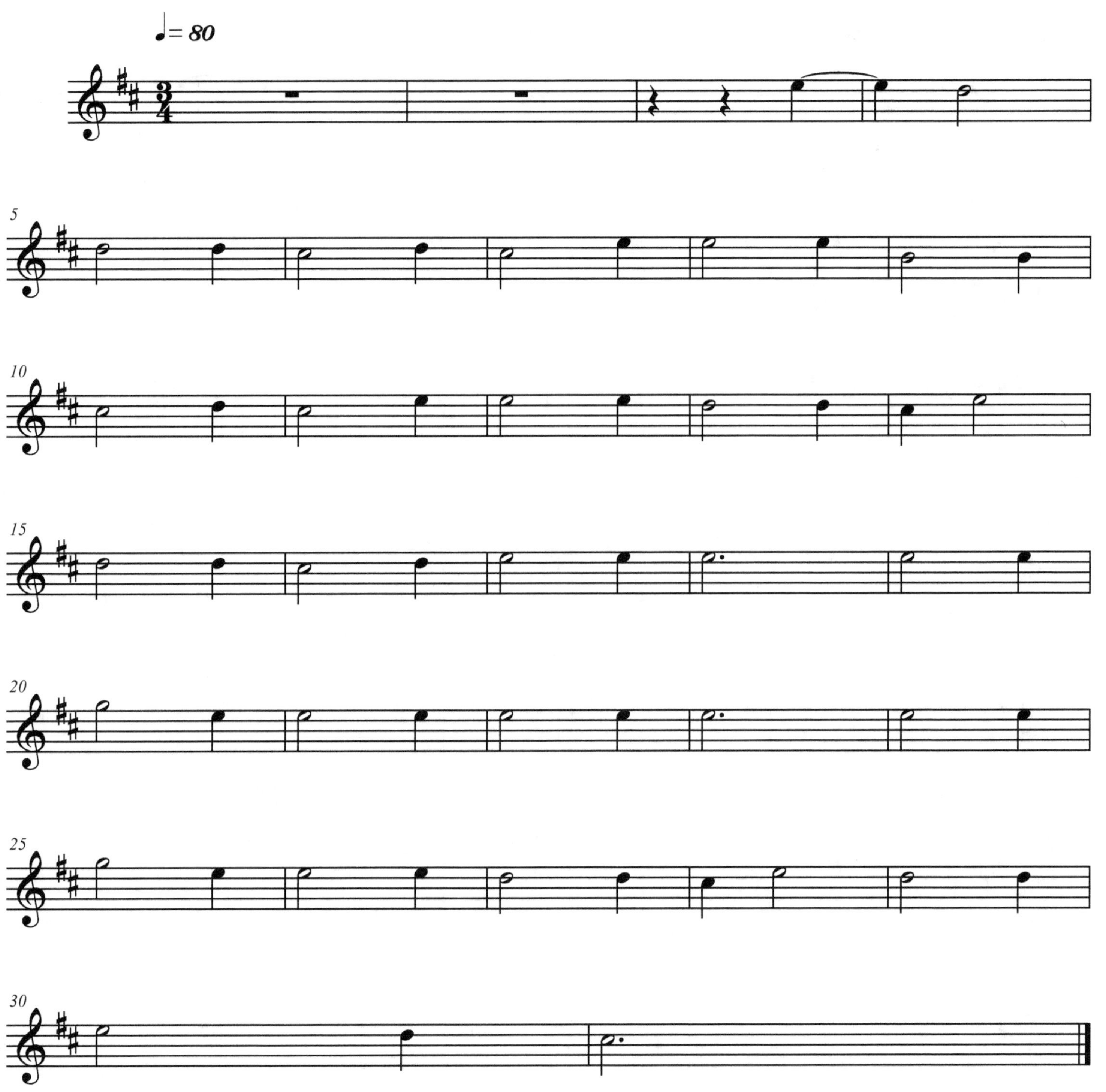

J

Part 4: Es Baritone Sax.

Joost de Gro

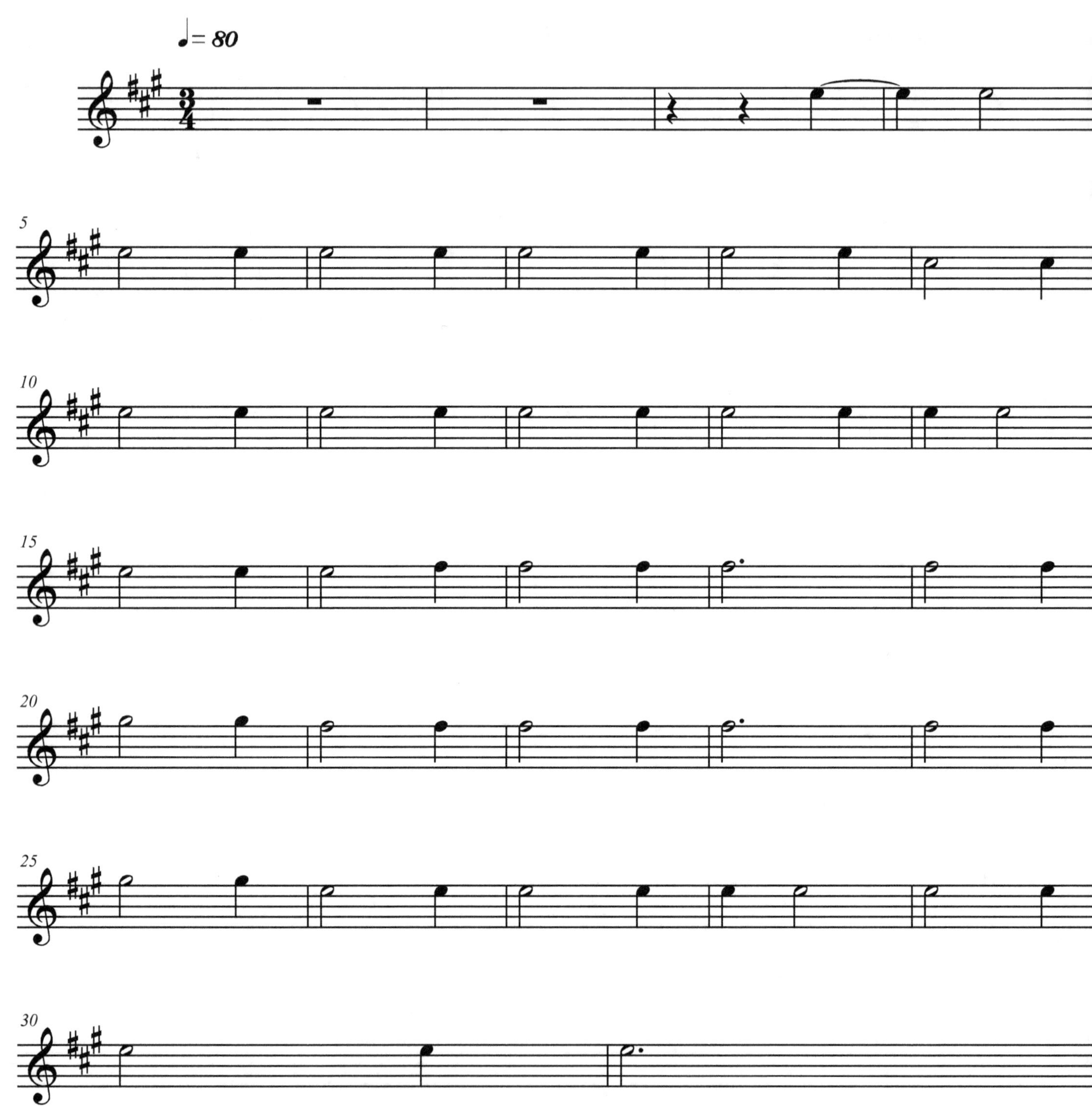

J

Part 1: Bes Trumpet 1

Joost de Groot

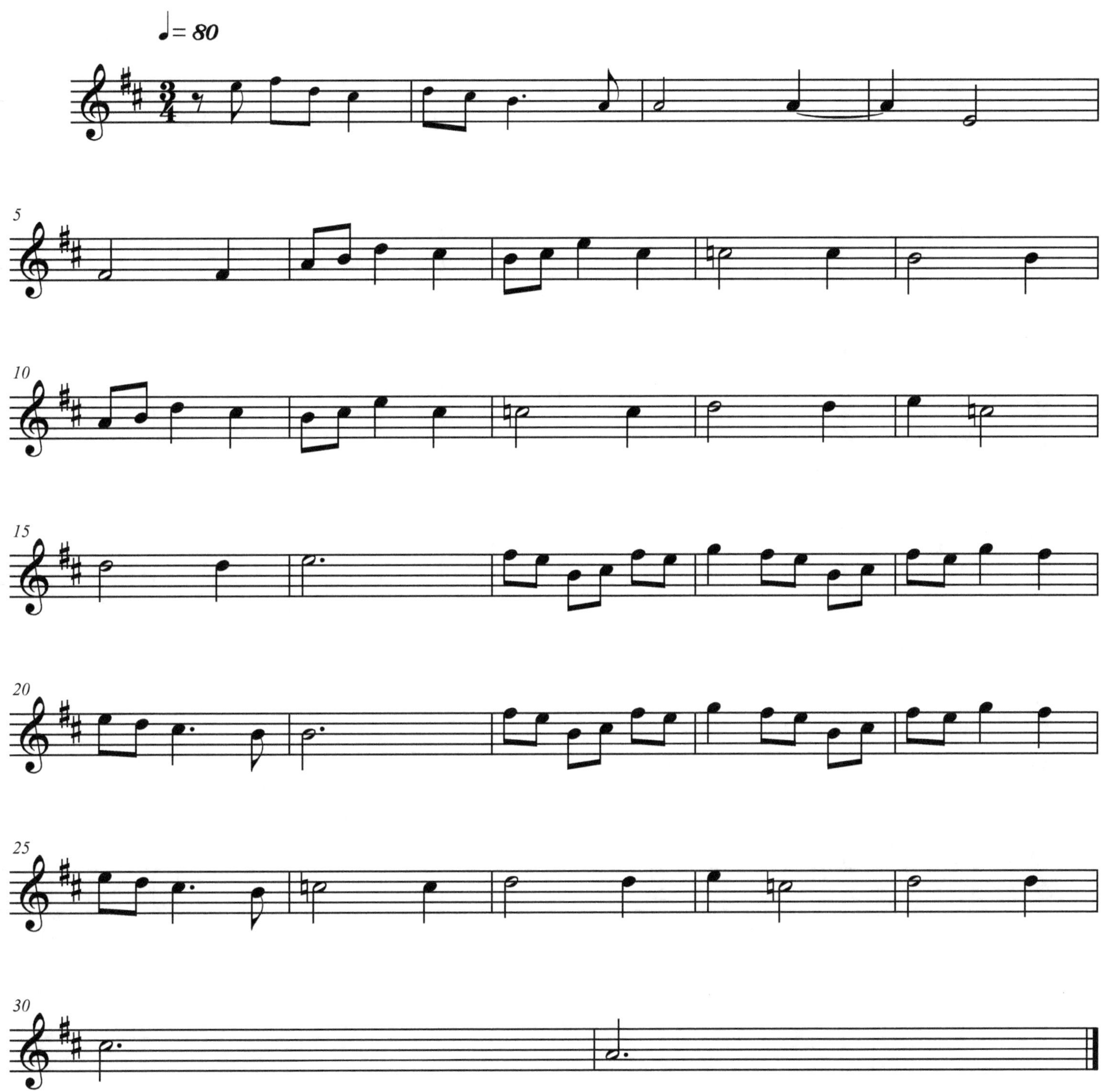

J

Part 2: Bes Trumpet 2 + 3

Joost de Gro

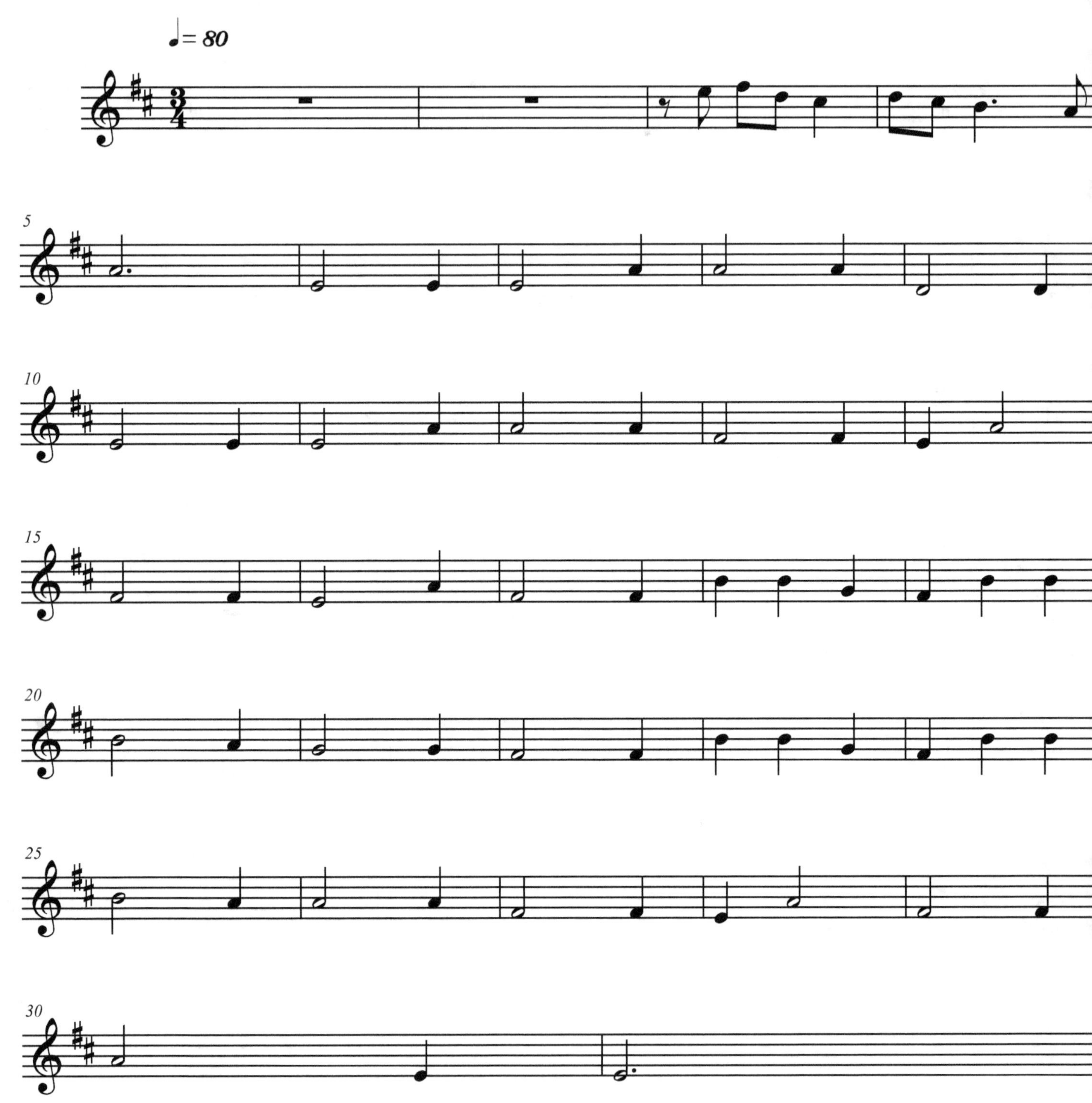

J

Part 2: F Horn 1 + 2

Joost de Groot

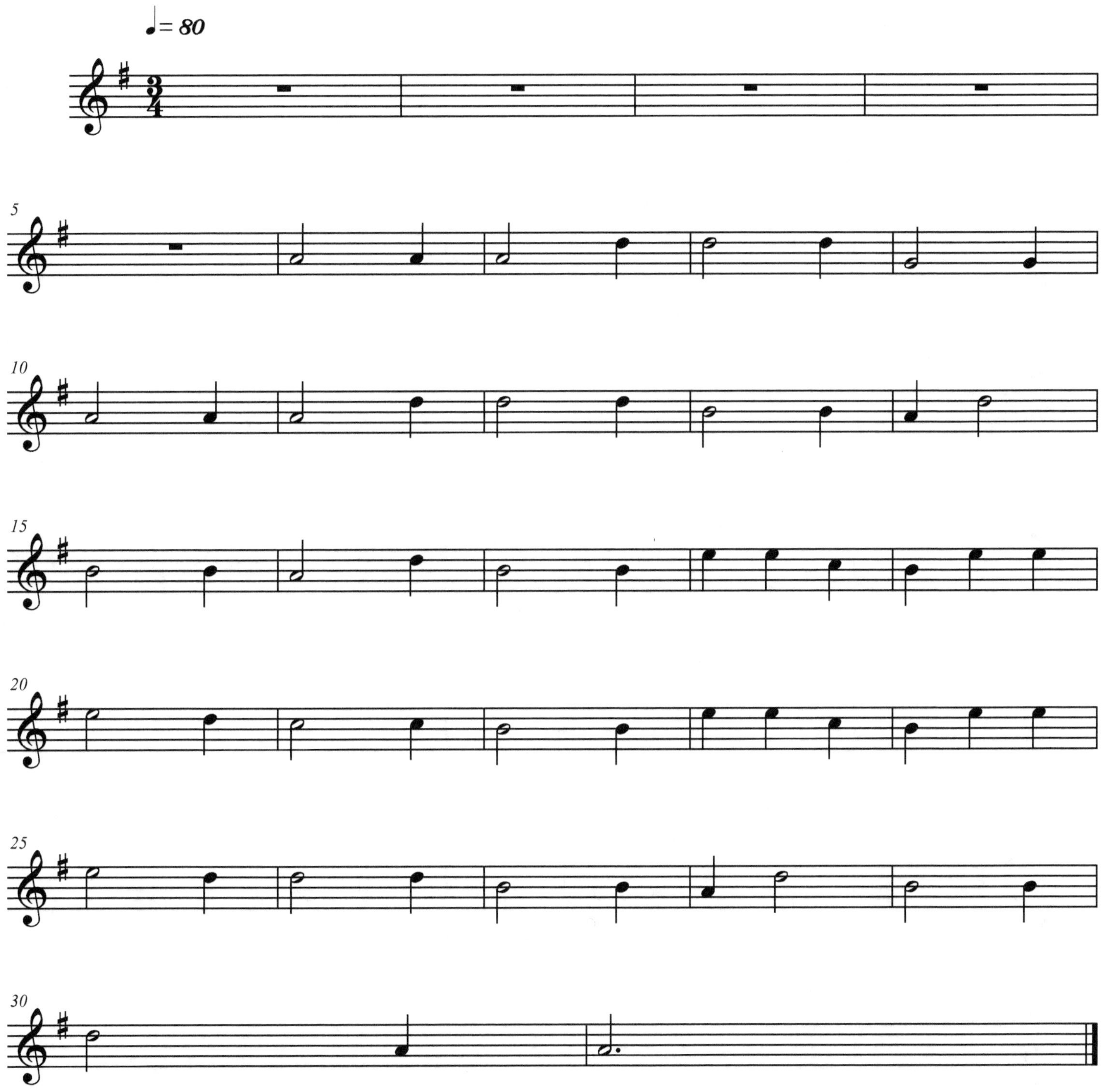

Part 3: F Horn 3 + 4

J

Joost de Gro

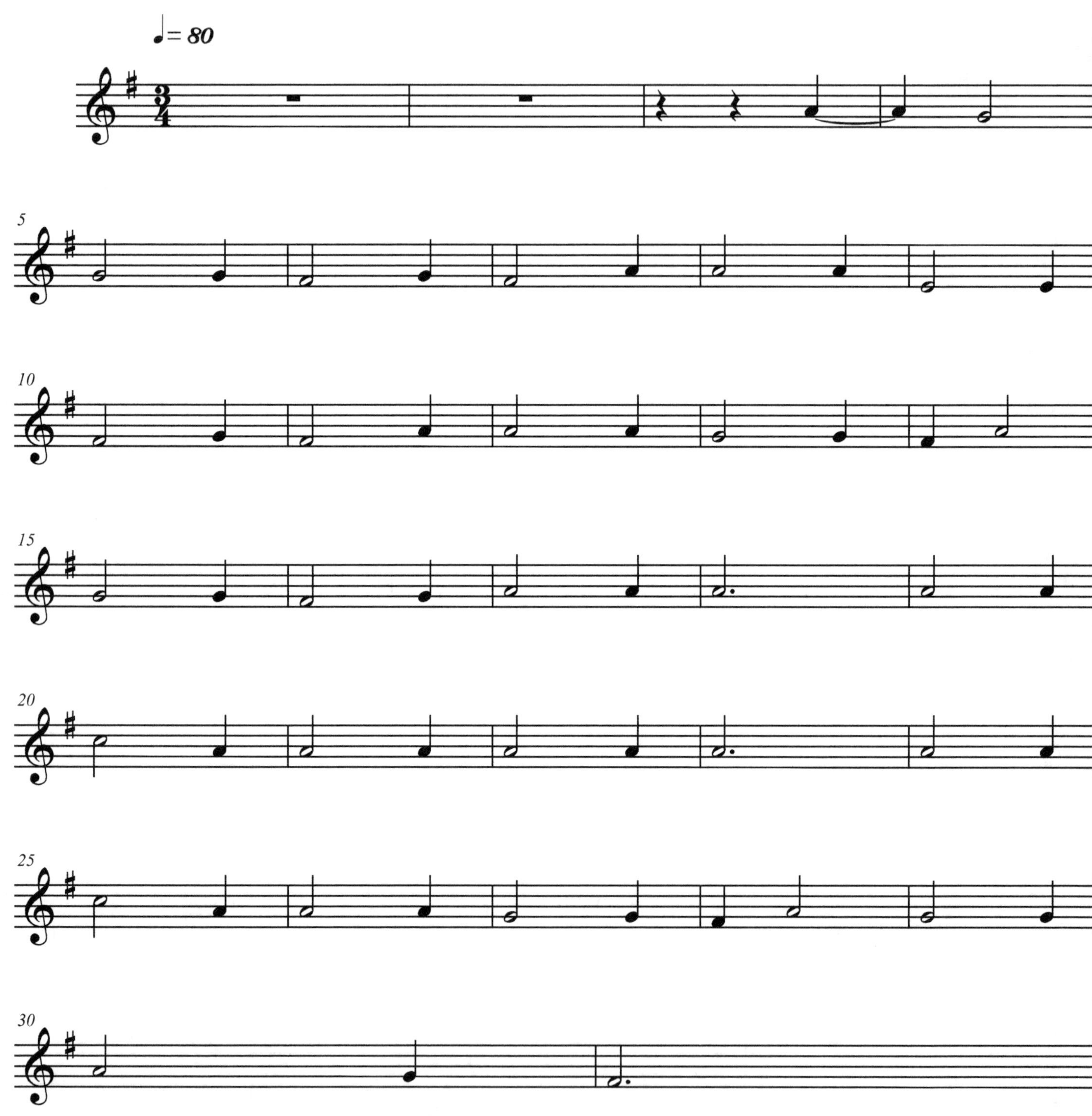

Part 3: C Trombone 1 + 2

J

Joost de Groot

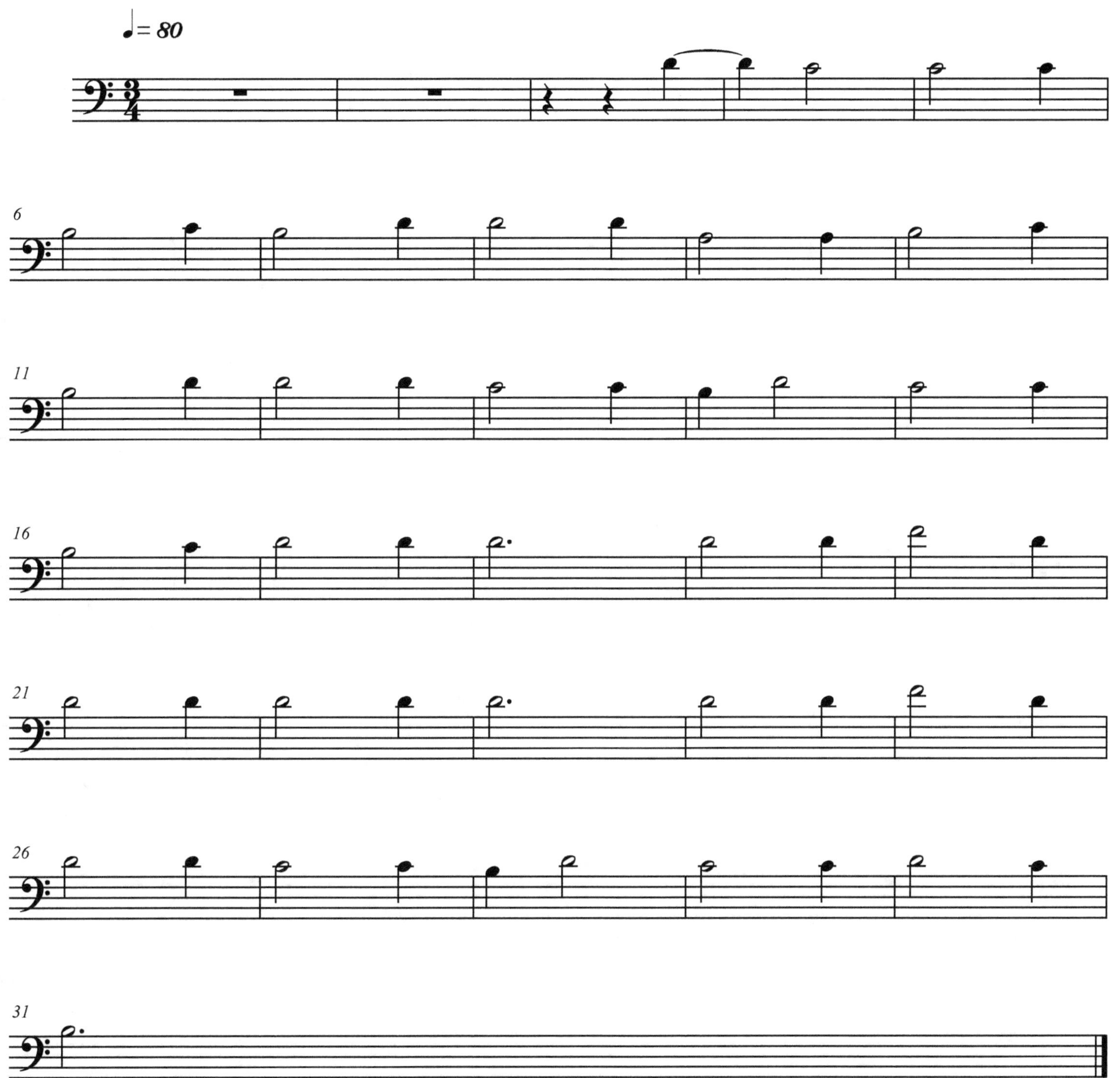

Part 4: C Bass Trombone

J

Joost de Gro

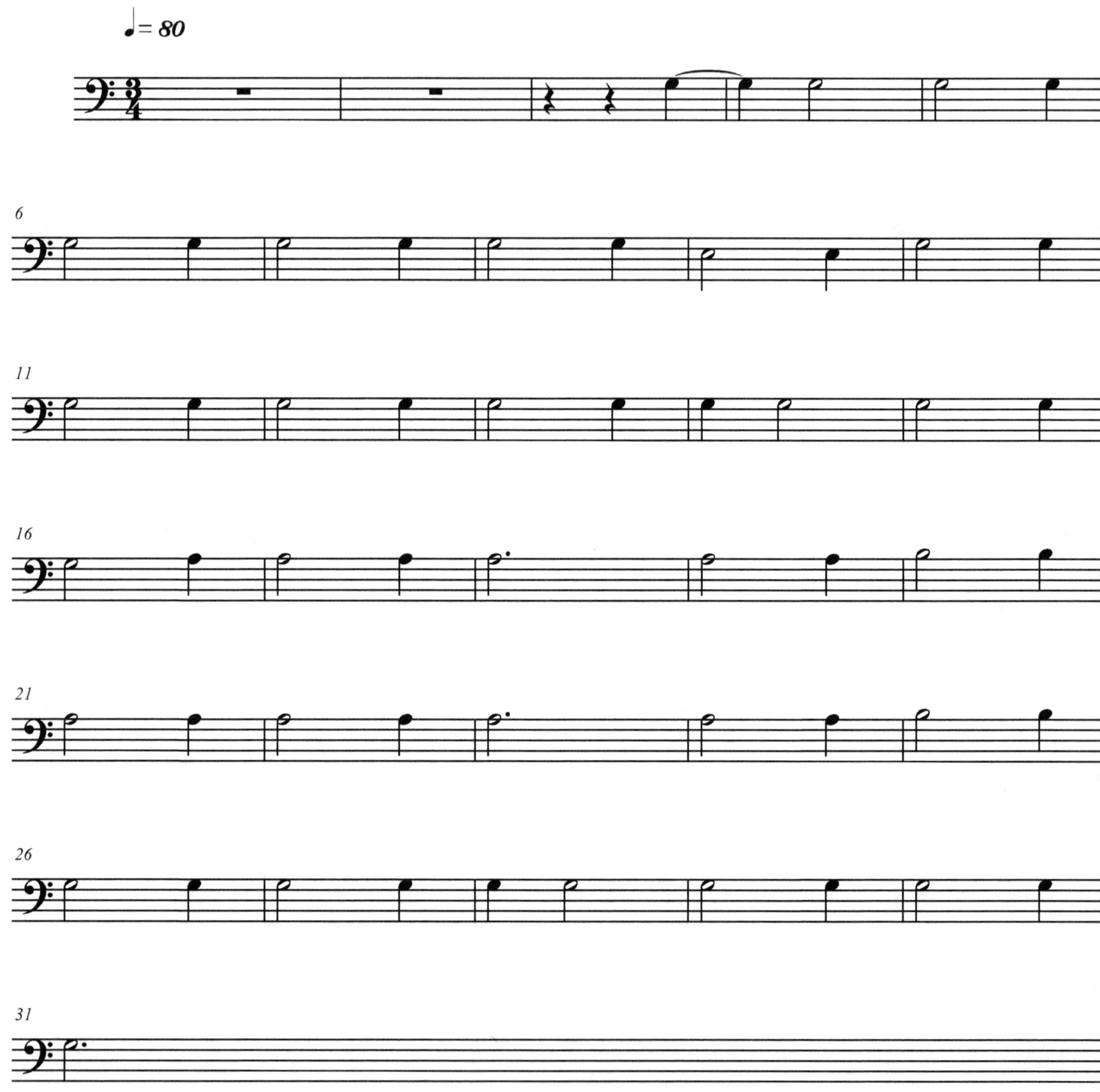

Part 3: C Baritone

J

Joost de Groot

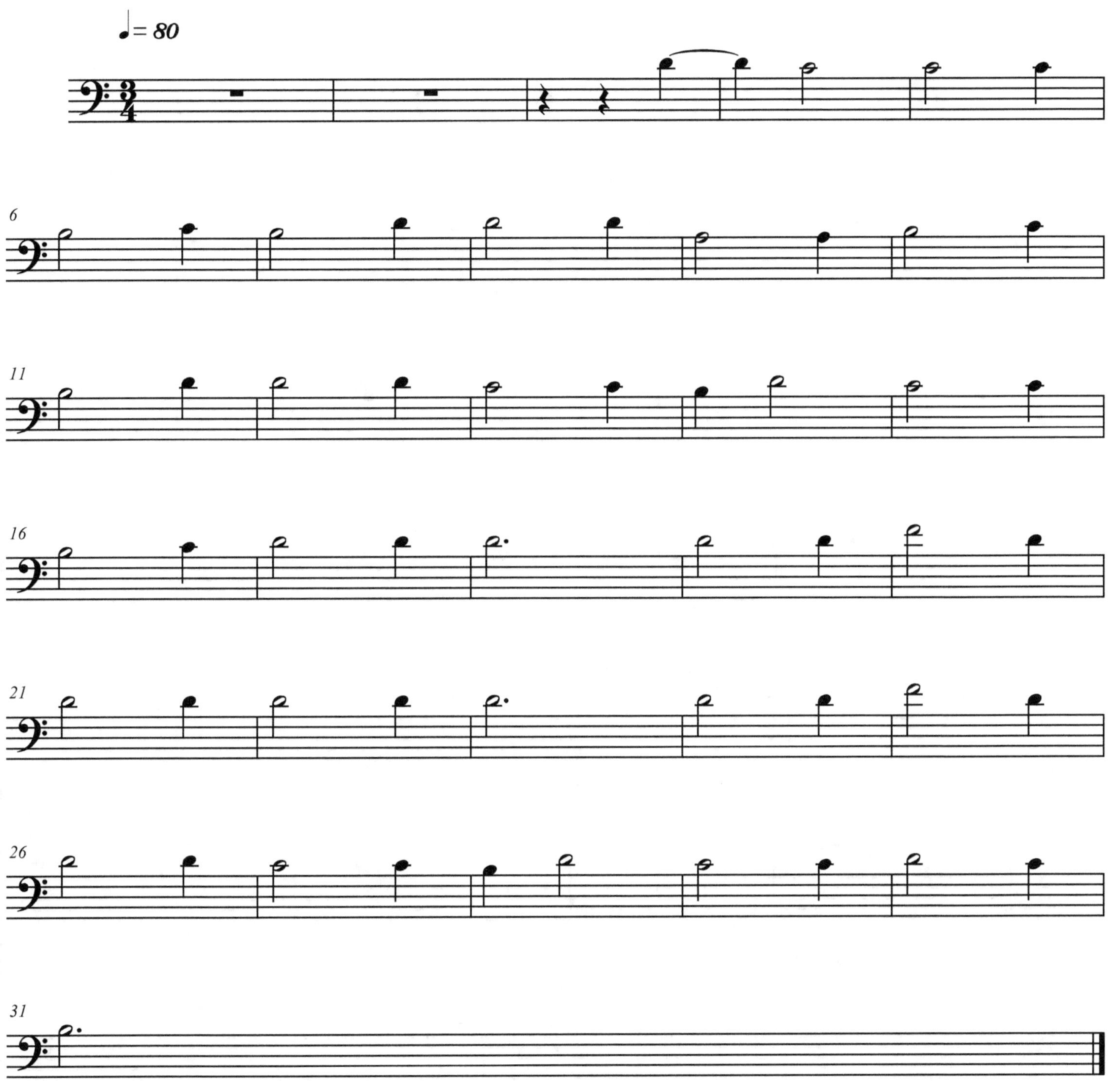

Part 3: Bes Baritone

J

Joost de Gro

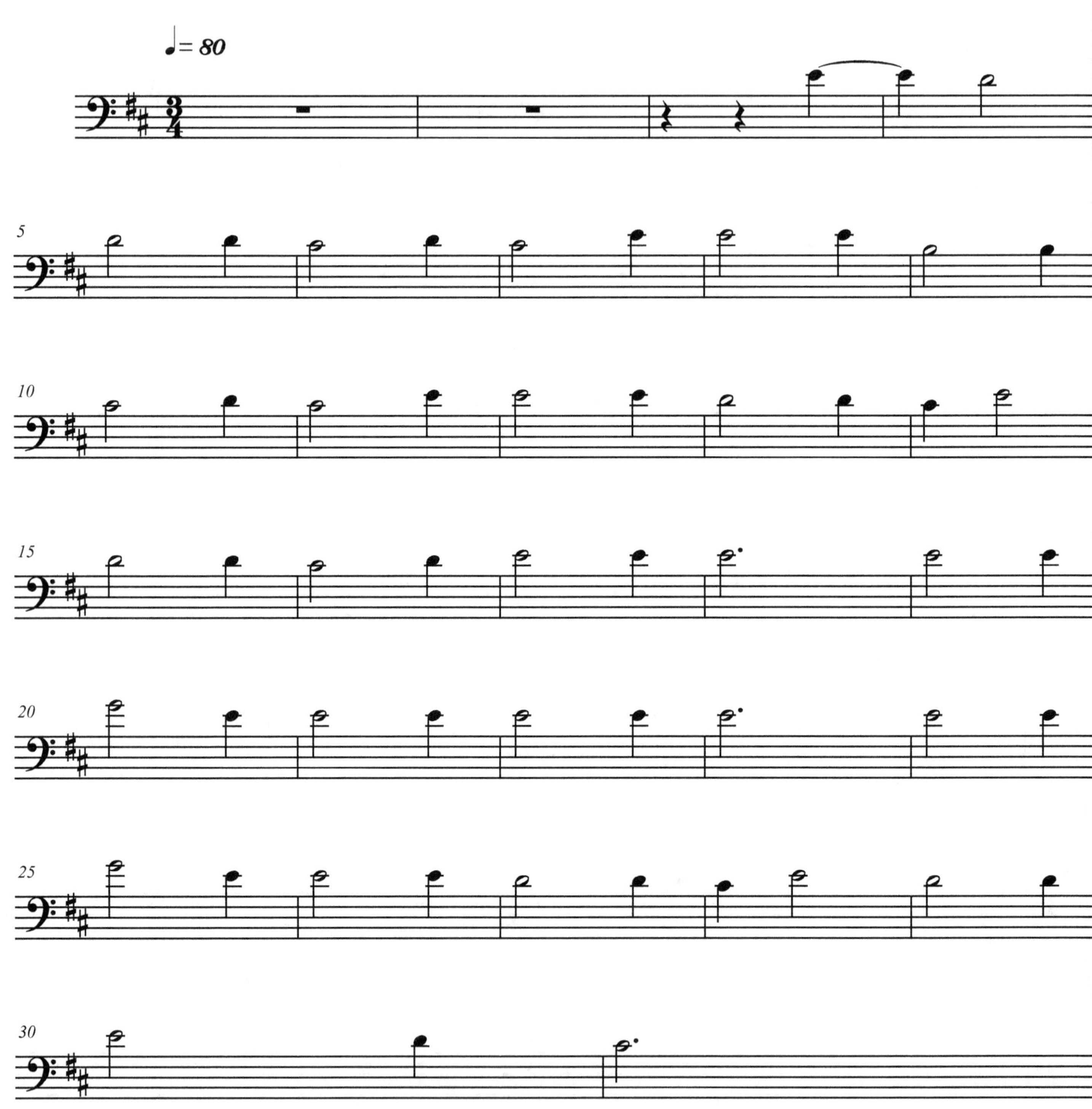

Part 3: Bes Baritone

J

Joost de Groot

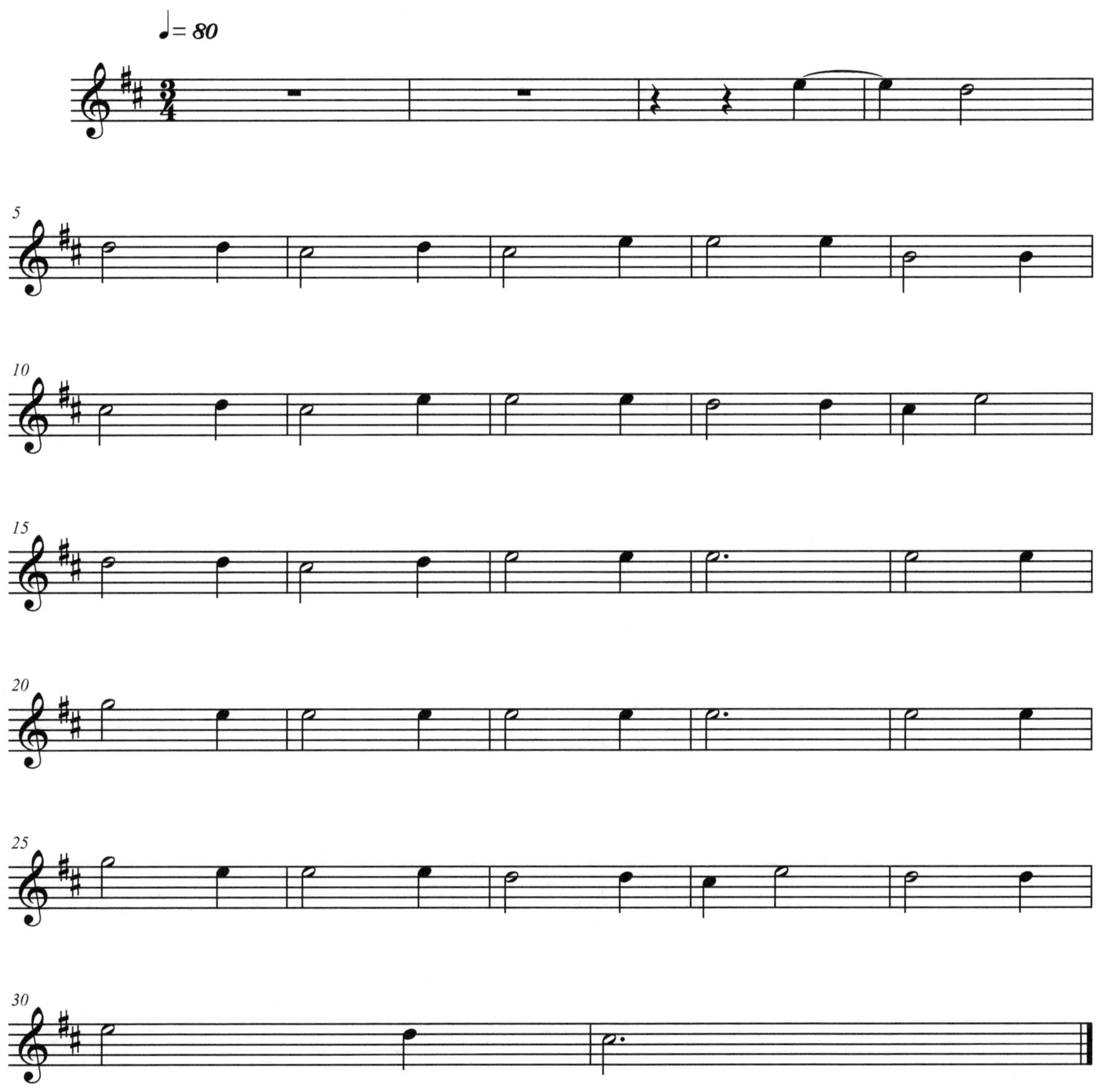

J

Part 4: C Bass Tuba

Joost de Gro

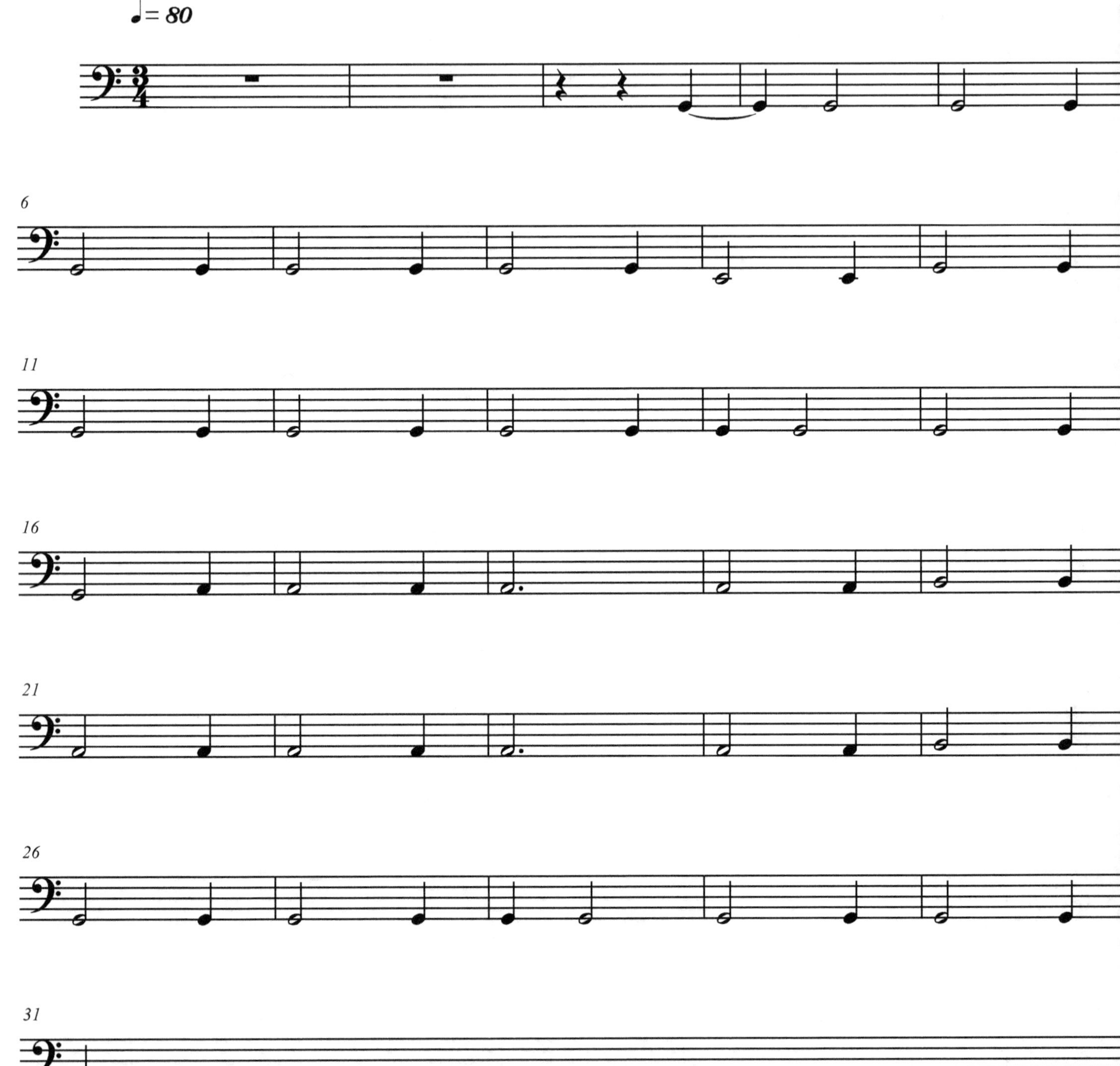

Part 4: Bes Bass Tuba

J

Joost de Groot

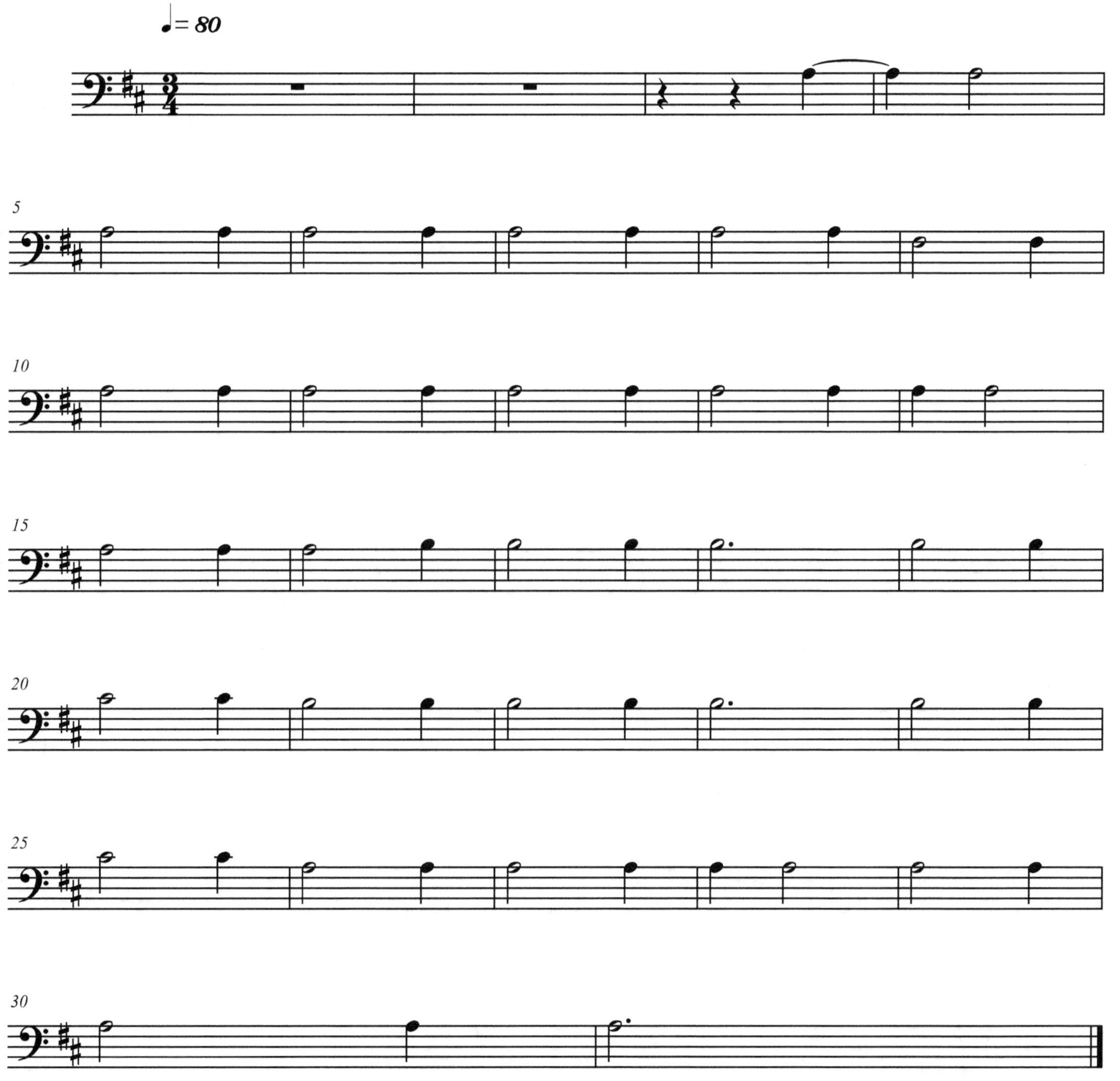

J

Part 4: Es Bass Tuba

Joost de Gro

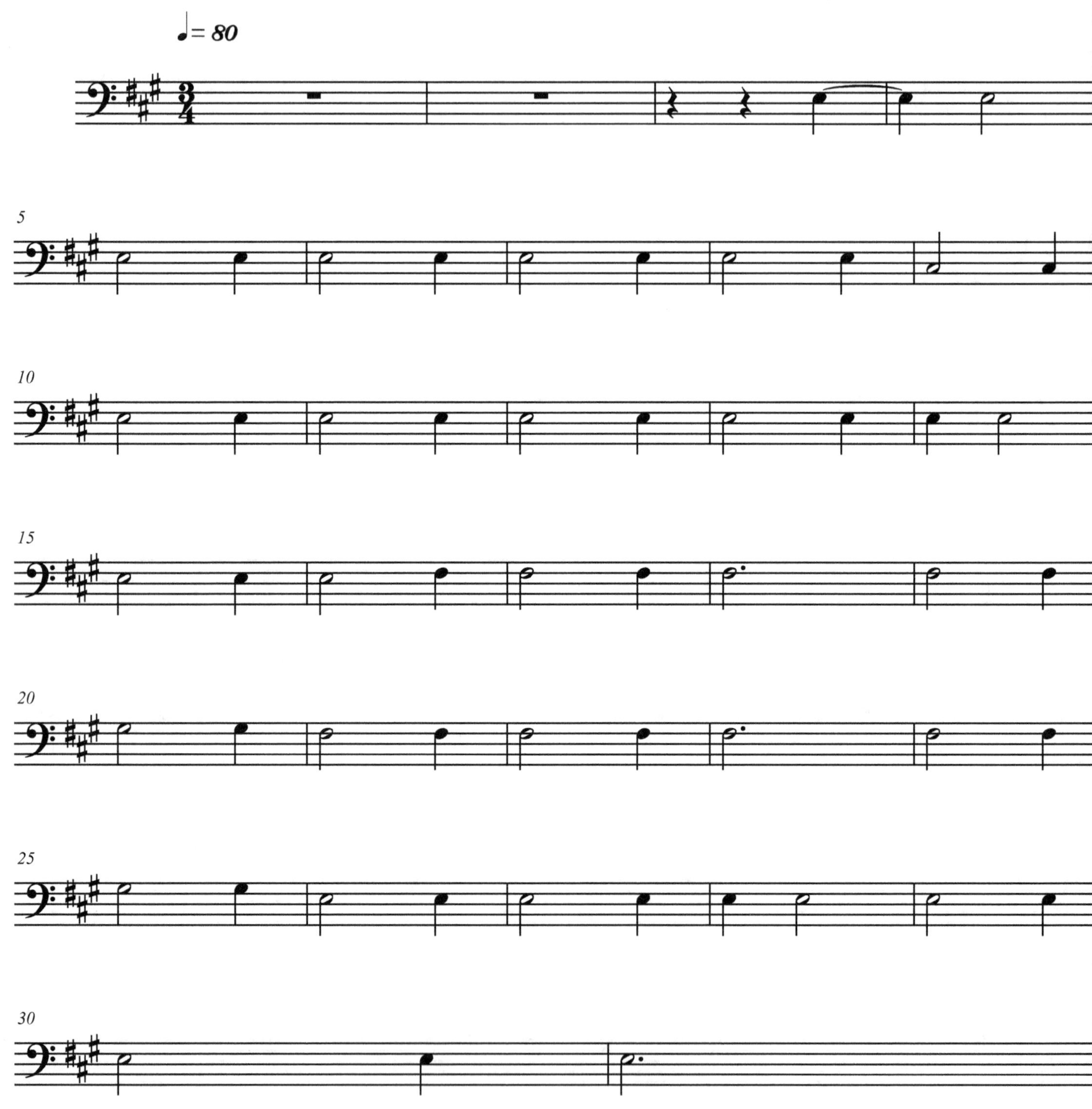

A

Part 1: C Flute

Joost de Groot

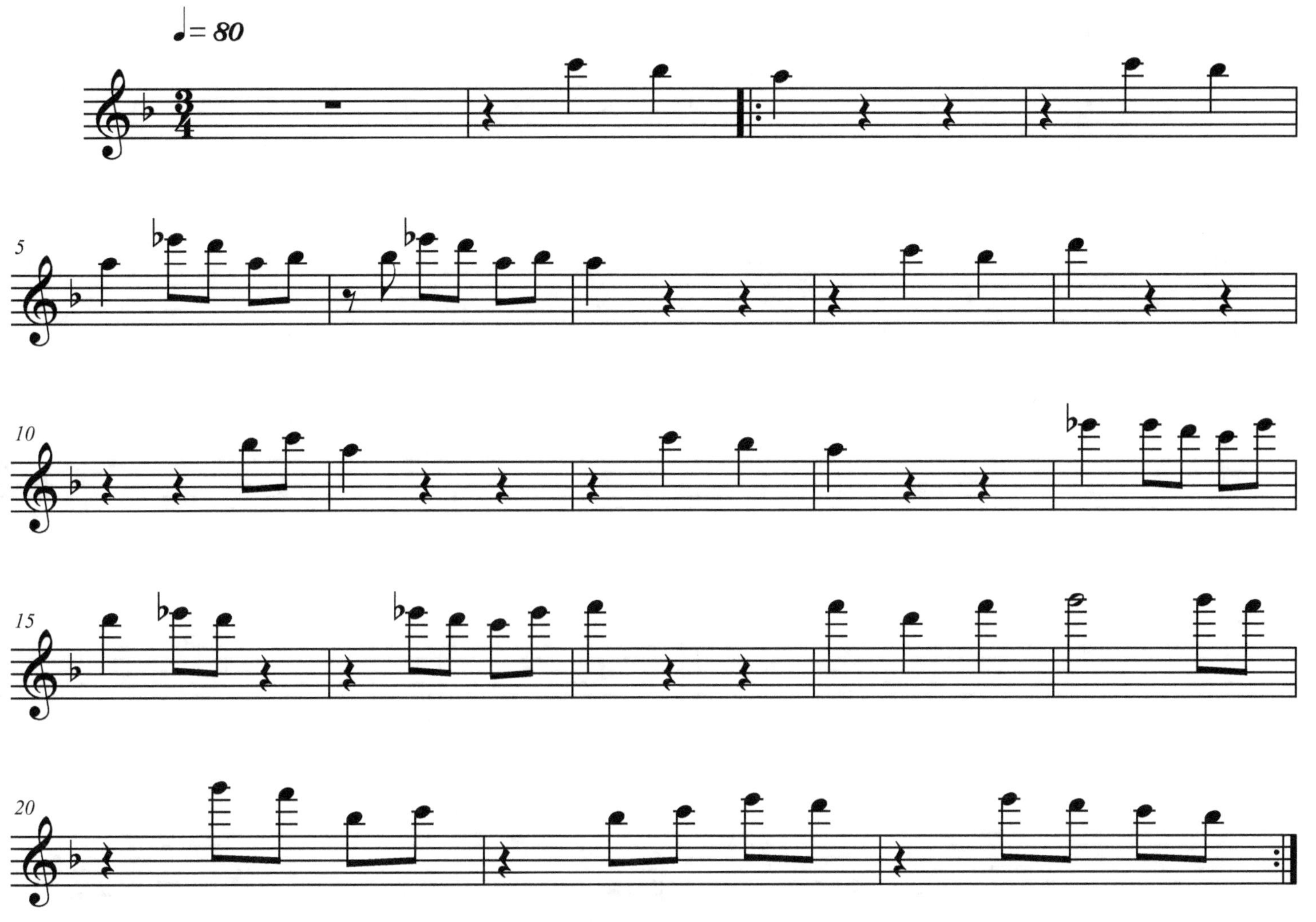

A

Part 1: C Oboe

Joost de Gro

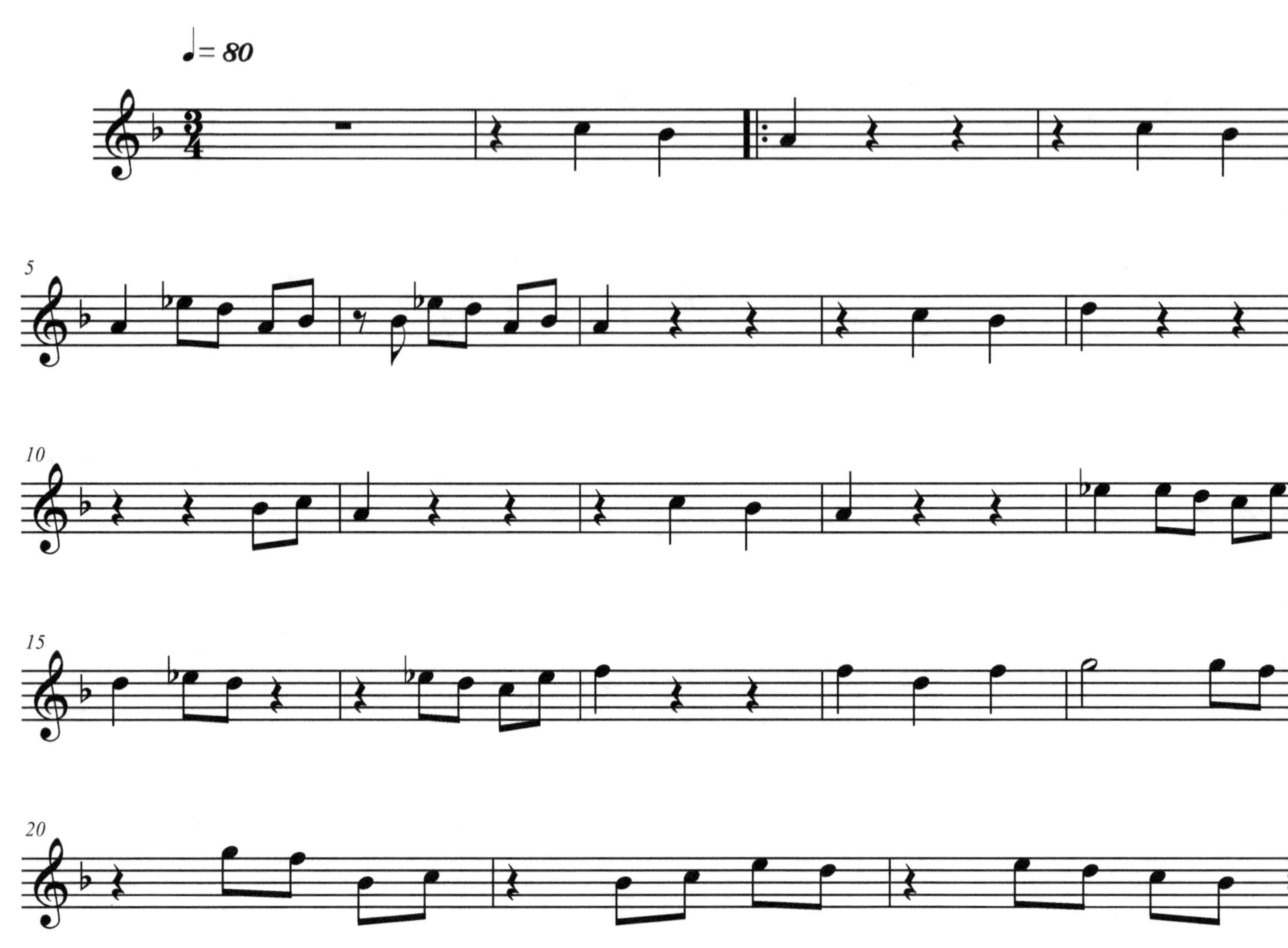

A

Part 4: C Bassoon

Joost de Groot

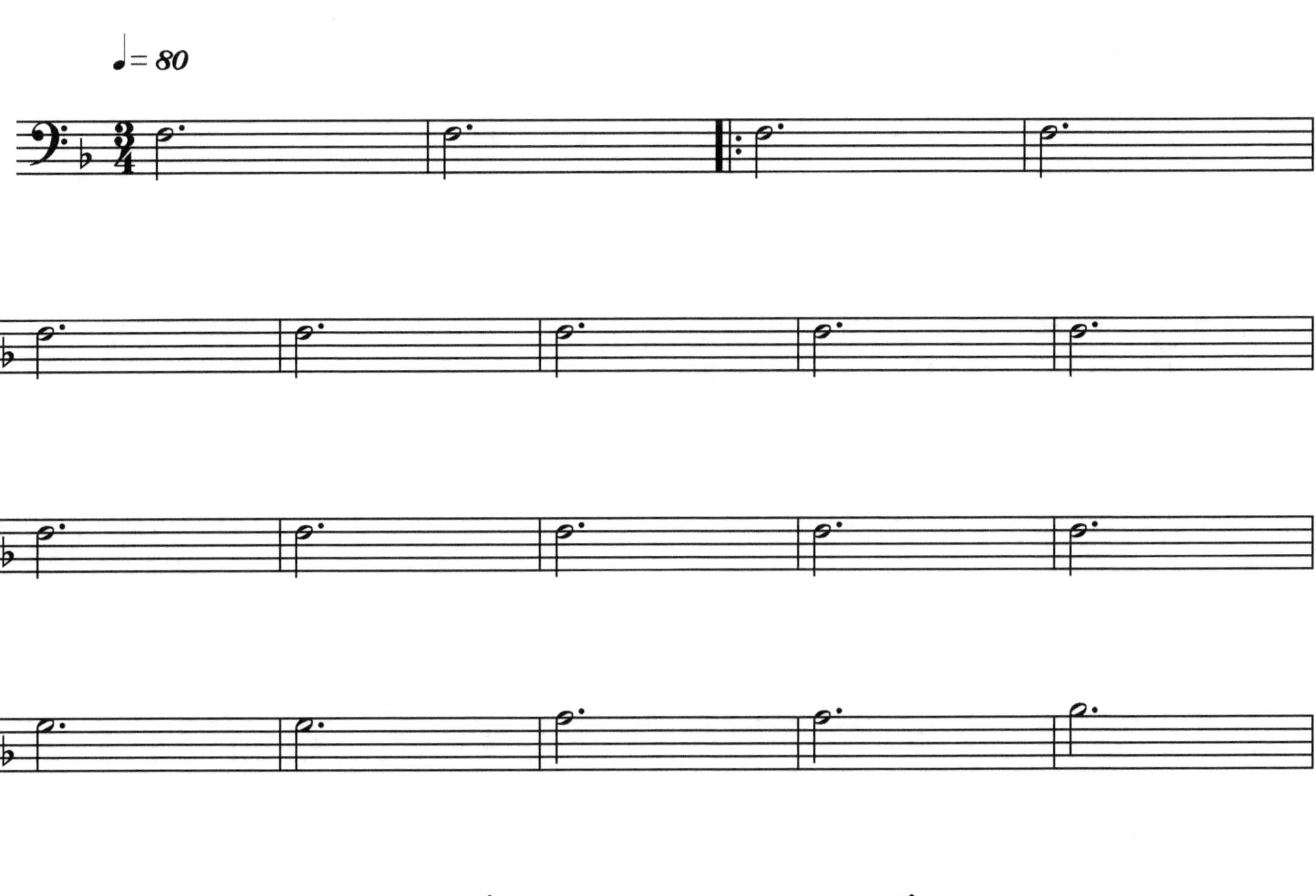

Part 1: Bes Clarinet 1

A

Joost de Gro

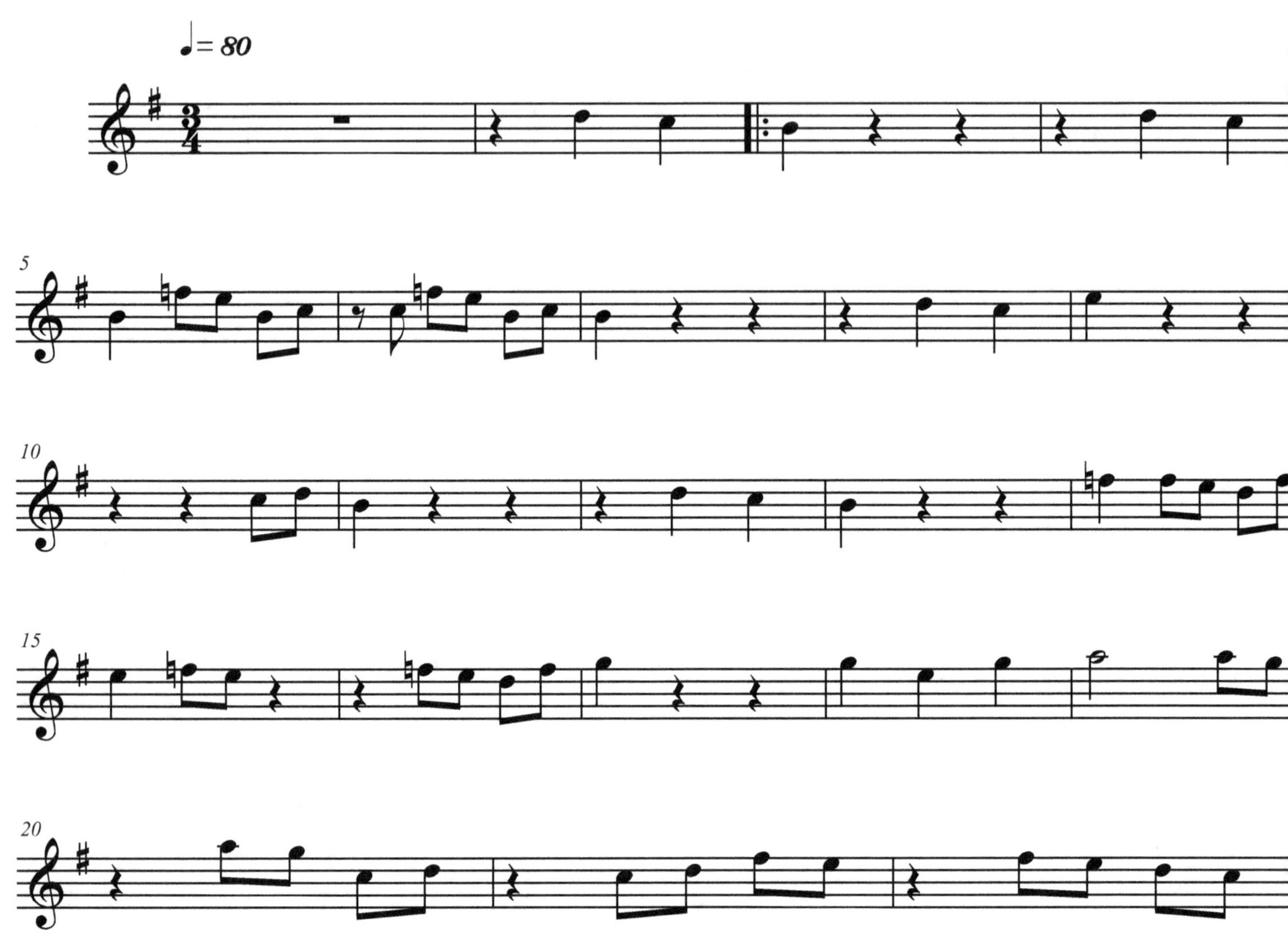

A

Part 2: Bes Clarinet 2 + 3

Joost de Groot

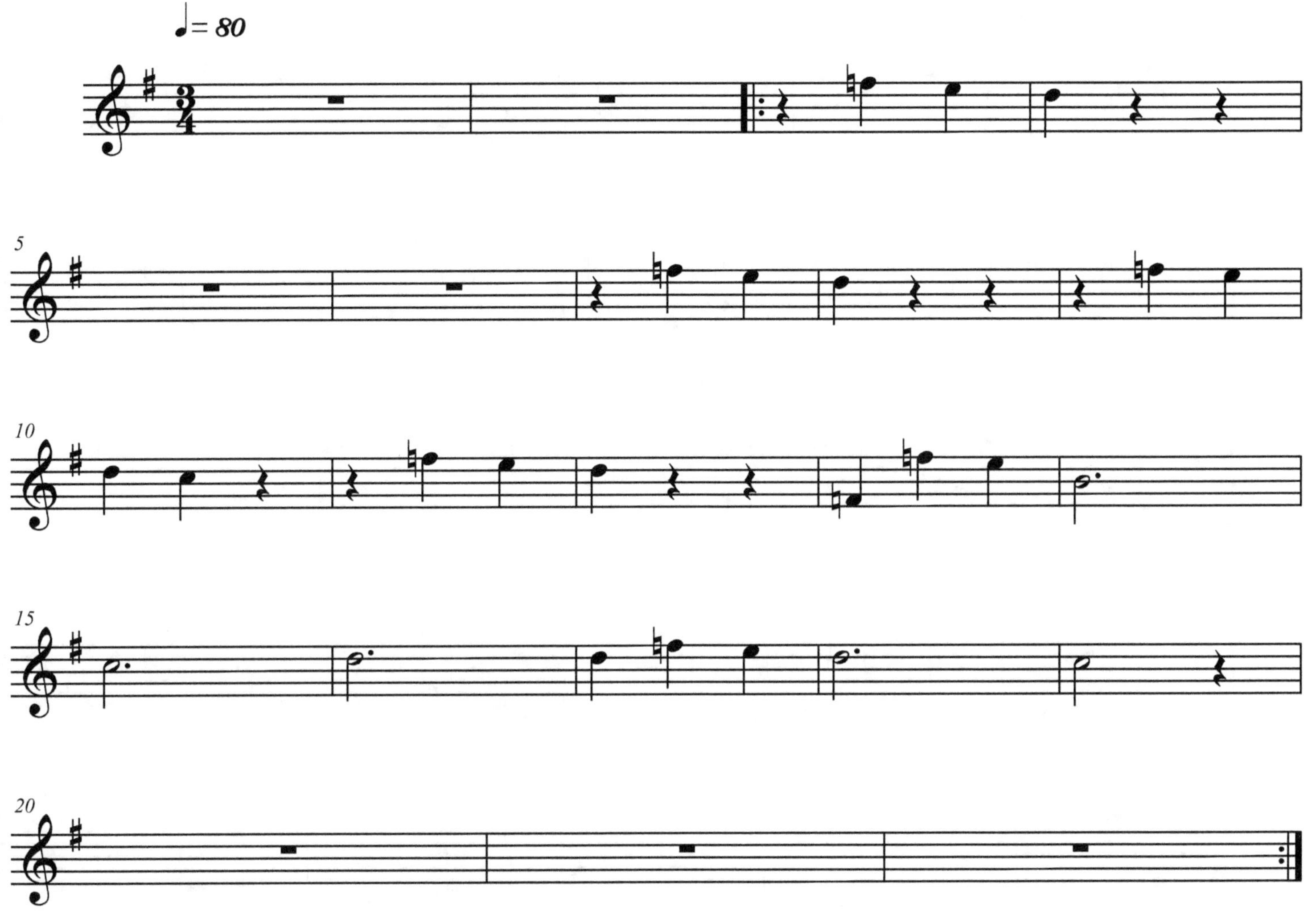

A

Part 3: Es Alto Clarinet

Joost de Gro

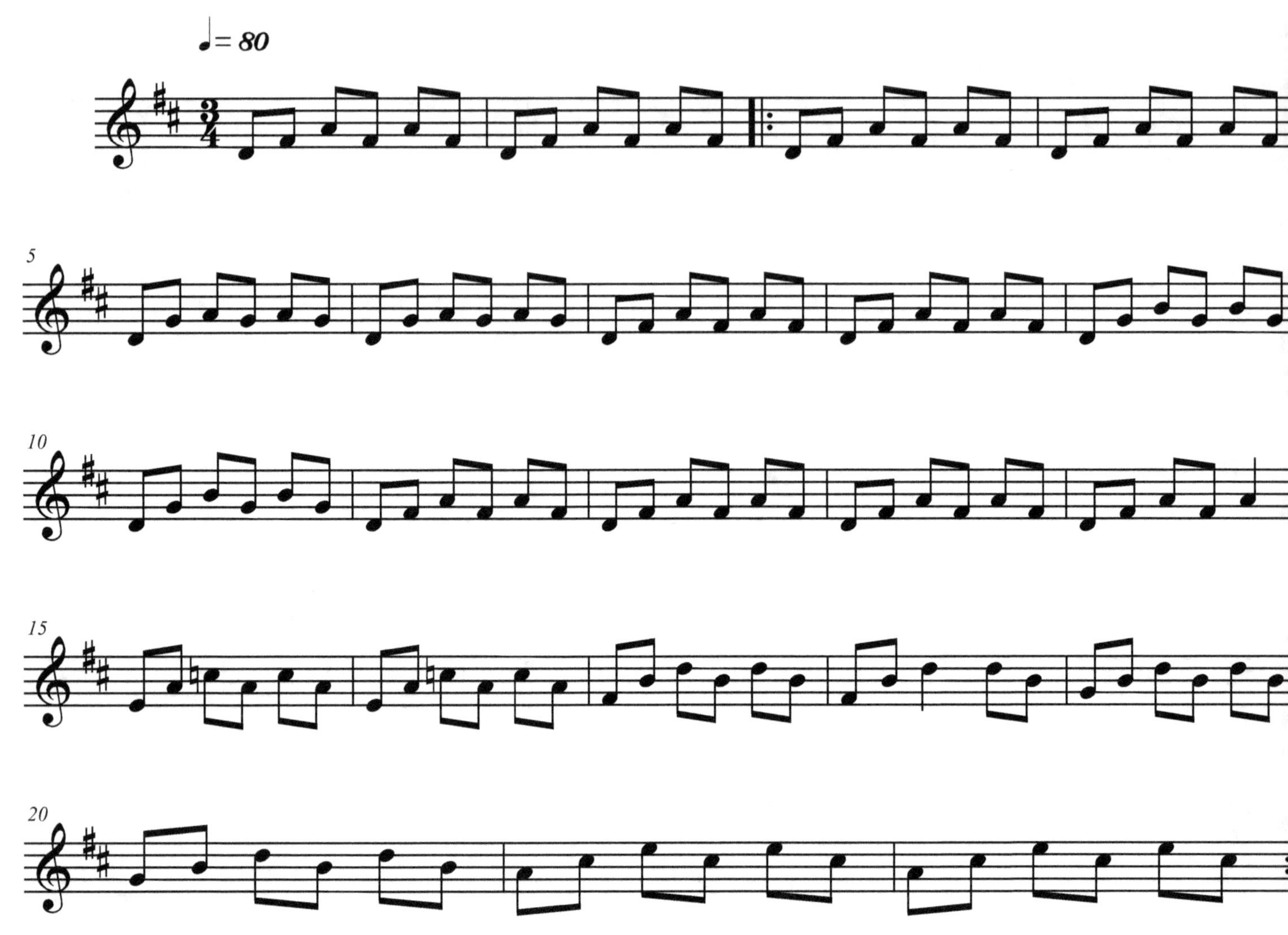

Part 4: Bes Bass Clarinet

A

Joost de Groot

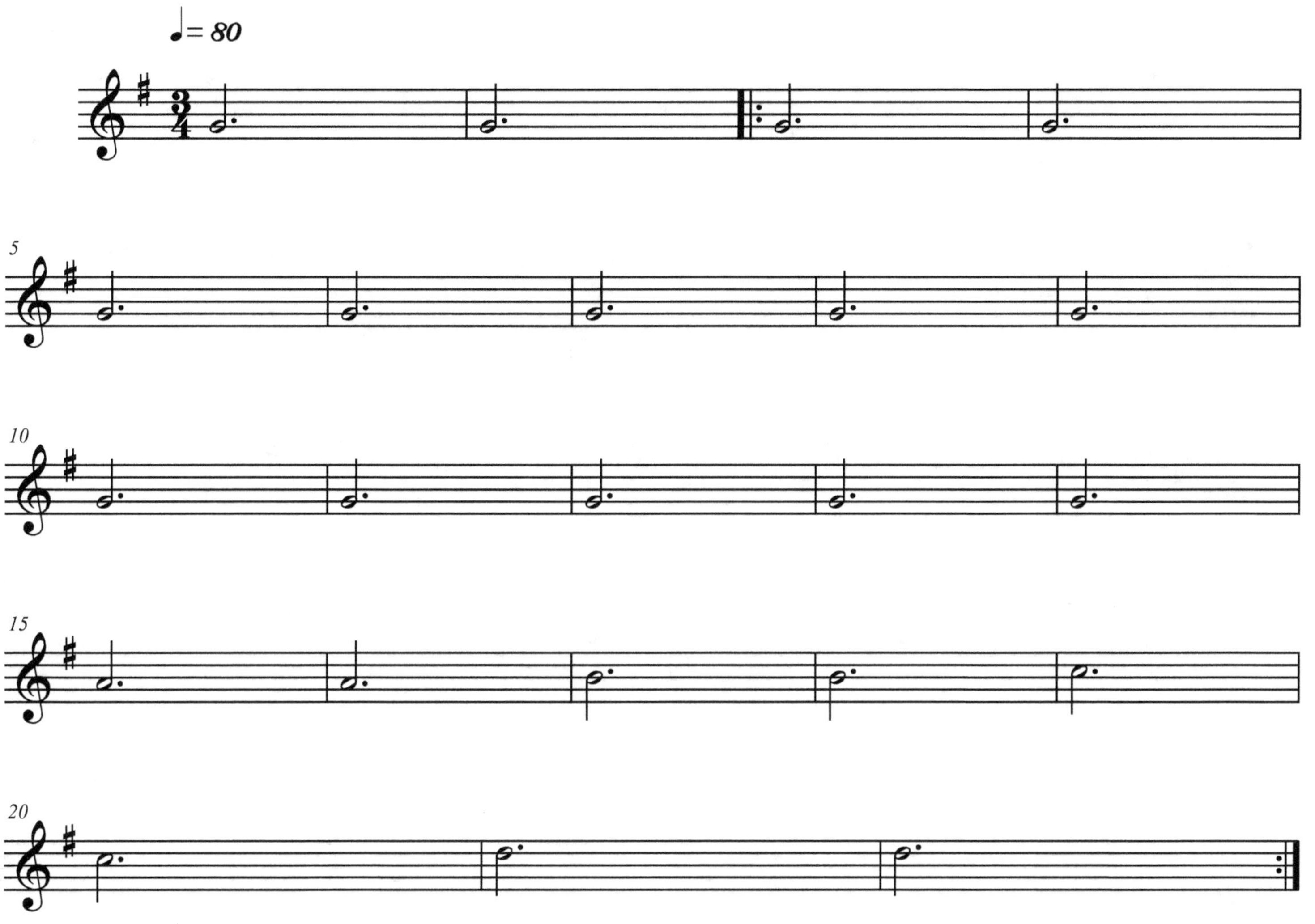

Part 2: Es Alto Sax.

A

Joost de Gro

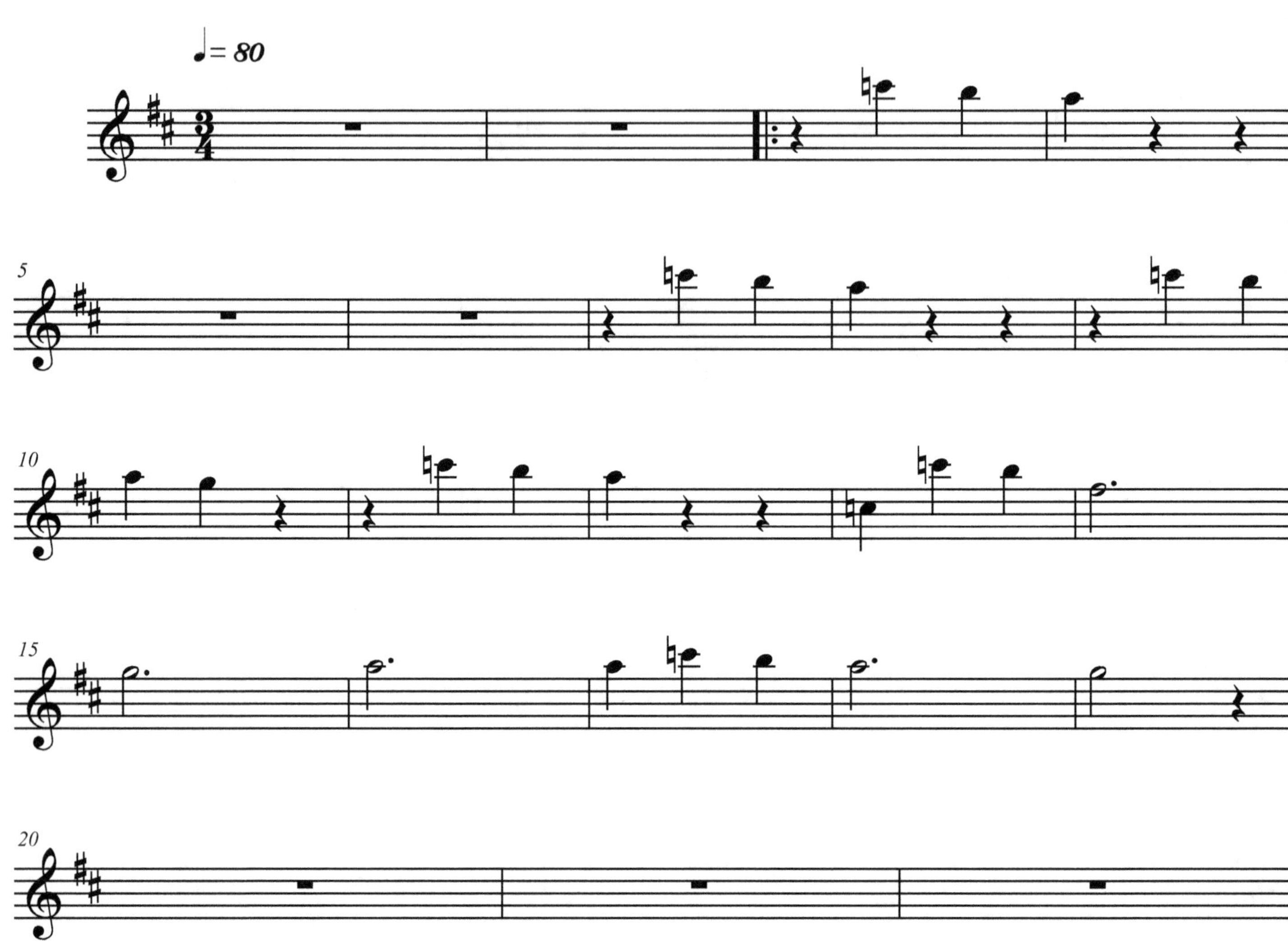

A

Part 3: Bes Tenor Sax.

Joost de Groot

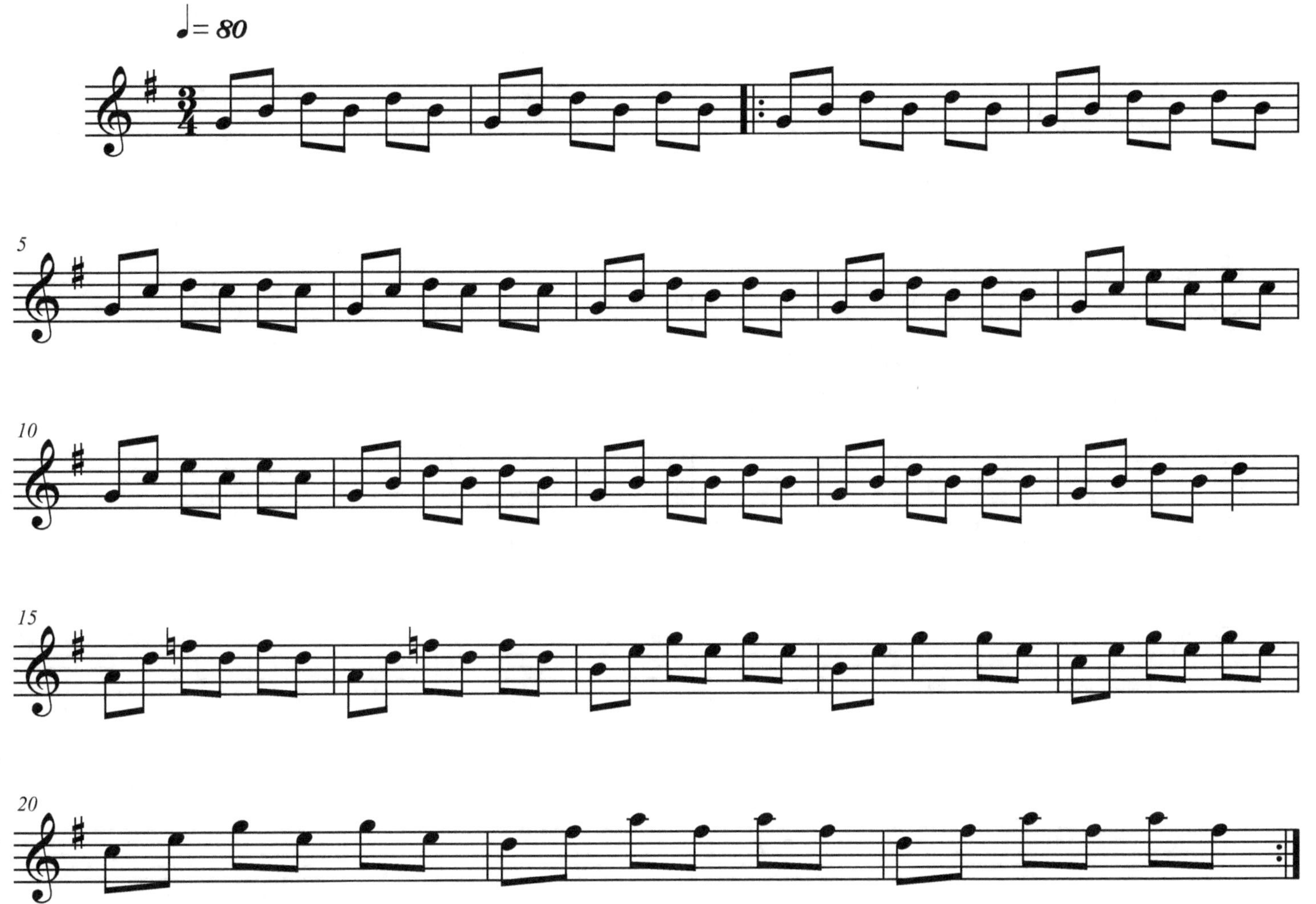

Part 4: Es Baritone Sax.

A

Joost de Groo

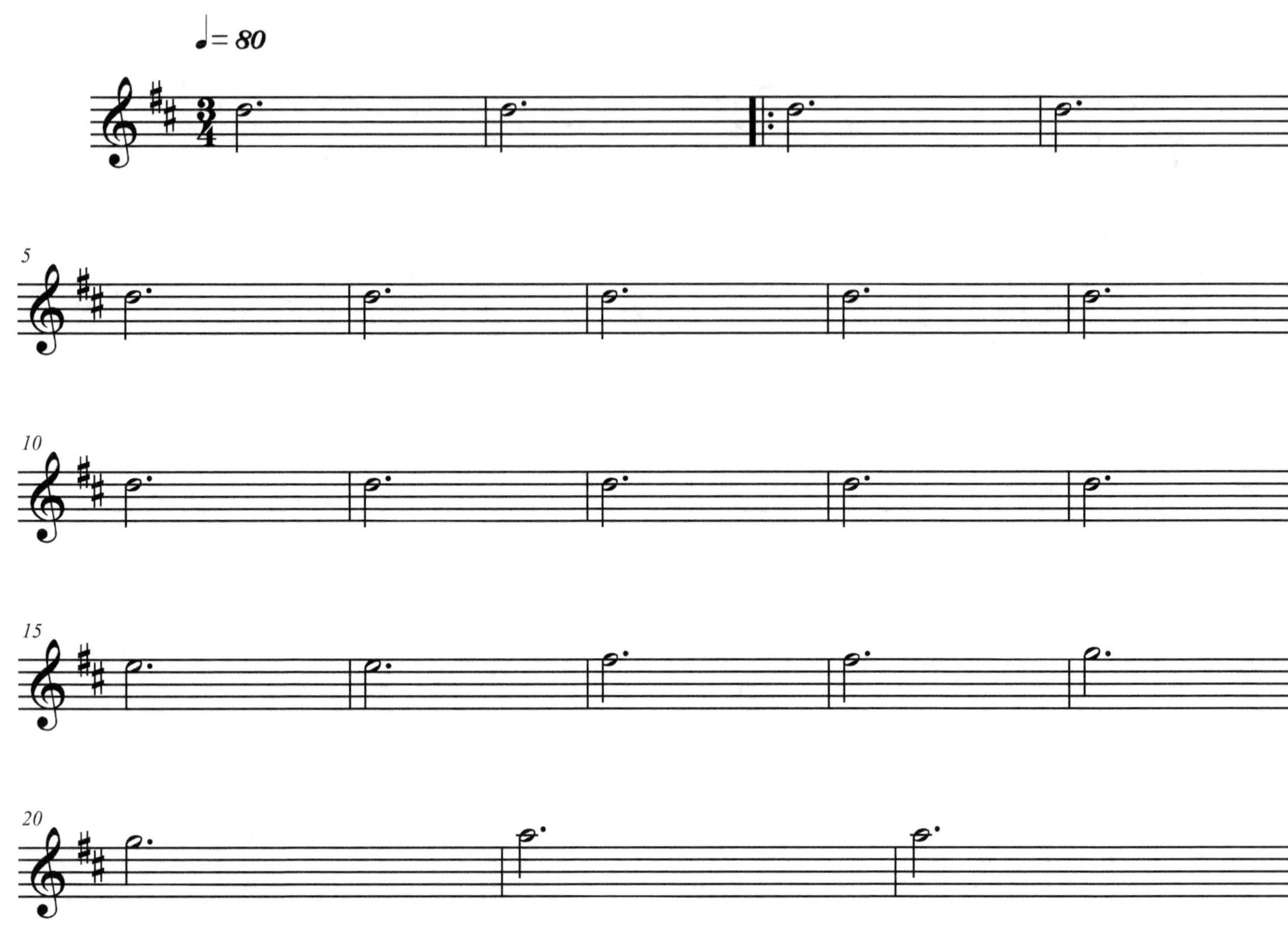

A

Part 1: Bes Trumpet 1

Joost de Groot

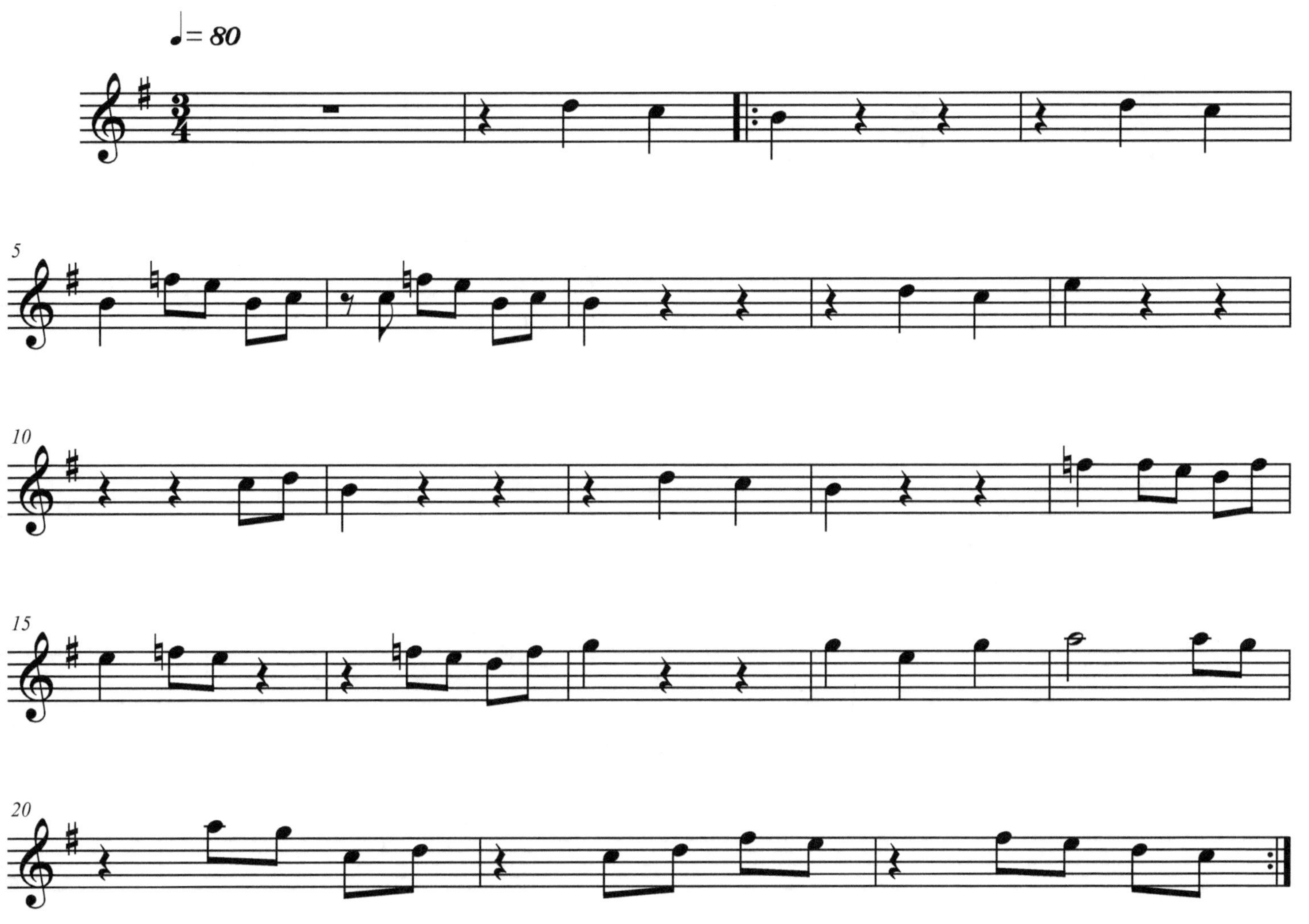

Part 2: Bes Trumpet 2 + 3

A

Joost de Gro

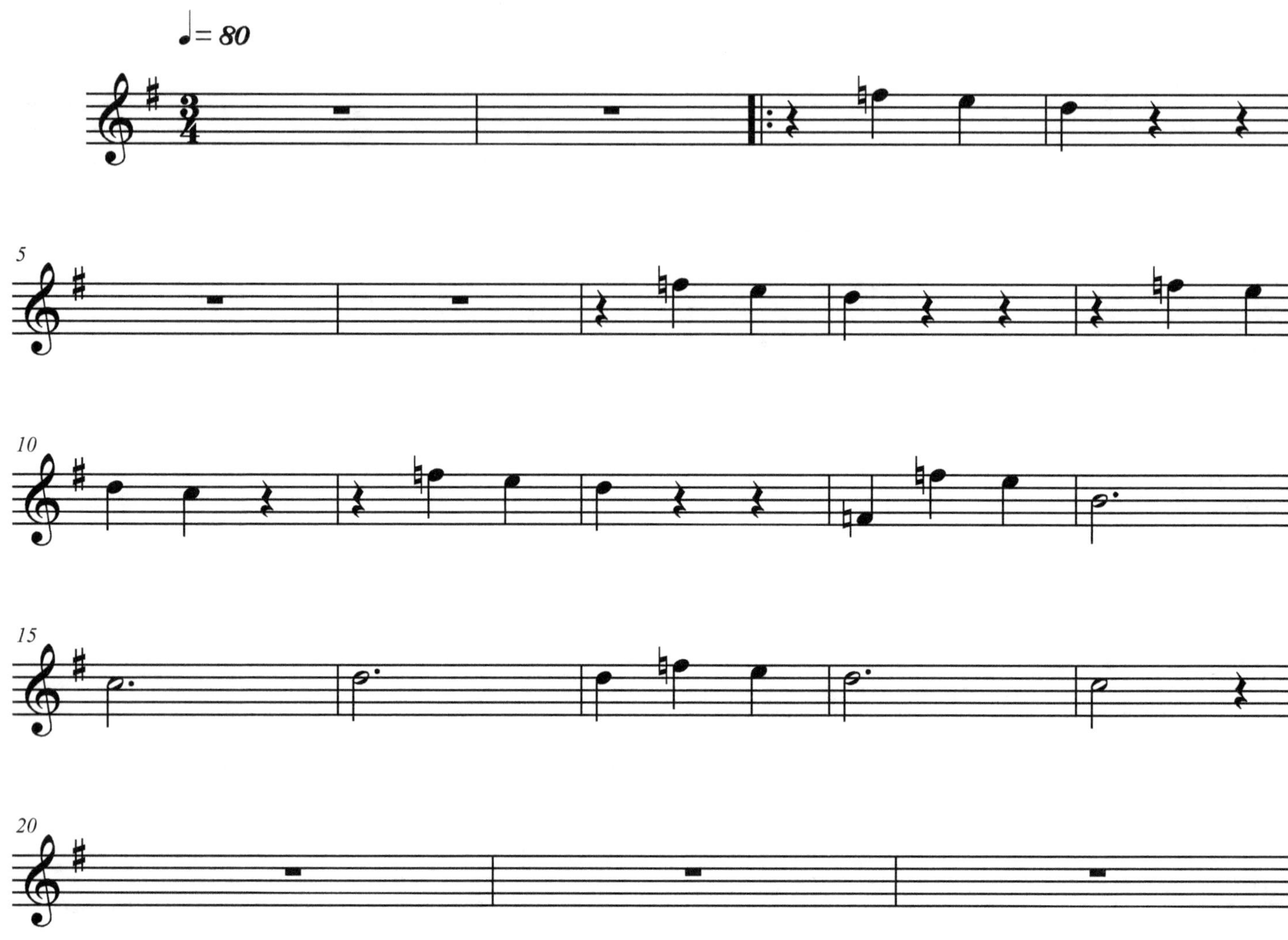

Part 2: F Horn 1 + 2

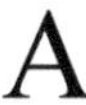

Joost de Groot

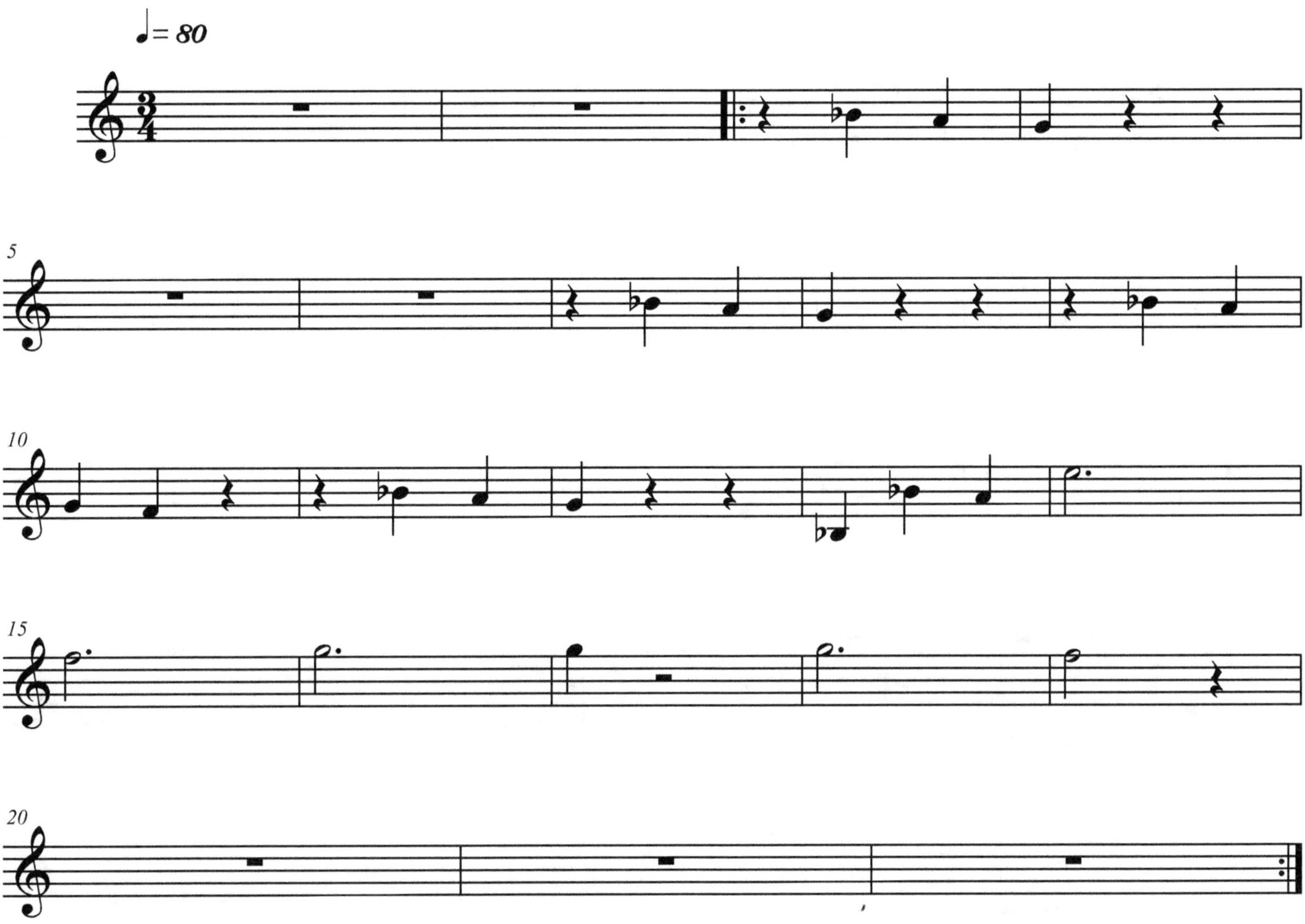

♩ = 80

Part 3: F Horn 3 + 4

A

Joost de Gro

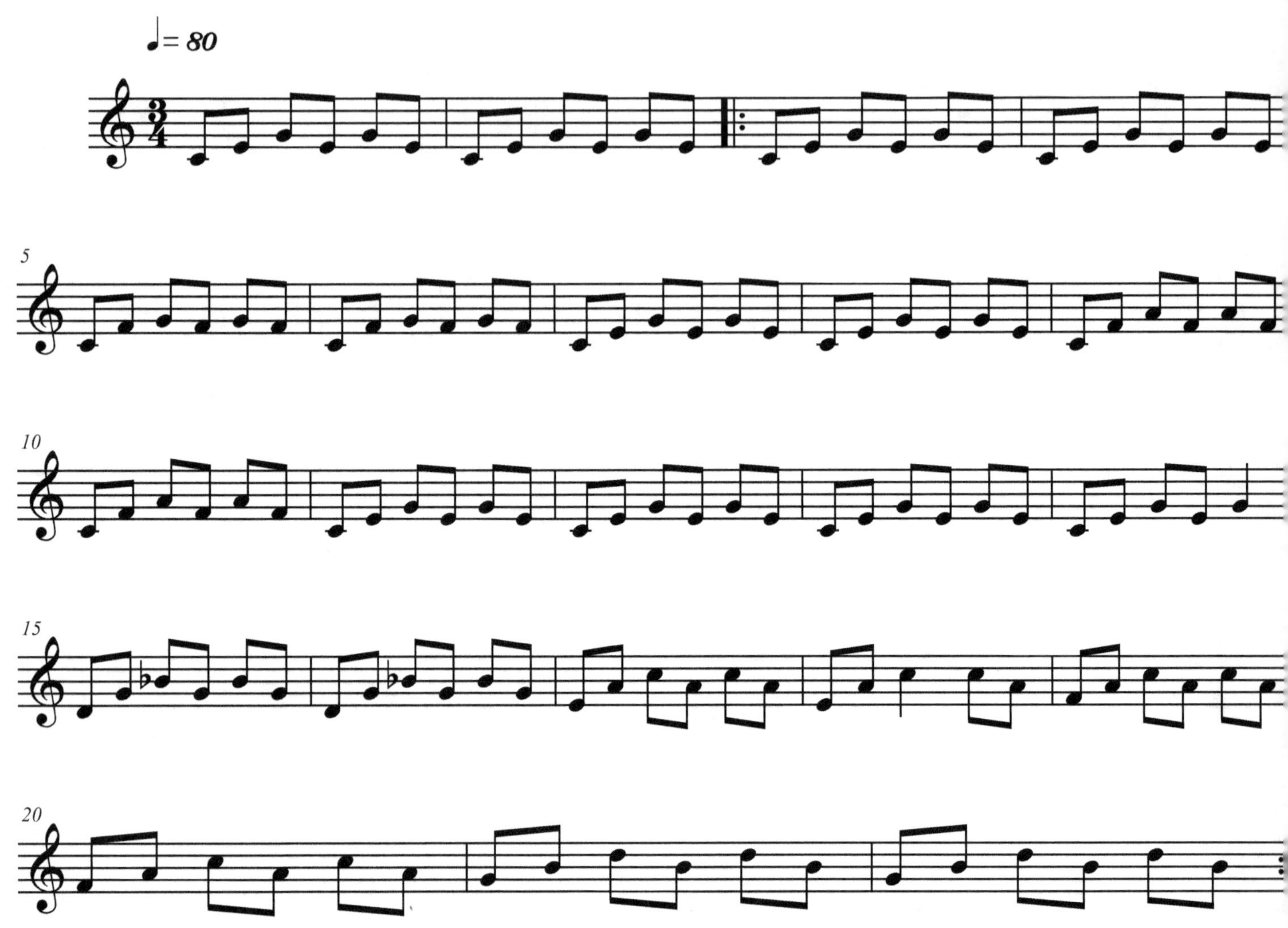

Part 3: C Trombone 1 + 2

A

Joost de Groot

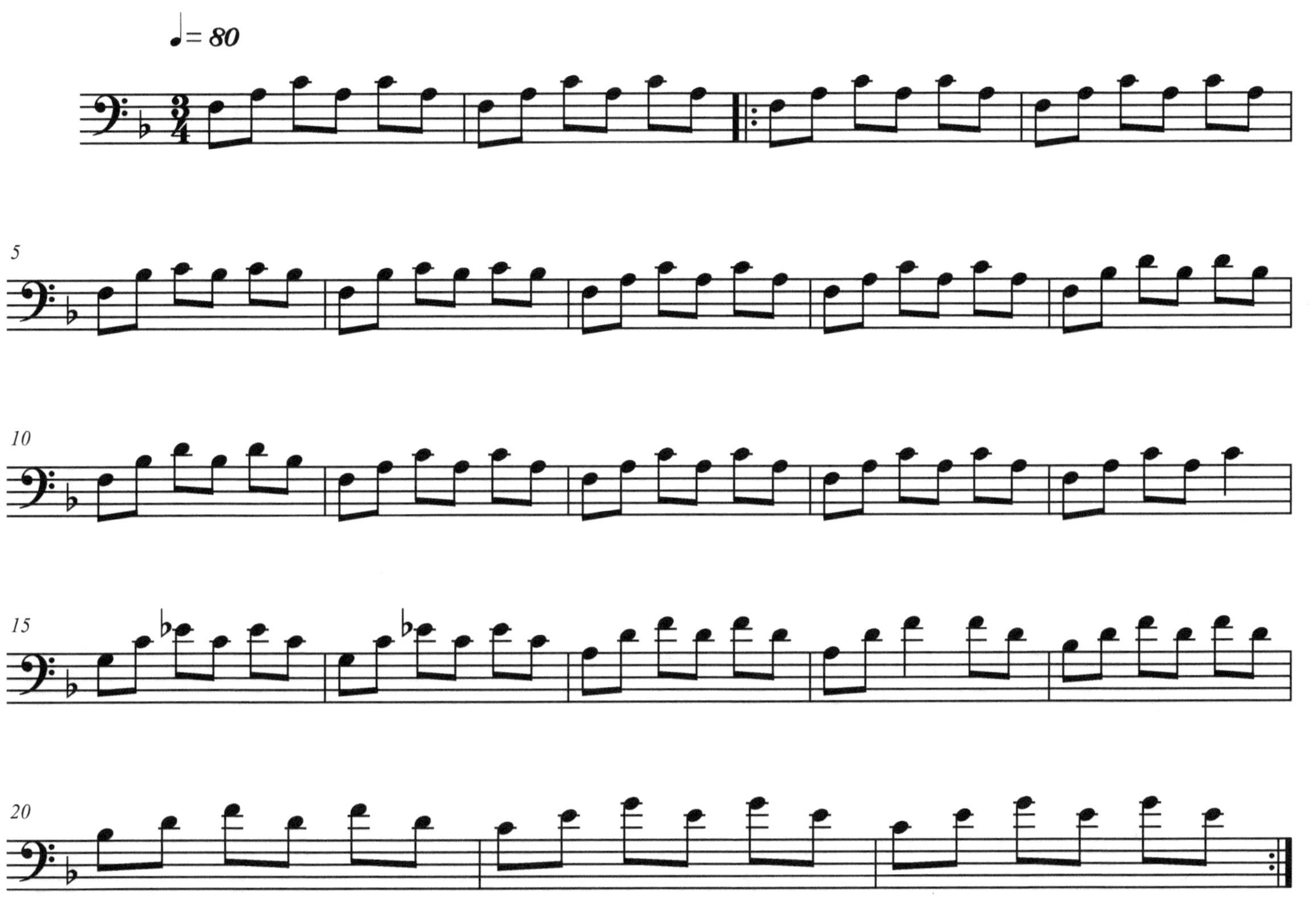

Part 4: C Bass Trombone

A

Joost de Gro

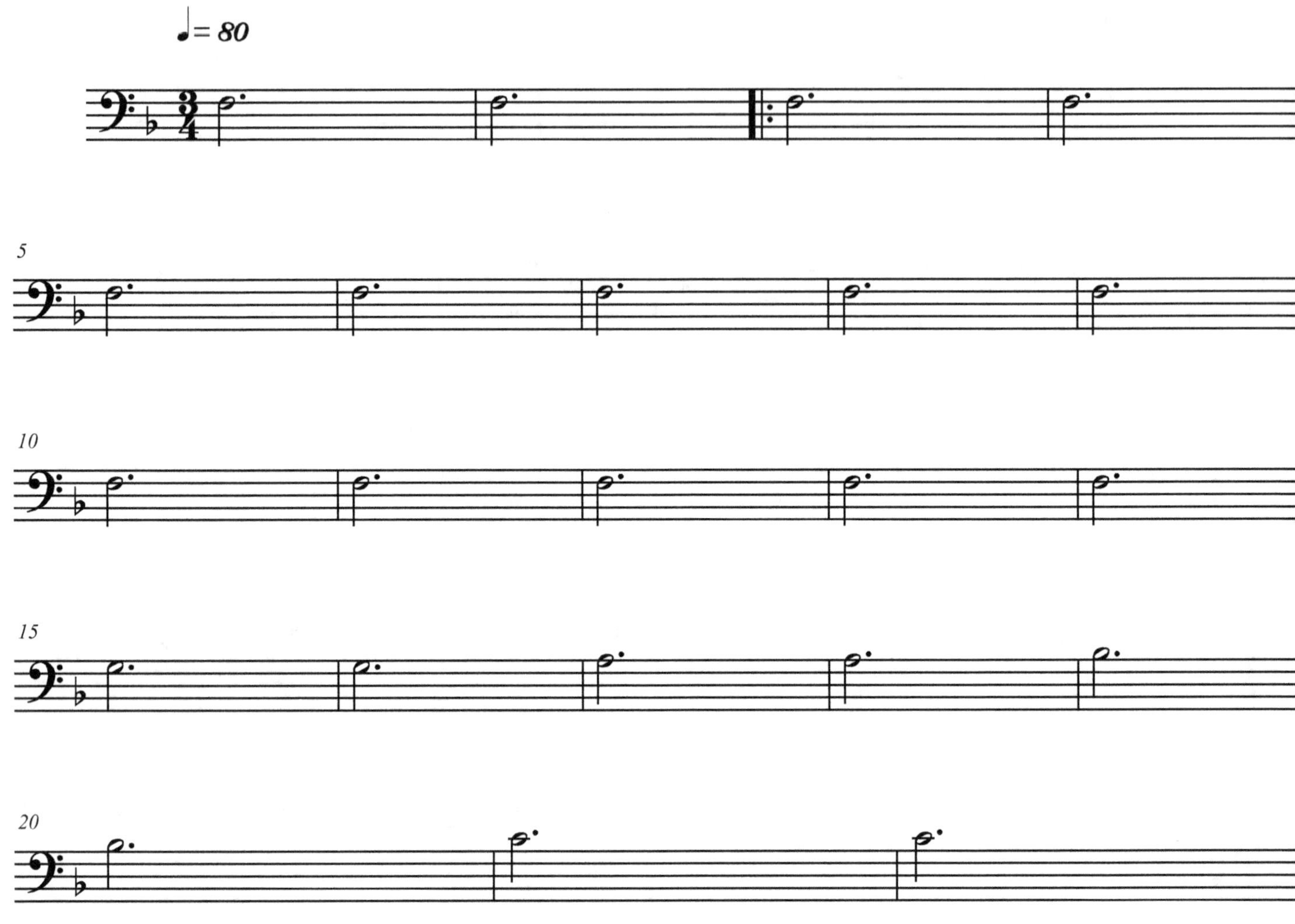

A

Part 3: C Baritone

Joost de Groot

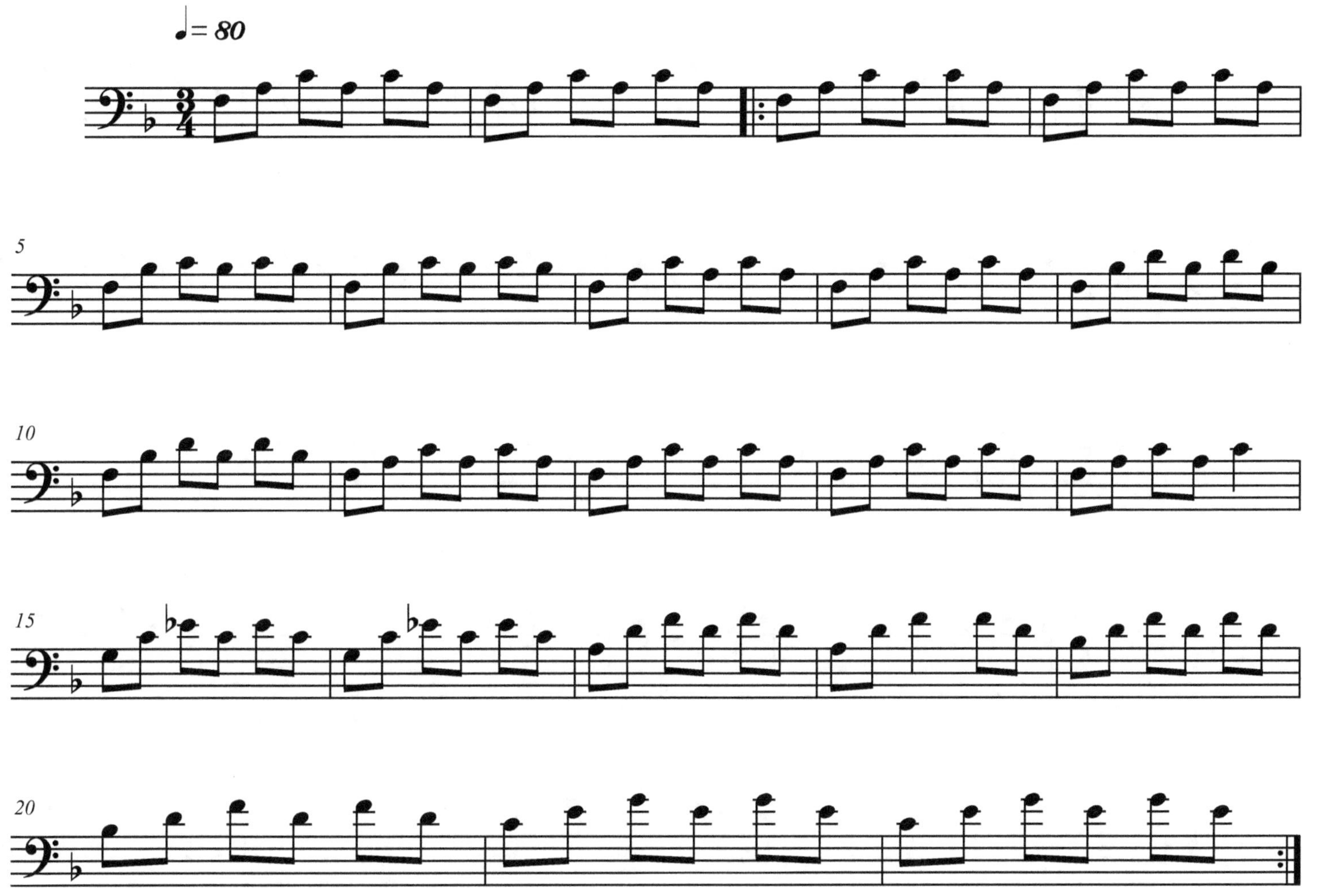

Part 3: Bes Baritone

A

Joost de Gro

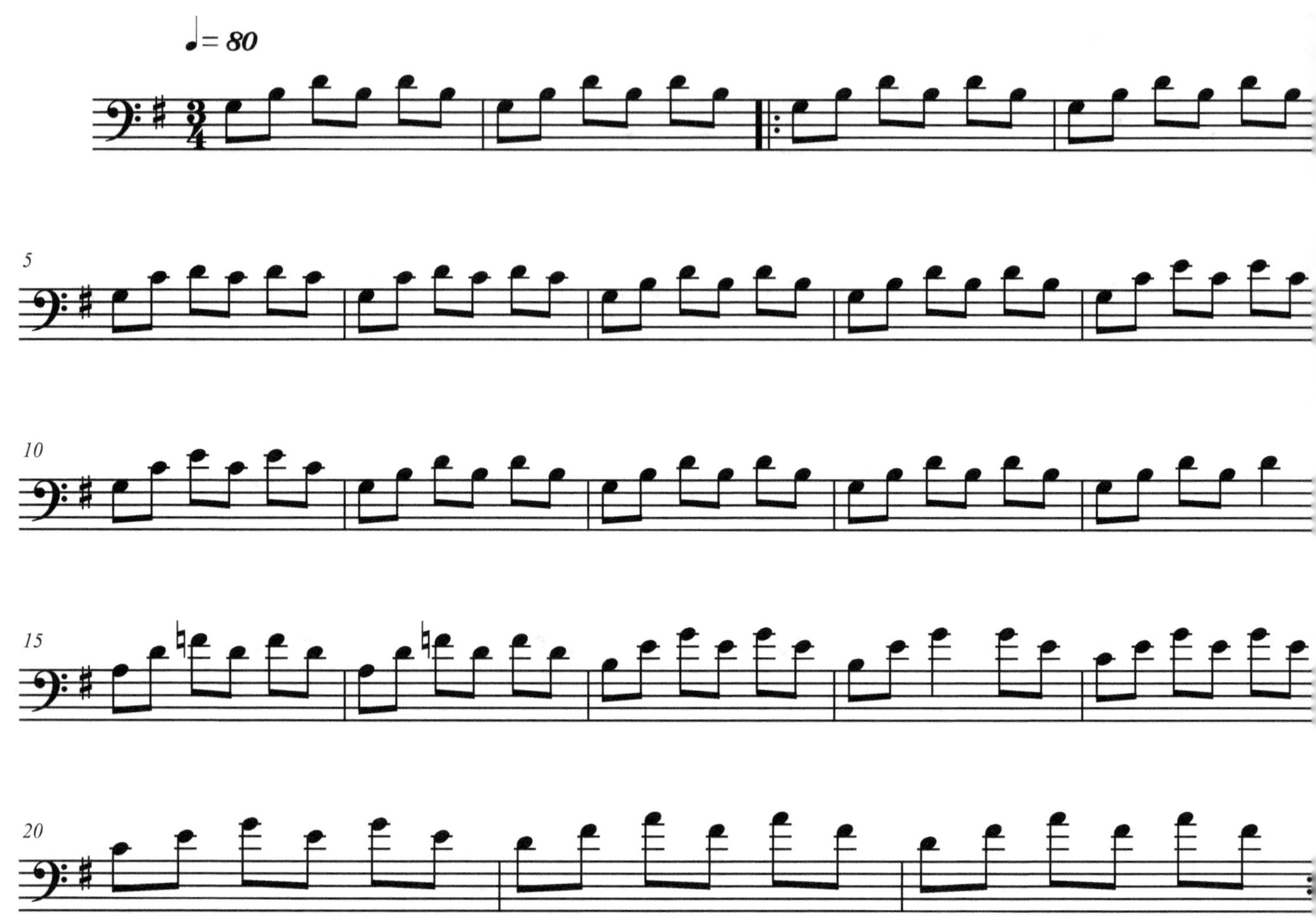

Part 3: Bes Baritone

A

Joost de Groot

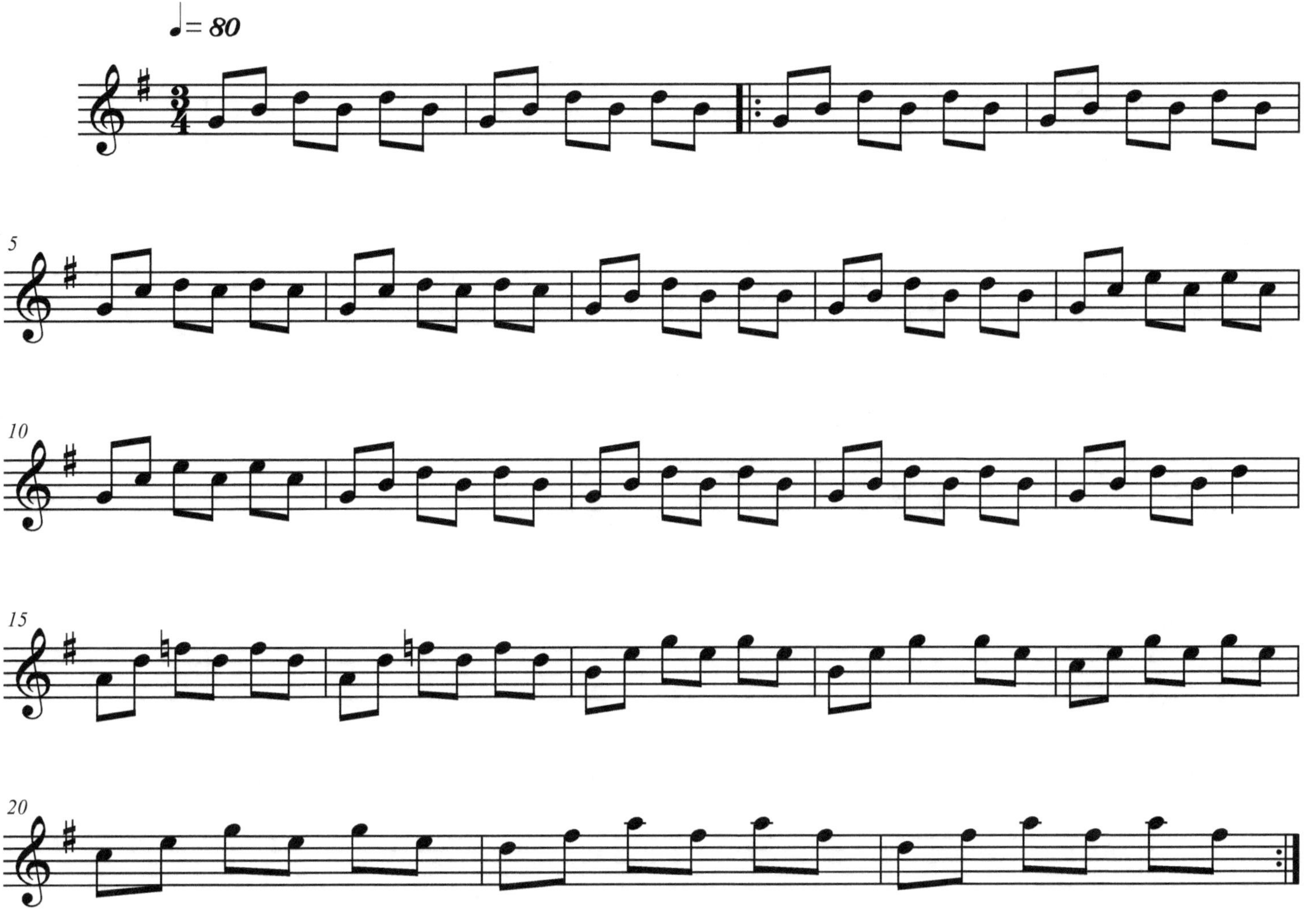

A

Part 4: C Bass Tuba

Joost de Gro

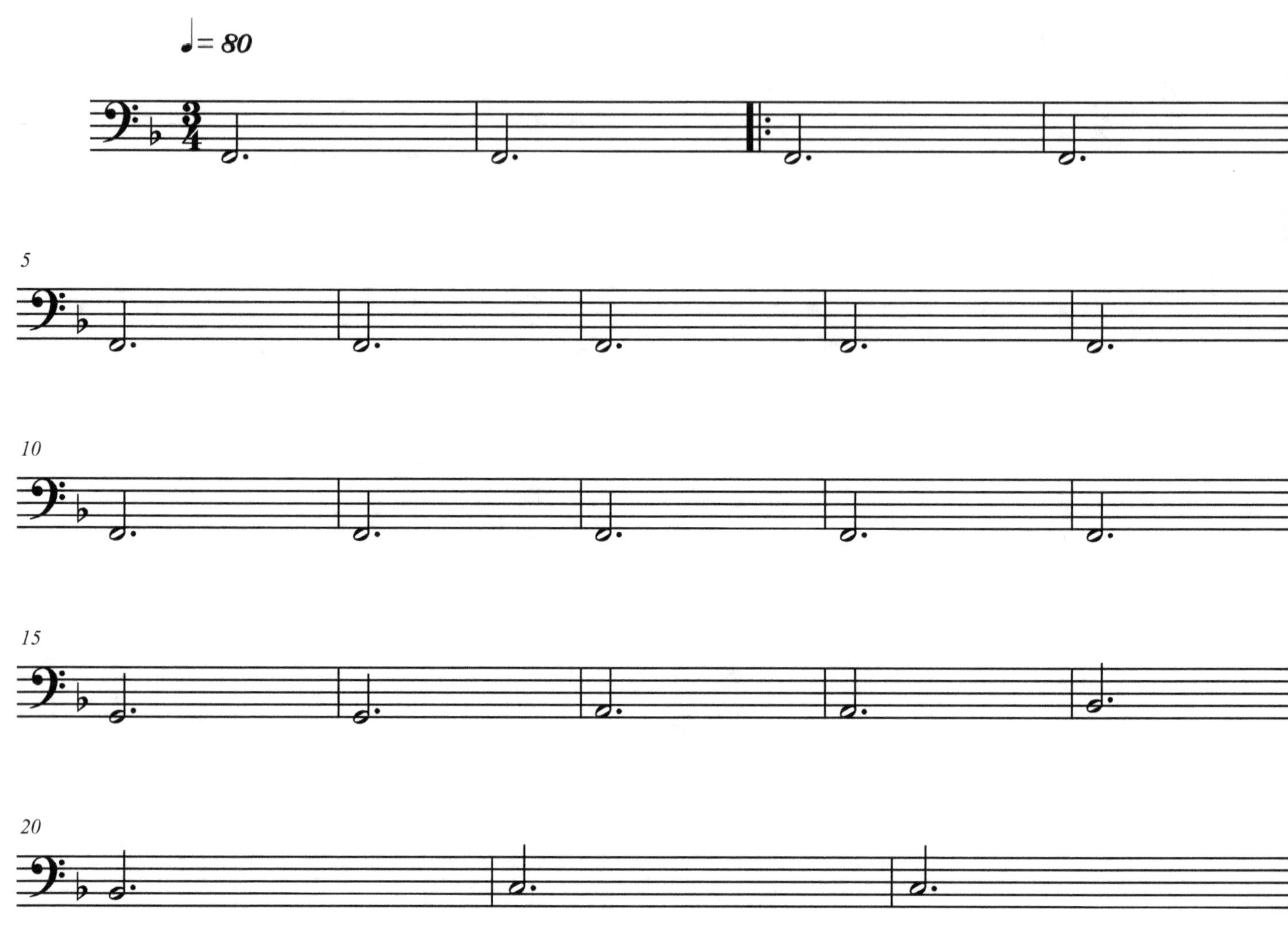

A

Part 4: Bes Bass Tuba

Joost de Groot

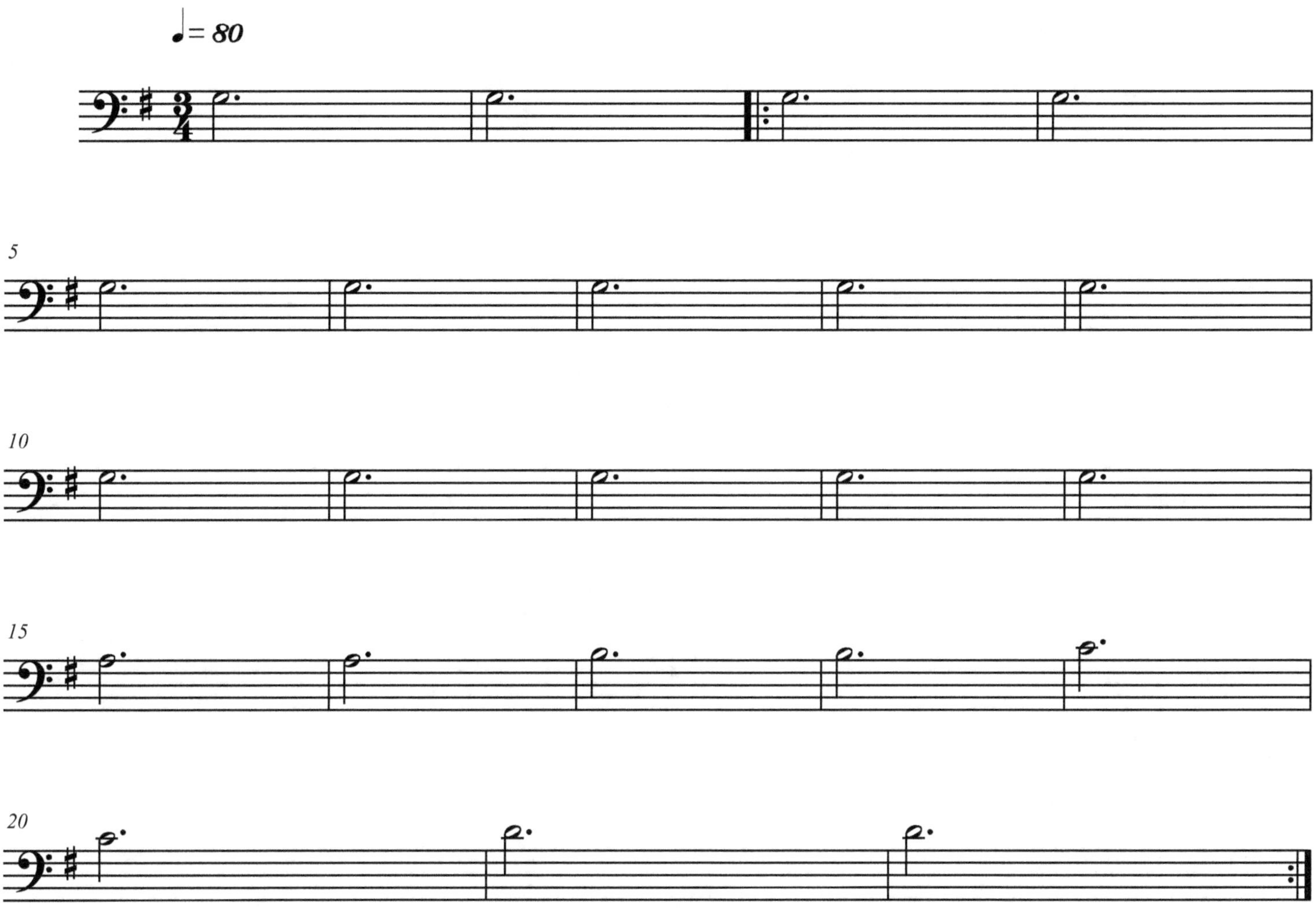

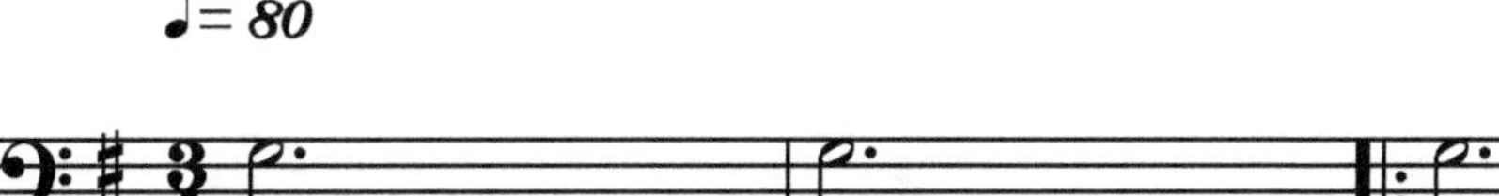

Part 4: Es Bass Tuba

A

Joost de Gro

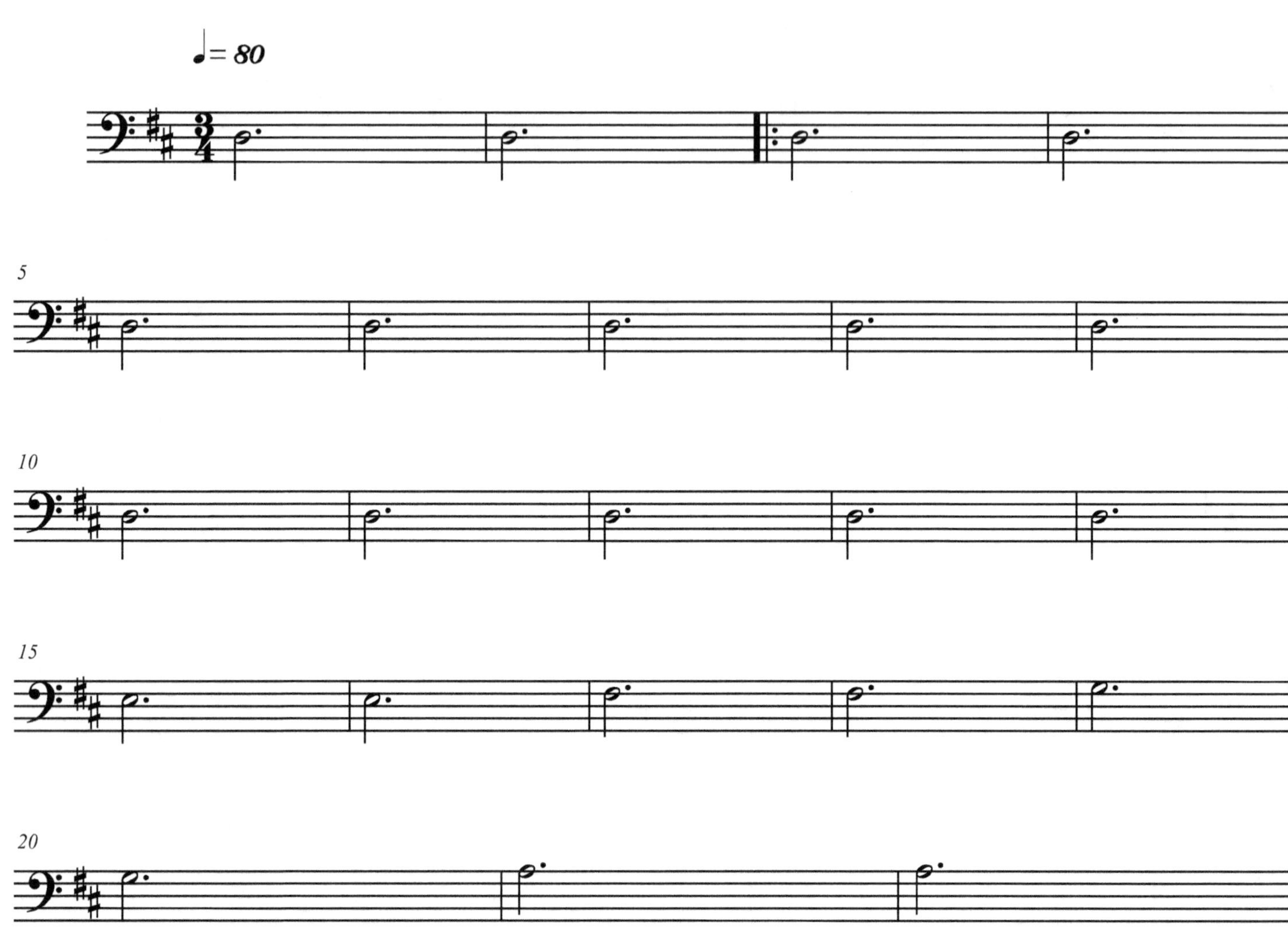

Part 1: C Flute

N

Joost de Groot

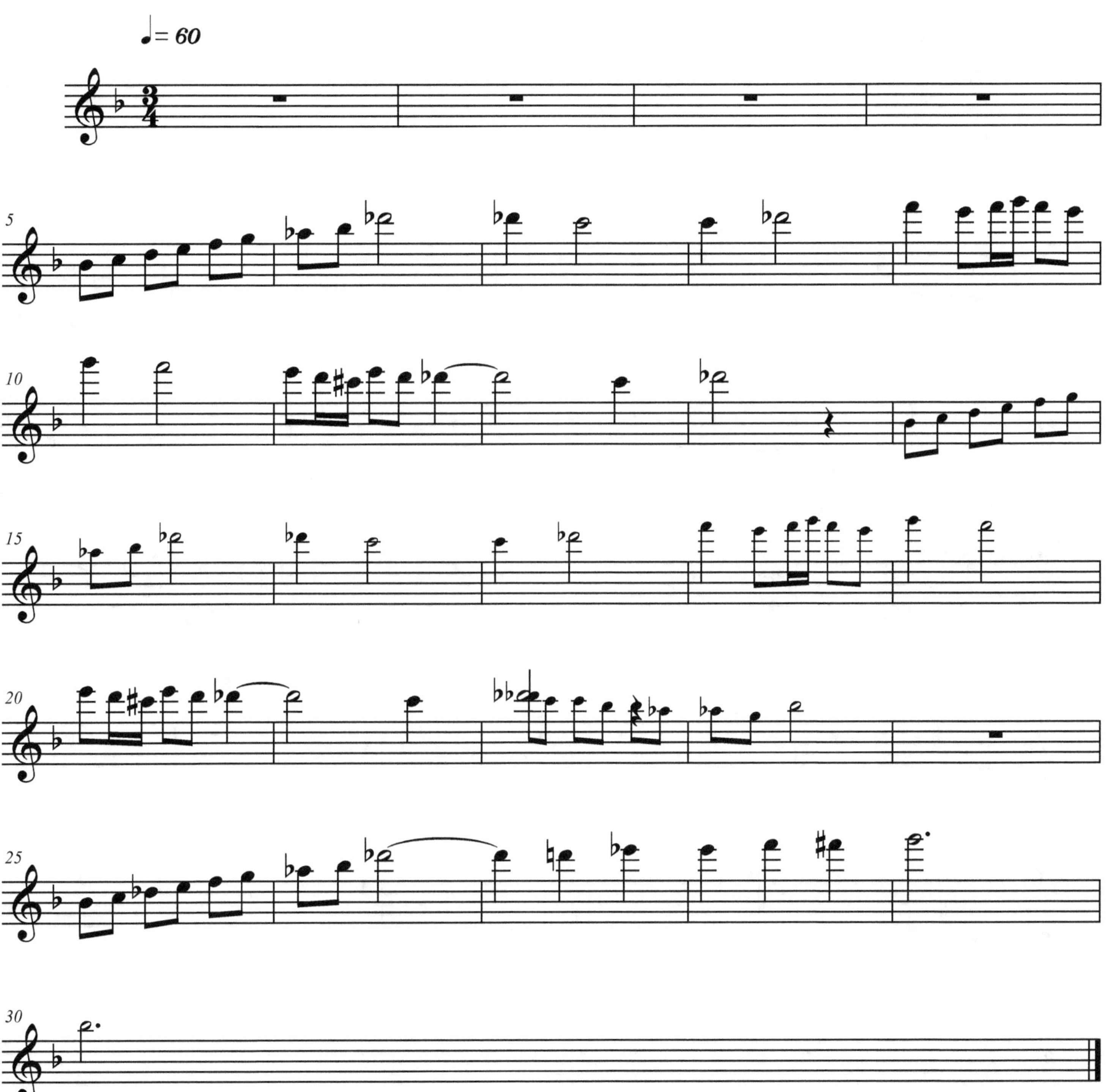

N

Part 1: C Oboe

Joost de Gro

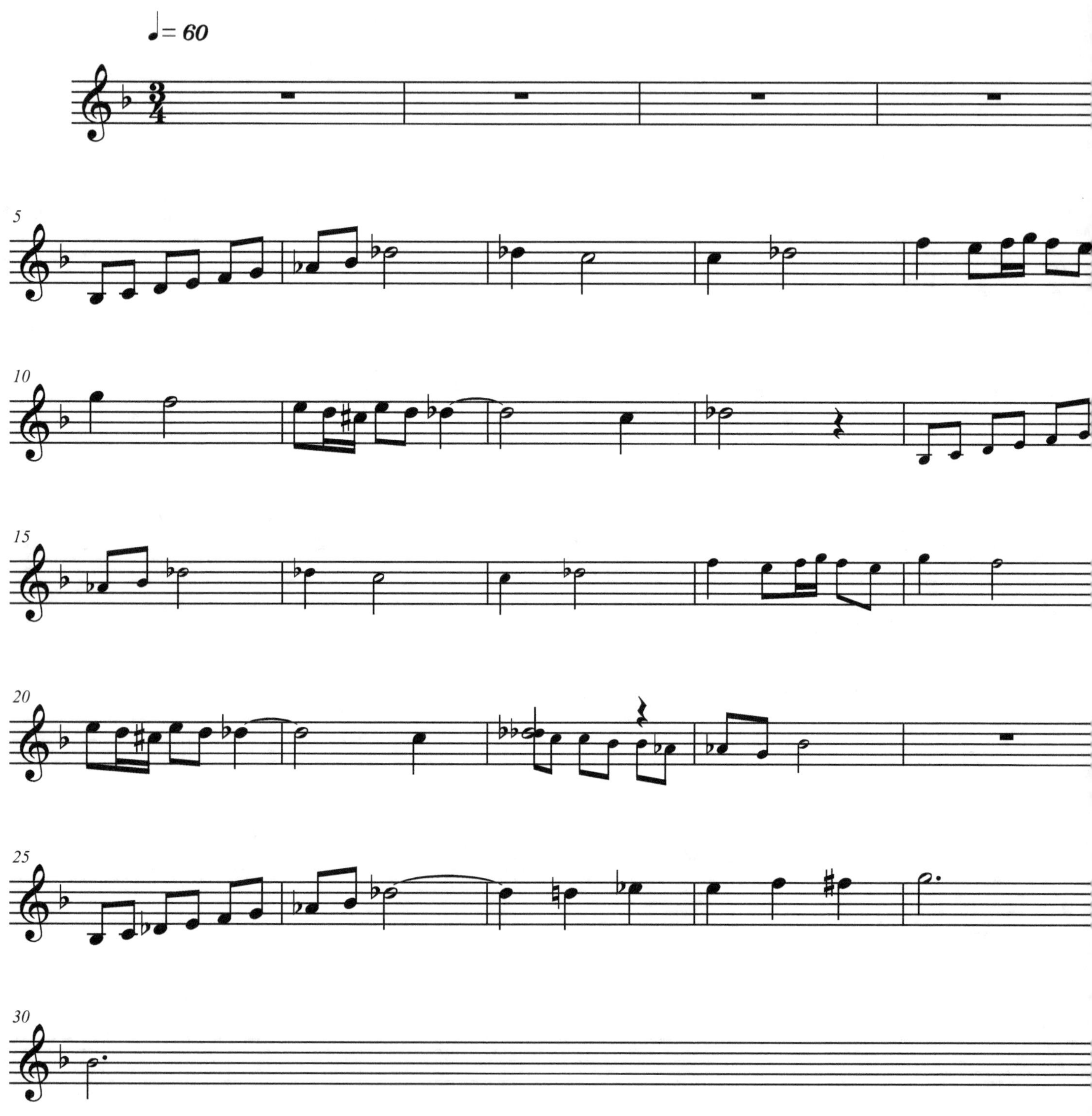

Part 4: C Bassoon

N

Joost de Groot

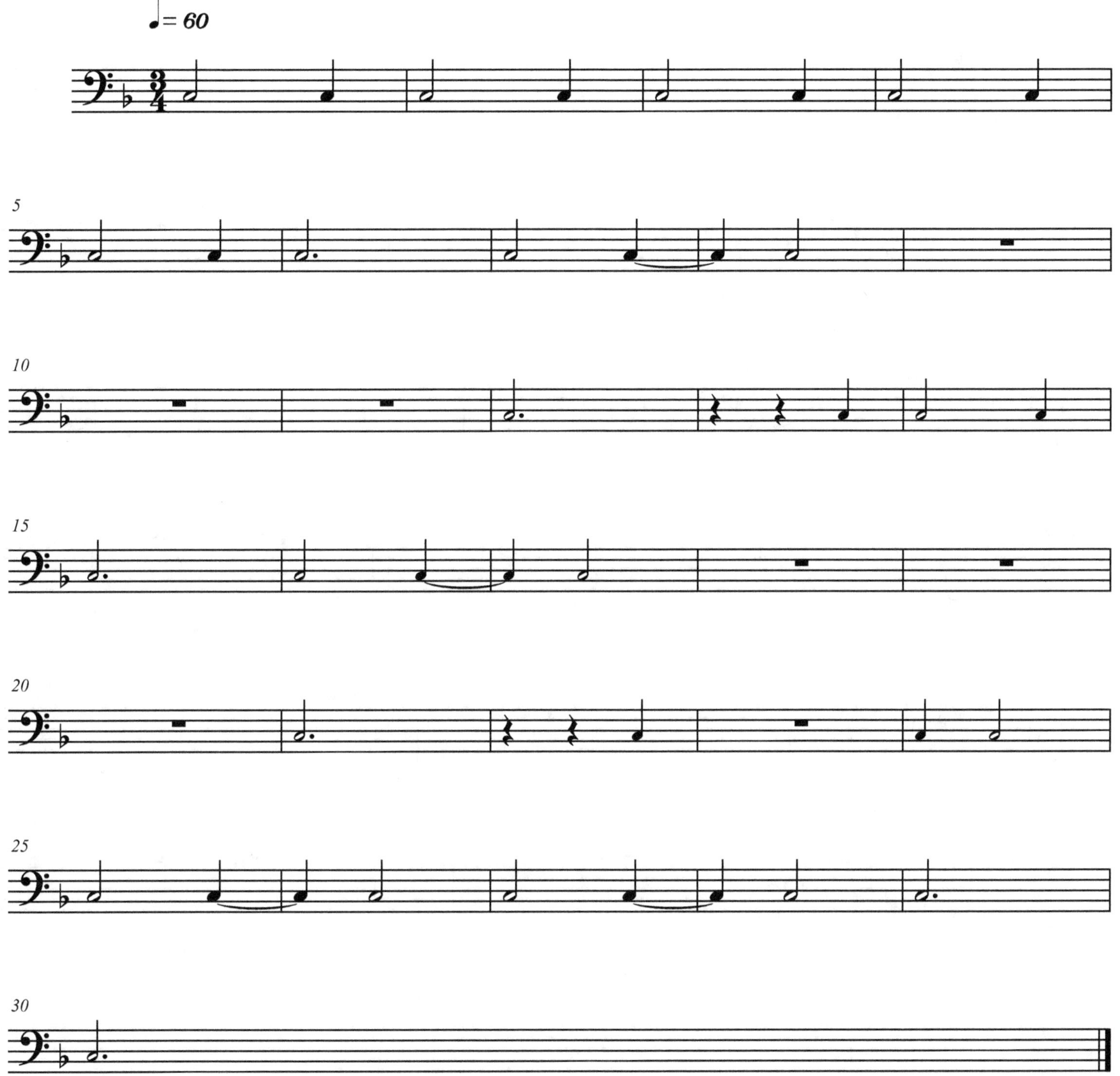

N

Part 1: Bes Clarinet 1

Joost de Gro

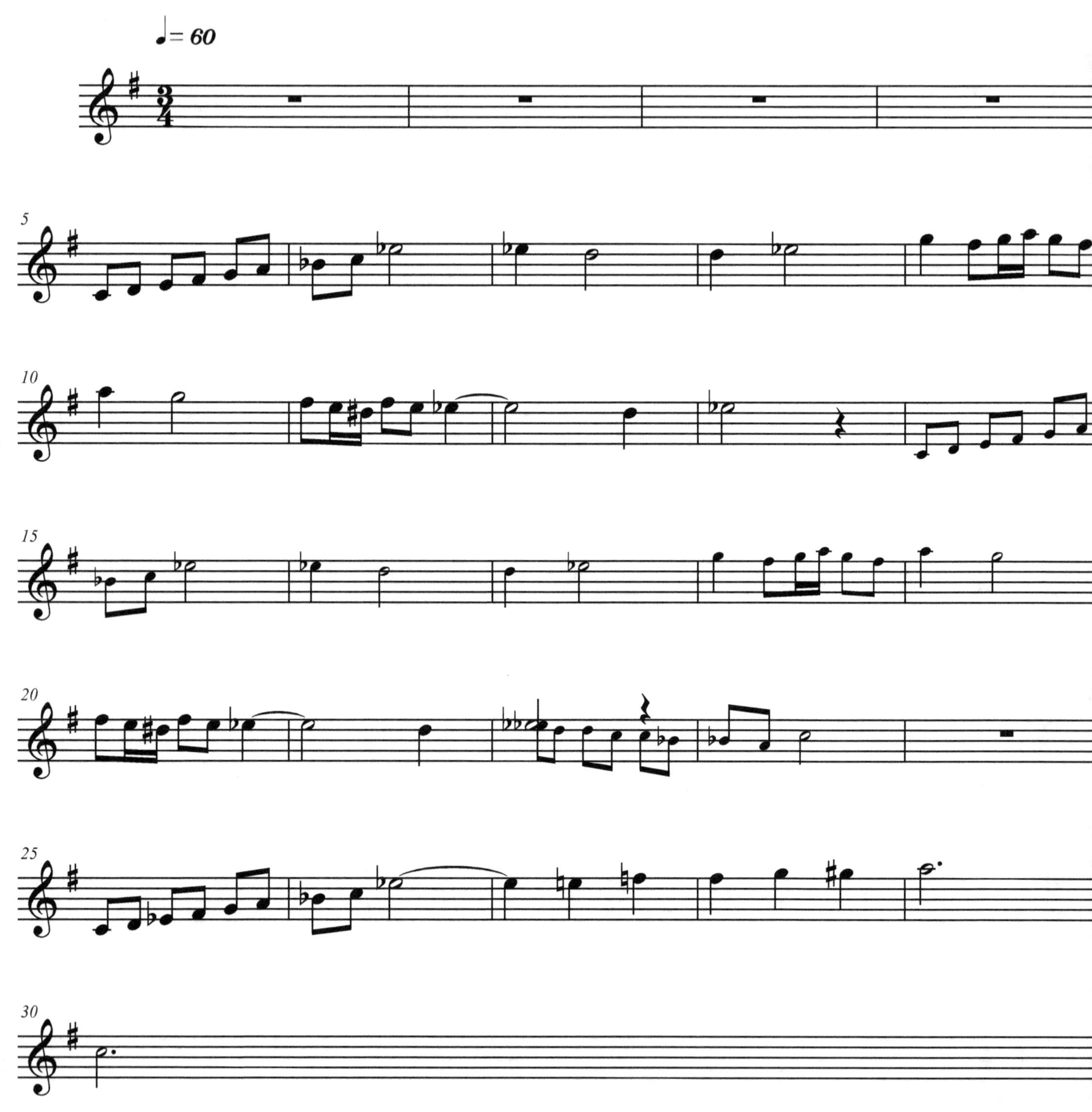

Part 2: Bes Clarinet 2 + 3

N

Joost de Groot

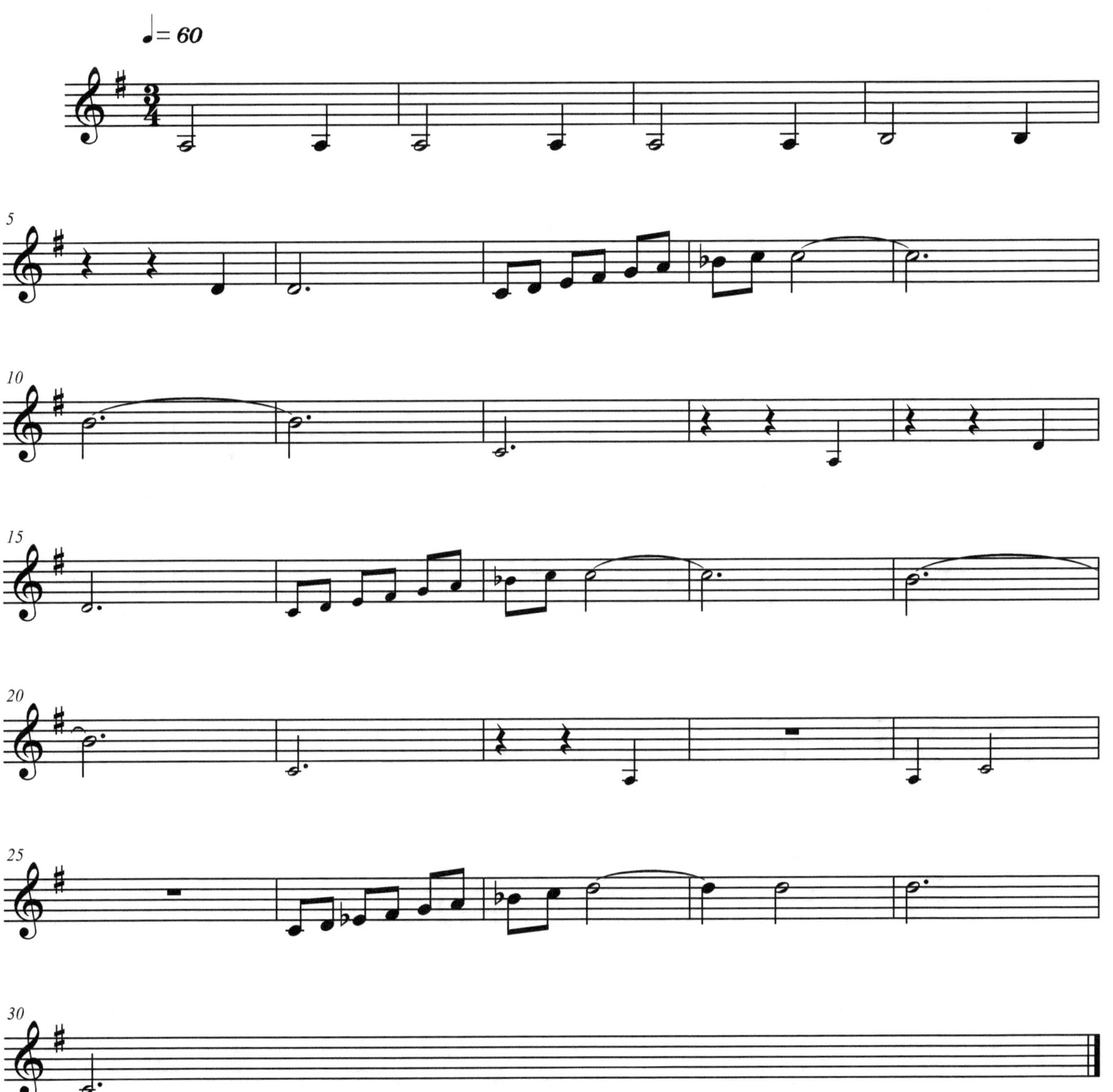

Part 3: Es Alto Clarinet

N

Joost de Gro

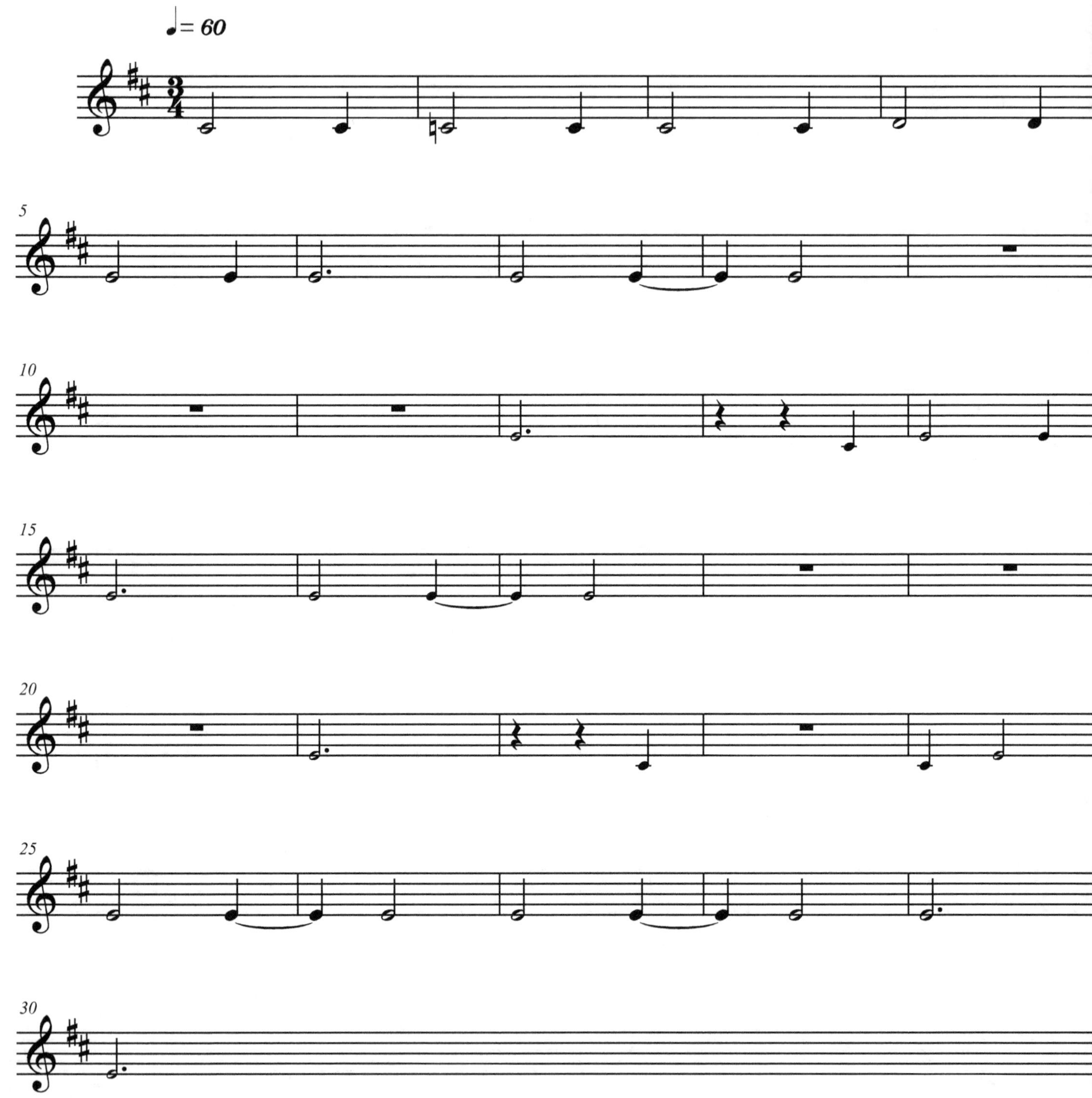

Part 4: Bes Bass Clarinet

N

Joost de Groot

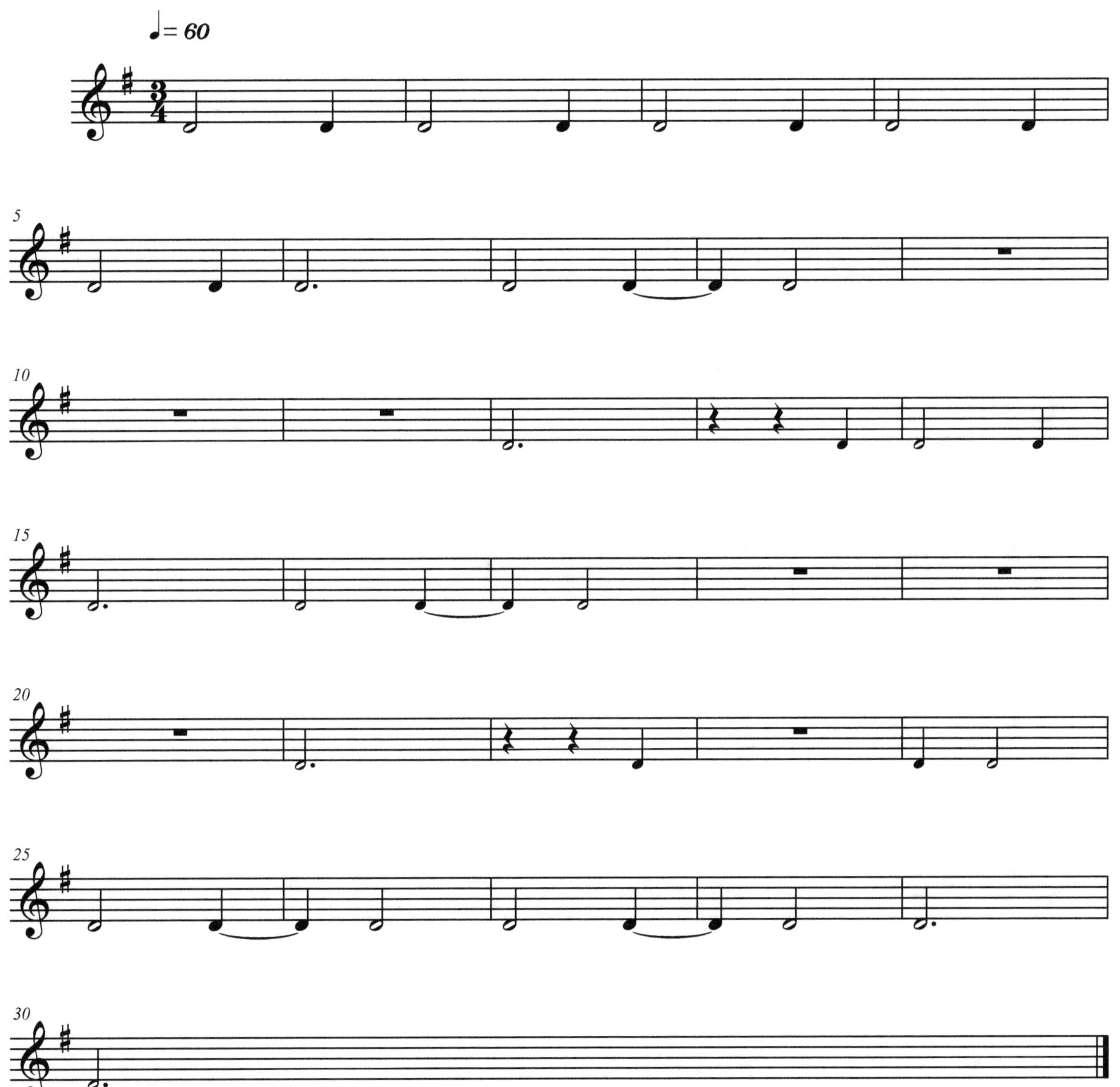

N

Part 2: Es Alto Sax.

Joost de Gro

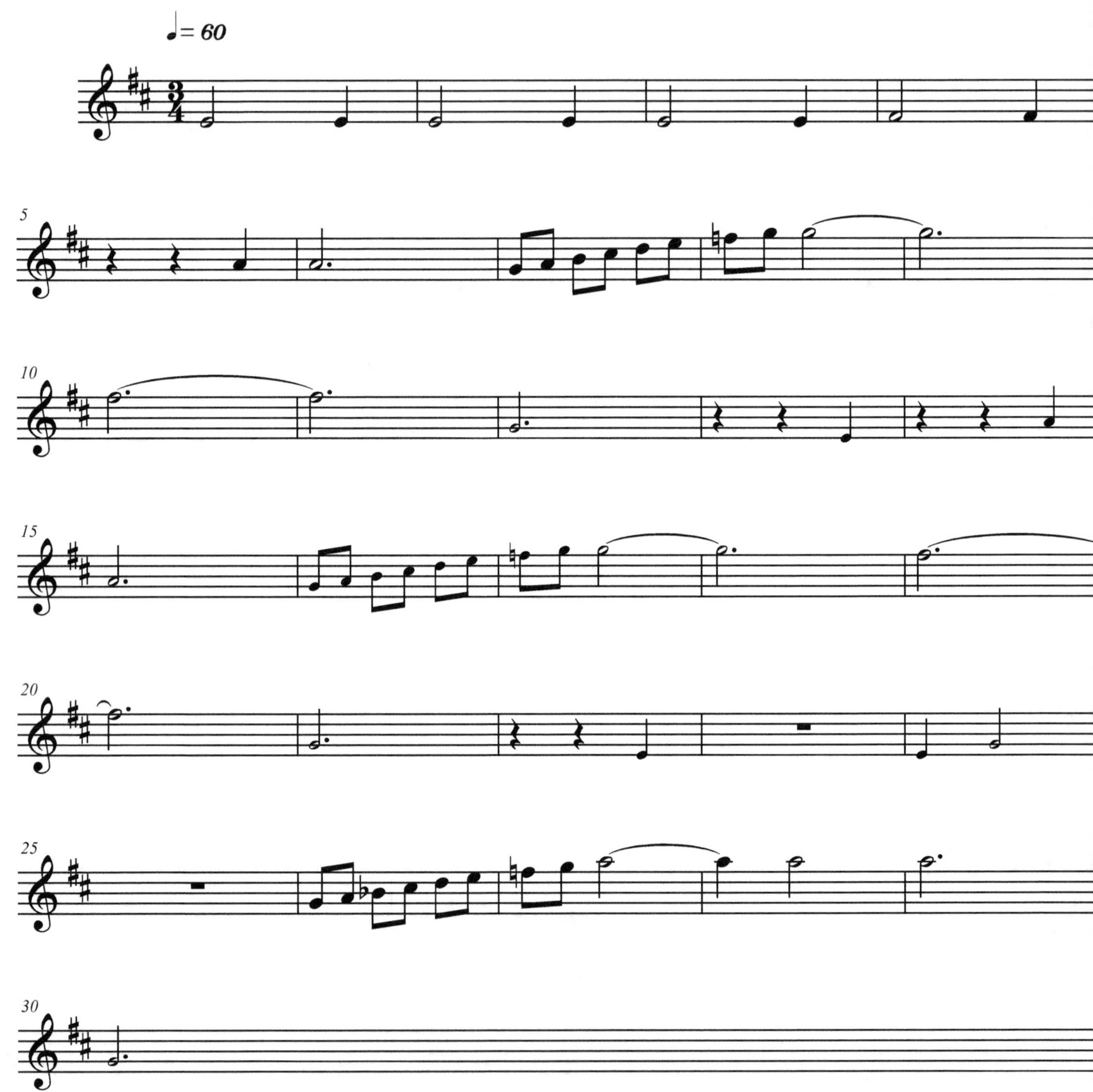

N

Part 3: Bes Tenor Sax.

Joost de Groot

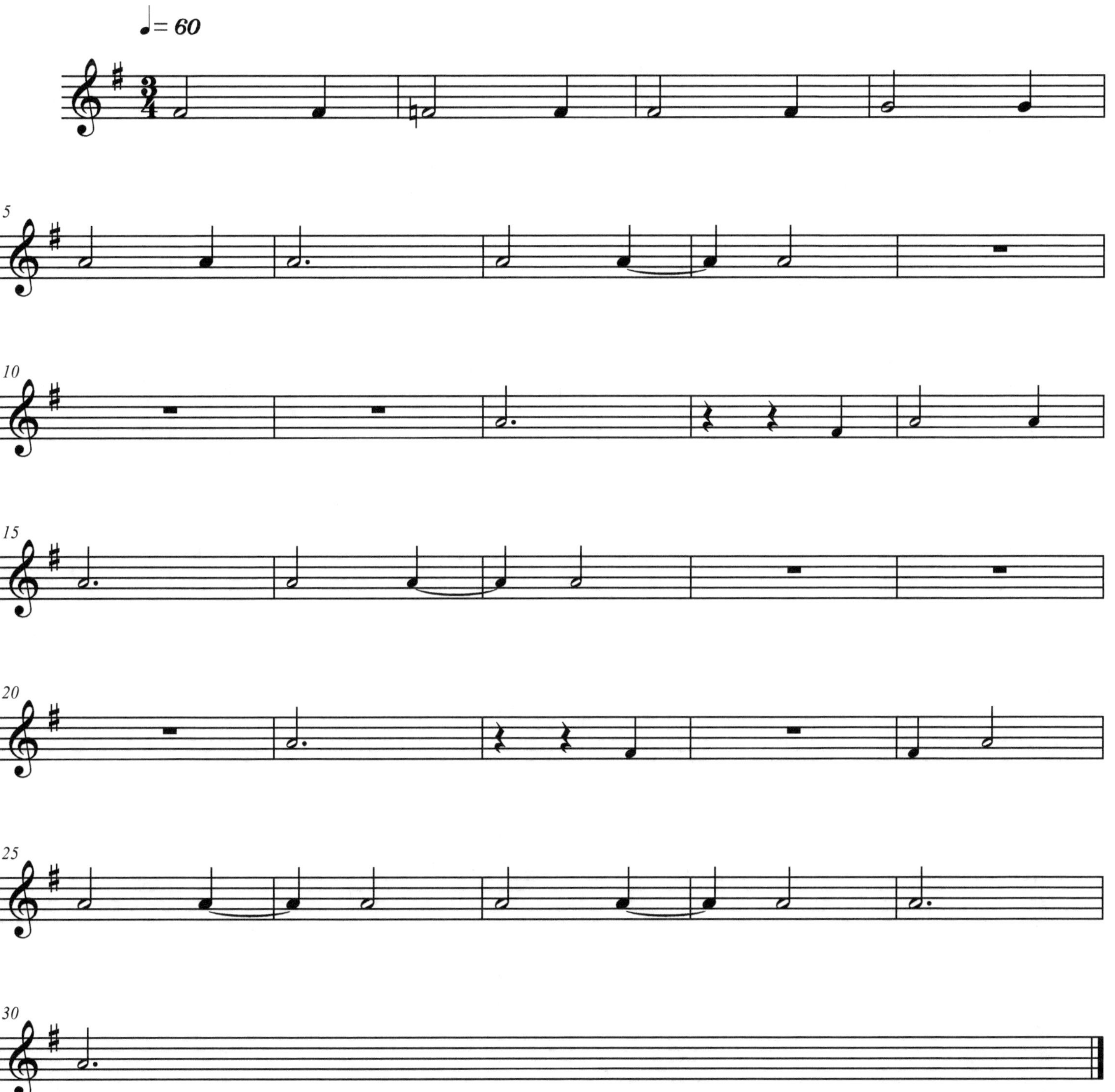

Part 4: Es Baritone Sax.

N

Joost de Gro

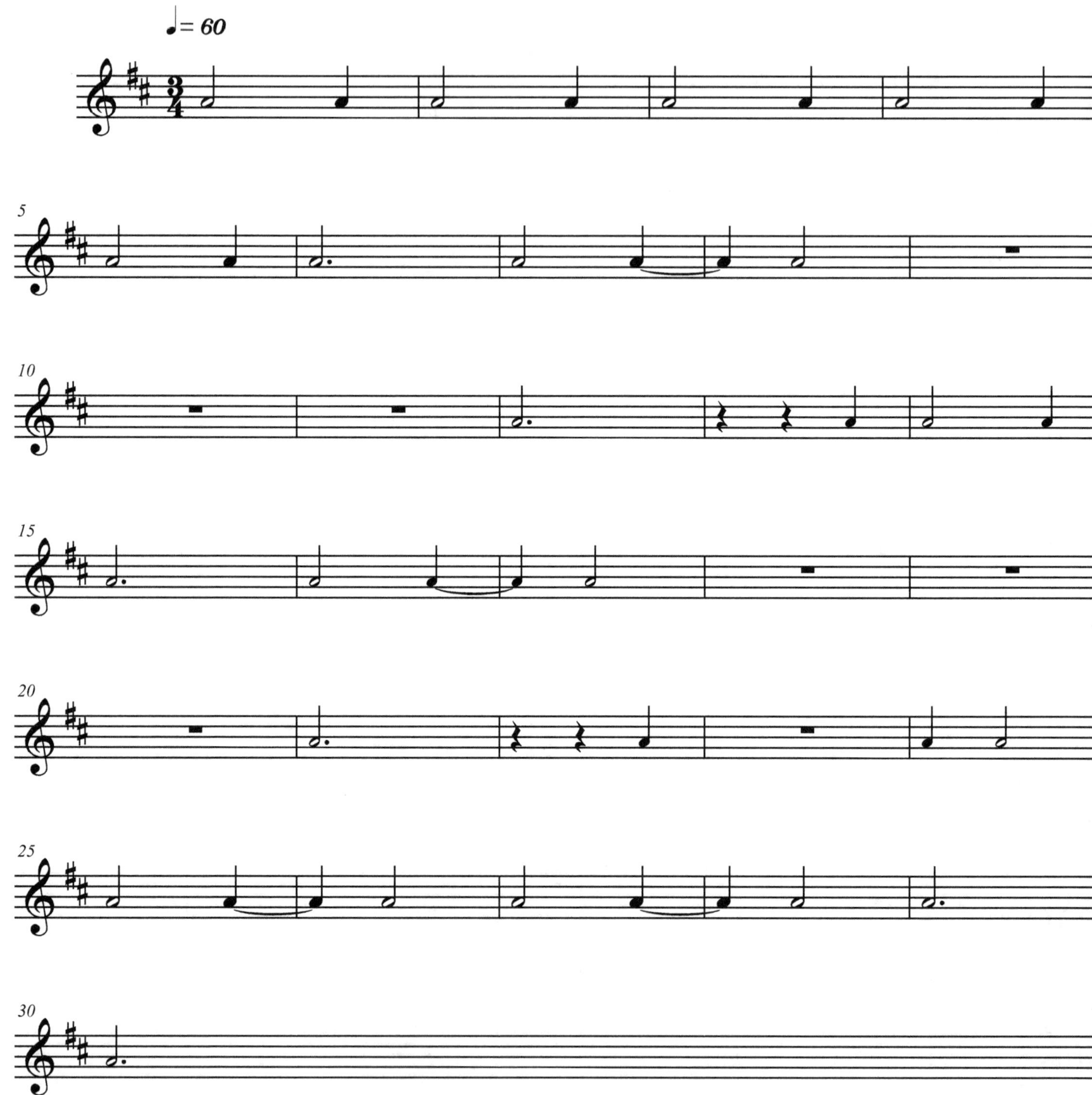

Part 1: Bes Trumpet 1

N

Joost de Groot

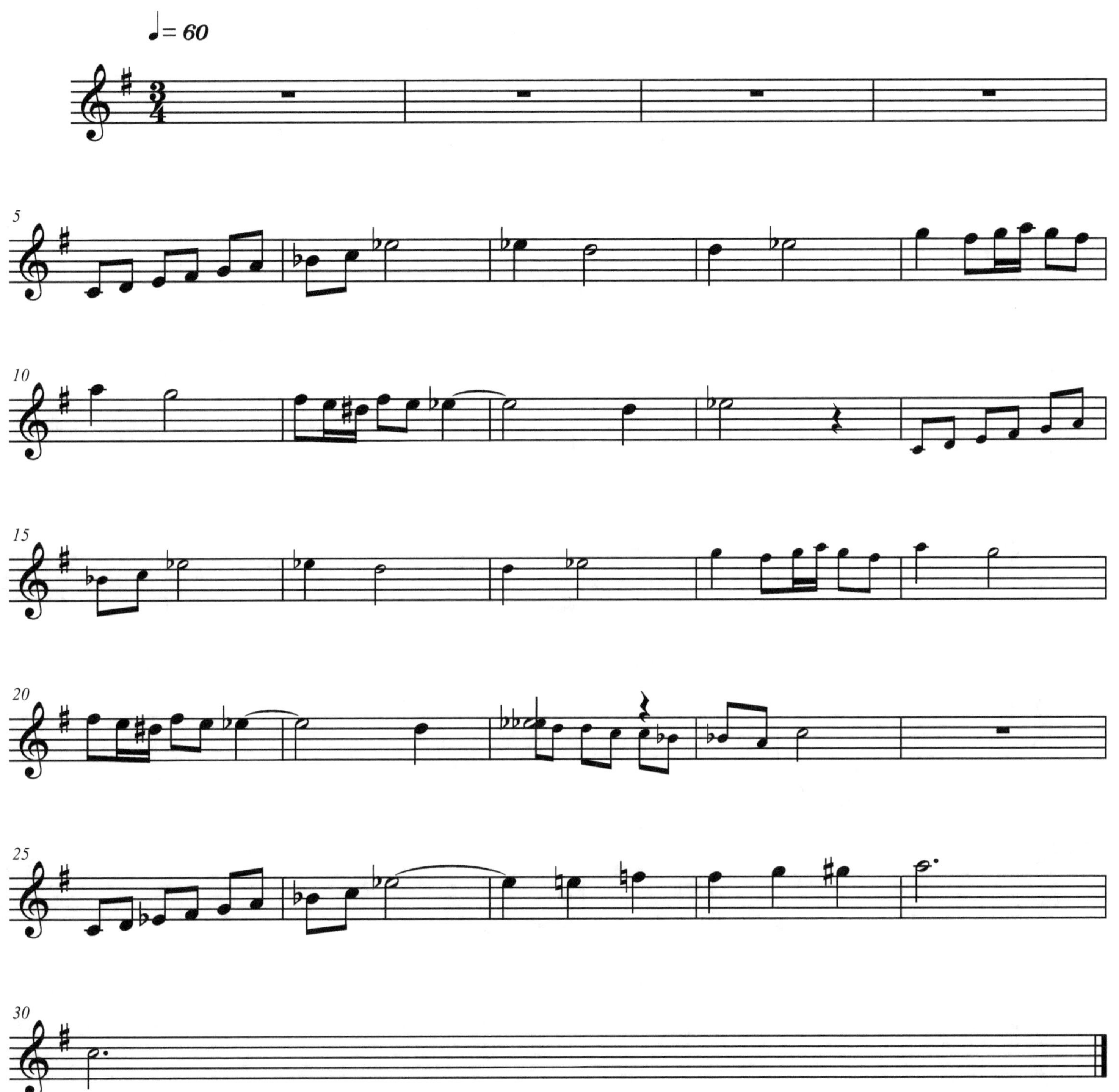

Part 2: Bes Trumpet 2 + 3

N

Joost de Gro

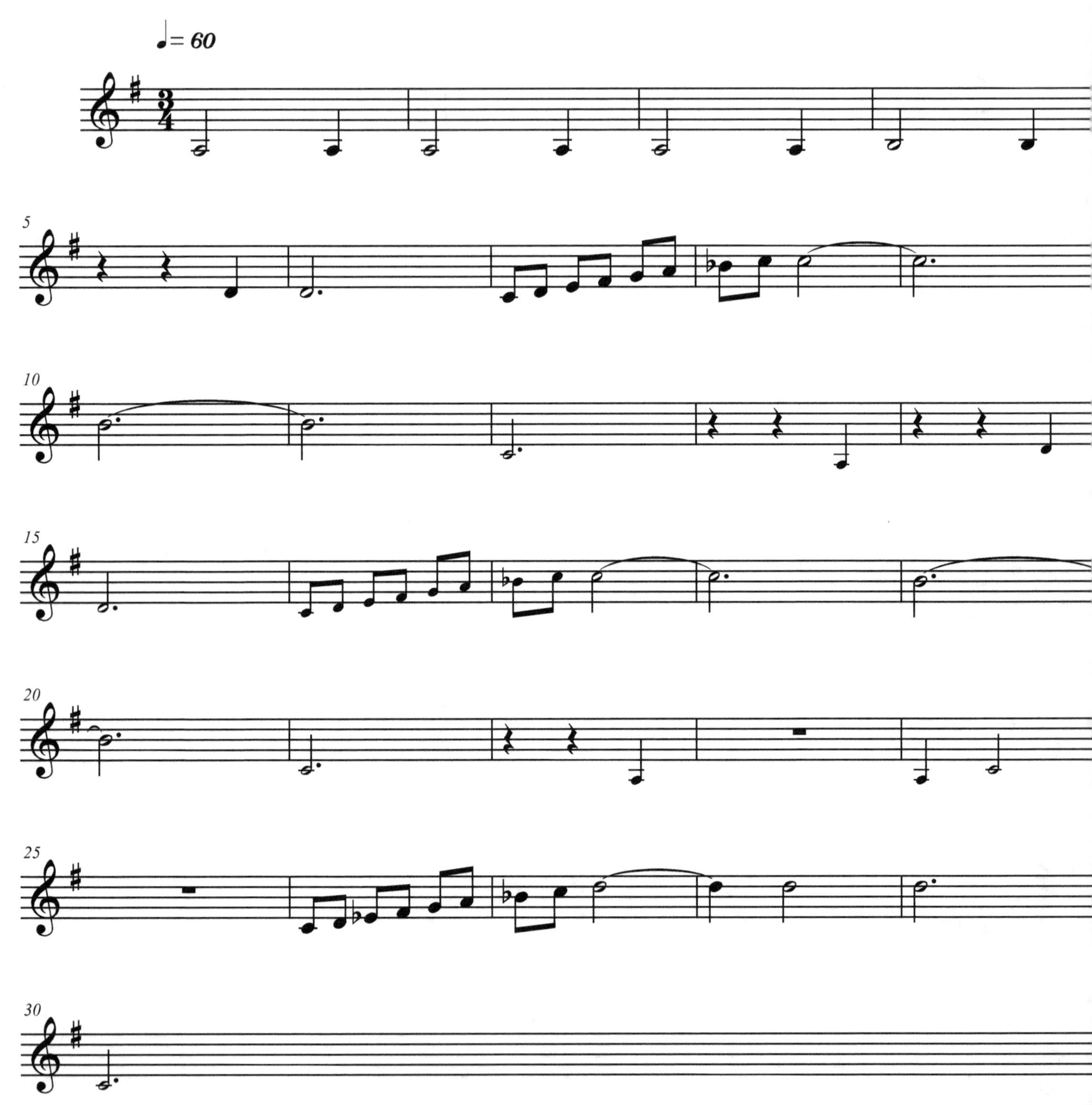

Part 2: F Horn 1 + 2

N

Joost de Groot

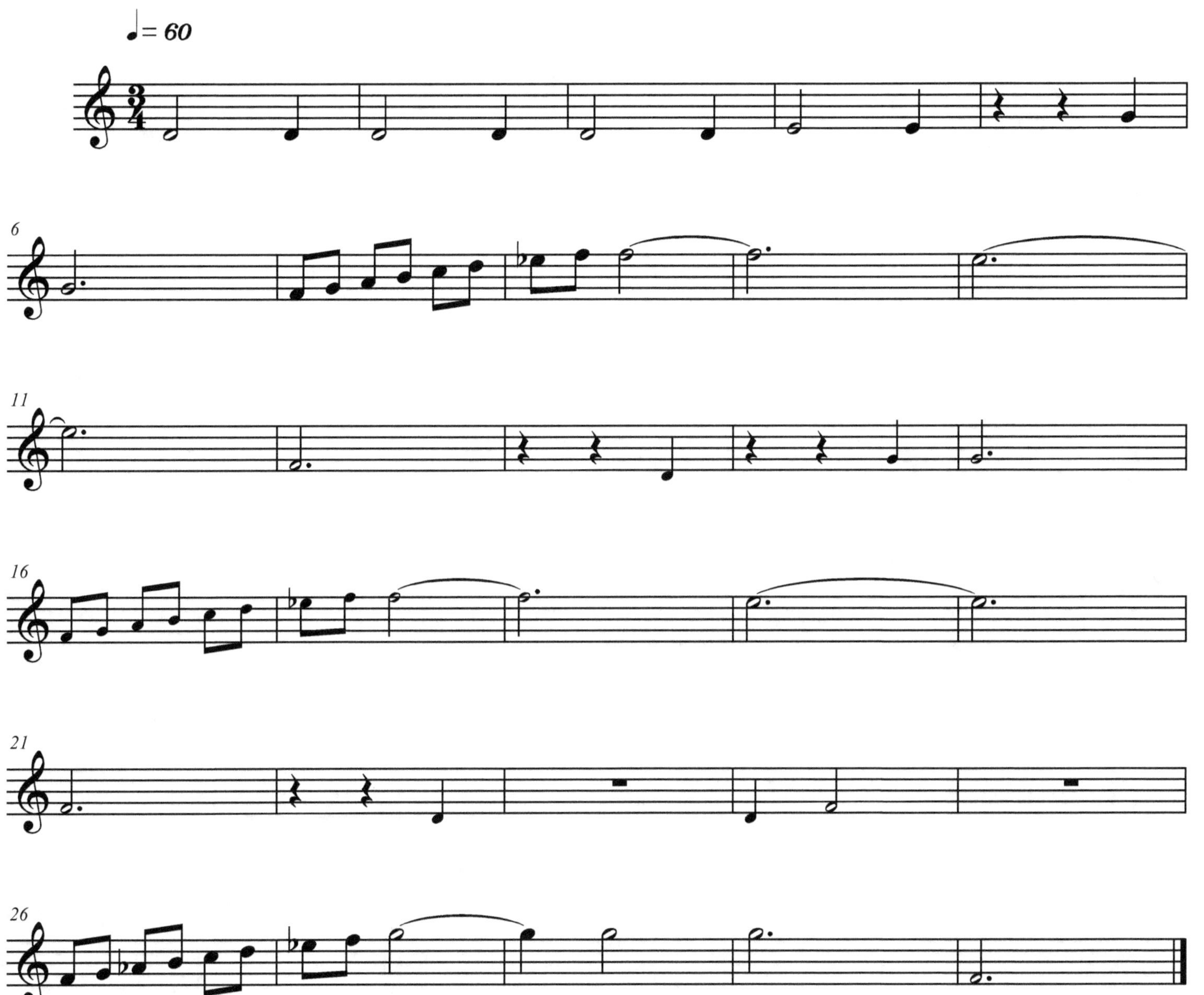

N

Part 3: F Horn 3 + 4

Joost de Gro

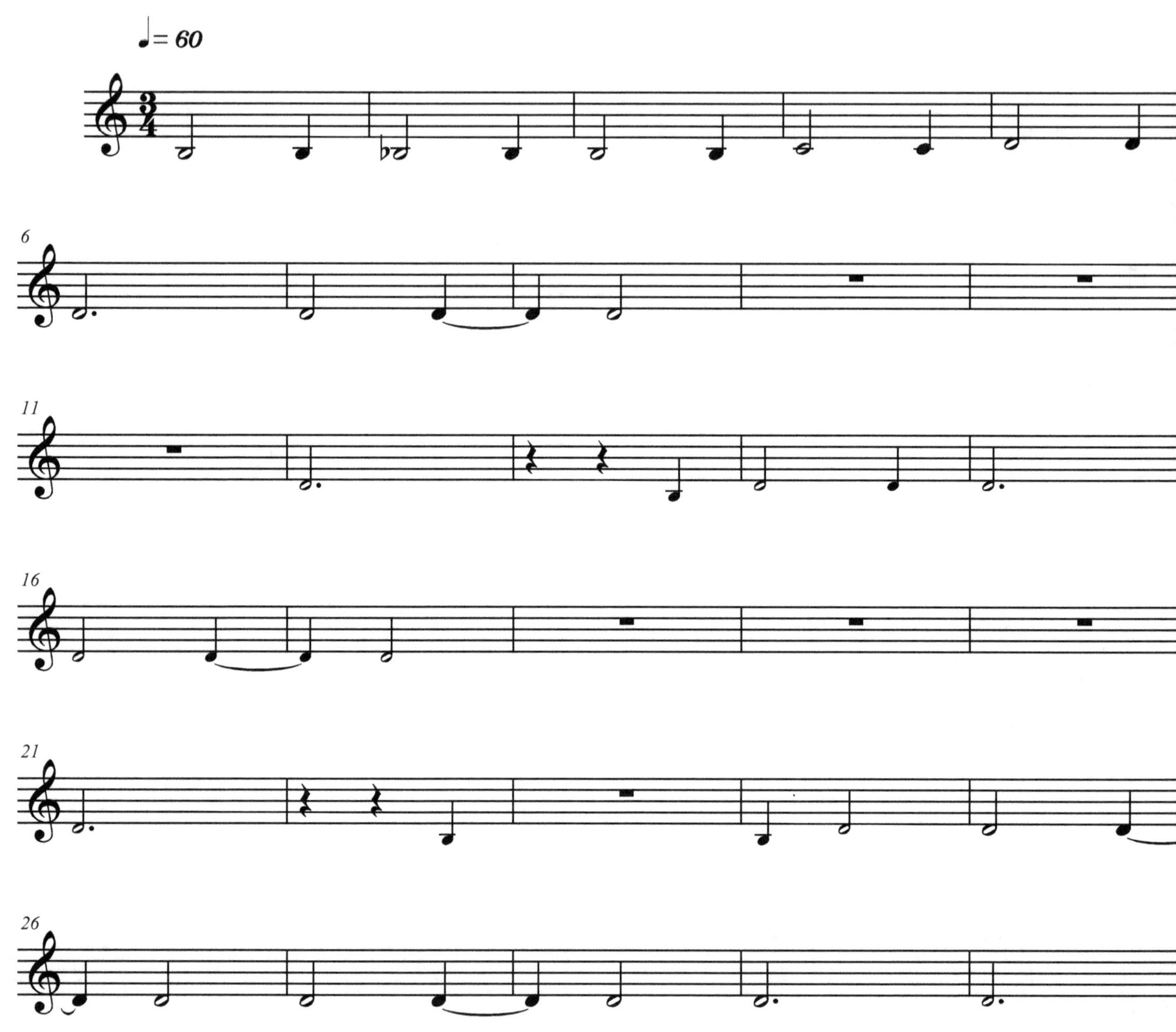

Part 3: C Trombone 1 + 2

N

Joost de Groot

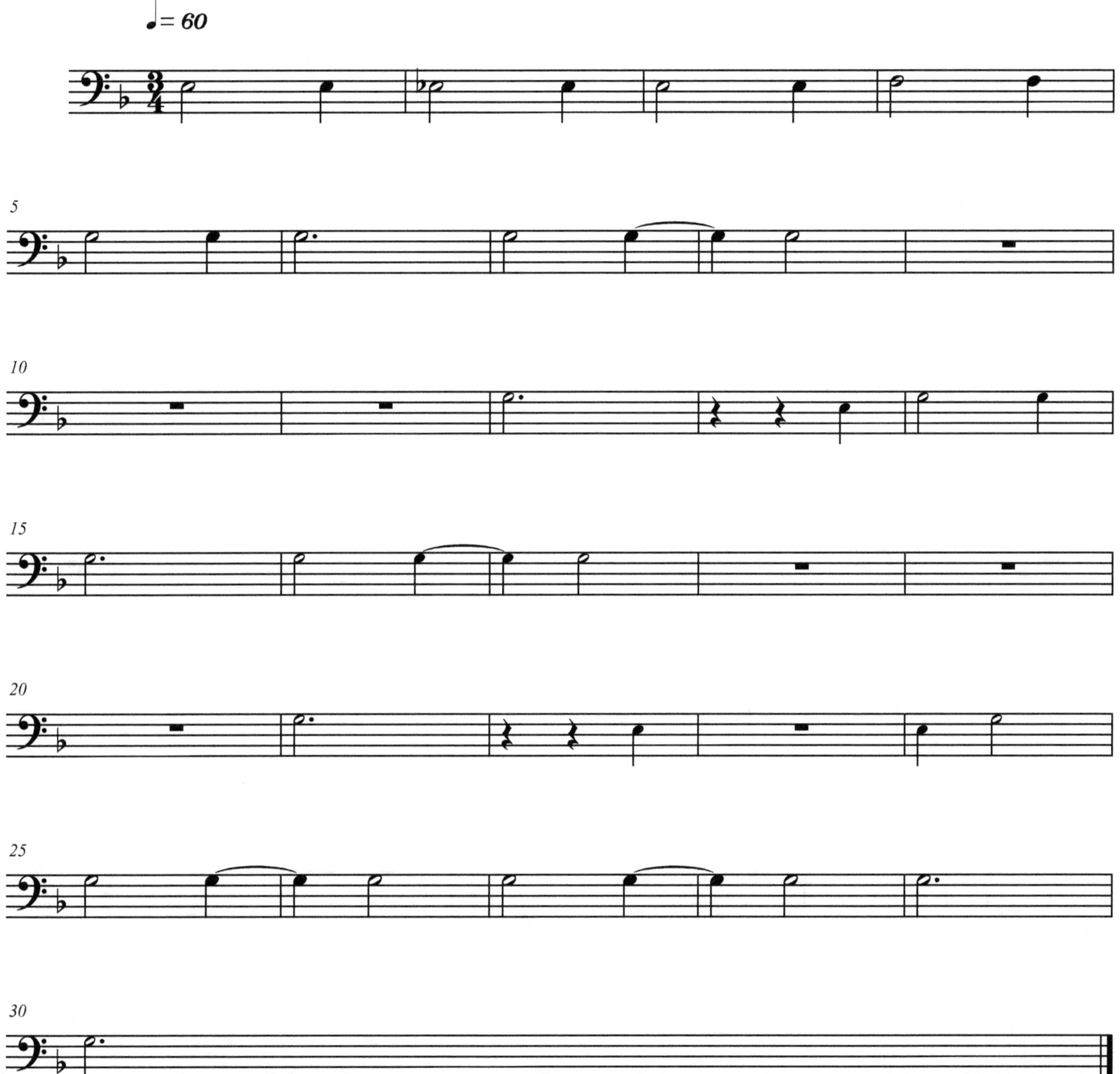

N

Part 4: C Bass Trombone

Joost de Gro[illegible]

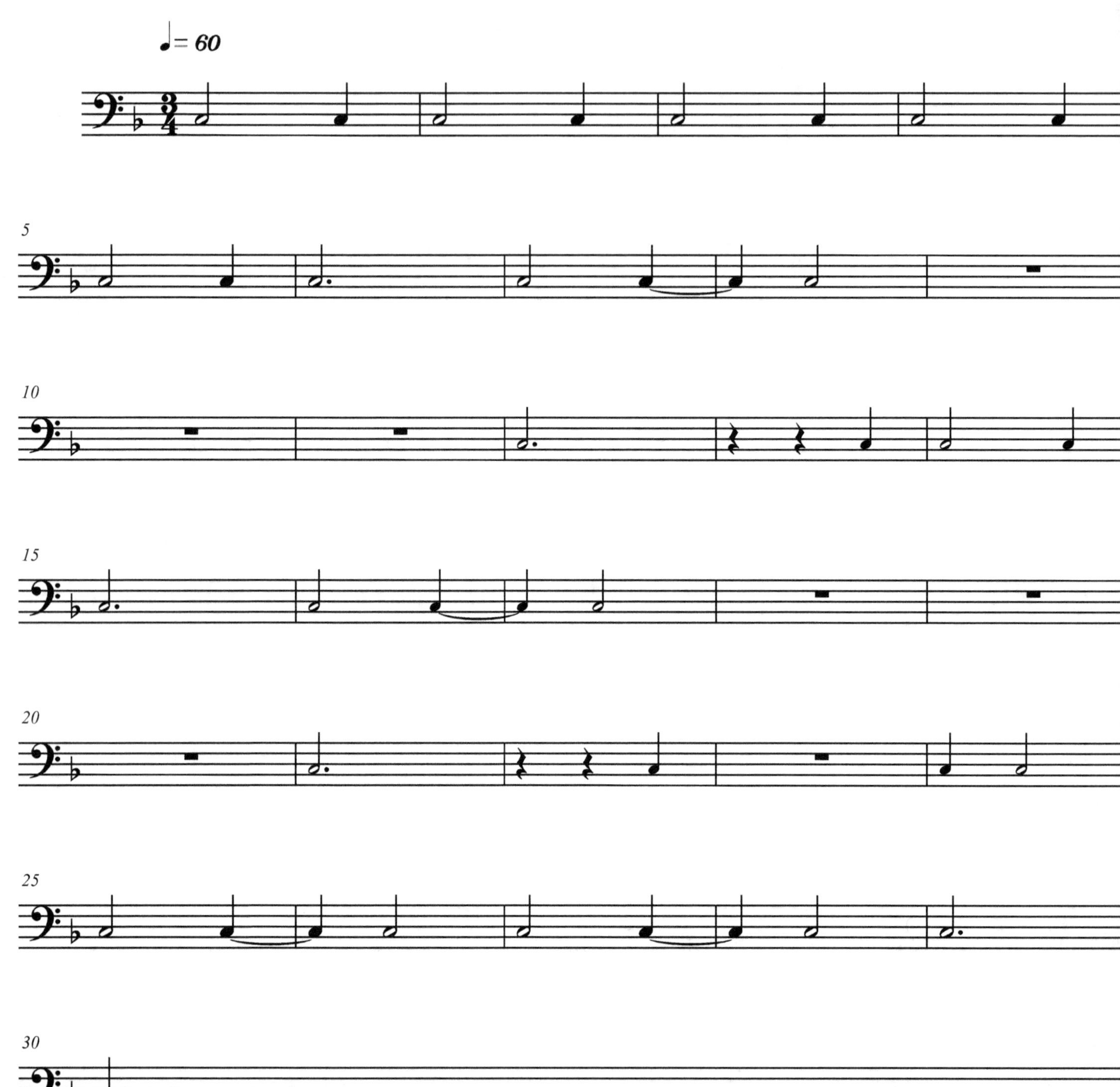

Part 3: C Baritone

N

Joost de Groot

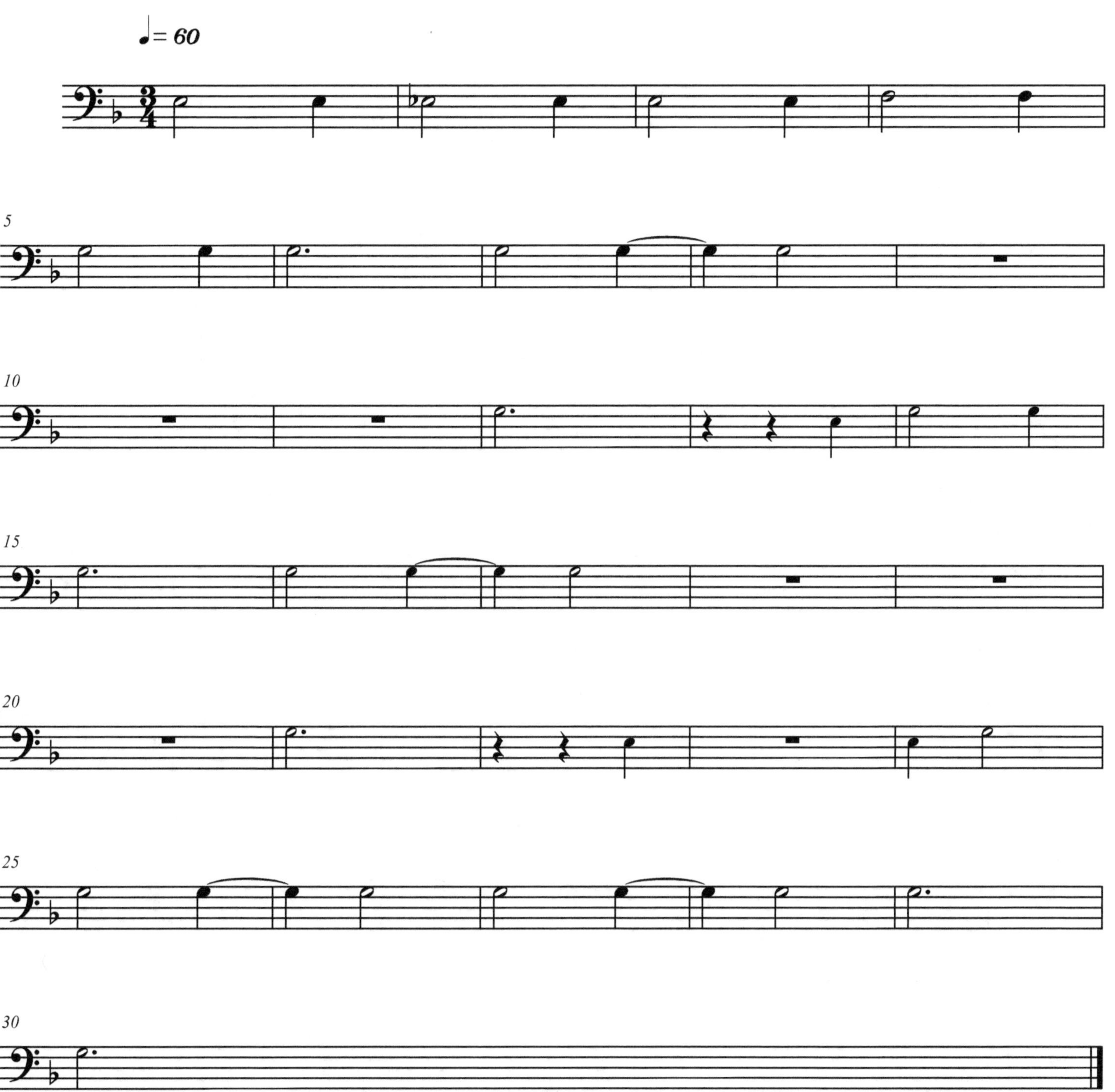

Part 3: Bes Baritone

N

Joost de Gro

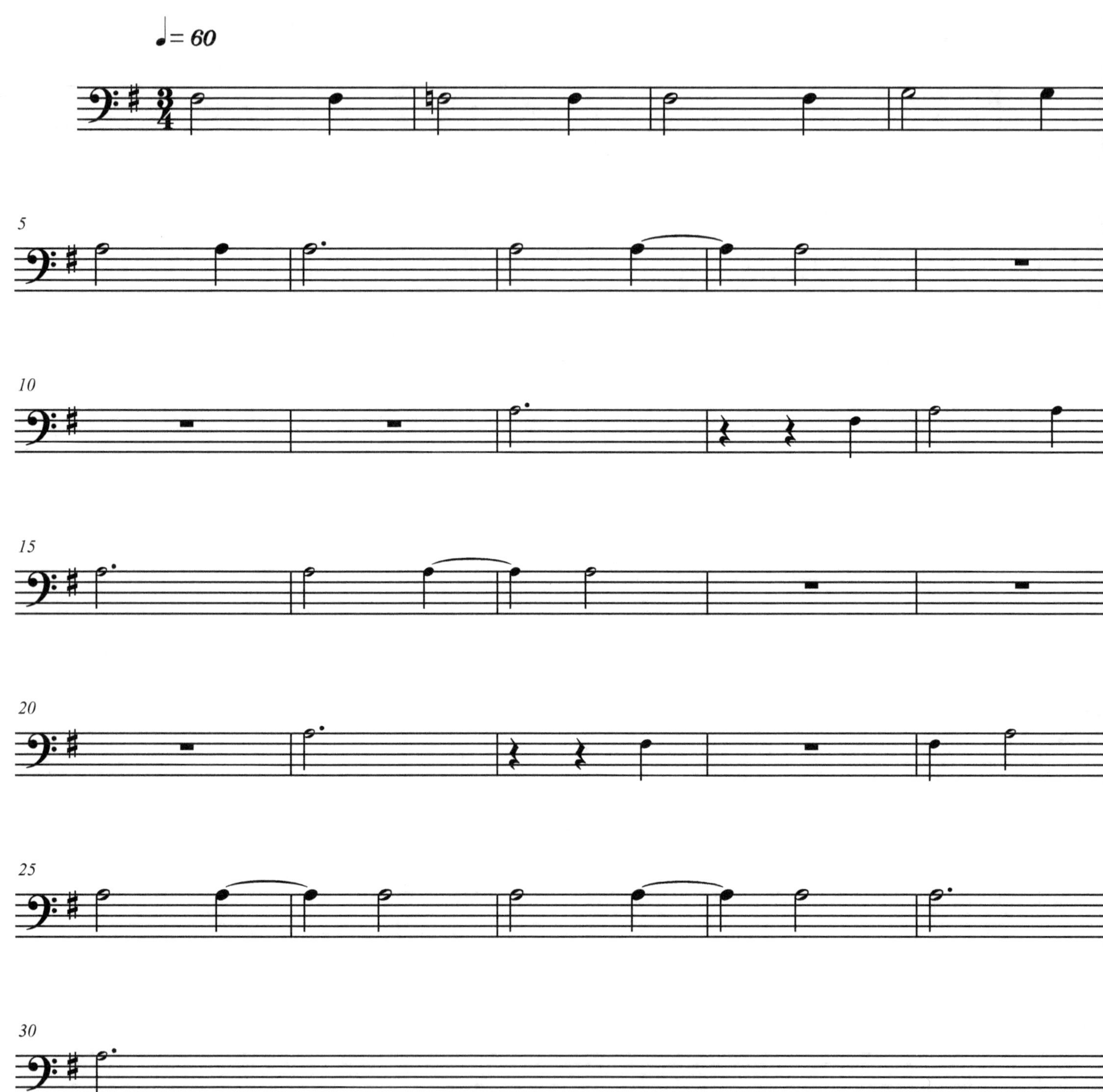

Part 3: Bes Baritone

N

Joost de Groot

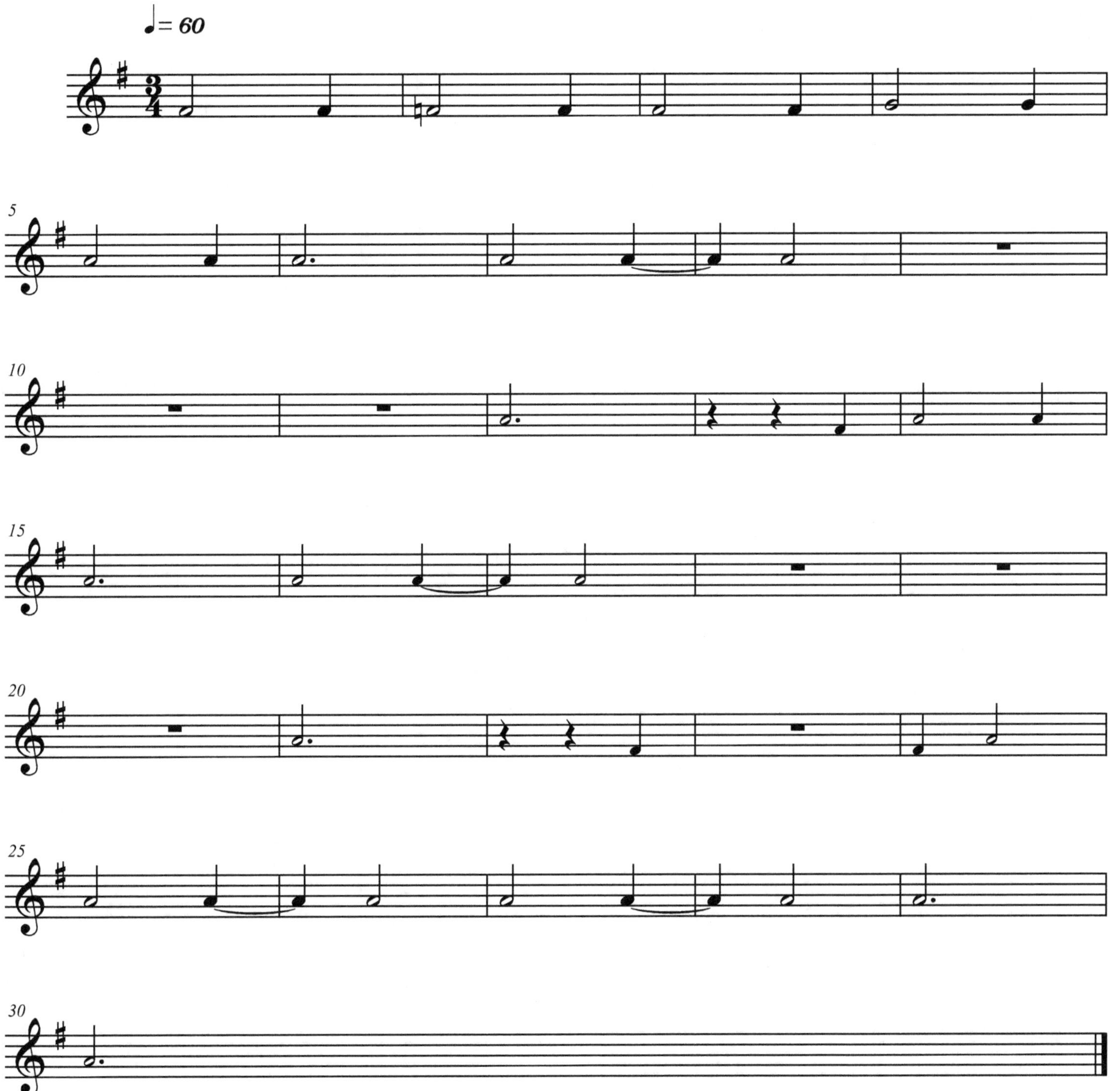

Part 4: C Bass Tuba

N

Joost de Gro

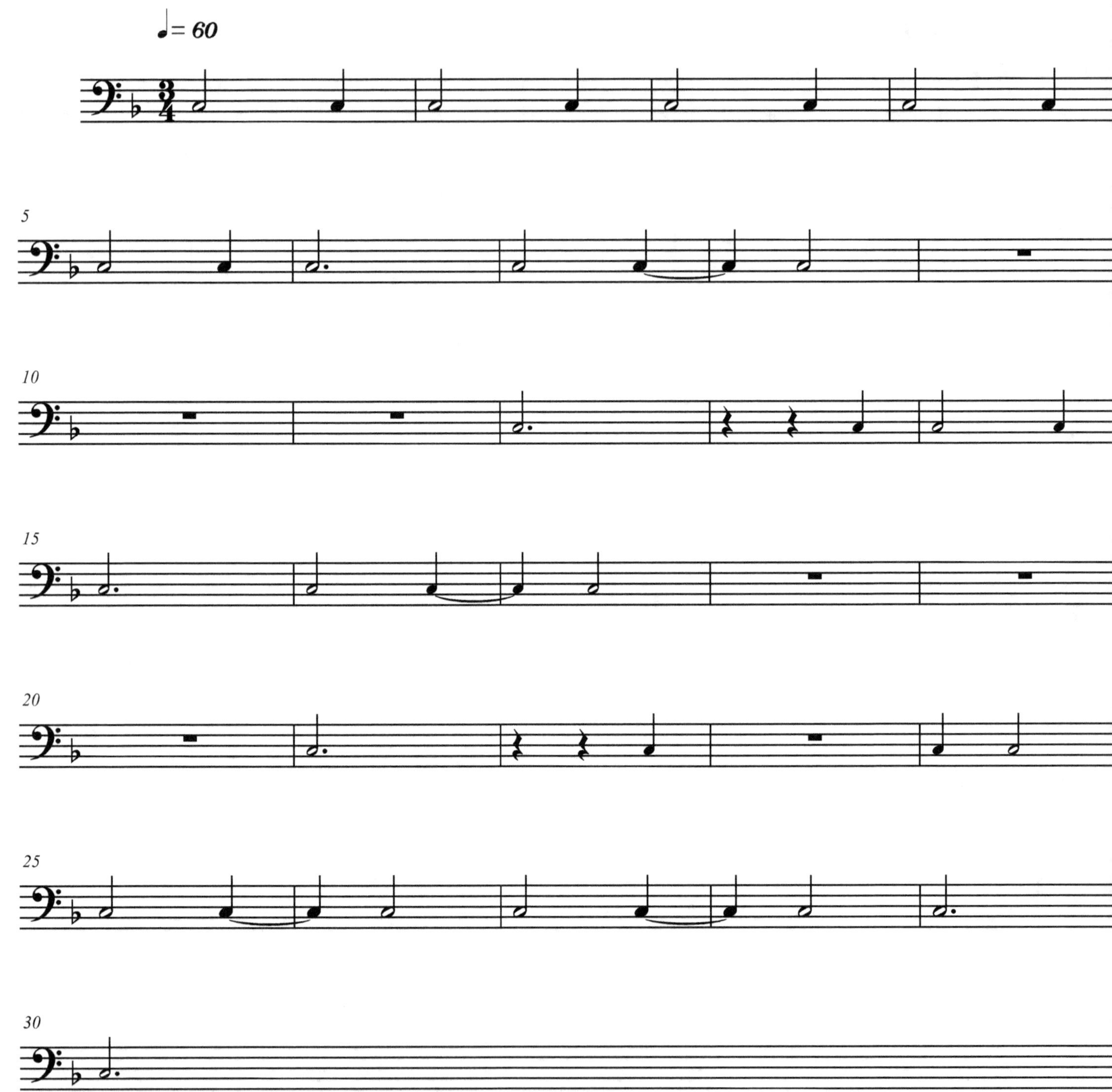

Part 4: Bes Bass Tuba

N

Joost de Groot

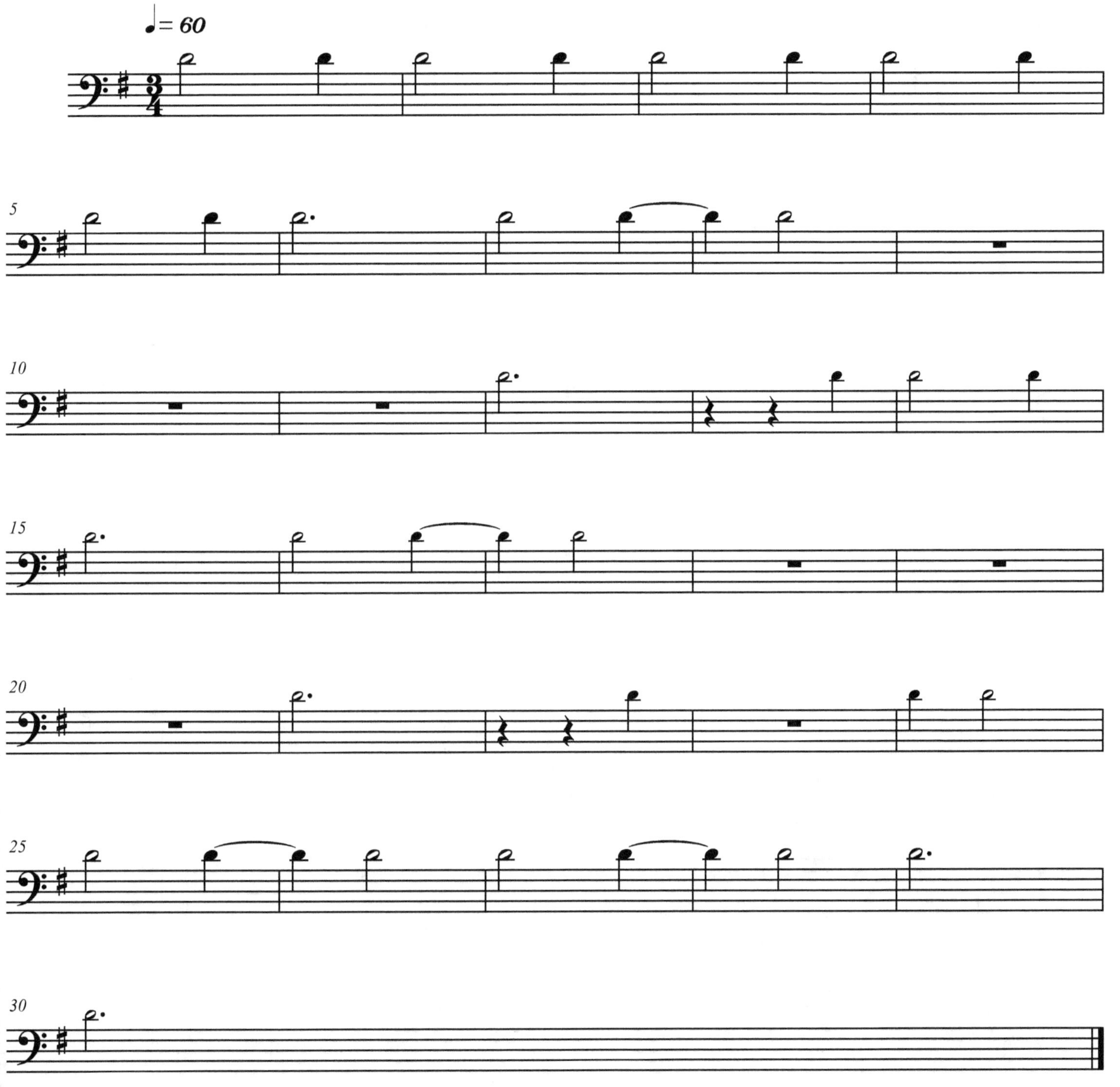

N

Part 4: Es Bass Tuba

Joost de Gro

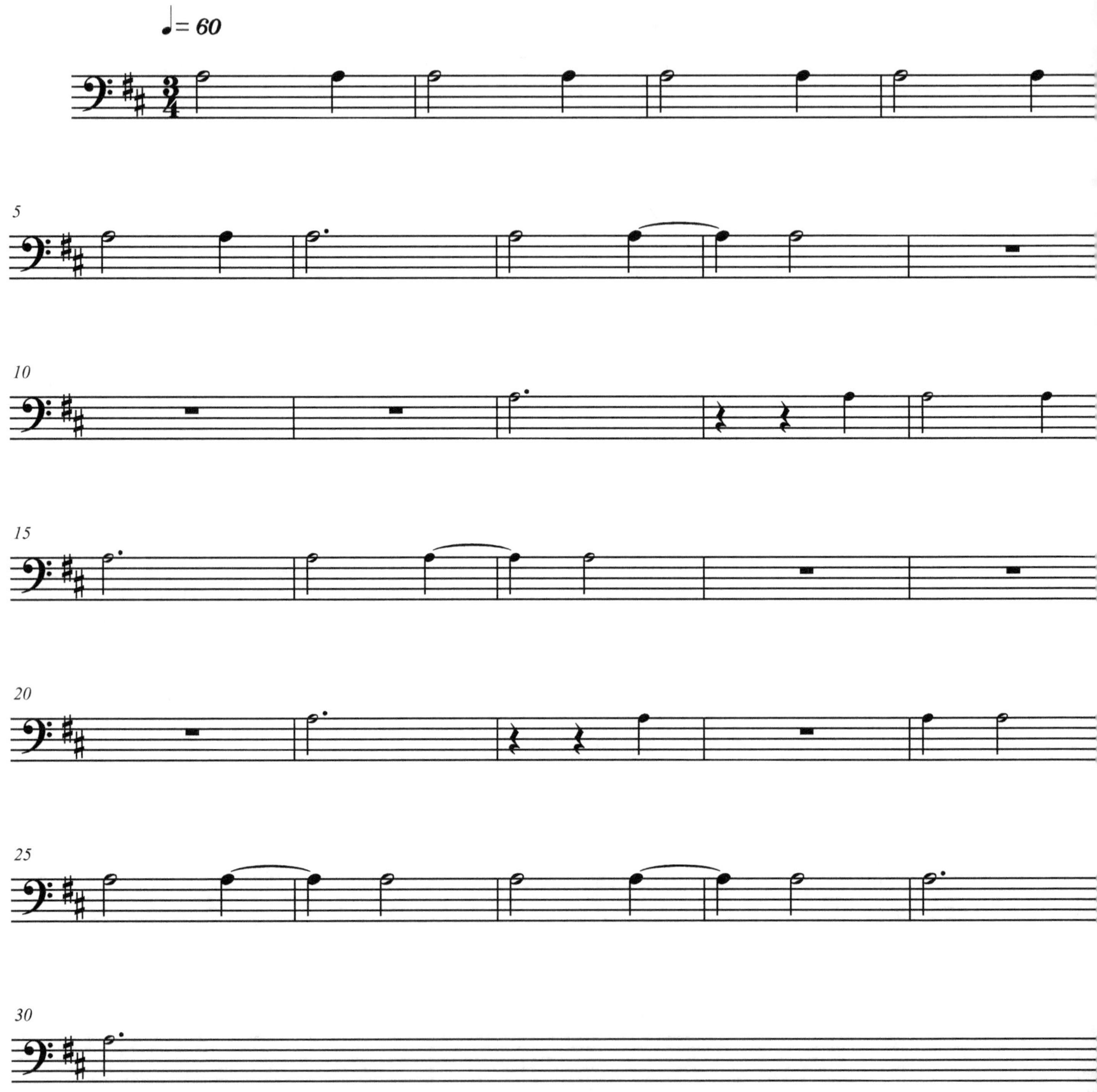

Part 1: C Flute

N

Joost de Groot

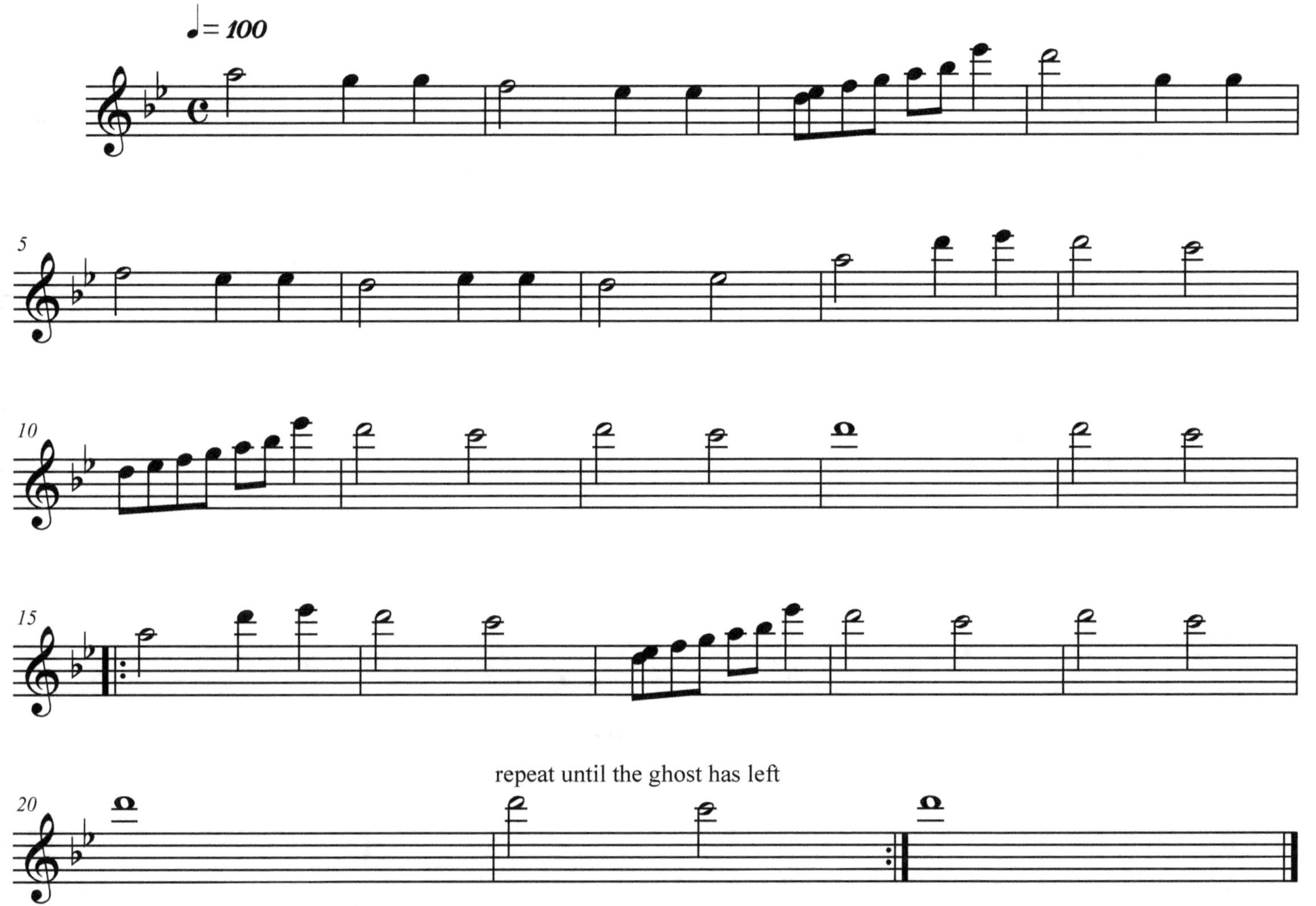

Part 1: C Oboe

N

Joost de Gro

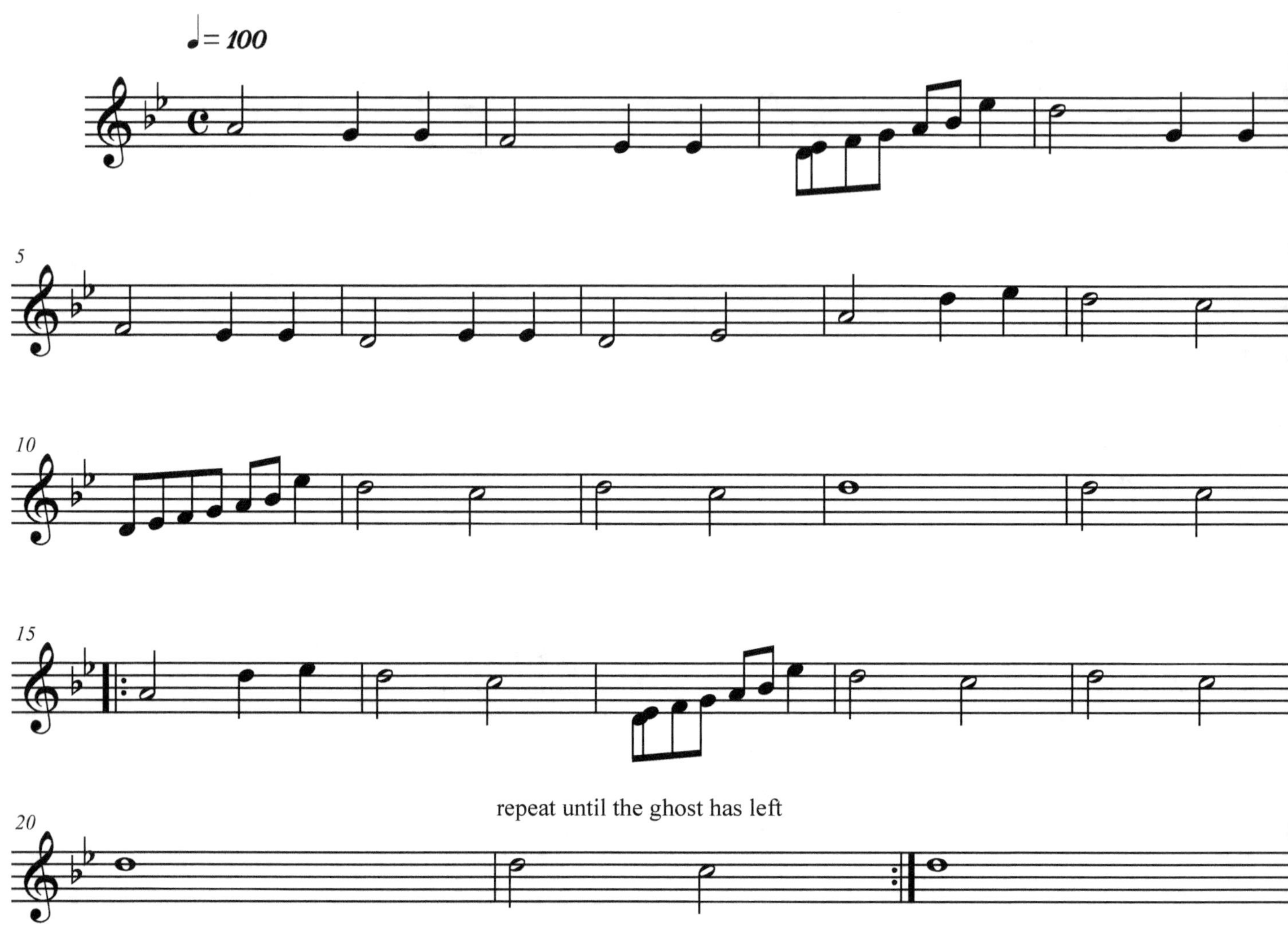

Part 4: C Bassoon

N

Joost de Groot

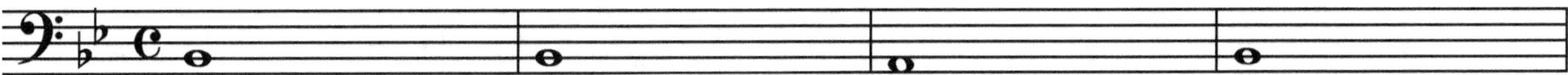

N

Part 1: Bes Clarinet 1

Joost de Gro

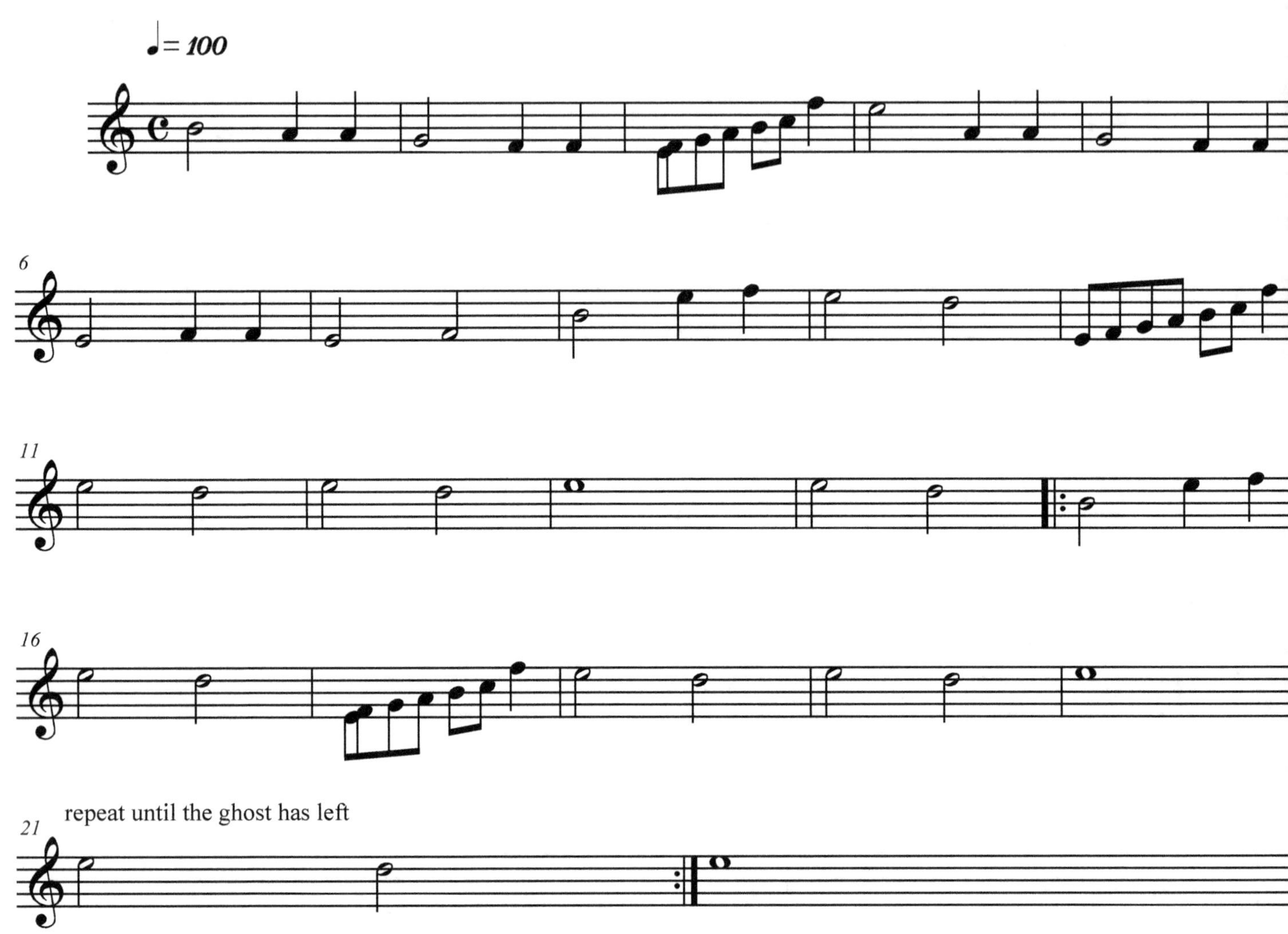

Part 2: Bes Clarinet 2 + 3

N

Joost de Groot

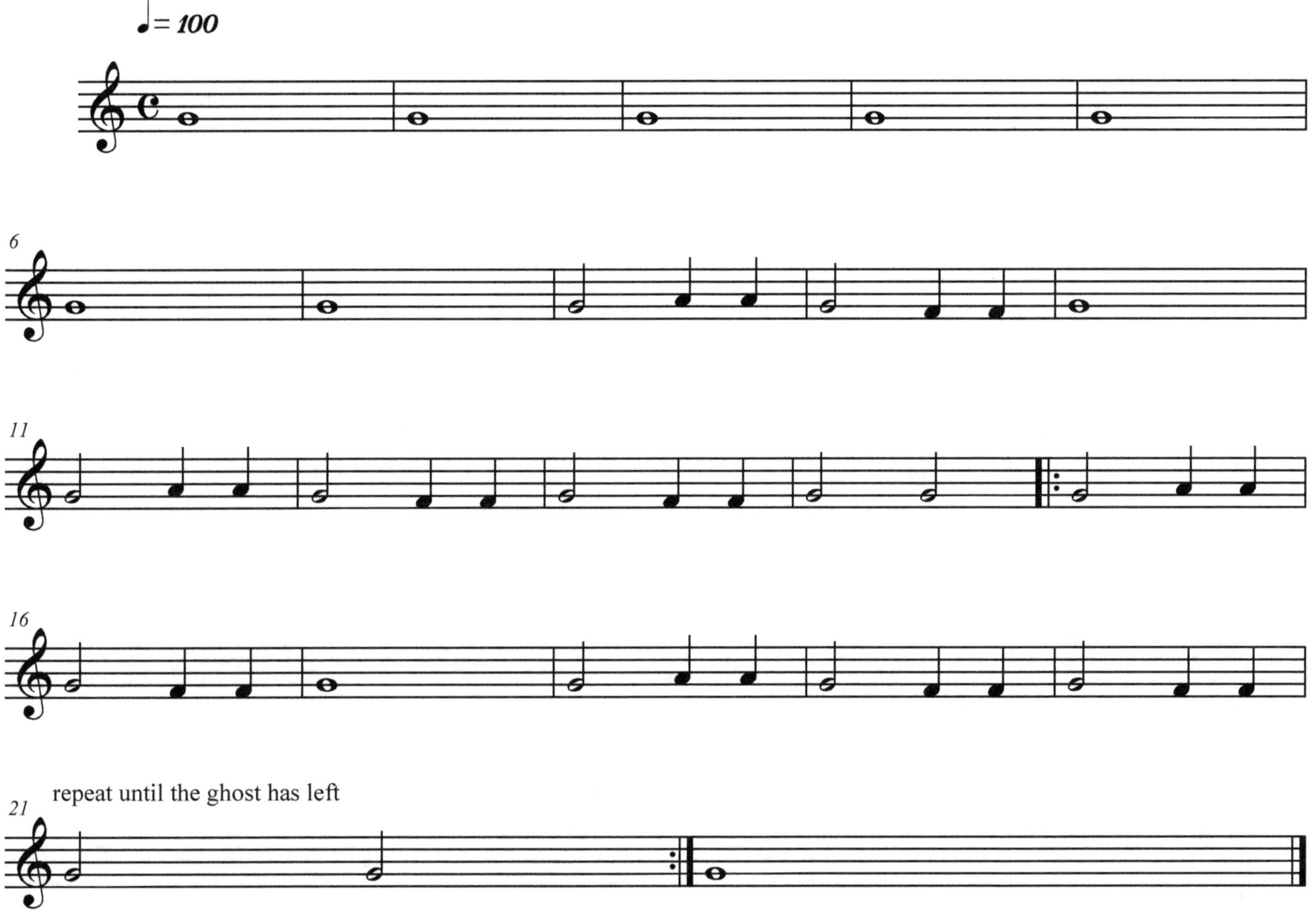

N

Part 3: Es Alto Clarinet

Joost de Gro

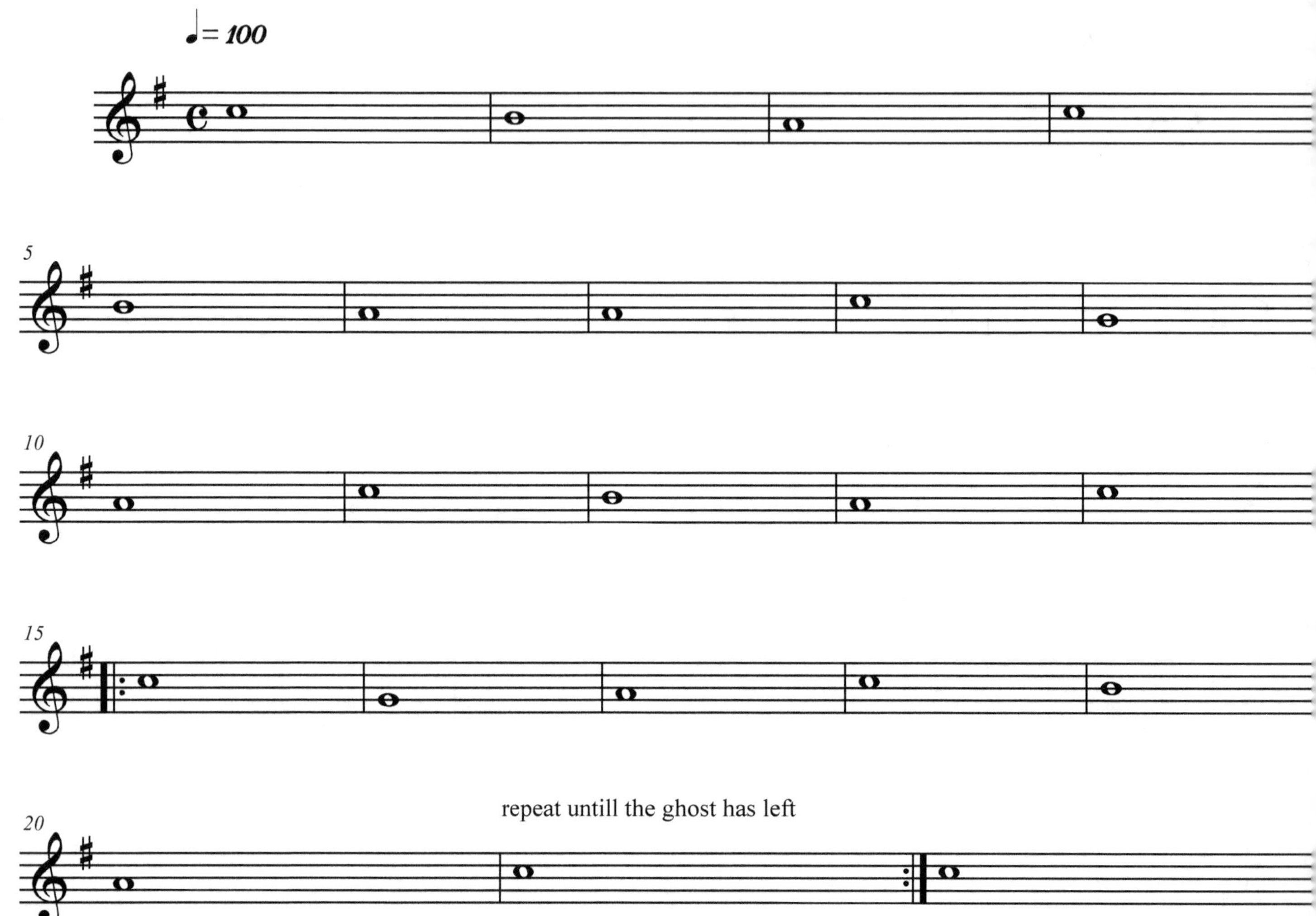

Part 4: Bes Bass Clarinet

N

Joost de Groot

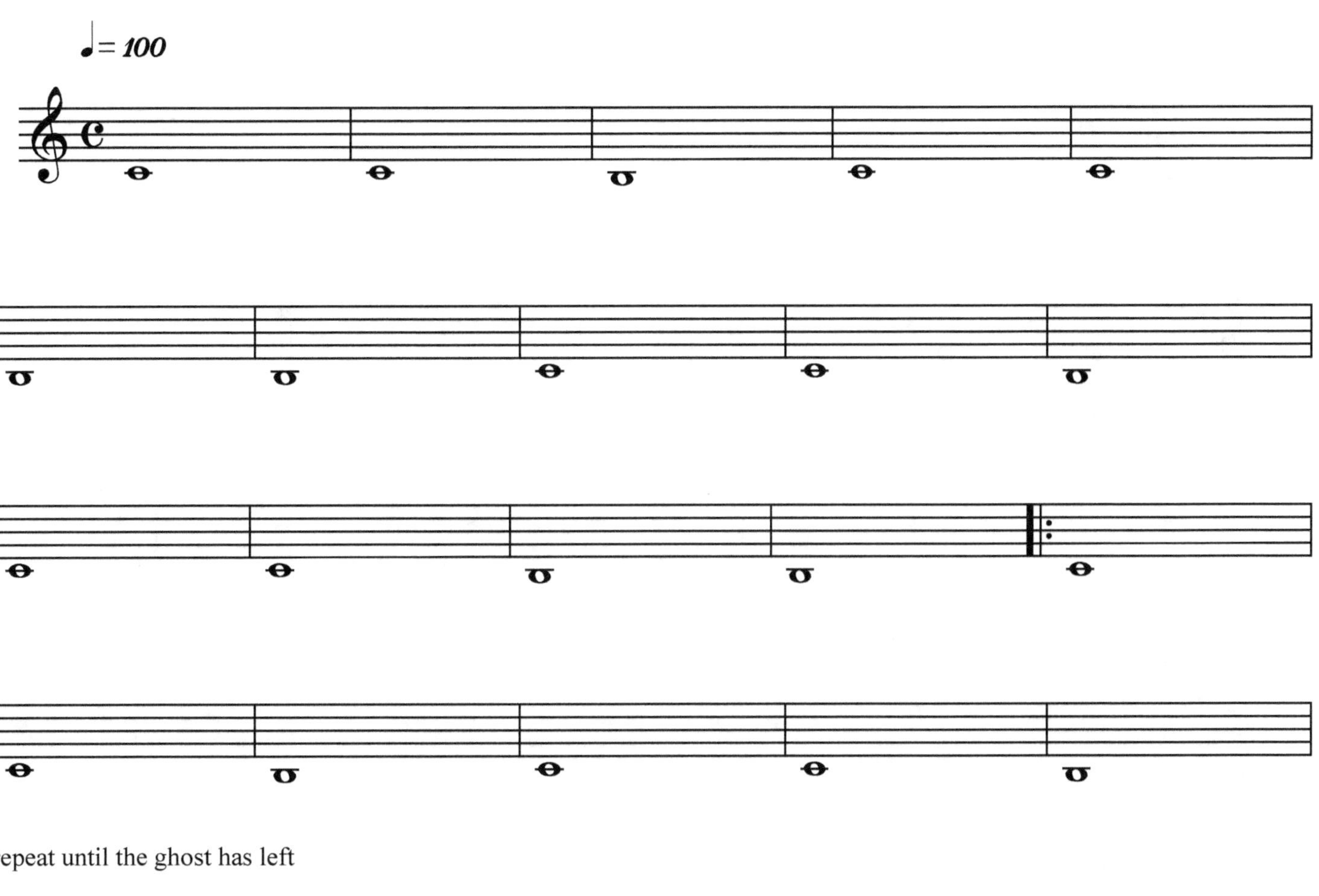

Part 2: Es Alto Sax.

N

Joost de Gro

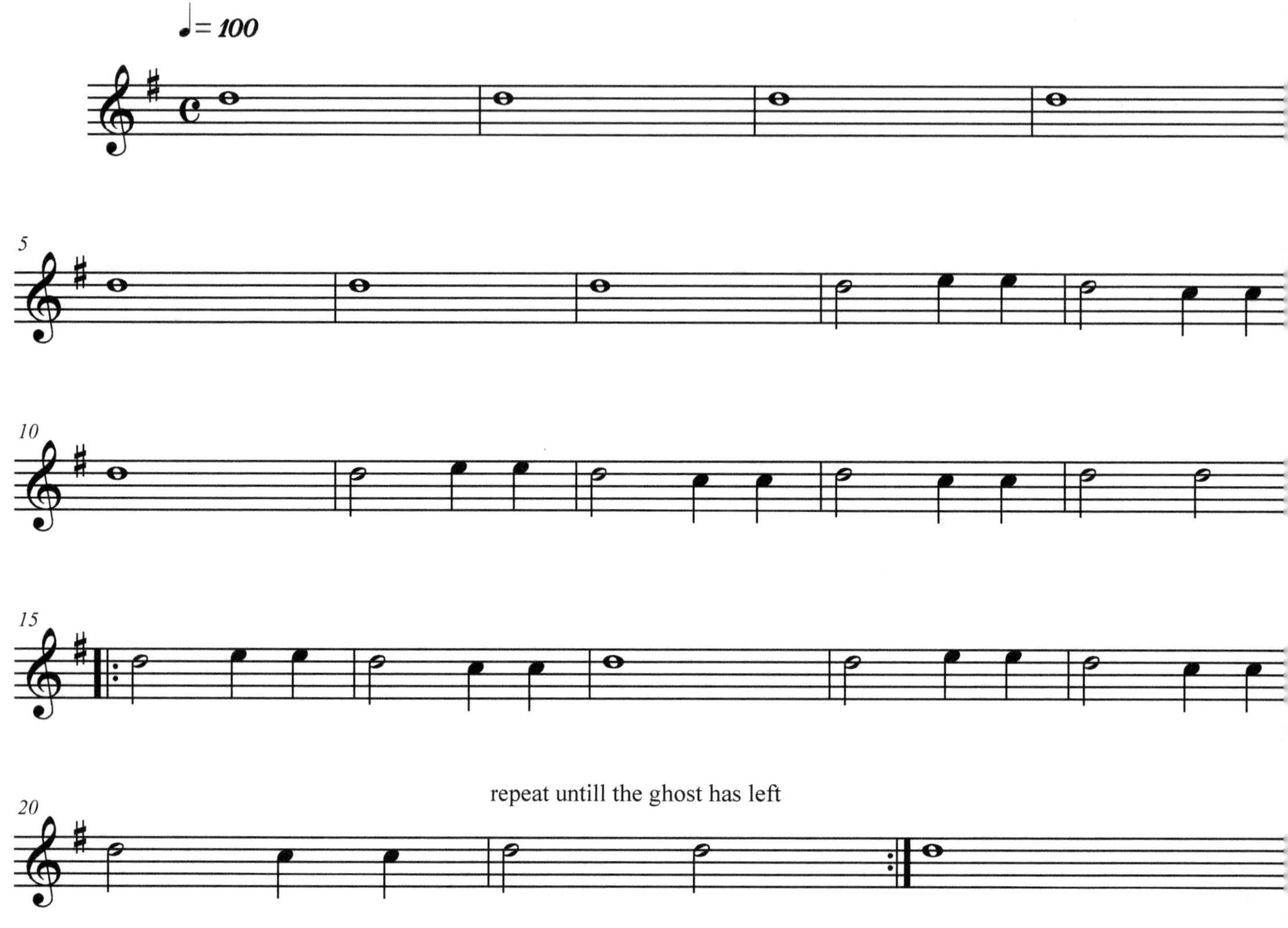

Part 3: Bes Tenor Sax.

N

Joost de Groot

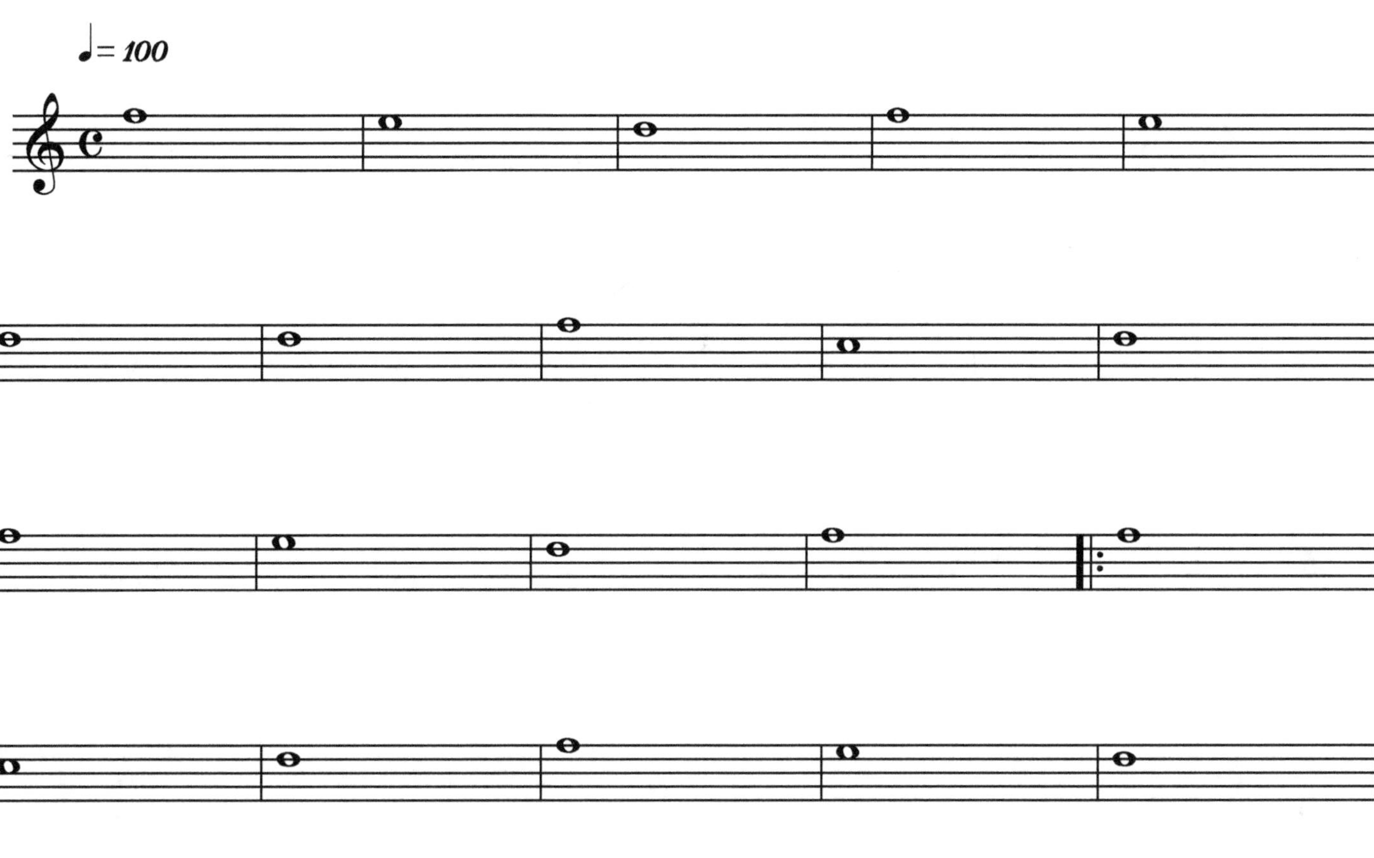

Part 4: Es Baritone Sax.

N

Joost de Gro

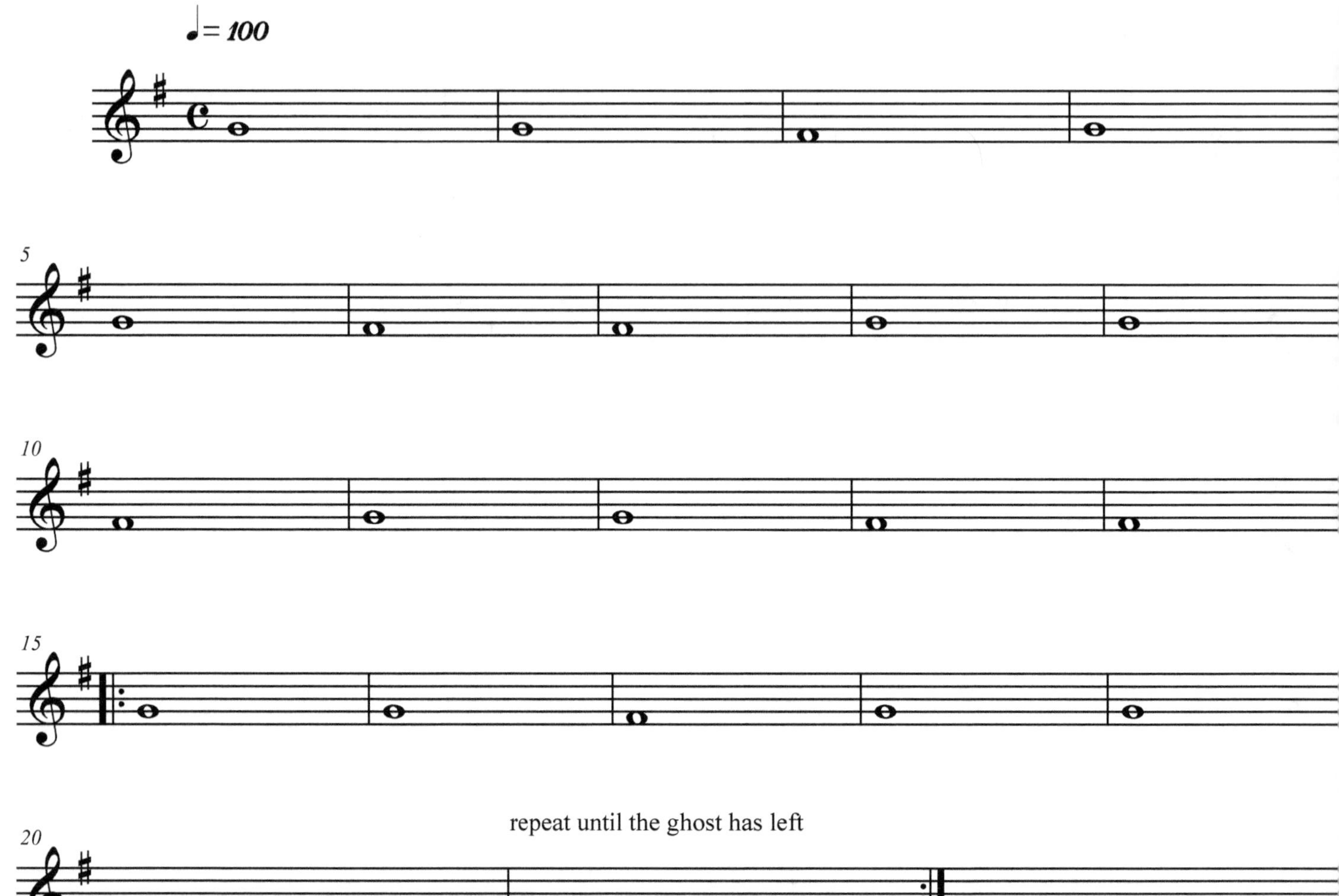

Part 1: Bes Trumpet 1

N

Joost de Groot

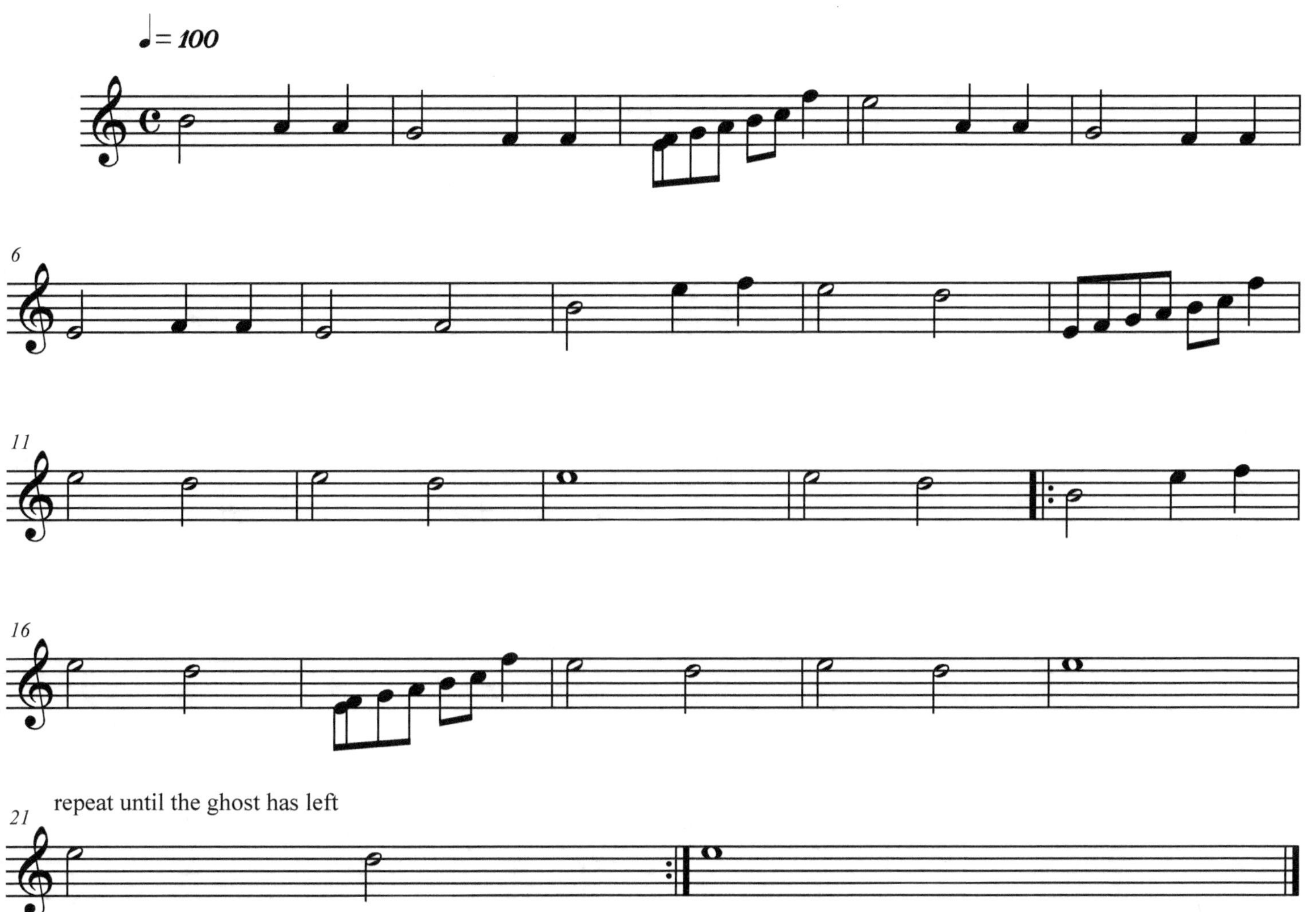

Part 2: Bes Trumpet 2 + 3

N

Joost de Gro

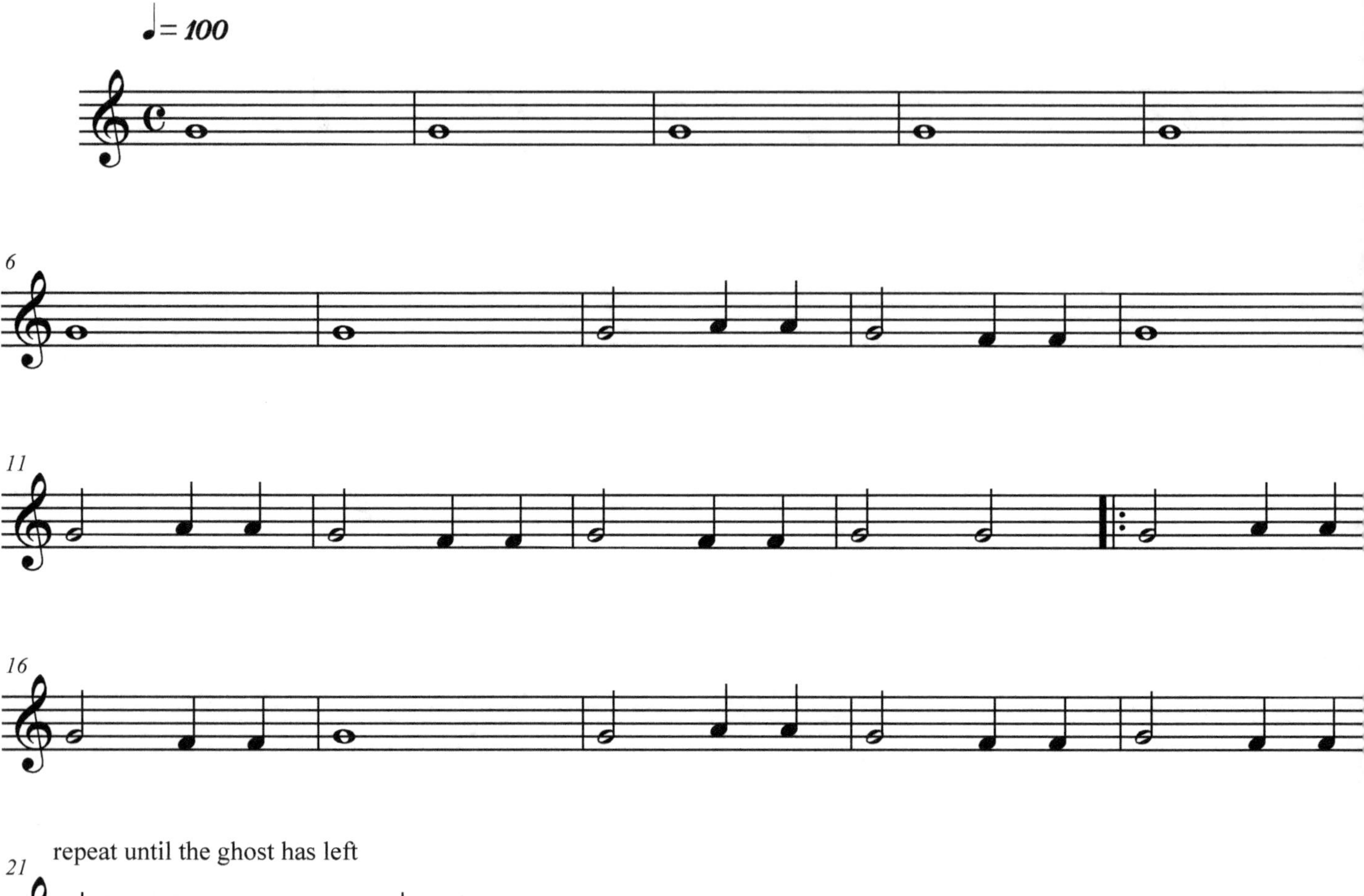

Part 2: F Horn 1 + 2

N

Joost de Groot

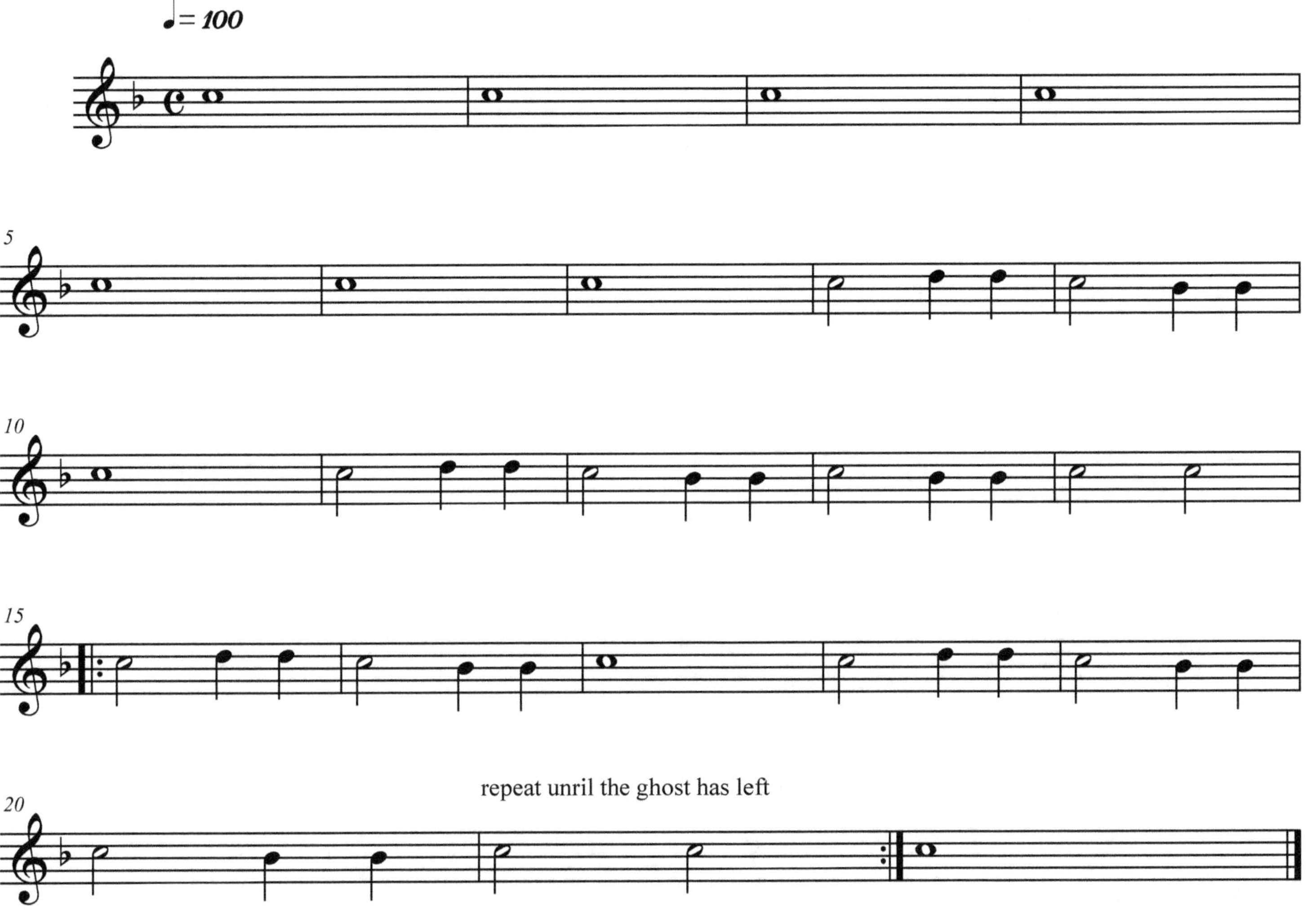

Part 3: F Horn 3 + 4

N

Joost de Gro

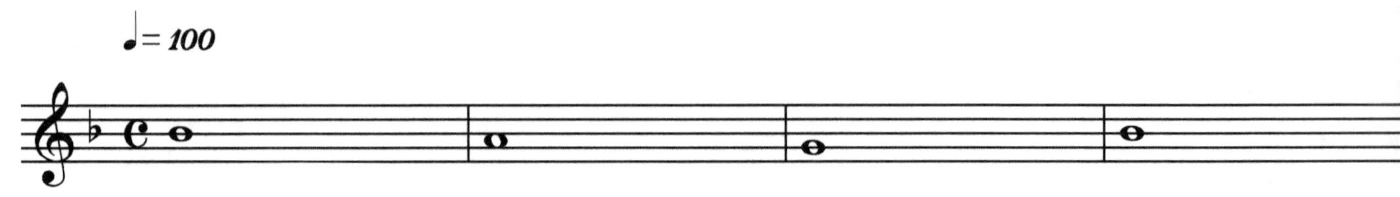

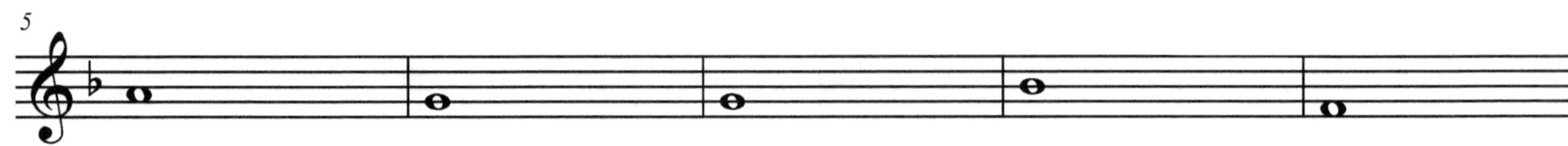

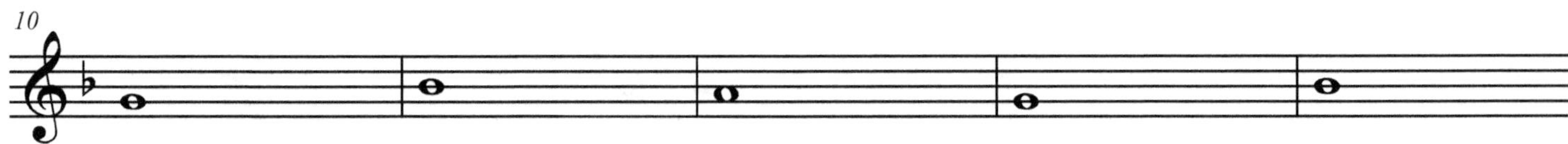

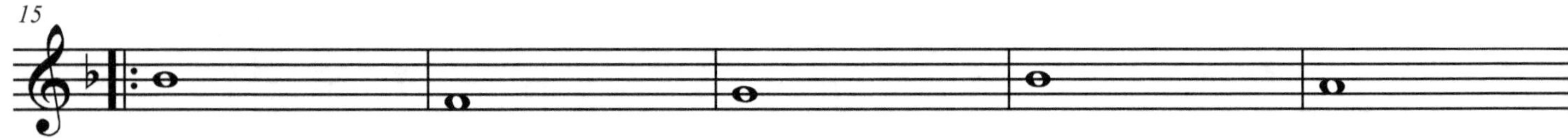

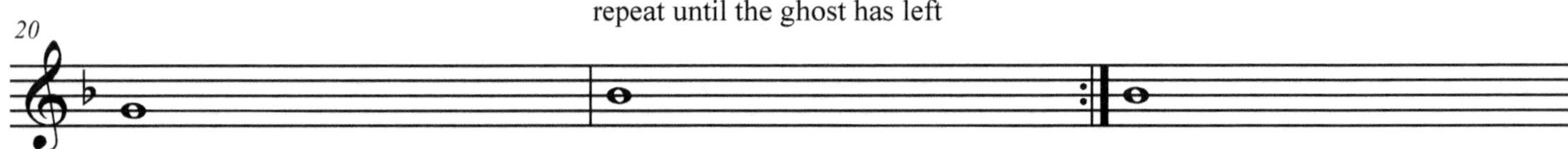

N

Part 3: C Trombone 1 + 2

Joost de Groot

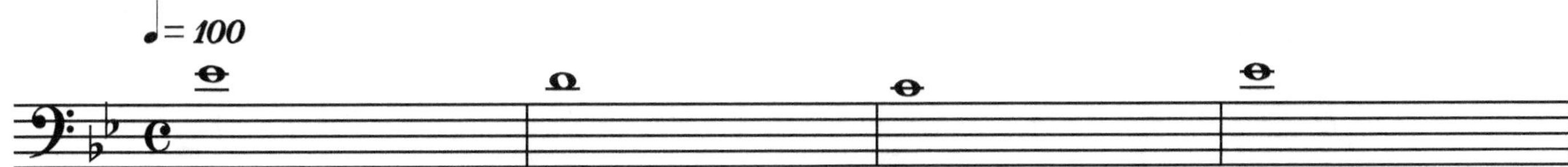

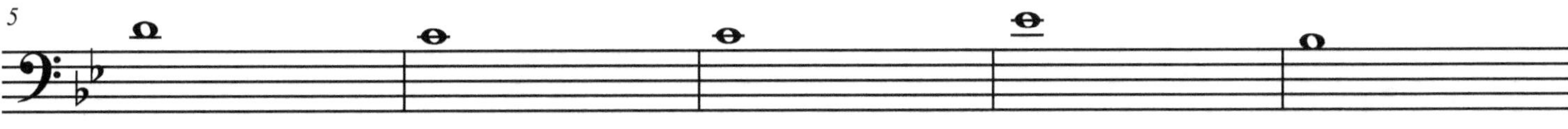

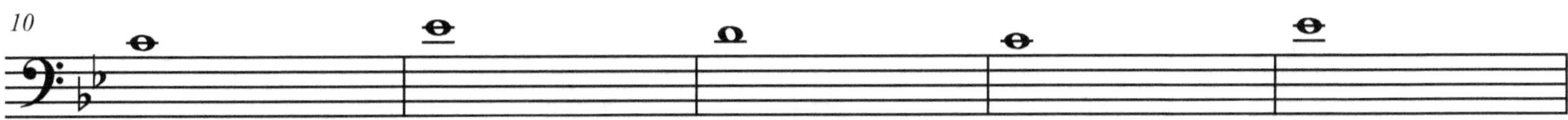

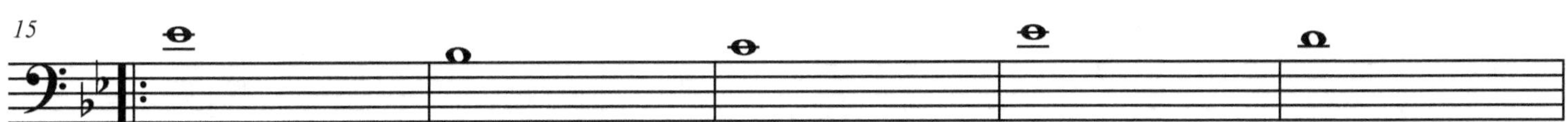

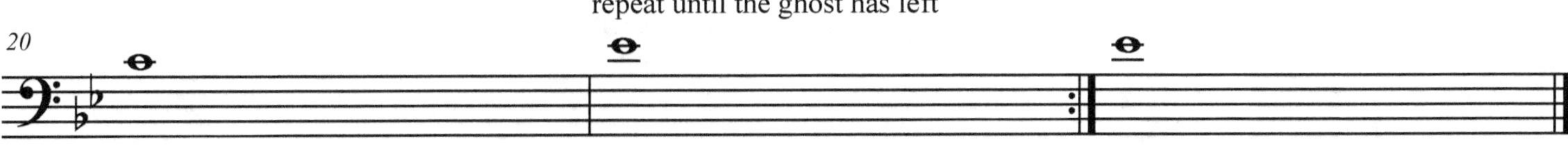

Part 4: C Bass Trombone

N

Joost de Gro

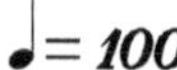

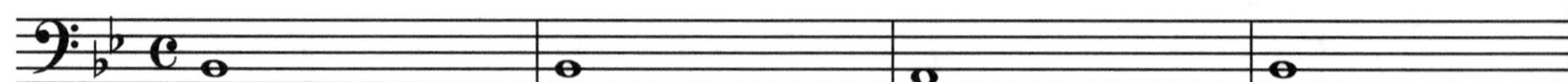

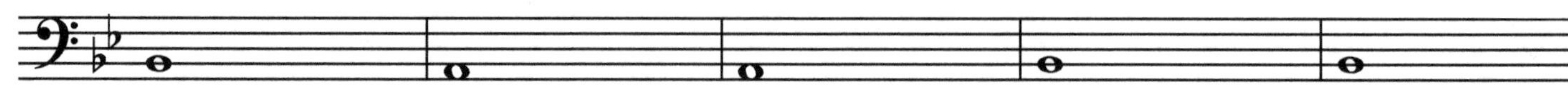

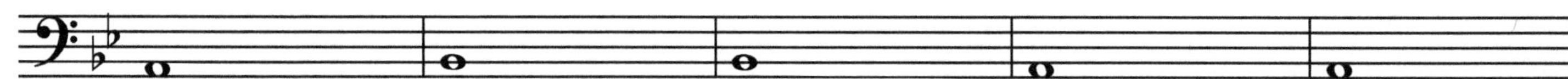

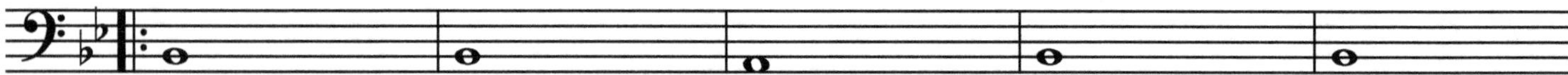

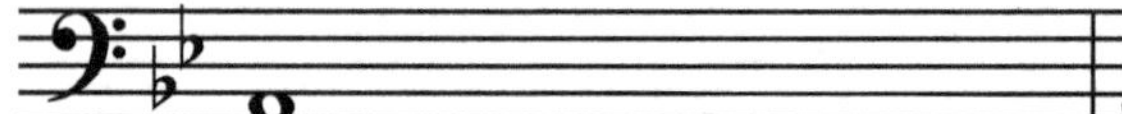

repeat until the ghost has left

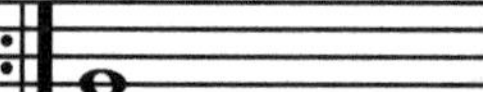

Part 3: C Baritone

N

Joost de Groot

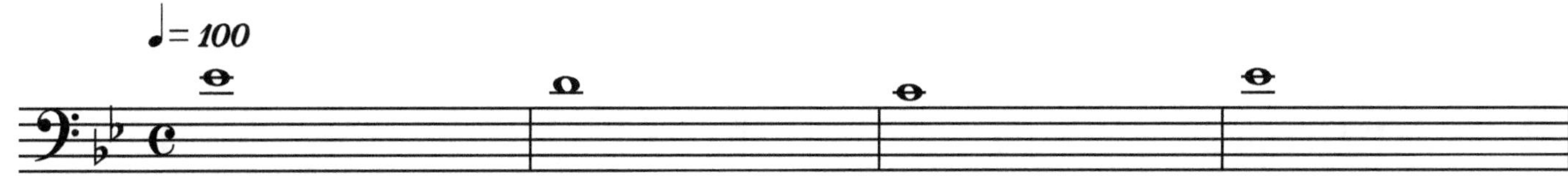

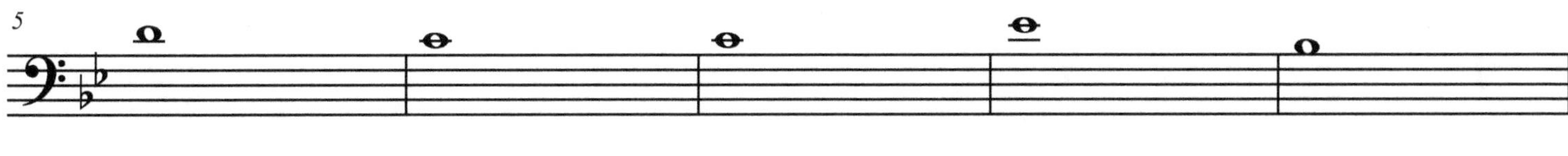

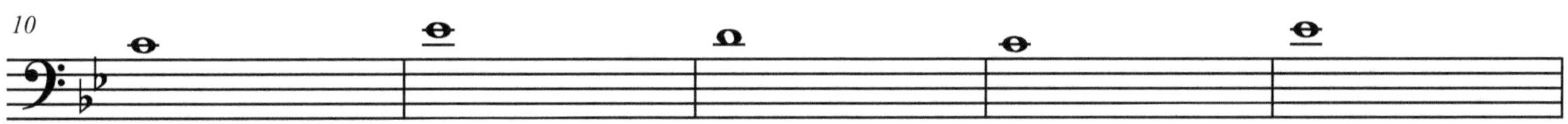

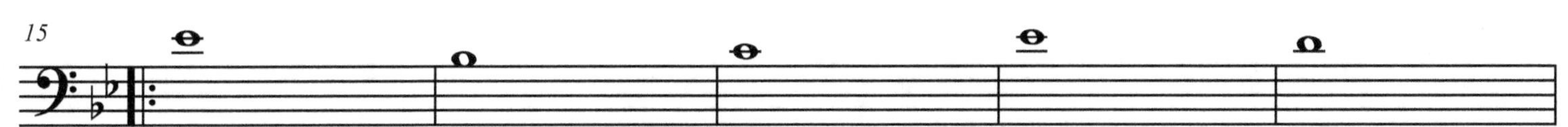

repeat until the ghost has left

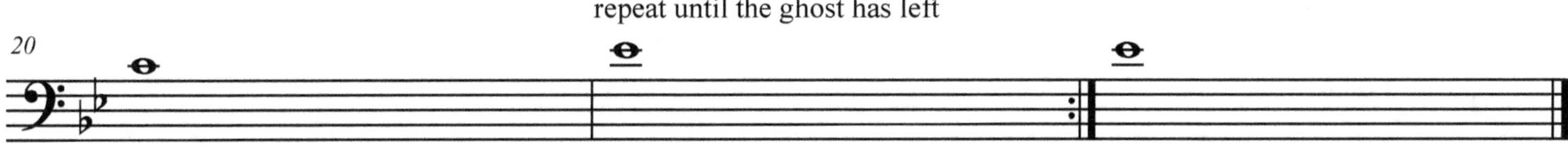

Part 3: Bes Baritone

N

Joost de Gro

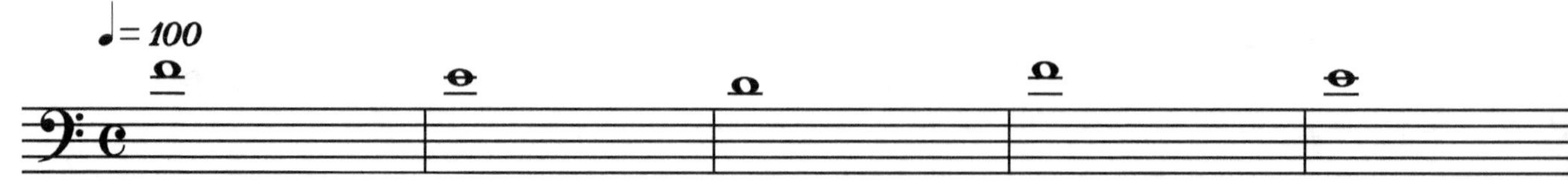

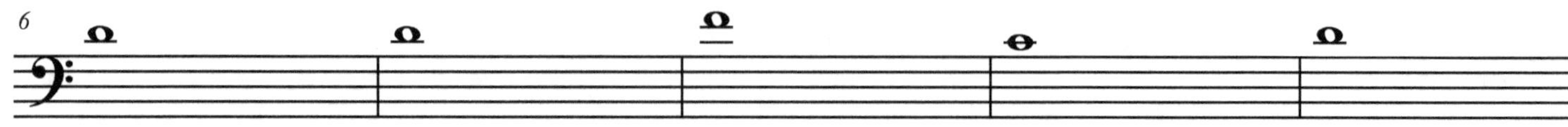

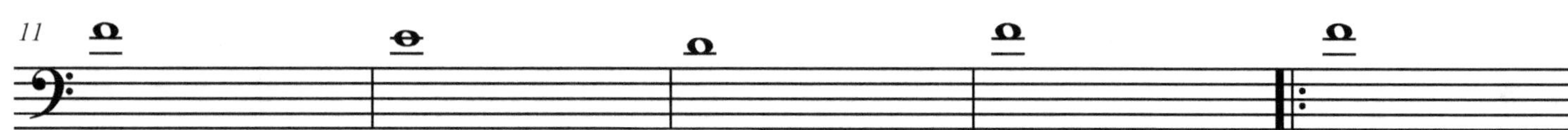

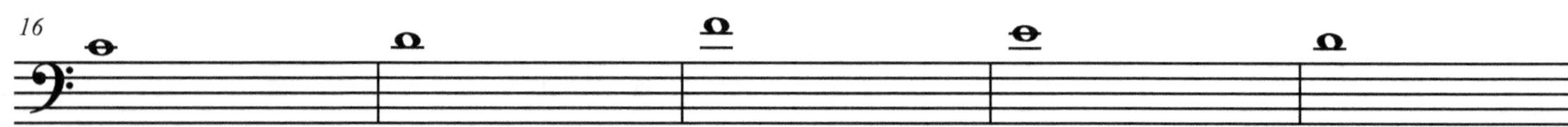

repeat until the ghost has left

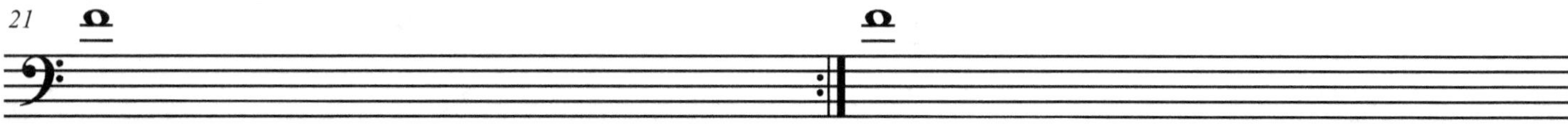

Part 3: Bes Baritone

N

Joost de Groot

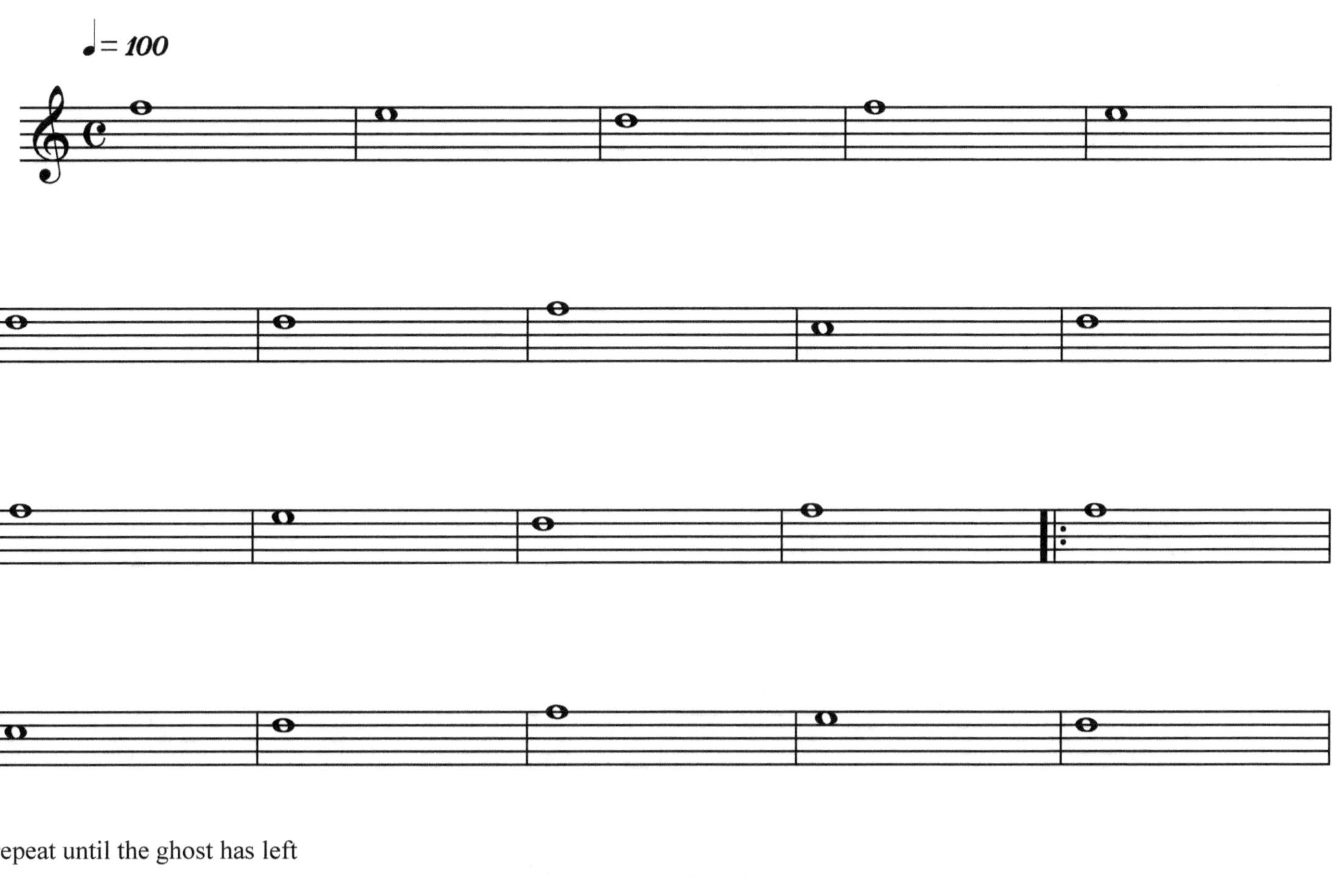

Part 4: C Bass Tuba

N

Joost de Gro

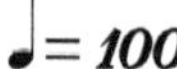

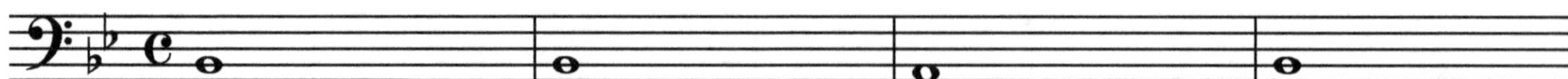

5

10

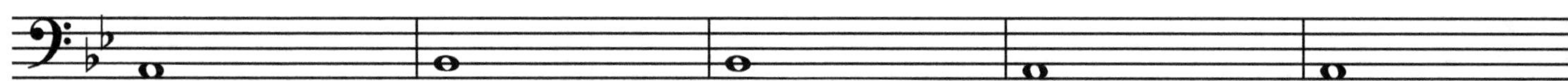

15

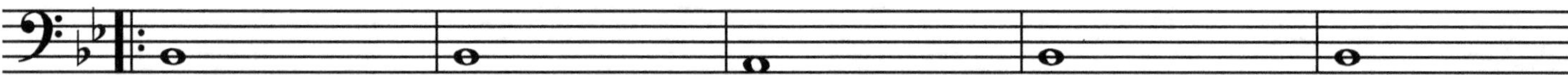

20

repeat until the ghost has left

Part 4: Bes Bass Tuba

N

Joost de Groot

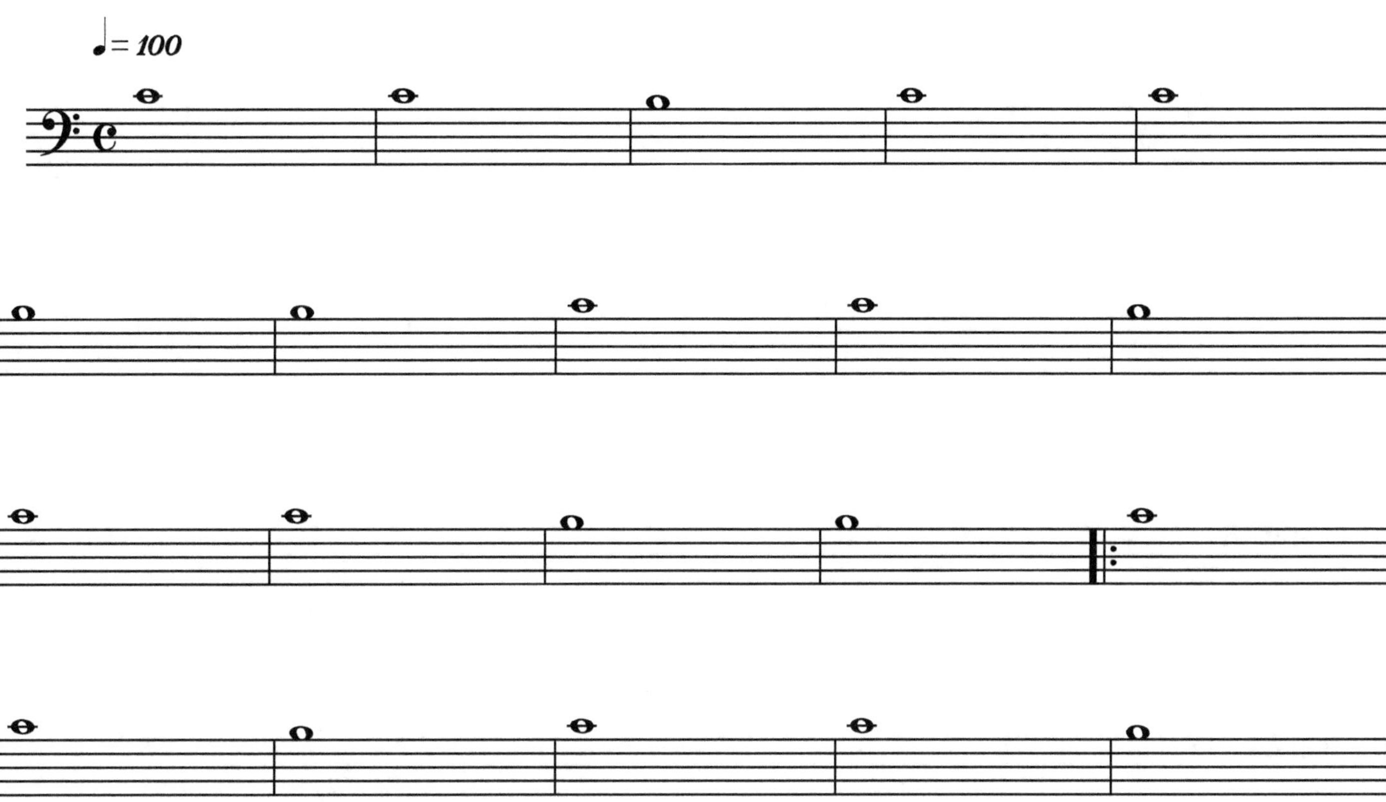

Part 4: Es Bass Tuba

N

Joost de Gro

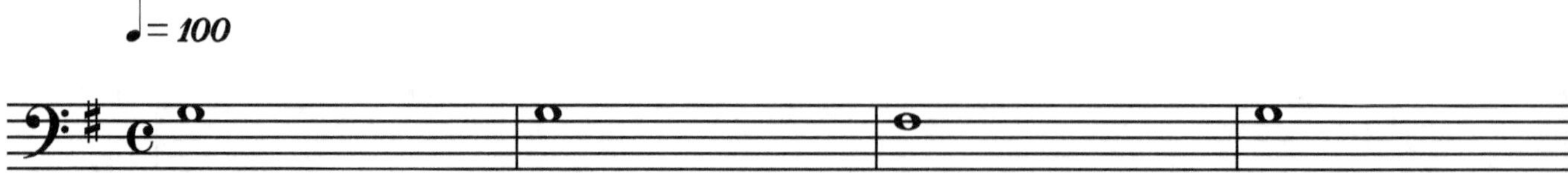

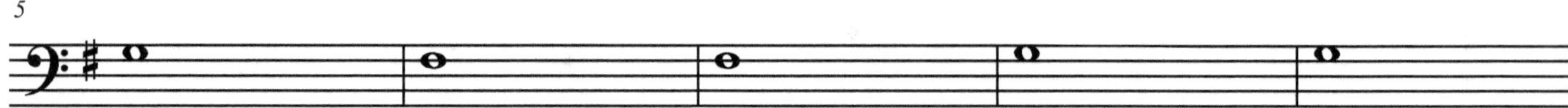

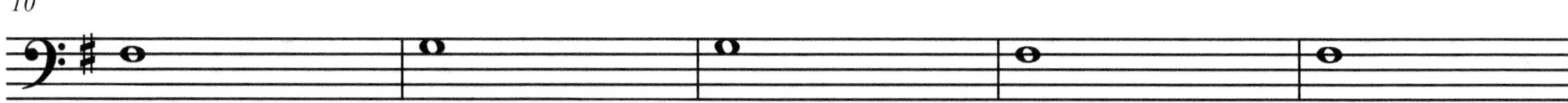

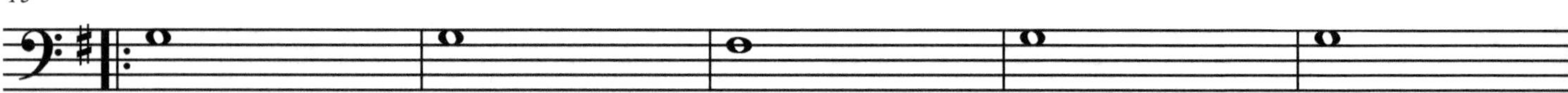

20

repeat until the ghost has left

Part 1: C Flute

I

Joost de Groot

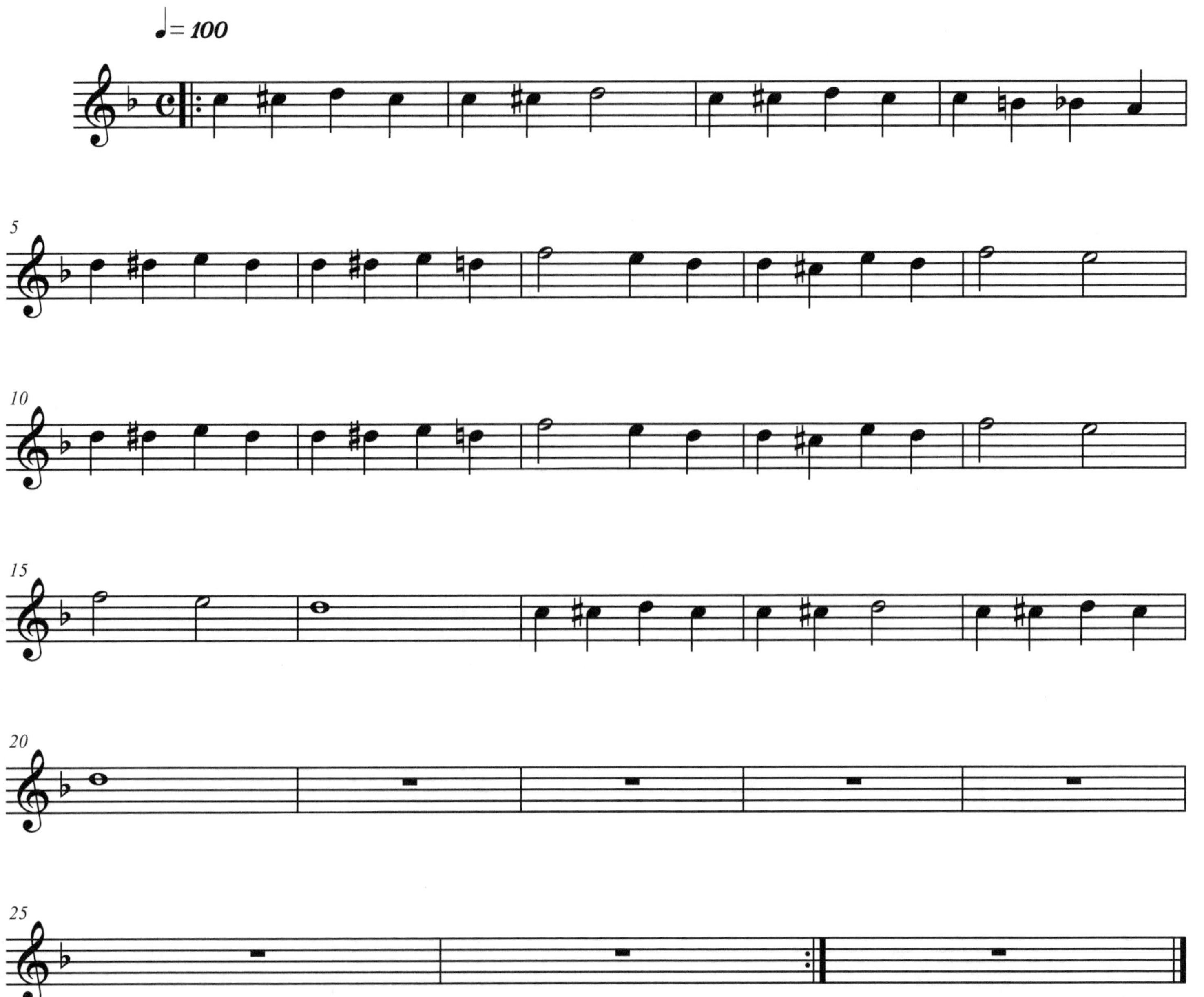

Part 1: C Oboe

I

Joost de Gro

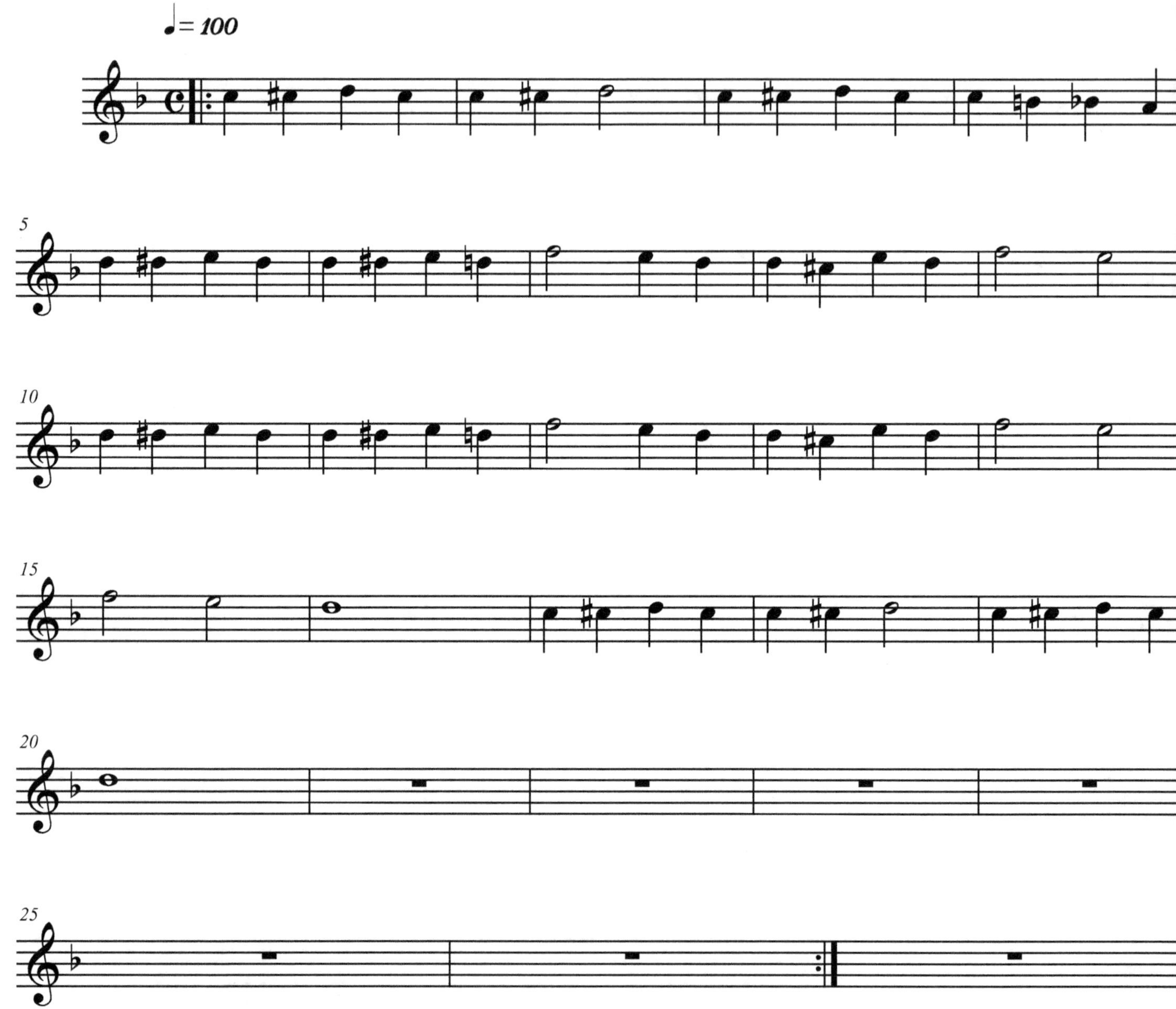

I

Part 4: C Bassoon

Joost de Groot

♩= 100

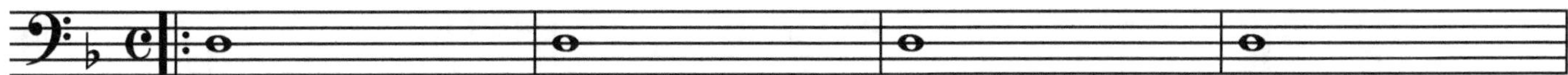

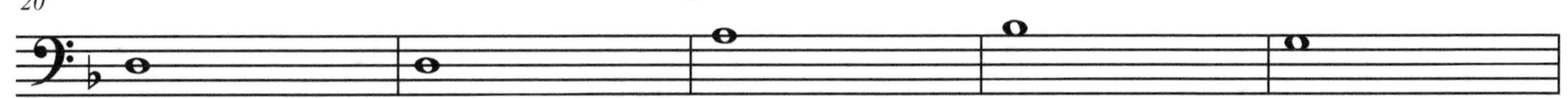

Part 1: Bes Clarinet 1

I

Joost de Gro[illegible]

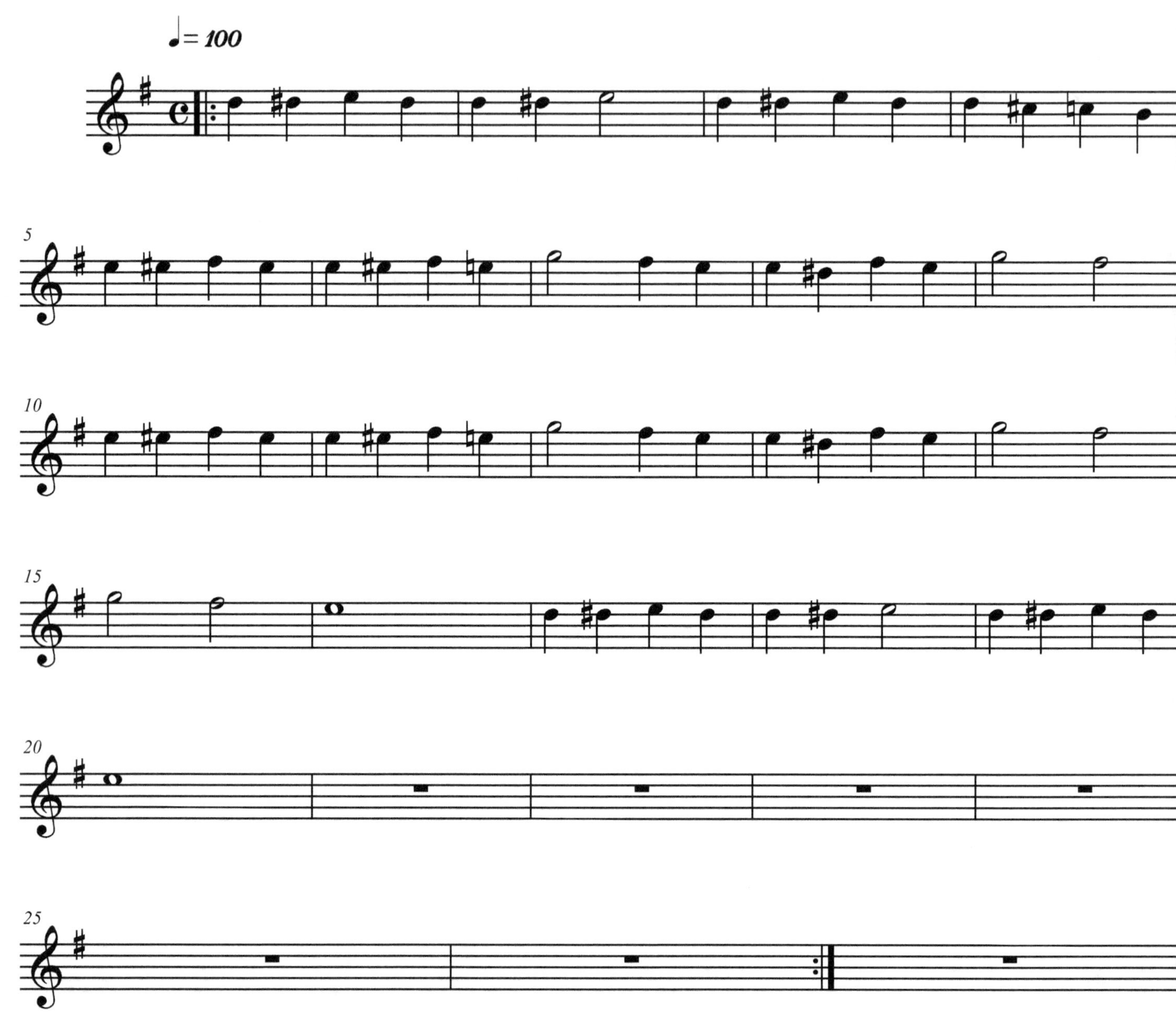

I

Part 2: Bes Clarinet 2 + 3

Joost de Groot

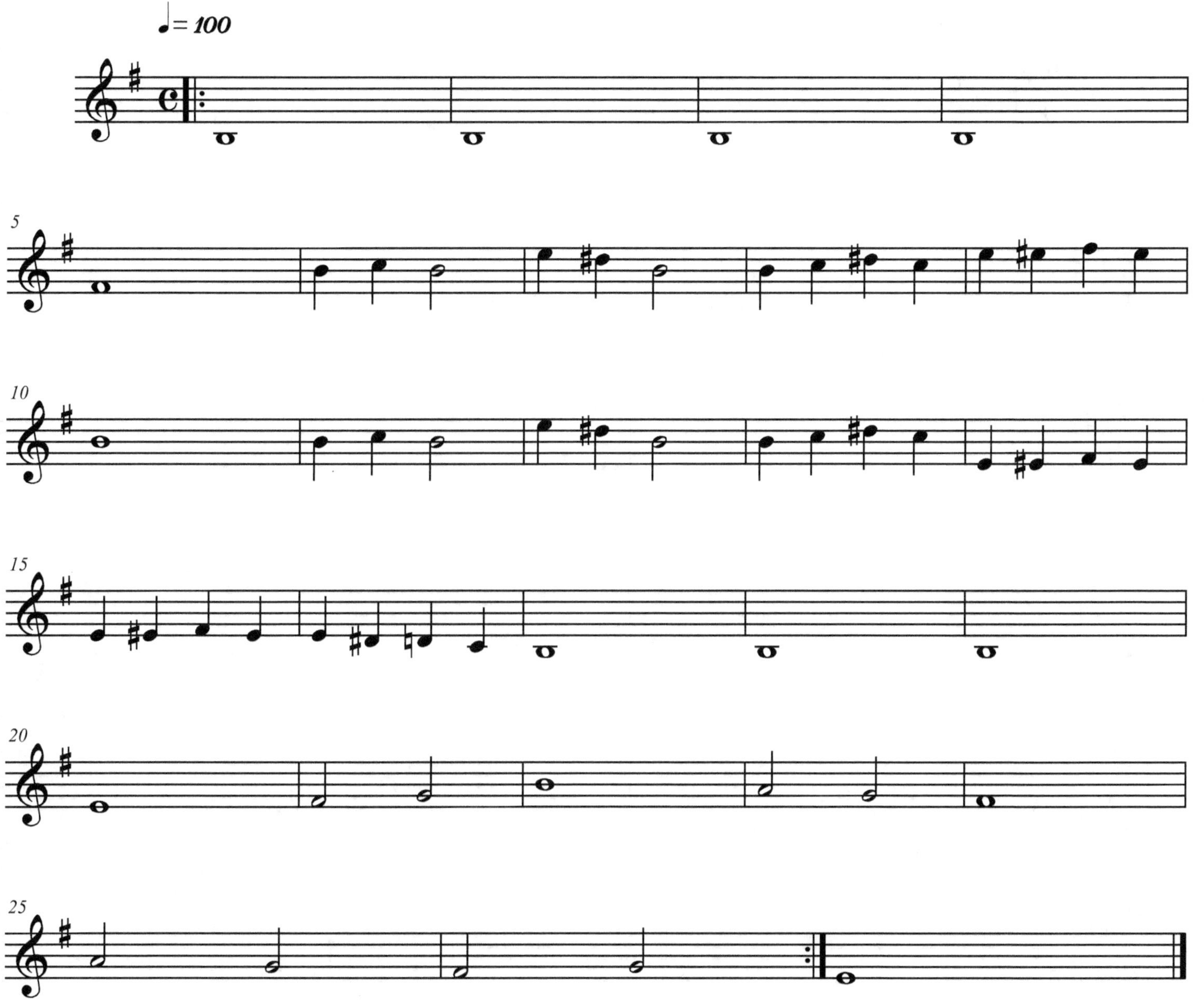

I

Part 3: Es Alto Clarinet

Joost de Gro

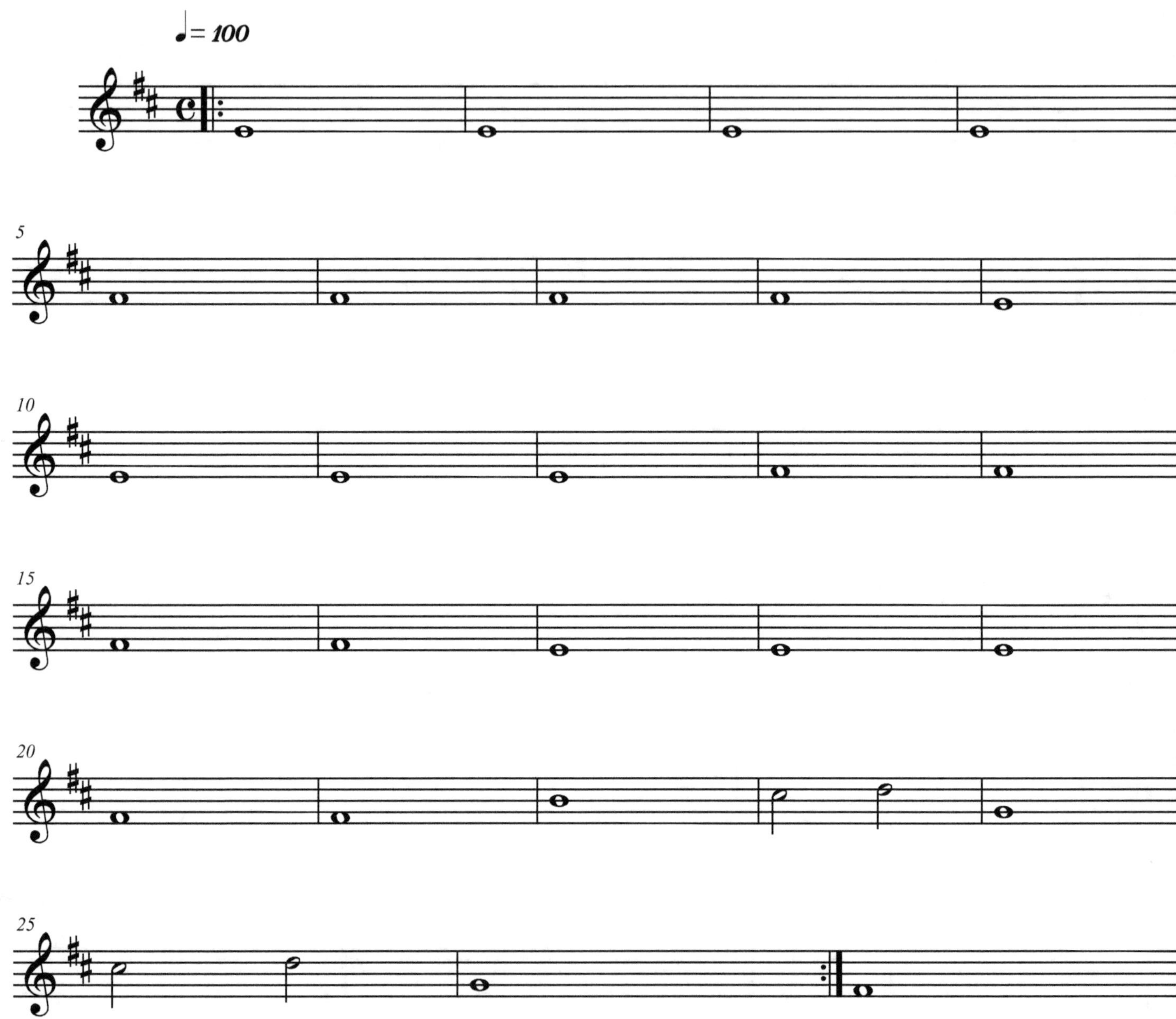

I

Part 4: Bes Bass Clarinet

Joost de Groot

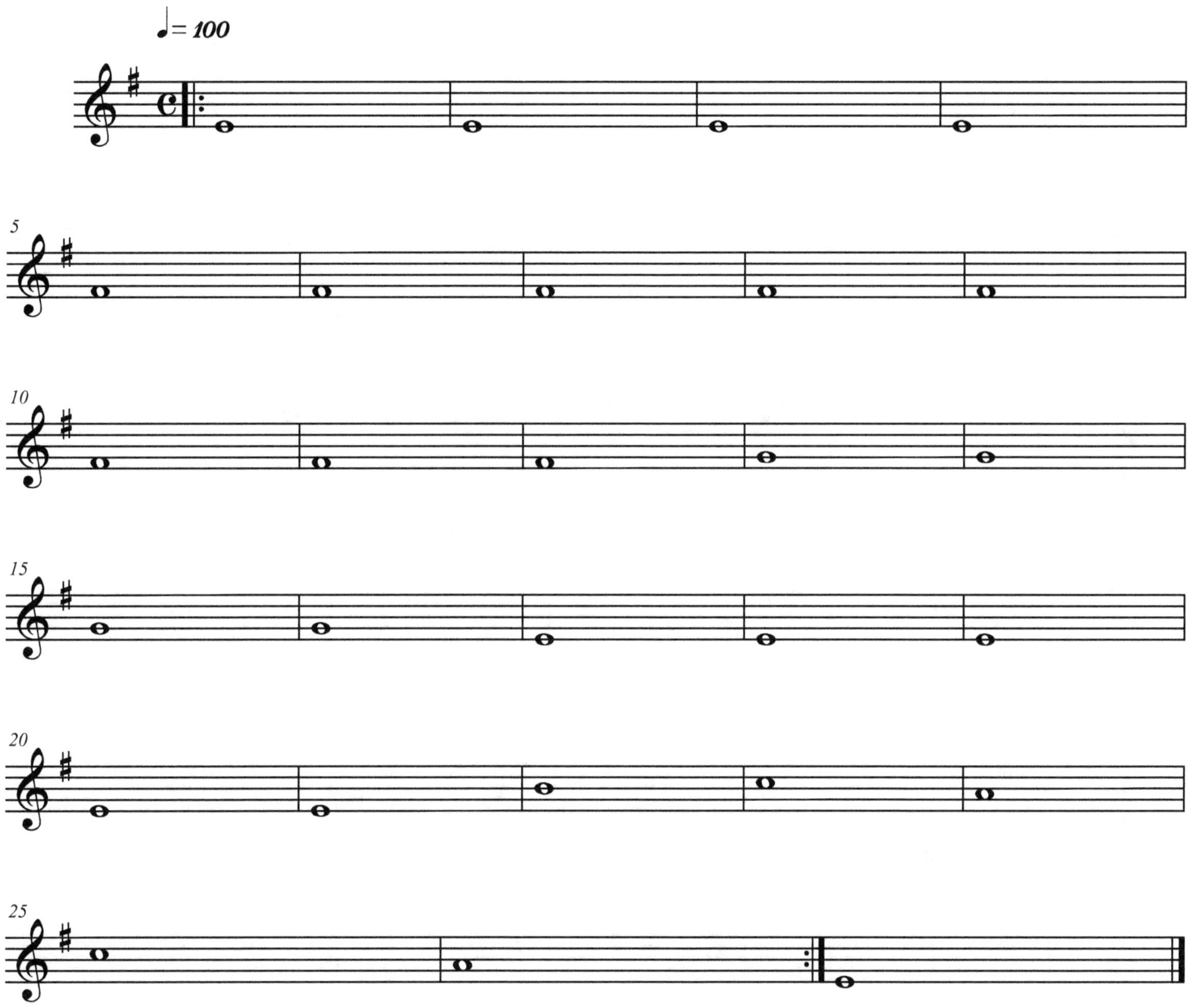

I

Part 2: Es Alto Sax.

Joost de Gro

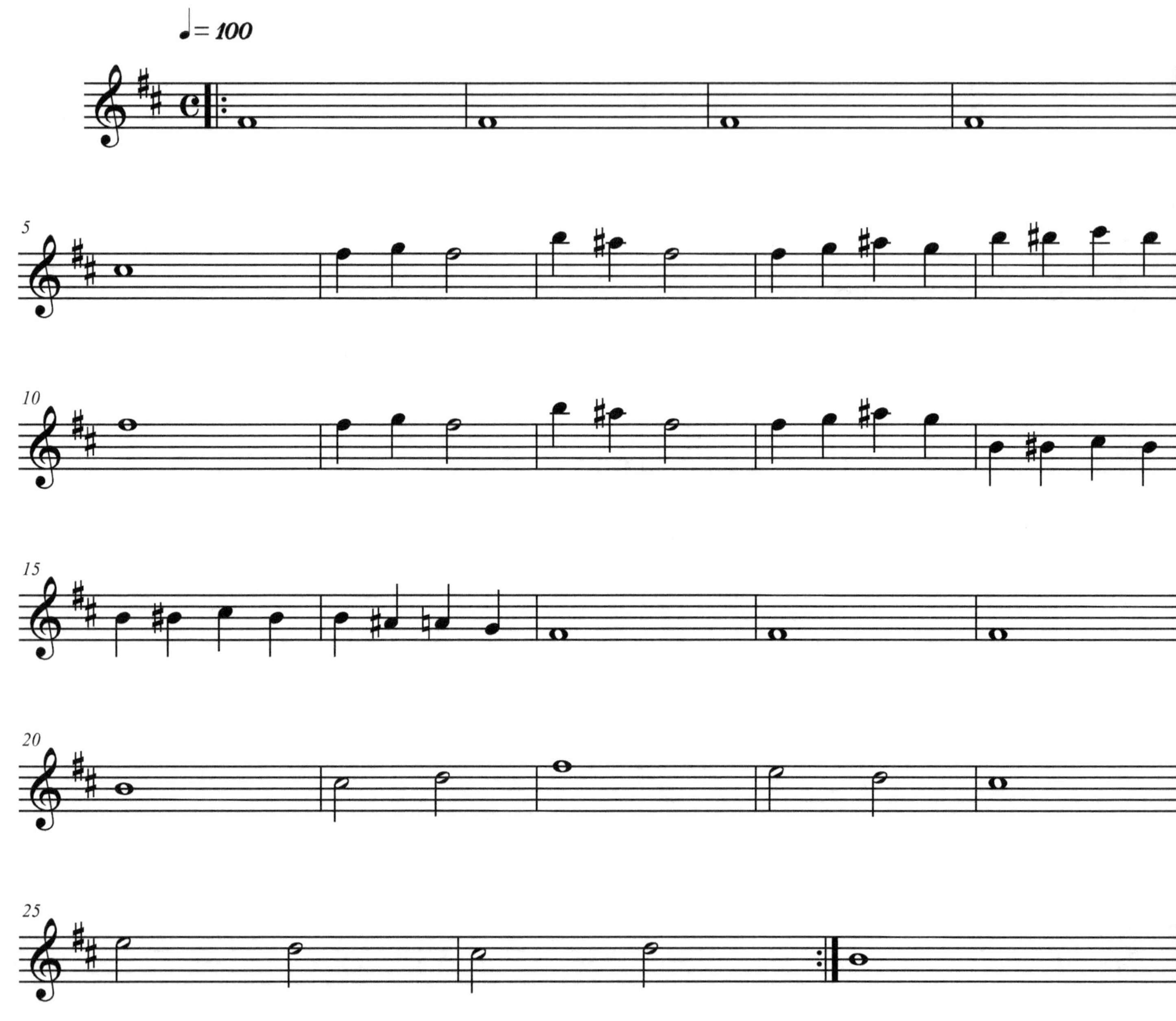

I

Part 3: Bes Tenor Sax.

Joost de Groot

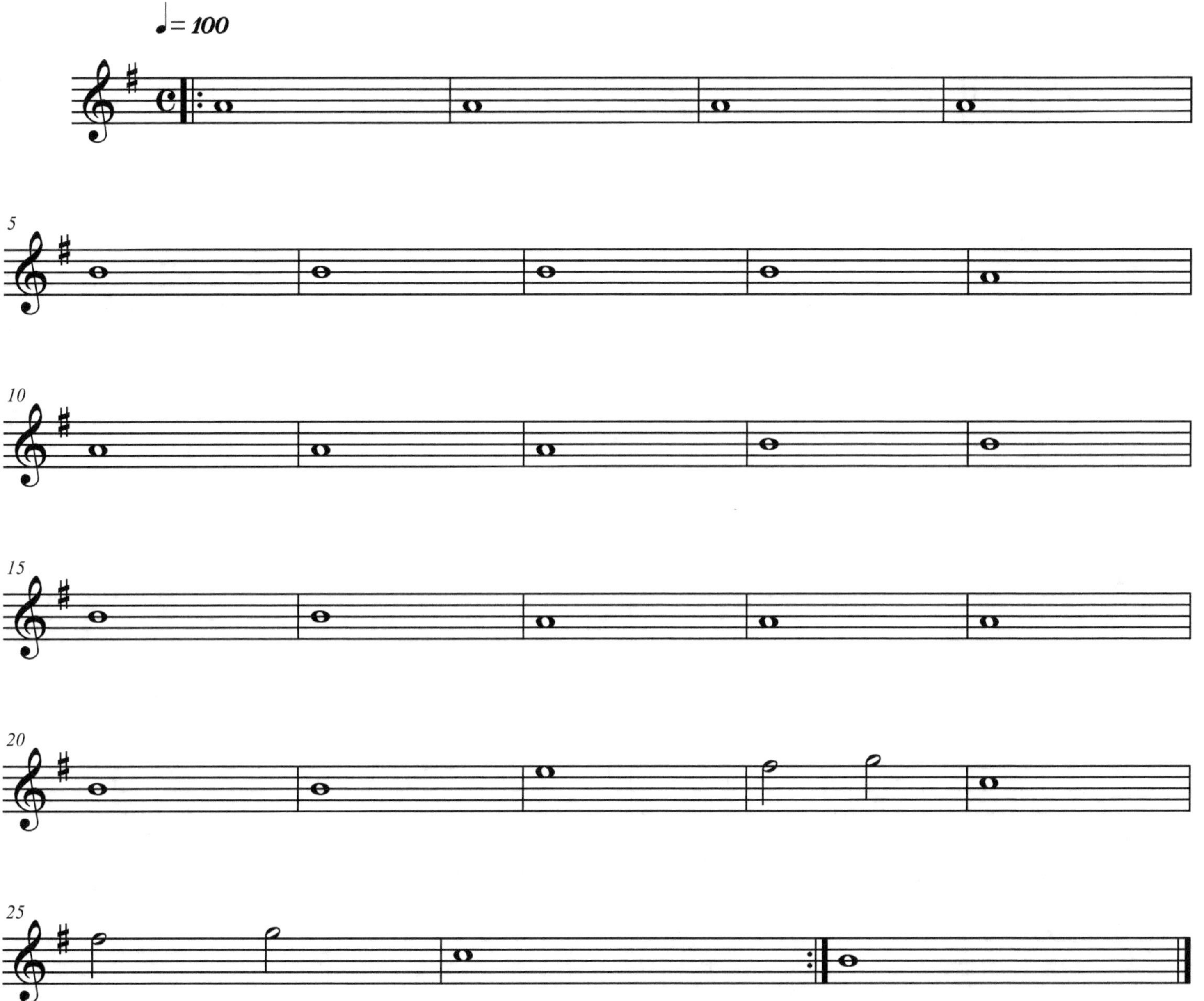

Part 4: Es Baritone Sax.

I

Joost de Gro

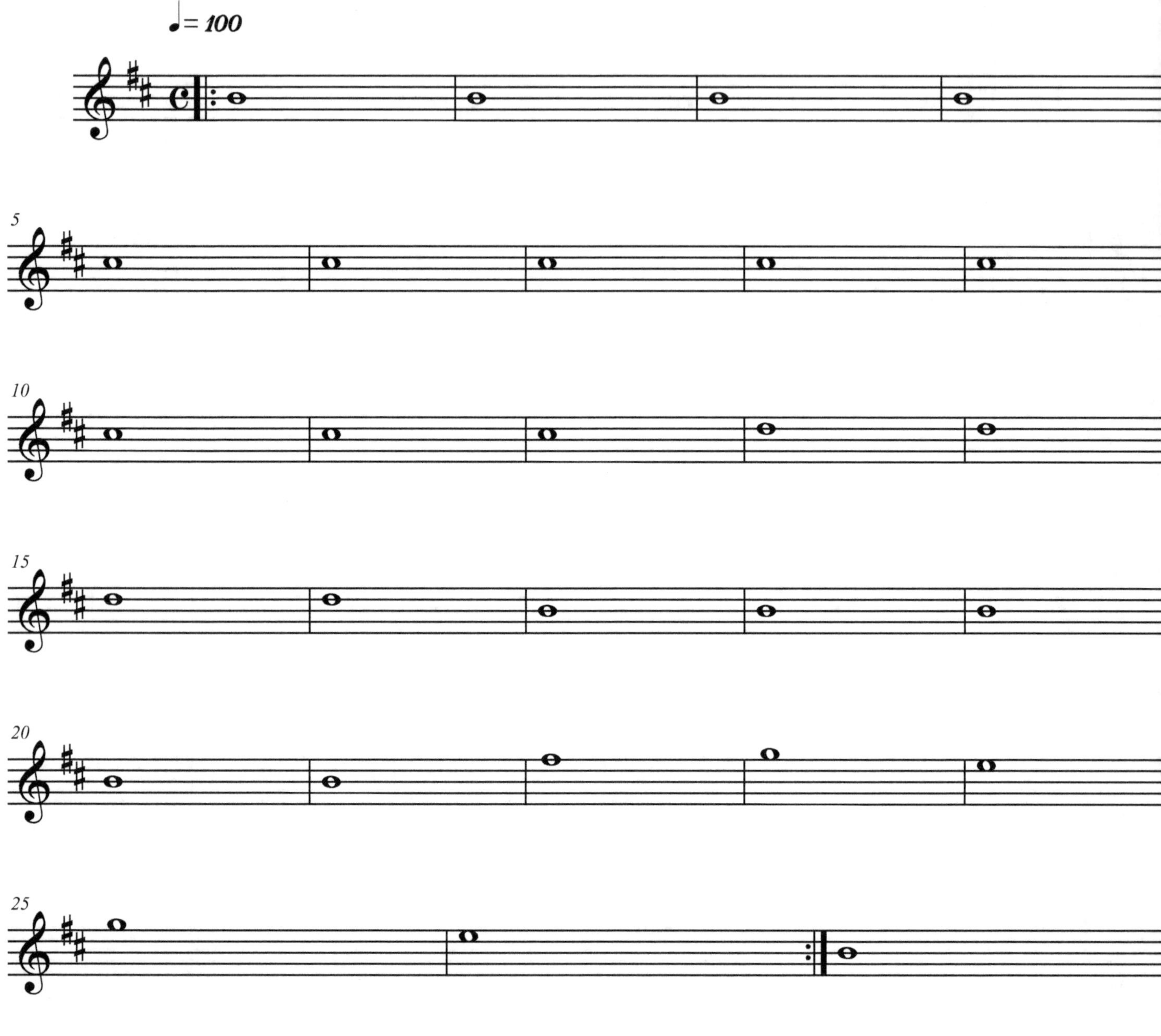

I

Part 1: Bes Trumpet 1

Joost de Groot

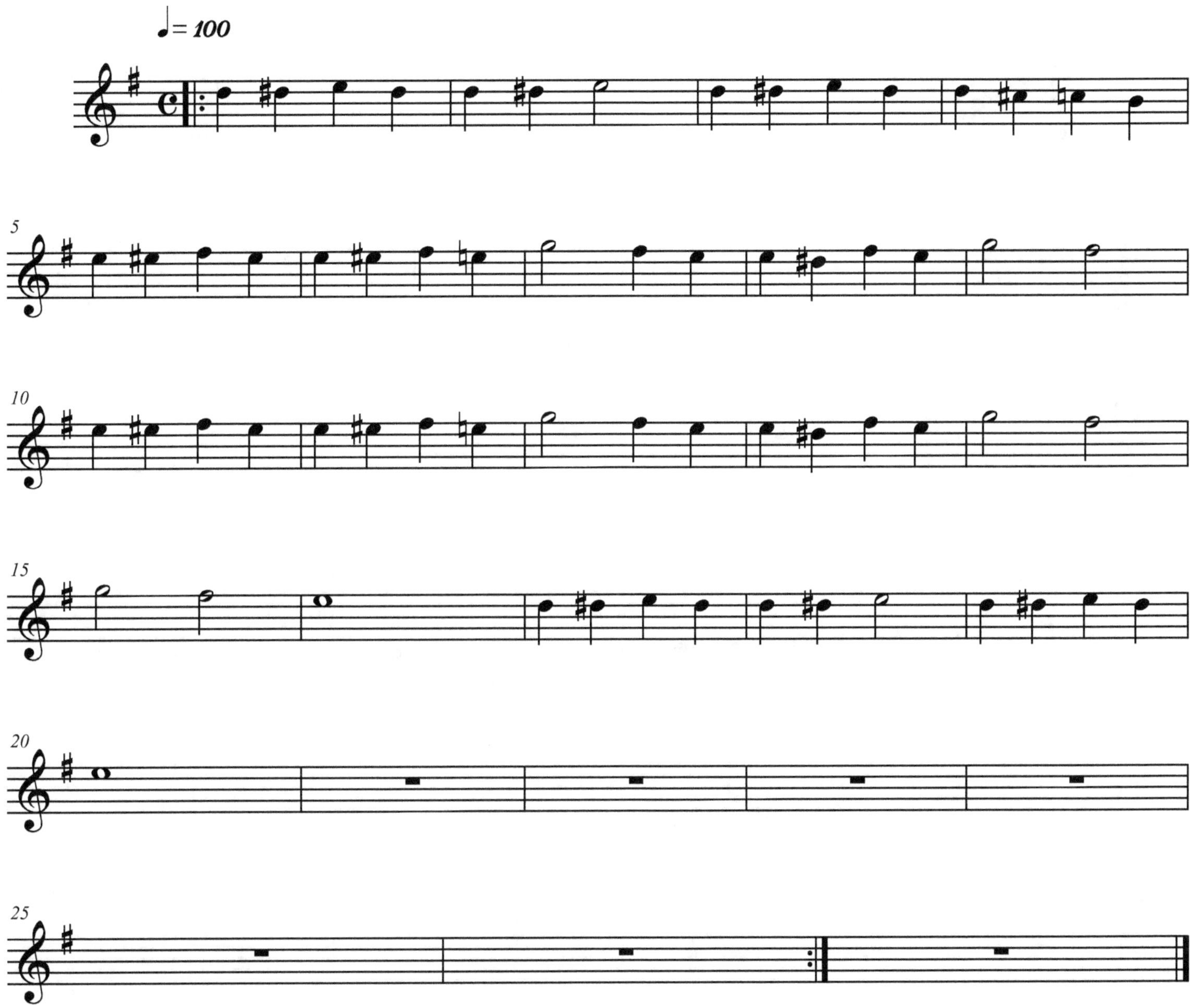

Part 2: Bes Trumpet 2 + 3

I

Joost de Groo

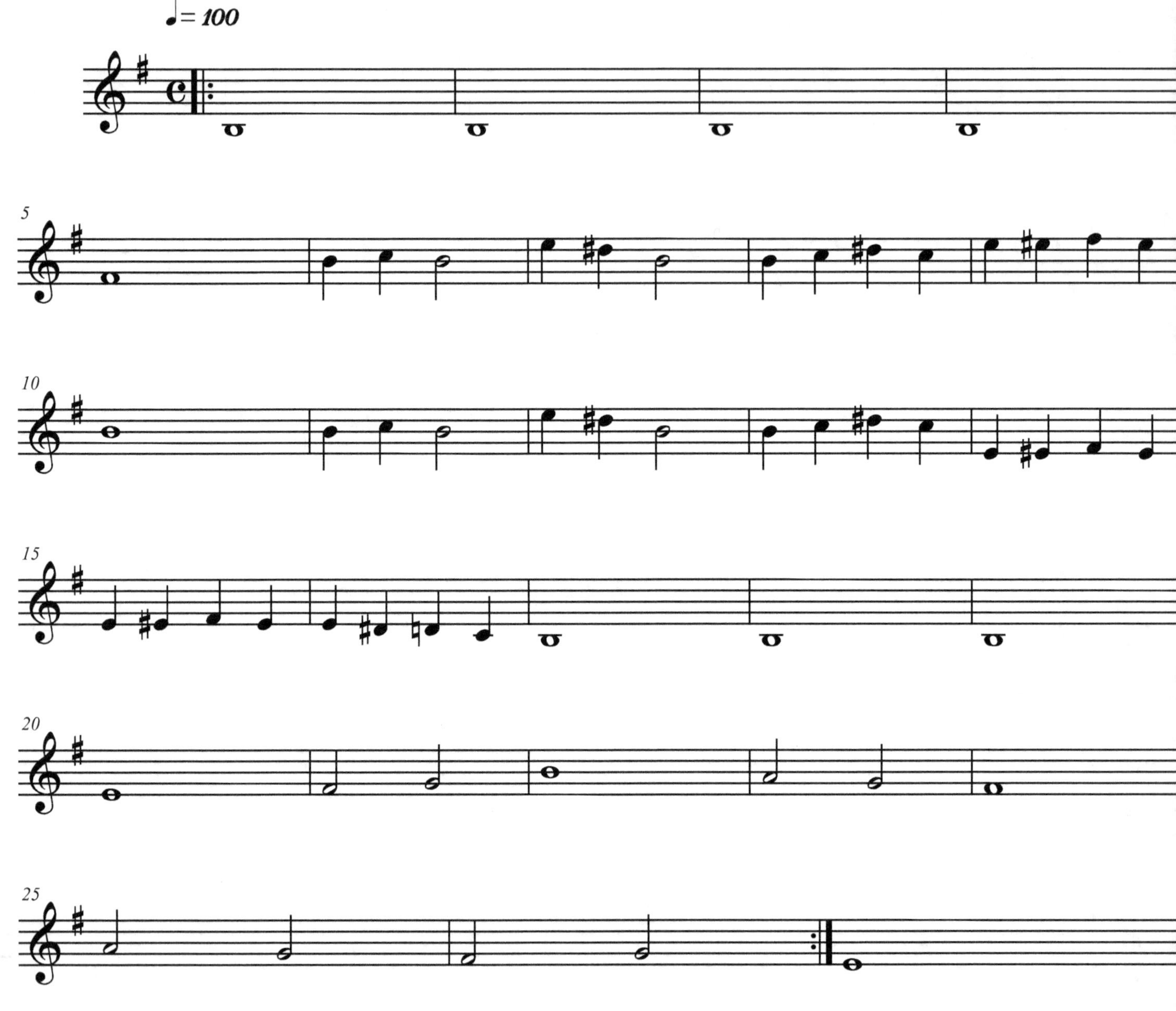

Part 2: F Horn 1 + 2

I

Joost de Groot

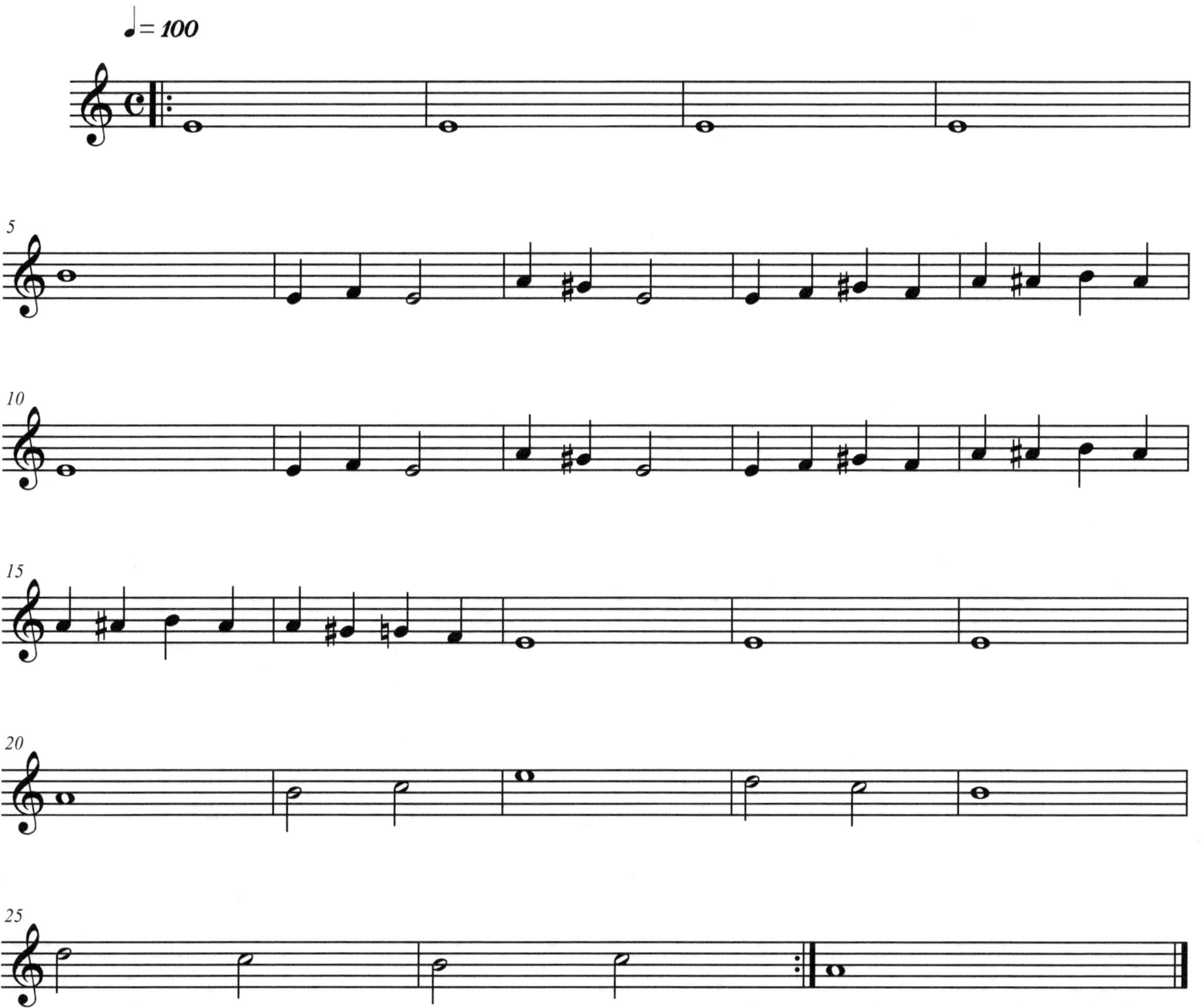

Part 3: F Horn 3 + 4

I

Joost de Gro

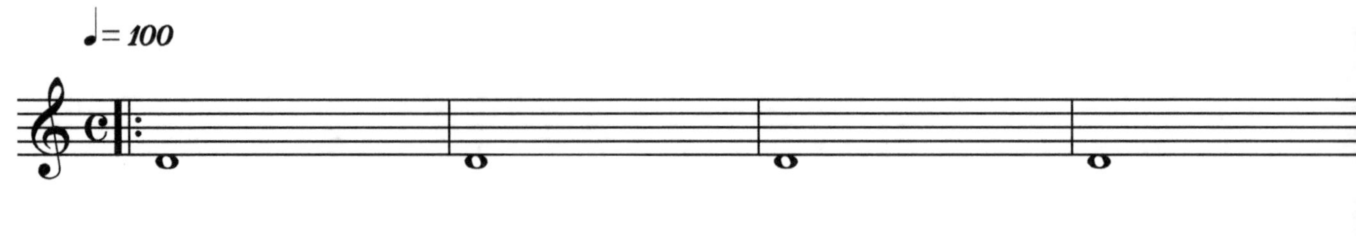

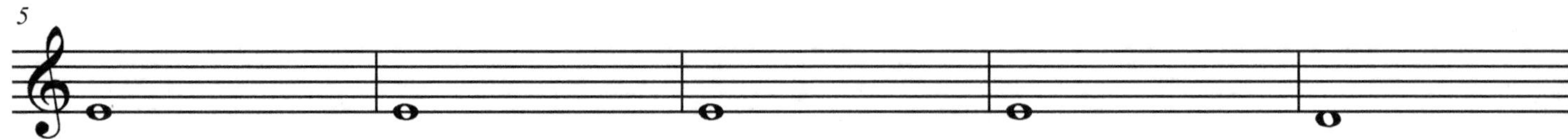

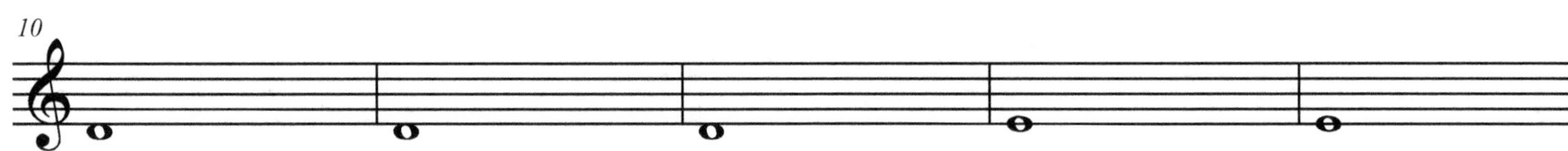

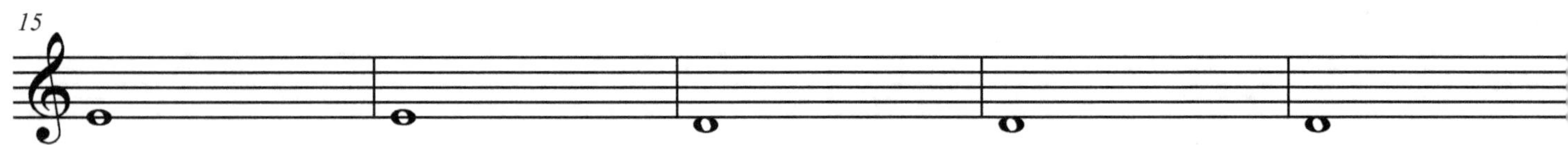

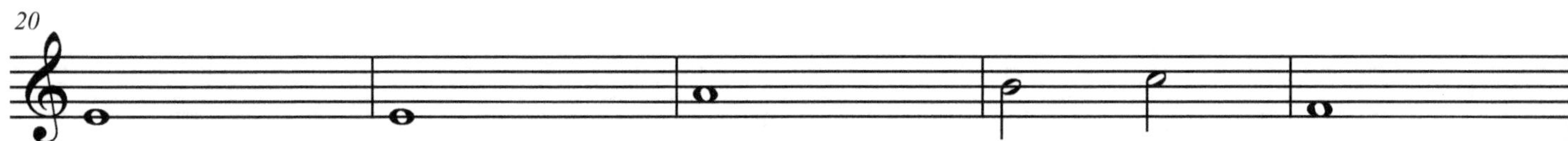

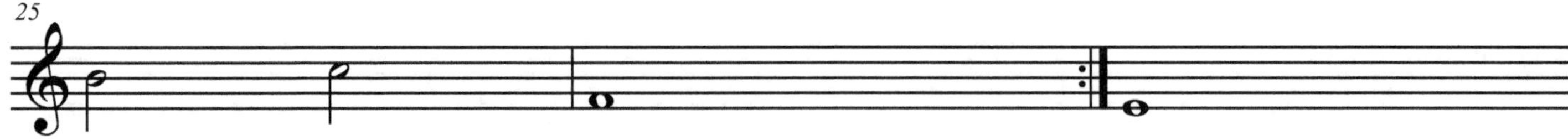

Part 3: C Trombone 1 + 2

I

Joost de Groot

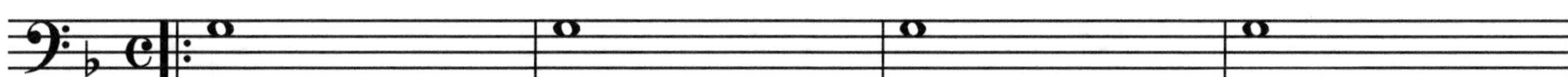

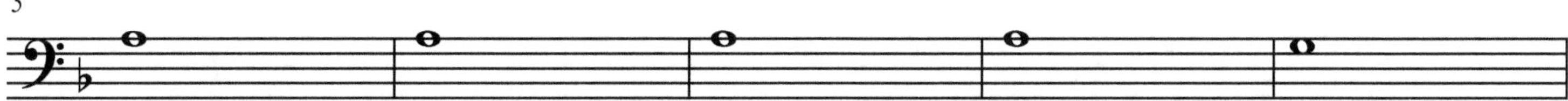

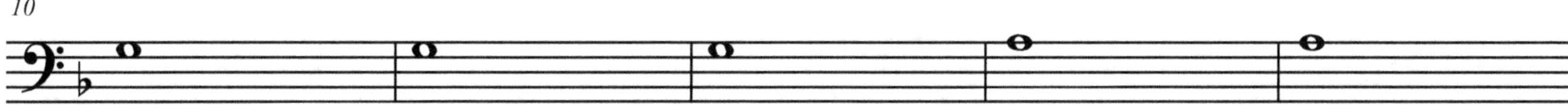

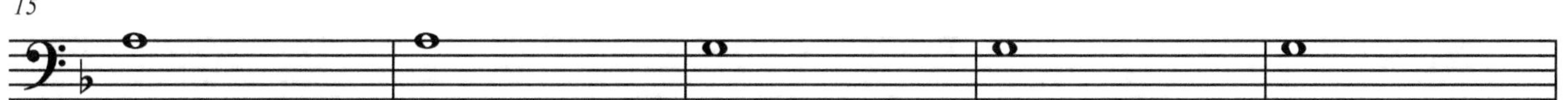

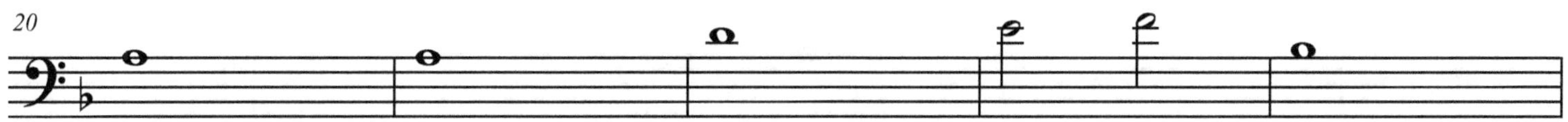

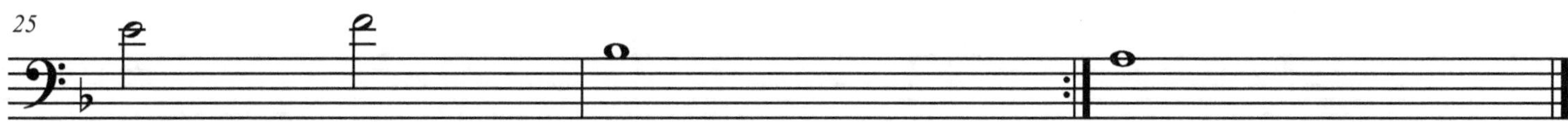

Part 4: C Bass Trombone

I

Joost de Groo

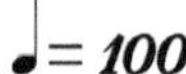

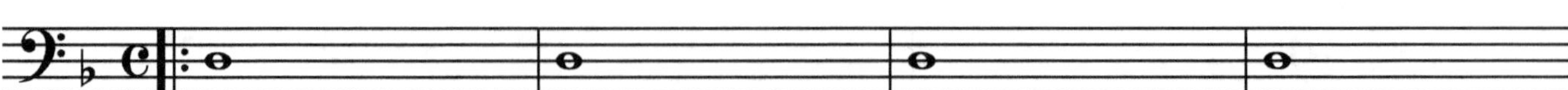

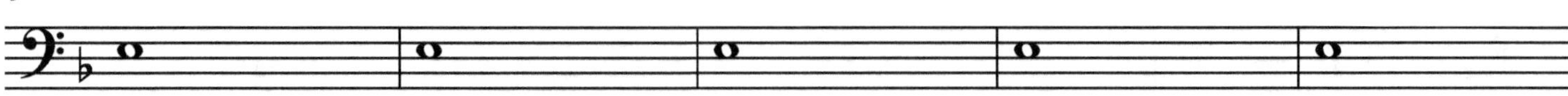

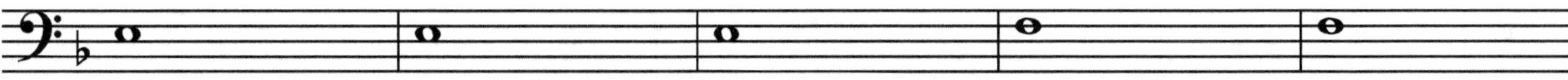

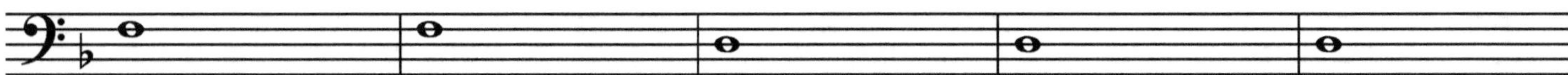

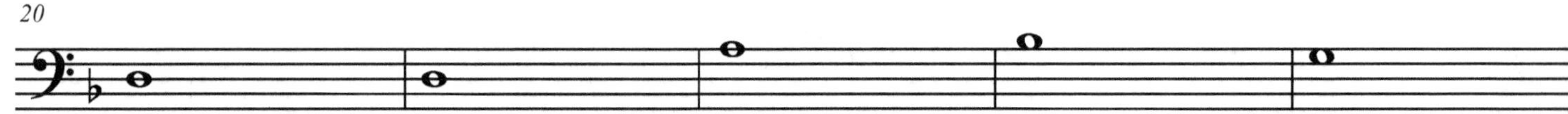

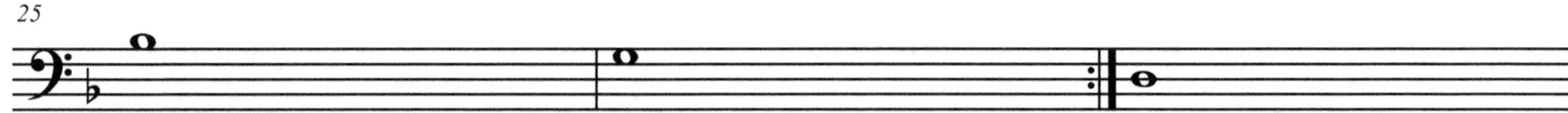

Part 3: C Baritone

I

Joost de Groot

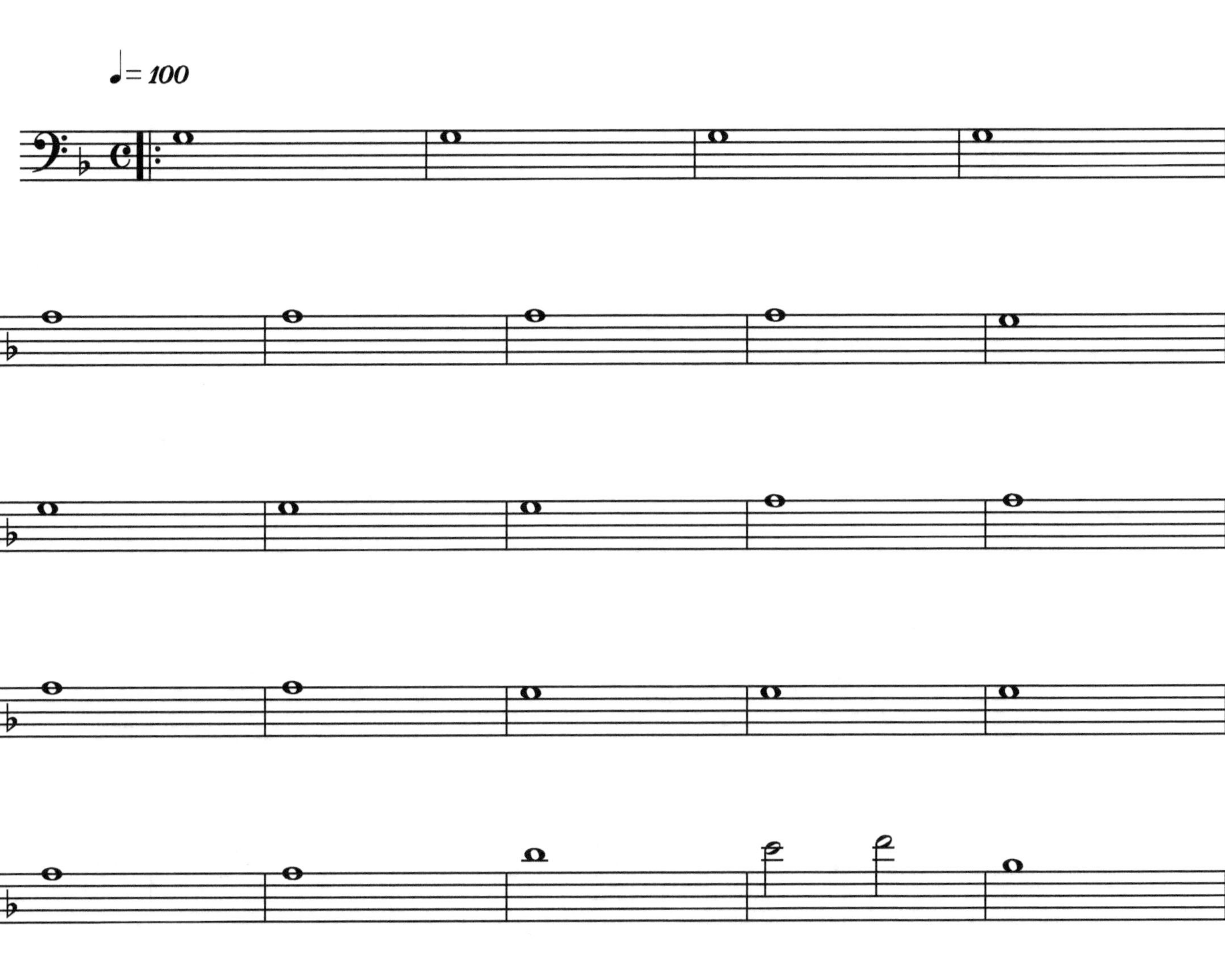

Part 3: Bes Baritone

I

Joost de Gro

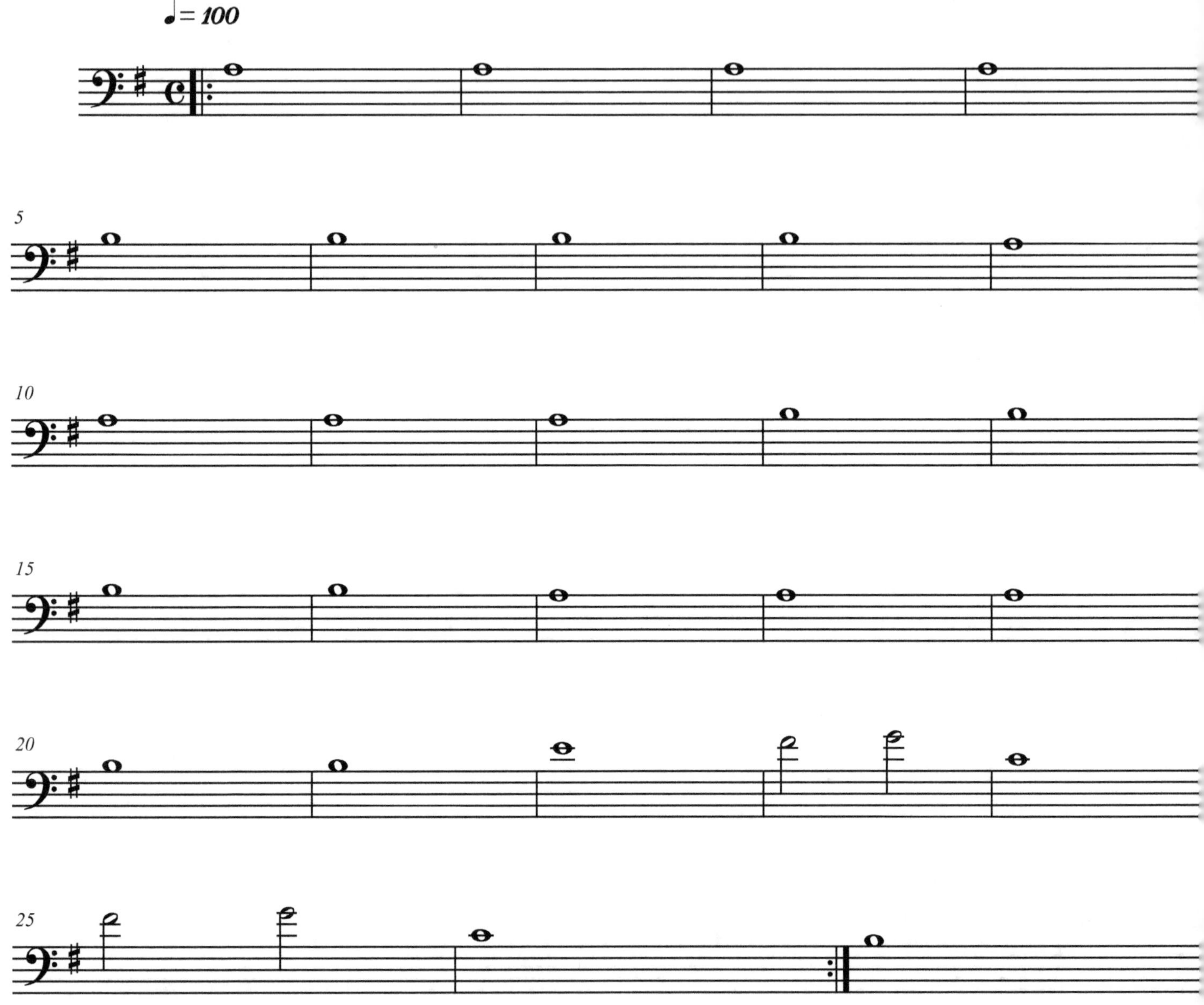

Part 3: Bes Baritone

I

Joost de Groot

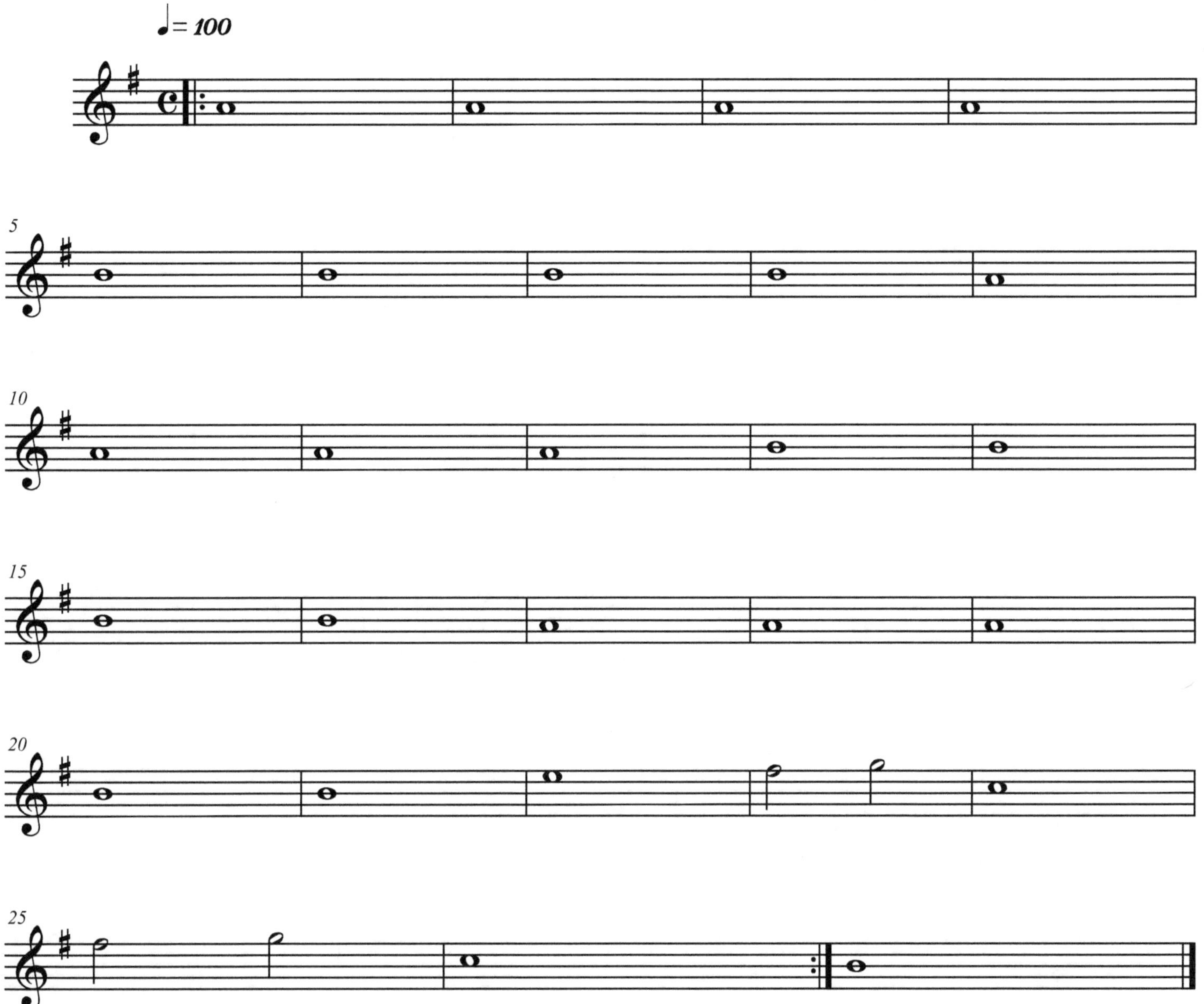

I

Part 4: C Bass Tuba

Joost de Groo

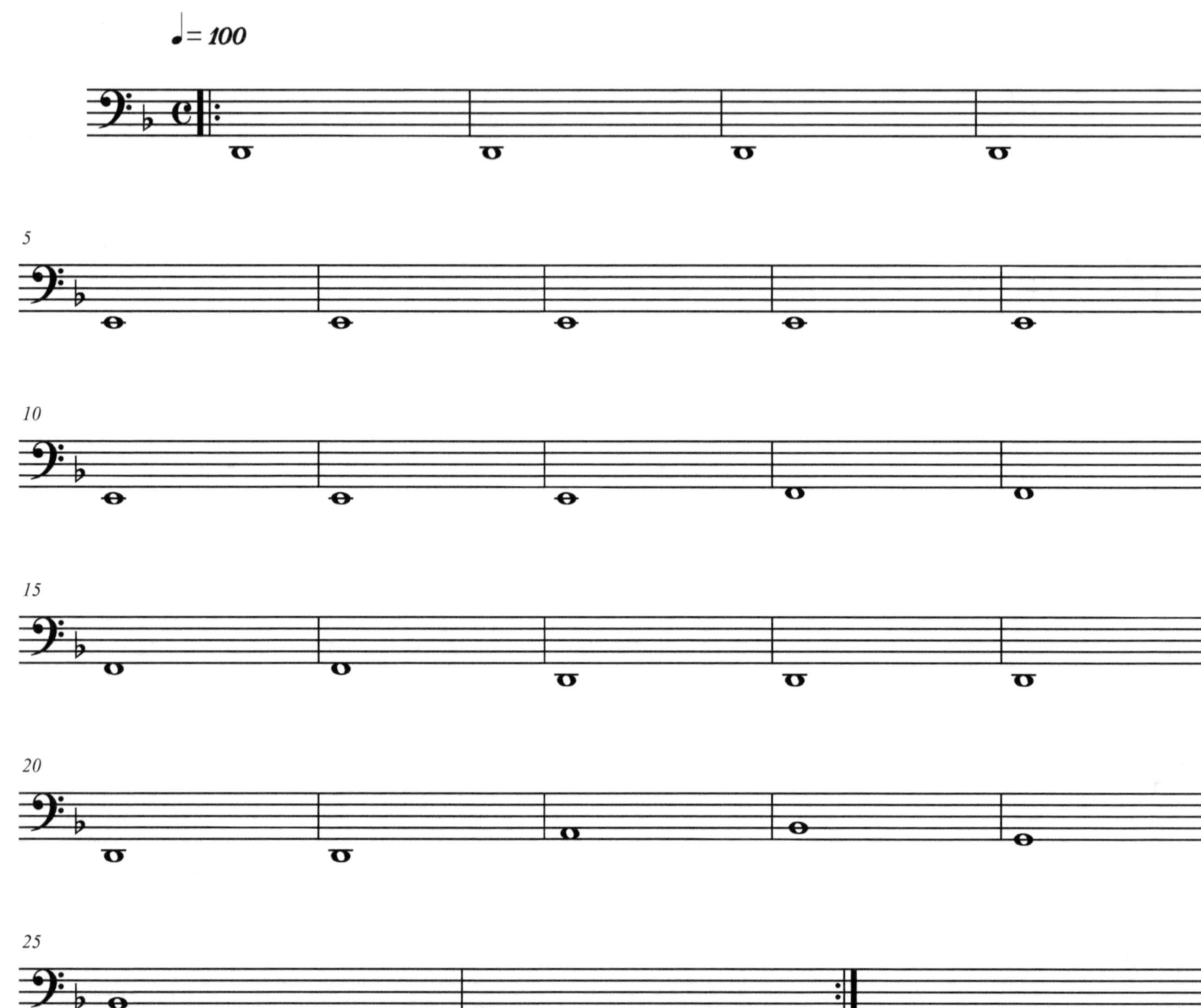

Part 4: Bes Bass Tuba

I

Joost de Groot

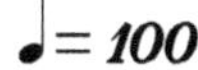

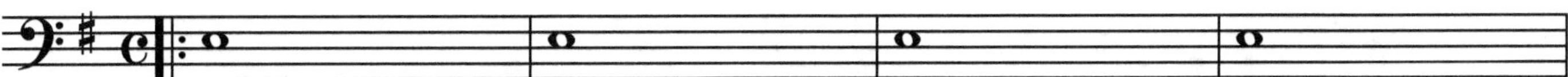

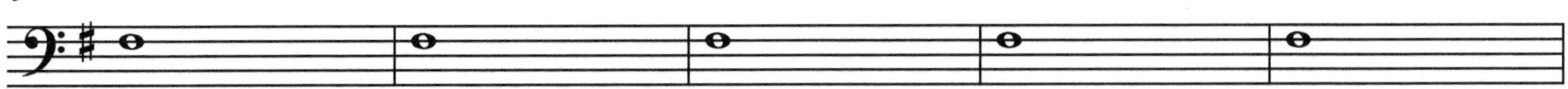

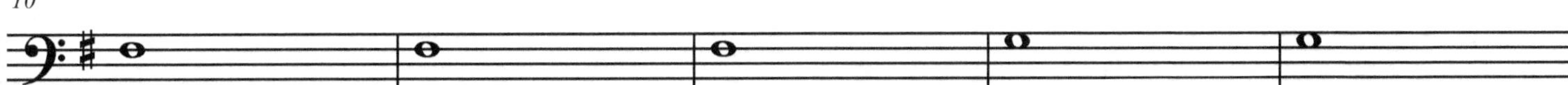

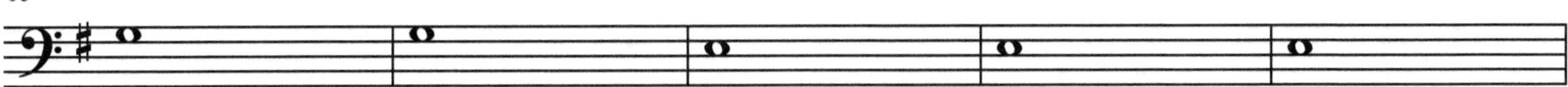

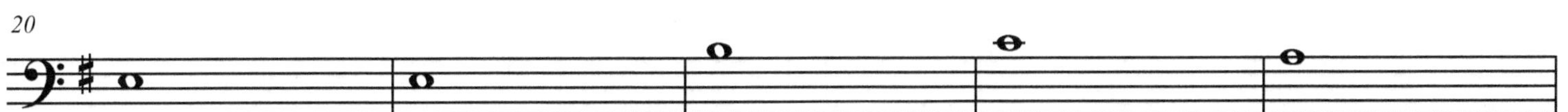

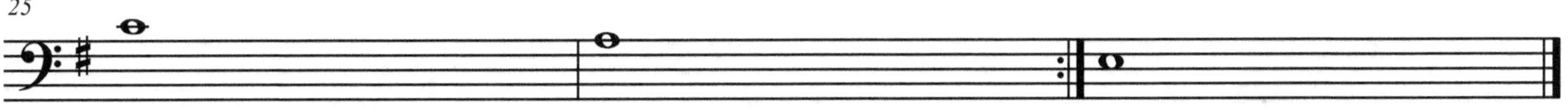

Part 4: Es Bass Tuba

I

Joost de Gro

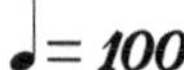

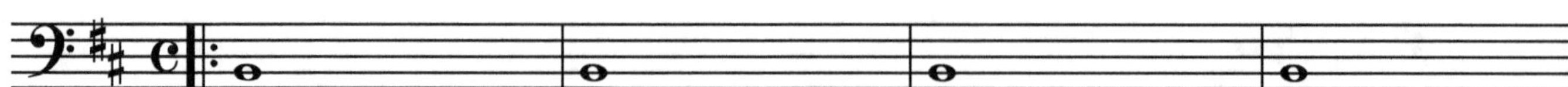

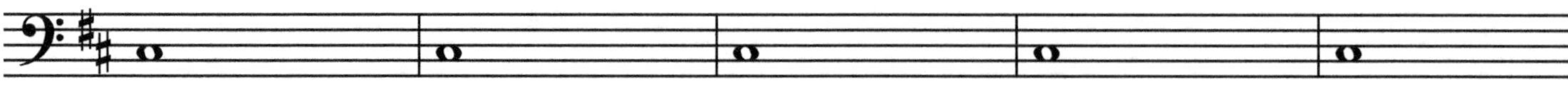

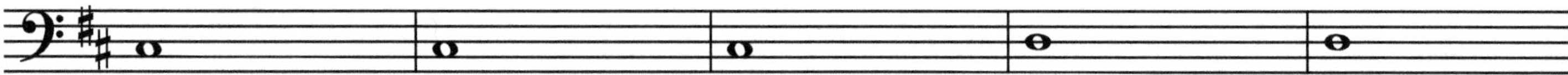

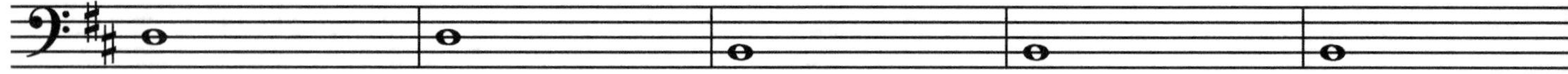

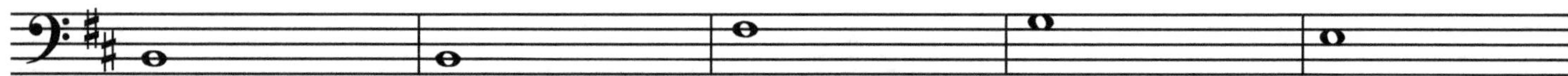

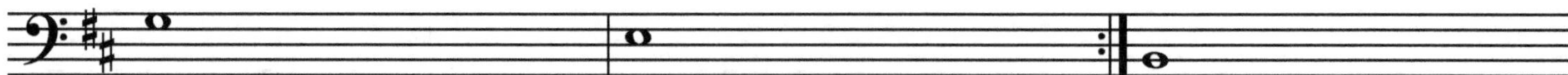

E

Part 1: C Flute

Joost de Groot

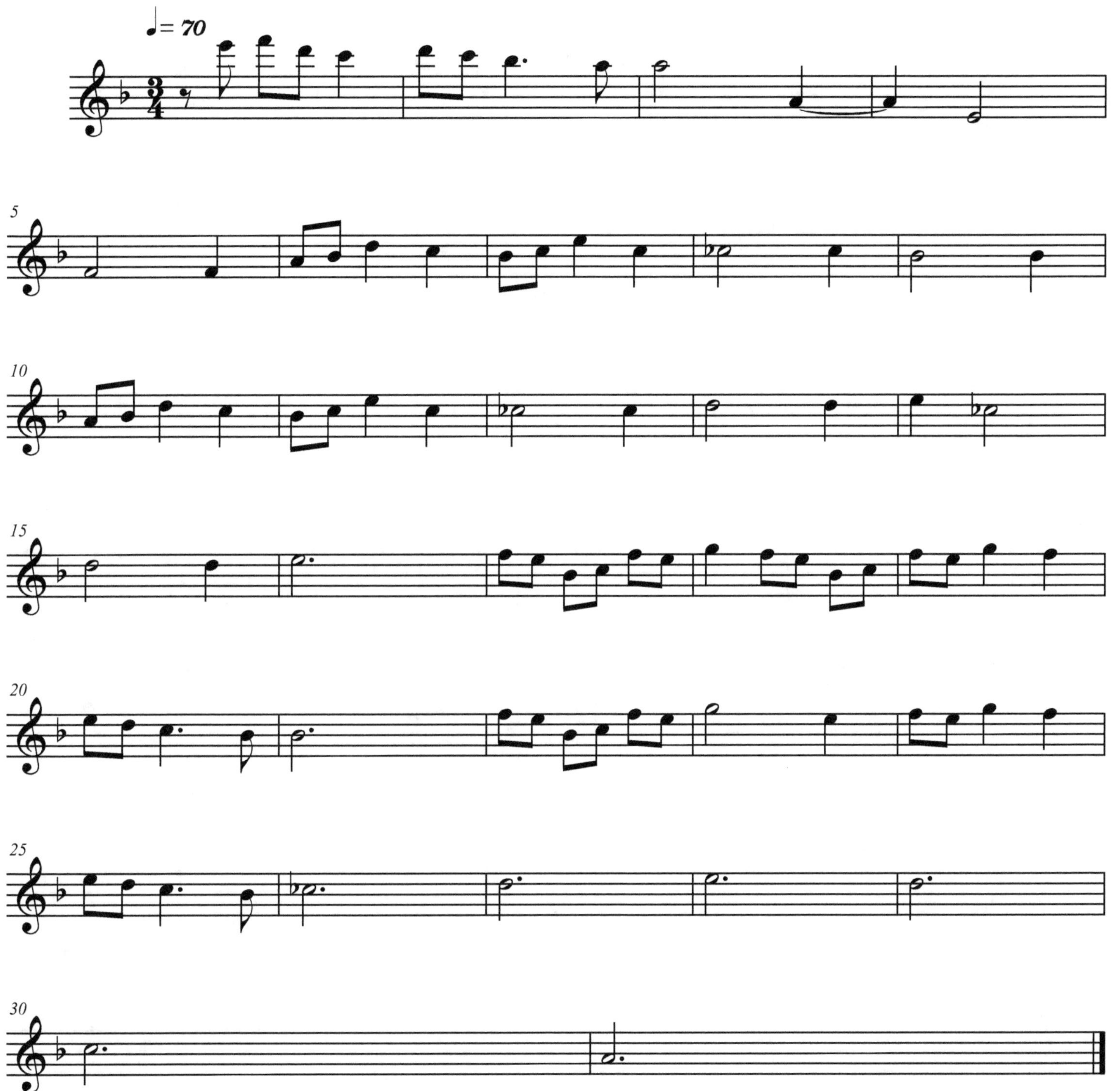

E

Part 1: C Oboe

Joost de Groo

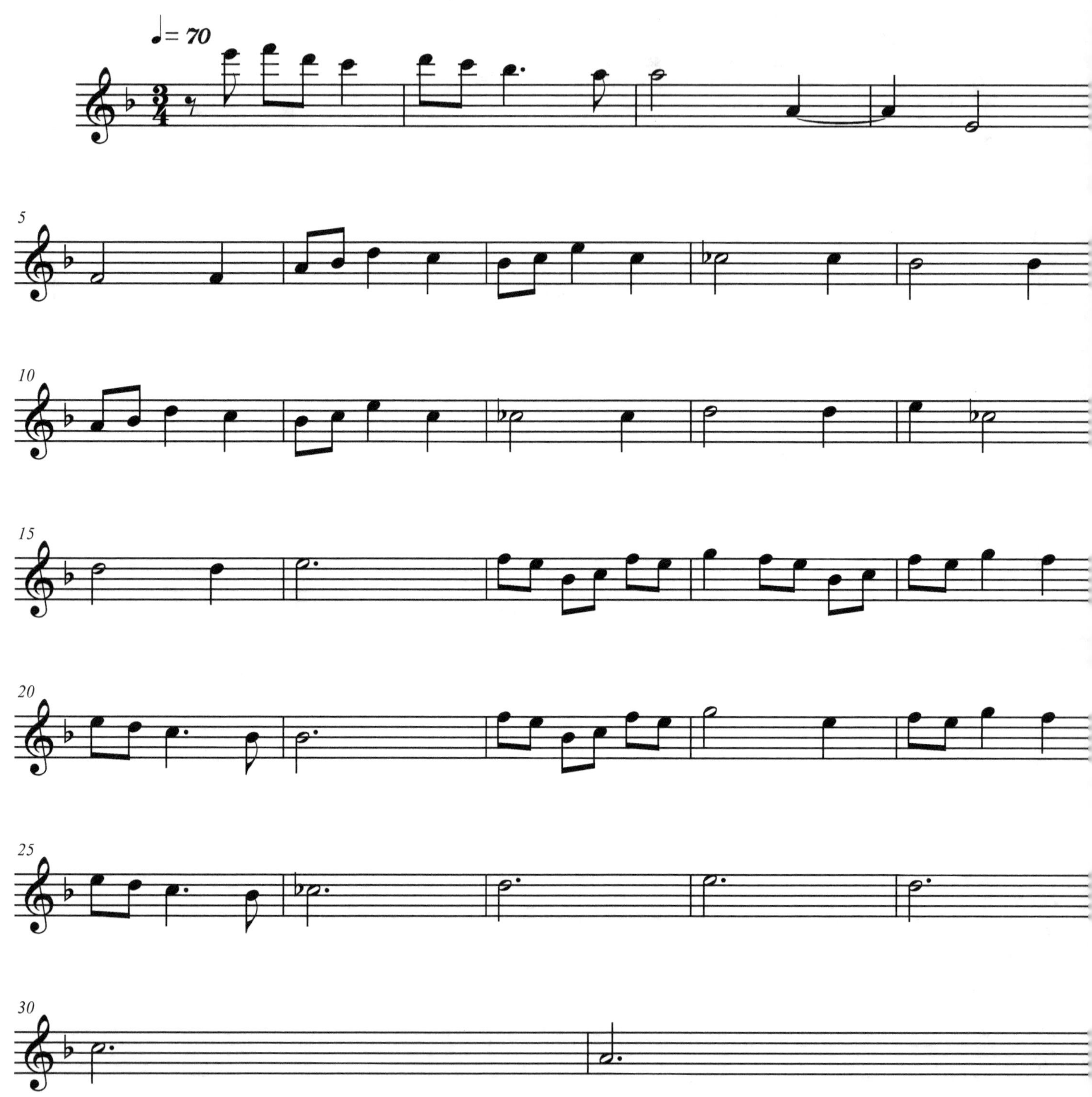

Part 4: C Bassoon

E

Joost de Groot

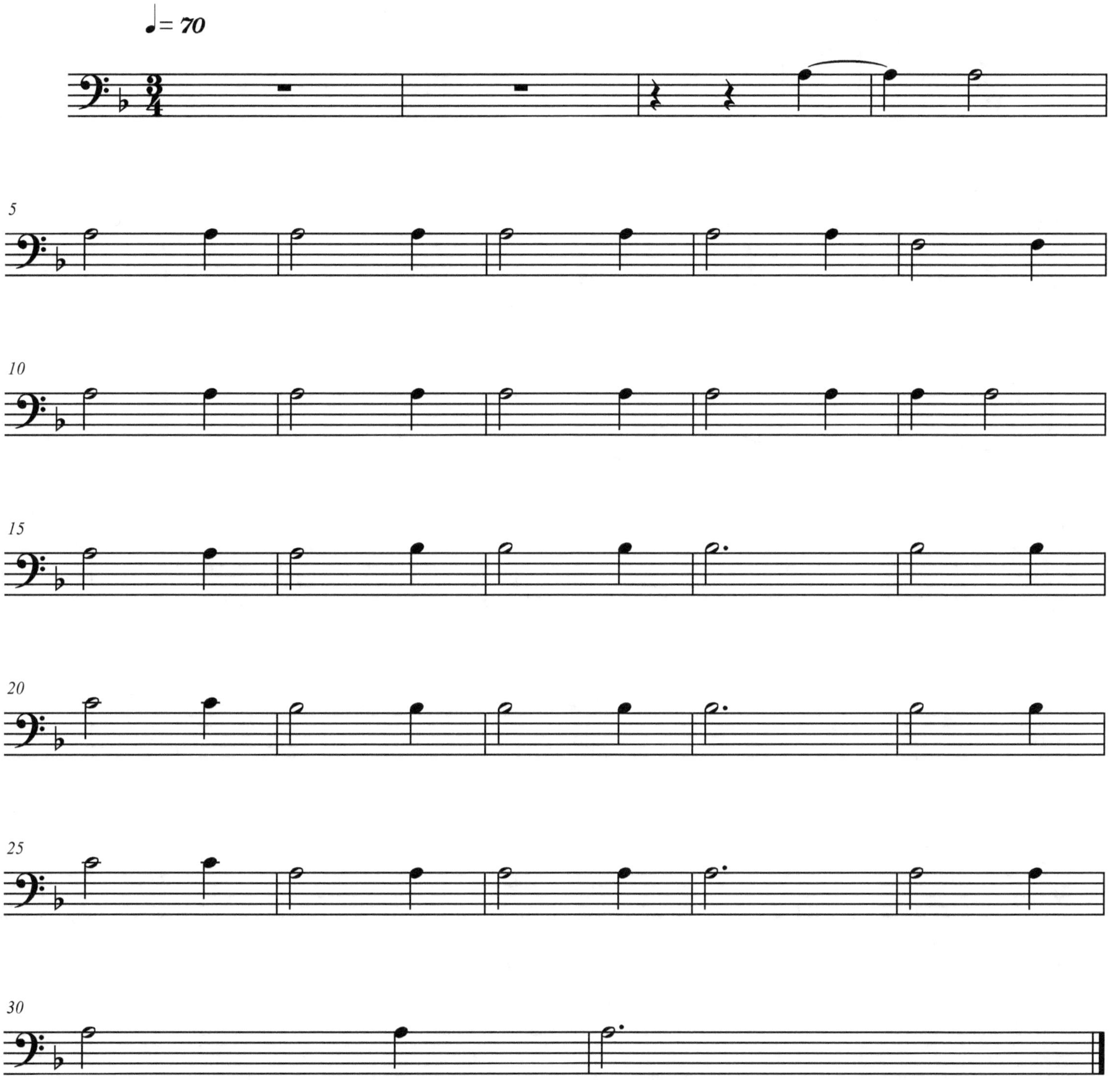

Part 1: Bes Clarinet 1

E

Joost de Gro

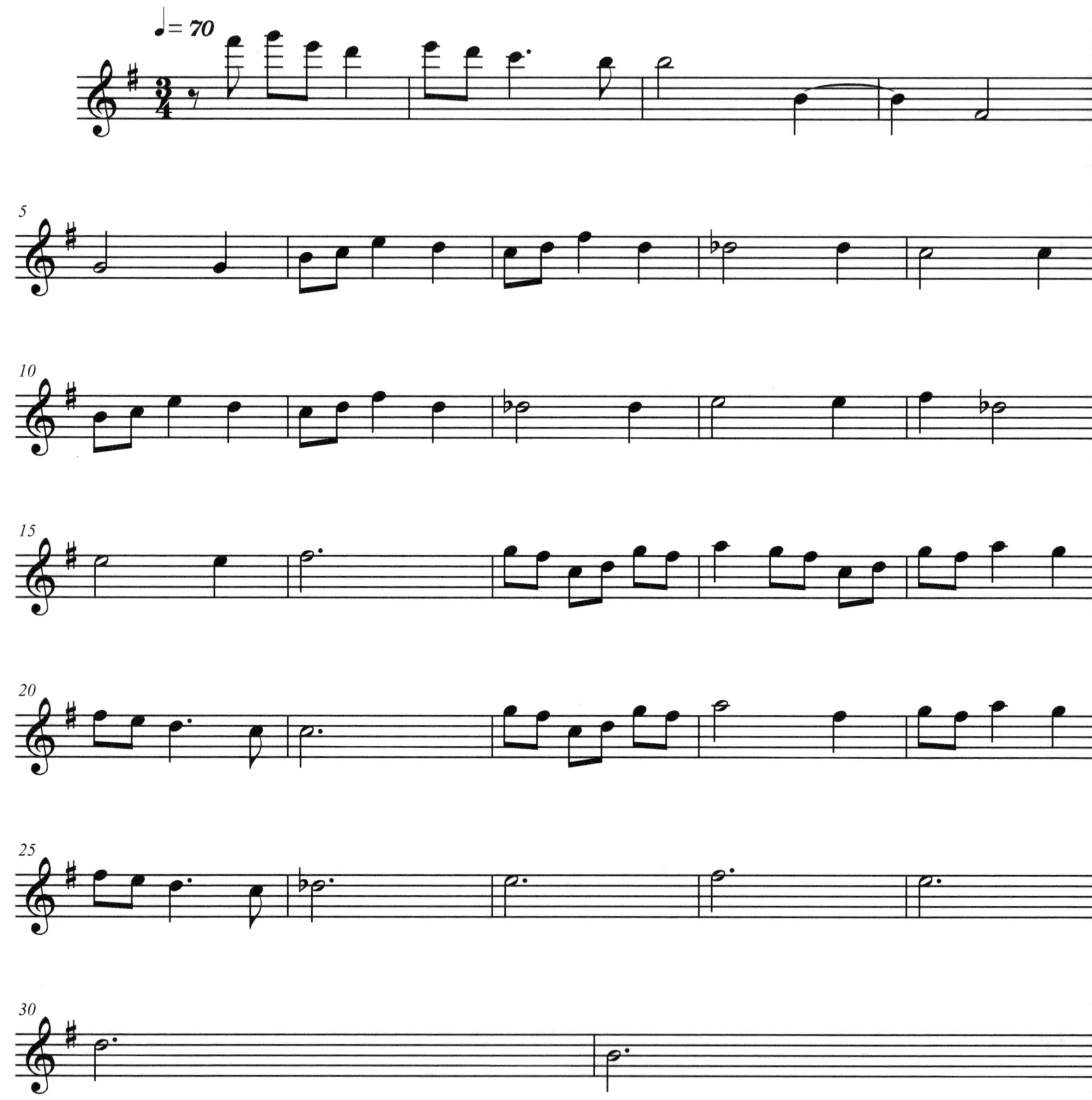

E

Part 2: Bes Clarinet 2 + 3

Joost de Groot

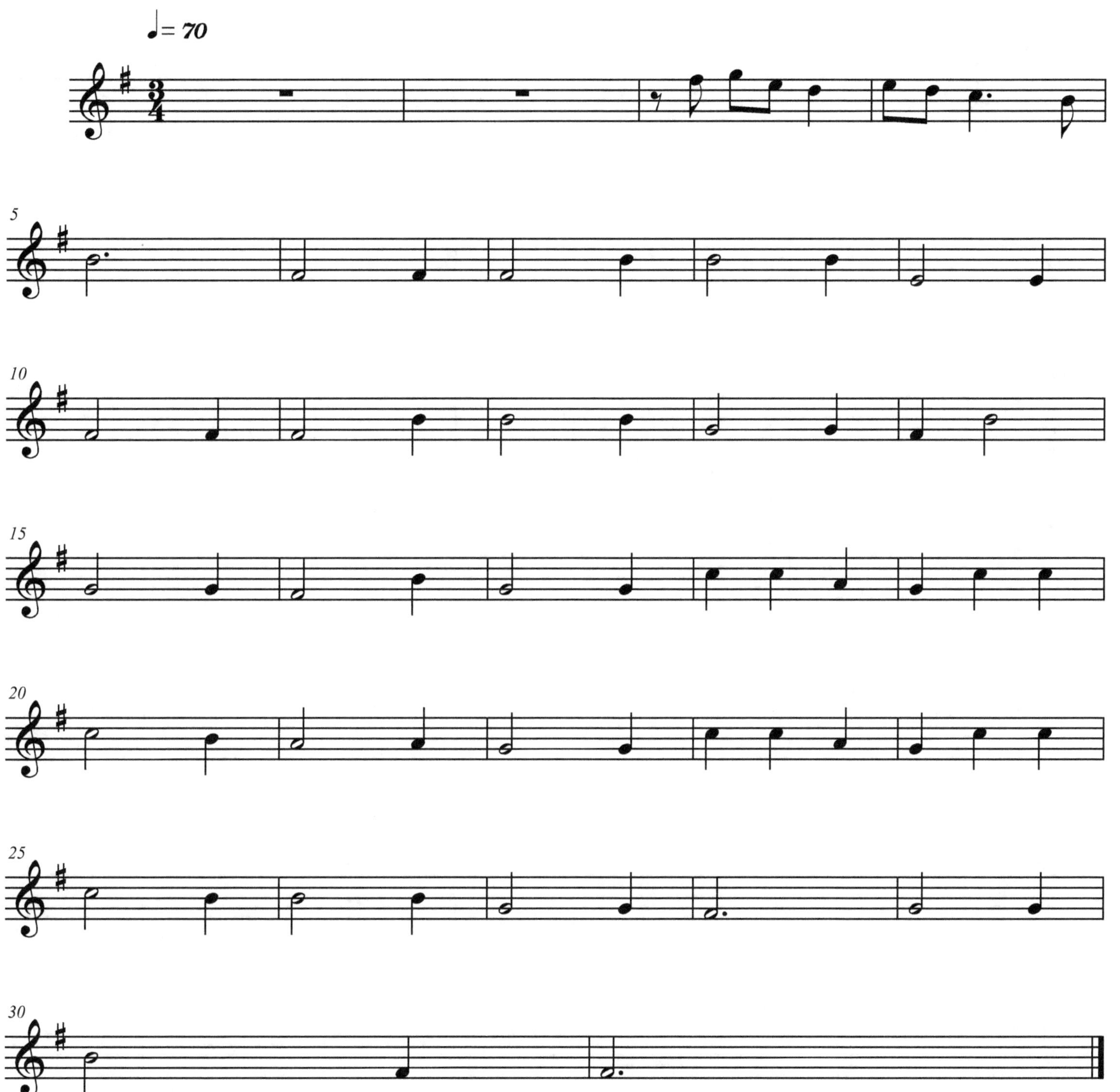

Part 3: Es Alto Clarinet

E

Joost de Groo

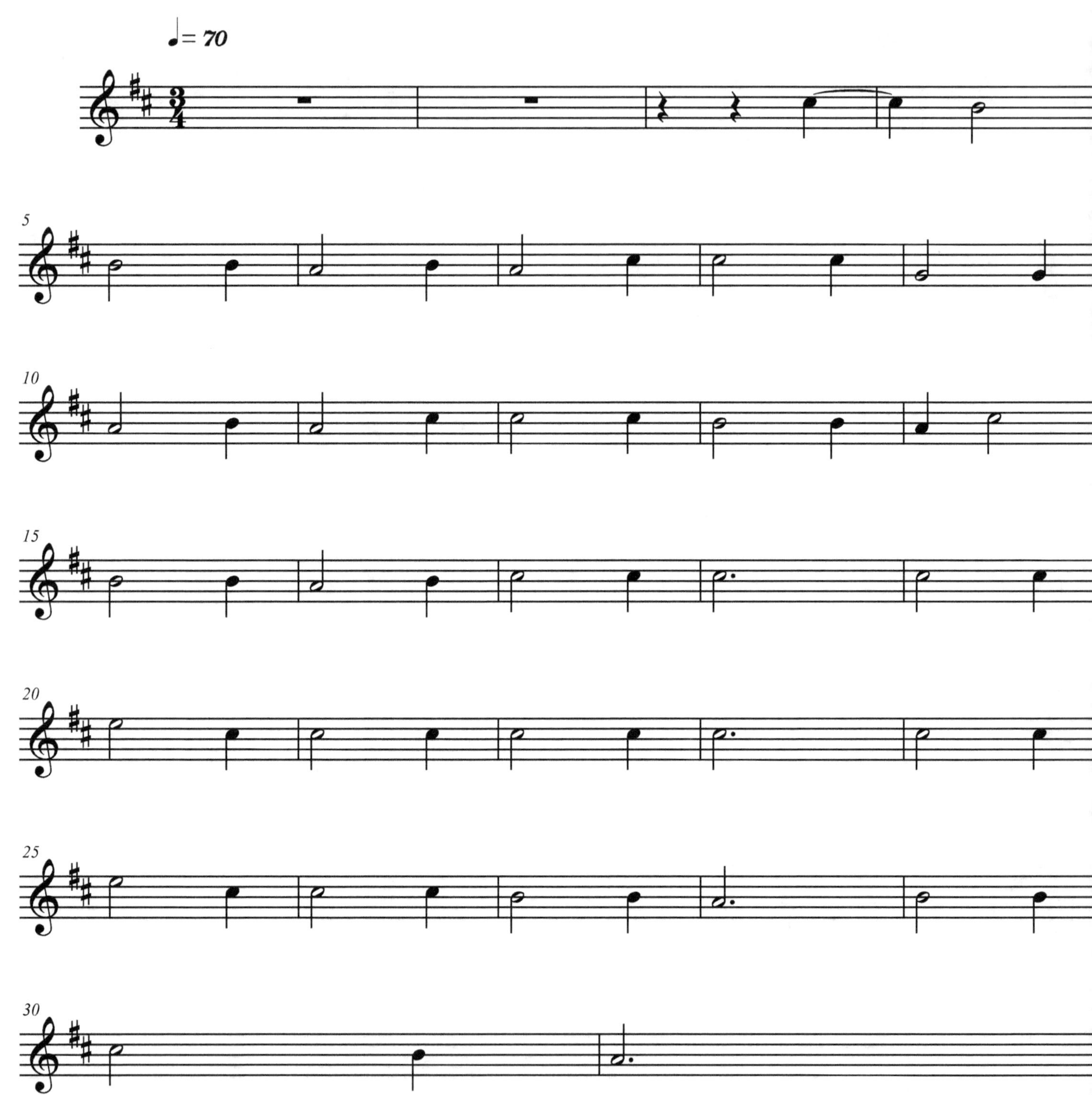

E

Part 4: Bes Bass Clarinet

Joost de Groot

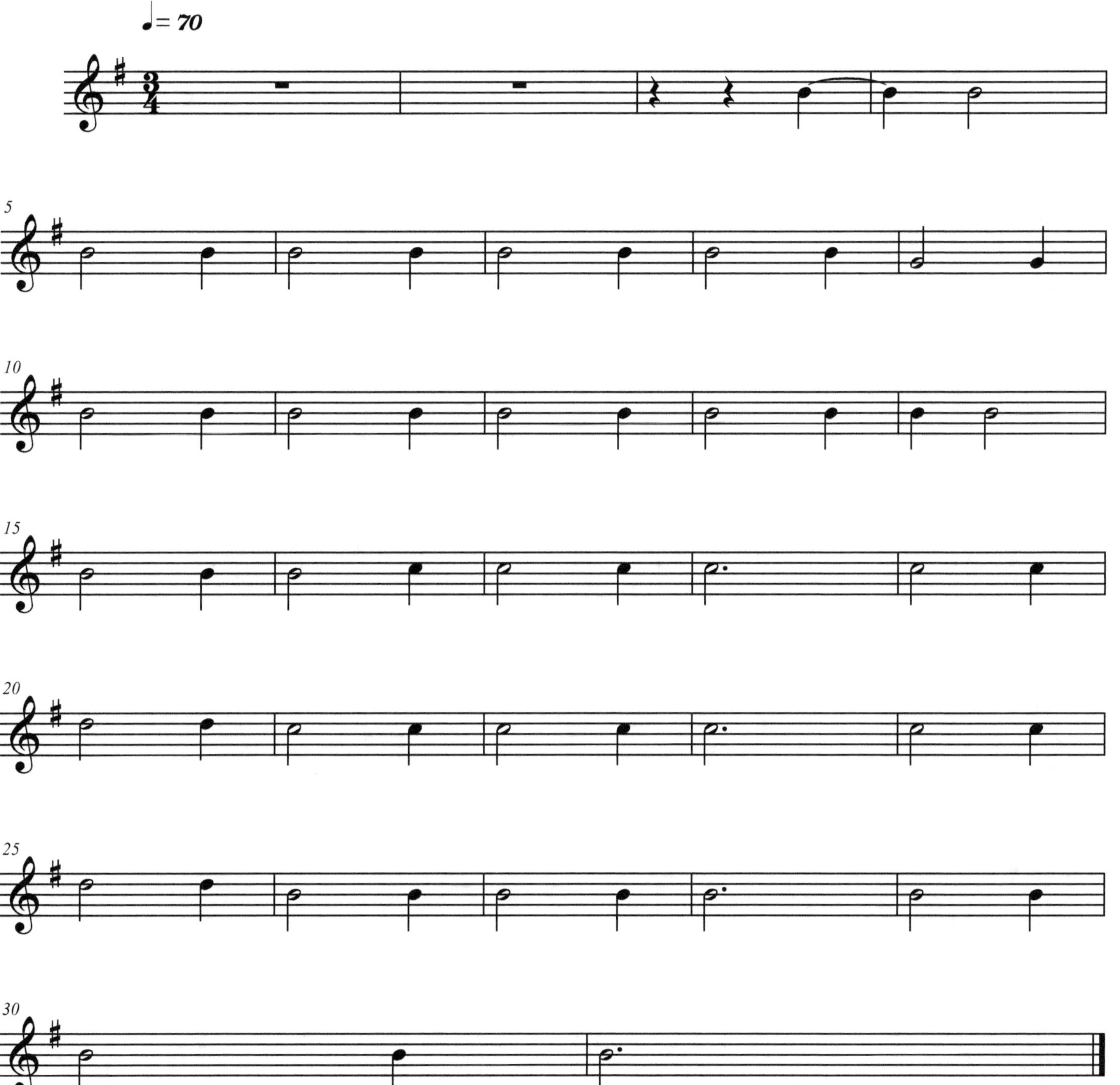

E

Part 2: Es Alto Sax.

Joost de Gro

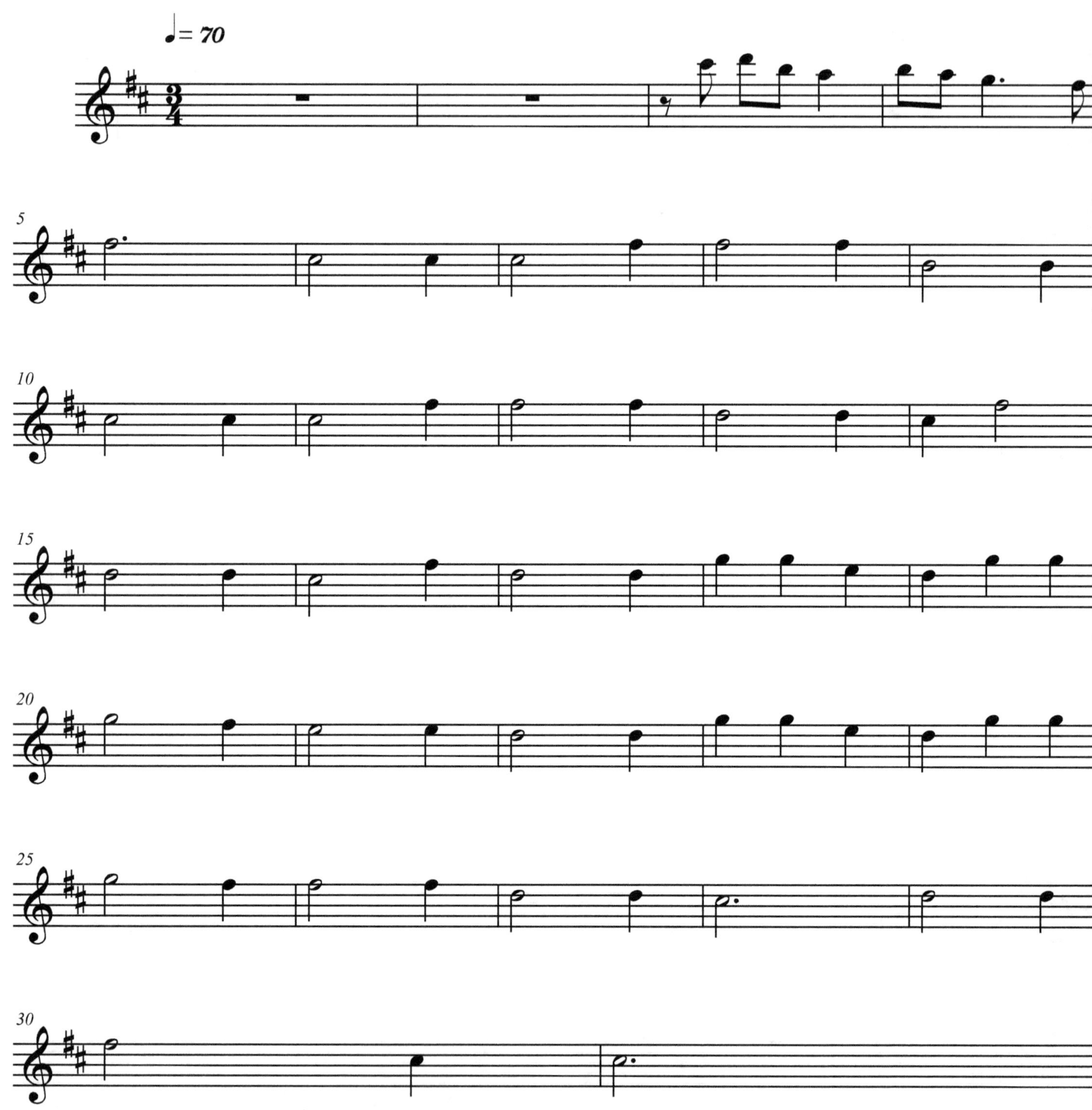

Part 3: Bes Tenor Sax.

E

Joost de Groot

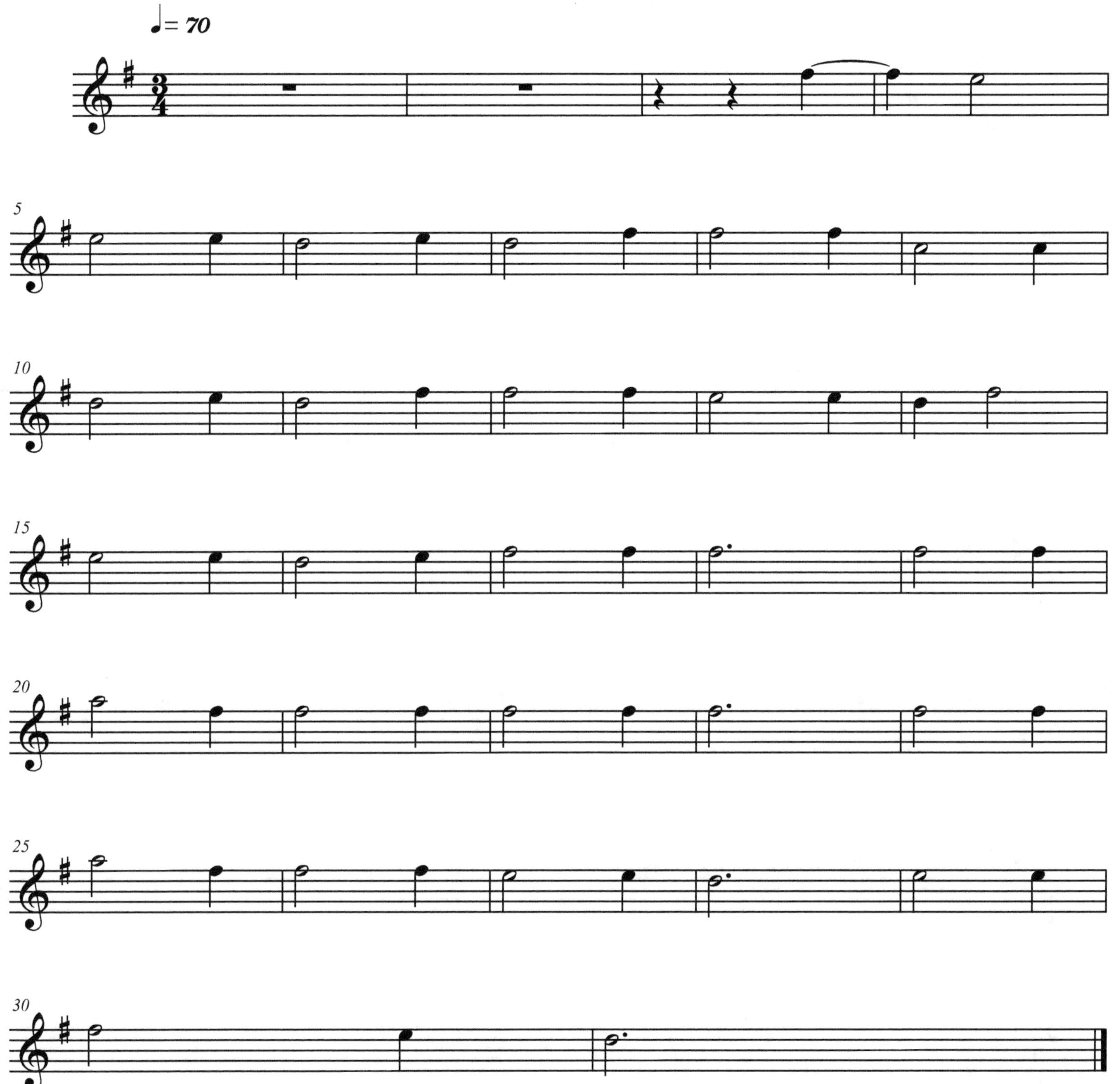

Part 4: Es Baritone Sax.

E

Joost de Groo

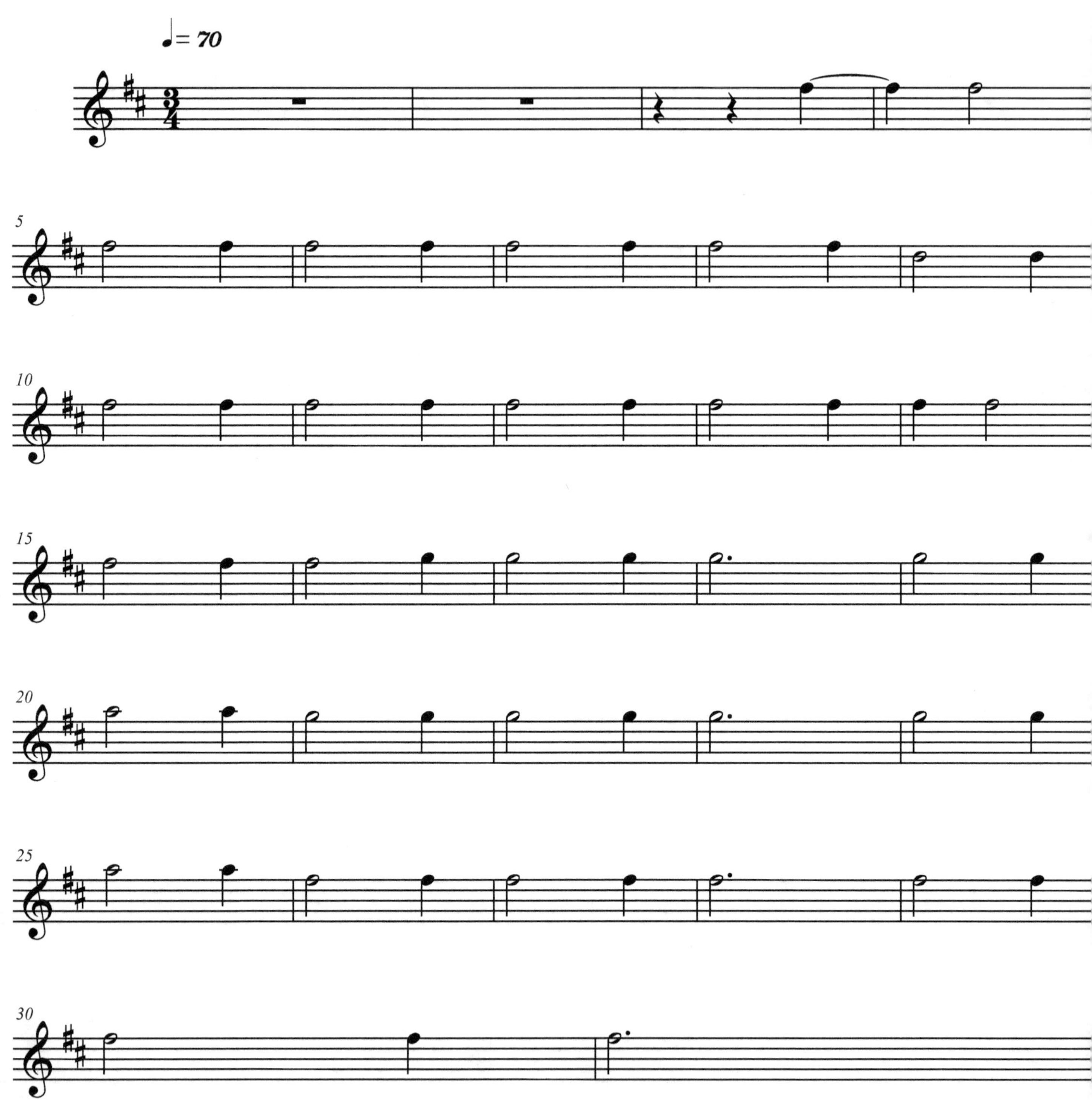

Part 1: Bes Trumpet 1

E

Joost de Groot

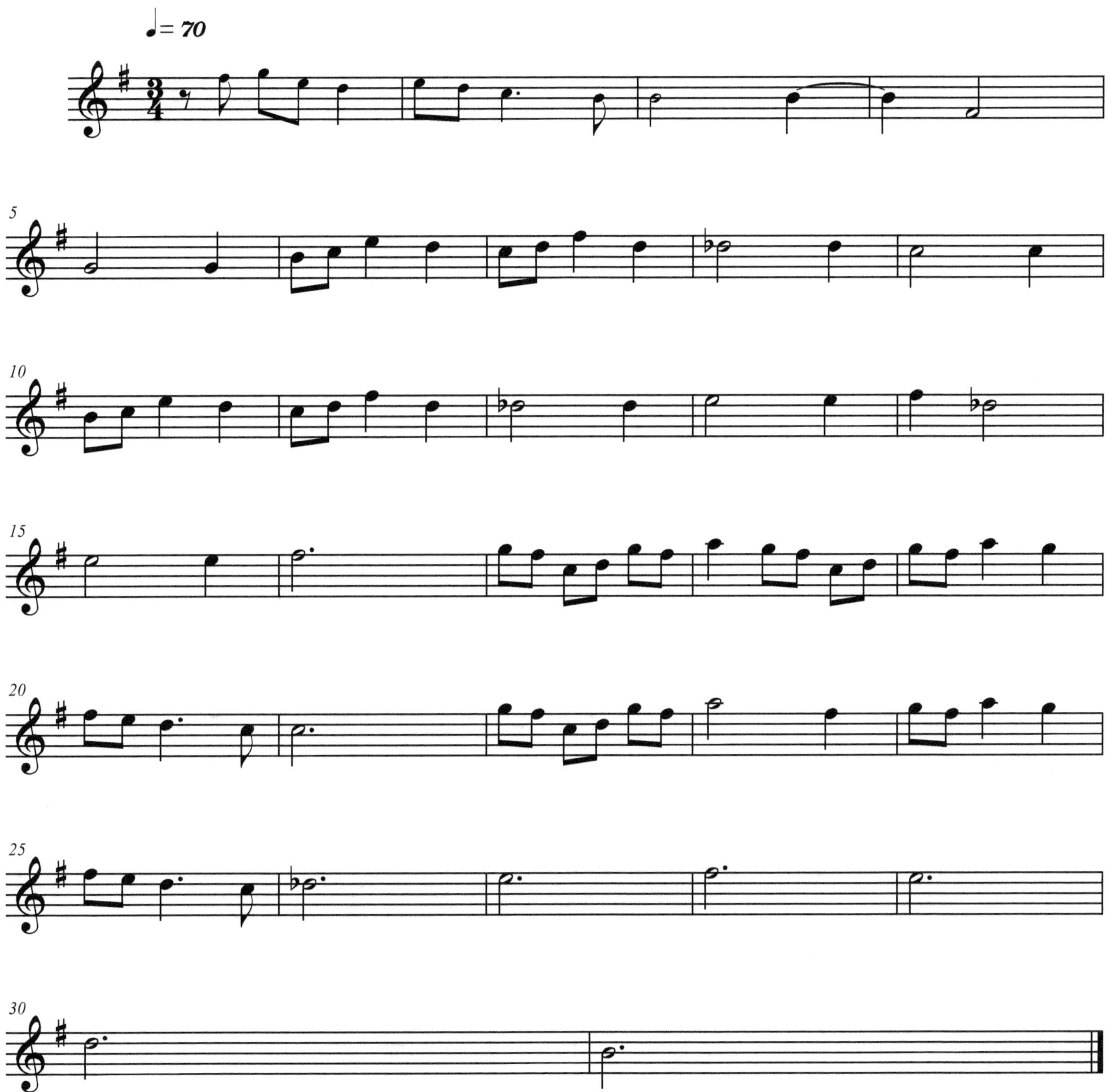

E

Part 2: Bes Trumpet 2 + 3

Joost de Gro

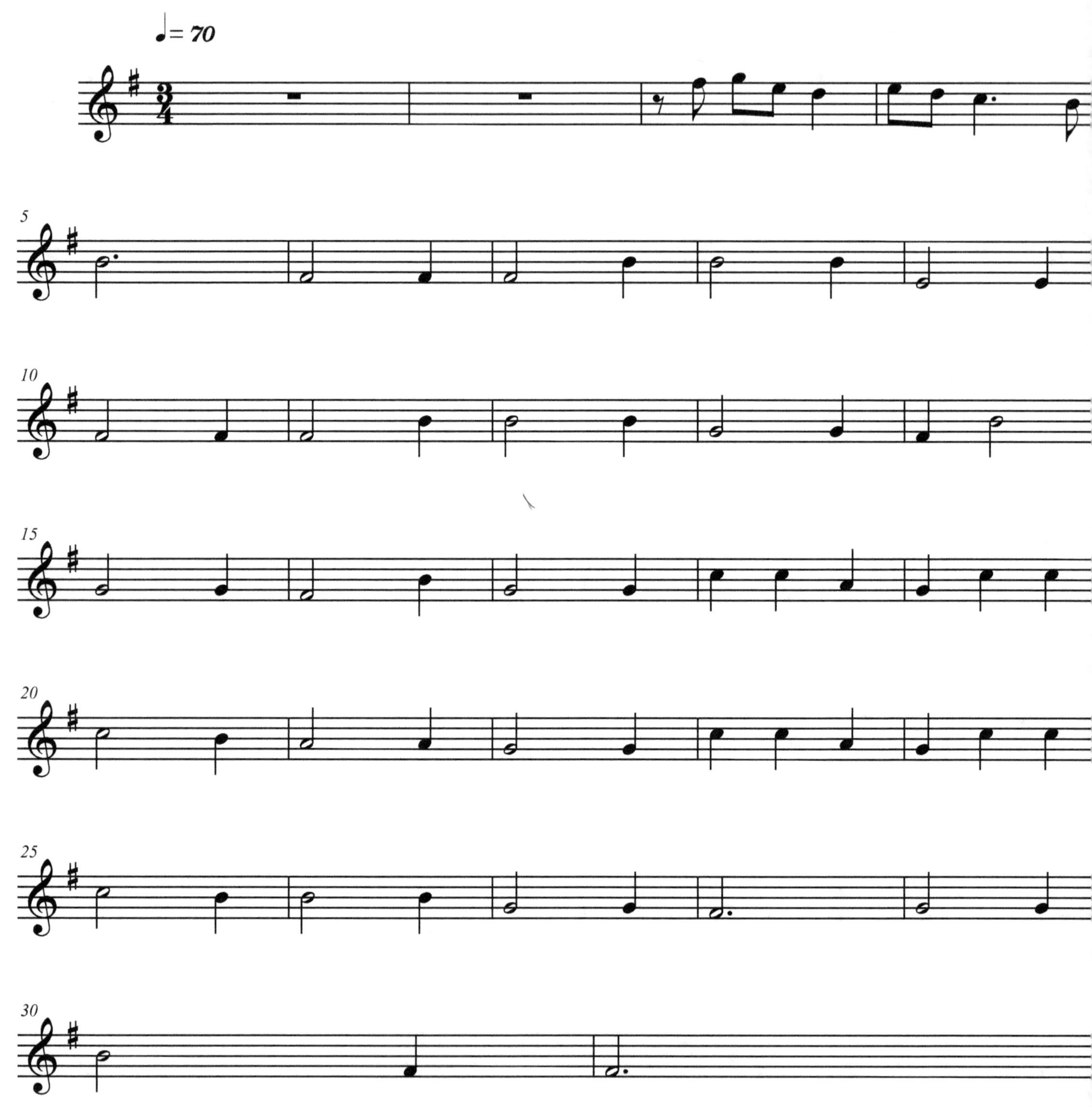

Part 2: F Horn 1 + 2

E

Joost de Groot

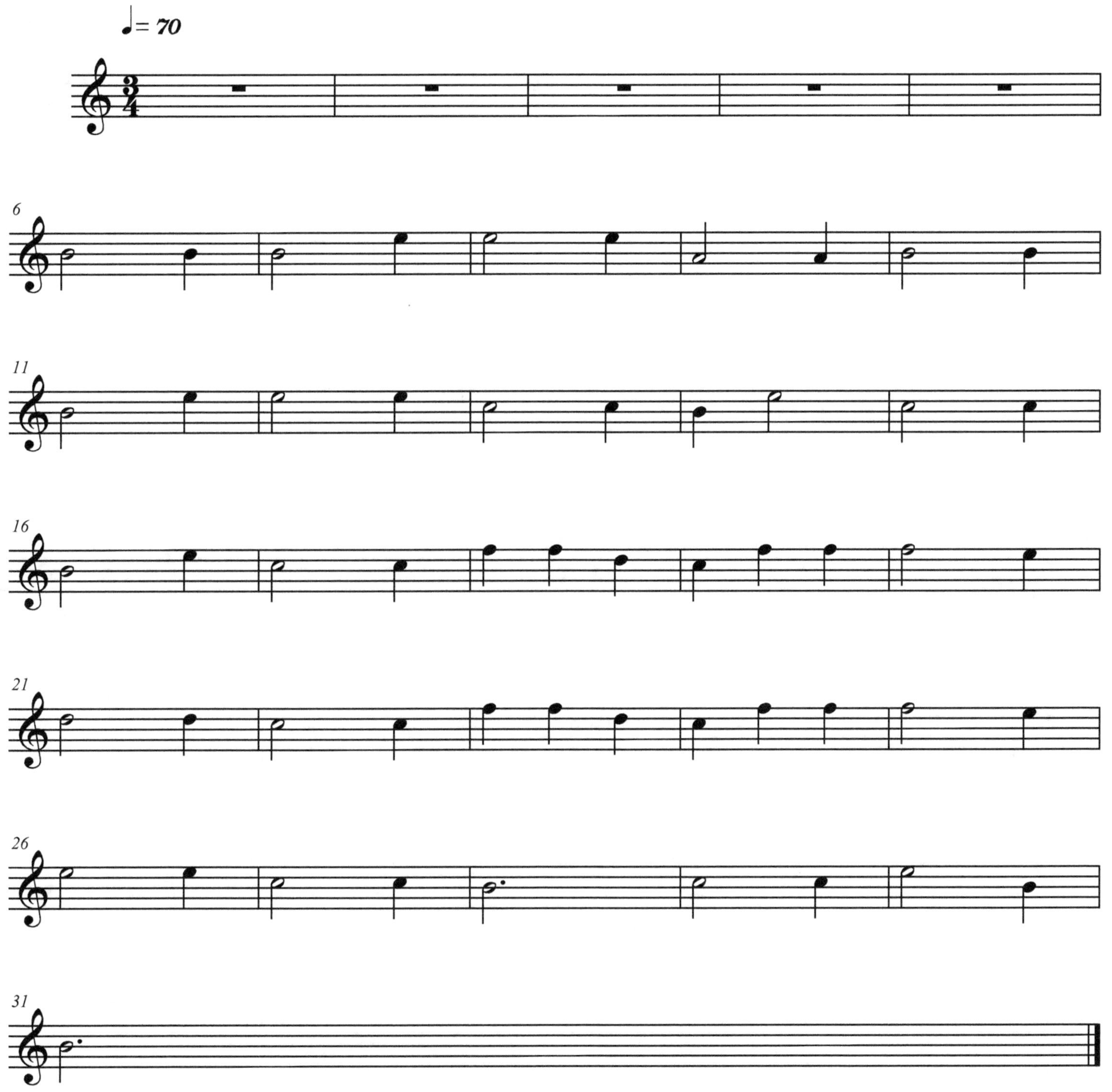

Part 3: F Horn 3 + 4

E

Joost de Groo

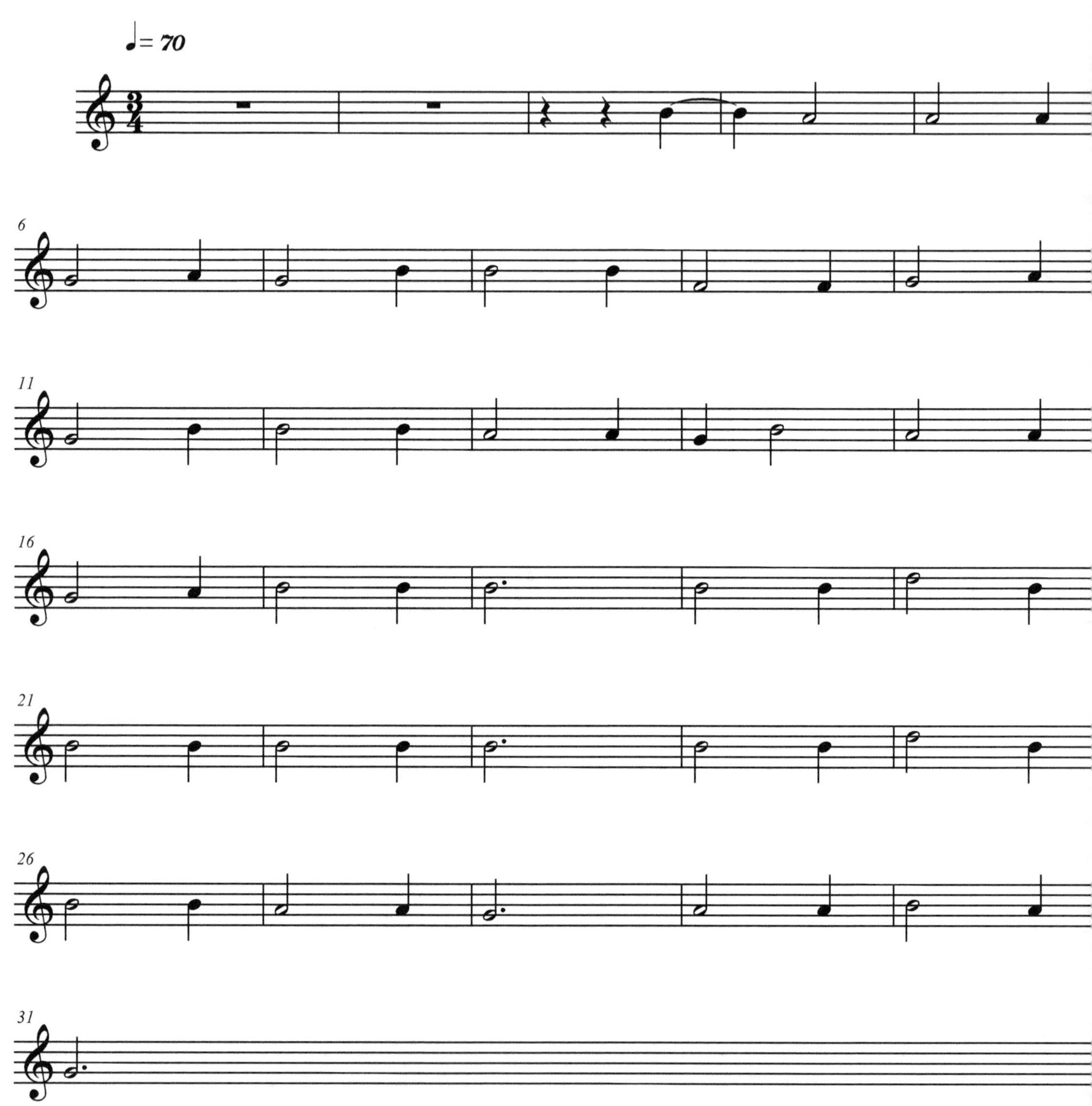

Part 3: C Trombone 1 + 2

E

Joost de Groot

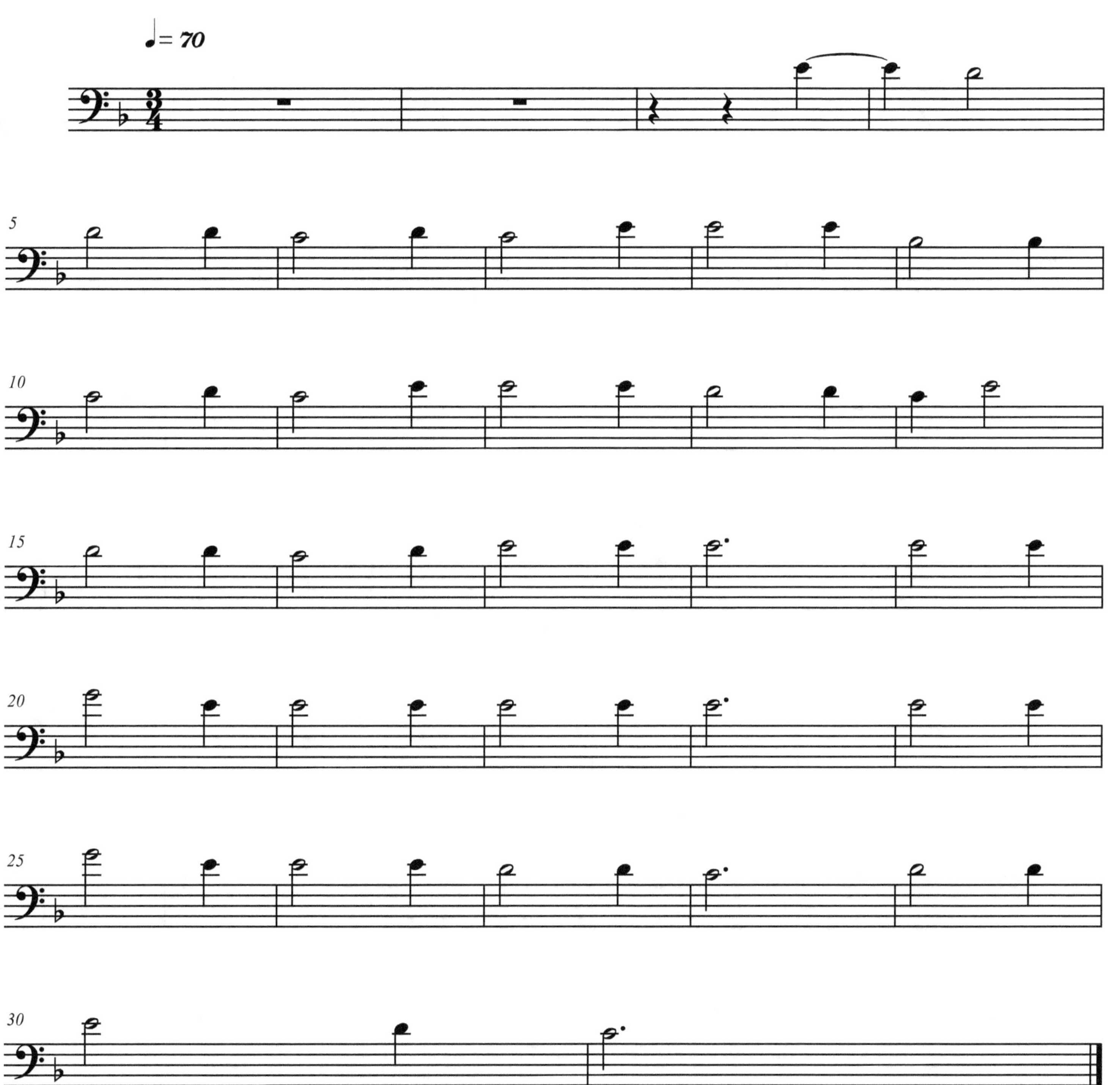

Part 4: C Bass Tombone

E

Joost de Gro

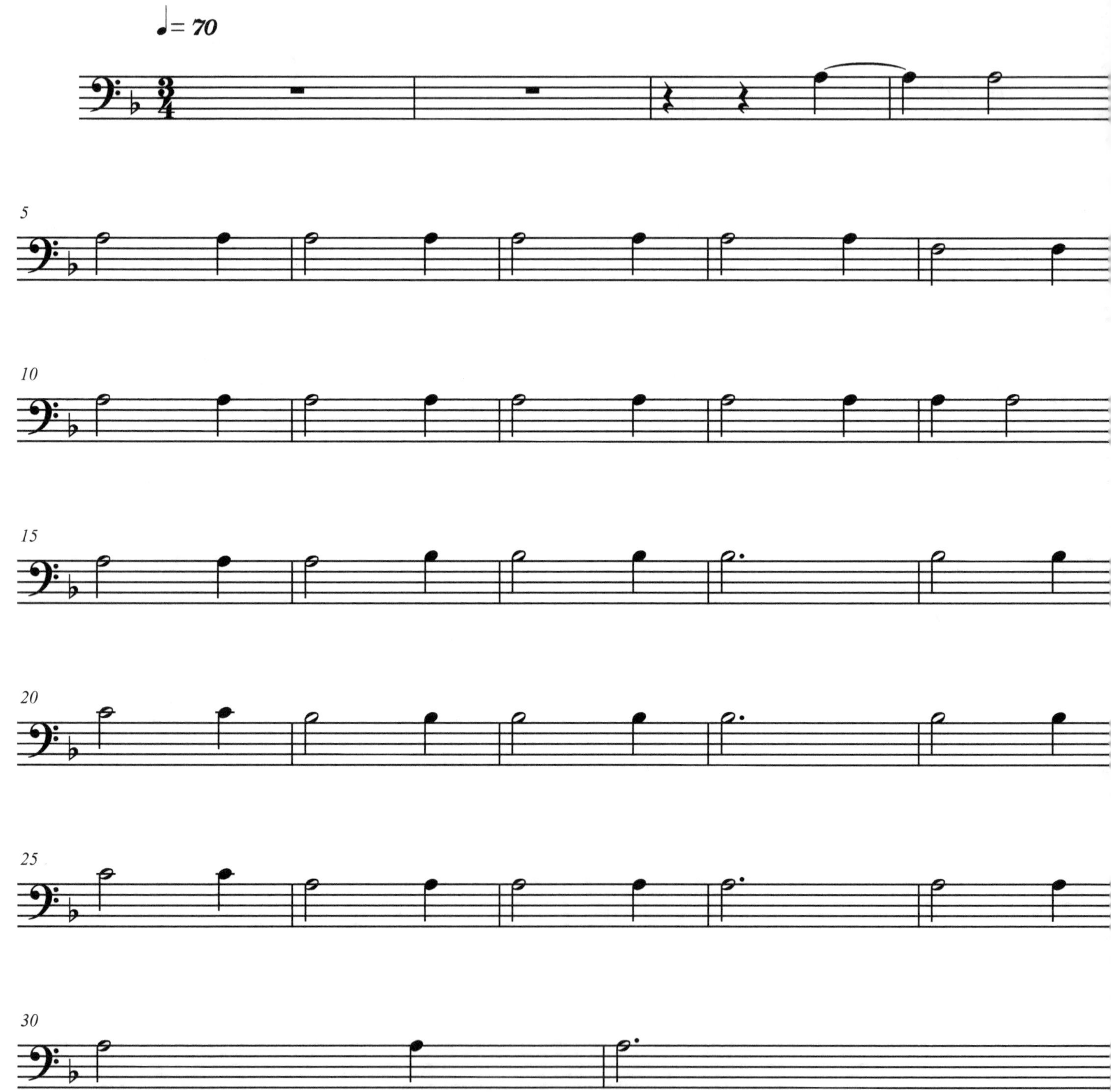

Part 3: C Baritone

E

Joost de Groot

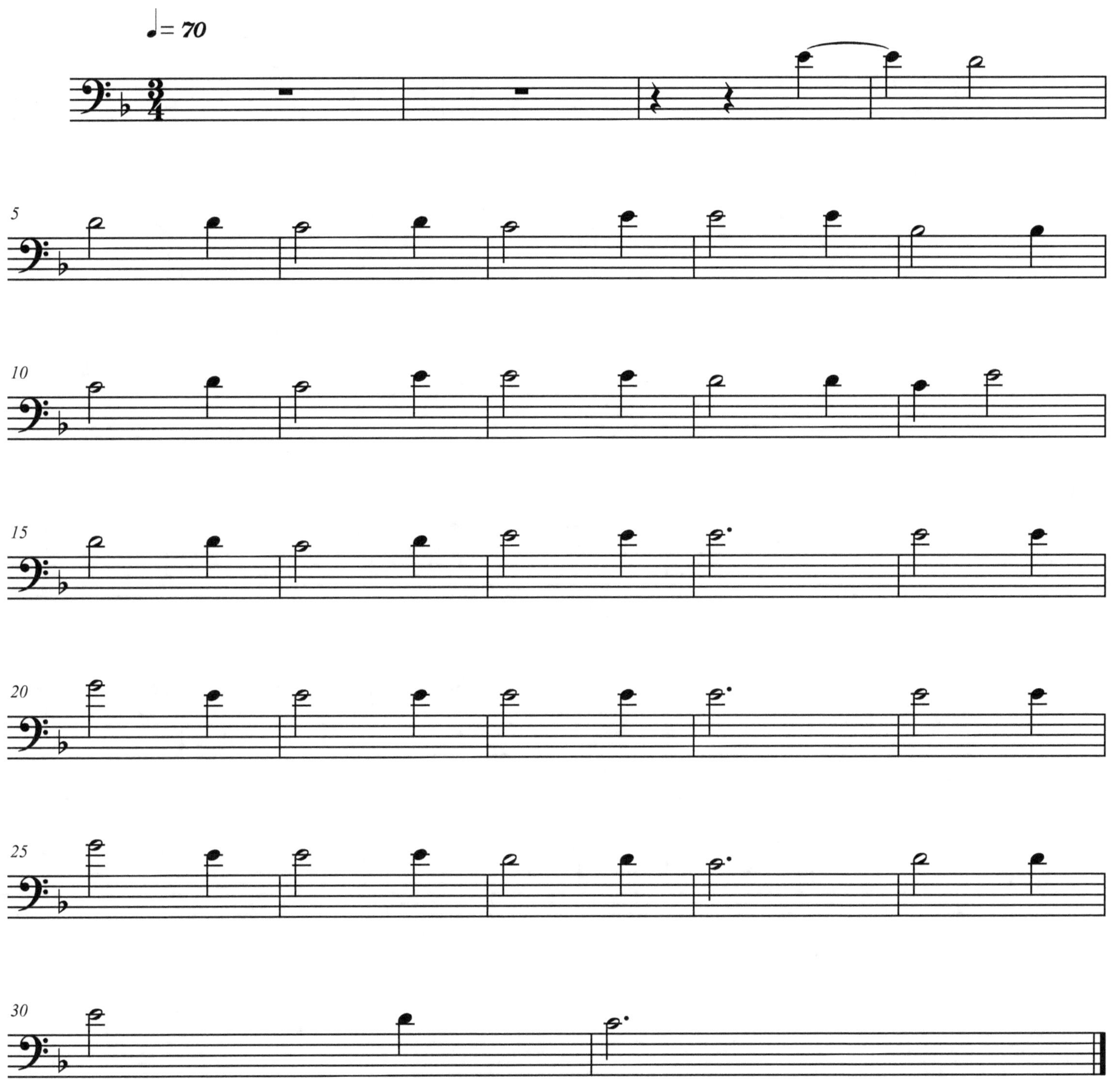

Part 3: Bes Baritone

E

Joost de Groo

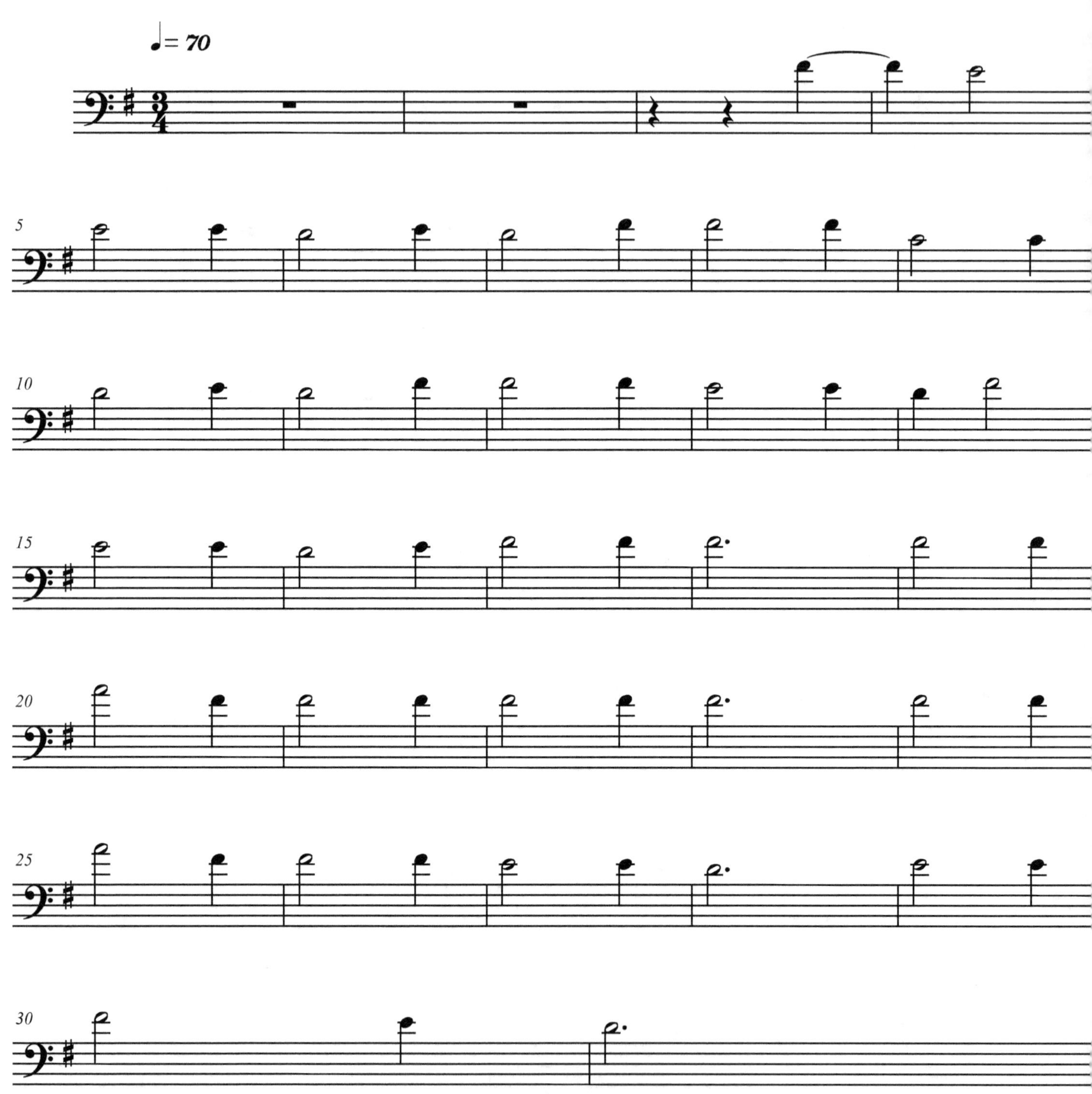

Part 3: Bes Baritone

E

Joost de Groot

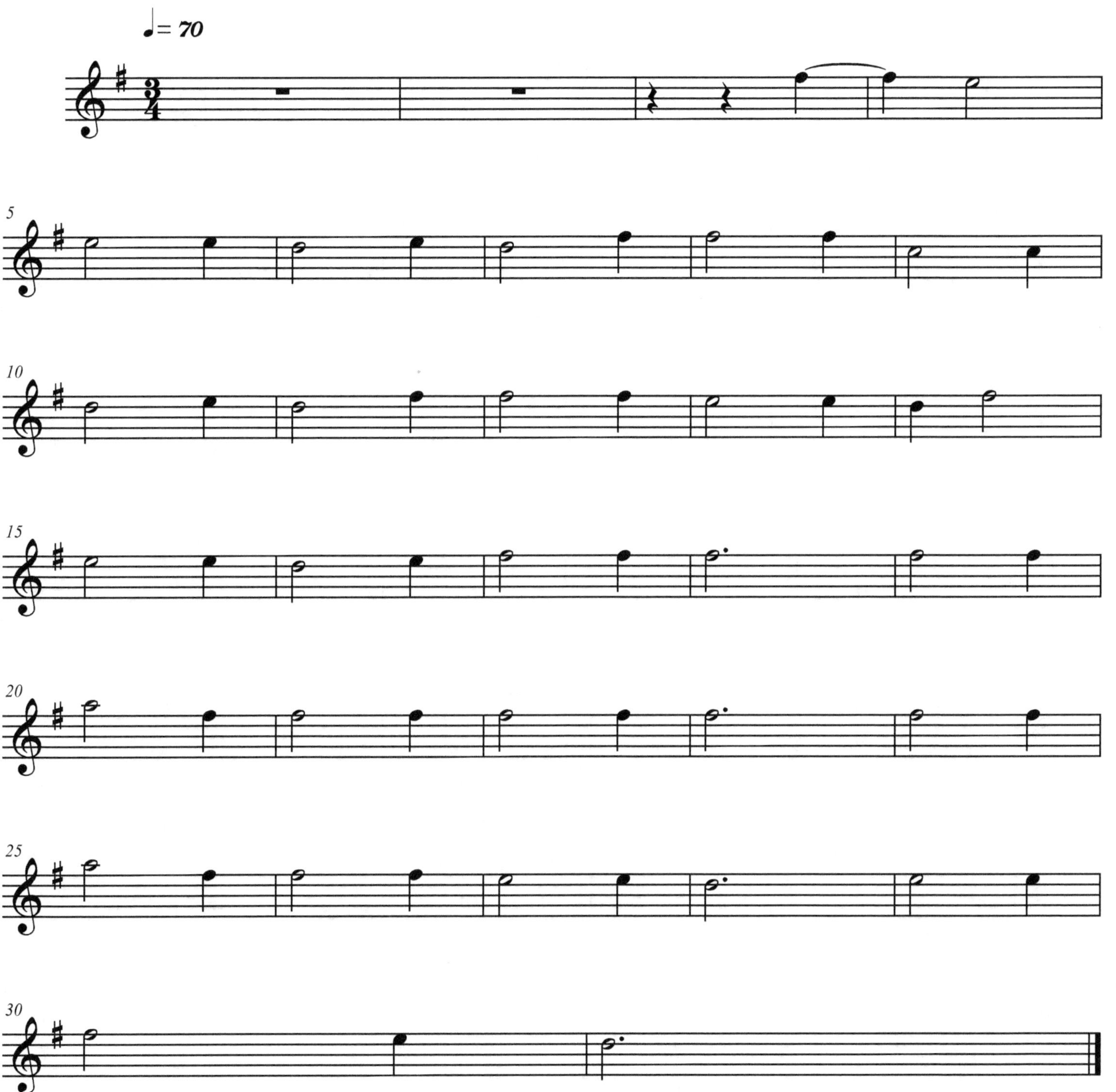

Part 4: C Bass Tuba

E

Joost de Gro

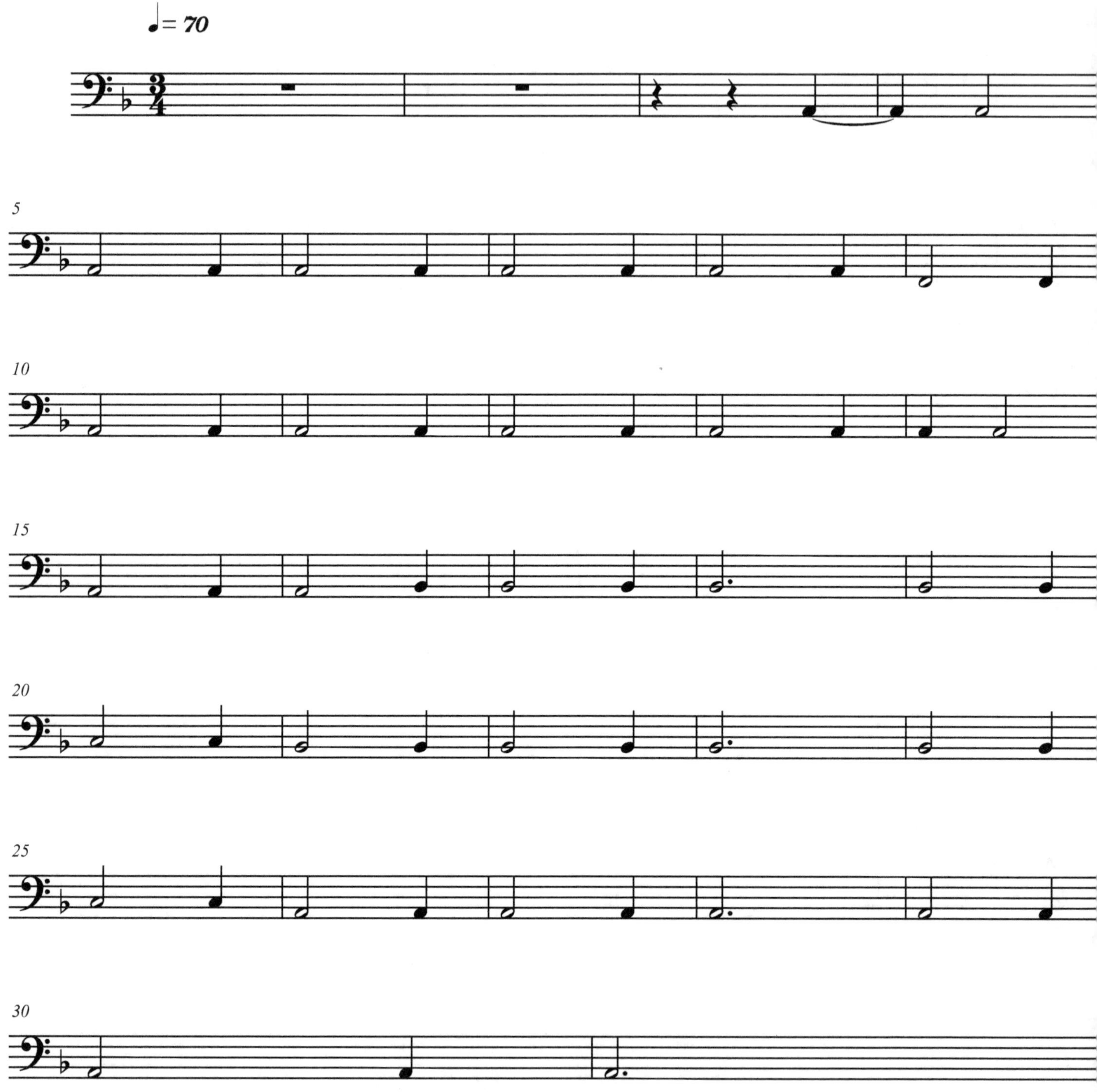

E

Part 4: Bes Bass Tuba

Joost de Groot

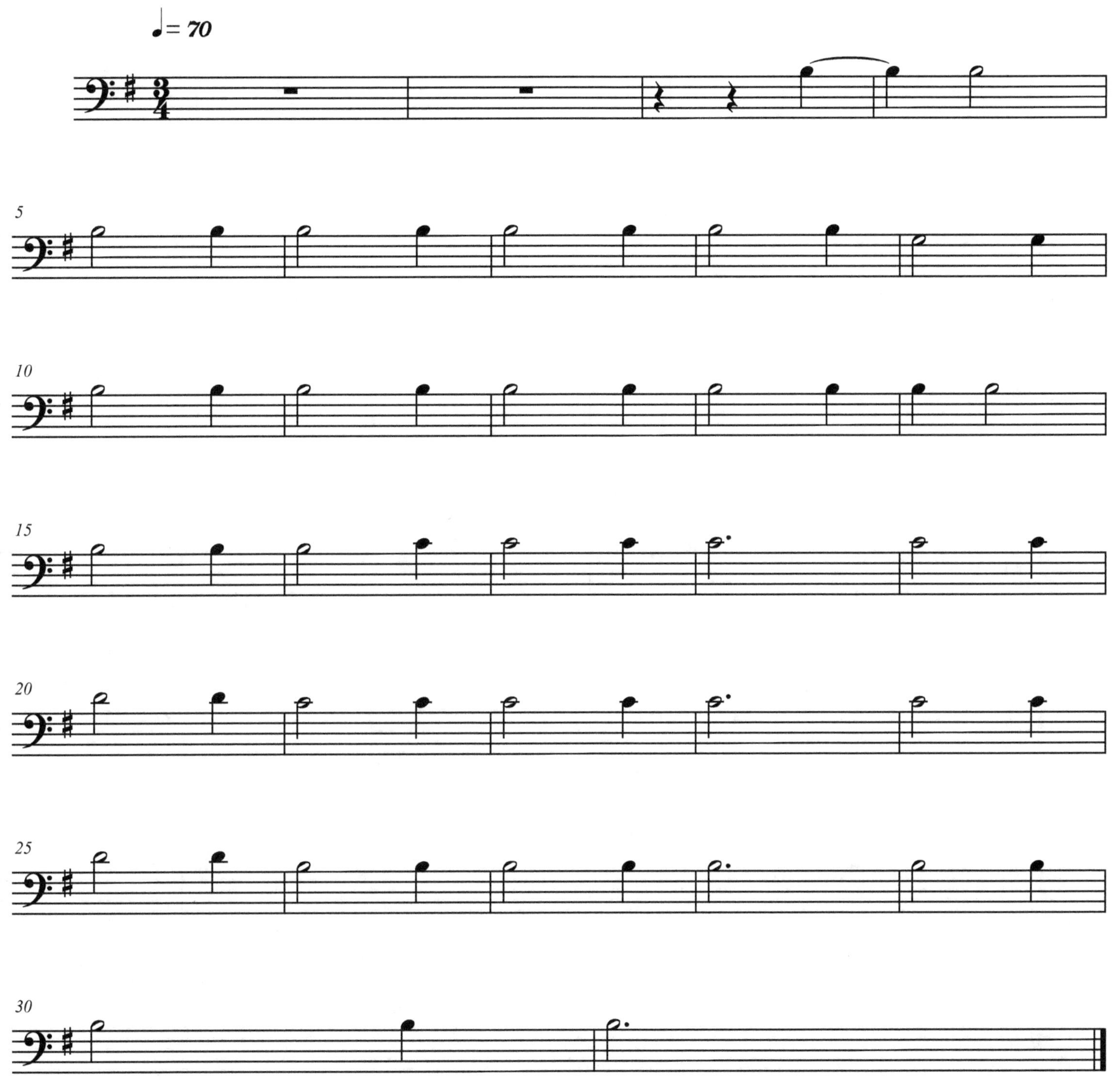

E

Part 4: Es Bass Tuba

Joost de Gro

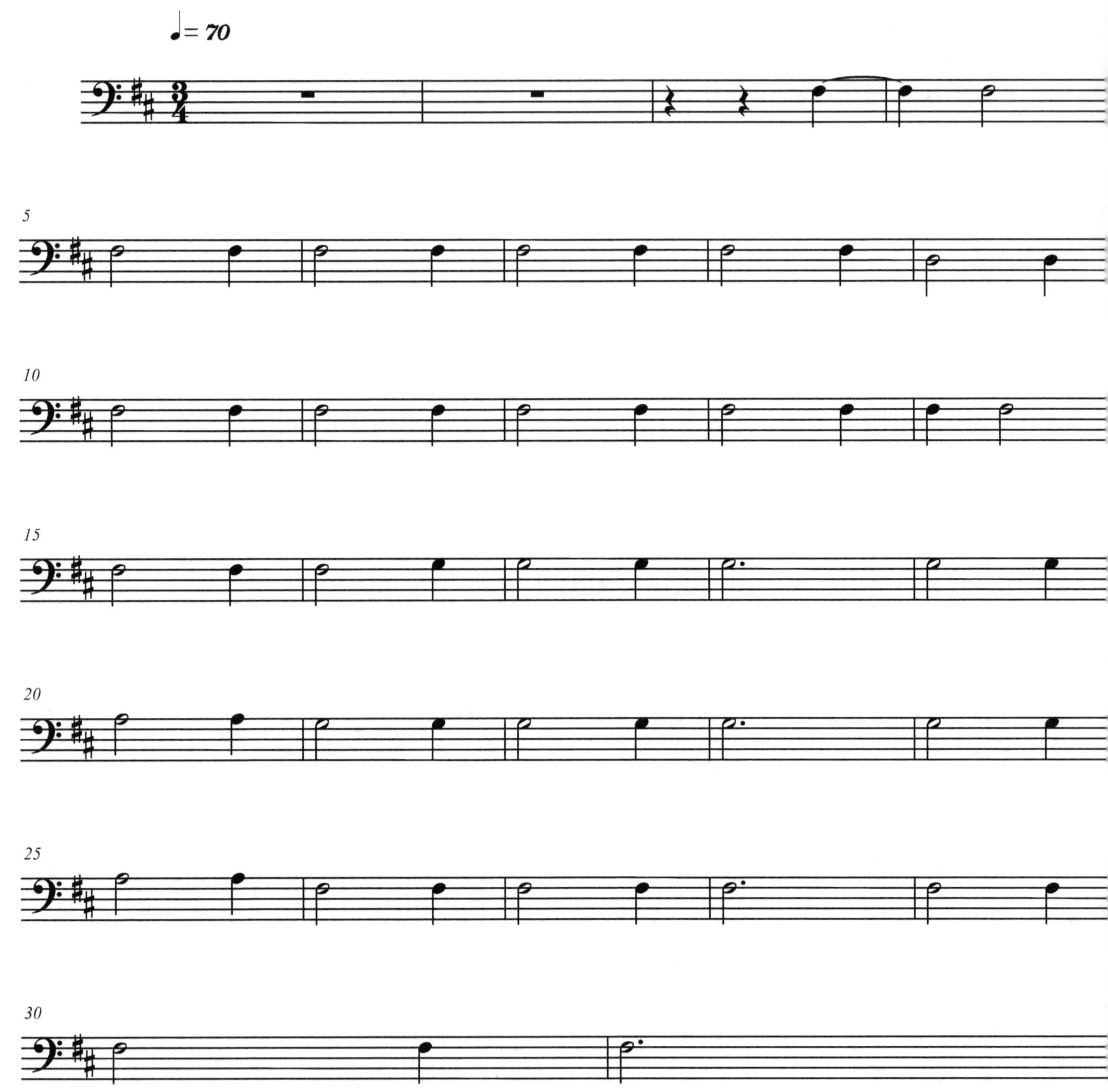

www.ingramcontent.com/pod-product-compliance
Lightning Source LLC
LaVergne TN
LVHW081149110826
845149LV00008B/1606
* 9 7 8 9 0 7 8 8 0 8 2 2 0 *